MEN OF LETTERS
AND THE ENGLISH PUBLIC
IN THE EIGHTEENTH CENTURY

INTERNATIONAL LIBRARY OF SOCIOLOGY AND SOCIAL RECONSTRUCTION

Editor : Dr. Karl Mannheim

MEN OF LETTERS AND THE ENGLISH PUBLIC IN THE EIGHTEENTH CENTURY

1660-1744, DRYDEN, ADDISON, POPE

by

ALEXANDRE BELJAME

PROFESSEUR ADJOINT À LA FACULTÉ DES LETTRES DE
L'UNIVERSITÉ DE PARIS
MAÎTRE DE CONFÉRENCES À L'ÉCOLE NORMALE
SUPÉRIEURE

Edited, with an Introduction and Notes
by BONAMY DOBRÉE

Translated by
E. O. LORIMER

LONDON
KEGAN PAUL, TRENCH, TRUBNER & CO., LTD.
BROADWAY HOUSE: 68-74 CARTER LANE, E.C.4

English Edition. First Published in 1948

Le Public et les Hommes de Lettres
en Angleterre au Dix-huitième Siècle
1660–1744
First Edition 1881
Second Edition 1897

To

MONSIEUR A. MÉZIÈRES

DE L'ACADÉMIE FRANÇAISE

PROFESSEUR DE LITTÉRATURE ÉTRANGÈRE

À LA FACULTÉ DES LETTRES

DE L'UNIVERSITÉ DE PARIS

A Tribute of Affectionate Respect

THIS BOOK IS PRODUCED IN COMPLETE
CONFORMITY WITH THE AUTHORIZED
ECONOMY STANDARDS

Printed in Great Britain by Butler & Tanner Ltd., Frome and London

CONTENTS

FOREWORD

Before embarking on my subject, it will be advisable briefly to define the words of my title.

By " Man of Letters " I mean a writer who lives by his pen and who is able by his works alone to achieve independence and, if he deserves it, distinction.

By " Public " I do not mean the public of theatre-goers so much as the body of intelligent people who are interested in the various forms of literature, the people who read and buy books.

So long as a nation lacks such a public, so long as education is the privilege of a chosen few, so long as the taste and habit of reading are not common to a considerable proportion of society, it is obvious that the sale of their works will provide writers with an income so uncertain and so inadequate that they cannot be " men of letters " in any sense of the term.

The starting-point of this study of mine is therefore the gradual growth of an enlightened and interested public.

How does such a public come into being ? By what degrees and by what means has it been formed ? What part have men played, and what influence have events had, in forming it ?

What influence has its development exercised on writers ? What effect has its existence had on their position in society ?

These are the questions I have tried to answer. It seemed to me that in a country like England, and in a literature like English literature, these questions were not unworthy of some attention.

The data for such a study as this really begin with a people's first literary efforts, and I might well have gone back to the origins of English literature. I preferred to confine myself within more modest limits, and to begin my study with the accession of Charles the Second in 1660. Many reasons moreover combined to make the choice of this date appear a wise one. What may be considered the modern period of English literature begins in fact with Charles II : documents become more and more numerous and more accurate, facts clearer and more precise. Above all, it is with the Restoration that the picture of literary life begins to assume peculiar interest : the public enters on the scene ; during the succeeding reigns we see it little by little developing and taking shape. We see at the same time the writers, after various trials and vicissitudes, begin to rise and take their place. ·

I have stopped at the death of Pope in 1744, because with Pope we reach the climax : with him a public has been established ; the writer's trade has become a liberal profession ; the man of letters has won for himself the place in society which he occupies to-day.

Moreover, even with these limitations, the field of study was sufficiently vast, comprising, as it does, from different points of view almost a whole century of English social history and of English letters. My bibliography offers sufficient proof of the distance to which my researches have led me.

I should like to record how greatly I have been aided in these researches by the staff of the British Museum. During the frequent and lengthy visits I paid to the admirable library in their charge, I was invariably received by them with goodwill and eagerness to help. It is a most pleasant duty here to express to them my thanks.

In England and the United States, in France and Germany, the press has given my book a cordial welcome, for which on the threshold of its second edition I should like to offer my cordial thanks.

To the present edition, purged of some inaccuracies, I have added an Index which will, I trust, prove useful to students.

PREFACE

The translation of this book has been no easy task, for it has had to be a work of interpretation as well as of idiomatic rendering, and has itself involved scholarship. It has, for instance, been no simple matter to know exactly what, in each instance, Beljame meant by the word *puritan*. Did he mean a Church of England man, a Dissenter, or simply " puritan " ? Again, the tracing of quotations in books which are no longer common reading has been no mean labour, one which has been indefatigably pursued. Often a phrase for which no reference was given had to be hunted up, here and there without result, because most of the work was done during the war when access to books and old periodicals was not easy, and sometimes impossible.[1] An editor can do no less than to give grateful thanks for the scholarly work that Mrs. Lorimer has carried out, as well as for a translation which is as spirited as it is exact. He would also like to thank Mr. Noel F. Sharp of the British Museum for most valuable help in looking up quotations and references not otherwise obtainable during the period when the Reading Room was closed. Thanks are also due to the Curator of the Hampton Court pictures for providing the new number of a portrait referred to by Beljame.

All Beljame's notes have been included in this edition, except such as gave the English of certain passages translated in his text : these have, of course, been transferred to the English text. Any extra notes added—and these have been kept down to a minimum—have been enclosed in square brackets and initialled, so that they are easily distinguishable from Beljame's.

Beljame's Bibliography has also been printed in full (with the excision of shelf numbers which are no longer all of them the same as they were seventy years ago). The bibliography has, however, been reorganized so as to make it more easily used, and to bring it into some conformity with modern practice. A certain number of additions have been made, not in any attempt to give a complete bibliography of the period—which would occupy an inordinate amount of room—but to enable

[1] Very few errors have been found, and these have been silently corrected, as have a few misprints and obviously wrong dates.

the reader who wishes to familiarize himself with more recent scholarship, either on the period or on individuals, to pick up the main strains. I have to thank Mrs. Dorothy Broughton for a great deal of help in this compilation ; indeed this part of the work is mainly hers, though it is I who must be responsible for any errors or omissions. Here again the additions are put in square brackets, but without initials, to enable the reader to know which are the books that Beljame used.

B. D.

INTRODUCTION

How did the people who lived by the pen between 1660 and 1740 earn their livelihood? That is the question, with its implications as to the kind of writing produced, which Beljame set himself to answer in this classic work of scholarship. The word classic is used advisedly, since no one interested either in the literature of the period, or in its social history, can afford to neglect it, if only to save himself a deterrent amount of initial spade-work. It is classic also by its form and its method : it is a model of how such things should be done. Moreover, the period chosen by Beljame is one of crucial interest, since it was during those years that a fundamental change in the status of the writer took place, a change which corresponded with the final emergence of society from its mediæval phase into the modern one.

The Revolution of 1688 was the political event which defined, gave legal status to, a profound social development bound to affect the position of the great writer, the man of letters (whom alone Beljame considers), as it also did that of the popular or Grub-Street writer ; the position of the author of sermons, or of polemical theology, however, remained largely unaltered. Beljame's work was thoroughly done ; and however much subsequent studies may have led to revision here and there, however much the attitude, both critical and general, may have varied since 1881—such processes go on continually—*le Public et les Hommes de Lettres en Angleterre au Dix-huitième Siècle* must always remain the groundwork of a similar study, should it ever be undertaken, and the constant recourse of the scholar or the curious.

But before plunging into this work, the reader, especially if he be a student, should perhaps ask himself what it is he is really reading about. A book such as this is commonly regarded as a part of literary studies, and the danger is that it may come to be accepted as a study of literature. It cannot be too plainly stated that a knowledge of the appurtenances of literature, of its social surroundings, of the soil in which it flourished, will not make a fig of difference to its value for us here and now— and it is that which matters. To have a notion of how a thing came about, to undergo the most minute explanation of its appearance, will not make you " understand " it any better, in the sense that a work of art is " understood " as opposed, say, to a piece of machinery. One may begin to wonder whether what is in some places studied as literature is indeed literature or something else ; for what the student of literature should aim at is to eat the bread, not analyse the chemical nature of the soil from which the wheat sprang. What the literary addict should do is to taste the bread, analyse how it is made, whether or not it is properly cooked, and how much it nourishes him. Anything else is another study, perhaps a paradise for the specialist, but not half so rewarding for the whole man.

Nevertheless, a study of this kind has enormous value, if properly used : it may remove certain barriers which prevent us from getting into intimate contact with the work of literature. Of course it has its value as a sociological study, but with such, as students of literature, we are not primarily concerned. Yet if we can discount the mental and moral trappings of an age, separate them from what is essential so that they need not distract us from our proper study of the work of art as such, a great deal has been gained. A generation or so ago such a statement would have been regarded as " mere æstheticism ", as perhaps a good many now may regard it, with a good deal of stress on the " mere " : but it is time to reconsider the position in view of the danger of the study of literature becoming a sub-department of sociology. This is not the place in which to argue the question—to anyone abreast of recent studies in psychology, education, or scientific philosophy it will need no arguing—but rather to see in what way a book such as Beljame's can be of use to us as students of literature itself.

How the writers earned their livelihood, that is, who paid them, must evidently have some effect upon what they wrote, and how they wrote it ; as Dryden, forestalling Dr. Johnson, put it :

> They who have best succeeded on the stage,
> Have still conformed their genius to their age ;

and what this book enables us to do is to see how far certain attitudes, methods, materials used, developments of attack, are common form, and have only an accidental connection with the essentials of that unique thing, a work of art. All art is an exploration of reality : and anything which helps us to discard the adventitious paraphernalia of that reality brings us closer to the work of art. To many who have read, say, Restoration drama, all the comedies, or all the tragedies, seem much the same because the reader has never penetrated beneath the paraphernalia, and so has been unable to see what each individual dramatist was presenting or probing. All the comedy writers of that time dealt with cuckoldry ; they had to, as Beljame shows : but just because they had to, that is what matters least in their plays. In the same way they all dealt with foppery, because they could hardly avoid it : what matters is the relation of these characteristics to a broader sense of life that each writer may exhibit. Read them carelessly, and they will all seem to say much the same thing : but take the symbols for granted and look to see what they symbolize, and something much more important will come through. It is much the same with the tragedy of the time : the impossible plots, the ravings of heroic love, the bombastic ranting, these again are common form. Once we have discounted these things, we find that Dryden does not say the same thing as Lee, nor Etherege the same thing as Wycherley.

Beljame shows us how these things became counters, so that we can take them for what they are. Yet it must be confessed that in the first part of this book Beljame often leaves the discussion at the point of common form : he seems to us, with another sixty years of scholarship behind us, too much to take the symbols for the reality, and is inclined to handle the counters as though they were all of equal value. If the writers in question treated of certain matters, they did actually treat of them, and did not merely present crude " fact ". Nor is it quite certain that their material and their attitude was altogether imposed upon them from without, as Beljame suggests ; they may to some extent have shared the likes and prejudices of their audiences. Moreover, we shall probably think that Beljame sees the period a little too black ; and a little too naïvely, perhaps, accepts the statements of satirists as police-court evidence. The royal circle was hardly ideal ; no one will suggest that it was even decent according to our standards ; all would agree with Macaulay that Plato was no doubt a far better man than Sir George Etherege. But the Restoration Court did not invent literary licentiousness ; poetry knew it before in such things as *The Loves of Hero and Leander*, published in 1651 at the very height of the puritanical Commonwealth ; and editors of school editions of our classics have sometimes experienced certain

difficulties with Shakespeare himself. Men cannot live in the
sort of world presented by the satirists, and cuckoldry would
not have been comic had it not also been painful. There is a
real moral basis to Restoration comedy, which laughs at, rather
than with.

Nor was the drama of this period a sudden invention of the
time. Just as you can trace back much of Restoration comedy,
the themes and the manner alike, to earlier work, through
Davenant, Wilson and Brome back to Shirley, Massinger and
Marston, so you can trace Restoration tragedy not only back
to late Jacobean romantic comedy, but to early Jacobean
tragedy. Where would one suppose the following to come
from? One might easily say, at first reading, Dryden or Lee,
or possibly Orrery :

> *Tullia.* I am no wife of Tarquin's, if not King ;
> Oh ! had Jove made me man, I would have mounted
> Above the base tribunals of the earth,
> Up to the clouds for pompous sovreignty.
> Thou art a man : oh ! bear my royal mind,
> Mount heaven, and see if Tullia lag behind.
> There is no earth in me, I am all fire ;
> Were Tarquin so, then should we both aspire.

It is actually from Thomas Heywood's *Rape of Lucrece*, and was
written in about 1604.

Nor was the licentiousness of the stage a fashion which
appeared suddenly. Listen to what Ben Jonson, writing in 1607,
had to say about the stage of his time. Does it not seem exactly
like what Collier was to say about a hundred years later of the
then popular drama ? Jonson tells us in the dedication of
Volpone " that now, especially in dramatic, or, as they term it,
stage poetry, nothing but ribaldry, profanation, blasphemy, all
license of offence to God and man is practised ". And he adds
a little later : " For my particular, I can, and from a most clear
conscience, affirm, that I . . . have loathed the use of such
foul and unwashed bawdry, as is now made the food of the scene."
Jonson, whether he wished to be so or not, was here a satirist ;
and the danger is that if you argue from literature to life, and
then back again from life to literature, you are performing a
very pretty circle, but you are not getting very much further.
It is a danger which, we feel, Beljame does not always escape.

The courtiers whom he dismisses so easily were not, we will
be inclined to judge, quite such contemptible literary figures as

he makes them out to be. Sir Robert Howard, for example, could argue well on dramatic form, and the debt English prosody owed to Waller is not to be ignored. Beljame, indeed, is a little inclined to be certain that a good writer could not have been well born, and that conversely a well-born writer could not have been a good one : thus Etherege must be made out to spring from a social stratum higher than that of Dryden, a matter which is, to say the least of it, not proven. The reader, then, must be a little on his guard ; we know more about the period now than was possible for Beljame.

But however much—thanks, we may repeat, to the researches of the last sixty years—we may be able here and there to pick out a detail on which we can disagree with Beljame, this does not affect the validity of Beljame's main conclusion as to the way a man of letters made his living until the Revolution of 1688, and a little after : it was entirely by Court patronage ; and the public for the poet, the dramatist, the critic, was the Court. There was, of course, another public, that which devoured religious tracts, sermons, *The Pilgrim's Progress*, commercial treatises, political pamphlets and so on—and even poetry. But those who wrote for this public had another means of subsistence ; they were not primarily " men of letters ", and they wrote mainly for propaganda purposes.

But, little by little, the " general public " as opposed to the Court began to be catered for ; and at the same time this public became larger in its views, so began to appreciate what men of letters would write. It would seem to us that Beljame's version of the change, as exhibited in, say, 1710, presents too sudden a swing. It was not all due to Addison. Beljame, of course, was far too good a scholar to say that it was ; but it must be confessed that his emphasis is such that the careless or hasty reader will suppose that all the credit must go to Mr. Spectator. Beljame, in his admiration for Addison, out-Macaulay's Macaulay ; to-day our admiration is tempered. Addison was indeed a very good writer, a man of taste and discernment, of wide reading, and much worldly wisdom in the best sense. He was a good popular moralist, no doubt, but not the genius in moral thinking that Beljame would have us think ; he was, rather, as Matthew Arnold pointed out, provincial and trite. What made him, we are inclined to think, so notable a figure in the history of our literature, was his journalistic genius in seeing what was wanted, what would take, at exactly the right moment. He had a flair, and it made him almost great : but the question arises, was not the flair really Steele's ?

If one cannot ascribe to one man the change brought about in the relation between the man of letters and the public, it is impossible to say exactly what did bring it about. Such social changes are very complex, and we have not enough knowledge at our disposal. The patronage of the politicians who replaced the Court at the Revolution of 1688 was a lucky chance ; but it is possible that this only hastened a process which would in any event have taken place, namely, the writer as such achieving a social status. The more important process, that of the writer gaining a large middle-class audience ready to buy his work in sufficient bulk to support him, was already begun before the turn of the century, though only begun. This was largely owing to the rise of a new middle class. The middle class, as any student of history knows, is always rising—or has been hitherto—and this time it was the mercantilist-manufacturing middle class that was rising, the class represented by Defoe, between, say, 1690 and 1720, and sung by Dyer in *The Fleece* in 1757. There were two other causes, aptly commented on by Beljame ; the lapse of the Licensing Act, and the growth of the coffee-houses. Beyond this, there was the need which the large dissenting class in the middle stratum of society began to feel for some reading other than the long-winded and copiously documented effusions of sectarian protagonists. This public, incidentally, was being enlarged by the growth of dissenting elementary schools, which did not come under the Schism Act, and of the charity schools against which Mandeville was soon to inveigh precisely because they taught people to read when they should be hewing wood and drawing water. And when we consider that the City was largely dissenting, and that the main bulk of readers were townsmen, it is clear that there would be a considerable market for easy reading quite different in tone from what had diverted the Restoration Court. Nor should we ignore the influx of educated Huguenots who certainly helped to form and to influence the reading public.

Moreover, the women of this new group were beginning to join the ranks of readers ; they were becoming leisured, and were not averse from frivolities. The journalistic sense of Steele and especially Addison picked up this fact readily enough, and this will explain why so much of *The Spectator* is addressed to " the

fair sex ". Addison certainly wrote for the boudoir as much as
for the coffee-house : a paper has to be bought to be read in the
home, and this may partly account for Addison's enormous
sales.

The ground for a new kind of reading matter was well prepared before the appearance of *The Tatler* by, as Beljame tells
us, the various *Mercuries*,[1] and other publications of Dunton,
who, as a good if limited journalist, knew his job. These periodicals were not, we may think, so vapid as Beljame suggests.
There were, besides, such writers as Tom Brown, whom Beljame
too lightly dismisses as " flat ", and Ned Ward, not mentioned
at all in this volume. Their works ran into many editions in
the reign of Queen Anne (Ward, indeed, wrote on up till 1729),
and they had much the same idea as Addison had of civilizing
the public, in fact, in Ward's own words, " to expose vice and
encourage virtue ". Defoe, with his *Review*, also helped enor-
mously in preparing the way. Without Steele it is doubtful if
Addison would have achieved his resounding fame. Had there
been no *Tatler*, there would have been no *Spectator* ; and it was
Steele who launched *The Tatler* and created Sir Roger, just as
it was Defoe who had hit upon the idea of the Scandal Club.
Addison was in no way an innovator, nor had he a creative
mind : but he did what other people were doing, very much
better than they did. And that, at any time whatever, is no
mean achievement.

It is to be noted that such things as we have been discussing
were not aimed primarily at the more educated reading public,
the public that read Locke and Clarendon, D'Avenant's *Essay
on the Balance of Power*, Dampier's *Voyages*, the earlier works of
Berkeley, Shaftesbury and Mandeville, the critical works of Dennis
or Bysshe, or, possibly, *The Tale of a Tub*. Readers of such works
did not need the kind of civilizing influence that the great
journalists were so active in providing, though they too bought
The Tatler and its numerous progeny. And besides the above-
mentioned works, there were, as there had been in the Restoration period, innumerable works of theological controversy, now
more heretical than ever (Asgill, Toland, etc.), which together
with the usual routine flood of sermons, *The Practice of Piety* in
a diversity of forms, and so on, made up the bulk of published
matter, at least as revealed by the Term Catalogues. And no

---

[1] *Mercuries* appeared as early as 1644 ; but were not of much importance
until after the Revolution.

doubt readers of these latter works, anxious for relaxation, would patronize *The Spectator* which could hardly ever be accused of raising a blush in the cheek of any young person. Amongst all this reading there was also an intolerable deal of intolerable verse, and a little that was tolerable, but only a very thin trickle of poetry until Pope came to maturity.

Reading lists might be studied indefinitely without our gaining any real certainty as to what happened. What it is wished to do here is a little to gloss the too simplified picture that Beljame draws of an immoral Court calling forth corrupt or absurd literature, as opposed to a morally regenerated England demanding wholesome moralistic fare. The matter is by no means so simple as that. We may think, perhaps, that Beljame confines himself too much to a special class of writing, a special class of readers, and it is doubtful if one could to-day maintain his statement that Addison " increased the number and the quality of readers ". Nevertheless, the facts he adduces as causes are at least symptomatic ; they cannot be ignored ; and he points out the important fact that by the time of Addison's death in 1719 authors could to some extent rely on a general reading public to help keep body and soul together in some dignity, and were not entirely at the mercy of noble patrons. Yet it is well to insist that very few, if any, actually, did make their livelihood out of the reading public ; they were still, in varying degrees, dependent on political, and sometimes noble, patronage. In the age of the new Whig lords these were not always distinguishable : the lords often supported the men of letters out of the public pocket rather than their own. Certainly writers no longer had to grovel to peers who thought they knew something about poetry (some of them did know) : but it is difficult to point to a single writer above the scandalous or Grub Street level who made his living by his pen alone. Authors still had to make their terms with peers who had political power. Beljame makes this quite clear, but he a little discounts the purity of motive of some of the peers. Men such as Somers, " the all-accomplished ", Dorset, " the grace of courts, the muses' pride ", and Halifax who loved to be thought the Mæcenas of his age, really were concerned for literature ; and so long as writers did not make nuisances of themselves politically, did not mind to what party they belonged.

There is one matter which again Beljame seems to us to stress too strongly, namely, the purifying influence of Collier's diatribe,

A Short View, etc. Collier certainly voiced, if he exaggerated, the feelings of the new middle class, the members of which wanted to go to the theatre *en famille.* As a matter of sober fact the actual repertory of the theatre did not alter much as a result of his attack. Dryden, Wycherley, Mrs. Behn, and so on, continued to be acted ; we find Addison as late as the end of the first decade of the century reviewing Etherege's *Man of Mode,* and in a very solemn tone making a social criticism already implicit in what Etherege had written (see p. 282). Taste, of course, brought about a change. It was already beginning with Burnaby (fl. 1702) and made itself manifest in the sentimental comedy of Steele ; it was part of the social process which took the bite out of English comedy, and destroyed it for nearly two hundred years. Yet if, as far as one can judge, Collier had very little effect, he was a flamboyant symptom. He was himself a part of the reading public to whom *The Tatler* would later appeal : the translator of Marcus Aurelius would welcome something better written than the stuff Ned Ward could provide, based on a broader culture, and more representative of the newly-risen middle class which desired nothing better than to attain to the culture of the old aristocracy so long as it could retain something of its fierce and uncomfortable morality.

That we should on many points disagree with Beljame's critical opinions is only right and proper : the value of a work of literature (except perhaps for the very greatest), is relative to the experience any generation passes through. A state of society something analogous with that of the Restoration at one time made us see the point of dramatic work which Beljame believed for ever sunk below the horizon of appreciation : some writers to-day dislike Addison perhaps as much as Beljame adored him. It is not to cross critical swords, to oppose opinions, that objections against the author of this work are raised here and in the notes. What we are concerned to discover is how far, and in what way, a state of society influences writing. Beljame, in his admiration for Addison, ascribed too much to his influence : we are inclined to see Addison more as a product of his time than as its architect. Beljame's view of the personal relation between author and patron will seem to us a little vitiated by his not feeling the relations between the classes quite as we do. For instance, he finds it hard to understand why the political leaders should have been socially friendly with authors unless they had been afraid of them, or, alternatively, enlisting the support of their pens. It does not seem probable to him that, for instance, Congreve and Vanbrugh, or Gay, might have been drawn into close social relations with their patrons because they were good fellows, spoke the same language, had had much the same education. In the main the authors belonged to the same class as the patrons with whom they were friendly ; they were " the quality " ; though there were exceptions, such as Prior, which reflect the fluidity of the class system as it has always existed in England.

Scholar as Beljame was, we cannot but feel that here and there he was a little too much guided by his thesis ; his work seems to us slightly distorted by that unscholarly thing, a point of view. It is this, of course, which gives his book life. You cannot be completely disinterested about human affairs and be a whole human being in the workaday or the moral world. Thus Beljame occasionally lets himself be carried away by his argument, and if we are not on our guard we may obtain a slightly false impression. But only if we are not careful, and fail to read his footnotes, or the paragraphs he himself inserts, as a good scholar must, to redress the balance, though these, perhaps, he presents a little too shyly. For instance, he gives to Addison all the credit for what the *Tatlers* and *Spectators* accomplished ; only the careful reader will note that he tells us that for simplicity's sake he has used the name Addison throughout to cover the work of Steele as well ; only a reader who checks references will observe that certain essays quoted in glorification of Addison are actually by Steele.

In the same way he paints in too gloomy colours the fate that befell authors when Walpole came into power. It is true that the golden age of authorship was over, and many sad stories are truly told of starving poets. But when we see who these poets were we cannot wonder at their fate—Savage and Boyse, for instance. Many are simply unreadable. But after all, a good many poets and writers managed to live, at least partly if not all of them wholly, by their pens, without patronage, or by the aid of subscription lists : Defoe in his last years, Thomson, Dyer, Shenstone, Akenside, Mrs. Haywood. A certain reading public had indeed come into being, and was prepared to support the authors who gave it what it wanted. After all, it is not in conformity with experience to suggest, as Beljame does, that every young, untried author should be able to make a living out of writing. How many young authors in any country have ever been able to do so? Take this country; take France. How many authors in France since the Revolution have been able to live without either some modicum of private means or a civil service job? How many of our own distinguished poets or men of letters—as opposed to best-selling novelists—live, or have lived in this century without private means, a civil service post, or employment in a publisher's firm? Beljame, we feel, asked for too much. So we must not too readily accept this part of his analysis, especially as here again he is apt to rely a little too much on evidence afforded by the satirists, such as Fielding in his farces. Once more we feel that the picture is a little too simplified. The whole question is, in fact, infinitely complicated.

Beljame's was a great pioneer attempt, the first thoroughly documented attempt of its kind: and because it was so well documented it can never be altogether superseded. Nobody can write with authority about the period covered in this book without having read it, sifted it, found out not only where he disagrees with the conclusions, but why he does so. The main picture is clear, and just enough: it needs amending in detail, and here and there some fresh considerations may have to be introduced. One question, suggested in the previous paragraph, is whether Beljame has not made too rigid a demarcation between the professional writer and the amateur. In this country we have never had that respect for letters that they have so long had in France: we have, indeed, been a little over-proud of our amateur status, an attitude of mind not without its benefits to literature, though they are too easily overrated. That is the kind of point that must be kept in mind when reading this work. It is masterly, it stands the test of time, but it is, naturally, not beyond criticism: nevertheless, it is so well done that it demands the most fundamental criticism. It is with the certainty that this is so that this work is offered in English to the English-reading public, and in the hope that it may find imitators. It has, indeed, been the forerunner of similar works, but it still stands head and shoulders above most of them, and it is doubtful if any has yet equalled it for erudition and thoroughness.

BONAMY DOBRÉE.

BIOGRAPHICAL NOTE

In 1864, when Alexandre Beljame was twenty-two years old, he undertook an English course at the Lycée Louis-le-Grand. He found that English studies were very little considered, in no way regarded as being an important part of humane scholarship. He set himself to remedy this state of affairs, and in 1881 produced *Le Public et les Hommes de Lettres en Angleterre* to establish the dignity of English studies in France on a level with those in the classics. He proved by this masterly book that they involved as much real hard work, as much scrupulous thinking, and as fine a critical acumen as were needed in the time-honoured schools of Greek and Latin.

His efforts were rewarded with the success due to them. He was the first lecturer in English to be appointed at the Sorbonne, and in 1902 the Sorbonne Chair was founded that he might occupy it, which he did until his death some five years later.

The school grew rapidly under him, both in numbers and in prestige, thanks to his single-hearted devotion, his high culture, his deep knowledge, and his loving and fastidious scholarship. He soon attracted brilliant pupils and disciples, to whom he gave a large proportion of his time and energy. It can be said that he was virtually the founder of the English studies which now flourish in French Universities, and it is to him that we are indebted for such noted scholars as Émile Legouis, Louis Cazamian, to name only two, and so many monographs by distinguished scholars which are standard books for English studies in England.

An admirable brief account of his life, work and influence may be found in *Dernière Gerbe*, by Émile Legouis (Paris, Henri Didier, 1940).

CHAPTER I

JOHN DRYDEN AND THE THEATRE
(1660–1680)

· I

The Restoration of 1660 : King Charles II, the Court.—Anti-Puritan
reaction.—Gaming, wine, gallantry, profligacy.—Religion, morals

The story goes, that during his short and unhappy reign amongst the Scots in 1650, Charles II had been subjected by the strict Presbyterians to a severe discipline. Forced to sign their Covenant and to adopt their worship, he was first placed under the surveillance of a committee of stern and vigilant ministers. These fierce Argus-eyed guardians compelled him perpetually to attend interminable prayers, appointed fast-days for him and sometimes doomed him to listen to as many as six sermons running. He was lucky when these sermons were not exclusively pointed at the crimes of his family and his personal impiety. All pleasures were forbidden, including dancing and card-playing. On Sunday he might not take a walk, or smile ; the slightest ill-judged gesture, the slightest facial expression of boredom brought down on him terrible reproof. One day he had allowed himself to chat innocently with a woman. One of these austere fanatics came and delivered him a long and solemn reproof on the enormity of his sin, and closed by advising him always to keep the windows shut.[1]

The whole of England had been subjected by the Puritans to the same superhuman discipline. After more than eleven years of it, the country felt stifled for lack of air. When Charles II came back, she flung all windows open—wide. She opened them too wide. The Restoration reacted against exaggerated rigour by exaggerated licence.

In this the King took the lead. After a long exile, a wandering and miserable life, he suddenly ascended one of the leading thrones in Europe amid the acclamation of the whole nation. He was 30, with a graceful figure, seductive manners, a love of pleasure and an admirable constitution. Up to this point he

---

[1] Clarendon, book XIII ; Burnet, *History of my Own Times*, vol. I, pp. 91, 92 ; Malcolm, p. 154.

had always been short of money ; now he was going to have as much as ever he liked, and with it all, companions well able to gratify his wishes and themselves eager for enjoyment.

London in those days was everything. Lacking easy communication with the Capital [2], the provinces did not count, and lived an obscure life of their own. London being the whole of England, the Court was the whole of London. Convicted of Puritanism, the middle classes of the city were rudely brushed aside, or ceased to count ; the Court took the only place in the sun and everyone fell into line and adopted its tastes and amusements.

It is easy to formulate the programme followed by the Court : it did everything which the Puritans had forbidden. They had worn short hair and banned every refinement of dress ; the Court adopted long wigs in the Louis XIV style, and dress became one of the main preoccupations of people of fashion. [3] They had forbidden gaming : people gambled wildly and cheated into the bargain. [4] As for wine : they drank, they caroused, they got drunk [5] ; as for oaths : no one opened his

[2] See what Macaulay says about the difficulty of communications at this time (*History*, chap. III).

[3] " A *Town-Gallant* is a Bundle of *Vanity*, composed of *Ignorance and Pride, Folly* and *Debauchery* ; a silly *Huffing* thing, three parts *Fop* and the rest *Hector* (see note 10) : A kind of *Walking Mercers shop*, that shows one Stuff to-day and another to-morrow, and is valuable just according to the price of his *Suit*, and the merits of his *Taylor* . . . His first care is his *Dress*, and next his *Body*, and in the fitting these two together consists his Soul and all its Faculties " (*The Character of a Town-Gallant*, anonymous). Once for all, let me here state that in all my quotations I scrupulously preserve the original orthography which is in my opinion of historic interest. See also *The Man of Mode* ; or, *Sir Fopling Flutter*, a comedy by Etherege ; and *Tyrannus, or the Mode* by Evelyn, in *Memoirs Illustrative of the Life and Writings of John Evelyn, Esq.*, vol. II.
[Beljame is a little too inclined to accept a satirical picture as a sober statement. Since *A Town Gallant* is frequently referred to as authority for the social background, the reader must be on his guard. B. D.]

[4] Pepys : Feb. 14, 1667–8 ; Evelyn : *Diary*, Jan. 25, 1685 ; Butler : *Satire upon Gaming* (in *Genuine Poetical Remains*).—Loaded dice were known as *fulhams*.

[5] See, for example, Pepys, Sept. 23, 1667 : " The King and the Duke of York get drunk at a hunting-party ; the King kneels down to drink the Duke's health, and all the spectators kiss each other with tears." See also ibid.; Oct. 23, 1668. The poet Waller is quoted as an exceptional person because he had the art of being a good companion without drinking (Johnson, *Lives of the English Poets*, Waller).
[Since one of the objects of comedy is to ridicule divergence from the normal, or departure from what ought to be (as Vanbrugh put it : " the business of comedy is to show people what they should do, by representing

mouth without calling in one mood or another on God and the Devil.[6]

The reaction went further. The Puritans had vetoed all pleasures, even the most innocent : the Court plunged into every form of indulgence, even the most unmentionable. The Puritans had preached severity of manners : gallantry was enthroned at Court. Fashionable men called themselves " gallants " and thought of nothing but women and how to charm them.[7] They had set foot on a steep and dangerous slope ; they soon slid to the bottom. Their gallantry was at first pleasing and in good taste. Polished conversation and courtesy in social inter-course superseded biblical jargon and icy Puritanism ; but this stage was short-lived, and soon no restraint was observed. The King, the " Merry Monarch ", set the pace by openly keeping mistresses and exhibiting himself everywhere in their company. The Palace of Whitehall became a place blatantly consecrated to amorous intrigues ; prostitution flaunted itself without a blush, at Court, at the theatre, everywhere. Woman became accustomed to hearing everything, and those who preserved their own virtue consented to mix freely with those who had never pretended to any.[8]

---

them on the stage doing what they should not "), it is hardly fair to expect comedy at any period to paint a good parson. B. D.]

[6] " He admires the Eloquence of *Son of a Whore*, when 'tis pronounced with a good Grace, and therefore applyes it to *every* thing : So that if his *Pipe* be faulty, or his *Purge* gripe too much, 'Tis a *Son of a Whores Pipe*, or a *Spawn of a Bitches Purge* . . . he . . . may have a Patent for the sole use (as the first Inventer) of that Noble Complement, *Let me be Damn'd, my Body made a Gridiron to Broil my Soul on, to Eternity, If I do not Madam, love you confoundedly*" (*The Character of a Town-Gallant*).—One of the favourite oaths of Sir Samuel Hearty in Shadwell's *Virtuoso* is : "*your Nose in my Breech*". Here is a declaration of the Gallant, Wittmore : " Madam,—as Gad shall save me, I'me the Son of a Whore if you are not the most Bell Person I ever saw, and if I be not damnably in love with you, but a pox take all tedious Courtship, I have a free-born and generous Spirit, and as I hate being confin'd to dull cringing, whining, flattering, and the Devil and all of Foppery, so when I give my heart I'me an Infidel, Madam, if I do not love to do't frankly and quickly." (*Sir Patient Fancy*, by Mrs. Behn, II, 1.)

[7] " His trade is making of *Love*, yet he knows no difference between that and *Lust* ; and tell him of a *Virgin* at Sixteen, he shall swear then Miracles are not ceas'd. He is so bitter an Enemy to *Marriage*, that one would suspect him born out of *Lawful Wedlock* . . . But for the most delicious Recreation of *Whoring*, he protests a Gentleman cannot live without it . . ." (*The Character of a Town-Gallant*).

[8] See Dryden's *The Kind Keeper* and Walter Scott's note prefixed to this comedy ; and the relations of Theodosia with Mrs. Friske (in Shadwell's *The Humorists*): " A vain Wench of the Town, debauched and kept by Briske."

Men abandoned themselves to the most outrageous licence.[9]
One of their favourite pastimes was to scour the streets at night
after their orgies, thrashing the guard, threatening with death
belated passers-by, sometimes slitting their noses, detaining
women, on occasion hanging them upside down, overturning
sedan-chairs, breaking windows and filling the town with cries
and oaths.   Milton at this very moment was writing :

> In Courts and Palaces he also Reigns
> And in luxurious Cities, where the noyse
> Of riot ascends above thir loftiest Towrs,
> And injury and outrage : And when Night
> Darkens the Streets, then wander forth the Sons
> Of *Belial,* flown with insolence and wine. [10]

Some, and amongst them some of the most highly placed,
sank to the lowest depths of debauchery.   The Earl of Rochester,
one of the merry-makers of this gay Court and an intimate
favourite of Charles II, used to disguise himself as a porter or a
beggar to run wild through the suburbs (it is said that the King
often accompanied him).   One day when he and the Duke of
Buckingham had fallen into disgrace, Rochester hired an inn on
the Newmarket road, and they both settled in there, serving
drinks to the carters and debauching their wives and daughters.
The King, happening to pass that way, laughed and restored
him to favour.   Another time Rochester set up trestle tables in
the middle of London, played the astrologer and mountebank
and peddled medicines : " to relieve poor girls of all the ills
and all the accidents into which they may have fallen ".   On
his own confession he was continuously drunk for five con-

---

[9] Women no less.   See the exploits of the Court ladies in Hamilton :
Mémoires de Grammont, passim.—There was a society of " Ballers " which met
to dance naked (Pepys, May 30, 1668).

[10] *Paradise Lost,* I, 496 ff.—See Oldham, *Works,* vol. III, *A Satyr, in
Imitation of the Third of Juvenal* ; Shadwell : *The Scowrers* ; Etherege : *The
Comical Revenge,* I, 2 ; *The Character of a Town-Gallant* ; in *Poems on Affairs of
State,* 1703, vol. I, p. 147 : *On the Three Dukes killing the* Beadle *on Sunday
Morning,* Feb. the 26th, 1671.—There were, to use Macaulay's expression,
several dynasties of these terrible jokers : the *Muns,* the *Tityre Tus,* the *Hectors,*
the *Scourers* or *Skimmers* ; then the *Nickers,* the *Hawkubites,* the *Mohawks,* etc.
These last three were still flourishing in the days of Addison and Swift.—
Tope in Shadwell's *Scowrers* (I, 1) says : " Why I knew the Hectors, and
before them the *Muns* and the *Titire Tu's* : they were brave fellows indeed ;
in those days a man could not go from the *Rose Tavern* to the *Piazza* once,
but he must venture his life twice."—In *The Maid's Last Prayer* by Southerne
(II, 2) Drybubb speaks of " your Dammee-Boys, your Swashes, your
Tuquoques, and your Titire-Tues ".

secutive years. He ended by dying of old age at thirty-three.[11]

Sir Charles Sedley, whom Charles II used to call the Viceroy of Apollo, was supping one evening in a London tavern with Lord Buckhurst (later the celebrated Earl of Dorset) and Sir Thomas Ogle. Flown with good food and wine, all three went out on to the balcony, hailed and abused the passers-by and exhibited themselves in the most indecent attitudes. Finally, Sedley, in order to outdo his friends, presented himself stark naked and cut such grossly coarse Rabelaisian capers that the crowd rioted, threw stones, and tried to force an entrance in order to knock him down.[12] Fashionable though licence might be, there had been a public scandal and Sedley was consequently cited before Sir Robert Hyde, senior Judge of the Court of Common Pleas, and sentenced to a heavy fine. " I am the first," Sedley commented, " that has had to pay for doing what I did." [13]

Sedley disliked being fined, however, so he begged a friend, Henry Killigrew, to intercede with the King and get the fine remitted. This devoted friend begged the money for himself, obtained it, and pocketed it to the last penny.

That is how friendship was conceived of in those days. Every lofty, or merely delicate, sentiment was similarly debased. Needless to say, there was no longer any question of religion. After the reign of the " saints " it was good taste to be ungodly. It is true that people went to church, but to Anglican churches so as to score off the Presbyterians. The church-goers in any case attended the service without reverence,[14] and lost no oppor-

---

[11] Burnet, *Some Passages in the Life and Death of John, Earl of Rochester* ; Johnson, *Lives of the English Poets,* Rochester ; Hamilton, *Mémoires de Grammont,* pp. 245 ff. ; *Forgues, John Wilmot* ; letter of Saint-Evremond (?) prefacing the works of Rochester.

[12] à Wood, *Athenæ Oxonienses,* art. Sedley (Charles) states in unvarnished words : " Putting down their breeches they excrementiz'd in the street."

[13] à Wood quotes his reply more crudely : " He thought he was the first man that paid for shiting." Pepys, July 1, 1663, also records this fact. But his first editor, Lord Braybrooke, suppresses the most characteristic part of it. Mr. Mynors Bright and Mr. Wheatley who promised a more complete text, show the same lacuna at the same spot. It is regrettable that Pepys's *Diary* is not yet in its entirety accessible to the historian, who has no means of consulting the original shorthand manuscript.

[14] " *Wildish :* The Beaux are the most constant Church-men : you shall see Troops of 'em perk'd up in Galleries, setting their Cravats " (Shadwell, *Bury-Fair,* III, 1).—See also Pepys, Oct. 14, 1660.

tunity of showing the poor opinion they held of the officiating clergymen,[15] while the clergy for their part were in no mood to irritate their congregations by ill-directed zeal.[16] Preserved by the memory of the Puritans from any excessive enthusiasm or outbursts of piety, well satisfied to have dispossessed their enemies,[17] they were concerned to display courtesy and good manners,[18] and not to shock their flocks who might have amply supplied them with texts and unwelcome lessons for their sermons. " In short," said one of them, preaching in the King's presence " if you don't live up to the Precepts of the Gospel ; but abandon yourselves to your irregular Appetites, you must expect to receive your Reward in a certain Place which 'tis not good Manners to mention here." [19]

If religion was thus handled within a sacred building, it is not difficult to imagine what was made of it outside. People were atheists,[20] or rather called themselves atheists, for this also

[15] I doubt if there appears in all the dramas of this period, a single priest, Protestant or other, ancient or modern, who is not either odious or ridiculous.—See a characteristic scene in Pepys, Dec. 25, 1662 : the Bishop of Winchester is preaching in the Chapel of Whitehall against the pleasures of the Court ; his audience laughs while he is speaking.

[16] " I took a turn with Mr. Evelyn . . . talking of the badness of the Government, where nothing but wickedness, and wicked men and women command the King . . . that much of it arises . . . from the negligence of the Clergy, that a Bishop shall never be seen about him." (Pepys, April 26, 1667. See also ibid., Nov. 9, 1663, and Feb. 16, 1667–8.)

[17] In 1661 two thousand Presbyterian ministers were driven from their churches.

[18] John Stoughton, *The Church of the Restoration*, vol. I, especially pp. 470–3 and 507–12. When the Plague broke out the entire body of clergy fled from London (ibid., vol. I, p. 337).

[19] " What a fine thing it is to be well-manner'd upon Occasion ! In the Reign of King *Charles* the Second, a certain worthy Divine at *Whitehall*, thus address'd himself to the Auditory at the Conclusion of his Sermon : In short . . ." (Tom Brown, *Works*, vol. IV, p. 124 : Laconicks, *or New Maxims of* State *and* Conversation).—See also Pope, *Moral Essays*, Epistle iv, l. 150 and note.

[20] " . . . They professed themselves atheists, both in word and deed— smiling at the name of the devil, . . . and maintaining with oaths that there were no other angels than those in petticoats, denying any essential difference between good and evil, and deeming conscience a check suited merely to frighten children." (*Proteus Redivivus*, quoted by Malcolm, p. 167.)—" His religion (for now and then he will be pratling of that too) is pretendedly *Hobbian* : And he Swears the *Leviathan* may supply all the lost Leaves of *Solomon*, yet he never saw it in his life, and for ought he knows, it may be a *Treatise* about catching of *Sprats*, or new Regulating the *Green-land* Fishing Trade. However, the Rattle of it at *Coffee-houses*, has taught him to . . . maintain that there are no *Angels* but those in *Petticoats* : And therefore he defies *Heaven* worse than *Maximin* (one of Dryden's characters, see p. 41) ; imagines *Hell*, only a *Hot house* to Flux in for a *Clap*, and calls the *Devil*, the

was a matter of fashion : you professed atheism for the same reason as M. Jourdain wore his embroidered flowers, upside down.[20a] These people were not even sceptics : they denied, so as not to be taken for Roundheads, and to save themselves the trouble of thinking ;—just as ready to believe a thing one minute as they had been to deny it the moment before. Rochester suddenly became edifying when he felt his end approaching ; after having paid court to the Muse of gallantry up to the age of eighty, Waller took to writing pious verses [21]; Charles II on his deathbed surreptitiously received the Eucharist at the hands of a Roman Catholic priest ; a large number verted to Roman Catholicism on the accession of James II.

In short, the sole aim of this Court was pleasure. In Rochester's words :

> Our Sphere of Action is Life's Happiness
> And he who thinks beyond, thinks like an Ass.[22]

The Puritans saw human life as a vale of tears, a road strewn with trials and struggles by which man purchased life eternal. Their successors contented themselves with the present life. But to enjoy it properly—and to make up for the fasting under the Republic a man had to take two mouthfuls at a time—and merrily to perform life's pilgrimage, nothing embarrassing could be tolerated, all impedimenta had to be scrapped. Whence do we come ? Whither are we going ? What matter ! Here we are ; that's enough. Virtue, modesty—lies ! Pity, honour, courage [23]—prejudices of petty men ! You tell me some women are virtuous ? Those are the ones who sell their favours dear. You say some men are honest ? They are either liars or fools.[24]

Parsons *Bugbear*, and sometimes the *Civil Old Gentleman in Black* " (*The Character of a Town-Gallant*).

[20a] Molière, *Le Bourgeois Gentilhomme*, II, 5.

[21] Johnson, *Lives of the English Poets*, Waller.

[22] Rochester, *Satire against Man*, Works, vol. I, p. 5. " She was a Woman of Sense, and by consequence a Lover of Pleasure " (The History of the *Life* and *Memoirs* of Mrs. Behn, By one of the Fair Sex. Prefacing the edition of her novels).

[23] " . . . all men would be Cowards, if they durst " (Rochester, *Satire against Man*, Works, vol. I, p. 7). We shall see that he dared.—The Duke of Buckingham had a duel with Lord Ossory ; he gave him Chelsea Fields as the rendezvous and went off to await him elsewhere (Cobbett, *Parliamentary History*, I, 342).

[24] " He denies there is any Essential Difference betwixt *Good* and *Evil*, deems *Conscience* a thing only fit for *Children*, and ascribes all *Honesty* to *simplicity* and an unpractisness in the *Ways* and *Methods* of the *Town* " (*The Character of a Town-Gallant*).

Men of wit were not taken in by such nonsense. So when he wanted money, the King of England thought it quite natural to sell himself to France.[24a] Those around him were no less unscrupulous. Aubrey de Vere, Earl of Oxford, was in love with an actress who rejected his advances ; to get his way he agreed to marry her but brought a soldier disguised as a priest to perform the ceremony. When she discovered the base trickery of which she had been the victim, she flung herself at the King's feet demanding justice. To the King, however, her betrayer's conduct seemed perfectly natural and he decreed that an annual pension was quite adequate compensation.[25] Villiers, Duke of Buckingham, lover of the Countess of Shrewsbury, killed her husband in a duel, while she, in the dress of a page-boy, held his horse's bridle. Buckingham boasted that she granted him her caresses before he had removed his blood-stained clothes.[26] Incidents of this type were common. The morals of the day are summed up in the following maxim, borrowed from one of the heroes of a contemporary novel :

A man of Wit cou'd not be a Knave or Villain.[27]

When pleasure called him nothing halted him.

II

Art, literature : songs etc. satires, novels

Literature and the arts naturally took their place among the pleasures, since the Puritans had banned them. Their Parliament had decreed that all pictures in the royal collection which represented the second person of the Trinity or the Virgin Mary, should be burnt, and the rest sold.[28] They were no less

---

[24a] [The politics of this transaction are not so simple as would appear from this statement. In so far as Louis and Charles both wished to re-establish absolute monarchy in England, Charles might well regard Louis as his ally, and honourably accept funds from him. Louis might possibly guess that Charles was double-crossing him, but that is another story, not rare in politics. B. D.]

[25] Hamilton, *Mémoires de Grammont*, pp. 220-1.

[26] *Biographia Britannica*, Villiers.—" 'Tis said the duke slept with her in his bloody shirt " (Spence, p. 164).

[27] *Oroonoko, or the Royal Slave*, by Mrs. Behn ; in the volume of her novels.

[28] Cromwell succeeded nevertheless in preserving for England the Raphael cartoons which are now in the South Kensington Museum (Lecky, vol. I, p. 528).

insensitive to music.[29] As for literature, they had neither the taste nor the time to read any but polemical writings, and the drama had been rigorously put on their index of forbidden works.[30] So the new Court restored the arts to favour. Painters were encouraged (Lely,[31] Kneller, Cooper the miniaturist) and musicians also (Grabut, Purcell), while everyone took to writing literature. You could not be a gallant without being a man of wit : the two epithets became synonymous. The most fashionable men, the most brilliant courtiers were critics, authors, connoisseurs of literature : the Earl of Rochester, Sir Charles Sedley, Villiers Duke of Buckingham, the Earl of Mulgrave, Sir Car Scroop, Edmund Waller, Lord Buckhurst, the Duke and Duchess of Newcastle and innumerable others.[31a]

Since women were the main preoccupation of the day, they naturally set the tone, and gallant little verses composed for them were from the first the rage. All the poets of the Court set to work to sing of them.

It must be admitted that the singers' muse showed no overmastering inspiration. It was exhausted after a few strophes, or to be accurate after a few couplets, for it ran more to songs than to anything else, though it occasionally ventured on an elegy.[32] The Restoration Muse did not, it is true, aim very high, it sought neither lofty ideas nor style : its ideal was a slight, delicate thought in simple and harmonious form. Its poetry

[29] See an interesting chapter on Puritanism in relation to music in Chappell, vol. II, p. 401.

[30] Prynne's celebrated book, *Histrio-Mastix*, gives a good indication of the Puritans' views on questions of amusement. The book is rare and as there is no copy in the Bibliothèque Nationale I quote its full title in my bibliography. The title is instructive.

[31] Sir Peter Lely was knighted by Charles II.

[31a] [Waller and the Duke of Newcastle, and the Duchess had " taken to literature " well before the Restoration. See note 59a. B. D.]

[32] In his *Essay on Poetry*, Sheffield, Earl of Mulgrave (later Duke of Buckinghamshire), began with songs :

" First then, of *SONGS*, which now so much abound
Without his *Song* no Fop is to be found . . .
Tho' nothing seems more easie, yet no part
Of *Poetry* requires a *nicer* Art."

Then comes the elegy :

" Next *ELEGY* . . .
The Praise of *Beauty*, *Valor*, *Wit* contains
And there too oft despairing *Love* complains . . . "

Then the ode ; but he can quote no lyric belonging to the reign of Charles II.

was called " witty " [33] ; the most flattering term that could be
applied to it was to say that it was " ingenious ". The subjects
sung varied little. Poetry devoted itself wholly to " beauty "
and " beauties ". Lord Buckhurst on the eve of a great naval
battle against the Dutch covered himself with glory by writing
verses :

> To all you *Ladies* now at Land
> We *Men* at Sea indite ; etc.[34]

Confessions of love, disdain, desire, contempt, absence, sighs,
inconstancy—such are the usual themes which the poets em-
broider with their monotonous variations. They offer sweet
nothings to Chloris (Dorset) ; to Amoret, to Sacharissa (Waller) ;
to Celimene, to Phillis, to Celia, to Thireis, to Aurelia, to Amar-
anta (Sedley). They shrink neither from sentimentality nor
subtleties :

> While in this park I sing, the list'ning deer
> Attend my passion, and forget to fear :
> When to the beeches I report my flame,
> They bow their heads, as if they felt the same :
> To Gods appealing, when I reach their Bow'rs
> With loud complaints, they answer me in show'rs.
> To Thee a wild and cruel soul is giv'n,
> More deaf than trees, and prouder than the heav'n ! [35]

That is the sort of thing, when it does not descend into sheer
silliness. Waller inscribes verses to a " Lady who can do any
thing but sleep when she pleaseth " and others to a " Lady who
can sleep when she pleases ". He sings " Of a Tree cut in
Paper ", of a " Card that her Majesty tore at Omber ".[36] The
Earl of Roscommon, famed for the seriousness of his inspirations
in this frivolous century,[37] wrote stanzas " On a young Lady

---

[33] It is from this period that English dates the noun *witticism* : " *A mighty
Wittycism (if you will pardon a new word !) * "—Dryden, Preface to *The State
of Innocence.*

[34] Song, *Written at* Sea, *in the first* Dutch-War, 1665, *the Night before an
Engagement.* (Printed in the Works of Rochester, vol. II, p. 53.)

[35] Waller, *Works,* p. 42. *At* Pens-hurst.

[36] Waller, *The* Apology *of* Sleep, *Works,* pp. 17, 35 ; also pp. 144, 204.
[The title of a poem is not necessarily a good guide as to its merit. " On
a girdle " is not promising, but Waller's poem is one of the most famous
in the language. The poems on the tree and on the card are blameless
trivialities of " occasional " verse : but the ones on sleeping or sleepless ladies
have a certain poetic value. B. D.]

[37]   " Unhappy Dryden ! in all Charles's days.
    Roscommon only boasts unspotted lays." (Pope.)

who sung finely, and was afraid of a cold " or an elegy " On the Death of a Lady's Dog ".[38]

All these graces, however, all these poetic delicacies, were nothing but false coin. Scratch the elegant nobleman of those days and you find at once the ungoverned and shameless debauchee. The poet of the day is no better : his playful flirtation is wholly superficial ; if he is at pains laboriously to concoct little verses apparently tender and languorous, his main desire is to appeal to the physical senses, to excite desire, and to this end he does not hesitate to use the vivid, at need the coarsest phrase.[39]

But it was particularly in their satires that the " gentlemen-poets " gave a free rein to their pen in such matters. The satires, or as they were then called, the " lampoons ",[40] became in fact the refuge of those at Court who could boast neither wit nor poetic talent. To speak evil of your neighbour is within the powers of the meanest intelligence, and the satirists of those days aimed at nothing else. An old French poet wrote, " I bear no malice against fools, but against Folly."[41] The Restor-

---

[38] *Works*, pp. 53, 54.
[Beljame might have remembered that Apollo does not always keep his bow at full stretch. Roscommon was a good poet in his own line, the *Essay on Translated Verse* being justly well known. One wonders whether, if Beljame had been studying a later period, he would have commented adversely upon Gray for writing on a cat drowned in a bowl of goldfish. B. D.]

[39]   " For *Songs* and *Verses* mannerly obscene,
  That can stir *Nature* up by Springs unseen,
  And, without forcing Blushes, warm the Queen :
  Sedley has that prevailing, gentle Art,
  That can with a *Resistless Pow'r* impart
  The *Loosest* Wishes to the *Chastest* Heart,
  Raise such a Conflict, kindle such a Fire
  Betwixt declining Virtue and Desire ;
  Till the poor vanquish'd Maid dissolves away
  In Dreams all Night, in Sighs and Tears all Day."
      (Rochester, Horace's *Tenth Satire of the First Book
        imitated. Works*, vol. I, p. 10.)

Such was the poetic art of this type. To see it in practice the reader has only to choose amongst the verses of the fine gentlemen of that day.
[This again is something of an overstatement : the proposition is true only in the main. B. D.]

[40]   " *Lord Lampoon* and *Monsieur Song*
  Who sought her [the Muse's] love, and promis'd for't
  To make her famous at the Court."
      (Otway, *The Poets Complaint of his Muse*.)

[41] Du Lorens, 7th Satire : Je ne'en veux point aux sots, j'en veux à la sottise.

ation satirists laid no claim to such detachment ; they never rose to a general point of view ; they dreamt of nothing but personal attacks. They hurl abuse at people, and since poetry is all the fashion they hurl it in verse. From the King downwards, who often appears under the nickname of " Old Rowley ", no one is spared. With him everyone runs the gauntlet of a vocabulary drawn from the pigsty and the gutter. No one who has not read these lampoons could conceive the flood of mud and filth with which they unashamedly overflow ; having read them, you are driven to marvel how people could be found to write such stuff in such quantities, and readers to understand it when written, especially in a period so near our own time and in a country which has so great a reputation for reserve if not for prudery. But there is no use labouring this point. Apart from the fact that quotations from these satires would, to say the least, be difficult, the drama bears more revealing though weaker witness to the prevailing social conditions. At their worst, a few obscene writings, which may circulate privately and be read in a whisper, need not damn the moral reputation of a period. What a more numerous, more sensitive, more impressionable public openly listens to in a theatre, has far greater significance. Without saying more on the subject, it will suffice to cite as specimens of the coarseness of this satiric verse, Rochester's two satires on the King [42], Etherege's *The Lady of Pleasure* [43] and an imitation of Boileau's *Festin Ridicule* from the uninhibited pen of Villiers, Duke of Buckingham. [44]

Having said so much, it is only fair to recognize that these verses, never lofty and often insipid and coarse, have at moments a touch of elegance, and display a genuine feeling for harmony. [45] It should in justice be added that their noble authors have a real taste and feeling for literature, not very deep perhaps, not very

[42] A *Satire which the* King *took out of his Pocket*—*The Satire on the* King, *for which he was banished the* Court ; and *turned* Mountebank (*Works*, vol. I, pp. 20 ff. and pp. 24–5).

[43] *The* Lady *of* Pleasure. A Satyr. *By Sir* George Etheridge, Knight. Printed in the *Miscellaneous Works* of Buckingham (Villiers).

[44] Timon, a Satyr, *In Imitation of Monsieur* Boileau [*sic*] (in *Miscellaneous Works*). This satire is included also in the works of Rochester (vol. I, p. 126) under the title of *The Rehearsal. A* Satire. It is possible that the two friends collaborated to produce this charming work.—See also " A Faithful Catalogue of our most Eminent *Ninnies*, Written by the Earl of *Dorset* in the year 1683 " in the works of Rochester (vol. II, p. 23).

[45] For instance, Waller's " Go, lovely rose ! " and Sedley's " *Love* still has something of the Sea " both justly included in the anthologies.

acute, but on the whole worthy of note. The writers have an up-to-date acquaintance with French literature. They know the classic poets, the Latin poets at any rate, especially Horace. When they want something a shade better than usual they translate from the classics. The Earl of Roscommon makes an English verse translation of Horace's *Ars Poetica* [46]; Rochester imitates the tenth satire of the first book of Horace and the first satire of Juvenal [47]; Sedley translates in verse the fourth book of the *Georgics*. [48] It is of course a sign of weakness that they cannot escape from their own rut without other men's aid ; but it also demonstrates a degree of culture which must in justice be placed to the credit of their account.

After poetry came romantic fiction. It ran on the same lines ; it was gallant too. For years England had rejoiced in Mademoiselle de Scudéry. Her *Clélie* was translated in 1656 (the very year that it appeared in France). The first part of La Calprenède's *Cleopatra* had been translated as early as 1652. [49] Preoccupied as it was with women, the Restoration could not fail to take pleasure in these affected pretentious writings, and people continued to wander in the Land of Tender Sentiment. Ladies found their favourite reading in the most mawkish of these novels [50]; and in writing the dedication of his tragedy *Aureng-Zebe*, Dryden takes pains to defend his play to the ladies by quoting the example of *Le Grand Cyrus*. The theatre borrowed from this romantic literature a whole species of play, and every-day conversation was steeped in its style and vocabulary. A simple bookseller, John Dunton, married Miss Elizabeth Annesley in 1682. She was his " Beautiful Iris " and signed herself " Iris ", while he signed his letters " Philaret ". He called his wife " my beautiful conqueror " and " my dear captive " and published a portrait of " Iris " written by " Arsinda ", with a portrait of " Philaret " by the ingenious " Cleonta, sister of the Beautiful Iris ". [51] Mrs. Katherine Philips, " the matchless Orinda ", bestowed on her husband the name of Antenor, and

[46] *Works*, 1753.

[47] Horace's *Tenth Satire of the First Book imitated* (*Works*, vol. I, p. 10), *Imitation of the First Satire of* Juvenal (ibid., p. 15).

[48] The Fourth Book of Virgil (*Poetical Works*).

[49] See the Bibliography s.vv. Scudéry and La Calprenède.

[50] Pepys, Dec. 7, 1660 : " My wife in Great Cyrus till 12 at night."

[51] See The *Life and Errors of John Dunton*, pp. 75 ff.—Swift was still under this spell when he called Miss Waring " Varina ", Miss Esther Johnson " Stella " and Miss Vanhomrigh " Vanessa ".

on his friends the names Silvander, Cratander, Poliarchus, Lucasia, etc.[52]

The Restoration novel, then, drew its inspiration from Mademoiselle de Scudéry and her like. But the gallants of the day needed some livelier and less severe reading. They got exactly what they wanted from " the ingenious Madame Aphara Behn ", or as they called her " the admirable " or even " the divine Astræa ".

Her story of *Oroonoko, or the Royal Slave* written, amongst others, " at the command of King Charles II ", was so popular that more than thirty years afterwards the poet Southerne took it as the subject of one of his most successful tragedies.[53] Yet this famous story has not survived, and the same abyss of forgetfulness has swallowed all the romantic literature of the period. It is all the more necessary to dwell on it for a moment, since it reflects one whole facet of the Restoration spirit.[54]

[52] See her *Poems*, passim.

[The fashion recurs at intervals, and is not peculiar to this period, nor originated by it. It is not, perhaps, surprising that the Sidney circle, with Spenser, should have adopted it, as they seem to have done. It is more surprising that in 1730 John and Charles Wesley should, in a special circle, have been called respectively Cyrus and Araspes, while Mrs. Pendarves was known as Aspasia, and Ann Granville as Selina, etc. There is no special significance to be attached to this recurring social-literary game. B. D.]

[53] *Oroonoko* (1696).—Southerne borrowed the tragic part of *The Fatal Marriage* from another of Mrs. Behn's novels, *The Fair Vow-breaker* ; see his dedication.—Here is a trifling fact which shows the long-enduring popularity of the novel *Oroonoko*. The heroine of the story is called Imoinda. Now, in 1756 John Buncle met a young woman with whom he had been in love : " What (I said) *Miss Wolf of Balineskay* ? *O my Imoinda !* And snatching her to my arms, I almost stifled her with kisses." (*The Life of John Buncle, Esqr*, by Thomas Amory, vol. II, p. 183.)

[54] The oldest edition of Mrs. Behn's novels quoted by Lowndes is 1698 ; but *Oroonoko* must date from the beginning of the reign of Charles II, for it contains an allusion to the production of Dryden's *Indian Queen* in 1665 as to something recent. The 1705 edition is the earliest I have been able to find in the British Museum.

[Oroonoko is perhaps the earliest example of " the noble savage ", and the work had a great influence in France, being translated into French in 1745 and in 1788, possibly oftener. The book has been described as " the first English philosophical novel containing dissertations upon abstract subjects, such as the religion of humanity " (Sir Paul Harvey in *The Oxford Companion to English Literature*). Mrs. Behn's novels were edited by E. A. Baker in 1905, and her plays by Montague Summers in 1915. She was later the subject of a monograph by Miss V. Sackville-West. The revival in the interest in her works took place since this book was written, and Beljame could not now say that either she or her works are " forgotten ". The *D.N.B.* article suggests that she was to the writers of her day what George Sand was to the writers of France in the last century. B. D.]

Oroonoko is the grandson and sole heir of the King of Cormantin (Kormantine) on the Gold Coast, where the English go to fetch slaves for their colonies. The inhabitants of this country are children of Nature, whom the author compares to our first parents "before the Fall". Oroonoko, however, is a model of courtesy, honour and generosity; he knows French, English and Spanish and even a little history (he admires the Romans and grieves for the death of Charles I of England). It is unnecessary to say that he is handsome and capable of the loftiest sentiments, above all made to love and to be loved.

He meets Imoinda, as perfect in her way as he in his:

Having made his first Complements, and presented her an hundred and fifty Slaves in Fetters, he told her with his Eyes, that he was not insensible of her Charms; while *Imoinda*, who wish'd for nothing more than so glorious a Conquest, was pleas'd to believe, she understood that silent Language of new-born Love; and, from that moment put on all her additions to Beauty.

The Prince return'd to Court with quite another Humour than before; and though he did not speak much of the fair *Imoinda*, he had the pleasure to hear all his Followers speak of nothing but the Charms of that Maid, insomuch that, even in the presence of the old King, they were extolling her, and heightening, if possible, the Beauties they had found in her: so that nothing else was talk'd of, no other sound was heard in every Corner where there were Whisperers, but *Imoinda! Imoinda!*

So beautiful a love was bound to run unsmoothly. The old King (he was over a hundred years old) is fired by these descriptions and sends Imoinda the royal veil, which compels her on pain of death to attend at his harem. She can but obey, and the amiable monarch receives her at the bath.

Despair ensues for Oroonoko, and a painful conflict between respect for his sovereign-grandsire and his love. At last he calms himself and decides to hide his passion and his troubles, reassured by reflecting that in view of his age the King will be his rival rather in desire than deed.

The King who has not failed to get wind of his grandson's love has kept him somewhat at arm's length, but seeing him so calm and peaceful, supposes him cured, and invites him to a feast at which his lady-love is present. During the meal he leaves his guests to lead Imoinda into an adjacent room where his luckless rival sees: " a Bed of State made ready, with Sweets and Flowers for the Dalliance of the King ".

Oroonoko has meantime succeeded in getting into touch

with inmates of the harem ; he contrives to see Imoinda, to
tell her of his love and " ravished in a moment, what his old
Grandfather had been endeavouring for so many Months ".
Unfortunately he is surprised ; the King sends him back to the
army and has Imoinda sold as a slave, telling her lover that she
has been killed.

The youth is disconsolate, he heaves many sighs, weeps
copious tears, but comforts himself just enough to continue
living and overcome his country's enemy, Jamoan, " a Man
very gallant, and of excellent graces, and fine parts ", who,
after having been defeated, becomes his best friend.

After this victory Oroonoko, deceived by an English captain,
is treacherously seized and sold as a slave to Surinam. There
he commands the admiration of all by his merits, entrances
the English ladies by his grace, and finds among the slaves in
the colony the beautiful Imoinda, a slave like himself, hiding
herself under the name of Clemene. He is allowed to marry
her and the tale of their love so greatly touches the authorities
that they promise to set the couple free and send them both
back to their own country. There is delay in fulfilling this
promise, and Oroonoko who has once already been deceived
by a European, suspects new treachery, enlists the negroes'
interest in his case and organizes a general rising of the slaves
in the colony. The Deputy-Governor, alarmed, suggests discussion, and by fair words induces Oroonoko to lay down his
arms. No sooner is the over-trustful youth disarmed than he is
seized and flogged. The " royal slave " trembling with wrath
at such an outrage swears to be avenged. He flees to the woods
with his pregnant wife. That she may not fall into the white
men's power he kills her, and she is happy to die by his hand.
Imoinda dead, her lover lingers for two days weeping beside
her body. There he is found by the Deputy Governor's people
who have the greatest difficulty in approaching him. Finally,
however, they capture him and put him to death with refined
torture : cutting off his limbs one after the other. Calm and
heroic, he smokes his pipe till his last arm is amputated. " Thus
died," writes the author in conclusion :

this Great Man ; worthy of a better Fate, and a more sublime wit
than mine to write his Praise : Yet, I hope, the Reputation of my
Pen is considerable enough to make his Glorious Name to survive
to all Ages, with that of the Brave, the Beautiful and the Constant
Imoinda.

It is obvious that in the matter of fine sentiment and high-falutin language Mrs. Behn is a worthy rival of Molière's *Précieuses Ridicules*. She differs from them in two points, however : she does not impose such severe tasks on her readers (the volume of her novels contains eight other narratives besides the *Royal Slave*) and, secondly, she spices her gallantry with a dash of sensuality. Her heroes imitate the style of the Hotel de Rambouillet, but the style only ; none of them is inclined like Montausier to languish for fourteen years.

At other times, however, they wallow in the most utter bathos, for instance, as in *The Lover's Watch, or The Art of Courtship.*[55] Here is the " Argument ":

'*Tis* in the most Happy and August Court of the Best and Greatest Monarch of the World, that *Damon*, a young Nobleman, whom we will render under that Name, languishes for a Maid of Quality,[56] who will give us leave to call her *Iris* :

Their births are equally Illustrious ; they are both Young ; their Beauty such, as I do not too nicely particularize, lest I should discover (which I am not permitted to do) who these charming Lovers are. Let it suffice that *Iris* is the most fair and accomplisht Person that ever adorn'd a Court : and that *Damon* is only worthy of the Glory of her Favour ; for he has all that can render him lovely in the fair Eyes of the Amiable *Iris*. Nor is he Master of those Superficial Beauties alone, that please at first Sight ; he can charm the Soul with a thousand Arts of Wit and Gallantry. And in a word, may say, without flattering either, that there is no one Beauty, no one Grace, no perfection of Mind and Body, that wants to compleat a Victory on both sides.

The Agreement of Age, Fortunes, Quality and Humours in these two fair Lovers, made the impatient *Damon* hope, that nothing would oppose his Passion ; and if he saw himself every Hour languishing for the Adorable Maid, he did not however despair : And if *Iris* sigh'd, it was not for fear of being one day more happy.

Here we have the refinement of refinement. Iris has to go into the country. It is impossible for Damon to follow her. He consoles himself by writing her the sweetest letters in the world ; and she, in payment of a wager she had lost to Damon sends him " the watch ".

[55] This is an imitation of two gallant works of Balthazar de Bonnecorse, the author whom Boileau has linked with Pradon in the following epigram :

" Venez, Pradon et Bonnecorse,
Grands écrivains de même force . . ."

For the complete titles, see my Bibliography.

[56] Madame la comtesse d'Escarbagnas would have enjoyed reading these novels : all the characters are " persons of quality ".

The face of the watch shows no vulgar numerals, but instead indicates how a tender lover should employ each hour of his day, while a Cupid points the tip of his arrow to each successive hour :

Eight a Clock. *Agreeable Reverie.*—Nine a Clock. *Design to please no Body.*—Ten a Clock. *Reading of Letters.*—Eleven a Clock. *The Hour to Write in.*—Twelve a Clock. *Indispensible Duty.*—One a Clock. *Forc'd Entertainment.*—Two a Clock. *Dinner Time.*—Three a Clock. *Visits to Friends.*—Four a Clock. *General Conversation.*—Five a Clock. *Dangerous Visits.*—Six a Clock. *Walk without Design.*—Seven a Clock. *Voluntary Retreat.*—Eight a Clock. *Impatient Demands.*—Nine a Clock. *Melancholy Reflections.*—Ten a Clock. *Reflections.*—Eleven a Clock. *Supper.*—Twelve a Clock. *Complaisance.*—One a Clock. *Impossibility to Sleep.*—Two a Clock. *Conversation in Dreams.*—Three a Clock. *Capricious Suffering in Dreams.*—Four a Clock. *Jealousie in Dreams.*—Five a Clock. *Quarrels in Dreams.*—Six a Clock. *Accommodation in Dreams.*—Seven a Clock. *Divers Dreams.*[57]

He then gets up, to begin all over again.

In sending Damon the watch, Iris adjures him to guard it tenderly. Damon replies by pointing out that the watch had no case. He suggests the following scheme : the case for the watch should be in the form of a heart and be decorated with their initials and in addition the initials of the words : *Love Extream . . . Reciprocal Love . . . Constant Love . . . Secret Love.* The fastening of the case should be formed by two hands and inscribed with the motto : *Inviolable Faith.*[58]

Gallant reflections and rhymes are throughout intermingled with the tale. Such embroideries as : " These are little paths all strewn with roses."

Nor is this the end. Our author's imagination is not so quickly exhausted. To balance the watch Damon sends his lady love a mirror : " The Lady's Looking-Glass to dress Herself by : or, the Art of Charming. This speaks to her of *The Shape of* Iris . . . Iris's *Complexion* . . . Iris's *Hair* . . . Iris's *Eyes* . . . *The Mouth of* Iris . . . *The Neck of* Iris . . . *The Arms and Hands of* Iris . . . *The Grace and Air of* Iris . . . *The Discretion of* Iris . . . *The Goodness and Complaisance of* Iris . . . *The Wit of* Iris . . . *The Modesty of* Iris . . . Once started on this line there was

[57] Here the *ingenious* Mrs. Behn's imagination would seem to have given out : the adjective *divers* is not very gallant.
[58] Note that during the whole narrative it is not clear whether Damon and Iris are betrothed or are vulgar paramours. It is more delicate not to allude to marriage.

no reason why he should ever stop.   Let us leave him to continue
by himself.

III

So, what the fashionable society of the Restoration asked
first and foremost of literature, was gallant and sensual verse,
or free and romantic narrative.   But the writers of these things
were all wealthy people of high rank, for whom writing was
merely a recreation and a means of shining in society.   They
were amateurs, not authors.[59]

Side by side with them, however, there were others who were
forced to seek a livelihood by plying the author's trade on which
they depended for their living.   It is with these latter that this
book intends to deal.

The years of the Civil War and the Republic had been an
iron age for literature.   For eighteen years there had been an
interregnum in public taste.   No theatre, no books (except
polemics).[59a]

[59] All the writers so far quoted belonged to the aristocracy except Waller,
Etherege and Mrs. Behn.   But Waller and Etherege were rich and in favour
at Court.   As for Mrs. Behn, she was a political spy in the pay of Charles II,
and as a gallant lady she had other sources of income than her pen.   Her
writing, moreover, was not confined to novels.—See *Biographia Britannica*, under
Waller (Edmund), Etherege and Behn.

[59a] [Little theatre, true, till Davenant's *Siege of Rhodes* in 1656 ; yet some
surreptitious playing (See L. Hotson : *The Commonwealth and Restoration Stage*).
But reference to any compilation, such as the Oxford *Annals of English Literature*,
or the Tables in the relevant volume of the Oxford History of English Literature, will show that the output in books was as great in these eighteen years
as in the previous eighteen.   I name a selection, omitting all polemics.   1642.
Denham, *Cooper's Hill* ; Fuller, *Holy State*.   1643. Baker, *Chronicles of the Kings
of England* ; Browne, *Religio Medici* (authorized).   1644. Donne, *Biathanatos* ;
Quarles, *Barnabas and Boanerges*.   1645. Milton, *Poems* ;   Waller, *Poems* ;
Howell, *Epistolae Ho-elianae*.   1646. Browne, *Vulgar Errors* ;   Crashaw, Quarles,
Shirley, Suckling and Vaughan, various volumes of poems.   1647. Corbet,
Cleveland, Stanley, and More all published volumes of poetry.   1648.
J. Beaumont, *Psyche* ;   Herrick, *Hesperides* ;   Hooker, *Ecclesiastical Polity*, vi and
viii.   1649. D. of Newcastle, *The Country Captain* ;   Lovelace, *Lucasta* ;   Donne,
Fifty Sermons ;   Taylor, *Great Exemplar* ;   Lord Herbert, *Life of Henry VIII* ;
R. B., *Lachrymae Musarum* (poems by Dryden, Marvell, Herrick and Denham).
1650. Davenant, *Gondibert* ;   Vaughan, *Silex Scintillans* ;   Raleigh, *Essays and
Observations* ;   Taylor, *Holy Living*.   1651. Stanley, *Poems* ;   Vaughan, *Olor
Iscanus* ;   Donne, *Essays in Divinity* and *Letters* ;   Taylor, *Holy Dying* ;   Wotton,

Cowley and Denham were exiled with their sovereign ; Waller was awed into silence by the rigour of the puritanic spirit ; and even the muse of Milton was scared from him by the clamour of religious and political controversy, and returned, like a sincere friend, only to cheer the adversity of one who had neglected her during his career of worldly importance.[60]

When Charles II ascended his father's throne, writers could not contain themselves for joy. It seemed that after long wandering in the wilderness, they had reached at last the Promised Land. They dreamt of marvellous grapes, of rivers flowing with milk and honey, and they immediately vied with each other in trying to attract the attention and favours of the King. Panegyrics and dithyrambs poured in from all directions. Each one reckoned that the King would rain down on him gifts and sinecures.

Disillusionment was swift.

Even those who had quite special claims on the royal favour reaped nothing but indifference. Cowley, who had gone into exile to follow the Queen-Mother to Paris, who had devoted himself heart and soul to the Royalist cause and had endured prison in consequence : even he was brushed aside when the hour of recompense arrived. Yet he had not let himself be overlooked. He had celebrated the Restoration in a pindaric *Ode upon His Majesties Restauration and Return* [61] and requested to be made

---

Reliquiae Wottonianae ; Walton, *Life of Wotton.* 1652. Herbert, *Remains* ; Crashaw, *Carmen Deo Nostro* ; Greville, *Life of Sidney* ; Vaughan, *Mount of Olives.* 1653. Cleveland, *Poems* ; Basse, *Pastorals* ; Taylor, *Sermons* ; Urquhart, *Rabelais* ; Walton, *Compleat Angler.* 1654. Johnson, *History of New England* ; Orrery, *Parthenissa.* 1655. Poems by Marvell, Waller, and Philips ; Dugdale, *Monasticon Anglicanum* ; Fuller, three *Histories* ; Taylor, *Golden Grove* ; Vaughan, *Hermetical Physics.* 1656. Cowley, *Poems* ; Denham, *Destruction of Troy* ; Osborne, *Advice to a Son* ; Duchess of Newcastle, *Nature's Pictures.* 1657. Cleveland, *Poems* ; King, *Poems* ; Raleigh, *Remains* ; Taylor, *Discourses and Friendship.* 1658. Waller and Godolphin, *Passion of Dido* ; Browne, *Urn Burial* ; Ussher, *Annals of the World.* 1659. Further poems (posthumous) by Lovelace and Suckling ; Chamberlayne, *Pharonnida* ; Baxter, *Holy Commonwealth* ; Evelyn, *Character of England* ; More, *Immortality of the Soul.* This is only a selection from the usual lists. Besides such works, a number of the plays of the previous period were printed for the first time in these years. There was obviously plenty to read. Far from there being literary starvation, there was not even literary scarcity. B. D.]

[60] Walter Scott, *The Life of John Dryden* prefixed to his works. [Scott is not quite right here. Milton's early poems were published in 1645. He deliberately put poetry aside so as to serve, as a good citizen, the cause he believed in. Nevertheless, his sonnets were nearly all written in this period, and he probably began *Paradise Lost* in 1656. B. D.]

[61] *Works.*

Director of *The Savoy*,[62] a post which had been promised him both by Charles I and Charles II. Turned away, rejected, criticised,[63] he bitterly complained ; finally, weary of his devotion, " Melancholy Cowley ", as he called himself, withdrew from the World and the Court, and died in retreat seven years after the Restoration. When he was dead the King remembered him : " Mr. Cowley," he said, " has not left a better man behind him in England."[64]

Butler, whose poem *Hudibras* did good service to the Royalists by enlisting laughter on their side, was treated no better than Cowley. When the first three cantos of his burlesque epic appeared in 1663, Lord Buckhurst introduced the poem to the Court. It at once evoked general enthusiasm. The Presbyterian Don Quixote, setting out for war with his stable-boy Ralph, was hailed with shouts of triumphant laughter. People felt revenged on the *Saints* by this merciless satire on their ridiculous ways. The King was for ever quoting lines of *Hudibras* and the courtiers set about learning it by heart, so as to be able to quote it like their master. All eyes expectantly waited to see " the rain of gold " which was bound to be showered on the author. He himself, living at the time an obscure and precarious life, expected it no less eagerly than his admirers. The royal sky remained without a cloud.

The second part appeared in 1664. The nation's interest was kindled once again, and the author once more vaunted to the skies. Praise was his sole reward.[65] There is, it is true, a story that Clarendon who was then Lord Chancellor promised him posts, but the truth of this is questionable, and it is certain that Butler got nothing. There is another story that the King

[62] *The Savoy* was originally a hospital (now no longer existing) which had gradually become a refuge for professional beggars, a sort of *Cour des Miracles*. The post of Director which Cowley coveted was of course a sinecure. —See W. Thornbury, *Haunted London*, chap. VI.

[63] Amongst other things his *Cutter of Coleman-Street* was made a matter of reproach. It was supposed to be an attack on the Royalists. Cowley himself vigorously protested in his preface how unlikely it was that a man who had suffered for a lost cause would choose the day of its triumph to attack it.—See also his ode, *The Complaint*, in his *Works*.

[64] Johnson, *Lives of the English Poets* : Cowley.

[65] " Did not the celebrated Author of Hudibras bring the king's enemies into a lower contempt with the sharpness of his wit, than all the terrors of his administration could reduce them to ? Was not his book always in the pocket of his Prince ? And what did the mighty prowess of his Knight-Errant amount to ? Why—he died, with the highest esteem of the Court— in a garret ! " Cibber, Dedication to Steele of his tragedy *Ximena, or the Heroic Daughter*, 1719. Printed in Steele's *Correspondence*, vol. II, p. 535.

one day gave him three hundred guineas, but there is no proof of this outbreak of generosity.[66]

Wycherley, the writer of comedies, who was in great favour at Court, was astonished at the neglect of his unfortunate fellow-author. He was in the good graces of Buckingham, who at that time was all powerful, and he made representations to the Duke, pointing out how much the royal family owed Butler for having written *Hudibras* and what a disgrace it was to the Court that a man of his " loyalty " and " wit " should be left in penury and obscurity. Buckingham, who fancied himself as a patron of literature, promised to speak of the matter to the King. To strengthen him in these good intentions, Wycherley suggested introducing Butler to him. Buckingham agreed, and on the appointed day Butler and his friend arrived first at the rendezvous. The powerful patron turned up in due course, but as bad luck would have it, the door of the room where the meeting took place was not shut. Two beautiful ladies happened to pass, and catching sight of them the great man left the two friends sitting there, while he dashed out to play the gallant. He did not return, and that was the last Butler heard of His Grace the Duke of Buckingham.[67]

Nevertheless, though discouraged, and more and more forgotten, Butler published a third part of his poem in 1678. But he went no further : *Hudibras* remained unfinished.

Butler died without leaving enough to pay for his own funeral. One of his friends tried to raise a subscription to secure a tomb for him in Westminster Abbey, but without success. The friend had to bury him at his own expense.[68]

[66] Johnson, *Lives of the English Poets* : Butler.—*Biographia Britannica*, s.v. Butler.

[It is possible that Butler's extreme poverty has been exaggerated. According to the *D.N.B.* it seems that Butler may have had a pension of £100 a year (no mean sum when compared with the currency values of our day) during the last few years of his life. B. D.]

[67] Pack (Richardson), *Miscellanies in Verse and Prose*, p. 181 ; *Some Memoirs of William Wycherley, Esq.*

[This sort of gossip is hardly evidence ; and in any case the whole of these *Memoirs* is extremely suspect. B. D.]

[68] à Wood, *Athenæ Oxonienses*, s.v. Prynne (William).—*The Genuine Poetical Remains of Samuel Butler*, Preface.

"... you have ev'ry Day before your Face
Plenty of fresh resembling Instances :
Great *Cowley's* Muse the same ill Treatment had, ⎫
Whose verse shall live for ever to upbraid   ⎬
Th'ungrateful World, that left such Worth unpaid. ⎭

If loyal writers were thus treated it is not difficult to imagine how the others fared.

Bunyan, who was of course an apostle rather than a writer, lay twelve and a half years in prison for the crime of having preached in public. His works were too serious to be understood by the frivolous readers of those days. They were not collected till 1736 and such was the vacuum of scorn around him that as late as 1782 Cowper hesitated to name him in his verse.[69]

Great Milton, " on evil dayes though fall'n, and evil tongues ; in darkness, and with dangers compast round, and solitude ",[70] wrote his masterpiece for a scanty audience.[71]

Scant the audience, indeed, and scant their sympathy.

Waller himself may thank Inheritance
For what he else had never got by Sense.
On *Butler* who can think without just Rage,
The Glory and the Scandal of the Age ?
Fair stood his Hopes, when first he came to Town,
Met ev'ry where with Welcomes of Renown,
Courted, caressed by all, with Wonder read,
And Promises of Princely favour fed :
But what Reward for all had he at last,
After a Life in dull Expectance pass'd ?
The Wretch, at summing up his misspent Days,
Found nothing left but Poverty and Praise.
Of all his Gains by Verse, he could not save
Enough to purchase Flannel and a Grave :
Reduc'd to Want, he in due Time fell sick,
Was fain to die, and be interr'd on Tick :
And well might bless the Fever that was sent
To rid him hence, and his worse Fate prevent."
          (Oldham, *A Satire, Dissuading from Poetry, Works*, vol. III.)

Oldham was a contemporary ; he died in 1683 at the age of thirty-two.

[69] *Biographia Britannica*, s.v. Bunyan ; Watt, *Bibliotheca Britannica*, s.v. Bunyan.—The first edition of *The Pilgrim's Progress* is dated 1678 ; Bunyan died in 1688. Here are Cowper's lines :

" I name thee not, lest so despised a name
    Should move a sneer at thy deserved fame."
          (*Tirocinium : or, a Review of Schools.*)

We shall later see, however, that not every reader greeted his writings with indifference.

[70] *Paradise Lost*, VII, 28 ff.—His Book *Defensio Populi* had been burned by the hangman in 1660, and proceedings had been instituted against him. (Neal, *History of the Puritans*, vol. IV, p. 308).—See also Geffroy, pp. 204–9.

[71]   " . . . still govern thou my song,
    Urania, and fit audience find, though few.
    But drive farr off the barbarous dissonance
    Of *Bacchus* and his Revellers . . ."
          (*Paradise Lost*, VII, 32 ff.)

On April 27, 1667, the bookseller Samuel Symons bought the manuscript of *Paradise Lost* on conditions which deserve to be remembered.[72] He paid the poet five pounds sterling down ; if he sold 1,300 copies of the first edition he was to pay him another £5 ; a third £5 after the sale of the same number of copies of the second edition and a fourth payment of £5 after an equal sale of the third edition. None of the three editions was to exceed 1,500 copies.

At the end of two years Milton's right to the second payment of £5 matured, and he signed a receipt for this sum on April 26, 1669. So England bought 1,300 copies of *Paradise Lost* in two years.[72a] Neither the author nor his subject was of a type to win popular favour, nor his style either ; the Court compared his verse to the clatter of a wheelbarrow.[73] His brother poets themselves treated his biblical epic no better : Dryden turned it into an opera, *The State of Innocence and Fall of Man.* The publisher, in order to quicken attention, had eight times (perhaps more) renewed the title of the first edition.[74] He did not publish the second edition until 1674 and again made modifications ; the format of the volume was changed and the ten books of the poem were converted into twelve. Readers remained unmoved. The third edition did not appear till 1678, after the poet's death. The widow lost no time in selling her rights in it for £8. As for the bookseller Symons, who, despite the very modest price he had paid the poet, had probably made little enough profit from the bargain, he surrendered his rights to his colleague Brabazon Aylmer for the sum of £25.

It was not Symons who four years after *Paradise Lost* published *Paradise Regained* and *Samson Agonistes.* Milton was obliged to turn to another publisher, on what conditions we do not know. Perhaps he had himself to bear the cost of this double publication.[75]

[72] This contract which brought in so little to Milton was bought for 100 guineas by the banker-poet Rogers who presented it to the British Museum. Together with the receipts and contracts quoted below, it is reproduced in Professor Masson's excellent edition of Milton's poetical works.

[72a] [One wonders whether many more would be sold to-day, with a population many times larger, and far more literate. Seventh ed. : 1700 ! B. D.]

[73] Smith, quoted by Johnson, *Lives of the English Poets*: Philips (Appendix).

[74] It is interesting to see in Lowndes the detail of these various modifications.

[75] *The Poetical Works of John Milton*, edited by Professor Masson ; Introduction to *Paradise Regained*.

The great man in his poverty and obscurity continued to the end to write books which were not, and could not hope to be, read : a treatise on Logic in Latin, treatises on True Religion, on Heresy, on Schism, on Tolerance and the best methods of preventing the spread of Popery ; a volume of intimate letters in Latin with oratorical essays of his youth ; a history of Muscovy, etc.[76]

All these subjects accorded ill with " the barbarous dissonance of *Bacchus* and his Revellers ". Yet his funeral was attended by a great concourse of mourners, but his modest grave was left without an inscription.[77]

It is clear that the position of authors was not an easy one and no easier for the friends of the Court than for others.[78]

How did those writers manage, who contrived to live by their pen ?

When Charles II returned to England, John Dryden,[79] the most famous of them, had just published *A Poem upon the Death of his late Highness, Oliver, Lord Protector of England, Scotland and Ireland.* This did not prevent his joining in the poetic chorus which greeted the King's return.[80] He wrote a poem *Astræa*

---

[76] Geffroy, *les Pamphlets de Milton*, pp. 239 ff.

[77] Johnson, *Lives of the English Poets* : Milton and the notes of Cunningham.

[78] I am far from wishing to forget Andrew Marvell amongst the authors hostile to the Court. He was a friend of Milton's, a poet of great merit and one of the rare admirable characters of the period. But Marvell did not live by his pen. He represented the town of Kingston upon Hull in the House of Commons, and what his constituents paid him sufficed for his needs (he was the last Member of Parliament to be thus paid). Let us not mention his name without recording an episode which does him honour. Wanting to buy him over, Charles II sent him a thousand guineas by the hand of Lord Danby. Marvell's reply was to ask his servant : " Pray, what had I to dinner yesterday ? A shoulder of mutton, sir. And what do you allow me today ? The remainder hashed. And tomorrow, my Lord Danby, I shall have the sweet blade-bone broiled ; and when your lordship makes honourable mention of my cook and my diet, I am sure his majesty will be too tender in future, to attempt to bribe a man with golden apples, who lives so well on the viands of his native country." Lord Danby carried back the thousand guineas (Life of Marvell, *Works*, vol. III).

[79] On the subject of Dryden see his *Works* and the authors quoted under his name in my Bibliography. See in addition his life by Johnson in *Lives of the English Poets* and by George Saintsbury ; Macaulay's *History* ; *Biographia Britannica*, s.v. Dryden ; and an article in the *Quarterly Review* for Oct. 1878.

[80] Waller was equally untroubled by scruples. He had sung of Cromwell, he sang of Charles II. When he presented his verses to the King, Charles remarked that the verses in honour of the Protector were better than those the poet was offering him. Waller saved the situation by saying " Poets, Sir, succeed better in fiction than in truth." (Johnson, *Lives of the English Poets* : Waller.)

Redux, A Poem on the happy Restoration and Return of His Sacred Majesty, Charles the Second.

The next year he returned to the charge with a new offering : *To His Sacred Majesty, a Panegyric on his Coronation.* Then, not content with addressing the god, he also offered homage to his saints, and wrote verses to Hyde : *To my Lord Chancellor. Presented on New Year's Day 1662.*

The poet's position at the time was none too brilliant. If we are to believe his enemies, he took up his quarters with Herringman, the bookseller, paying for his board and lodging by writing prefaces, advertisements, etc.[81] There is probably some exaggeration in this, for Dryden had a private income. But this income was very small (about £40 sterling a year), and though it prevented his starving it did not relieve him of the need to work. It is certain that in his early days he led a very modest existence : " I remember plain John Dryden before he paid his court with success to the great," writes a disinterested observer of his fortunes, " in one uniform cloathing of *Norwich* drugget." [82]

Obviously he expected presents or at least promises of protection from the King and the Lord Chancellor. Did he get anything ? It is probable : for in those days it was customary to thank poets for their homage by a gift of money. But he certainly did not receive anything which seemed likely to make his future secure, for he set himself at once to try another line.

---

[81] " At first I struggled with a great deal of persecution, took up with a lodging which had a Window no bigger than a Pocket-looking-glass, Dined at a Threepenny Ordinary enough to starve a Vocation (vacation) Taylor, kept little Company, went clad in homely Drugget, and drunk Wine as seldom as a *Rechabite*, or the *Grand Seignior's* Confessor." (Tom Brown, *The Reasons of Mr. Bays Changing his Religion.*) It is Bays (that is to say Dryden) speaking.

> " He turned a Journey-man t'a *Bookseller ;
> Writ Prefaces to Books for Meat and Drink,
> And as he paid, he would both write and think.
> Then by th' assistance of a †Noble *Knight*,
> Th' hadst plenty, ease and liberty to write
> First like a *Gentleman* he made thee live
> And on his Bounty thou did'st amply thrive.

* *Mr.* Herringman, *who kept him in his House for that purpose.*
† *Sir* R. H. (Robert Howard), *who kept him generously at his own house.*"

(Shadwell (?), *The Medal of John Bayes*, pp. 8–9.)
[82] *The Gentleman's Magazine* ; letter of an old correspondent in the issue of Feb. 1745, p. 99.

He turned his attention where the attention of the Court was turned : to the theatre.

He was far from taking this step of his own choice.[83] His genius urged him towards epic and lyric poetry, and all his life his heart was there. But the times had little use for major works and a man had to live. He noted which way the wind was blowing and trimmed his sails accordingly. He decided to write for the stage and everyone else did the same : Otway, Shadwell, Lee, Crowne, Mrs. Behn, Settle, D'Urfey, Ravenscroft ; all writers, without exception, who lived by their pen, tried writing plays.[84]

Cromwell's Puritans had completely suppressed the theatre : the playhouse was a pleasure, and an impious, Royalist pleasure to boot. On February 11, 1647, Parliament had passed an Act by which

All Stage-Players are declared to be Rogues punishable by the Act of the 39th of Queen *Elizabeth* and 7th of King James . . . All Stages, Galleries, Seats and Boxes are ordered to be pulled down by Warrant of two Justice of Peace ; All Actors in Plays for time to come being convicted shall be publickly whipp'd, and find Sureties for their not offending in like manner for the Future ; and all Spectators of Plays for every offence are to pay Five Shillings.[84a]

The Puritan hatred of spectacles went so far as to make them prohibit bear-baiting, not from humanity or pity for the bear, but from horror at the pleasure of the spectators.[85]

[83] " For I confess my chief endeavours are to delight the Age in which I live. If the humour of this, be for low Comedy, small Accidents and Raillery, I will force my Genius to obey it, though with more reputation I could write in Verse. I know I am not so fitted by Nature to write Comedy . . ." (*A Defence of an Essay of Dramatique Poesie* . . . prefixed to *The Indian Emperour.* 1668.)

" I have never thought myself very fit for an employment, where many of my predecessors have excelled me in all kinds ; and some of my contemporaries, even in my own partial judgment, have outdone me in Comedy." (Dedication to *Aureng-Zebe.*)—See also his Preface to *An Evening's Love.*

[84] Sheffield's *Essay on Poetry*, already quoted, speaks of the theatre as the supreme goal of the writer's art. This is how he introduces it :

" Here rest, my *Muse*, suspend thy Cares a while,
A greater Enterprise attends thy Toil.
As some young Eagle . . .
The Muse inspires a sharper Note to sing . . .
On then, my Muse, adventurously engage
To give Instructions that concern the Stage."

[84a] Neal, vol. III, p. 478. Theatrical performances were first forbidden in 1642.

[85] On this subject see the curious information quoted by Macaulay : *History of England*, vol. I, chap. 2, p. 161.

Yet so lively was the taste for the drama, implanted in England by the Renaissance, that even under the Republic, despite the penalties incurred—and paid—theatrical performances continued surreptitiously from time to time.[86]

But these rare godsends had been like a few mouthfuls of food to a starving man ; they had kept the appetite alive without satisfying it. So when it became possible after weary years of deprivation again to indulge the taste without restraint, the playhouses reopened of themselves, as it were, and found at once actors and audience.

The King for his part, who was used to seeing the continental theatre held in honour, and forming the favourite recreation of princes and society, was bound to be as keenly interested in the matter as his subjects. The organization of the theatres was therefore one of the first affairs of state to which Charles II devoted his attention.

The King returned on May 29, 1660. In August he granted a warrant to establish a theatre to Thomas Killigrew, a former royal page of his father's whom he had appointed his own valet, and another to Sir William D'Avenant, a zealous Royalist whom Charles I had knighted after the battle of Worcester.[87] The company of the former called itself " The King's Servants ", the second took the name " The Duke's Company " (after the Duke of York, brother of Charles II, later King James II). A certain number of actors of the royal company were considered part of the Royal Household and were entitled " Gentlemen of the Great Chamber ".[88]

[86] See Disraeli, *Curiosities of Literature*, the chapter *The History of the Theatre during its Suppression.*—See also Malone : *Historical Account of the Rise and Progress of the English Stage*, pp. 97, 98, notes ; and Ebsworth, *Westminster Drolleries*, Introduction.

[87] See the Royal Warrant to the two Directors in Malone, *Historical Account*, pp. 311–14.—Political foresight had no doubt a word to say in the matter. These two privileged companies were easy to supervise. [The political explanation is curious. But see addition to next note. B. D.]

[88] Cibber, *An Apology*, etc., pp. 53 ff.—Under Elizabeth, James I and Charles I some actors had already received the title of Servants of the Queen or King (Malone, *Historical Account*, pp. 49, 55 (note 3), 61 and 62).

[From Elizabethan times, all actors, to save themselves from being treated as rogues and vagabonds, had to be somebody's " servants ". In Elizabeth's day there were Lord Strange's Men (or Servants), the Lord Chamberlain's Men (Strange became Lord Chamberlain), the Lord Admiral's Men, and also the Queen's Men. (See E. K. Chambers, *William Shakespeare*, vol. I.) In Jacobean times there were The King's Men, Queen Anne's Company, and so on. Prince Charles I had a company, as had Queen Henrietta, and Charles II himself had a company as Prince Charles. (See G. E. Bentley,

The King and his brother were not content merely to lend the two companies the protection of their name ; they took a personal interest in the theatre. Not only did they diligently attend performances,[89] thereby ensuring their success, but they considered no detail beneath their dignity. They condescended to smooth out the squabbles which arose, whether between the actors or between the two theatres. Even the costumes were an object of their royal solicitude. When D'Avenant's *Love and Honour* was being played, the King gave the actor Betterton the robe he had himself worn at his coronation. The Duke of York and Lord Oxford gave two other actors the costumes in which they had appeared at the same ceremony. Another time the Duchess of York gave her wedding dress to Mrs. Barry, and the Duke of Monmouth, one of the King's natural sons, offered his sword to the actor Nokes and himself buckled it on.[90]

Charles II took a personal interest in the actors (not to mention the actresses). The comic actor, Leigh, he called *his* actor,[91] and he took such a fancy to another comedian, John Lacey, that he had his portrait painted in three different rôles.[92]

It was on the King's recommendation that Mrs. Butler, whom he called by her Christian name of Charlotte, made her first appearance on the stage. Cibber, who records the fact, remarks that this was " a provident restitution giving to the stage in kind what he had sometimes taken from it ".[93]

There was also a private theatre at Court and members of the Royal Family were not too proud themselves to act and

---

The Jacobean and Caroline Stage.) So this was no scandalous innovation, but a resumption of what had long been the tradition, and a proper regularization. Under Charles II, besides the King's and the Duke of York's players, there were the Duke of Monmouth's Servants, and the Duchess of Portsmouth's Servants. See Montague Summers : *The Playhouse of Pepys*, Allardyce Nicoll : *Restoration Drama*, and for later history, *Their Majesties' Servants* by J. Doran. B. D.]

[89] This was an innovation. Charles II's predecessors did not go to the theatre. When the sovereign wished to see a play, he summoned the actors to him. Only Charles I's Queen, Henrietta Maria, once attended a public performance. (Malone, *Historical Account*, pp. 183–4 ; P. Cunningham, *The Story of Nell Gwyn*, p. 10.)

[90] Betterton, *The History of the Stage*, p. 17 ; Downes, *Roscius Anglicanus*, pp. 21 and 29.

[91] Cibber, *Apology*, pp. 91 and 92.

[92] à Wood, *Athenæ Oxonienses*, s.v. William Lacey.—This triple portrait, painted by Michael Wright, is now in the Hampton Court Museum where it bears the registered No. 847.

[93] *Apology*, p. 97.

to take lessons in the art of declamation from professional actors.[94]

The theatre being thus under royal patronage it became an act of "loyalty" to attend. (What a dream for the courtier !— to enjoy himself and pay his court at the same time.) This factor combining with the passion for pleasure which had taken possession of society, made dramatic performances *the* fashionable recreation.

IV

What the drama was :   actresses, production ;   dramatic opera.—Tragedy :
heroic plays.—Comedy

On its side, the theatre spared no trouble or expense to delight its audiences.

Hitherto women's parts had always been played by young boys.[95] A few tentative efforts had been made to introduce actresses to the stage, but these had always failed.[96]

Under Charles II the experiment could be renewed without fear of failure. As Cibber says : " We may imagine too that these actresses were not ill chosen, when it is well known that more than one of them had charms sufficient at their leisure hours to calm and mollify the cares of empire." [97]

Following the King's example, the gallants much appreciated this innovation and the new-comers were rapidly well established.

[94] Mrs. Betterton " had the honour to teach Queen Anne, when Princess, the part of Semandra in *Mithridates*, which she acted at Court in King Charles's time." (Cibber, *Apology*, p. 96.)
[It was nothing new for royalty to take part in theatricals at Court. Queen Ann of Denmark appeared in masques, though James I held aloof, while Charles I and Queen Henrietta Maria performed frequently. Such a custom was not unknown in France.   See Enid Welsford, *The Court Masque.* B. D.]
[95] It will be remembered how in *Midsummer Night's Dream*, Flute protests : " Nay, faith let me not play a woman : I have a beard coming." (Act I, sc. 2.)
[Perhaps such a reminder is unnecessary for English readers, all of whom will know that women did not normally act in plays until after the Restoration, the female parts being taken by boys, of whom the most famous, perhaps, thanks to his being celebrated by Ben Jonson, is " Salathiel " Pavy, who died at the age of thirteen. B. D.]
[96] Prynne, *Histrio-Mastix*, p. 215, speaks of French actresses who have made their appearance " not long since " at the *Blacke-friers* theatre. But he has no word for an actress : he uses only the expression " woman-actor ". In the same way Pepys always says " actor ", not " actress " ; see especially Dec. 27, 1666. Southerne (*The Wives' Excuse*, 1692, p. 48) still says " woman-actor."—On the subject of actresses, see Malone, *Historical Account*, pp. 128–42.
[97] *Apology*, p. 55.

There was not, however, a sufficient supply of actresses all at once, and in default the actor Kynaston, amongst others, still played a woman's part. One day when Charles II was in the theatre he was surprised at a delay in beginning the performance. " Sire," was the reply, " the queen is not yet shaved." The queen, that day, was Kynaston.[98]

The male actors, however, lost no time in giving up feminine rôles (except a few comic parts. Nokes was famous as the Nurse in *Romeo and Juliet* and was known by the nickname of " Nurse Nokes ") [99] and actresses took a larger and larger share. Soon they were indispensable. When D'Avenant re-wrote *Macbeth*, he lengthened the rôles of Lady Macbeth and Lady Macduff for no apparent reason except to have women longer on the stage.[100] Ere long the actresses even began to encroach. Men in the past had played women's parts, women now took men's. This was perhaps sometimes due to necessity or to some dramatic advantage. In the *Tempest*, for instance, arranged as a lyric comedy by Dryden and D'Avenant, a woman was entrusted with a young boy's part.[101] For the most part dramatic art had nothing to gain from these disguises. On October 28, 1661, Pepys went to the theatre. He saw an actress who, after having played a woman's part, reappeared on the stage in men's clothes.

[98] This Kynaston was a great favourite with the ladies of quality. They would often take him driving in their carriages in Hyde Park after the performance (which was then held in the afternoon) still wearing his actor's dress. (Cibber, *Apology*, p. 72.)

[99] Otway, *Epilogue* to *The History and Fall of Caius Marius*.

[100] See particularly Act I, p. 10, a whole scene added between Lady Macbeth and Lady Macduff : Lady Macbeth has to find an excuse for expediting Lady Macduff's departure, so as to be free to read Macbeth's letter.—Lady Macduff, who appears in only one scene of Shakespeare's play, is given in D'Avenant's arrangement one scene in the first, second and fourth acts and two scenes in the third.

[101] But then the Prologue took pains to point out to the audience the full piquancy of the situation :

> " But, if for *Shakespeare* we your grace implore,
> We for our Theatre shall want it more :
> Who, by our dearth of youths, are forc'd t'employ
> One of our Women to present a Boy.
> And that's a transformation, you will say,
> Exceeding all the Magick in the Play.
> Let none expect in the last Act to find
> Her Sex transformed from Man to Woman-kind
> What e're she was before the Play began,
> All you shall see of her is perfect Man.
> Or if your fancy will be further led
> To find her Woman, it must be a-bed."

He remarks that " she had the best legs that ever I saw ", and adds that he was very well pleased with it all.   All the males of the audience were of one mind with Pepys in such matters, and the theatre lost no opportunity of catering for their taste.[102]   A large number of prologues and epilogues were recited by women dressed as men, with the evident intention of giving pleasure to spectators who shared Pepys' taste.[103]   Sometimes, even, the women took complete possession of the theatre and carried a whole performance through, unsupported by a single male actor.   In such cases they chose the most outspoken plays, such as Thomas Killigrew's *Parson's Wedding*.[104]   On their lips, ambiguous words evidently had a more piquant flavour, and their acting threw indelicate situations into peculiar relief.   They were almost all dancers [105] as well as actresses, and they were given licentious songs to sing with which all plays, even the most tragic, were freely interspersed.[106]   In short, no opportunity of thus titillating the spectators' senses was missed.

[102] See Pepys, March 7, 1666–7.

[103] For instance, on the revival of Dryden's *Maiden-Queen*, the Prologue and Epilogue were spoken, the one by Mrs. Boutell, the other by Mrs. Reeves, both dressed as men.—In these and the following quotations " Mrs." is used of an unmarried, not a married woman.   The first unmarried actress who was called " Miss " was Miss Crow, who created the part of Miss Hoyden in Vanbrugh's *Relapse* (1697).   (Cunningham, *The Story of Nell Gwyn*, p. 14, note.)

[" Miss instead of Mrs. meant that she was a very young girl.   Six years was by no means an uncommon age for actresses to make their first appearance in a Prologue or Epilogue, or even as a page, as Mrs. Bracegirdle did in *The Orphan* when she was no older, according to Curll.   Seeing what these children had to say, this custom roused very natural moral opposition.   See the Epilogue to Farquhar's *Love and a Bottle*, 1699.

O Collier !   Collier !   thou'st frighted away Miss Cross.

But she returned on Jan, 2, 1705, to dance and sing in *The Careless Husband* at Drury Lane." B. Dobrée.   Notes on *The Relapse*.   Nonesuch Ed.   B. D.]

[104] *The Parson's Wedding* (1664).—See Pepys, Oct. 11, 1664.

[105] " Mrs. *Johnson* in this Comedy (Shadwell's *Epsom Wells*) Dancing a Jigg so Charming well, Loves power in a little time after Coerc'd her to Dance more Charming else-where."   (Downes, *Roscius Anglicanus*, p. 33.)

[106] Here, for instance, is a song recited by *Betty* in the presence of *Lady Ancient*, Penelope, and Tim, Penelope's betrothed (D'Urfey, *The Fool turn'd Critick*, IV, 2) :

" I

I found my *Caelia* one night undrest,
a precious Banquet for languishing Love,
the charming object a flame increast,
Which never, ah never, till then I prov'd ;

Simultaneously with the advent of the actresses came the arrival of scenery. Previously, the sole decoration consisted of

> her delicate skin, and starry eye,
> made me a secret bliss pursue,
> but with her soft hand she still put it by,
> and cry'd. Fie, *Amintor* what would you do?
>
> ### 2
>
> Her words and blushes so fir'd my heart,
> I pulled her to me and clasp'd her around,
> And though with Cunning she play'd her part :
> Yet fainter, and fainter, her threats I found.
> But when I least thought on her, least I desir'd,
> My love a forebearance should allow,
> A touch of her hand, my heart so inspir'd :
> My Passion melted I know not how.
>
> ### 3
>
> Which when fair *Caelia's* quick eye perceiv'd,
> And found by my calmness my passion's decay,
> Her Fate she inwardly seem'd to grieve :
> That Fool'd her and Cool'd her, so base away.
> She sigh'd and look'd pale to see me dull,
> And in her heart, this oath she swore,
> She never again would slight an address ;
> Nor the critical minute refuse no more."

When the song was finished, Tim, the fiancé, found it not " bawdy " enough.

See another song recited by Francisca in Mrs. Behn's *Dutch Lover* (II, 4) and another specimen in Dryden's *Marriage à-la-Mode* (IV, 3).

I have said that the most tragic subjects did not exclude such spicy seasonings. Here is a song recited at the banquet of Atreus in Crowne's tragedy of *Thyestes* :

> ### " 1
>
> A Lovely pair endowed by Fate
> With Loves and Beauties whole Estate ;
> At the sweetest game have been,
> You know, you know what I mean,
> You know, you know what I mean.
>
> ### 2
>
> For Kisses first the Lovers play'd
> The pleasant sport provok'd the Maid . . .
>
> ### 4
>
> To deeper Play, they now begin,
> The happy young man's hand is in,
> Both have stak'd down all their joys,
> But she loses, for she cryes :
> See ! she cryes ! Oh ! see she cryes !
>
> ### 5
>
> But now the Bride, oh ! tempting sight !
> Has won her lapful of delight,

curtains stretched across the background of the stage (when the walls were not left bare).[107]   Sir William D'Avenant was the first to introduce the English public to movable scenery painted in perspective.   Before the Restoration he had already shown his skill as a decorative artist [108] in a play which as an exceptional case Cromwell had authorized for political reasons.   But it was not until restrictions were removed that he was able to give free rein to his talent.   Through him the whole theatre fell under the spell of scenic effects.   Battles and sacrifices were shown on the stage, aerial spirits who rose winging into the air, genii,[109] phantoms, sorcerers.[110]   The Temple was seen on fire in the *Destruction of Jerusalem* [111] ; in the *Empress of Morocco* [112] there was a river covered with a fleet, a tempest of hail and a rainbow ; in Lee's *Sophonisba* [113] a sky of blood was suddenly displayed with two suns shining in it ; in the same author's *Rival Queens* [114] a battle of crows and ravens took place in the air ; in the middle of this

---

To deeper Play, she urges on ;
But, alas, his stakes are gone,
But, alas, his stakes are gone.

6

And now she locks her Cabinet,
But he'll play another set,
When his hand again is in.
You know, you know what I mean,
You know, you know what I mean."

[107] Malone, *Historical Account*, pp. 85–115 and p. 348.
[108] " *The Cruelty of the Spaniards in Peru.* Exprest by Instrumentall and Vocall Musick, and by Art of Perspective in Scenes . . . 1658."—He had previously given : " *The Siege of Rhodes.* Made a Representation by the Art of Prospective in Scenes . . . 1656."—See *Biographia Dramatica* ; s.vv. Sir William Davenant, and The Cruelty of the Spaniards in Peru.
[It was really the tradition of the masque, especially from the time of Inigo Jones, which gave the impetus to elaborate scenery, and new knowledge of the Italian theatre : but even during the Jacobean period there was sometimes no lack of stage effects in the ordinary theatre.   In about 1610–12 some plays of Heywood's required much stage contraption. (See Montague Summers, *The Restoration Theatre*, p. 191.)   The scenery of *The Siege of Rhodes* was much restricted by the size of the stage at Rutland House.   Davenant certainly did much to bring in scenery and " machinery ". (See Montague Summers, *The Playhouse of Pepys*, chap. I.)   B. D.]
[109] *The Indian Queen* by Dryden and Sir Robert Howard.—See Evelyn, Feb. 5, 1664.
[110] Tate's *Brutus of Alba* ; *Œdipus* by Dryden and Lee.
[111] By Crowne, last act.
[112] By Settle.
[113] Last scene of Act II.
[114] Act II, 1.

battle an eagle and a dragon fought a strange fight in which the eagle was defeated.

Horror played no less a part in these performances : in Dryden's *Amboyna* the English were tortured on the stage by the Dutch. In the same author's *Indian Emperour* Montezuma was handed over to the executioner, and during his torments a Catholic priest conducted a religious discussion with him. In Ravenscroft's *Titus Andronicus* a curtain is drawn aside to show the head and hands of Demetrius and Chiron hung on the wall, while their corpses in chairs are covered with bloodstained cloths.[115]

Songs and dances were introduced wherever possible [116] ; the songs were such as we have seen ; the dances were sometimes strange. In Crowne's *Juliana* two queens, two nuns, two phantoms and two crowned angels danced together. They made an odd company ; but the aim was to strike the eye.

The taste for the spectacular preponderated to the point of giving rise to a peculiar type of play in which decoration, machines, costumes, dance, song and music combined to please both eye and ear. They were called " Dramatic Operas " [117] and corresponded approximately to our pantomimes, except for the difference of subject matter.

These new plays which enjoyed extraordinary success,[118] carried the elaboration of scenery to marvellous heights of magnificence. When Shadwell's *Psyche* was played, the decorations alone cost " more than £800 sterling ".[119] The description of the first production of *The Tempest, or the Enchanted Isle* by Dryden and D'Avenant [120] will give an idea of the degree of costly elaboration attained :

[115] Acted in 1678 (Genest, I, 233) but not published till 1686 or 1687. The dates of the performance and the publication of these plays do not always tally. In such cases I quote here the date of performance according to Genest, and in my bibliography the date of the first edition, or if this is not ascertainable, the date of the oldest edition I have been able to consult.— " A Curtain drawn discovers the heads and hands of *Dem.* and *Chir.* hanging up against the wall. Their bodys in chairs in bloody Linnen." (Act V.) [Professor Allardyce Nicoll gives date of first performance *c.* Dec., 1686. B. D.]

[116] In Mrs. Katherine Philips's translation of Corneille's *Pompée*, songs are inserted and at the end " A Grand Masque is Danc'd before Caesar and Cleopatra ".

[117] Cibber, *Apology*, p. 57.

[118] Pepys, July 4, 1661.

[119] Downes, *Roscius Anglicanus*, pp. 35 and 36.

[120] Played in 1667.

ACT I.

First Tableau.

The front of the stage is opened, and the band of twenty-four violins, with the harpsicals and theorbos which accompany the voices, are placed between the pit and the stage. While the overture is playing, the curtain rises, and discovers a new frontispiece, joined to the great pilasters, on each side of the stage. This frontispiece is a noble arch, supported by large wreathed columns of the Corinthian order ; the wreathings of the columns are beautified with roses wound round them, and several Cupids flying about them. On the cornice, just over the capitals, sits on either side a figure, with a trumpet in one hand, and a palm in the other, representing Fame. A little farther, on the same cornice, on each side of a compass-pediment, lie a lion and a unicorn, the supporters of the royal arms of England. In the middle of the arch are several angels, holding the king's arms, as if they were placing them in the midst of that compass-pediment. Behind this is the scene, which represents a thick cloudy sky, a very rocky coast, and a tempestuous sea in perpetual agitation. This tempest (supposed to be raised by magick) has many dreadful objects in it, as several spirits in horrid shapes flying down amongst the sailors, then rising and crossing in the air. And when the ship is sinking, the whole house is darkened, and a shower of fire falls upon them. This is accompanied with lightning, and several claps of thunder, to the end of the storm.

Second Tableau.

In the midst of the shower of fire, the scene changes. The cloudy sky, rocks, and sea vanish ; and, when the lights return, discover that beautiful part of the island, which was the habitation of PROSPERO : 'Tis composed of three walks of cypress-trees ; each side-walk leads to a cave, in one of which PROSPERO keeps his daughter, in the other HIPPOLITO : The middle-walk is of great depth, and leads to an open part of the island.

And this is only the beginning of the play with five more acts to come ! The whole performance was on this level of magnificence, varied by surprises from time to time. There were choirs of demons. In the Fourth Act a table rose out of the ground and four spirits entered who danced as they set the table with wine and viands. When the dance was over, bottles and dishes vanished and the table sank again into the ground. But all these marvels culminated in the *apotheosis* of the Fifth Act. Here appeared an arcade of rocks and calm sea. Music being played on the rocks. Neptune, Amphitrite, Oceanus and Tethys drove in a chariot drawn by sea-horses ; on each side of the chariot were sea gods and goddesses, Tritons and Nereids. There followed songs and dances the list of which filled four quarto pages.

Authors protested against this invasion of the intellectual sphere by merely decorative effects. Prologues and Epilogues are filled with their wailing.[121] But they complained in vain. Aristocratic taste was against them and in this, as in everything else, it prevailed. Authors were not in a position to put up a fight ; they did not even try. They confined themselves to protests, and even while protesting continued to supply plays of a type to gratify both in form and matter the tiresome preferences of their audiences.

As regards matter, the influence to which authors were subjected was not propitious either.

When the theatres first reopened, they were caught unprepared and they began by simply reverting to the rich repertoire of old : Shakespeare, Ben Jonson, above all Beaumont and Fletcher and some plays of D'Avenant that had already been acted.[122] But

---

[121] The Prologue to Dryden's *Limberham, or the Kind Keeper* says, for instance :

> " True wit has seen its best days long ago ;
> It ne'er looked up, since we were dipt in show."

Shadwell's Prologue to *The Squire of Alsatia* complains :

> " Then came Machines, brought from a Neighbour Nation ;
> Oh how we suffered under Decoration ! "

Here is another protest against the importance assumed by music (the *Timon* alluded to is Shadwell's, 1678) :

> " How was the Scene forlorn and how despis'd,
> When *Tymon*, without Musick moraliz'd ?
> *Shakespeare's* sublime in vain entic'd the Throng,
> Without the charm of *Purcel's* Syren Song."
> (Epilogue to *The Jew of Venice* : a Comedy by George
> Granville, Lord Lansdowne ; produced 1701.)

[122] See Genest, vol. I, *passim*.—" Dryden in his *Essay on Dramatick Poesie* records that they used to play two of Beaumont and Fletcher's plays for one of Shakespeare's (or Jonson's). This proportion is the most conclusive proof of the decadence of the theatre and the change in public taste. To prefer Beaumont and Fletcher to Shakespeare, is to prefer the amusement arising from complicated intrigues and novel subjects to the noblest emotions of dramatic art. Their plays are full of beautiful lines ; like the Spanish poets, they dazzle the eye by a series of brilliant scenes ; but they have neither created a character nor composed a complete drama. Everything they write bears the mark of improvisation. They linger over the portrayal of no feeling ; they skate over the surface touching no moral or psychological problems which the drama raises. Theirs is just the kind of superficial play which suited the courtiers of the Restoration ; avid of enjoyment, eager to vary their pleasures and incapable of any sort of serious concentration.

they soon felt that they could not rest content with these revivals, and frankly set out to replough the old furrows. A plot well worked out, characters vigorously drawn, daring and logical endings, made the theatre a weariness and not a recreation. Downes [123] tells us that people could not long put up with seeing Romeo and Juliet dying ; James Howard altered the play to give it a happy ending and it was acted one day as a tragedy and on the morrow as a tragi-comedy. Waller changed the last act of Beaumont and Fletcher's *Maids Tragedie* to let it end as a comedy. [124] The whole repertoire of the old theatre was out of tune with the new taste. A break was therefore made with the glorious tradition of Elizabeth's day, and people devoted themselves to writing tragic and comic plays in the new fashion. [125]

In the tragic plays two influences are observable, equally

Beaumont and Fletcher also offered them voluptuous situations to titillate their senses. On all these grounds they were bound to please, and please they did." (A. Mézières, *Shakespeare, ses œuvres et ses critiques*, pp. 165–6.)

[Shakespeare's comedies were on the whole neglected ; the tragedies were often, but not always altered, as much in the interests of new critical theories as to form as of those of sentiment ; the histories were popular, and not much tampered with. (See Allardyce Nicoll, *Restoration Comedy*.) The Duke of Marlborough said he got his knowledge of English history chiefly from the plays of Shakespeare, which he probably saw rather than read. The preference for Fletcher (Beaumont should not be included in these strictures ; while he lived there was bone in the plays) dates from the days of Charles I, when the theatre became more courtly, puritanism keeping the good bourgeois away. B. D.]

[123] Downes, *Roscius Anglicanus*, p. 22. The play has not been published.

[124] *Biographia Dramatica*, s.v. The Maid's Tragedy. By Edm. Waller, 1690.—The play had been acted in its remodelled form from 1682 onwards.

[125] " I saw *Hamlet, Prince of Denmark* played," writes Evelyn (*Diary*, Nov. 26, 1661) ; " but now the old plays began to disgust this refined age, since his Majestie's being so long abroad."—For Pepys " *Romeo and Juliet* . . . is a play of itself the worst that I ever heard in my life " (Mar. 1, 1661–2) ; " *Midsummer Night's Dream* . . . is the most insipid ridiculous play that I ever saw in my life " (Sept. 29, 1662) ; " the so much cried-up play of *Henry the Eighth* . . . is so simple a thing made up of a great many patches . . ." (Jan. 1, 1663–4) ; " reading *Othello, Moore of Venice* . . . but having so lately read *The Adventures of Five Houres* (by Sir Samuel Tuke) it seems a mean thing " (Aug. 20, 1666) ; " *The Tempest* . . . has no great wit . . ." (Nov. 7, 1667).—The Bibliothèque Nationale in Paris possesses a copy of the 1623 edition of Shakespeare which bears this manuscript note beside the title of *The Tempest* : " Much better in Dryden."—To see into what discredit Shakespeare had fallen, see Malone, *Historical Account*, pp. 338–42 and 354–8, and Ingleby, pp. 242 ff.

[Pepys is not a reliable witness as to general taste. The critics and playwrights of the period had an extremely high opinion of, even veneration for, Shakespeare, but they were not " bardolators ", and criticized him according to the standards of criticism of their day—as we do. B. D.]

strong, equally deplorable : the influence of women and the influence of the King. The King who had seen French tragedy in all its glory with Corneille, had brought back to England a passion for French ideas and great difficulty in understanding a theatre different from what he had grown accustomed to during his exile. The Earl of Orrery wrote to a friend : " I have now finished a Play in the *French* Manner ; because I heard the King declare himself more in favour of their Way of Writing than ours : My poor attempt cannot please his Majesty, but my Example may incite others who can."[126]

The things which had particularly impressed him in French tragedy were the externals such as the unity of place, the consistent dignity of the characters and the rhymed verse. As was natural, the King made converts and his taste was unopposed, with grave injury to English drama. No more than formal homage could be paid to unity of place, for it could ill be reconciled with the new methods of production. But dramatists adopted rhyme, which, while it seems necessary to the rhythm of French verse, turns English verse into a lyric chant, quite intolerable in a work of any length, and obviously at variance with the genius of English drama. Rhyme had been dethroned by Marlowe in the sixteenth century, and the Restoration poets succeeded only in giving it an artificial life of a few years, after which it disappeared for ever from the English theatre.[127] They also adopted the convention of showing on the stage only kings and queens, heroes and princesses, and tolerating no discussion of lesser problems than the possession of a crown or the overthrow of an empire.

This tendency to sustained majesty—which is perhaps to be regretted in the classical drama of France—was encouraged and accentuated in England by the influence of women and their preference for gallant and romantic literature.[128] The joint

---

[126] Quoted in the Preface to *The Dramatic Works of Roger Boyle, Earl of Orrery*.

[127] When Waller rewrote the conclusion of *The Maids Tragedie* he wrote the Fifth Act in rhymed verse though the preceding four acts were in blank verse. No. 39 of the *Spectator* discusses the use of rhyme in drama. Addison finds that a rhymed play produces on him the same effect as a Greek or Latin tragedy in hexameters.

[But he ended the Acts of *Cato* with passages in rhyme. B. D.]

[128] " This faulty Manner (Luxury of splendid Words) took its rise from the numerous Romances that were the great delight of Gentlemen and Ladies, after the return of king Charles." (Blackmore, *Essays*, vol. II, p. 266.)—Dryden, in his Essay on *Heroic Plays* (prefixed to the *Conquest of Granada*), claims

effect of these two influences gave birth to a new type of play which was known as the Heroic Play.

The mere titles are sufficient indication of their source of inspiration : *Secret-Love, or the Maiden-Queen* [129] ; *Tyrannick-Love, or the Royal Martyr* [130] ; *Love and Revenge* [131] ; *The Rival Queens, or the Death of Alexander the Great* [132] ; *Theodosius, or the Force of Love* [133] ; *Abdelazer, or the Moor's Revenge* [134] ; *The Rival Kings, or the Loves of Orondates and Statira* [135] ; *Ibrahim, the Illustrious Bassa.* [136] No subject is worthy of treatment, if it is of less import-ance than the Conquest of Mexico or Granada, [137] the siege of Memphis, [138] the destruction of Jerusalem, [139] or similarly august events which allow the chief actors to display themselves in circumstances worthy of their distinguished birth and noble soul. The women, almost all crowned on the steps of the throne, [140] have characteristic names ; they are called Roxolana, [141] Zempoalla, Orazia, [142], Almeria, Cydaria, [143] Melissa, [144] Alma-hide, Lyndaraza, [145] Almavanga, Alcinda. [146] Rosalinda, [147] Inda-mora. [148] The men-folk, lofty in rank, [149] and lofty in sentiment,

---

to have borrowed many features of one of the characters, Almanzor, from the Artaban of " Monsieur Calprenède ". The serious part of his *Marriage à-la-Mode* was furnished by *le Grand Cyrus*.

[129] By Dryden ; borrowed from *le Grand Cyrus*.

[130] By Dryden ; *l'Amour tyrannique* is the title of one of Mademoiselle de Scudéry's tragedies.

[131] By Settle.

[132] By Lee ; inspired by La Calprenède's *Cassandre*.

[133] By Lee ; borrowed from Gomberville's *Pharamond*.

[134] By Mrs. Behn.

[135] By Bankes ; borrowed from La Calprenède's *Cassandre*.

[136] *Ibrahim, ou l'Illustre Bassa* is the name of one of Mademoiselle de Scudéry's novels.

[137] *The Indian Emperour, or the Conquest of Mexico by the Spaniards ; Almanzor and Almahide, or the Conquest of Granada ;* by Dryden.

[138] *The Siege of Memphis, or the Ambitious Queen,* by D'Urfey.

[139] *The Destruction of Jerusalem by Titus Vespasian,* by Crowne.

[140] *The Indian Queen* (by Sir Robert Howard and Dryden) ; *The Empress of Morocco* (by Settle) ; *Juliana, or the Princess of Poland* (by Crowne), etc.

[141] *In Mustapha,* by the Earl of Orrery (1668).

[142] In *The Indian Queen,* by Sir Robert Howard and Dryden.

[143] In *The Indian Emperour,* by Dryden.

[144] In *The Maiden-Queen,* by Dryden.

[145] In *Almanzor and Almahide, or the Conquest of Granada,* Part II, by Dryden ; Mademoiselle de Scudéry wrote a novel called *Almahide.*

[146] In *The Conquest of China, By the Tartars,* by Settle.

[147] In *Sophonisba, or Hannibal's Overthrow,* by Lee.

[148] In *Aureng-Zebe,* by Dryden.

[149] Now, it is Suleiman the Magnificent (in Lord Orrery's *Mustapha* and Settle's *Ibrahim*) ; now, the Great Mogul (in Dryden's *Aureng-Zebe*) ; now, some hero of antiquity dressed up for the occasion.

are genuine heroes of romance, full of love, full of honour, full of courage. Or can we justly speak of love, honour or courage? Are there any words to express such amazing passions, such exalted and extraordinary virtues? Their love is the distilled essence of sentimentality, insipid to the last degree and at the same time to the utmost limit impetuous and violent—a little stream flowing with a gentle murmur or a raging torrent unleashed. Their honour is a blend of delicacy and impulse, both equally incomprehensible; their courage is heroic lunacy. They outdo even the models which gave them birth. Aided by the theatre and by rhyme, they push their chivalrous sentiments to the limit of intensity and clothe them in sonorous tirades that hurl defiance at Gods and men and common sense.

When Maximin is informed that " the gods have claimed " Valeria, he exclaims :

> What had the Gods to do with me or mine?
> Did I molest your heaven?
> Why should you then make Maximin your foe
> Who paid you tribute, which he need not do?
> Your altars I with smoke of gums did crown,
> For which you leaned your hungry nostrils down,
> All daily gaping for my incense there,
> More than your sun could draw you in a year.
> And you for this these plagues on me have sent!
> But by the Gods, (by Maximin, I meant,)
> Henceforth I, and my world,
> Hostility with you and yours declare.
> Look to it, Gods ; for you the aggressors are.

This master ranter is mortally wounded ; his self-confidence remains unshaken :

> And shoving back this earth on which I sit,
> I'll mount, and scatter all the Gods I hit. (*Dies.*) [150]

If they feel themselves so mighty in face of the gods, it is clear that nothing in Nature is going to halt them :

> . . . Where is Clarona gone? (*Grows mad.*)
> Aloft !—I see her mounting to the Sun !—
> The flaming Satyr towards her does roul,
> His scorching Lust makes Summer at the Pole.
> Let the hot Planet touch her if he dares !—
> Touch her, and I will cut him into Stars,
> And the bright chips into the Ocean throw.[151]

---

[150] Dryden's *Tyrannick Love*, V, i.

[151] Phraartes, in *The Destruction of Jerusalem*, by Crowne, Part II, Act V.

Another declares :

> If she were dead, I would restore her breath,
> And she should live,
> Spight of her self, spight of the gods, and Death.
> My Pow'r's unlimited, as is their own :
> My smile brings Life, and death attends my frown.[152]

After that, who among men could resist them? What dangers or threats could move them? Wounds and death have no terror for them. Every blow struck at them must give them new strength, each limb smitten from their body must become yet another hero.[153] Demetrius is threatened with death :

> Come Villains, level me right against the Clouds,
> And then give fire, discharge my flaming soul
> Against such saucy Destinies as those
> As dare thus basely of my life dispose ;
> Then from the Clouds rebounding I will fall,
> And like a clap of thunder tear you all.[154]

They carry off Porphyrius to cut off his head. What cares he? Dead, he will still pursue the enemy who strikes him. To Maximin he cries :

> Where'er thou stand'st, I'll level at that place
> My gushing blood, and spout it at thy face.
> Thus, not by marriage, we our blood will join ;
> Nay more, my arms shall throw my head at thine.[155]

Bombast can hardly go further. Almanzor and Maximin,

---

[152] Nero speaking in Lee : *The Tragedy of Nero* (V, 1). The character is conceived in this style throughout.

In *The Destruction of Troy* by Bankes, Achilles beside the corpse of Troilus similarly says :

> " Here by thy Side for ever I'le remain
> Close, till I've hatched thee into Life again."
>   (*Actus Quartus*, Scena Prima.)

[153]   " *Almanzor :* Cut piecemeal in this cause,
> From every wound I shou'd new vigor take :
> And every Limb should new Almanzors make."
>   (*The Conquest of Granada*, by Dryden, Part II, v.)

[154] *Juliana, or the Princess of Poland*, by Crowne, Act IV.

[155] Dryden's *Tyrannick Love* (IV, 2). Let us quote yet another sample from Dryden's *Conquest of Granada* (Part I, iii). Almanzor speaking :

> " If I would kill thee now, thy fate's so low
> That I must stoop, e're I can give the blow.
> But mine is fix'd so far above thy Crown,
> That all thy Men,
> Pil'd on thy back can never pull it down."

See also a passage from Lee's *Alexander* quoted in No. 438 of the *Spectator*.

the two model heroes of this type, strike us to-day as two lunatics escaped from their asylum. Yet the Court of Charles II, so subtle, so fastidious, with so many claims to wit—some of them not unjustified [156]—accepted it all, applauded it all, revelled in it all. These bombastic declamations, for which English has the special name of " ranting ", were the delight of the audience, [157] and no dramatic works were more popular than those in which this roaring rhetoric had free play.

It is easy to imagine the kind of intrigues amidst which these superhuman heroes thread their way. Every sort of vicissitude, every imaginable complication multiplies around them ; battles dog their footsteps ; ambuscades await them at every turn ; hurricanes hurl themselves with fury at the ship that carries them ; everywhere there lurks the enemy, the traitor, the assassin.

[156] No one could criticize these Heroic Plays with more wit and judgment than the Duke of Buckingham in his *Rehearsal*, a work too often forgotten. Rochester also expressed himself admirably on the subject to Nathaniel Lee, one of the masters of this balderdash (Horace's *Tenth satire of the First Book*, imitated, *Works*, I, p. 11).—Amongst professional authors there was scarcely one, save Butler and Shadwell, who lodged a protest against this bombast. See Butler's amusing parody " Reparties between Cat and Puss at a caterwauling, in the modern Heroic Way ", in the *Genuine Poetical Remains of Samuel Butler*. Shadwell's protest is less well known and deserves to be quoted here :

> " How have we in the space of one poor Age,
> Beheld the Rise and Downfal of the Stage !
> When, with our King restor'd, it first arose,
> They did each Day some good old Play expose ;
> And then it flourish'd : Till, with Manna tir'd,
> For wholesome Food ye nauseous Trash desir'd.
> Then rose the whiffling Scribblers of those days,
> Who since have liv'd to bury all their Plays :
> And had their Issue full as num'rous been
> As *Priam's*, they the Fate of all had seen.
>   With what prodigious scarcity of Wit
> Did the new Authors starve the hungry Pit ?
> Infected by the *French*, you must have Rhime,
> Which long, to please the Ladies Ears, did chime.
> Soon after this came ranting Fustian in,
> And none but Plays upon the fret were seen :
> Such Roaring Bombast stuff, which Fops would praise,
> Tore our best Actors Lungs, cut short their days.
> Some in small time did this distemper kill ; ⎫
> And had the savage Authors gone on still, ⎬
> Fustian had been a new Disease i' th' Bill . . ." ⎭
>   (Prologue to *The Squire of Alsatia*.)

[157] See Cibber, *Apology*, pp. 63 and 64.—In the Dedication to his *Indian Emperour* Dryden writes : " The favour which heroic plays have lately found upon our theatres, has been wholly derived to them from the countenance and approbation they have received at court."

Dame Fortune is proverbially fickle ; the adjective is here in-adequate ; in their case she displays a ubiquitous caprice that defeats all foresight, overturns all plans. But nothing disconcerts these champions ; their mere presence routs an enemy [158] ; their enemies bite the dust ; those whom their sword does not lay low are conquered by the greatness of their soul [159] ; if they are surprised by ambushed foes, singlehanded they annihilate them in the twinkling of an eye [160] ; if they are thrown into prison you know that some unexpected miracle [161] will set them free to perform new exploits and recover their mistress.

For these valiant men are tender-hearted, true knights errant that they are. Dryden's Montezuma confesses : " My lion's heart is captive in the toils of love." [162] They are captive and they take captive. When Cortez arrives in Mexico, Cydaria falls in love with him at first sight, Mexican and Spaniard, forth-with consumed by the same fire, exchange their declarations *secundum artem*.[163] All the rules of the game are observed, here, as in the romance. It involves neither love nor affection, it is pure gallantry in the approved form :

> In tedious Courtship we declare our pain
> And ere we kindness find, first meet disdain.[164]

In Dryden, Adam and Eve whom we normally picture to our-selves as less sophisticated, conduct their courtship on the same lines. Eve says to Adam :

> But some restraining thought, I know not why,
> Tells me, you long should beg, I long deny.[165]

The whole is interspersed with the inevitable coquetries and jealousies. So inevitable, that—odd as it may seem—Eve is jealous :

> Or like my self, some other may be made ;
> And her new Beauty may thy heart invade.[166]

---

[158] " But I would give a Crown in open day,
And when the Spaniards their Assault begin
At once beat those without and these within."
(Dryden, *The Conquest of Granada*, Part I, iii.)

[159] Dryden : *The Indian Emperour* (I, 2).—We have seen pretty much the same sort of thing occurring in the romance of *Oroonoko*.
[160] Settle : *The Empress of Morocco* (IV, 2).
[161] Dryden : *The Indian Emperour* (IV, 4, and V, 2).
[162] Ibid. (I, 2).   [163] Ibid. (I, 2).   [164] Ibid. (II, 2).
[165] *The State of Innocence* (II, 2).—This play was never acted.
[166] Ibid. (II, 1).

Sometimes too, in due deference to the convention, love indulges in savage ravings. To the lovely Almahide who is betrothed to another, Almanzor says :

> . . . then a ghost I'll be ;
> And from a ghost, you know, no place is free.
> Asleep, awake, I'll haunt you everywhere ;
> From my white shroud groan love into your ear :
> When in your lover's arms you sleep at night
> I'll glide in cold betwixt, and seize my right.[167]

It was this gallant strain in the Heroic Plays which was evidently counted on to be particularly attractive to audiences of the time. Women, so much exalted, so much sought after, could not but find pleasure in the sight of these proud conquerors humbly prostrate at the shrine of Beauty.[168] Men who prided themselves on their gallantry and eloquence could not but listen with pleasure to these amorous scenes, where action was suspended that the poet might at leisure display his talent for making pretty speeches. Devoted to literature, sensitive to wit, they were carried away by plays written for wit alone and in the rhymed verse they loved.[169] A high-sounding couplet excuses many things, and those which to-day sound the most extravagant to us, must have had for their first hearers the supreme merit of expressing in reverberating language ideas then by no means

---

[167] *The Conquest of Granada*, Part I, iv, 2.—See similar threats of Roxana to Statira in Lee's *Rival Queens* (III, 1).

[168] " As our heroes are generally lovers, their swelling and blustering upon the stage very much recommends them to the fair part of their audience. The ladies are wonderfully pleased to see a man insulting kings, or affronting the gods, in one scene, and throwing himself at the feet of his mistress in another. Let him behave himself insolently towards the men, and abjectly towards the fair one, and it is ten to one but he proves a favourite of the boxes. Dryden and Lee, in several of their tragedies, have practised this secret with good success." (*Spectator*, No. 40.)

In the Dedication of his *Mithridates*, Lee himself claims to have represented Ziphares " for the ladies " as ardent, tender, and passionately in love.

[169] The author pauses every moment to bring in a purely poetic simile or metaphor. In Lee's *Sophonisba*, for instance (V, 1), in a scene of less than twenty lines between Lælius and Scipio, eleven lines are taken up by two similes. In Otway's *Orphan* (V, 1), Monimia and Castalio find occasion for three similes in four small pages. Buckingham wittily makes mock of this practice in his *Rehearsal*.

" *Bayes*. . . . Now, here, she must make a *simile*.
Smith. Where's the necessity of that, Mr. *Bayes* ?
Bayes. Because she's surpris'd. That's a general Rule : you must ever make a *simile* when you are surpris'd ; 'tis the new way of writing." (II, 3.)
See the notes on this passage quoted in the Arber edition, p. 56.

commonplace. It must also be noted that the Heroic Plays were adopted by a poet, a real poet, Dryden himself, who lavished on them the treasures of a luxuriant style and brilliant versification.[170] We must remember too that these plays lent themselves to pompous declamation, and to the elaborate scenery which played so important a part in the dramatic art of the time.

However that may be, the Heroic Plays satisfied only some of the tastes of the day : they reflected the elegance of high society, its external graces, its good manners. Now, we have seen what lay below the surface of this society. This deceptive veneer concealed licentious souls whom tragedy, even rouged and bejewelled, could not wholly satisfy.

At this point my task as a historian becomes delicate. So far I have revealed only the more respectable aspects of the period I am attempting to portray, those where a relative reticence is observed. Now I must show it as it was, and from the glimpses already permitted, the reader can foresee that no edifying sights await him. Ought the historian in such a case to refrain ? If he does, is he not playing false to that truth to which he owes his duty ? If he does not, must he endeavour by subtleties of phrase and style to convey things difficult to speak of openly ? But if he does not quote his evidence, has not the reader a right to question his interpretations ? And in trying merely to hint at his full meaning, does he not incur the danger of allowing too little to be understood, or, perchance, too much ? It seems to me that the most honourable and the safest course is neither to conceal, nor to take refuge in euphemisms, but to state the facts simply and frankly, without over-emphasizing them, without evading them, with moderation no doubt, with such reserve as respect for a modern reader imposes, but at the same time with the sincerity due to the overriding claims of historic truth.

Tragedy suffered from the grave defect of not being amusing. Comedy was. Good-bye to the sonorous phrase, the grandiloquent language, the fine sentiment, the poetry. In Comedy : reality and prose. Love is no longer gallantry but

---

[170] Even in his normal dramas, the least admirable of his works (except *All for Love*, and *Don Sebastian*), passages occur of rare and lasting beauty. From Voltaire down to Macaulay, people have often quoted Nourmahal's lines about life (*Aureng-Zebe*, IV, 1). But was Dryden's public appreciative of what we of to-day admire in his plays ? We may fairly doubt it.

[Why should we doubt it ? The great Duchess of Marlborough, for instance, frequently quoted those lines, which she had probably heard at an early performance, and read later. And she was no great reader. B. D.]

lust.[171] It goes straight to the point : " To make sure of one good night is as much in reason, as a man should expect from this ill world." [172] So the men run after the women, and the women after the men, by no roundabout route. " Give me leave to lie with you," says one to a woman in front of her husband.[173] There was no more to it than that. Or else : " Come, there is a bed adjacent." [174] The women do not refuse these gentle invitations.[175] The sequel is within an ace of taking place on the stage.[176] For that matter, it might nearly as well. The author wishes us to lose as little as possible. If he consents to screen his heroes from us for a moment, he is at pains to let us know at once what takes place behind the scenes. For fear of any mistake, the actors remaining on the stage are ready at need to supply ample details.[177]

If the women are not attacked, they attack first. Lady Love-All in *The Parson's Wedding* [178] is " An old Stallion-hunting Widow ". Lady Vain in Shadwell's *Sullen Lovers* is a " whore " ; Lady Gimcrack in the same author's *Virtuoso* hires Hazard, and makes explicit suggestions to boot to both Bruce and Longvil, who ask nothing better than to take her at her word.[179] In Dryden's *Kind Keeper* three women at once are a-hunting Woodall, a man whom they have scarcely had time even to see.[180] It

[171] " *Lodwick.* How, love another ? in what quality and manner ?
Wittmore. As a Man ought to love, with a good substantial Passion without any design but that of right-down honest Injoyment." (Mrs. Behn, *Sir Patient Fancy*, IV.)
" *Stanmore.* My Mistress is not here neither ; her Folly has a little cool'd my Love ; but I have a most abominable lust to her, the wiser Passion of the two ; and no despair : Though that Rogue *Selfish* has her Mind, I do not doubt but to get her Body ; which is worth two of it for my use." (Shadwell, *A True Widow*, IV, 1.)
[172] Dryden : *The Maiden-Queen*, II, 1 (comic part).
[173] Thomas Killigrew : *The Parson's Wedding*, 1664, (IV, 2) in *Comedies and Tragedies.*
[174] Wycherley : *The Plain-Dealer* (IV).
[175] See Dryden : *The Kind Keeper* (II, 2).
[176] See Mrs. Behn : *Sir Patient Fancy* (III and IV) ; Wycherley : *The Plain Dealer* (IV).
[177] " *Pandarus.* There was a creake ! there was a creake : they are both alive and alive like ; there was a creake : a ha boyes ! " (Dryden : *Troilus and Cressida*, III, 2.)—See also Dryden's *Kind Keeper* (III, 1).
[But the curious reader might like also to see Shakespeare's *Troilus and Cressida*, III, ii. B. D.]
[178] By Thomas Killigrew.
[179] " *Lady Gimcrack.* . . . I know not why we Ladies should not keep, as well as Men, sometimes " (III).
" *Hazard.* . . . I am kept by her, as I know you are by him " (IV).
[180] Mrs. Saintly, Mrs. Tricksy, Mrs. Brainsick.

might certainly be argued that these are nothing but vulgar intrigues of no significance. Note, however, that Lady Love-All, Lady Gimcrack and Lady Vain are all members of the aristocracy. Even when intentions are " strictly honourable " the tone is no more delicate.

The naval lieutenant Freeman is seeking the widow Black-acre in marriage : " What mean you, sir ? " she asks. " Why, faith, (to be short) to marry you, widow." . . . " You are an impertinent person ; and go about your business." " I have none, but to marry thee, widow." " But I have other business." . . . " But you have no business a-nights, widow ; and I'll make you pleasanter business than any you have. For a-nights, I assure you, I am a great man of business ; for the business. . . ." " Go, I'm sure you're an idle fellow." [181]   Marcella and Cornelia, desiring to win the hearts of two attractive striplings, escape from their uncle's house and pass themselves off as prostitutes. They thus succeed in marrying the husbands of their choice.[182]

Handsome Celadon marries Florimel :

Celadon. None of my privileges to be infringed by thee, Florimel, under the penalty of a month of fasting nights.

Florimel. None of my privileges to be infringed by thee, Celadon, under the penalty of cuckoldom.

Cel. Well, if it be my fortune to be made a cuckold, I had rather thou should'st make me one, than any one in Sicily ; and for my comfort, I shall have thee oftener than any of thy servants.

Flo. Look ye now, is not such a marriage as good as wenching, Celadon ?

Cel. This is very good ; but not so good, Florimel.[183]

And they marry.

It is not easy to see why.

---

[181] Wycherley, *The Plain Dealer* (imitated from *le Misanthrope*), Act II. —A moment later the widow says to Freeman :

" Thou art a foul-mouthed Boaster of thy Lust, a meer Bragadochio of thy strength for Wine and Women . . . I say you are a worn-out Whore-master, at five and twenty, both in Body and Fortune : And cannot be trusted by the common Wenches of the Town, lest you shou'd not pay 'em, nor by the wives of the Town, lest you shou'd pay 'em," etc.

[182] *The Feign'd Curtizans* by Mrs. Behn.

[183] Dryden, *The Maiden-Queen* (V, last scene).—In Etherege's *Man of Mode* (V, 2) Bellair says to the Chaplain who has come to officiate at his son's marriage : " Please You, Sir, to Commission a young Couple to go to Bed together a God's name ? "—In Mrs. Behn's *Sir Patient Fancy* (IV), Sir Credulous Easy says to Lodwick : " Dost thou know I am to unty the Virgin Zone tomorrow, that is barter Maiden-heads with thy Sister, that is to be married to her . . . ? "

Such is the consistent picture of "love" in these dramas.
There is nothing between the fatuously sentimental and pom-
pously extravagant gallantry of the Heroic Plays, and the barefaced sensuality of the comedies.   You cannot find in all the
comedies a single husband who is not a figure of fun, not a single
married woman who has not a lover (or several) or, at best, is
trying to secure at least one.   You may search them for a maiden :
in vain.   The young girls who should be such, command a
strange vocabulary.[184]   They chatter continually of their maiden-
head, but not as virgins.[185]   Gertrude in Shadwell's *A True
Widow* is described as a fool and " whorish ".[186]   Timorous, in
speaking of Isabella, says :   " and therefore I have reason to love
her the longest day I have to live ".   Isabella, who is present,
interjects :   " Ay, and the longest night too, or you are to blame.
And you have one argument I love you, if the proverb be true,
for I took you almost in your bare shirt." [187]

Parents talk of their daughters with the same looseness.
One mother, Melissa, frankly says :   " Well, I'll be bold to say
it, 'tis as easy to bring up a young lion without mischief, as a
maidenhead of fifteen, to make it tame for an husband's bed." [188]
Another mother tries to wean her daughter from a preference
for regular marriage, and persuade her to let herself be kept.[189]
Children are no less outspoken with their parents :   When Mrs.
Blackacre gives her son the good advice :   " Do not go to ordin-
aries and bagnios, good Jerry," the young man retorts :   " Why,
have you had any dealings there ? you never had any ill by

[184] " I will cuckold thee, look to 't ; I will most damnably," says Isabella
to a suitor whom she dislikes (*Sir Patient Fancy*, by Mrs. Behn, V).—Here is
a scrap of conversation between young Pleasance and Mrs. Tricksy, a kept
woman :

" *Pleasance :*   Let but little *Minx* go proud, and the dogs in *Covent-Garden*
have her in the wind immediately ; all pursue the Scent.
Mrs. Tricksy :   Not to a Boarding-house, I hope !
Pleasance :   If they were wise, they wou'd rather go to a Brothel house,"
etc. (*The Kind Keeper*, by Dryden, III, 1).

In Shadwell's *Virtuoso*, Miranda says to Old Snarl : " Such as you should
be destroyed, like Drones that have lost their Stings, and afford no Honey."
He replies : " Marry come up, you young Slut ! Are you so liquorish after
the Honey of Man ? " (I).
[185] In Mrs. Behn's *Sir Patient Fancy* Isabella says to Lucretia : " Thou
may'st lay thy Maiden-head upon't . . ."—See also Dryden's *Maiden-
Queen*, III, 1, and IV, 1.
[186] In the list of *Dramatis Personæ*.   [187] V, 3.
[188] Dryden, *The Maiden-Queen*, IV, 1.
[189] Lady Cheatly, backed up by Lady Busie, in *A True Widow*, by
Shadwell (II).

them, had you ? " [190]   Another youth lives incognito for five acts with his father, a loquacious old debauchee, in order to take advantage of his sorry revelations. [191]

No one would believe that human imagination could thus run riot if he had not the documents under his very eyes. For all this is solely the product of imagination. We are not dealing with the spontaneous exuberance of youth, unconsciously over-flowing all bounds, nor with a rude expansive gaiety frankly finding laughter and merriment in highly-spiced jesting. We have to do with a perverted and deliberate search for the smutty and the bawdy ; with a cold-blooded, intentional study of the lewd and licentious, with a refinement of unwholesome thinking on the part of debauchees who have drunk of life too deeply. [192]

Are we at least compensated by interesting situations, by humorous observation, by skilful character-studies ? Not at all. Obscenity is the least of the failings, which mark the comedies of this period. It would obviously be too much to say that none of them have either wit or zest. But the zest (which is rare) is used to serve worthless intrigues which scarcely deserve to be called farces, [193] in which the same gallants and the same coquettes [194] court each other in the same way. The wit is

[190] Wycherley, *The Plain Dealer*, IV. Later on, she informs him— untruthfully—that he was born out of wedlock. To which he replies : " What, what ? Am I then the Son of a Whore, Mother ? "

[191] Woodall, in Dryden's *Kind Keeper*.

[192] No one will accuse Voltaire of prudery, yet though he admired and even imitated Wycherley's *Plain Dealer*, he says of it : " The manners portrayed are so shameless that you might suppose the scene set in a house of ill fame adjacent to a guard room." (Foreword to *la Prude*.)—See also his note on Act III, 7, and the beginning of his Letter 19 on the English ; the picture he paints is not overdrawn. *La Prude* is an imitation of *The Plain Dealer*, which title Voltaire translates as " l'Homme au franc procédé ".

[193] In Dryden's *Wild Gallant* Constance puts a pillow under her dress to make her father believe that she is pregnant and she succeeds in persuading him that he himself is on the point of having a child.

[This may have been a topical allusion. Genest quotes a story of a certain " Dr. Pelling, Chaplain to Charles II, who having studied himself into the disorder of mind called the hyp . . . between the age of forty and fifty imagined himself to be pregnant." The illusion is not unique : Marshal Blucher, of Waterloo fame, was also its victim. B. D.]

[194] " *Character* they supply with a smutty *Song, Humor*, with a Dance, and Argument with *Lightning* and Thunder, which has oft repriev'd many a scurvy Play from *Damning*. A huge great Muff, and a gaudy Ribbon hanging at a Bully's backside, is an excellent Jest : and new-invented curses, as, *Stap my Vitals, Damn my Diaphragm, Slit my Windpipe, Sink me Ten thousand fathom deep*, rig up a new Beau, tho' in the main 'tis but the same everlasting Coxcomb . . ." (Tom Brown, *Amusements Serious and Comical, The Play-House. Works*, vol. III.)

the author's purely verbal wit, never provoked by the situation. It is always the author who is speaking, never his characters [195] ; he constantly interrupts the play to let the characters assail each other with repartee and to display to the admiring gallery the skill with which he can parry the thrusts he makes himself. [196] Nothing could be more fatal to dramatic effect, nothing so monotonous, nothing so wearisome as these " compositions where everything is blue, everything is pink, everything is the author ".[197] So we do not find a single living part, a single real character : all these concoctions are artificial, cast in the same conventional mould, the fashionable mould of the day.[198] The most you can hope for is occasionally to see a figure or a type which makes you laugh.[199] You are lucky if the wit does not consist wholly of lewd jests " to make the Ladies look they know not how ".[200]

[195] See Macaulay, *Essays* : The Comic Dramatists of the Restoration.

[196] See, for instance, the dialogue between Courtine and Sylvia in the 5th Act of Otway, *The Souldiers Fortune*. This type of thing was called " slap-dash ". (Lee, *The Princess of Cleve*, II, 2.)—" This, Sirs, might properly enough be call'd a prize of Wit ; for you shall see 'em come in upon one another snip snap, hit for hit, as fast as can be. First one speaks, then presently t'other's upon him slap, with a Repartee ; then he at him again, dash with a new conceipt : and so eternally, eternally, I gad, till they go quite off the Stage." (Buckingham, *The Rehearsal*, III, 1.)—Dryden himself says : " As for Comedy, repartee is one of its chiefest graces ; the greatest pleasure of an audience is a chase of wit, kept up on both sides, and swiftly managed." (*An Essay of Dramatick Poesie*.)

[197] Preface to *le Mariage de Figaro*.

[198] Yet they had models and were acquainted with them. But see what Wycherley makes of Alcestis and of Agnes (*The Plain Dealer* and *The Country Wife*).

[199] The widow *Blackacre*, in *The Plain Dealer* ; *Sir Samuel Hearty* in Shadwell's *Virtuoso*.

[200]
　　" Here's nothing you will like ; no fustian Scenes,
　　　And nothing too of—you know what he means ;
　　　No double *Entendrés*, which your Sparks allow ;
　　　To make the Ladies look they know not how."
　　　　　　　　　(Prologue to Dryden's *Love Triumphant*.)

　　" Alas ! 'tis a meer out-of-fashion Play ;
　　　No Bawdy in 't to make the Ladies glow . . ."
　　　　　　　　　(Prologue to Dogget's *Country-Wake*.)

I suppose the ladies must have looked " they know not how " at passages like this :

" *Young Jorden :* Sure there is no woman so necessitated to venture on him.
Cureal : O, many.
Young Jorden : Not she that wears a stiff Busk to keep down a great belly, and is to pass for a Maid still ; or she that is forc'd to come to a Play in a Vizard-Mask to pick up a gallant to give her a Supper.
Cureal : Ha, ha, ha.

As a consequence this whole comic drama has been expunged

Young Jorden : Nay, not she that has lived to be a stale Maid, and is convinc'd by her own imperfections that she shall never know any pleasure, but what her own art and industry can create, but would think her self cast away on him."

(Ravenscroft, *The Citizen turn'd Gentleman*, II, 1.)

I should not venture to assert that there were any ladies who did not understand.

As further samples of this kind, see the character of Sir Jolly Jumble in *The Souldiers Fortune* by Otway ; Mrs. Behn's play *The Town-Fopp*, where one scene is laid in a brothel, and the mistress of the establishment initiates us into the details of her management ; the scene in Dryden's *Kind Keeper* where Aldo receives the town prostitutes ; or rather, see the whole play : note that it had been *softened down* before being printed.

All the comedies of the time should be quoted. Let it suffice to call attention to some conversations in Etherege's *Comical Revenge*, IV, 5, and still more to others in Shadwell's *Humorists* and *Virtuoso*. In the former of these two plays note particularly the first act and the character of Crazy ; in the latter the scenes between old Snarl and Mrs. Figgup. Here is a specimen :

" *Snarl :* . . . Where are the instruments of our Pleasure ? Nay, prethee do not frown, by the Mass thou shalt do 't now.
Figgup : I wonder that should please you so much, that pleases me so little ?
Snarl : I was us'd to 't at *Westminster*-School, I cou'd never leave it off since.
Figgup : Well, look under the Carpet then if I must.
Snarl : Very well, my dear Rogue. But dost hear, thou art too gentle. Do not spare thy pains. I love Castigation mightily.—So, here's good provision. (Pulls the Carpet, three or four Rods fall down.)" (Act III.)

Contemporary tragedy is not free from similar touches, witness the following taken from the works of Lee :

" *Titus :* Sir, I am marry'd.
Brutus : What, without my knowledge ?
Titus : My Lord, I ask your Pardon ; but that *Hymen*—
Brutus : Thou ly'st ; that honorable God would scorn it.
Some bawdy Flamen shuffled you together ;
Priapus lock'd you, while the *Bacchanals*
Sung your detested *Epithalamium*.
Which of thy blood were the curs'd Witnesses ?
Who would be there at such polluted Rites
But *Goats*, *Baboons*, some chatt'ring old *Silenus*
Or *Satyrs* grinning at your slimy Joys ? "

(*Lucius Junius Brutus*, I, 1.)

" *Ascanio Sforza* : . . . Would he were *Pope*,
Head of the Christian World, and I his Engine,
His particular member, to bring, to cast,
To throw, disperse, convey the warmest
Sprinklings of his benediction."

(*Caesar Borgia*, I.)

See also the same author's *Theodosius* (II, 1) where two women, Pulcheria and Julia, are present.

from English literature.[201] If Dryden's name is still held in high honour, it is because he wrote other things beside comedies. As for Shadwell, Ravenscroft, Mrs. Behn, Etherege and even Wycherley, their names have become mere memories ; their works are read only by the curious and by those who seek in them information about the characters they depict, and the people for whose pleasure the writers wrote.

These people had reason to be well satisfied, for everything was made according to their favourite recipe. Reflecting the manners of society, offering its members everything that could allure them, sparing no pains to devise new inventions, patronized by the King, the theatre was the great relaxation of people of fashion. They could not do without it. It was with extreme reluctance that they resigned themselves to its closing during the terrible Plague of 1665. While people were still dying of the scourge, they importuned the Bishops to hasten a Day of Thanksgiving for the Cessation of the Plague, that the playhouses might be re-opened.[202]

V

Dramatists' difficulty in satisfying the audience.—Audience limited in numbers ; perpetual demand for something new ; collaboration and adaptation. —Frivolity of the audience : Prologues and Epilogues

It might seem that in such circumstances the profession of drama-writer would have been one of the most brilliant and well recompensed. Nothing of the sort.

In the first place the number of enthusiastic theatre addicts was very limited. The City remained Puritan, horrified at the manners of the day and the audacity of the plays ; the citizens

---

[201] As early as 1749, Otway's comedy *Friendship in Fashion* was hissed because of its " obscenity " and driven from the stage (Johnson, *Lives of the English Poets*, Otway).—In 1818 Wycherley's *Country Wife* was still being played ; but the character of Horner no longer appeared " as Wycherley made him " (Hazlitt, *Lectures*, part II, p. 101).

[It is, of course, no longer true to say that this whole comic drama has been expunged from English literature. Much of it is reprinted in the Mermaid Series and the World's Classics. The Phœnix Society, a private society which employed professionals, revived many of the plays as such in the twenties of this century, and some have become part of the public repertoire. They are, one need hardly say, studied in the universities. B. D.]

[202] Pepys, Nov. 20, 1666.—" Nay, she (Lady Cartaret) told me they have heretofore had plays at Court, the very nights before the fast for the death of the late king." (Ibid., Oct. 15, 1666.)

did not attend the performances at all, or very rarely.[203]   " The
playhouse was abhorred by the Puritans, and avoided by those
who desired the character of seriousness or decency. A grave
lawyer would have debased his dignity, and a young trader
would have impaired his credit, by appearing in those mansions
of dissolute licentiousness." [204]   Even works composed to flatter
the political views of the citizenry could not break down this
aloofness.[205]   This meant that a large part of the normal theatre
audience was excluded, and perhaps the better part, people
sufficiently cultured to appreciate, and at the same time sufficiently unsophisticated and naïve, to recognize honest laughter
and genuine emotion, and be carried away by them.[206]

Theatre-goers were thus reduced to the Court and the tribe
of officials and idlers who revolved round the King. The fact
that the audience was thus limited, and always the same, made
it impossible to repeat the same plays with any frequency. A
play which had a run of ten consecutive performances was
counted a huge success.[207]   More often it was played only three
to six times.[208]   For the same reasons, revivals could not be
counted on. *Sir Martin Mar-all* by the Duke of Newcastle and
Dryden, and Etherege's *Comical Revenge,* two great successes of the

---

[203] See the Epilogue to Wycherley's *Gentleman Dancing Master.*

[204] Johnson, *Lives of the English Poets* : Dryden—" Of late the play-
houses are so extremely pestered with vizard-masks and their trade (occasion-
ing continual quarrels and abuses) that many of the more civilised part of
the town are uneasy in the company, and shun the theatre as they would a
house of scandal." (Wright, *Historia Histrionica,* 1699, p. 6 ; quoted by
Malone, *Historical Account . . .* p. 127.)   Despite the date 1699 Malone says
that this applies to " after the Restoration ".—" Men of *Figure* and Consideration are known by seldom being there (in the theatre) and Men of
Wisdom and Business by always being absent." (Tom Brown, *The Play-
House,* in Amusements *Serious and Comical, Works,* vol. III.)

[205]   " Our Popes and Fryars on one Side offend,
         And yet alass the City's not our Friend :
         The City neither likes us nor our wit,
         They say their Wives learn *ogling in the Pit ;
         They'r from the Boxes taught to make Advances,
         To answer stolen Sighs and naughty Glances . . ."
                    (Shadwell, Epilogue to *The Lancashire Witches.*)

         * A foolish word among the Canters for glancing.

[206] Even at the time people were well aware of this. " And he (T. Killigrew) tells me plainly that the City audience was as good as the Court ;
but now they are most gone." (Pepys, Feb. 12, 1666–7.)

[207] Downes (p. 37), speaking of the *Œdipus* by Dryden and Lee, says :
" it took prodigiously, being *Acted* 10 Days together ".

[208] See Genest, vol. I, *passim.*

day (they were played for a month), were revived after several years, the former being then played three times, the latter twice.[209] Authors were therefore compelled to write without ceasing ; since the audience could not be, the repertoire had to be, constantly renewed, and the paucity of spectators compensated by the abundance of plays.[210] Between 1662 and 1680 Dryden produced eighteen plays, one of which was in two parts, making in all ten acts ; the others were of five acts and most of them in verse. In some years his output ran to three : in 1678, for instance, *All for Love*, *The Kind Keeper* and *Œdipus* : ten acts in verse and five in prose. As a natural consequence, an author had to work fast : Dryden wrote *Tyrannick Love* in seven weeks [211] and *Amboyna* in a month.[212] Shadwell wrote *The Miser* in less than a month.[213] In his preface to *The Libertine* the same author tells us : " I must applaud my good Fortune, to have pleased with so little pains : there being no Act in it, which cost me above five days writing ; and that the last two (the Play-House having great occasion for a Play) were both written in four days, as several can testifie." [214] Ravenscroft wrote a five-act play in seven days.[215]

These demands of the theatre compelled authors to have recourse to two expedients : collaboration (of the bad kind which springs, not from community of literary interests, but from consideration of self-interest) and *adaptation*, which later became the ruin of English drama.[216] Dryden collaborated with D'Avenant to rewrite *The Tempest* ; with Lee in *Œdipus* and

---

[209] Genest, vol. I, pp. 75, 76, 123, 124.

[210]   " He still must write ; and Banquier-like, each day
            Accept new Bills, and he must break, or pay."
                                (Dryden, Epilogue to *An Evening's Love*.)

[211] See the Preface.
[212] See the Dedication.
[213] " 'Tis not barrenness of wit or invention, that, makes us borrow from the *French*, but laziness ; and this was the occasion of my making use of *l'Avare*. This play . . . was wrote in less than a month." (Notice of *The Miser*.)
[214] Preface to *The Libertine*.
[215] " In three dayes time, the Three first Acts were Made, Transcrib'd, and given them (the actors) to write out in Parts.—The Two last Acts took me up just so much time : one Week compleated it." (*The Careless Lovers* : The Epistle to the Reader.)
[216] *Adaptation* consists in taking a foreign play, transferring the scene to England and giving the characters English names. Allusions are modified, touches of wit in the original are replaced by local jests, and the play is finished. An older English play is *adapted* by modernizing it.

The Duke of Guise. Crowne and an unknown collaborator brought out a spiritless reproduction of *Andromache*, partly in verse, partly in prose. The plays of Shakespeare and his contemporaries were rewritten ; the French and Spanish drama were plundered. In addition to *The Tempest* Dryden pirated *Troilus and Cressida* and staged *l'Étourdi* as *Sir Martin Mar-All*. D'Avenant combined *Measure for Measure* and *Much Ado about Nothing* into *The Law against Lovers* and concocted an opera out of *Macbeth*. Wycherley borrowed his *Gentleman Dancing Master* from Calderon, his *Plain Dealer* from Molière's *Misanthrope*, and blended *l'École des Maris* with *l'École des Femmes* into *The Country Wife*. Otway's *History and Fall of Caius Marius* is nothing but *Romeo and Juliet*.[216a] Molière supplied Otway with *The Cheats of Scapin* ; Racine provided him with *Titus and Berenice*. Tate remodelled *King Lear*. Shadwell rewrote Shakespeare's *Timon* and Molière's *l'Avare*. Lacey converted *The Taming of the Shrew* nto *Sauny the Scott*, manufactured *The Dumb Lady* out of *le Médecin malgré lui* and *l'Amour Médecin*, and *Sir Hercules Buffoon* out of Massinger's *City Madam*.[217] Mrs. Philips translated Corneille's *Pompée*[218] and an anonymous author *le Menteur*.[219] This list might be considerably extended. Almost the whole of Molière was lifted.

All authors of the time borrowed more or less. There was

[216a] [It is not true to say that Otway's *Caius Marius* " is nothing but *Romeo and Juliet* ". The play is about Marius, Otway's sources being the usual ones, such as Plutarch, Shakespeare's play providing the sub-plot.

The whole paragraph needs some comment. The way the Restoration dramatists treated other people's plays, and turned them to their own use was not an invention of their own, and the practice has luckily not been discontinued. All playwrights, when they need to, borrow and " improve ", or at least adapt to their own country and society. If *Sir Martin Mar-All* came from *L'Étourdi*, *L'Étourdi* itself was an adaptation of drama foreign to France. These playwrights, like Molière himself, took their good things where they could find them. B. D.]

[217] In *Sir Hercules Buffoon*, Lacey makes one of his characters rightly remark : " Now Poets are turned cobblers ; they vamp and mend old plays." (II, 4.)

[That was in the good old tradition, for it was also the practice of the Elizabethan-Jacobean playwrights, including Shakespeare, to the despair of editors and the delight of writers of Ph.D. theses. With the earlier playwrights also, collaboration often sprang from considerations of self-interest rather than from a community of literary interests, so this harmless practice was no monstrous innovation of the amoral Restoration dramatists. B. D.]

[218] *Pompey*, 1663. The translation was made at the request of the Earl of Orrery. See *Biographia Dramatica*, s.v. Pompey.

[219] *The Lyar*, 1661. See *Biographia Dramatica*, s.v. Mistaken Beauty, or *The Lyar*.

even one who did almost nothing else, a certain Edward Ravenscroft. He is nowadays almost completely forgotten, but for a long time he and his dozen plays held a certain position in the theatre world. He rehashed Shakespeare's *Titus Andronicus*, and pieced together his comedy *The Citizen turn'd Gentleman* from *le Bourgeois gentilhomme*, *Monsieur de Pourceaugnac* and *l'Avare*. *The Careless Lovers* was constructed from such fragments of *Monsieur de Pourceaugnac* as he had not been able to work into his *Citizen*, and a third fine-combing of the same play provided him with his *Canterbury Guests*. *Le Mariage Forcé* combined with the *Fourberies de Scapin* and the unused passages of *le Bourgeois gentilhomme*,[220] yielded yet another play, and so on.

It will be realized that the audiences of those days had an unholy appetite for plays and gave little respite to their suppliers. But this was not their only annoying characteristic. The author's sorrows were not over when his play was ready. We must never forget that people's sole idea was to have a good time, in whatever way and by whatever means they could contrive it.[221] So theatre-goers did not come in the best mood to pay serious attention. They came not so much to enjoy the play as to make merry at the play's expense. They came to look and to listen, but also to be seen.[222] They were more taken up with

[220] " Scaramouch a Philosopher, Harlequin a Schoolboy, Bravo, Merchant and Magician."—See *Biographia Dramatica*, s.v. Ravenscroft (Edward) and my bibliography.

[221] They even made merry over affairs of state : " At the daily meeting of the Council, when the great Lord Chancellor, Clarendon, wearing one of the magnificent periwigs of the period, was gravely expounding to Charles II his lengthy and carefully thought out opinions, Buckingham would post himself behind the Chancellor's armchair, mimicking the speaker's attitude and gestures, stretching out his arm and tapping with his foot in time with his model." (Geffroy, p. 199.)

[222] " He fears not Sparks who with brisk Dress and Mien,
Come not to hear or see, but to be seen.
Each prunes himself, and with a languishing Eye,
Designs to kill a Lady, by the by."
(Shadwell, Epilogue to *The Squire of Alsatia*.)

" . . . you, the fine, loud gentlemen o' th' Pit,
Who damn all Plays ;
Now, you shrewd Judges, who the Boxes sway,
Leading the Ladies hearts and sense astray,
And for their sakes, see all, and hear no Play :
Correct your Cravats, Foretops, Lock behind ;
The Dress and Breeding of the Play ne'er mind.
(Wycherley, Prologue to *The Plain Dealer*.)

themselves and with the theatre itself than with what was happening on the stage. For women, theatre-going has always
been an opportunity for dressing up : *spectatum veniunt, veniunt
spectentur ut ipsae.*[223] They naturally continued the custom :
they came in order to be admired by the men, as the men came
in order to be admired by them. " Really," says Selfish in
Shadwell's *True Widow*, " I never come to a Play, but upon
account of seeing the Ladies." [224] They had more than enough
to choose from. It was customary for women to come masked
to the performances, which made it impossible to distinguish
honourable women from the others.[225] The masks were a subject
of much interest for the gallants :

> . . . when vizard-mask appears in pit,
> Straight every man who thinks himself a wit
> Perks up, and, managing his comb with grace,
> With his white wig sets off his nut-brown face ;[226]
> That done, bears up to the prize, and views each limb,
> To know her by her rigging and her trim ;
> Then, the whole noise of fops to wagers go,—
> " Pox on her, 't must be she " ; and—" Damme, no ! " [227]

It was evidently the masked women who particularly attracted
these gentlemen to comedy at the theatre. People dined at
about 1 or 2 o'clock p.m. and went on to the theatre where the
performances began about half-past three.[228]

---

[223] Ovid, *Artis Amatoriæ*, I, l. 99.—" Here the Ladies come to shew
their Cloaths." (Tom Brown, *Amusements Serious and Comical, The Play-House,
Works*, vol. III.)

[224] Act IV, 1.

[225] " . . . By that Mask of modesty which Women wear promiscuously
in publick ; they are all alike, and you can no more know a kept Wench
from a Woman of Honour by her looks than by her Dress . . ." (Wycherley,
Dedication to *The Plain-Dealer*.)

> " Audacious Vizards too, so fast do grow,
>   You hardly can the Virtuous from 'em know."
>   (Crowne, Epilogue to *Sir Courtly Nice*.)

> " The proper Use of Visors once was made,
>   When only worn by such as own'd the Trade :
>   Tho' now all mingle with 'em so together,
>   That you can hardly know the one from t' other."
>   (Otway, Epilogue to *Titus and Berenice*.)

[226] A brown complexion was all the fashion, for Charles II's was brown.

[227] Dryden, Prologue to the Second Part of *The Conquest of Granada*.

[228] Dryden, Original Prologue to *The Wild Gallant*. See also Malone,
Historical Account . . ., p. 158.

... A Town Gallant ...
... repairs to th' Play to meet a sinner :
And here with Burgundy and brisk sableé
Inspir'd, with vizard-Masque holds reparteé.[229]

Here is a picture of the gallant's arrival :

He advances into the middle of the *Pit*, struts about a while, to render his good parts Conspicuous, pulls out his *Comb*, Carreens his *Wigg*, *Hums* the *Orange-Wench* to give her her own rates for her China-fruit, and immediately *Sacrifices* the fairest of them, to the shrine of the next *Vizor Mask*. Then gravely sits down, and falls half *asleep*, unless some *petulant Wench* hard by, keep him awake by treading on his *Toe*, or a wanton Complement ; Yet all on a sudden to shew his *Judgment*, and prove himself at once a *Wit* and a *Critick*, he starts up and with a Tragical Face, *Damns the Play* though he have not *heard* (at least understood) two Lines of it. However when 'tis done, he picks up a Miss, and pinching her fingers in a soft Tone, and looks abominably *Languishing*, he Whispers, " *Damn me, Madam ! If you were but sensible, and all that of the Passion I have for you ; and the Flames which your irresistable Charms, and all that have kindled in my Breast, you would be merciful, and Honour me with your Angelical Company, to take a Draught of Loves Posset at next Tavern.*" But if he finds her honest and cannot prevail, then he cries aloud, *Damn ye for a Puritanical Whore, what make you in the Pit here : The Twelve penny Gallery with Camlet-Cloaks and Foot-boys is good enough for you.* And so raises his Seige, and leaves her.[230]

If the masks were few or uninteresting the gentlemen amused themselves by playing practical jokes on their neighbours. They dug them in the back with their fists or threw their hats into the air. Squabbles and fisticuffs ensued. They shouted ; they criticized the play at the top of their voice ; they teased the orange-women ; they moved from the pit to the gallery and from the gallery to the pit. They thought nothing of turning their back to the stage ; they played cards in the boxes ; they munched fruit while the performance was going on. Everyone had songs, epigrams or satires in his hand.[231]

[229] Ravenscroft, Epilogue to *The Citizen turn'd Gentleman* :
" Leave coming here, when you do not intend
To see the Play, but pick up a she-friend.
Leave sharping for your selves, and pay your Guinny
For Procuration there to honest Jenny."
(Prologue, Spoken in *Lent*. Preceding Ravenscroft's *Titus Andronicus*. Jenny Cromwell was a well-known procuress.)

[230] *The Character of a Town-Gallant.*—In one of Hogarth's engravings we see two of the " orange-women " here mentioned.

[231] " They (the young men of this age) are vitious illiterate foolish Fellows, good for nothing but to roar and make a noise in a Play-house. To

This picture reveals an audience anything but attentive. But these were only the minor incidents common to every performance ; matters sometimes went further. One day some young men, over-stimulated by a heavy meal, burst into the theatre with lighted torches and flung them at the actors, loudly

be very brisk with pert Whores in Vizards . . . And when Whores are not there, they play Monkey-tricks with one another . . .'' (Shadwell, *The Virtuoso*, II, 2.)

> " Our Gallerys too, were finely us'd of late,
> Where roosting Masques sat cackling for a Mate :
> They came not to see Plays but to act their own,
> And had throng'd Audiences when we had none.
> Our Plays it was impossible to hear,
> The honest Country Men were forc't to swear :
> Confound you, give your bawdy prating o'er
> Or Zounds, I'le fling you i' th' Pitt, you bawling Whore.''
> (Crowne, Epilogue to *Sir Courtly Nice*.)

> " The empty Head, that never thought before,
> But on New Fashions, or a fresh new Whore :
> Who without us no Afternoon could spend,
> Nor shew Himself, nor meet a secret Friend ;
> Whom mounting from the Pit we use to see
> (For dangerous Intrigues) to th' Gallery ;
> Where stead of Maidenheads 'tis oft his hap
> By bold advent'ring to atchieve a Clap
> Or down he comes, and lolls i' th' Orange-wenches lap.
> For News he now walks gravely up and down," etc.
> (Shadwell, Prologue to *The Woman-Captain*.)

> " He who comes hither with design to hiss
> And with a bum revers'd to whisper Miss,
> To comb a Perriwig, or to shew gay cloathes,
> Or to vent Antique non-sence with new oaths,
> Our poet welcomes . . . ''
> (D'Urfey, Prologue to *The Fool turn'd Critick*.)

" Thou shalt . . . after Noon at the Theatre exalted in a Box, give Audience to ev'ry trim amorous twiring Fop of the Corner, that comes thither to make a Noise, hear no Play, and show himself ; thou Shalt, my *Bona Roba*.''
(Otway, *Friendship in Fashion*, V.)

> " . . . Flutt'ring Hectores on the Vizard fall
> One half o' th' Play they spend in noise and braul.''
> (Lee, Epilogue to *Sophonisba*.)

In the Prologue to St. Serfe's comedy, *Tarugo's Wiles, or The Coffee House* an actor says : " it may scare the Ladies from eating their fruit.''

The fourth Act of Shadwell's *True Widow* is laid in a theatre. Here are a few phrases culled from it : " Several young Coxcombs fool with the Orange-women.'' A *Bully* says : " What Play do they play ? some confounded Play or other.'' Another exclaims : " A Pox on't, Madam ! What should we do at this damn'd Play-house ? Let's send for some Cards, and Play at Lang-trilloo in the Box.'' There are literary discussions, there are intrigues, and a gentleman who refuses to pay the Door-Keeper for his seat, hurling abuse against the Duchess of Portsmouth.[232] On another occasion one of the spectators insulted another of the King's mistresses, Nell Gwyn, who was present ; a young gallant [233] took up her defence, and one half of the public drew swords against the other. It even happened that concurrently with the tragedy being enacted on the stage, a real tragedy was taking place in the pit as when Sir Thomas Armstrong one day stabbed and killed Mr. Scroop.[234]

An audience of this kind, irresponsible, temperamental and riotous, was easy neither to attract nor to retain. Strive as they might to cater for its taste, authors were not always successful in combating its wayward caprices. A troup of marionettes was enough completely to empty two theatres and an appeal had to be made to the King to protect them against such dangerous rivalry.[235]

At all costs some means must be devised to satisfy tastes so little interested in drama proper, to fix the wandering attention

---

but will not leave. One of the audience complains of his neighbours : "These Fellows will be witty and trouble us." Another : "See how kind the Ladies are to me : Pretty Rogue ! Let me repose my Head in thy soft Bosom." Another uses insulting words (Whore, etc.) to a mask who does not answer. Another "Raps People on the Backs, and twirls their *hats, and then looks demurely, as if he did not do it.*" Thereupon there is a fight ; swords are drawn, the actors vanish and the women scatter screaming.

Tom Brown represents *Country Gentlemen* in the theatre loudly discussing the hunt. "A *Bully Beau* comes drunk into the Pit, screaming out : *Damn me*, Jack, '*tis a Confounded Play, let's to a Whore and spend our time better.*" (*The Play-House* ; *Works*, vol. III. Amusements Serious and Comical.)

See also *The Tatler*, No. 1 ; Epilogue to Otway's *Titus and Berenice* ; Prologue to Lee's *Rival Queens* ; Prologue to Southerne's *Disappointment* (attributed to Dryden) ; Pepys, Nov. 2, 1667 ; Prologue, *Spoken in Lent* prefixed to Ravenscroft's *Titus Andronicus* ; *Prologue Against the Disturbers of the Pit* by Rochester (*Works*, I, p. 56) ; Prologue to Dryden's *Cleomenes*.

[232] Malcolm, p. 177.

[233] William Herbert, later Earl of Pembroke and first plenipotentiary at Ryswick. This incident is recorded by M. W. Thornbury, *Haunted London*, p. 461, and by Dr. Doran, *Their Majesties' Servants*, p. 21. Neither quotes his authority.

[234] *Makbeth*, a Tragedy ; which was reviv'd by the Dukes Company, and re-printed with Alterations and New Songs, 4°, *Lond.*, 1674 (this is D'Avenant's arrangement). . . . "At the Acting of this Tragedy, on the Stage, I saw a real one acted in the Pit ; I mean the Death of Mr. *Scroop*, who received his death's wound from the late Sir *Thomas Armstrong*, and died presently after he was remov'd to a House opposite to the Theatre, in *Dorset-Garden* (Langbaine, I, p. 460). See also Dryden's Epilogue for the Union of the Two Troops in 1682 (Christie, pp. 457–8).—Reresby tells (Jan. 8, 1679) how one of his friends was nearly wounded in the theatre by a drunken neighbour who had drawn his sword.

[235] Cibber, *Apology*, p. 57.

of gallants and rowdies, to counter the attractions of prostitutes,
interrupters and marionettes. To meet the case, recourse was
had to prologues and epilogues.

The function of the prologue was, not so much to introduce
the author or the play, as to summon the audience as bells call
the faithful to church and to compensate them in advance if
the play was " dull ".   In proportion as the play was " dull " [236]
—that is to say serious—the prologue had to be lively and highly
spiced.

" . . . you think yourselves ill used," says Dryden to his
audience,

> When in smart prologues you are not abused.
> A civil prologue is approved by no man ;
> You hate it as you do a civil woman.
> Your fancy's palled, and liberally you pay
> To have it quickened ere you see a play.
> Just as old sinners, worn from their delight
> Give money to be whipped to appetite.[237]

Such was the task assigned to the prologue.

The epilogue's business was to amuse the public and more
especially, while feigning to crave indulgence, to offer some
broad jokes to make good any tediousness or difficulty of the
play. The prologue was the appetizer before the meal, the
epilogue a liqueur to aid digestion.

Prologue and epilogue both discharged their duty conscien-
tiously. The author racked his brains to provide the attraction
of novelty and originality. The prologue to *The Indian Queen* [238]

---

[236]   " Prologues, *like Bells to Churches, toul you in*
              With Chimeing Verse ; till the dull Playes begin . . . "
                                (Dryden, Prologue to *The Assignation*.)

[237] Prologue to *Secret-Love*, or *The Maiden-Queen* ; Lee's Epilogue to
Gloriana expresses the same idea more vividly :

> " We'l deal with you, Gallants, in your own way,
> And treat you like those Punks that love for pay ;
> *Cartwright* and I, dress'd like two thund'ring Whores,
> With rods will stand behind the Play-house doors,
> And firk you up each day to pleasure duly,
> As *Jenny Cromwell* does, or *Betty Buly*."

It was the actor Haines who spoke this epilogue ; Cartwright was one
of his fellow-actors. Jenny Cromwell, already mentioned, and Betty Buly
were two procuresses.—There had been prologues before, but how different
were those of Shakespeare and Ben Jonson. The epilogue was unusual before
the time of Charles II. (Malone, *Historical Account* . . . pp. 123, 124.)

[238] By Sir Robert Howard and Dryden.

was spoken by " two Indian children ", the epilogue to *The Indian Emperor* by " a Mercury ". The original prologue to *The Wild Gallant* brought " two astrologers " on to the stage, that of *Troilus and Cressida* the " ghost " of Shakespeare.[239] Popular actresses were entrusted with the speaking. The prologue of Sir Robert Howard's *Duke of Lerma* was spoken by Mrs. Ellen (Gwyn) and Mrs. Nepp.[240] We have already seen that on such occasions they were often dressed as men. Sometimes prologues and epilogues were sung.[241] Surprises were introduced : now, two prologues at a time on the stage [242] ; now, after about twenty lines the speaker went off to return a moment later crying :

> I had forgot one half, I do protest,
> And now am sent again to speak the rest . . .[243]

But the triumph of this type of thing was the prologue spoken by Nell Gwyn in a large hat. The credit for this invention belongs to the actor Nokes, of the Duke's Company. He was the first to have the bright idea of appearing surmounted by a hat with an enormous brim. It seems that this novelty—the salt of which has perhaps somewhat lost its savour nowadays —was considered extremely witty and made a palpable hit. But it was reserved for Dryden to exploit Nokes's idea to the full. He got a hat made with a brim " as large as a cart-wheel " and presented it to Nell Gwyn who masqueraded in it to speak the prologue to the first part of the *Conquest of Granada*. It was a stroke of genius : " the entire theatre fell into convulsions ; the King nearly choked with laughter ". Tradition adds that it was in this headgear that Nell Gwyn first attracted the attention of her royal lover : Charles II, swept off his feet with admiration, sought her out behind the scenes and carried her off that very day.[244]

Note that this preposterous kit was used not for the prologue to a comedy but to a tragic drama. Imagine a musician who

---

[239] These three plays are Dryden's.

[240] Obviously Pepys's friend Mrs. Knipp.

[241] *The Man is the Master*, a comedy of D'Avenant's : " The prologue but poor, and the epilogue little in it but the extraordinariness of it, it being sung by Harris and another in the form of a ballad." (ballet ? —E. O. L.). (Pepys, March 26, 1667–8.)

[242] Dryden's *Rival Ladies*.

[243] Dryden's *Secret-Love, or the Maiden-Queen*.

[244] Downes, *Roscius Anglicanus*, edited by Thomas Davies, Appendix, pp. 14 and 18.

would allow a medley or a pom-pom-pom to be played as the
overture to a tragic opera. Nothing less was customary in
those days. Everyone—audience and authors alike—unanimously refused to take anything seriously. The author not
only took care to warn his audience in advance against any
genuine emotion which his work might evoke, but when the
play was over was the first to laugh at it. Like Penelope he
hastened to unravel in his epilogue the fabric laboriously woven
in his five acts.[245]   In Sir Robert Howard's *Vestal Virgin* all the
chief characters perished at the close. After this murderous
climax, the comic actor Lacey entered *ex abrupto* and chattered
nonsense to the audience whom the dramatist had just plunged
into grief. Later the climax was altered : only one character
was sacrificed. Lacey arrived and finding everybody alive but
one, complained that he was no longer wanted and that they
had completely ruined his epilogue.[246]

Better still. At the close of Dryden's *Tyrannick Love*, Princess
Valeria kills herself rather than marry an unloved husband.
Her lifeless body remains stretched out upon the stage and people
come to carry it away. But as one of the bearers draws near
to raise the corpse, the dead woman cries out :

> Hold ! Are you mad ? You damn'd confounded Dog !
> I am to rise and speak the epilogue.

It was Nell Gwyn who, flinging aside her character of
princess, became herself again and took the public into her
confidence :

> I come, kind gentlemen, strange news to tell ye,
> I am the ghost of poor departed Nelly.
> Sweet ladies, be not frighted ; I'll be civil ;
> I'm what I was, a little harmless devil . . .
> O poet, damned dull poet, who could prove
> So senseless, to make Nelly die for love !
> Nay, what's yet worse, to kill me in the prime
> Of Easter-term, in tart and cheese-cake time !
> I'll fit the fop ; for I'll not one word say,
> To excuse his godly, out-of-fashion play ;
> A play, which, if you dare but twice sit out,
> You'll all be slandered, and be thought devout . . .[247]

---

[245] See what No. 338 of the *Spectator* has to say about the effect of these
comic epilogues to tragedies.

[246] Sir Robert Howard's volume : *Five New Plays* contains both versions
and both epilogues.

[247] Dryden tells us that he wrote *Tyrannick Love* in praise of piety.

As for my epitaph when I am gone,
I'll trust no poet, but will write my own :—
Here Nelly lies, who, though she lived a slattern,
Yet died a princess, acting in St. Catherine.[248]

Highly uplifting and highly favourable to tragic emotion !
But to be given information about the more interesting personalities of the stage ; to hear the back stage gossip was almost
as amusing as unveiling masked faces, and so the audience
listened. The authors, who knew the type of mind they were
catering for, were careful, by prologue and epilogue, to keep
the gentlemen informed of the ways and doings of the actress
ladies. One poet pleads with his audience that they shall :

Think him not duller for this year's delay ;
He was prepared, the women were away ;
And men, without their parts, can hardly play.
If they, through sickness, seldom did appear,
Pity the virgins of each theatre :
For, at both houses, 'twas a sickly year !
And pity us, your servants, to whose cost
In one such sickness nine whole months are lost.[249]

Or it might be an actress [250] who would come to complain of
her lovers :

Who wou'd have thought such hellish times to 've seen
When I shou'd be neglected at eighteen ?

We are justified in considering these prologues and epilogues
not exactly models of reserve. Yet those so far quoted are
anything but the most outspoken. Their usual tone is similar
to that we have already noted in the songs and satires. Indecent
allusions, phrases with a double meaning, often, too, words of
incredible coarseness so abound that it is difficult to give the
reader an idea of them in any language suited to his ears. Here,
however, is a prologue of Dryden's which it is just possible to
quote, as a sample of the type. It introduces *An Evening's Love* :

---

[248] St. Catherine is one of the characters in the play.—The epilogue
to Otway's *History and Fall of Caius Marius* was similarly spoken by Mrs.
Barry who had just been playing Lavinia :

  " A Mischief on't ! though I'm agen alive
  May I believe this Play of ours shall thrive ? " etc.

[249] Dryden, Epilogue to the first part of *The Conquest of Granada*.
[250] Mrs. Currer in Mrs. Behn's Prologue to *The Feign'd Curtizans*.

When first our poet set himself to write,
Like a young bridegroom on his wedding-night,
He laid about him, and did so bestir him,
His Muse could never lie in quiet for him :
But now his honey-moon is gone and past,
Yet the ungrateful drudgery must last,
And he is bound, as civil husbands do,
To strain himself in complaisance to you :
To write in pain, and counterfeit a bliss,
Like the faint smacking of an after-kiss.
But you, like wives ill pleased, supply his want ;
Each writing Monsieur is a fresh gallant :
And though, perhaps, 'twas done as well before,
Yet still there's something in a new amour.
Your several poets work with several tools,
One gets you wits, another gets you fools :
This pleases you with some by-stroke of wit,
This finds some cranny that was never hit.
But should these jaunty lovers daily come
To do your work, like your good man at home,
Their fine small-timbered wits would soon decay ;
These are gallants but for a holiday.
Others you had, who oftener have appeared,
Whom for mere impotence you have cashiered :
Such as at first came on with pomp and glory,
But, overstraining, soon fell flat before ye.
Their useless weight with patience long was borne,
But at the last you threw them off with scorn.
As for the poet of this present night,
Though now he claims in you an husband's right,
He will not hinder you of fresh delight.
He, like a seaman, seldom will appear,
And means to trouble home but thrice a-year ;
That only time from your gallants he'll borrow ;
Be kind to-day, and cuckold him tomorrow.

It is not hard to see why ladies took the precaution of wearing a mask when coming to hear such pretty verses. But the limit had not yet been reached : the final triumph was to put the grossest indecencies into women's mouths, ignoring the possibilities of euphemism. But further quotation is impossible.[251]

[251] [Beljame's last sentence reads in the original " But further translation is impossible ". He makes the following note. B. D.] Yet quote I must, for these are historical documents. First, some fragments from the epilogue to Duffett's *Spanish Rogue* spoken by Mrs. Kneppe :

" . . . Kind Women, new *French* Words, and Fashions got :
And finding all *French* Tricks so much did please,
'T oblige you more, They got—ev'n their Disease . . .

VI

Courtiers' literary pretensions.—Authors compelled to seek courtiers' favour :
Dedications.—Incidents : Dryden and Sir Robert Howard, the Duke of
Newcastle, the Duke of Buckingham, the Earl of Rochester

When an author had succeeded in satisfying the clamorous
impatience of the theatres, and had overcome the frivolity of
his audience, he had still not surmounted all his difficulties.
One of the most serious remained. The courtiers naturally did
not surrender in favour of the theatre their pretensions to being
men of wit. On the contrary, it was in the theatre that they
most enjoyed displaying their wit. Those who were able to
rise above songs and satires could not resist the craving to hear
their names bandied about by a larger, though more dangerous,
public than that of the drawing-room. Villiers, Duke of
Buckingham, Sir Charles Sedley, the Honourable Sir Robert

O 'tis so gente ! So modish ! and so fine !
To shrug and cry, Faith *Jack* ! I drink no wine :
For I've a swinging Clap this very time," etc.

Read the epilogue to Wycherley's *Country Wife* in the same taste, also
spoken by a woman ; read also Dryden's prologue written for the revival
of *The Wild Gallant* and his Epilogue to *The Assignation*. The works of
Dryden and Wycherley are easily come by ; the plays from which I take
the following quotations are less accessible.

Epilogue to Settle : *The Empress of Morocco* :

" This play like Country Girls come up to Town
Long'd t'appear fine, in Jewels and rich Gown ;
And so,
              Hoping it's Pride your Courtiers would support,
To please You, lost its Maiden-head at Court . . .
A generous Gallant though tired and Cloy'd,
Should still speak well of what he has enjoy'd.
Should you damn this you would your selves reproach,
'Tis barb'rous to defame what you debauch.
Nay, now you've Cast it off, yet do not Frown : ⎱
Though like the Refuge of a *Miss* o'th' Town   ⎬
It is turn'd Common, Yours for half a crown . . . ⎰
Thus your applause resembles your Amours,
Have we not seen (*Oh loves almighty Powers*) !
A *Wench* with tallow-looks and winter-Face,
Continue one Man's Favourite seven Years space :
Some Ravishing knack i'th' sport and some brisk motion,
Keeps the gilt *Coach* and the gallants Devotion . . ." etc.

Epilogue to Ravenscroft's *Citizen turn'd Gentleman* :

" . . . Tow'rds morning, when they think of going home,
Each Gallant on a Couch in the next room,
In's turn, takes gentle solace with his Punk ;
Drops her a Guinney, and sends her home half-drunk.

Howard, the Earl of Orrery, the Duke of Newcastle, Sir Robert
Stapylton, Gentleman Usher of His Majesty's Most Honourable
Privy Chamber, Sir Francis Fane, Knight of the Bath, Sir
William Killigrew, the Queen's Vice-Chamberlain, Sir Samuel
Tuke, the Earl of Bristol, etc., wrote plays and had them
produced.[252]   Rochester re-wrote Beaumont and Fletcher's
Valentinian [253] ;   Waller and Lord Buckhurst tried their hand
at a translation of Corneille's *Pompée* [254] ;   Sir John Denham
helped Mrs. Philips, " the matchless Orinda ", to handle the
same author's *Horace* [255] ;   the Earl of Mulgrave re-modelled
Shakespeare's *Julius Cæsar*.[256]   Those who, like the Earl of
Roscommon [257] and Sir Car Scroop [258] were aware that they
possessed no spark of dramatic genius, sought at least to provide
the theatre with songs or prologues.   The ordinary man of
fashion contented himself with theorizing and posing as *arbiter
elegantiarum*.   The most insignificant little coxcomb assumed,
with his fine clothes and his Chedreux wig, the right of passing

---

. . . Ladies, our Author trusts in you.
He is a man as modest for his age,
As most you've seen, who know him dare engage
That he has kept 'till now his pusillage."

Epilogue to Lee's *Nero* :

" . . . May each Gallant that has an assignation,
Be jilted after four hours expectation ;
Or if the masked Gentlewoman come
Spight of long Scarff, may she be dogg'd from home :
May ye—
In height of Titilation hear a rapping
And then the jealous Cuckold take ye napping."

I give it up.   But that is not to say that the mine is exhausted.

A point to note in this shameless writing is that all reverence for childhood is lacking.   Read for instance this passage from Mrs. Behn's *Abdelazer*,
" Spoken by little Mis. *Ariell* " :

" Your kindness, Gallants, I shall soon repay . . .
Your last Applauses, like refreshing showrs,
Made me spring up and bud like early Flow'rs ;
Since then I'm grown at least an Inch in height,
And shall e're long be full blown for delight."

[252] See my Bibliography.
[253] See my Bibliography, s.v. Wilmot (John).
[254] *Biographia Dramatica*, s.v. Pompey the Great.
[255] Ibid., s.v. *Horace*.
[256] His version is printed in his *Works*.
[257] Prologue to *Pompey* : *A Tragedy* . . . *Translated from the* French *of
Monsr.* Corneille, by *Mrs.* Katherine Philips (in her *Miscellaneous Works*,
p. 3).
[258] Prologue for Lee's *Rival Queens* ; song for Lee's *Mithridates* ; prologue
for Etherege's *Man of Mode*.

authoritative judgment on literary questions [259] ; and it was to comedy that he devoted his severest and noisiest condemnations. At the theatre, writes a contemporary, the gallant " resigns himself to sleep, but roused suddenly proclaims his pretensions to wit and criticism, by loudly damning the play, with a most tragical face ".[260] The spectators whom Shadwell introduces in *A True Widow* noisily express their opinions on what is being acted.[261]

These individual sharpshooters were merely annoying folk who might be tiresome but were not greatly to be feared. There were others more dangerous ; those who were known as *Flagwits*,[262] comparing them with the admiral's flagship whose signals govern the movements of the whole fleet. As one epilogue puts it :

> . . . And where a lot of smilers lent an ear
> To one that talked, I knew the foe was there.
> The club of jests went round ; he who had none,
> Borrowed of the next, and told it for his own.[263]

These " leading Voters of the Pit " [264] with their following of friends and flatterers always ready to take their lightest expression of opinion as an order to fight, were a serious menace, and in a period when literature was the correct and fashionable thing, there were many of them. The most insignificant scribbler who borrowed a gleam of importance from his rank, his profession or his position near the King, became a literary sun round whom revolved a whole system of inferior planets. All writers of standing had their little courts, their flatterers, their coteries, and became the dispensers of success. Woe to the author who displeased them ! The hounds were unleashed against him,[265]

---

[259] " How often have I heard true wit call'd stuff,
        By Men with nothing in their Brains but Snuff ?
        Each Shante Spark, that can the Fashion hit. ⎫
        Place his Hat thus, role full (,) forsooth(')s a Wit ; ⎬
        And thinks his Cloaths allow him judge of it." ⎭
                        (Crowne, Epilogue to *Sir Courtly Nice*.)

[260] *Proteus Redivivus, the Art of Wheedling*, a little work written in the reign of Charles II, quoted by Malcolm, p. 167. See p. 59, my quotation from *The Character of a Town Gallant* couched in almost identical terms.

[261] See also Pepys, Oct. 4, 1664, and Feb. 18, 1666–7.

[262] St. Serfe, Prologue to *Tarugo's Wiles*.

[263] Dryden, Epilogue to *An Evening's Love*.

[264] Lee : Prologue to *Lucius Junius Brutus*.

[265] " . . . It Met with the clamorous opposition of a numerous party, bandied against it, and resolved, as much as they could, to damn it, right

cat-calls [266] and hisses were the order of the day. When Colonel
Henry Howard's *United Kingdoms* was being performed, the Duke
of Buckingham, who was the declared enemy of the heroic style,
organized a regular attack upon the play. Like a commander-
in-chief he disposed his forces throughout the theatre, urged
them on and gave the signal for whistles. But the author knew
his world and had forces of his own at his disposal and the two
parties nearly came to blows. An ambush was laid at the exit
of the theatre to manhandle the Duke.[267]

Authors of commoner stock had no such resources at their
command. They could neither arm others in their defence nor
themselves draw sword against their enemies, as their aristocratic
colleagues so readily did.[268] They were driven therefore to
diplomacy in order to propitiate the capricious deities of success
with whom it was impossible to contend. This required tact
and resourcefulness. The great lords considered wit and taste
as the prerogative of birth ; every author who bore an honoured
name had a claim to their admiration or at worst to their
tolerance [269] (I know of none save Buckingham who drew the

---

or wrong, before they had heard or seen a word on't." (Shadwell, Preface
to *The Humorists*.) See Langbaine, s.v. *Shadwell*.

> " I'm told that some are present here today,
> Who e're they see, resolve to Dam this Play."
>
> (Lee, Prologue to *Nero*.)

[266] One way of expressing disapproval in the theatre was to imitate
the mewing of a cat (Malone, *Historical Account* . . . p. 186, note 7).—
" *Banditti* or *A Ladies Distress*, a Comedy acted at the Theatre-Royal, printed
in quarto, *Lond.*, 1686. This Play was affronted in the Acting by some who
thought themselves Criticks, and others with Cat-calls, endeavour'd at once
to stifle the Author's Profit, and Fame : which was the occasion, that through
Revenge he dedicated it to a certain Knight under this Ironical Title, " To
the extream Witty and Judicious Gentleman, Sir *Critick-Cat-call*." (Langbaine, s.v. Thomas Durfey.)

[267] He contrived to elude the author's partisans.—See Arber's reprint
of *The Rehearsal*, pp. 46 and 90.

[268] " . . . Some . . . of our Modern Fops, that declare they are
resolv'd to justifie their Plays with their Swords . . . such as peep through
their loopholes in the Theatre, to see who looks grum upon their Playes :
and if they spy a Gentle Squire making Faces, he poor soul, must be *Hector'd*
till he likes 'em . . . " (Shadwell, Preface to *The Sullen Lovers*.)—" *Tutor*.
When you come to a new Play and know the Author is no fighter, and you
may venture to abuse him ; first sit grave and unconcern'd, and be sure to
cast an eye upon some fam'd wit of the town and take him for your pattern."
(Arrowsmith, *The Reformation* II, 2.)

[269]
> " From the Court party we hope no success,
> Our Author is not one of the Nobless,
> That bravely does maintain his Miss in Town,
> Whilst my great Lady is with speed sent down,

sword against his friends). A commoner who dared to meddle
in the writing business was looked on with another eye ; there
was no need to spare his feelings. You must note in the many
verses Rochester devotes to ordering literature about, the very
different tone in which he speaks of writers who are well-born
and of those who are not. The plebs had to sue for permission
to be witty.

A few succeeded almost without taking thought. Etherege,
man of the world, elegant, supplied by an advantageous marriage
with ample funds, was, like Waller, speedily accepted by fashionable young men as a social equal.[270] Wycherley, a simple law
student, owed the favour of the Court to his distinguished
appearance. Pope assures us that he had a "nobleman look".[271]
The Duchess of Cleveland, "mistress of the King and of everybody else ",[272] took a fancy to him. Seeing him one day in
the Ring, she put her head out of the carriage window and was
clearly heard to say in a loud voice : "Sir, you are a rascal ;

> And forc'd in Country Mansion house to fix,
> That Miss may rattle here in Coach and six.
> If one of these the Author was, perchance
> You'd join your int'rest, and the Play advance ;
> For tho' you great ones and you Courtiers be
> Not o'er good natur'd, you've civilitie. '
> (Ravenscroft, Epilogue to *The Citizen turn'd Gentleman*.)

[270] *Biographia Britannica*, s.v. Etherege (George).—

> "E'en gentle *George* (flux'd both in tongue and purse)
> Shunning one Snare, yet fell into a worse.
> A man may be reliev'd once in his Life,
> But who can be reliev'd that has a Wife ? "
> (Villiers, Duke of Buckingham, *A consolatory Epistle
> to Captain Julian the Muses News-Monger in his
> Confinement,* in his *Miscellaneous Works*.)

Rochester, in his *Scession of the Poets* (*Works*, I, 133) also calls him " Gentle
George ".

[Etherege's marriage, if anything, closed his social career. His last
play, *The Man of Mode*, appeared in 1676, and he was regarded as newly
married in 1680. (See the Preface of his *Works* edited by F. Brett Smith.)
Whether he married wealth to obtain a knighthood, or obtained a knighthood
to marry wealth is not clear. As the quotation shows, he only just escaped
bankruptcy, so it was not his wealth that made him a playwright acceptable
to society. Waller had always been rich, and accepted in society, and,
from his teens had been an M.P., in those days an acknowledgment of rank.
He was first cousin to John Hampden, and it was not considered at all odd
that he should court a daughter of the Earl of Leicester. There is no reason
to suppose that she refused him on account of his unequal birth. He published long before the Restoration. B. D.]

[271] Spence, p. 284.
[272] Taine, II, p. 486.

Sir, you are a villain : Sir you are a . . . " and she used a word which, according to Macaulay, " might most justly have been applied to her own children ".[273] He became her lover and dedicated to her his first play, *Love in a Wood.* In it he carefully introduced an allusion to the gallant way in which their acquaintance opened.[274] Without ado she presented him at Court. Charles II, resigned to defeat, developed an affection for him, visited him in person when he was ill, and wanted to entrust him with the education of the Duke of Richmond, one of his natural sons. Buckingham, at that time the King's Minister and Master of his Horse, had been one of the lovers of the indefatigable Duchess. He showed himself at first less complaisant than his master and looked askance at this new rival. But he in turn fell under the spell of Wycherley's good looks and conversation, made friends with him, and gave him not only a regimental commission but a post as equerry in the King's household. Thus introduced and welcomed, the fortunate young man had to do nothing but carry on. His plays were successful. Lord Buckhurst, now Earl of Dorset, made the success of *The Plain Dealer* his personal concern,[275] and forced it on a public at first unappreciative. Thereafter his progress was as easy as Etherege's.[276]

Both men happened to share a qualification which commended them to their noble friends : neither pursued literature for a livelihood.[277] Etherege's private means and Wycherley's emolu-

---

[273] Essays, *The Comic Dramatists of the Restoration.*

[274] In the first Act, Lady Flippant recites a song against marriage, which closes with these lines :

" Great Wits, and great Braves,
Have always a Punk to their Mother."

[275] " Butler owed it to Him (Dorset), that the Court tasted his *Hudibras :* Wicherley [sic], that the town liked his *Plain Dealer.*" (Prior, Dedication of *Poems on Several Occasions* to the Earl of Dorset's son.)

[276] Pack, *A New Collection,* etc., p. 113 : Some Remarkable Passages in the Life of Mr. *Wycherley* by *Mr. Dennis.*—Spence, pp. 16–17.

[277] " Brawny *Wycherley* was the next Man shew'd his Face ;
But *Apollo* e'en thought him too good for the Place
[amongst the royalty of Parnassus]
No Gentleman-Writer that Office should bear,
'Twas a Trader in Wit the Laurel should wear."
(Rochester, *A Scession of the Poets, Works,* I, 133.)

[Wycherley was a gentleman of means too narrow to permit of Court life. But he was a law student, not because he wanted to become a barrister or a solicitor, but because in those days a study of the law was still the natural ments placed them beyond the reach of want. They wrote, like aristocratic amateurs, pleasantly to occupy their leisure, the former composing three plays, the latter four.

The ordinary run of authors, as we have seen, had of necessity to be more active. They had, moreover, to learn how to steer clear of dangers which never threatened the favourites of Fortune. The method was somehow to continue to enlist the interest of some great man possessing influence both at Court and in the world of letters. When Dryden accepted his fate and took to writing drama he approached the theatre only after enlisting as an ally Sir Robert Howard, good courtier and writer of plays, whose favour he won by praising in verse his " excellent poems ".[278] Every person of importance who stood well at Court and fancied himself in literature, became a target for the poetry-writing tribe. Authors swarmed round them to beg for their good offices.

Some of the poets, like D'Urfey, were none too fastidious in their approach. He wrote gallant songs which he recited to the applause of society circles. Having thus introduced himself, he soon proceeded to become the professional jester and recognized buffoon of all the young scatter-brains of Charles's Court. He took part in all their pranks, even the King's. Thanks to

---

conclusion of a gentleman's education ; it enabled him to look after his estates. After the death of his wife, the Countess of Drogheda, he relapsed for some years into a debtor's prison, from which he was finally rescued by the king. We have already glanced at Etherege's position. As for the remark quoted below by Beljame, you cannot argue to a man's opinions from something that he puts into the mouth of one of his characters. B. D.]
" Writing Madam's a Mechanick part of Witt ! A Gentleman should never go beyond a Song or a Billèt." (Etherege, *The Man of Mode*, IV, 1.)

" *Sir Courtly* : I write like Gentleman, soft and easie.
Servant : Does your Honour write any Plays ?
Sir Courtly : No, that's Mechanick ; I bestow some Garniture on Plays, as a Song or a prologue."
(Crowne, *Sir Courtly Nice*, III.)

[278] " *To my Honored Friend*, SIR ROBERT HOWARD, On his Excellent Poems." (Signed : John Driden.) Dryden's verses are prefixed to Sir Robert's poems.
[Beljame's remarks again give the wrong emphasis. Dryden and Howard were friends for a long time, Dryden marrying Howard's sister. Howard was an interesting writer, and thinker on literary matters, and in the controversy he had with Dryden over *The Duke of Lerma*, Dryden did not carry off all the laurels. (See the edition of *The Duke of Lerma* by D. Arundell.) As regards birth, Dryden was well qualified to move in Court circles. He was the grandson of a baronet (his uncle succeeded to the title), and was equally well connected on his mother's side. B. D.]

his versatility and accommodating gifts, his adaptable and unscrupulous gaiety, Tom D'Urfey, as his friends called him, was in high favour, if low esteem, with the fashionable world. The question of esteem did not worry him overmuch.[279]

Not all his fellow-poets were inclined to such excess of good nature, and a writer seeking patrons usually had need of more tact and better manners. The height of his art was to infiltrate quietly into high society, posing as a weak and timorous soul who needed the company of superior beings in order to improve himself. He had to worm his way in by the charm of his conversation, to know when to speak and when to hold his tongue, to make himself unobtrusively agreeable until he became the indispensable guest at every gathering and at every banquet.[280] It was particularly important for him not to embarrass those who honoured him with their intimacy by too profuse a display of his own gifts. Without appearing to do so, he must render

[279]   *Biographia Dramatica*, s.v. D'Urfey (Thomas).
        " And Sing-Song D'Urfey, placed beneath abuses,
            Lives by his impudence, and not by the Muses."
    (Buckingham, *Epistle to Captain Julian*, etc., already quoted, note 270.)
    " I myself remember King *Charles* the Second leaning on *Tom D'Urfey's* Shoulder more than once, and humming over a Song with him." (*The Guardian*, No. 67. This number was by Addison.)—Jeremy Collier speaks of D'Urfey with marked contempt. In *A Short View*, etc., p. 208, he says : " His way is rather to cultivate his Lungs, and Sing to other Peoples Sense : For to finish him in a word, he is *Vox et praeterea nihil*." Dunton also writes : " Mr. *Durfey* has but a low *Genius* and yet some of his *Farces* wou'd make a Body laugh." (*Life*, p. 238.)—See also Langbaine, s.v. Thomas Durfey.
            " And all Retreats except *New-Hall* refuse
            To shelter *Durfey* and his Jocky Muse ;
            There to the Butler and his Grace's Maid,
            He turns, like *Homer*, Sonnetteer for Bread ;
            Knows his just bounds, nor ever durst aspire
            Beyond the swearing Groom and kitchin fire."
                    (A Satyr upon the Poets, being a Translation
                    out of the 7th Satyr of Juvenal. In *Poems
                    on Affairs of State*, vol. II, 1703, pp. 138 ff.)
[280] " We have . . . our Genial Nights, where our discourse is neither too serious nor too light ; but alwayes pleasant, and, for the most part, instructive : the raillery neither too sharp upon the present nor too censorious on the absent ; and the Cups only such as will raise the Conversation of the Night, without disturbing the Business of the Morrow." (Dryden, Dedication of *The Assignation* " to my most honour'd Friend, Sir Charles Sedley, Baronet.)
    " . . . My greatest Satisfaction is, that I have the Honour of his Friendship, and my Comedies have had his Approbation, whom I have heard speak more wit at a Supper than all my Adversaries, with their Heads join'd together, can write in a Year." (Shadwell, Dedication of *A True Widow* to the Same.)

discreet assistance with their productions,[281] while welcoming their most trifling suggestions with exuberant expressions of admiration and gratitude. He must give them the credit for any merit in his works and finally succeed in imperceptibly identifying the interests of protégé and patron. Dryden's fortune was secure once he was so high in favour of Sedley and Mulgrave that he could venture publicly to proclaim himself their friend.[282] Titled critics would have made but one mouthful of plain John Dryden, but when they could attack him only across the body of one of their own kind, they thought twice, and did not dare.

" The Criticks ", says Shadwell frankly to the Duke of Newcastle of his new play, " . . . will not dare to use it roughly, when they see Your Grace's Name in the beginning . . ." [283] Dryden proudly replies to those " cavillers " who failed to appreciate his *Don Sebastian* : " I will give them and their fellows to understand that the Earl of Dorset was pleased to read the tragedy twice over before it was acted, and did me the favour to send me word, that I had written beyond any of my former plays, and that he was displeased anything should be cut away." [284] It would have needed a brave critic to continue the attack after that.

For the ordinary courtier to differ from the literary judgment of a Court favourite, was to forgo his patronage and the hope of a good job. But the overriding consideration which restrained them all, was that the whole body of courtiers saw their interest in preserving intact the reputation for good taste which each had severally acquired. Every nobleman was by birth infallible in such matters. To question the views of one, was to cast a doubt on the infallibility of the rest. If even one was mistaken the others might be too.

The author therefore takes care to efface himself and shelter behind his patron. He never introduces himself to his readers

---

[281] " *Bayes. Mr. Johnson,* How d'e like that Box ? Pray take notice of it, 't was given me by a *Person of Honour* for looking over a Paper of Verses . . ." (Prior and Charles Montague, *The Hind and the Panther Transvers'd* p. 22.)—D'Alembert called this, being " décrotteur bel esprit ". (Letter to Voltaire, Dec. 26, 1772.)

[282] Dedications to *The Assignation* and to *Aureng-Zebe*.

[283] " And I doubt not, but that Generosity wherewith Your Grace has always succour'd the Afflicted, will make You willing (by suffering me to use the Honour of Your Name) to rescue this from the bloody Hands of the Criticks, who etc." (Dedication of *The Sullen Lovers*.)

[284] Preface. The play appeared in 1690 ; but Dorset retained his literary influence unimpaired under William III.

without the protection of a dedication addressed to some great man.[285]   Like a naughty child he seems to cry : " Please, it isn't me."   He gets his play read before its appearance on the stage.   He gets it approved at the cost, if need be, of a few alterations, and he loudly proclaims how little credit he, the author, deserves for its excellence.   Settle owes the subject of his *Empress of Morocco* to the Earl of Norwich.[286]   In the Dedica-tion of *A True Widow* Shadwell thanks Sedley for having revised his play.[287]   Dryden's *Aureng-Zebe* was corrected by the Earl of Mulgrave ;   his comedy, *The Assignation*, before being played, had been read " by the best judges ".[288]   To Sir Robert Howard Dryden writes of his *Annus Mirabilis* :

It is not long since I gave you the trouble of perusing a play for me ; and now, instead of an acknowledgement I have given you a greater in the correction of a poem . . .   I must leave my poem to you with all its faults, which I hope to find fewer in the printing by your emendations . . .   'Tis but reason I should do you that justice to the readers to let them know, that, if there be anything tolerable in this poem, they owe the argument to your choice, the writing to your encouragement, the correction to your judgment, and the care of it to your friendship.[289]

The share remaining to the author is small indeed.

To humble himself still further, the author raises his protector to the seventh heaven.   Shadwell writes to Sedley : " You have

---

[285] Otway's *Souldiers Fortune* is probably the only play of the period which is not dedicated to a person of quality.   He dedicated it to his book-seller, Mr. Bentley.

[286] " . . . The *Story* . . . I owe to your Hands, and your honourable Embassy into *Africa*."   (Dedication.)

[287] " . . . This Comedy, which had the benefit of your Correction and Alteration, and the Honour of your Approbation."

[288] Dedications.

[289] " An Account of the ensuing Poem, in a Letter to the Honourable Sir Robert Howard " prefixed to *Annus Mirabilis*.   Dryden is careful to date his letter " From Charlton in Wiltshire ", the country house of Lord Berkshire, Sir Robert's father.

[Dedication to noble patrons was no new thing ; some of the Jacobean playwrights indulged in the practice, e.g. Webster's dedication of *The Duchess of Malfy* to Lord Berkeley.   The language used in this period was courtly to the stage of being, to our minds, ridiculous ; but the statements were not altogether devoid of justification, and the noblemen were not addressed merely because they were " by birth infallible in literary matters ".   It is possible that Settle did get his material from Lord Norwich, who knew Africa.   Mulgrave (John Sheffield, afterwards Duke of Buckinghamshire) had set himself to study literature, and if his shorter poems are merely agree-able if skilful trifles, his verse essay on criticism still repays reading.   Howard was a fellow-author of distinction, as was Sedley.   B. D.]

in the *Mulberry Garden* shown the true Wit, Humour and Satyr of a Comedy ; and in *Anthony and Cleopatra* the true Spirit of a Tragedy ; the only one (except two of *Johnson's* and one of *Shakespear's*) wherein *Romans* are made to speak and do like *Romans*." (Dedication to *A True Widow*.)

Crowne's patron, the Earl of Orrery, was also honoured by Dryden's praise. Amongst other things His Lordship had written eight plays, a novel and some poems as well as *A Treatise of the Art of War* [290] which went with him to the grave. When dedicating his rhymed tragedy, *The Rival Ladies*, to this champion of rhyming drama, Dryden says to him :

> Who could so severely judge of faults as he, who has given testimony he commits none ? Your excellent poems have afforded that knowledge of it to the world, that your enemies are ready to upbraid you with it, as a crime for a man of business to write so well. Neither durst I have justified your lordship in it, if examples had not been in the world before you ; if Xenophon had not written a romance,[291] and a certain Roman, called Augustus Caesar, a tragedy and epigrams.

William, Duke, Marquis and Earl of Newcastle, one of the faithful adherents of Charles II who had followed him into exile, was a poet by conviction. Versifying was not his only passion : horses and poetry divided his heart between them. He wrote several plays and devoted two magnificent folio volumes to the art of riding. His *System of Horsemanship* is adorned with engravings depicting His Grace on horseback in every possible attitude and in every conceivable costume, and finally prancing triumphantly on Pegasus and rising towards Olympus from the midst of a circle of horses who gaze on him with admiration and respect.[292] By great good fortune this high-born enthusiast had found a wife after his own heart. The Duchess is the author of philosophic essays, of letters, of discourses, and of nineteen plays, eight of which are in two parts. At night she kept a servant ready to come at her first summons to record in writing

[290] See my Bibliography.

[Orrery was a serious writer ; his rhymed tragedies are by no means despicable, and are not disagreeable reading. *Mustapha* might even be recommended. It was not absurd to dedicate works to him, or even to praise him. B. D.]

[291] This romance is no doubt the *Cyropædia*.

[292] See my Bibliography.—" Newcastle and's Horse for entrance next strives . . ." (*The Scession of the Poets, to the Tune of Cook Lawrel*, in *Poems on Affairs of State*, vol. I, p. 209.)

her lightest inspiration.[293] This noble pair formed a natural target for dedications. Flecknoe dedicated *The Damoiselles à la Mode* to them both, and his *Love's Kingdom* to the Duke. Settle inscribed to the Duke his tragedy, *Love and Revenge.* Shadwell dedicated to him his *Virtuoso*, his *Libertine*, *The Sullen Lovers* and *Epsom-Wells* while commending *The Humorists* to the Duchess's protection. Dryden presented *An Evening's Love* to the poet-horseman in a dedication in which no virtue of either spouse is overlooked :

Methinks I behold in you another Caius Marius, who, in the extremity of his age, exercised himself almost every morning in the Campus Martius, amongst the youthful nobility of Rome. And afterwards in your retirements, when you do honour to poetry, by employing part of your leisure in it, I regard you as another Silius Italicus, who, having passed over his consulship with applause, dismissed himself from business and the gown, and employed his age, amongst the shades, in the reading and imitation of Virgil.

In which, lest any thing should be wanting to your happiness, you have, by a rare effect of fortune, found, in the person of your excellent lady, not only a lover, but a partner of your studies ; a lady whom our age may justly equal with the Sappho of the Greeks, or the Sulpicia of the Romans ; who, by being taken into your bosom, seems to be inspired with your genius.

Lee wrote to Dorset : " Your writing dazzles with Clearness and Majesty . . . Whate'er you stamp as Royal, other Pretenders to Satire but file and wash : they live by the Clippings of your Wit, and dip their Silver in your Bath, to make it pass for Gold." [294] He appealed to Rochester in these terms : " From the Criticks . . . I appeal to your Lordship as the Saint did to *Cæser*. To you whose Judgment vies remark with your Grandeiur, who are as absolutely Lord of Wit as those prevaricators are its slaves. To you . . . whose sayings astonish the Censorious, and

[293] To summon him, she would call : " John, I conceive . . . ".—She was more or less mad ; the ragamuffins of London used to run after her carriage when she drove out. (Pepys, April 11, 1667 ; April 26, 1667 ; May 10, 1667.)—See H. Walpole : *A Catalogue*, etc., vol. III, s.v.v. Margaret, Duchess of Newcastle and William Cavendish, Duke of Newcastle.

[It is true that the Newcastles appear slightly ridiculous to us, but that is only because they took literature too seriously in view of their own accomplishment. Nobody seems to read their works now, but they were considered capable judges then. In a sense the Duke was Dryden's collaborator ; at least he gave him the translation of Molière's *l'Étourdi*, from which Dryden made *Sir Martin Mar-All*. Why it should be considered a crime in a man who had been a cavalry leader in the Civil War to write two works on horsemanship and horsemastership is not quite clear. B. D.]

[294] Dedication of *Mithridates*.

whose Writings are so exactly ingenious ; Princes treasure them
in their Memory, as things Divine." [295] In his *Discourse concerning Satire* Dryden simply says to Dorset : " In tragedy and
satire . . . this age and the last, particularly in England, have
excelled the ancients in both these kinds ; and I would instance
in Shakespeare of the former, of your Lordship in the latter
sort." [295a]

This was flattery laid on with a trowel. It was sometimes
applied with greater restraint and subtlety. In his *Essay of
Dramatick Poesie*, for instance, Dryden introduces Sir Charles
Sedley, Sir Robert Howard and Lord Buckhurst, in a long and
interesting discussion, under the transparent pseudonyms of
Lisideius, Crites and Eugenius. [296]

Though the poets aimed their flatteries by preference at
literary aristocrats they by no means omitted to cultivate the
influential men of the time who were not writers. Literature
was in fact so much the fashion in the higher strata of society
that it was always possible, whatever the occasion, to find some
pretext for a flattering dedication designed effectively to impress
the public by the use of a great name. Dryden dedicated *Troilus
and Cressida* to the Earl of Sunderland, chief Secretary of State,
and his *All for Love* to the Lord Treasurer, the Earl of Danby.
He was even mindful of the City, greatly though its influence had
waned, and dedicated his poem *Annus Mirabilis* " to The Metropolis of Great Britain, the Most Renowned and Late Flourishing
City of London, in its Representatives the Lord Mayor and Court
of Aldermen, the Sheriffs and Common Council of it ".

But the *ne plus ultra* of an author's ambition was to enlist
the benevolent attention of the supreme judge and patron [297] :
an arduous and delicate undertaking. Etiquette forbade a

---

[295] Dedication of *Nero*.

[295a] The *Discourse* is prefixed to Dryden's translation of Juvenal, dedicated
to the Right Honourable Charles Earl of Dorset and of Middlesex, etc.

[296] [Dryden was guilty of no special flattery in his choice of persons
for the *Essay of Dramatick Poesie*. They were all people keenly interested
in the drama, Sedley and Howard being themselves playwrights. Buckhurst,
later Lord Dorset, had certain literary qualifications. It seems likely that
these four men had often had similar discussions, which Dryden now put
into form. We know, for instance, that Howard did hold the views imputed
to him in the *Essay*. When Mr. T. S. Eliot wrote a conversation on dramatic
matters as an introduction to a new edition of the *Essay*, he stated that much
of the matter came out of conversations with his friends. This would seem
to be the way in which Dryden worked. B. D.]

[297] " The Lord of Hearts, and President of Wit " (Otway, Prologue
to *The History and Fall of Caius Marius*).

work being dedicated to the King without permission. It was impossible boldly to march to the attack and sue for the royal approval ; a repulse would have spelt disaster. So the wise author trod warily, digging trenches at a respectful distance and advancing slowly, patiently and discreetly. The minor out-works leading to the citadel were first captured. Dedications were addressed to the Duchess of Monmouth, wife of the King's natural son, then to the Duke himself, finally to the King's brother or to his Duchess.[298]

Since you could not speak to the King, you lost no opportunity of speaking about him in the hope that something of what you said would reach his ear. Settle writes to the Duke of Newcastle : " Providence has justly lengthened out your happy life to see the prosperous Raign of a Great, a Pious, and Gracious *Monarch*." [299] Dryden, in addressing the Duke of York, says : " I have always observed in your royal highness an extreme concernment for the honour of your country ; it is a passion common to you with a brother, the most excellent of kings ; and in your two persons are eminent the character which Homer has given us of heroic virtue ; the commanding part in Agamemnon, and the executive in Achilles ".[300]

You thus swing the censer round the King's circle praying Heaven that some odour of incense will reach the royal nostrils. Then suppose that the King should learn the name of the burner of incense, that he should remember it, and that one day his august lips should let fall an opinion flattering for his worshipper, in what an ecstasy of happiness the favoured being will trumpet his triumph abroad !

Dryden was frequently reproached for having stolen his plays, a reproach which (we may note in passing) all authors

[298] In 1665 Dryden dedicated *The Indian Emperour* to the Duchess f Monmouth ; in 1668 *Tyrannick-Love* to the Duke ; in 1669 *Almanzor and Almahide* to the Duke of York, the King's brother. The gradation of dates is significant.—This is how he writes to the Duke of York : " Heroic poesy has always been sacred to princes, and to heroes . . . It is from this consideration, that I have presumed to dedicate to your royal highness these faint representations of your own worth and valour in heroic poetry : Or, to speak more properly, not to dedicate, but to restore to you those ideas, which in the more perfect part of my characters I have taken from you . . . You shone to us from afar . . . " In 1674 he dedicated *The State of Innocence* to the Duchess of York. To her he writes : " We think not the day is long enough when we behold you . . . Your person is a paradise, and your soul a cherubim within, to guard it."

[299] Dedication of *Love and Revenge*.

[300] Dedication of *Almanzor and Almahide, or the Conquest of Granada*.

of his day deserve at least as much as he. Hearing someone voice this accusation the King very sensibly retorted, so Dryden tells us : " that he only desired that they who accused me of theft, would always steal him Playes like mine ". It is worth seeing how great was Dryden's delight at this and how, while feigning modesty, he enjoyed quoting the royal saying and therewith firmly stopping the critics' mouths.[301] Crowne's *Calisto* pleased Charles II and the King condescended to mention this to the author. The playwright lost no time in ostentatiously parading the approval of the King " to whose Pleasure all our endeavours ought to be devoted ". Joyously he exclaimed : " the devouring Critick must cease his pursuit, for the poor Sinner is out of his Fangs, and safe in Glory ".[302]

On another occasion the King's intervention was more direct. He liked giving advice to authors. It was on a suggestion of his that Sir Samuel Tuke borrowed from Calderon his *Adventures of Five Hours*.[303] It was also the King who supplied Crowne with the plot of *Sir Courtly Nice* [304] (the rumour even ran that he had actually helped in its composition).[305] One day he suggested a correction to Dryden who hastened to give his play the benefit of the alteration. The poet naturally did not fail to boast of Charles's collaboration and in his enthusiasm applied to him *Si fractus illabitur orbis* . . . [306] But the great day, the day of glory was the day when the royal patron claimed *The Maiden-Queen* as *his* play. Then the entire preface was devoted to singing the praises of a monarch who displayed such good

---

[301] Preface to *An Evening's Love*.

[302] " It (*Calisto*) attained the felicity for which it was made, to afford some delight to His Royal Mind, to whose Pleasure all our endeavors ought to be, and this more particularly was devoted. And of this I have full assurance by the best and to me most pleasing testimony of it, that of His most Princely Bounty. Having said this, the devouring Critick, etc." (Crowne, Preface to *Calisto*.)

[303] The " Prologue at Court " has the following note : " This refers to the Authors purpose of Retirement, at that time when his Majesty recommended this Plot to him."

[304] " This Comedy was Written by the Sacred Command of our late most Excellent King, of ever blessed and beloved Memory . . . The greatest pleasure he had from the Stage was in Comedy, and he often Commanded me to Write it, and lately gave me a *Spanish* Play called *No Puedeser* (*Non pued esser*) : Or, It Cannot Be out of which I took part o' the Name) and design o' this (dedication)."—See also Dennis, *Original Letters*, etc., vol. I, pp. 51 ff.

[305] Crowne showed the King each scene as he wrote it. (Langbaine, manuscript note of Oldys, p. 96.)

[306] *Aureng-Zebe*, Dedication.

taste. The happy author recalls that plays have been dedicated to the Kings of France, and that he has good reason to follow this precedent,

it having been own'd in so particular a manner by His Majesty that he has graced it with the Title of " His Play " . . . But though a character so high and undeserv'd, has not raised in me the presumption to offer such a trifle to his most serious view, yet I will own it my vanity to say, that after this glory which it has receiv'd from a Soveraign Prince, I could not send it to seek protection from any subject. Be this poem then sacred to him without the tedious form of a Dedication, and without presuming to interrupt those hours which he is daily giving to the peace and settlement of his people.

Nevertheless, the King while adopting his play took exception to one episode in it : the poet humbly bowed to the royal judgement :

" But though the artifice succeeded, I am willing to acknowledge it as a fault, since it pleas'd His Majesty, the best Judg, to think so."

Boileau felt no shame in flattering his royal master either, but on a literary issue he would not so readily have waived his own opinion in favour of the Great King's.[306a]

To gain access to the " Merry Monarch ", there was a surer road than that leading via his family and his favourite courtiers : the road via his mistresses. Men in those days scorned no path that led to success, and writers were no more scrupulous than others. Dryden addressed verses to the Duchess of Portsmouth (Mademoiselle de Kéroualle) [307] and to Lady Castlemaine.[308] He at least confined himself to ephemeral verses of limited circulation. His fellow-authors were less fastidious : Crowne openly dedicated his *Destruction of Jerusalem* to the Duchess of Portsmouth with the words : " I fix then Your Grace's Image at this *Jewish* Temple Gate, to render the Building sacred." Lee offered the same lady his tragedy of *Sophonisba* and praised not only her beauty but " the immortal splendours of an elevated soul ". Duffett went even further. He dedicated his *Spanish*

[306a] [The phrase " although the artifice succeeded " should be enough to indicate how much Dryden (or any other poet) was talking with his tongue in his cheek. Charles II would probably be amused enough to condone the *lèse-majesté*. B. D.]

[307] *The Fair Stranger, A Song* (*Works*, edited by Walter Scott and George Saintsbury, vol. XI, p. 167).

[308] She had been a patron of his early days when he was producing *The Wild Gallant* (*Works*, Scott and Saintsbury, vol. XI, p. 20). He compared her to Cato : to Cato's disadvantage.

Rogue to Nell Gwyn, the least reputable of the royal mistresses, who, as all London well knew, had begun life as barmaid in a brothel and had later been the mistress of Hart, the actor (amongst others),[309] before winning the King's heart in the circumstances already related. This was the person to whom Duffett wrote : " . . . Next to your Beauty, these Virtues are the greatest Miracle of the Age. If I am the first that has taken the boldness to tell you this, in Print, 'tis because *I* am more ambitious than all others, to be known by the Title of, *Madam, Your Admirer and humblest Servant*, T.D." [310]—" Boldness " was certainly the right word.

Authors, as we see, omitted no precaution, neglected no skill, to remedy the weakness of their position *vis-à-vis* an omnipotent Court consumed with vanity. Once embarked on this course, they availed themselves of every facility offered by the period in which they lived.

Their utmost care, however, did not always suffice to steer their fragile bark safely past the rocks. However zealously they practised humbug and self-humiliation, they could not always make themselves sufficiently insignificant and obscure to be invisible amidst the clash of conflicting vanities ; they received in consequence their share of bruises.

Let us first consider some minor misadventures.

After having insinuated himself into the good graces of Sir Robert Howard, Dryden collaborated with him in *The Indian Queen*, which was notably successful. But his noble friend, having done him the honour of borrowing his ideas and his style, studiously omitted all mention of him, and the play appeared under Sir Robert's name alone. *Sic vos non vobis* . . .[311]

309 She used to tell anyone who would listen that Charles II was *her* Charles III (Burnet, *History of my Own Times*, vol. I, p. 457). On the subject of Nell Gwyn, see Pepys, Oct. 26, 1667 ; Etherege, *The Lady of Pleasure*, already mentioned, p. 12 ; Betterton, *History of The English Stage*, pp. 55 and 111 ; Downes, with the Appendix by Davies, pp. 11–20 ; Cunningham, *The Story of Nell Gwyn*.

310 Mrs. Behn dedicated her comedy *The Feign'd Curtizans* to Nell Gwyn too, saying : " When you speak, men crowd to listen with that awfull reverence as to Holy Oracles or Divine Prophesies, and bears [*sic*] away the precious words to tell at home to all the attentive family the Gracefull things you utter'd . . . etc." But the two were colleagues.

311 The first edition which was printed in Sir Robert's *Four New Plays*, is there entitled : " *The Indian-Queen*, a *Tragedy. London*, Printed for H. Herringman . . . 1665."—The title of the second edition in Sir Robert's *Five new Plays* is : " *The Indian-Queen, a Tragedy*. Written by the Honourable Sir Robert Howard. London . . . DDCXCII." No mention of Dryden. The play is now printed among Dryden's works.

Similar experience with the Duke of Newcastle. The illustrious scribbler handed Dryden a word-for-word translation of
Molière's *l'Étourdi*. Dryden took the trouble of working over
and modifying the play to suit current taste and created from
it *Sir Martin Mar-all*. Only the Duke's name was mentioned.[312]
The titled jays refused to flock with the vulgar peacock whose
plumage they borrowed. " If together they create a new work,"
writes Count Almaviva, " it is understood that the nobleman
will contribute his name, the poet his talent." [313]

In the case of Sir Robert Howard, Dryden was able to some
degree to retrieve the situation. He had the happy idea of
writing, without a collaborator, a sequel to *The Indian Queen*,
and his *Indian Emperour* benefited from its predecessor's success
and drew serious attention to the young playwright.[314] About
the same time he married his patron's sister, Lady Elizabeth
Howard. This marriage of a young noblewoman with a poet
—one of the despicable crew who lived by their pen and had
no means of livelihood save an uncertain income from the
theatre and presents, scrounged here and there in return for
sycophantic dedication—may well cause surprise. Various indications suggest that its background was not entirely honourable.[315]
Dryden hoped perhaps to gain a surer footing in good society

[312] " To the Duke's playhouse, where we saw the new play acted
yesterday, ' The Feign Innocence, or Sir Martin Marall ' ; a play made
by my Lord Duke of Newcastle, but, as everybody says, corrected by Dryden "
(Pepys, Aug. 16, 1667).—" Sir *Martin Marral*, The Duke of *Newcastle*, giving
Mr. *Dryden* a bare Translation of it, out of a Comedy of the Famous *French*
Poet, *Monseur Moleiro* [sic] " (Downes, p. 28).—The first edition bears no
author's name (see my Bibliography). The play was registered at Stationers'
Hall, June 24, 1668, as the Duke's work without allusion to Dryden (Malone,
Life of Dryden, p. 93). *Sir Martin Mar-all*, like *The Indian Queen*, is now
printed amongst Dryden's works. Thus the collaborator so disdainfully
treated by these grand gentlemen has preserved their names for posterity.
[313] *Mariage de Figaro*.
[314] When *The Indian Emperour* was being acted, Dryden was shrewd
enough to furnish the spectators of the first performance with a printed
slip : " Connexion of *The Indian Emperour* to *The Indian Queen*." There is
an allusion to this in *The Rehearsal*.
[315] The marriage took place on Dec. 1, 1663. It would seem that
before marrying Dryden, the Lady Elizabeth had had dubious relations
with the Earl of Chesterfield. On this point consult Mr. Christie, one of
Dryden's biographers. Dryden's enemies phrased the matter more crudely.
Here are some verses attributed to Somers :

> " Hear me, dull Prostitute, worse than my Wife,
> Like her the Shame and Clog of my dull Life . . .
> Against my Will, I marry'd a Rank Whore :

and so to better his position as a writer. If so, he had gravely miscalculated, a fact of which he was promptly made aware. The poet soon discovered that, though he had married the daughter of the house, he had by no means become one of the family.

In dedicating his *Rival Ladies* to the Earl of Orrery, Dryden had boasted of the superiority of rhymed plays. Sir Robert suddenly proclaimed himself the champion of blank verse, and in a preface [316] attacked rhyme, making an exception of the Earl of Orrery's works but pointedly abstaining from any praise of his brother-in-law's. The latter, in his *Essay of Dramatick Poesie* introduced Sir Robert Howard—under the pseudonym of Crites—amongst the distinguished persons taking part in the discussion, reserving to himself—as Neander—the pleasure of refuting his arguments. Sir Robert was shocked at Dryden's not leaving him the last word. In his notice of the *Duke of Lerma*, he set out to demonstrate the gulf which had always lain between them and combated the views of his sister's husband in the bored and disdainful tone of a great nobleman who condescends. [317]

Dryden replied with a *Defence of an Essay of Dramatick Poesie*, [318]

> After two Children, and a third Miscarriage
> By Brawny Brothers Hector'd into Marriage," etc,
> (*Satyr to his Muse;* by the author of *Absalom and Achitophel.*)

This satire is attributed to Somers.

Dryden came of good family : Sir John Driden was his uncle ; his mother was a granddaughter of Sir Gilbert Pickering. Nevertheless he was a commoner and worked for his living. One of his brothers was a London tobacconist and two of his sisters had married small tradesmen.

[316] Notice of *Four New Plays*. Two of these are in rhyme.

[317] " I suppose I need not trouble the Reader with so impertinent a delay to attempt a farther Confutation of such ill-grounded reasons, then thus by opening the true state of the Case . . . I will not . . . pretend to say, why I writ this Play, some Scenes in blank Verse, others in Rhime, since I have no better a reason to give then Chance, which waited upon my present Fancy ; and I expect no better a reason from any ingenious person . . ." He does not even name Dryden ; he calls him " the Author of an Essay of Dramatick Poesie " and " that Author ". The reply is very short.

[318] Prefixed to the second edition of *The Indian Emperour*. There he says : " To begin with me, he gives me the Compellation of *The Author of a Dramatique Essay* . . . therefore, that I may not be wanting to him in civility, I return his Complement by calling him *The Author of the Duke of Lerma.*" The Dyce Collection in the South Kensington Museum contains a copy of this second edition with a note by Dyce to say that when Dryden was reconciled to Sir Robert Howard, *The Defence* was suppressed, and was now rarely to be met with.

[The *Defence*, both a spirited piece of writing and admirable criticism, contenting himself with quietly aiming a few barbed phrases at Sir Robert without departure from good taste. Nevertheless, his brother-in-law did not forgive him for having dared to defend his own opinion and an estrangement resulted which for some time furnished lively entertainment to the satirists.

Throughout the whole affair Dryden preserved his right to retort, despite the aristocratic scorn with which he was treated. He countered when attacked. It was a duel of equals. The other side might have the advantage of birth ; he had the advantage of talent. Worse might be in store for him. He might be taken at a disadvantage and still more vigorously attacked when unable to defend himself, as in fact befell him with the Duke of Buckingham.

In 1671 Buckingham presented *The Rehearsal* which he had written, so it is believed, with the very effective assistance of Butler, and of his chaplain Sprat,[319] and of Matthew Clifford, Master of Charterhouse. Three other unfortunates to whom fell the toil but not the credit ; their names were not mentioned. *The Rehearsal* is an extremely clever and witty parody of the Heroic Plays and it appeared most opportunely at the very moment when these extravagant plays were at the zenith of their popularity. However small Buckingham's own share in *The Rehearsal*, it does honour to his wit and to his literary courage, for he was the only man to dare openly to speak his mind about the prevailing fashion and swim against the stream when the current was at its swiftest. His boldness was all the more praiseworthy in that he was challenging a style in which many fellow members of the aristocracy, the Howards, the Orrerys, and so forth, had won distinction. The play itself was an all-round parody and in so far we can applaud it without reserve. But, by the Duke's express intention, the character of Bayes

---

is now to be found in every edition of Dryden's plays or prose works. It is not easy to agree with Beljame that Howard's tone is condescending, but one can certainly agree that Dryden treats him as an equal. B. D.]

[319] His duty as chaplain must have been, as M. Forgues wittily points out, " a curious sinecure ".

[But of course the duties of a chaplain in a ducal household were not confined to ministering to the spiritual needs of the duke. Thomas Sprat, afterwards Bishop of Rochester, the historian of the Royal Society, and an acknowledged poet, at that time probably had to conduct the services in the Duke's private chapel, and carry out all the duties with respect to births, deaths and marriages, and consolation in sickness, to a fairly large establishment. It may be doubted whether the post was, after all, such a sinecure. B. D.]

became a personal caricature of Dryden. Buckingham himself took endless pains to coach the actor Lacey, and taught him to reproduce the voice, the gestures and the very mannerisms of the poet. He even went so far as to dress him like Dryden so that there could be no possible mistake.[320] The mockers had scored their point. For the rest of his life Dryden was saddled with the nickname of Bayes.

Some hundred years later the actor-author Foote was planning to impersonate Dr. Johnson on the stage. Johnson happened to be dining with Thomas Davies, the bookseller, when he first heard of Foote's intention : " What ", he promptly asked his host, " is the common price of an oak stick ? "—" Six-pence," was the reply. " Why then, Sir, give me leave to send your servant to purchase me a shilling one. I'll have a double quantity ; for I am told Foote means *to take me off*, as he calls it, and I am determined the fellow shall not do it with impunity." When Foote learned of Johnson's preparations he decided not to risk incurring the Doctor's wrath. He was wise. " Sir," said Johnson to Boswell, " fear restrained him. He knew I would have broken his bones. I would have saved him the trouble of cutting off a leg ; I would not have left him a leg to cut off." [321]

Dryden for his part said not a word.[322] Not only did he fail to wield an oaken stick, he did not even allow his pen to take up the defence of his reputation as a writer. Yet his pen did first-class service whenever it was allowed to turn on his enemies, and many of the wounds his satire inflicted still retain their sting. Nor was the Duke of Buckingham's hide invulnerable to epigrams. This was later proved and more than proved. But what would you ! The Duke was at that time the cherished favourite of Charles II, and Dryden durst not risk annoying the King and bringing at one blow the whole edifice of his literary success tumbling about his ears merely for the pleasure of

---

[320] Spence, p. 63.—Arber's Edition of *The Rehearsal*.

[321] Boswell, vol. V, p. 233, and vol. III, p. 96.

[322] In his *Discourse Concerning Satire*, written in 1693, Dryden gave very inadequate reasons for his silence : " I answered not *The Rehearsal*, because I knew the author sat to himself when he drew the picture, and was the very Bayes of his own farce : because I knew that my betters were more concerned than I was in that satire : and, lastly, because Mr. Smith and Mr. Johnson (two characters in the play), the main pillars of it, were two such languishing gentlemen in their conversation, that I could liken them to nothing but to their own relations, those noble characters of men of wit and pleasure about the town."

avenging himself. So *Bayes* held his tongue and waited ten long years till his tormentor had fallen from grace and lost his unassailable position. Then it was possible to exact a tooth for a tooth. When Dryden drew Zimri's portrait in *Absalom and Achitophel*, it was clear that he had forgotten nothing, and if he had hitherto held his peace this indicated neither indifference nor disdain, nor yet lack of ample material for a reply.

But Dryden's long-suffering was to be put to still more painful tests.

John Wilmot, Earl of Rochester, was one of those noblemen whom it was most difficult, and yet most important, to conciliate. Young, elegant, witty, keen and capricious, without shame or scruple, he lived on a footing of complete equality with the King. He was thus all-powerful. Prolific author of satires which respected no one, not even his royal master, he was a man to fear.[323] A leader of pleasure and fashion, he sought to be also a leader of taste, and as he did nothing by halves, he would fain have ruled as dictator over wit in every form.[324]

One day a new actress, Mrs. Barry, made her appearance on the stage. After three unfortunate attempts of hers all the connoisseurs maintained that she was no good and was utterly unqualified to play a part in tolerable style. Thereupon Rochester, merely " to shew them he had a Judgment superiour ",[325] fired up on her behalf and loudly asserted that she would be ere long the best actress on the English stage. Not to see this prophecy belied, he devoted six months to teaching her himself. The task is said to have been no easy one, but he persisted in it, and when he thought his pupil sufficiently prepared,

[323] " In satire, no pen so ruthless as was his . . . the most dangerous enemy in the world." (Hamilton, p. 206.)

[324] In dedicating his first play, *Nero*, to Rochester, Lee tells him that he is " absolutely Lord of Wit ".—Sir Francis Fane calls him " the most accomplish'd of all Mankind that I ever Knew, read, or heard of, by Humane Testimony . . . " and he adds this amazing eulogy : " I never return from your Lordships most Charming and Instructive Conversation, but I am inspir'd with a new Genius, and improv'd in all those Sciences I ever coveted the Knowledge of : I find my self, not only a better Poet, a better Philosopher ; but, much more than these, a better Christian : your Lordship's miraculous Wit, and intellectual pow'rs being the greatest Argument that ever I could meet with for the immateriality of the Soul ; they being the highest exaltation of humane Nature ; and under Divine Authority much more convincing to suspicious Reason, than all the Pedantick proofs of the most Learnedly peevish Disputants ; so that, I hope, I shall be oblig'd to your Lordship, not only for my Reputation of this World, but my future Happiness in the next . . ." (Dedication of *Love in the Dark*).

[325] Betterton, p. 14.

he invited the King with the Duke and Duchess of York to come and applaud her. Such august judges could not be wrong : she proved a great success and Rochester shared her triumph.[326]

Dryden took great care not to ignore a man of so much influence, whose self-conceit was backed by so much passion and perseverance. In 1673 he dedicated his comedy *Marriage à-la-Mode* to " The Right Honourable, the Earl of Rochester " with this significant quotation : ·

> Quidquid sum ego, quamvis
> Infra Lucilli censum ingeniumque, tamen me
> Cum magnis vixisse invita fatebitur usque
> Invidia, et fragili quaerens illidere dentem
> Offendet solido.[327]

His dedication is a laborious piece of work in which he painstakingly endeavours to flatter from every angle the vain person whose smiles he covets. The long-winded elaborate eulogies make it weary and heavy reading. But the very long-windedness, the insistent flatteries, the pains the poet takes to humble himself, the literary importance of the patron he addresses, make the document interesting and worth quoting almost in full, as one of the most remarkable specimens of its type.

My Lord,
 I humbly dedicate to your Lordship that poem, of which you were pleased to appear an early patron, before it was acted on the stage. I may yet go farther, with your permission, and say, that it received amendment from your noble hands ere it was fit to be presented. You may please likewise to remember, with how much favour to the author, and indulgence to the play, you commended it to the view of his Majesty, then at Windsor, and by his approbation of it in writing, made way for its kind reception on the theatre . . . I am sure, if there be anything in this play, wherein I have raised myself beyond the ordinary lowness of my comedies, I ought wholly to acknowledge it to the favour of being admitted to your Lordship's conversation. And not only I, who pretend not to this way, but the best comic writers of our age, will join with me to acknowledge that they have copied the gallantries of court, the delicacy of expression, and the decencies of behaviour, from your Lordship, with more success than if they had taken their models from the court of France. But this, my Lord, will be no wonder to the world, which knows the excellency

---

[326] " . . . He made her Rehearse near thirty times on the Stage, and about twelve in the Dress she was to Act it in . . . The Dutchess of *York* . . . made her a Present of her Wedding-Suit . . . " (Betterton, pp. 15-17).
[327] Horace, *Satires*, II, 1.

of your natural parts and those you have acquired in a noble education. That which, with more reason, I admire, is, that being so absolute a courtier, you have not forgot either the ties of friendship or the practice of generosity.   In my little experience of a court (which, I confess, I desire not to improve), I have found in it much of interest, and more of detraction : Few men there have that assurance of a friend, as not to be made ridiculous by him when they are absent.   There are a middling sort of courtiers, who become happy by their want of wit ; but they supply that want by an excess of malice to those who have it. And there is no such persecution as that of fools : They can never be considerable enough to be talked of themselves ; so that they are safe only in their obscurity, and grow mischievous to witty men, by the great diligence of their envy, and by being always present to represent and aggravate their faults . . .   These are the men who make it their business to chase wit from the knowledge of princes, lest it should disgrace their ignorance.   And this kind of malice your Lordship has not so much avoided, as surmounted.   But if by the excellent temper of a royal master, always more ready to hear good than ill ; if by his inclination to love you ; if by your own merit and address ; if by the charms of your conversation, the grace of your behaviour, your knowledge of greatness, and habitude in courts, you have been able to preserve yourself with honour in the midst of so dangerous a course ; yet at least the remembrance of those hazards has inspired you with pity for other men, who, being of an inferior wit and quality to you, are yet persecuted, for being that in little which your Lordship is in great.   For the quarrel of those people extends itself to anything of sense ; and if I may be so vain to own it, amongst the rest of the poets, has sometimes reached to the very borders of it, even to me.   So that if our general good fortune had not raised up your Lordship to defend us, I know not whether anything had been more ridiculous in court than writers.   It is to your Lordship's favour we generally owe our protection and patronage, and to the nobleness of your nature, which will not suffer the least shadow of your wit to be contemned in other men.   You have been often pleased, not only to excuse my imperfections, but to vindicate what was tolerable in my writings from their censures ; and, what I never forget, you have not only been careful of my reputation, but of my fortune.[328]   You have been solicitous to supply my neglect of myself ; and to overcome the fatal modesty of poets, which submits them to perpetual wants, rather than to become importunate with those people who have the liberality of kings in their disposing, and who, dishonouring the bounty of their master, suffer such to be in necessity who endeavour at least to please him, and for whose entertainment he has generously provided, if the fruits of his royal favour

---

[328] Is this not a delicate invitation to Rochester to show his generosity in the present case ?

[Dedications were not mere idle flattery, but were written chiefly for the purpose of receiving a handsome acknowledgment in cash in return for the compliment.   But see Beljame later, and the article on Dryden in the *D.N.B.* B. D.]

were not often stopped in other hands.[329] But your Lordship has given me occasion, not to complain of courts whilst you are there. I have found the effects of your mediation in all my concernments ; and they were so much more noble in you, because they were wholly voluntary. I became your Lordship's (if I may venture on the similitude) as the world was made, without knowing him who made it, and brought only a passive obedience to be your creature. This nobleness of yours I think myself the rather obliged to own, because otherwise it must have been lost to all remembrance ! For you are endued with that excellent quality of a frank nature, to forget the good which you have done.

But, my Lord, I ought to have considered, that you are as great a judge as you are a patron ; and that in praising you ill, I should incur a higher note of ingratitude, than that I thought to have avoided. I stand in need of all your accustomed goodness for the dedication of this play ; which, though perhaps it be the best of my comedies, is yet so faulty, that I should have feared you for my critic, if I had not, with some policy, given you the trouble of being my protector. Wit seems to have lodged itself more nobly [330] in this age than in any of the former ; and people of my mean condition are only writers, because some of the nobility, and your Lordship in the first place, are above the narrow praises which poesy could give you. But, let those who love to see themselves exceeded, encourage your Lordship in so dangerous a quality ; for my own part, I must confess, that I have so much of self-interest, as to be content with reading some papers of your verses, without desiring you should proceed to a scene, or play ; with the common prudence of those who are worsted in a duel, and declare they are satisfied, when they are first wounded. Your Lordship has but another step to make, and from the patron of wit, you may become its tyrant [331] ; and oppress our little regulations with more ease than you now protect them. But these, my Lord, are designs, which I am sure you harbour not, any more than the French king is contriving the conquest of the Swissers. It is a barren triumph, which is not worth your pains ; and would only rank him amongst your slaves who is already,

My Lord,

Your Lordship's most obedient,

And most faithful servant,

JOHN DRYDEN.

Rochester would have been hard indeed to please if he had not been gratified. He would seem to have expressed his pleasure in a letter of some literary pretensions, to which Dryden replied by yet further abasing himself before the genius of the noble Lord. Rochester's reply dazzled him ; he professes himself conquered with his own weapons.

[329] An obvious allusion to the Poet-Laureate's salary which Dryden should be receiving, but which, as we shall see, was very irregularly paid.

[330] How elegantly the noble habitation is indicated !

[331] O my prophetic soul ! (*Hamlet*, I, 5.)

I find [he adds] it is not for me to contend any way with your
Lordship, who can write better on the meanest subject than I on the
best. . . . My only relief is, that what I have written is publique,
and I am so much my own friend as to conceal your Lordship's letter ;
for that which would have given vanity to any other poet has only
given me confusion. . . . You are that *rerum natura* of your own
Lucretius :
  Ipsa suis pollens opibus, nihil indiga nostri.[332]

It looked as if everything were turning out for the best.
Unfortunately Rochester was not content with offerings of
frankincense unless they burned for him alone and were denied
to others. Dryden, busy winning many patrons for himself,
had not foreseen this dilemma. He thought himself fortunate
in having gained the friendship of Sheffield, Earl of Mulgrave :
a friendship which cost him innumerable vexations.

After having been on the best of terms with Mulgrave,[333]
Rochester had had a duel with him from which he emerged
with scant honour by feigning sudden illness and declaring
himself in no condition to fight.[334] His opponent was at little
pains to keep the matter secret, and it can well be imagined that
Rochester was not over-grateful for his indiscretion. Mulgrave's
friendly relations with Dryden further embittered him. To see
the man who had snatched from him the palm of courage now
stretching out his hand to grasp the palm of wit, was wounding
to his vanity. Moreover, Dryden's talent and reputation
threatened to cross his own literary ambition ; this was salt
in the wound. Rochester determined to avenge himself and
began hostilities at once : against the poet only. He recommended Elkanah Settle to the King, that Settle might play
towards Dryden the part of Pradon against Racine.

Poor Settle, whose works are long since studiously un-read,
whose name survives only as the synonym of ridiculous presumption and ludicrous anticlimax [335], had produced his first tragedy
in 1666. *Cambyses, King of Persia*, is a miserably bad play, but

---

[332] *Works*, edited by Scott and Saintsbury, vol. XVIII, pp. 91 ff.—
Rochester had translated fragments of Lucretius. See his *Poems on Several
Occasions*, p. 45.

[333] Witness some verses entitled *An Epistolary Essay from Lord Rochester
to Lord Mulgrave upon their mutual poems*. See *The Works of the English Poets*,
edited by Chalmers, vol. VIII, p. 244.

[334] See *Memoirs of His Grace* John *Duke of* Buckingham. *Written by
himself*, pp. 8, 9, 10 in vol. II of *The Works of John Sheffield*.

[335] For Settle, see Nichols, *Literary Anecdotes*, vol. I, p. 41, note, and
Dryden's biographers.

thanks to good acting it had succeeded in achieving six performances.[336] This modest success drew Rochester's attention to him
as the suitable instrument for the plan he had in mind. At the
instance of the outraged aristocrat, Settle's new tragedy, *The
Empress of Morocco*, made its first appearance in the Palace of
Whitehall : an honour which had never been accorded to
Dryden, Poet Laureate though he was. To make Dryden's
humiliation the more complete, the cast was drawn from ladies
and gentlemen of the Court. Caring not a whit for the rebuff
to his protégé, Mulgrave wrote the prologue for the first performance, and Rochester, to underline his interest in the matter,
the prologue for the second.[337]

The play had sore need of every adventitious aid. It would
not be easy to conceive a more extravagant and complicated
plot nor a cruder, more fatuous style.

The Empress of Morocco is a criminal hussy who has skilfully
poisoned her husband and is plotting to get rid of the young king,
her son, to plant her lover Crimalhaz on the throne. While
her people picture her plunged in grief mourning her husband's
death, she is carrying on with the said Crimalhaz and the two
are discovered by Muly Hamet, Commander in Chief of the
royal forces, sleeping side by side. The young king hears the
tale and immediately believes it ; but his mother, without
turning a hair, accuses Muly Hamet of having attempted to
seduce her and persuades her credulous son to throw him into
prison on the spot and later send him into exile.

Virtuous Crimalhaz meanwhile is appointed Royal Treasurer
and loses no time in making off to the mountains with the army
and the treasure. There, with his mistress's co-operation, he
tries to lure the king into an ambuscade. Not succeeding in this,
he feigns a reconciliation with the king, returns to court and to
celebrate his return to favour, he offers his royal master a ballet
whose subject—somewhat surprising in Morocco—is Orpheus
descending to Hell to seek Eurydice. Now thanks to the
machinations of the queen-mother the part of Eurydice is played
by the young queen, her daughter-in-law, without the king's
knowledge. He, for his part, has disguised himself as Orpheus

[336] " The first new Play that was Acted in 1666 was : *The Tragedy of
Cambyses, King of Persia*, wrote by Mr. *Settle* : Cambyses, was perform'd by
Mr. Betterton : . . . All the other Parts, being perfectly well Acted, it
succeeded six Days with a full Audience." (Downes, p. 27.)

[337] These prologues are prefixed to the printed text of *The Empress of
Morocco*.

to escape from Crimalhaz who—so he has been told—seeks his
life.   The young queen has been persuaded that Orpheus is no
other than Crimalhaz and at the moment when Orpheus is
preparing to carry off Eurydice, she slays with a dagger the
husband to whom, after a thousand misadventures, she has just
been united.

Crimalhaz becomes king.   But without revealing it, he has
been secretly in love with the young queen.   He offers her his
hand to avenge her husband's death.   After some hesitation she
accepts it and is confronted by the queen mother.   Suspecting
nothing, the latter urges her lover to put the young widow to
death.   But it is she herself who is seized by his bodyguard.
Seeing herself thus a prisoner, she begs mercy of her young rival,
throws herself on her knees before her and then suddenly leaping
up, pierces her with a dagger and tries to fling herself on her
treacherous lover.   Baulked of this, she kills herself.

While the two queens are breathing their last, Crimalhaz
learns that his army has been defeated by General Muly Hamet
who returns from exile in the nick of time to round off the play.
He seizes the usurper and has him put to death.   The last scene
shows the villain and his accomplices dangling hanged against a
wall ornamented with hooks.

The foregoing is only the main plot of the tragedy, but as if
it were insufficiently complicated there are subsidiary intrigues :
amongst others the love of Muly Hamet for the lovely Mariamne,
a princess of the royal family.   She is also beloved by her gaoler,
Hametalhaz.   He is a tool in the hand of Crimalhaz, but when
bidden to bring her head to his master he announces *ex abrupto* :
" . . . I have . . . the pride to be her Jaylor . . . and her
Slave." [338]

The whole play is a tissue of similar surprises.   It would
seem that the only chord in us which the author seeks to strike
is stupefaction.   Thus, in the first Act, while the royal prince
—who will in the second Act be king—is groaning in his chains,
his love, Morena, comes to tell him that his father consents to
their union.   He is transported with joy.   " Yes," she continues,
" we are to be united in death." [339]

[338] Act V.
[339]   " I come to tell you that your Father's kind,
                And has our mutual Happiness design'd, etc.
  Muly Labas :   This does disperse my Fears, checks my Despair :
                And has my Father . . .   Shall we then . . . and are
                Our Loves and Hopes . . .   Oh my unruly Joy, etc.

When General Muly Hamet in his turn is disgraced and
sent to prison (everyone in the play is sooner or later flung into
gaol for a bit), Mariamne comes to bring him his sword.

Mariamne : . . . You are free ; fly !
Muly H : And must I from my Princess presence fly ?
Mariamne : No, stay.
Muly H : Kind Stars !
Mariamne : Yes, in my Memory.[340]

There is one scene in particular in the last Act where the
surprises are oddly piled up. Muly Hamet enters the capital
as conqueror ; fair Mariamne greets her lover from a balcony.
Suddenly Crimalhaz appears beside her, and vows to slay her
hic et nunc if life and crown are not secured to him. She is about
to die when in his turn the tender-hearted gaoler, Hametalhaz,
pops up on the balcony, disarms Crimalhaz, proclaims his love
for Mariamne and forthwith generously resigns her to his rival
Muly Hamet. The latter is struck—as well he may be—by so
much magnanimity and in testimony of his esteem offers Muly
Hamet a crown : duly accepted.

Language and style are on the same lofty level as the plot.

I shed my Tears, as Rain in Egypt falls,
Sent for no common cause, but to foretell
Destructions, Ruins, Plagues and Funerals.
I ne'er draw Tears but when those Tears draw Blood.[341]

As he sets forth to banishment, Muly Hamet is overtaken
by a hail shower, an unprecedented phenomenon in Morocco.
In his amazement he questions a priest (a bogus priest of course) :

Muly H : Though show'rs of Hail Morocco never see,
  Dull Priest, What does all this Portend to me ?
Hametalhaz : It does Portend . . .
Muly H : What ?
Hametalhaz : That the Fates . . . designe . . .
Muly H : To tire me with Impertinence like thine.[342]

Such was the rival set up to outclass Dryden. It is difficult
to believe that in this Rochester was inspired by a pure passion
for literature. So intelligent a man and especially one so sensitive to the ridiculous in others, could have been under no

---

Morena : Know then, to grant our Souls a stricter Tye,
  He has decreed . . . we shall together Dye."

(I, 1).

[340] III, 2. [341] III, 2. [342] IV, 2.

misapprehension. It is obvious that he used the first rhymester he could lay hands on, to make clear in the right quarter that if there were other patrons than Rochester, there were also other poets than Dryden. And no doubt he was glad to find a man unlikely to endanger his own literary fame.

Such as it is, *The Empress of Morocco* was a great success. Apart from the quite exceptional welcome accorded it by the Court, it is fair to admit that the play had extrinsic merits which carried weight in its day. The settings and scenery were varied and magnificent. The hail shower just mentioned fell from a stormy sky with a brilliant rainbow. There was a great river covered with a "magnificent" fleet, there were cannon shots and fanfares, an ambush, choruses, Moors dancing round a palm tree and hell itself opening on the stage.

After having been performed at Court the play was acted continuously for a month by the Duke's Company. The unfortunate Settle's head was turned. He published his tragedy with "sculptures" (it was the first to be illustrated by engravings). On the title-page his name was followed by the words "Servant to His Majesty" [343] clearly proclaiming his rivalry with Dryden whom he attempts to ridicule in his dedication.[344]

Dryden committed the supreme folly of getting angry. With two of his colleagues, Shadwell and Crowne, he wrote *ab irato* some *Notes and Observations on The Empress of Morocco* [345] into which he poured more passion than good taste. Having called Settle "this upstart illiterate scribbler" and "so contemptible a wretch" he goes on : "His king, his two empresses, his villain, and his sub-villain, nay his hero, have all a certain natural cast of the father ; one turn of the countenance goes through all his children. Their folly was born and bred in them ; and something of the Elkanah will be visible." At some length he discusses two of his lines, fastidiously analysing his words and concludes : "Sure the poet writ these two lines aboard some smack in a storm, and, being sea-sick, spewed up a good lump

---

[343] See my Bibliography.—When he published his tragedy, *Ibrahim The Illustrious Bassa* in 1677, Settle resumed the title "Servant to His Majesty" in apparent rivalry to Dryden's title of Laureate.

[344] "But my Lord, whilst I trouble you with this kind of discourse, I beg you would not think I design to give rules to the *Press*, as some of our Tribe have done to the *Stage* ; No, that's a trick I do not pretend to." (An unmistakable allusion to Dryden's *Essay of Dramatick Poesie*.) See below, note 417, another passage of this dedication, evidently aimed at Dryden.

[345] Reprinted in part in the *Works* of Dryden.

of clotted nonsense at once." Dryden sums up his opinion thus : " In short he is an animal of a most deplored under-standing, without reading and conversation : his being is in a twilight of sense, and some glimmering of thought, which he can never fashion either into wit or English."

In a Billingsgate battle the better man is always the loser. The fool is more skilled in bandying abuse than argument. Settle replied to the *Remarks* in ninety-five quarto pages in the style in which he had been challenged, and easily proved him-self superior in its use. He called Dryden a thief and had the last word.[346] Dryden had succeeded only in prolonging his rival's success.

Settle, however, did not long enjoy his fame. Jealous of his success, Rochester took pleasure in humbling him and transferred his favour to John Crowne. At his suggestion [347] the King commanded Crowne to write the *Masque of Calisto* which was acted at Court in 1675.[348] This was a new and direct blow at Dryden, more cruel than the first. For one of his duties as Poet Laureate was to supply this type of court poetry. He tried to regain a footing by humbly offering an epilogue, but Rochester was on the alert and the epilogue was rejected.[349]

After having tried his hand at the novel,[350] Crowne had so far written only three plays for the theatre : *Juliana, or The Princess of Poland*, a tangled jungle of complications ; *Charles VIII of France, or the Invasion of Naples*, a poor tragedy which he was

[346] " . . . With very little Conjuration, by those three remarkable Qualities of *Railing*, *Boasting* and *Thieving*, I found a *Dryden* in the frontispiece." (*Notes and Observations*, etc.)

[347] " His (Crowne's) Writings soon made him known to the Court and Town. Yet it was neither to the Favour of the Court, nor of *Wilmot* Lord *Rochester*, one of the shining Ornaments of it, that he was indebted for the Nomination which the King made of him for the writing the Mask of *Calypso* [*sic*] but to the Malice of that noble Lord, who design'd by that preference to mortify Mr. *Dryden* (Dennis : *Original Letters*, etc., vol. I, p. 49).—See also Saint-Evremond (?), *Lettre à la duchesse de Mazarin*, prefixed to the works of Rochester.

[348] See my Bibliography.—In the Preface he says : " I was invaded, on the sudden, by a Powerful Command, to prepare an Entertainment for the Court . . . it was done by Command." And in his Dedication to " The Lady Mary, Eldest Daughter of His Royal Highness the Duke," he writes : " This Poem, made like the first Man, by the Command, and for the Service of a Divinity . . ."

[349] This epilogue, which was to have been spoken by Lady Henrietta Maria Wentworth who was acting Jupiter, is to be found in Scott and Saints-bury's edition of Dryden's *Works*, vol. X, p. 332.

[350] *Pandion and Amphigenia*. See my Bibliography. It is a romance of 307 pages in Scudéry style.

careful to dedicate to Rochester, and a comedy called *The Countrey Wit*. He had also collaborated in a miserable imitation of Racine's *Andromaque*, half-verse, half-prose. *Calisto* has added nothing to his posthumous fame. The seduction of the nymph Calisto by Jupiter in the guise of Diana, as Ovid tells the story, was a risky subject for the stage. Not that this would in those days have been an objection. But Crowne, diluting his meagre material to spread it over five long acts, yet stopped short of the seduction. In his play Jupiter is converted to virtue by Calisto's resistance and to guard himself against future temptation he gallantly addresses her :

> I then entreat you will (to end this War !)
> Accept the small dominion of a Star.[351]

The most noteworthy thing about the play was the rank of the actors taking part in it : amongst others, the two daughters of the Duke of York, Mary and Anne, both of them later to be Queens of England (Mary played Calisto), the Countess of Sussex, natural daughter of the King, and Mrs. Sarah Jennings, destined to become Duchess of Marlborough. The Duke of Monmouth and other nobles danced with ladies of the Court.[352]

A work thus staged, with scenery and costumes in keeping with the actors, was bound to succeed and did in fact prove a success : it was played more than twenty times at Court, and won for Crowne the King's signal favour.[353]

Dryden swallowed this fresh affront without a word ; but in the same year when dedicating his tragedy of *Aureng-Zebe* to Mulgrave he could not conceal his vexation and discouragement. He speaks of " those unhappy people, whom, in our own wrong, we call the great ". " Neither am I formed," he adds, " to praise a court, who admire and covet nothing, but the easiness and quiet of retirement . . . I desire to be no longer the Sisyphus of the stage ; to roll up a stone with endless labour . . . which is perpetually falling down again." And he dreams anew of epic poetry.

Rochester, meanwhile, growing more and more capricious, was growing weary of Crowne also (on account of the success

---

[351] Act V.

[352] When the play was printed, Crowne gave the names of noble actors and dancers in great detail.

[353] The *Dramatic Works of John Crown*, 1873–76. See the Preface and the note prefixed to *Calisto*.

of his new play, *The Destruction of Jerusalem*) [354] and was commending Thomas Otway to Charles II and his royal brother.

Otway at this time was twenty-five. He had failed to make
a success of an actor's career,[355] but his ready wit and pleasant
manners won him the society of some gay young nobles,[356]
amongst whom were Lord Falkland and the Earl of Plymouth—
a natural son of Charles II—who had been fellow-students of
his at Oxford. When the need to earn a livelihood became
pressing, Plymouth's influence secured him a cornetship in the
army. But he was no more successful as a soldier than an
actor. Before a year was up, he sold his commission and returned penniless to London. He made his début as an author
in 1675 with his tragedy, *Alcibiades*, which, combined no doubt
with his value as a boon companion—for the play is a masterpiece of insipidity—drew the attention of Rochester. Thanks
to Rochester's patronage, his *Don Carlos*, an incomparably better
play than *Alcibiades*, was a great success. In his Preface, the
young poet, hitherto little accustomed to good fortune, effusively
thanks his patron for his good offices with the King and the
Duke of York, and to please him permits himself a sneer at
Dryden.[357] He also dedicated his next tragedy, *Titus and
Berenice*,[358] to Rochester.

[354] " When *Crown's Hierusalem* had met with as wild, and unaccountable
Success, as the *Almanzors*, his Lordship withdrew his Favours, as if he would
still be in Contradiction to the Town." (Saint-Evremond (?), Letter prefixed
to the works of Rochester.)

[355] Downes, p. 34.

[356] " Gay Coxcombs, Cowards, Knaves and prating Fools,
　　Bullies of o're-grown Bulks, and little Souls,
　　Gamesters, Half-wits, and Spendthrifts (such as think
　　Mischievous midnight Frollicks bred by Drink
　　　　　Are Gallantry and Wit,
　　Because to their lewd Understandings fit)
　　Were those wherewith two Years at least I spent . . ."
　　　　　(Otway, *The Poets Complaint of his Muse*.)

[357] " Though a certain Writer, that shall be nameless (but you may
guess at him by what follows) being ask'd his Opinion of this Play, very
gravely cock'd, and cry'd, *I gad* (a favourite exclamation of Dryden's, also
reproduced in *The Rehearsal*) *he knew not a Line in it he would be Author of*. But
he is a fine facetious witty Person, as my Friend Sir *Formal* has it ; and to be
even with him, I know a Comedy of his, that has not so much as a Quibble
in it that I would be Author of. And so, Reader, I bid him and thee Farewel."
(*Works*, 1712. The edition of 1695, the earliest possessed by the British
Museum, does not contain the Preface.)

[358] See Johnson, *Lives of the English Poets*, Otway ; Otway's *Life* prefixed
to his *Works*, 1712 ; E. W. Gosse : Otway, in *Seventeenth Century Studies*,

But Rochester was born to put everyone out of countenance. He wrote *A Session of the Poets*, and amidst the more or less vulgar shafts aimed at all poets—except aristocrats—he speaks thus of his latest pet :

> *Tom Otway* came next, Tom Shadwell's dear Zany,
> And swears, for Heroicks, he writes best of any :
> *Don Carlos* his Pockets so amply had fill'd,
> That his Mange was quite cur'd, and his Lice were all kill'd.
> But *Apollo* had seen his Face on the Stage,
> And prudently did not think fit to engage
> The Scum of a Play-House for the Prop of an Age. [359]

As if this were not enough, the noble Earl circulated anonymously—but everyone perfectly well knew the author—Horace's *Tenth Satire of the First Book imitated* in which he sneers at everybody : Dryden whom he is the first to call "Poet Squab" [360]; "blund'ring Settle" . . .; "Crown's tedious Scenes" ; "puzzling Otway".[361]

We can guess what Dryden must have suffered from all these blows and from feeling himself the plaything of the fantastic whims of a conceited ass in face of whom his tongue was tied as surely as in face of Buckingham. How often he must have reread his dedication to " The Right Honourable, the Earl of Rochester " and smiled wryly at his futile flattery of the man whom he had prophetically warned : " Your Lordship has but another step to make, and from the patron of wit, you may become its tyrant " !

But these trials did Dryden good service. From this period, so mortifying to the man, the poet emerged stronger and with greater respect for his own talent. Up to this point he had written to please others : he would now, to use his own ex-

---

pp. 269–305.—*Don Carlos* is dedicated to the Duke of York. The success of this play was so great that Settle, already infuriated at having been supplanted by Crowne, could bear no more and is said to have challenged Otway to a duel.

[359] *Works*, vol. I, p. 135.

[Beljame refers to the poem usually printed in Rochester's *Works* (e.g. in Chalmers or Hayward) as " A Trial of the Poets for the Bays ". In the edition Beljame used, it appears to have been called " A Scession of the Poets ". B. D.]

[360] " He was as plump as Mr. Pitt," said Pope (Spence, p. 261).

[361] *Works*, vol. I, pp. 10–11.—Otway in disgust gave vent to his resentment against Rochester in some bitter lines of *The Poets Complaint of his Muse*.

pression, write something to please himself,[362] and *All for Love* was the result. This play, Dryden's first real drama (and written under Charles II) is perhaps the only claim Rochester can make on the gratitude of posterity. But for his insolence and disdain, the poet might perhaps never have found himself again and given this tragedy to the world. Defying fashion, he returns to genuine drama and to genuine style ; he forsakes rhyme,[363] he brings real people to life and breathes into them something of Shakespeare's spirit.[364]

The play itself is a reply to the pretensions of the puppet-rivals who had been set up against him, and a happier reply than that recently to Settle, for not one of them felt strong enough to retort. The Preface disposed not less happily of their patron's pretensions. It is easy to recognise the portrait veiled behind words like these :

Men of pleasant conversation (at least esteemed so), and endued with a trifling kind of fancy, perhaps helped out with some smattering of Latin, are ambitious to distinguish themselves from the herd of gentlemen, by their poetry—

Rarus enim fermè sensus communis in illâ Fortunâ.

And is not this a wretched affectation, not to be contented with what fortune has done for them, and sit down quietly with their estates, but they must call their wits in question, and needlessly expose their nakedness to public view ? Not considering that they are not to expect the same approbation from sober men, which they have found from their flatterers after the third bottle. If a little glittering in discourse has passed them on us for witty men, where was the necessity of undeceiving the world ? Would a man who has an ill title to an estate, but yet is in possession of it, would he bring it of his own accord to be tried at Westminster ? We who write, if we

---

[362] " But it (*The Spanish Fryar*) was given to the people ; and I never writ any thing for my self but *Anthony* and *Cleopatra*." (Preface to *The Art of Painting*.) Anthony and Cleopatra are hero and heroine of *All for Love*.

[363] Lee followed his example and gave up rhyme in the same year with *Mithridates* ; Otway followed suit with *The Orphan* in 1680.

[364] The title with its " Written in Imitation of *Shakespeare's* Stile ", and the Prologue, betray the poet's joy in reverting to wholesome inspiration :

> " He fights this day unarmed,—without his rhyme— . . .
> His hero, whom you wits his bully call,
> Bates of his mettle, and scarce rants at all . . .
> I could name more : a wife, and mistress too ;
> Both (to be plain) too good for most of you :
> The wife well-natured, and the mistress true."

want the talent, yet have the excuse that we do it for a poor subsistence ; but what can be urged in their defence, who, not having the
vocation of poverty to scribble, out of mere wantonness take pains to
make themselves ridiculous ?   Horace was certainly in the right,
where he said, " That no man is satisfied with his own condition."
A poet is not pleased, because he is not rich ; and the rich are dis-
contented, because the poets will not admit them of their number.
Thus the case is hard with writers : If they succeed not, they must
starve ; and if they do, some malicious satire is prepared to level them,
for daring to please without their leave.   But while they are so eager
to destroy the fame of others, their ambition is manifest in their concernment ; some poem of their own is to be produced, and the slaves
are to be laid flat with their faces on the ground, that the monarch
may appear in the greater triumph.

Dionysius and Nero had the same longings, but with all their
power they could never bring their business well about.   'Tis true,
they proclaimed themselves poets by sound of trumpet ; and poets
they were upon pain of death to any man who durst call them otherwise.   The audience had a fine time on 't, you may imagine ; they
sat in a bodily fear, and looked as demurely as they could : for it was
a hanging matter to laugh unseasonably . . . but when the show was
over, and an honest man was suffered to depart quietly, he took out
his laughter which he had stifled, with a firm resolution never more
to see an emperor's play though he had been ten years a-making it.
In the meantime the true poets were they who . . . had wit enough
to yield the prize with a good grace, and not contend with him who
had thirty legions.   They were sure to be rewarded, if they confessed
themselves bad writers, and that was somewhat better than to be
martyrs for their reputation.   Lucan's example was enough to teach
them manners ; and after he was put to death, for overcoming Nero,
the Emperor carried it without dispute for the best poet in his
dominions.

These arrows were barbed and struck home.   Indignation
inspired Dryden better than flattery.

Rochester, however, had not yet said his last word.

In Molière's *Médecin malgré lui*, when Lucas is recalling
Jacqueline to the respect due to her master, it is Géronte,
unhappily placed between the two, who receives every blow
with which the outraged husband reinforces his exhortations
to his wife : Mulgrave and Rochester were at war, and it
was Dryden who was hit.   Things were about to take a tragic
turn.

Round about November, 1679, Mulgrave began to circulate
in manuscript an *Essay upon Satyr* he had written.   It was a
fairly crude attack on everybody ; on the King, his mistresses,
Dorset, Sedley and more particularly on Rochester, to whom

a long tirade was devoted, the celebrated duel with Mulgrave forming the main theme.[365]

In view of his relation to the author, it is possible that Dryden may have somewhat touched up Mulgrave's inspired satiric lines.   This is one of the accusations that was habitually levelled at poets who cultivated the friendship of lettered amateurs. But it seems probable that the verses owed nothing to him, for Mulgrave expressly asserts that Dryden had nothing to do with

[365]   " Nor shall the Royal Mistresses be nam'd,
            Too ugly, or too easy to be blam'd ;
            With whom each rhyming Fool keeps such a Pother,
            They are as common that way, as the other.
            Yet sauntering *Charles* between his beastly Brace, ⎫
            Meets with Dissembling still in either place,   ⎬
            Affected Humour, or a painted Face.   ⎭
            In Loyal Libels we have often told him,
            How one has jilted him, the other sold him :
            How that affects to laugh, how this to weep ;
            But who can rail, so long as he can keep ? . . .
            Thus *D—et*, purring like a thoughtful Cat,
            Married ; but wiser Puss ne'er thought of that ;
            And first he worried her with railing Rhyme . . .
            Then for one night sold all his Slavish Life,
            A teeming *Widow*, but a barren *Wife* ;
            Swell'd by contact of such a fulsome Toad,
            He lugg'd about the Matrimonial Load ;
            Till Fortune blindly kind as well as he,
            Has ill restor'd him to his Liberty.
            Which he would use in all his sneaking way,
            Drinking all Night, and dozing all the Day . . .
                 And little *Sid—y* for *Simile* renown'd
            Pleasure has always sought, but never found :
            Tho' all his Thoughts on Wine and Women fall,
            His are so bad, sure he ne'er thinks at all,
            The Flesh he lives upon is rank and strong ;
            His Meat and Mistresses are kept too long . . .
            No Nastiness offends his skilful Nose ;
            Which from all Stink can with peculiar Art
            Extract Perfume and Essence, from a *F—t* :
            Expecting Supper is his great Delight ;
            He toils all Day, but to be drunk at Night :
            Then o're his Cups this Night-bird chirping sits,
            Till he takes *Hewet* and *Jack Hall* for Wits.
                 Rochester I despise for want of Wit . . .
            For while he Mischief means to all Mankind,
            Himself alone the ill Effects does find . . .
            False are his Words, affected is his Wit,
            So often he does aim, so seldom hit ;
            To ev'ry Face he cringes while he speaks,
            But when the Back is turn'd, the Head he breaks.
            Mean in each Action, lewd in every Limb,
            Manners themselves are mischievous in him . . .

them [366] and the widowed Countess later printed them in the complete edition of her husband's works.[367]

Be this as it may, Rochester well knew who was responsible, for he called Mulgrave to account not long afterwards, chaffing him at length in a set of verses entitled " Rochester's Farewell " about an expedition he had led to Tangier. In them he takes the opportunity of accusing Mulgrave of lack of courage.[368] But he thought it more convenient to pose in public as believing that Dryden alone was the author of the satire. Far from belying the accusation of cowardice that had been flung at him, Rochester further justified it by a vile, cold-blooded ambuscade.

For (there's the Folly that's still mixt with Fear) ;
Cowards more blows than any Hero bear.
Of fighting-Spraks (Sparks), some (Fame ?) may her Pleasures say,
But 'tis a bolder thing to run away.
The World may well forgive him all his Ill,
For ev'ry Fault does prove his Penance still :
Falsly he falls into some dangerous Noose,
And then as meanly labours to get loose.
A Life so infamous is better quitting,
Spent in base Injury, and low submitting," etc.

> (*An Essay upon Satyr, By the Earl of* Mulgrave.
> In *A New Collection of* Poems relating to
> State Affairs . . . MDCCV, pp. 133 ff.)

[366] See below, note No. 375.

[367] Malone (pp. 129–34) and Walter Scott (pp. 167–72) in their biographies of Dryden have no hesitation in affirming that these verses are not his. Their argument—though it has since been disputed—seems to me irrefutable. Walter Scott's opinion (reinforcing Johnson's) has great weight on the literary side ; and the other considerations which he advances are, like Malone's, extremely cogent, especially this : that the Poet Laureate would not have taken the risk of attacking the King and his mistresses. Mulgrave, on the other hand, was at the time in the Opposition and such attacks were part of his rôle, besides being less dangerous for him than they would have been for Dryden. Mr. Bell, who believed in Dryden's authorship, stresses the fact that they contain a eulogy of Mulgrave which he could hardly have written himself. But isn't this obviously a device to throw the hounds off the scent ? Mulgrave moreover blows his own trumpet in the *Essay on Poetry* which is unquestionably his.

[368] " First, then, the *Tangier Bullies* must appear,
With open Brav'ry, and dissembled Fear.
Mulgrave, their Head . . .
Had it not better been, than thus to roam,
To stay and tie the Cravat-string at Home ?
To strut, look big, shake Pantaloon, and swear
With *Hewet, Dam me*, There's no action there.
Had'st thou no Friend, that would to *Rowley* write,
To hinder this thy eagerness to fight ?
That without Danger thou a Brave might'st be . . ." etc.

> (Rochester's *Farewell, Works*, I, pp. 161–2.)

You write me word [he wrote to a friend] that I'm out of Favour with a certain Poet, whom I have ever admir'd for the disproportion of him and his Attributes : He is a Rarity which I cannot but be fond of, as one would be of a Hog that could fiddle, or a singing Owl. If he falls on me at the Blunt, which is his very good Weapon in Wit, I will forgive him, if you please, and leave the Repartee to *Black Will*, with a cudgel.[369]

And thus it was done. One evening on his way home, Dryden was waylaid in Rose Street near Covent Garden by three men posted there, who first overwhelmed him with vulgar abuse, then flung him to the ground and belaboured him with blows.

Dryden, and for that matter everybody else, knew perfectly well who was behind this dastardly attack, but witnesses were lacking. The poet offered £50 reward for anyone who would help to trace the culprits [370] ; but in vain. Apart from the fact that episodes of this kind were not infrequent and roused little indignation,[371] Rochester was too highly placed for a mere author to reach him.

Dryden had to abandon hope of obtaining justice and once again decided to keep silence. The whole town, not least his fellow-authors, took sides against him. It seemed that it was

[369] Rochester, *Familiar Letters*, etc., p. 5.

[370] " Whereas *John Dreyden*, Esq. ; was on Thursday, the 18th instant at night barbarously assaulted and wounded in *Rose-street* in *Covent Garden*, by divers men unknown. If any Person shall make Discovery of the said Offenders to the said Mr. *Dreyden*, or to any Justice of the Peace—he shall not onely receive Fifty pounds, which is deposited in the hands of Mr. *Blanchard Goldsmith*, next door to *Temple Bar*, for the said Purpose ; but if he be a Principal or an accessory in the said Fact himself, His Majesty is graciously pleased to promise him his pardon for the same." (*London Gazette*, from Wednesday, Dec. 24, to Monday, Dec. 29, 1679.)

[371] In 1669 the House of Commons proposed to put a tax on theatres. The Court party opposed the motion saying that the actors were the King's Servants and part of his pleasures. Thereupon Sir John Coventry, M.P., asked whether the King's pleasure was in the actors or the actresses. That evening he was assailed in the street by men who cleft his nose to the bone and left him there. No one doubted that this attack was arranged by the King or one of his entourage (probably the Duke of Monmouth) and the House of Commons passed an Act condemning the criminals to banishment, adding that the King should have no power to pardon them. Needless to say they were not found. (Burnet, *History of my Own Times*, I, pp. 468–70.) —See also Pepys, July 29, 1667, and Feb. 1, 1669.—The *Athenæum* of April 17, 1875, quotes a curious document in which Charles II proclaims pardon to his " faithful and well-beloved cousin and counsellor " the Duke of Buckingham for several " murders, treasons and other crimes ". The same monarch held in high favour the celebrated Colonel Blood, who had daringly tried to steal the Crown Jewels and to kidnap the Duke of Ormond.

E

he who had been guilty of a disgraceful act and who had lost his honour. From this time onwards the cowardly assault of which he had been the victim was constantly cast in his teeth. The satire of Rose-Alley, the ambush of Rose-street, Dryden's good health, became ever-recurring jests at the luckless author's expense and were considered in the best of taste. It is unnecessary to mention that Rochester, far from feeling regret—still less, remorse—joined in the chorus. At the close of some verses in which he reviews the disgraces of his time he can find nothing better for a final line than : " Who'd be a Wit, in Dryden's cudgell'd skin ? " [372]

Otway, whom Rochester had preferred to Dryden, Otway, who had accused Dryden of having said of *Don Carlos* that " I gad, he knew not a line in it he would be Author of ",[373] Otway was alone in defending his hapless colleague, and in the Epilogue to *Venice Preserv'd* he nobly expressed his opinion about ambuscades and those who laid them.[374]

[372] " Who'd be a *Monarch,* to endure the Prating
    Of NELL and sawcy OGLETHORPE in Waiting ?
    Who would SOUTHAMPTON's driv'ling Cuckold be ?
    Who would be YORK, and bear his *Infamy* ? . . .
    Who'd be a Wit in DRYDEN's cudgell'd skin ? "
    (*An Imitation of the First Satire of Juvenal, Works,* I, 15–16.)

[373] Preface to *Don Carlos* quoted above, note No. 357.

[374] " Poets in honour of the Truth shou'd write,
    With the same Spirit brave men for it fight ;
    And though against him causeless hatreds rise, ⎫
    And dayly where he goes of late, he spies ⎬
    The scowles of sullen and revengeful eyes ; ⎭
    'Tis what he knows with much contempt to bear
    And serves a cause too good * to let him fear :
    He fears no poison from an incens'd Drabb—
    No Ruffian's five foot-sword, nor Rascal's stab ;
    Nor any other snares of mischief laid,
    Not a Rose-alley Cudgel-Ambuscade,
    From any private cause where malice reigns,
    Or general Pique all Block-heads have to brains."

    * The defence of the King and the Duke of York.

But *Venice Preserv'd* was acted in 1682 and Rochester had died in 1680.— In the Prologue to Maidwell's comedy, *The Loving Enemies* played in 1680, there is a defence of Dryden :

    " Who dares be witty now, and with just rage
    Disturb the vice and follies of the Age ?
    With knaves and Fools, Satyr's a dang'rous fault,
    They will not let you rub their sores with salt.
    Else *Rose-Streets* Ambuscade shall break your head,
    And life in Verse, shall lay the Poet dead.

Mulgrave, who at the start of this long-drawn-out and disastrous quarrel of which he was the cause, had written a prologue to the play of the rival who was supplanting his protégé, preserved to the end the same haughty detachment. When he wrote his *Essay on Poetry* he found nothing more appreciative to say of Dryden than :

> Tho prais'd and punish'd for another's Rhimes
> His own deserve as great Applause sometimes . . .

and he calmly adds a footnote : " A Libel, for which he was both applauded and wounded, tho entirely innocent of the whole matter." [375] Pope, who revised the poem later,[376] did Mulgrave the service of suppressing both the couplet and the note.[377]

This was the last of Rochester's exploits. He died the following year, worn out with wine and debauchery and—it was said—reconciled with Heaven. Having to mention his name some years later, Dryden's sole revenge was to call him " an author of . . . quality whose ashes I will not disturb ".[378]

VII

Writers' profits : from the theatre, from sale of their books, from gifts

All this makes a sorry tale, and it shows the humiliating moral dependence of the writer on those who called themselves, and whom he called, his patrons. If he had even enjoyed financial independence in return ! But he did not. The income which he drew from his writings was small and precarious, and

---

> Since therefore such unequal Judges sit,
> Who for suspicion punish men of Wit,
> 'Twill be self-preservation to be dull,
> It cracks the credit but preserves the skull."

[375] " The * Laureat here may justly claim our Praise,
Crown'd by † Mac-Fleckno with immortal Bays
Tho *prais'd* " etc.

    * Mr. *D—n.*   † A famous Satirical Poem of his.

[376] Spence, p. 292.
[377] They are omitted in the edition of his books published by his Widow in 1723. See vol. I, p. 137.
[378] *Discourse concerning the Original and Progress of Satire* prefixed to his translation of Juvenal (1693).

[For Rochester's reconciliation with Heaven, see Burnet's *Some Passages in the Life and Death of the right honourable John Earl of Rochester*, 1680. Rochester was a more interesting character than Beljame would have us think. See the *Cambridge History of English Literature*, or the Preface to his *Works* edited by John Hayward, and Professor V. de S. Pinto's biography. B. D.]

it was this problem of a livelihood which placed him so completely at the mercy of a frivolous society and its capricious leaders.

The rewards which a professional writer might hope for were of three kinds :

1. profits from the theatre,
2. sale of his works to booksellers,
3. gifts.

All three were, as we shall see, very modest and most uncertain.

The rights of an author, as the theatre understands them to-day, were then unknown.   All the payment that a playwright could claim for a play's being acted was the profit on the third performance.   This profit was his—if there was a third perform-ance ; but plays did not always survive so far.   For the occasion, the author himself went round selling tickets and was obliged actively to solicit the presence of his patrons and their friends at his benefit performance.[379]

If after all these efforts the third performance yielded him £70 he thought himself incredibly lucky.[380]   If his play had a long run, its success benefited the theatre alone ;   the author had no further share in it.

In view of the popularity the theatres enjoyed, and their brilliant well-attended performances, it seems amazing that they should not have paid their authors more adequately.   But closer inquiry explains the phenomenon.   First, the brilliant performances were not achieved without immense expenditure

---

[379] ". . . you brought in Her Royal Highness just at the exigent time, whose single Presence on the Poet's Day, is a Subsistence for him all the Year after."   (Dedication of Lee's *Theodosius* to the Duchess of Richmond.)

[380] Malone, *Historical Account*, etc., p. 178 note 5.—This was evidently a maximum rarely reached ; for Spence (p. 262) records Pope as saying that it was very good if the third performance brought in £50 to the author. This estimate is confirmed by a passage of Otway's :

> " But which among you is there to be found,
> Will take his Third Day's Pawn for Fifty pound ? "
> (Epilogue to *The History and Fall of Caius Marius*.)

Those were fortunate who made even £50.   D'Urfey speaks of £20 :

> " He who now, in hopes of equal gain,
> Will needs be Pris'ner . . .
> He melts in durance half his Grease away,
> To get, like us, poor twenty Pounds a day."
> (Prologue to *The Injured Princess*.)

The same lines recur in the Epilogue to *The Fool turn'd Critick* by the same author, with £13 instead of £20.

on scenery and costumes [381] ; to cover this, the management would have needed the guarantee of full houses over a long period. But we have seen how small in number was the regular clientèle of the theatre and how little they could in fact be relied on, for all their enthusiasm. New plays had therefore to be continually provided and fresh expense incurred. Wrestling with these problems, the directors of the theatre did not grow rich : D'Avenant died bankrupt. [382] This was the first reason for offering writers derisory fees. A second factor lessened the commercial value of a play : the nobleman's very passion for drama. It is obvious that when men like Sedley, Buckingham, Orrery, or Howard, gave their plays to the theatre, they were aiming at honour and glory and were little concerned about a financial return. [383] The directors had thus a double induce-

[381] ". . . Scenes, which had been a little before introduced upon the publick stage by Sir William Davenant, at the Duke's old Theatre in Lincolns-inn-fields, but afterwards very much improved, with the addition of curious machines by Mr. Betterton in Dorset Garden, to the great expense and continual charge of the players. This much impaired their profit o'er what it was before . . ." (*Historia Histrionica*, 1699, quoted by Ebsworth, *Westminster Drolleries*, p. xxvi.)

[382] Chalmers, *Biographical Dictionary* : Sir William Davenant.—See also *Sir William D'Avenant's voyage to the other World*, etc., by Richard Flecknoe, quoted by Malone, *Historical Account*, etc., p. 250 ff.

[383]   " The *Poet* and the *Whore* alike complains
    Of trading Quality, that spoils their Gains ;
    The Lords will Write, and Ladies will have Swains." }
               (Lee, Prologue to *Constantine the Great*. This
               Prologue is printed also in Otway's works.)

" You've seen what Fortune other Poets share :
View next the Factors of the theatre :
That constant Mart which all the year does hold,
Where staple Wit is barter'd, bought and sold ;
Here trading Scriblers for their Maintenance
And Livelihood, trust to a Lott'ry chance :
But who his Parts would in the Service spend,
Where all his Hopes on vulgar Breath depend ?
Where ev'ry sot, for paying half a Crown,
Has the Prerogative to cry him down.
Sedley, indeed may be content with Fame,
Nor care, should an ill-judging Audience damn.
But *Settle* and the rest that write for Pence,
Whose whole Estate's an Ounce or two of Brains,
Should a thin House on the third Day appear,
Must starve, or live in Tatters all the Year.
And what can we expect that's brave and great, }
From a poor needy Wretch, that writes to eat ? }
Who the Success of the next Play must wait }

ment to accept their plays : the rank of the author, which ensured the interest of an audience that was almost exclusively aristocratic, and his indifference to money. The professional writer could not compete on either line, and the market, as economists would say, being flooded with goods easily disposed of and offered for nothing, the inevitable result was a fall in prices.

It should be said that authors enjoying the favour of the public were not content with the fluctuating fee of the third performance and dictated other conditions. Thus, after the success of *The Indian Emperour* and *The Maiden-Queen*, Dryden concluded a special agreement with the King's Company, by which he was entitled to one and a quarter shares in the profits of the theatre. But in return he pledged himself to furnish the playhouse with three plays a year. Since all comedies were in five acts and often in verse this meant immense labour, and labour ill-rewarded. The players reckoned the poet's share at £300 to £400 a year, *communibus annis*. The meanest Dryden of modern times would turn up his nose at such a sum—even allowing for the greater value of money in those days.[384] Yet even these figures are certainly an over-estimate. We possess in fact a document [385]

For Lodging, Food and Cloaths, and whose chief Care,
Is how to spunge for the next Meal and where ? "
　　　　(Oldham, *A Satire, Dissuading from Poetry.*
　　　　Works, vol. III.)

Sedley handed over the third performance of *Bellamira* to a friend, probably Shadwell (see his Preface).

[384] Money was then worth approximately three times what it is to-day (i.e. 1897. What of 1947 ? E. O. L.).

[385] " Whereas upon Mr. Dryden's binding himself to write three playes a-yeere, hee the said Mr. Dryden was admitted and continued as a sharer in the king's play-house for diverse years, and received for his *share and a quarter* three or four hundred pounds, *communibus annis* ; but though he received the moneys, we received not the playes, not one in a yeare. After which the house being burnt, the company in building another, contracted great debts, so that shares fell much short of what they were formerly. Thereupon Mr. Dryden complaining to the company of his want of proffit, the company was so kind to him that they not only did not presse him for the playes which he so engaged to write for them, and for which he was paid beforehand, but they did also at his earnest request give him a third day for his last new play called *All for Love* ; and at the receipt of the money of the said third day, he acknowledged it as a guift, and a particular kindnesse of the company. Yet notwithstanding this kind proceeding Mr. Dryden has now, jointly with Mr. Lee (who was in pension with us to the last day of our playing, and shall continue), written a play called *Œdipus*, and given it to the Duke's company, contrary to his said agreement, his promise, and all gratitude, to the great

in which the actors complain how little the author has done in return for all the advantages they have secured for him. So it is probable that their calculation is considerably exaggerated and that, as Malone believed, we must reduce his maximum receipts to £200.[386] We must also deduct the proceeds of the third performance which seem to have been cancelled by the new agreement,[387] and take account of the continual fluctuation of profits in any undertaking which is so much of a gamble as a theatre exposed to the whims of fashion as well as to the risks of every commercial venture. In 1671, for instance, the building in which the King's Company acted was destroyed by fire, and the shares, to Dryden's great vexation, fell considerably in value.[388] This agreement was in any case only temporary and according to Malone [389] Dryden benefited under it only from 1667 to 1680.

Other authors were employed on similar terms by the players who thus ensured themselves a supply of acting plays. Crowne would seem to have received an annual salary of £112 from the Duke's Company, and Lee to have had some like agree-

---

prejudice and almost undoing of the company, they being the only poets remaining to us. Mr. Crowne, being under the like agreement with the duke's house, writt a play called *The Destruction of Jerusalem*, and being forced by their refusall of it, to bring it to us, the said company compelled us, after the studying of it, and a vast expence in scenes and cloathes, to buy off their clayme, by paying all the pension he had received from them, amounting to one hundred and twelve pounds paid by the king's company, besides near forty pounds he the said Mr. Crowne paid out of his owne pocket.

These things considered, if notwithstanding Mr. Dryden's said agreement, promise, and moneys freely given him for his said last new play, and the many titles we have to his writings, this play be judged away from us, we must submit.

> (*Signed*) Charles Killigrew ;
> Charles Hart ;
> Rich. Burt ;
> Cardell Goodman ;
> Mic. Mohun."

(Malone, *Historical Account*, etc., pp. 192, 193.) Malone attributes this document—probably addressed to the Lord Chamberlain or to the King—to the year 1678 or thereabouts.

[386] *Life of Dryden*, pp. 444–8. He calculates that each share would have brought in not more than £160 a year.—According to Malone, Dryden's receipts from the theatre between 1665 and 1670 and from 1676 to 1685 did not exceed £100 a year.

[387] See the document quoted above, note No. 385.

[388] See the same.

[389] Life of Dryden, pp. 70–6.

ment with the King's.[390]   Others no doubt enjoyed similar advantages.

But, when all is said and done, authors were most reasonably dissatisfied with their income from the theatre.   Dryden never made more than £100 with any one of his most successful plays, and this includes not only the profits of the third performance but also the Dedication and the sale of his manuscript to the bookseller.[391]   The conclusion authors had arrived at by the end of Charles II's reign, was that the actors had been buying their goods too cheap,[392] and that they were being doomed like Sisyphus " to roll up a stone with endless labour, which, to follow the proverb, gathers no moss ".[393]

That Otway shared this opinion is shown by the quotation which he prefixed to *The Orphan*.[394]   Shadwell was of the same mind and expresses himself thus in the Dedication of his *Virtuoso* : " That there are a great many faults in the conduct of this Play, I am not ignorant.   But I (having no pension [395] but from the Theatre, which is either unwilling, or unable, to reward a Man sufficiently for so much pains as correct Comedies require) cannot allot my whole time to the writing of Plays, but am forced to mind some other business of Advantage." [396]   Lee

---

[390] Document quoted note No. 385.—". . . After the Restoration, when the two houses struggled for the favour of the town, the taking poets were secured to either house by a sort of retaining fee, which seldom amounted to more than 40s. a week, nor was that of any long continuance." (Gildon, *Laws of Poetry*, 1721, quoted by Malone, *Historical Account*, etc., p. 191.) Malone adds that he seems to have underestimated their profits. These cannot in any case have been large for according to the document above quoted (note No. 385) Crowne appears to have had only £112 a year.

[391] Life of Southerne, prefixed to his Works : Johnson, *Lives of the English Poets* : Dryden.—Mr. Gosse also says that Otway made only £100 by *The Orphan*.

[392] Life of Southerne.

[393] Dedication of *Aureng-Zebe*.

[394]   " Qui Pelago credit, magno se fœnore tollit ;
               Qui pugnas et Castra petit, præcingitur Auro ;
               Vilis adulator picto jacet Ebrius Ostro ;
               Et qui sollicitat Nuptas, ad præmia peccat :
               Sola pruinosis horret Facundia pannis
               Atque inopi lingua desertas invocat Artes."
                                          (Petronius Arbiter, *Sat.*)

[395] An allusion to the pension which Dryden drew, or was supposed to draw, as Poet Laureate.

[396] The same author in his Preface to *The Sullen Lovers*, says : " Look upon it, as it really was, wrote in haste, by a Young Writer, and you will easily pardon it ; . . . Nor can you expect a very correct *Play*, under a Years pains at the least, from the Wittiest Man of the Nation ; It is so difficult to

indulges in similar bemoaning of the unfortunates condemned to count on the uncertain profit of a third-day performance, and to die of hunger.[397] Though Crowne was patronized by the King to the point of being honoured by his advice he calls poetry " a pleasant but barren country ".[398]

It is true that the theatre offered one other source of income to poets : prologues and epilogues were the indispensable garniture of every play and distinguished authors like Dryden [399] were often asked for them. On all-important occasions, for the production of a new play or the revival of an old one, or when the theatre wished to pay tribute to the presence of some highly-placed personage, Dryden was called in. Though he was without a rival in this line, he never got more than five guineas for a set of verses of this sort.[400] This was obviously a source of revenue that could not be counted on. It must further be noted that this represented a real hardship for authors whose own

---

write well in this kind. Men of Quality, that write for their Pleasure, will not trouble themselves with exactness in their *Playes* ; and those, that write for profit, would find too little encouragement for so much *paines*, as a correct *Play* would require."

[397] " What think ye meant wise Providence, when first
　　　Poets were made ? I'd tell you, if I durst,
　　　That 'twas in Contradiction to Heaven's Word,
　　　That when its spirit o're the Waters stir'd,
　　　When it saw All, and said that All was good,
　　　The Creature *Poet* was not understood.
　　　For, were it worth the Pains of six long Days ⎫
　　　To mould Retailers of dull Third-Day-Plays, ⎬
　　　That starve out threescore Years in hopes of Bays ? ⎭
　　　'Tis plain they ne're were of the first Creation,
　　　But came by meer Equiv'cal Generation.
　　　Like Rats in Ships, without Coition bred ;
　　　As hated too as they are, and unfed . . .
　　　Therefore, all you that have Male-Issue born
　　　Under the starving sign of *Capricorn* ;
　　　Prevent the Malice of their Stars in time,
　　　And warn them early from the Sin of Rhyme :
　　　Tell 'em how *Spenser* starv'd, how *Cowley* mourn'd,
　　　How *Butler's* Faith and Service was return'd . . ."
　　　　　　　　　　　(Prologue to *Constantine the Great*.)

We hear the same wailings by Lee in his Dedication of *The Rival Queens* and in the Prologue to his *Theodosius*.

[398] " Your Grace has been a Princely patron and encourager of Poetry ; a Pleasant but Barren Country where my Genius and inclination has cast me." (Dedication of *Sir Courtly Nice* to the Duke of Ormond.) [Cf. Heine : " Brotloseste der Künste, Poesie." E. O. L.]

[399] It was the custom to have them printed and sold for a penny at the theatre door before the first performance (see Genest, I, p. 236).

[400] *Life of Southerne*, prefixed to his works.

obscurity compelled them to ask a prologue or epilogue from a more famous colleague, for they had to pay him out of their own pocket.

A writer had little more to hope for from the publication of his works. Publishing firms as we know them did not exist : " publishers " were both printers and booksellers and often paper-makers and binders into the bargain.[401] There were, moreover, very few of them. An act passed after the Restoration limited the number to twenty for the whole of England.[402] Of this scanty number not all were at the service of pure literature ; we must deduct the printers who specialized in books on medicine, law, theology and the like. A petition presented to Parliament in 1666 reveals that there were in that year only 140 " working printers ".[403] It is true that the law limiting the number of printers would seem not to have been very strictly enforced, for the aim of the petitioners was to exclude intruders. But if their number increased, the increase must have been slight, if we may judge by the number of publications. We possess a catalogue (one of the first ever printed in Britain) of " Books, Printed in England Since the Dreadful Fire of London MDCLXVI. To the End of *Trinity Term* MDCLXXX " (that is to say from 1666 to June 12, 1680),[404] and this is how an excellent judge [405] analyses the information yielded by a careful study of this interesting document :

A great many—we may fairly say one-half of these books, are single sermons and tracts. The whole number of books printed during the fourteen years from 1666 to 1680, we ascertain, by counting, was

---

[401] They were still called " stationers ".

[402] Hallam, *Constitutional History of England*, vol. III, p. 4, and Keble, I, pp. 1306 and 1322.—The Act fixing the number of printers at twenty is known as 14 Car. 2, c. 33. It was valid for a limited time but was renewed by Parliament until 1679. The same Act imposed on books a censorship exercised by the Licenser, and limited the number of type-founders to *four* with *two* apprentices. No printer was allowed more than two presses at a time ; at the very most three. The text of the Act will be found in Keble, vol. II, pp. 1250 ff. In 1637 a decree of the Star Chamber had already limited the number of printers to twenty and of type-founders to four. See my Bibliography, s.v. Star-Chamber.

[403] Knight, *Shadows of the Old Booksellers*, p. 307.—Timperley, p. 543. According to Timperley there were in London in 1831, 3,628 printers, that is twenty-five times as many as in 1666.—I have myself seen the above-mentioned petition : see my Bibliography, s.v. Printers.

[404] See my Bibliography, s.v. Clavell.

[405] Knight, *Shadows*, etc., p. 308. Knight speaks with peculiar authority since he was himself a publisher.

3,550, of which 947 were divinity, 420 law, and 153 physic,—so that two-fifths of the whole were professional books ; 397 were school books, and 2,653 on subjects of geography and navigation, including maps. Taking the average of these fourteen years, the total number of works produced yearly was 253 ; but deducting the reprints, pamphlets, single sermons and maps, we may fairly assume that the yearly average of new books was much under 100.

It is a remarkable fact—which strengthens the impression produced by these figures of the very limited book trade at the beginning of Charles II's reign—that almost no information beyond the name has come down to us about any one of the booksellers of the time. We know that Henry Herringman " at the Blew-*Anchor* in the Lower Walk of the New-Exchange " was Dryden's first publisher. We know that William Cademan published Settle's plays, and so on. But that is all. Not one of them occupies more space in the history of literature than is taken up by his name on the front page of the books he sold. Jacob Tonson was the first bookseller to acquire personal, inde-pendent importance. He made his first timid entry on the scene when, in 1678 he published a tragedy of Tate's, *Brutus of Alba*. In 1679 he took unto himself a partner, Abel Swall, in order to print Dryden's *Troilus and Cressida*, not feeling his financial position sound enough to let him shoulder single handed a commitment of £20, the fee due to the author for his play.[406]

We must admit that the booksellers had every reason to be cautious, for the sale of books was anything but a safe venture.

> To read was not then [says Samuel Johnson] a general amusement ; neither traders, nor often gentlemen, thought themselves disgraced by ignorance. The women had not then aspired to literature, nor was every house supplied with a closet of knowledge. Those, indeed, who professed learning, were not less learned than at any other time ; but of the middle race of students who read for pleasure or accomplish-ment, and who buy the numerous products of modern typography, the number was then comparatively small.[407]

Many facts bear out Johnson's words and prove that education was not sufficiently widespread in any class to make a taste for reading anything but an exception. We have letters from people in high society which show that they possessed a curiously

---

[406] Disraeli, *The Case of Authors Stated*, in *Calamities of Authors* ; Knight, *Shadows*, etc., p. 52.
[407] *Lives of the English Poets* : Milton.

imperfect knowledge of their own tongue.[408] Milton's eldest
daughter could not write,[409] and Dryden's wife, though belonging
by birth to a great and noble family and married to the most
famous writer of the day, displays an ignorance of English
grammar and spelling which to-day would make her maidservant
blush.[410] So unenlightened a society was ill calculated to make
booksellers enterprising. This explains why their publications
were so infrequent and, I might add, why so few copies of an
edition were printed. From Milton's contract with Symons we
have seen that no printing of *Paradise Lost* was to exceed 1,500
copies. There is every reason to believe that most books did not
reach even this figure. We have no precise statistics ; it is a
subject on which publishers have at all times been very reticent.
Failing fuller information, a trustworthy clue is supplied us
by the price at which books were sold.

Roger North informs us that a small octavo volume which
could be read in an hour and a half was currently sold at six
shillings,[411] which, allowing for the difference in money values,

---

[408] Towards the close of Pepys's Diary, see the letter addressed to him
by the Duchess of Norfolk, *née* Lady Mary Mordaunt, daughter of the Earl
of Peterborough.—When the fashionable Will Honeycomb was anxious to
play the author, the *Spectator* was obliged " to rectify some little orthographical
mistakes " (*Spectator*, No. 499).

[409] Masson, *The Poetical Works of John Milton*, I, pp. 64, 65, 74.—She
puts her cross as signature to a document. Her two sisters learned to write,
but in very imperfect fashion. Deborah signs her name " Deboroh ".

[410] " He (your father) is much at woon as to his health, and his defnesse
is not wosce . . . you doe but Gust make shift to live wheare you are, and
soe I hope you may doe heare ; for I will Leaf noe Ston unturn'd to help
my belov'd Sonns . . . I hope I may have some better thinges against
you come, than what is sent you in that box ; there being nothing Considur-
abell but my deare Jackes play, who I desire in his next to me to give me a
true account how my deare Sonne Charlles is head dus ; for I cane be at
noe rest till I heare he is better, or rather thourely well, which I dally pray
for." (Malone, *Prose Works of John Dryden*, vol. I, part II, pp. 58, 59.)

[411] " It may not be amiss to step a little aside to reflect on the vast
Change in the trade of books, between that Time and ours (i.e. between
1666 and 1683). Then little Britain was a plentiful and perpetual Emporium
of learned Authors ; and men went thither as to a Market. This drew
to the Place a mighty Trade, the rather because the shops were spacious,
and the learned gladly resorted to them, where they seldom failed to meet
with agreeable Conversation. And the booksellers themselves were knowing
and conversible men, with whom, for the sake of bookish knowledge, the
greatest Wits were pleased to converse . . . But now this Emporium is
vanished and the Trade contracted into the Hands of two or three Persons,
who, to make good their Monopoly, ransack, not only their Neighbours of
the Trade that are scattered about Town, but all over England, aye and
beyond Sea too, and send abroad their Circulators, and in that Manner
get into their hands all that is valuable. The rest of the Trade are content

would represent 17 or 18 shillings nowadays. Twenty years later the normal price of a similar volume was five shillings.[412] The texts of plays fetched a shilling or eighteenpence, but with their dirty common paper, their coarse type and faulty printing, they would to-day be counted dear at half that price. Now, it is an axiom of economics that supply accommodates itself to probable demand and that the price of goods rises or falls according to their scarcity or abundance on the market. Books are no exception to the rule. We note to-day that books addressed to a necessarily limited number of specialists are issued in smaller editions and cost more than those which appeal to what we call " the general public ". From the price of books at this period we can deduce two things : first, that few copies were printed and, secondly, that buyers were few. We can draw a third conclusion, which follows naturally from the first two : that the booksellers could offer very inadequate payment for the books they printed, when they consented to print them at all.

We have already seen what a meagre sum was paid for the manuscript of *Paradise Lost* and what trouble Symons had to take to sell out the first edition, wooing readers by frequent changes of the title. No doubt the nature of the poem accounted for part of the difficulty, but literary works of the type that was then fashionable were scarcely more eagerly sought after by booksellers or readers.[413] The price at which a bookseller

---

to take their Refuse, with which, and the fresh Scum of the Press, they furnish one Side of a Shop, which serves for the sign of a Bookseller, rather than a real one ; but instead of selling, deal as Factors and procure what the Country Divines and Gentry send for ; . . . And it is wretched to consider what pickpocket work, with Help of the Press, these Demi-booksellers make. They crack their brains to find out selling subjects, and keep hirelings in garrets, on hard meat, to write and correct by the grate ; so puff up an octavo to a sufficient thickness, and there is six shillings current for an hour and a half's reading, and perhaps never to be read or looked upon after. One, that would go higher, must take his Fortune at blank Walls and Corners of Streets, or repair to the sign of *Bateman*, *Innys* and one or two more, where are best Choice and better pennyworths. I might touch other abuses, as bad Paper, incorrect printing, and false advertising ; all of which and worse is to be expected if a careful Author is not at the heels of them." (*The Life of the Honourable and Reverend Dr. John North*, pp. 241 ff. In the same volume as *The Life of the Honourable Sir Dudley North*.) [Beljame's figures refer to 1881, when this book was first published. Prices have risen considerably since then. B. D.]

412 Knight, *Shadows*, etc., p. 309.

413 Many dramatic works of this period have not come down to us, which suggests that they were perhaps not even printed. (Genest, I, pp. 64, 108, etc.)

bought a successful author's play did not exceed £20 or £25 [414] and he did not always find it easy to sell his copies. The people who read plays were naturally the same, with few exceptions, as those who went to see them and these, as we know, were not a large number. From their frivolous temperament we may assume that they were little inclined to go and seek in the printed play the beauties which might have escaped them in the actual performance. [415] Of those who had seen a play on the stage, it was, in fact, only a small proportion who bought it when published. "I have often heard the stationer sighing in his shop," writes Dryden, "and wishing for those hands to take off his melancholy bargain which clapped its performance on the stage." [416]

An attempt was made to allure readers by adding some new attraction when the play was published. In addition to the obligatory Dedication, it might be reinforced by a Preface handling some literary theme, or perhaps a literary discussion would be introduced with the Dedication. These additions had for the author the merit of swelling the size and consequently raising the price of his manuscript [417] ; but the main advantage

[414] Malone, *Historical Account*, etc., p. 178, note 5. This is the fee Dryden received at the height of his popularity, and what Otway and Lee got for their best plays.—Pope quotes a smaller figure still. He speaks of "ten broad pieces" (Spence, p. 262).—The *broad piece* was worth 24*s.*, say, therefore, £12.—Gentlemen of quality paid to have their plays printed (*The Tatler*, No. 224).

[415] "His whole Library consists of the *Academy of Complements*, *Westminster Drollery*, half a dozen *Plays*, and a Bundle of *Bawdy* Songs *in Manuscript* . . ." (*The Character of a Town-Gallant*).

[416] Dedication of *The Spanish Fryar*.—A play was rarely published until its success in the theatre was exhausted. Dryden's *Tyrannick Love*, acted at Easter, 1669, was not "entered in the Stationers' books" until July, 1670.

". . . Few Plays gain Audience by being
In Print, a fewer women get Husbands by
Being too much known."
(Sedley, *The Mulberry-Garden*, III, 2.)

[417]   " Read all the prefaces of Dryden,
For these our critics much confide in ;
Though merely writ at first for filling,
To raise the volume's price a shilling."
(Swift, *On Poetry. A Rhapsody. Works*, XIV, p. 336.)

In his Dedication of *The Empress of Morocco*, Settle introduces a bookseller saying to a poet : " Sir, Your Play has had misfortune, and all that . . . but if you'd but write a Dedication, or Preface . . . the Poet takes the hint, picks out a person of Honour, tells him he has a great deal of Wit, gives us an account who writ Sence in the last Age, supposing we cannot be Ignorant was that they persuaded many people to buy the printed play who would otherwise have let it lie at the bookseller's.

D'Avenant was the first to have the idea of prefixing a literary preface to a poem, his *Gondibert* (1651).[417a] Next Flecknoe in 1664 accompanied his play *Love's Kingdom* [418] with " A short Treatise of the *English Stage* ". While following Dame Fashion, Dryden had the genius to carry to perfection her every vagary. He saw all the opportunities, literary and pecuniary, that this innovation offered, and took advantage of it to produce some of the first critical studies which the English language can boast.[419] To *The Conquest of Granada* he added an " Essay on Heroic Plays " ; to *The State of Innocence*, " The Author's Apology for Heroic Poetry and Poetic Licence " ; to *Troilus and Cressida*, a discourse on " The Grounds of Criticism in Tragedy ", etc. And in 1667 he even published by itself (for the theatres were closed on account of the Plague and the Fire of London) his *Essay of Dramatick Poesie*. Their intrinsic value apart, these essays were amazingly well adapted to the readers of the day. The fashionable world talked literature, or aspired to talk it. To embark, however amateurishly, on literary conversation you must have opinions and arguments, and to press an argument home you must have authorities. It was necessarily only a small minority amongst society people who were qualified or inclined to seek enlightenment about the drama at first hand from Aristotle or even Horace. Dryden saved them the trouble of going so far afield, and in his literary prefaces he made them a gift of neat

---

who writes it in This ; Disputes the nature of *Verse*, Answers a Cavil or two, Quibles upon the *Court*, Huffs the *Critiques*, and the work's don. 'Tis not to be imagin'd how far a sheet of this goes to make a *Bookseller* rich, and a *Poet* famous."

[417a] [This preface is interesting also for the further reason that it gave occasion for a reply from Hobbes. See *Critical Essays of the Seventeenth Century*, ed. Spingarn. B. D.]

[418] *Love's Kingdom*. See my Bibliography.

[419] The following paragraph which I borrow from an article on Dryden in the *Quarterly Review* of October, 1878, perfectly sums up the state of literary criticism in England before Dryden : " The treatises of Wilson, Gascoign, Sidney, Webbe, Puttenham, Campion and Daniel ; the occasional discursions of Ascham in his ' Schoolmaster ', and of Ben Jonson in his ' Discoveries ' ; and the incidental remarks of Cowley, Denham, and Davenant—may be said to sum up all that had hitherto appeared in England on this important province of literature." See also Drake, *Essays . . . Illustrative of the Tatler*, II, pp. 121–142.

[Cowley and Davenant wrote more than " incidental remarks ", and Hobbes might be added, both for his answer to Davenant and his Preface to Homer. But in the main the statement is fair enough. B. D.]

little treatises, not too difficult to read, on special aspects of dramatic and poetic art, complete with the opinions of the chief authorities, with quotations and arguments all to hand, everything in short which a gentleman could need to cut a creditable figure in drawing-room conversation.[420] So these prefaces were warmly welcomed ; but though they swelled the author's profits, the total of his gains from theatre and bookseller combined was slight enough.

We now come to the writer's third source of income : gifts. The aim of the dedications was not solely—as the reader will no doubt have divined—to secure patronage and success for the poet. The incense so liberally expended had other functions : to loosen the strings of a well-lined purse as well as to pay homage to an aristocratic name. D'Urfey, making no bones about it, dedicated his tragedy, *The Siege of Memphis*, " to the truly generous Henry Chevers, Esquire ". Such tactful hints were superfluous : there was a tacit understanding between the flattered and the flatterer. The recognized reply to a dedication was a purse sent to the author : the reflex action was automatic. The custom was an old one, going back to Shakespeare's day and surviving under Charles II. In his Dedication of *Aureng-Zebe* Dryden thanks Mulgrave for " the care you have taken of my fortune ". He tenders similar recognition to Sir Robert Howard for having been " careful of my fortune ", in the Introduction to his poem *Annus Mirabilis*. This theme perpetually recurs.

Poets like Dryden confined themselves to adding a dedication to each of their works ; others added books to their dedications : their books were written solely to provide a pretext for a dedication. The poet, Payne Fisher, or as he learnedly subscribed himself Paganus Piscator—incidentally he was a graduate of Oxford and a prolific writer of Latin verse—used to go round knocking at everyone's door, whenever he was planning a new book, showing a specimen of the eulogies he was prepared to address to the highest bidders. When the book appeared he added the coats of arms on the copies supplied to the most generous. If the day of publication was delayed (and we can well believe that this sometimes happened) he would repeat his visits and try to *borrow* small sums from those who had swallowed

---

[420] His *Grounds of Criticism in Tragedy* quotes Aristotle, Euripides, Lebossu, Rymer (who had published critical comments on the English theatre the year before), Rapin, Homer, Racine, Sophocles, Æschylus, Terence, Plautus, Plato, Longinus and discusses the works of Shakespeare, Fletcher and Ben Jonson.

the bait of his praise.[421] Others who specialized in occasional verse kept poems in stock ready for every possible contingency. Was the Duke of York setting sail at the head of some expedition? their accommodating and fertile pen composed simultaneously a victory song to greet his glorious return and a mournful elegy to lament his death. They were thus sure not to be caught napping, and were equally prepared to welcome reward for their poetic inspiration from the triumphant prince himself or from his inconsolable widow.[422]

What sum in cash did these gifts amount to that formed the patron's response to the offerings of flattery?

We have seen that at best the average which Dryden made from a play was £100 sterling. Now, from the information quoted above, we may fairly reckon that the proceeds of the Third-Day performance brought him in £70 and the sale of his manuscript some £20 or £25 : this would leave between £5 and £10 as the probable yield from the dedication. This estimate can naturally be approximate only : we can at most take it as a rough average. Obviously the size of these gifts will have varied with the wealth and generosity of the patron [423] and also according to the importance of the author and of his work.

When the Earl of Ossory died, his death gave the poet Flatman inspiration for a Pindaric ode for which the bereaved father, the Duke of Ormond, gave him a diamond ring worth 100 guineas.[424] On the other hand, when Paganus Piscator challenged Pepys's generosity by asking an advance of twenty shillings, Pepys—official of the Admiralty though he was—made no scruple of sending him only ten.[425] Since, by its very nature, this

---

[421] Pepys, July 14 and 28, 1660 : à Wood, *Athenæ Oxonienses*, s.v. Payne Fisher.

[422] Dryden, *Essay Of Dramatick Poesie*.

[423] ". . . To a person of higher Rank and Order, it (the dedication) looks like an Obligation for Praises, which he knows he does not deserve and therefore is very unwilling to part with ready Money for." (Otway, Dedication of *The Souldiers Fortune*.)—" Epistles Dedicatory, and long Prefaces are of late much in Request ; no Person of Quality, how remote soever, can escape the Impertinences of *Poets* ; . . . But this is excusable in them that Write for *Bread*, and Live by *Dedications*, and *Third-Dayes*. If once in a Year they meet not with a good Audience, or a Bountiful *Mæcenas*, we are to expect no Play from them the next ; because they want Money to keep the great Wits company ; from whose Conversation, once in Twelve Months, they pick up a Comedy." (Ravenscroft, *The Careless Lovers*, Epistle to the Reader.)

[424] à Wood, *Athenæ Oxonienses*, s.v. Thomas Flatman.

[425] Pepys, July 28, 1660.—See below, note No. 440.

source of revenue was even more variable and uncertain than the others, I mention it only that it may not be overlooked. The point to remember is that the author's custom of begging and accepting alms in return for obligatory flattery—though it certainly did not seem so shocking in those days as it now does to us—was bound to lessen still further the scanty respect in which he was held.[426]

Compared with his fellow-authors, Dryden was particularly fortunate from the financial point of view. First, his talent assured him an absolutely supreme position ; then he had wealthy and influential patrons ; but in addition he had the good fortune to succeed D'Avenant in 1670 as Poet Laureate, and James Howell as Historiographer Royal. Each of these posts was worth £100 a year, payable quarterly, and the Laureate's also brought a tierce of Canary wine from the King's cellars. It would therefore seem that these salaries, added to his income from theatre and bookseller, ought to have set him at least at ease, and Dr. Johnson [427] appears to have felt little sympathy with the wails of which he is so lavish about the state of his finances.[428] Perhaps there was in truth some exaggeration in his plaints. Poets have at all times been inclined to rate themselves very highly, and as a natural consequence to believe themselves insufficiently appreciated. But Johnson is reviewing his whole life which extended over several reigns, while we are here considering only the early days of his career under Charles II, and it is clear that we must not judge his financial circumstances from outward appearances. His

---

[426]   The writers themselves were well aware of this :

> " A Poet would be dear, and out o'th'way,
> Should he expect above a Coachman's Pay :
> For this, will any dedicate and lie,
> And daub the gaudy Ass with flattery ?
> For this, will any prostitute his Sense
> To Coxcombs, void of Bounty as of Brains ?
> Yet such is the hard Fate of Writers now,
> They're forc'd, for Alms, to each great Name to bow :
> Fawn, like her Lap-dog, on her tawdry Grace . . .
> Sneak to his Honour, call him witty, brave,
> And just ; tho' a known Coward, Fool or knave . . . "

> (Oldham, *A Satire. Dissuading from Poetry*,
> Works, vol. III.)

[427] *Lives of the English Poets :* Dryden.

[428] See, for example, the Dedication of *Aureng-Zebe*, where he speaks of " the lowness of my fortune ".

Laureate's salary, of which Shadwell was so jealous,[429] was like all other debts of the Merry Monarch, most irregularly paid [430] ; any trifling accident at Court would even completely stop it. Mulgrave fell into disgrace in 1680 and by a sort of ricochet Dryden ceased to receive his pay.[431] We shall see that in 1684, at a moment when he was rendering the King most signal service, it was already four years in arrears. He wrote on the subject to the First Lord of the Treasury a letter, the feeling in which seems anything but feigned. If we further consider that neither he nor his family indulged expensive vices, and that he worked and produced without respite, we must conclude that his distress was genuine.

As for the other writers of the time, there cannot be the slightest doubt about their financial position. The greater number led a hand to mouth existence. We have already seen their complaints. Some like Otway [432] and Lee [433] lived in

[429] See note No. 395 above.

[430] Pepys, Dec. 19, 1666, April 4, 1667, and *passim* ; Reresby, May 15, 1679; Bell, *Life of Dryden*, prefixed to his *Works*, p. 38, note.—Dryden frequently complains of his salary's being irregularly paid, in his Dedication, for instance, of *Marriage-à-la-Mode* and in his *Discourse concerning the Original and Progress of Satire*. He might have applied to himself with even greater emphasis Corneille's lines :

> Grand roi, dont nous voyons la générosité
> Montrer pour le Parnase un excès de bonté
> Que n'ont jamais eu tous les autres,
> Puissiez-vous dans cent ans donner encor des lois
> Et puissent tous vos ans être de quinze mois
> Comme vos commis font les nôtres.

> Great King, whose liberality doth flow
> And on Parnassus bounties great bestow
> For which no other king e'er found the treasure,
> May you a hundred years our laws dictate,
> Your every year set in full three months late
> As ours does, at your clerks' good pleasure.

[431] *Biographia Britannica :* Sheffield, note M.

> " Thy pension lost . . .
> That lost, the Visor chang'd, you turn about,
> And strait a True Blue Protestant crept out ;
> The Fryar now was writ : and some will say
> They smell a Male-Content through all the Play."
> (*The Laureat*, anonymous.)

[432] " There was a time when *Otway* charm'd the Stage,
> *Otway* the Hope, the Sorrow of our Age ;
> When the full Pit with pleas'd attention hung,
> Wrapt with each accent from *Castalio's* Tongue,
> With what a Laughter was his *Souldier* read !
> How mourn'd they when his *Jaffier* struck, and bled !

abject poverty.   Oldham took the trouble to write a long poem
to dissuade any from poetry who might have felt tempted to
become his fellow-poets.   Besides, contemporary opinion on the
professional author's earnings was unambiguous.   Here is what
a great Lord, the Duke of Buckingham, has to say on the subject
in a letter addressed to an odd character of the time, Captain
Julian [434] :

> . . . Poetry has been so much your friend :
> On that thou'st liv'd and flourish'd all thy Time ;
> Nay more, maintain'd a family by Rhime ;
> And that's a Mark that Dryden ne'er could hit.
> He lives upon his Pension, not his Wit :
> E'en gentle George (flux'd both in tongue and purse)
> Shunning one Snare, yet fell into a worse.
> A Man may be reliev'd once in his Life,
> But who can be reliev'd that has a Wife ?

> Yet this best Poet, tho with so much ease,
> He never drew his Pen but sure to please ;
> Tho Lightning were less lively than his Wit,
> And Thunder-Claps less loud than those o' th' Pit,
> He had of 's many Wants much earlier dy'd,
> Had not kind Banker *Betterton* supply'd,
> And took for Pawn the Embryo of a Play,
> Till he could pay himself the next third Day."
>> (A Satyr upon the Poets, being a Translation
>> out of the 7th Satyr of Juvenal.—In *Poems
>> on Affairs of State*, vol. II, 1703, pp. 138 ff.)
>> Cf. the quotation from Otway, note No.
>> 380 above.

[433] See *Biographia Britannica*, s.v. Lee.

[434] This Captain Julian, who called himself " Secretary of the Muses "
used to haunt Will's Coffee House, and distribute on the quiet manuscript
copies of each new " lampoon ".   (See Dryden's *Works*, edited by Scott
and Saintsbury, XV, p. 217.)   In a period so prolific of satires, this occupation
lent him a certain importance and his name frequently recurs in contemporary literature, notably in the *Poems on Affairs of State*.

> " Now Fop may dine with Half-wit ev'ry Noon,
> And read his Satyr, or his worse Lampoon.
> *Julian's* so furnished by these scribbling Sparks
> That he pays off old Scores and keeps two Clarks."
>> (Ravenscroft, Prologue to *The London Cuckolds*.)

" The conscious Tub. Tavern can witness, and my *Berry-Street* Apartment testifie the solicitations I have had, for the first Copy of a new Lampoon,
from the greatest Lords of the Court :   though their own folly and their
Wives Vices were the subject . . .   And the Love of Scandal and native
Malice that Men and Women have to one another, made me in such request
when alive, that I was admitted to the Lord's Closet, when a Man of Letters
and Merit wou'd be thrust out of doors."   (Tom Brown, *Letters from the
Dead to the Living :* From Julian, Late Secretary to the Muses, to Will. Pierre
of Lincolns-Inn Fields *Play-House*.)

Otway can hardly Guts from Gaol preserve,
And, tho he's very fat, he's like to starve :
And Sing-song Durfey (plac'd beneath abuses)
Lives by his impudence, and not the Muses :
Poor Crown too has his third days mix'd with Gall,
He lives so ill, he hardly lives at all.
Shadwell and Settle both with Rhimes are fraught,
But can't between them muster up a groat :
Nay, Lee in *Beth'lem* [435] now sees better days,
Than when applauded for his bombast Plays ;
He knows no Care, nor feels sharp want no more,
And that is what he ne'er could say before :
Thus while our Bards are famish'd by their Wit
Thou who hast none at all, yet thriv'st by it. [436]

Now hear what the commoner, John Dunton, bookseller,
has to say : " Mr. Settle . . . But alas ! after all, when I see
an Ingenious Man set up for a *meer Poet* . . . I give him up as
one *prick'd down by Fate*, for misery *and misfortune.*" [437]

VIII

Conclusion : As yet, neither public, nor men of letters

Neither money, nor honour—such in a couple of words was
the plight of authors after the Restoration.

Need we be surprised ? What else could they expect from
the sorry society they had to do with ? Their fate was all the
sadder because this society had inspired them with eager and
apparently well-founded hopes, and they had trusted it. How
natural that they should be taken in ! The King, young and
all-powerful, took a pride in being a connoisseur of the beautiful,
the great Lords were so much in love with literature that they
felt bound to write themselves and thus become in some sort
fellow-authors. Surely all this was full of promise ? But the
promise was not kept : authors were given nothing but hope.

The fact is that truly to encourage literature you must love
her for herself. Now society folk in those days loved her solely
for their own sakes. Essentially frivolous, thinking only of having
a good time, their one merit is that they counted literature
among their pastimes ; but she was for them a pastime only,

---

[435] He was for many years insane.
[436] A Consolatory Epistle to Captain *Julian* The Muses News-Monger,
in his Confinement. (In the *Miscellaneous Works* of George Villiers, Duke
of Buckingham.)
[437] *The Life and Errors of John Dunton*, Written by Himself, etc., p. 241.

and that in the most literal sense of the word. So they cared only for verses and the theatre ; the verses had to be of the lightest kind, and what they asked of the theatre was luxurious scenery, brilliant versification and licentious characters. When fashionable people dabbled in writing or posed as judges of literature, it was merely for personal satisfaction : to gratify their vanity, to please the ladies, to parade a veneer of culture, or to add a few flattering epithets to their name.

What conception could they have of literature who were so preoccupied with themselves ? What feeling would they be capable of ? Obviously they would disdain its loftier aspects, having disqualified themselves for attaining to them. They might be stirred by the superficial quality of a couplet, by harmony, by a neat turn of phrase. At a pinch they might be able to criticize the choice of words, the conduct of a plot ; in a word they would concentrate on outward form. But the soul and spirit would be beyond their ken, and they would carefully guard themselves against too lively an emotion and shrink from being stirred to genuine admiration. They would ban every serious inspiration, every careful delineation of character or passion, everything which might touch the heart or quicken the mind. Even love they would tolerate only on the condition that it should be treated as a sentiment of no depth and of no importance. On the other hand, they would welcome the lightest and most frivolous works, however far they went in frivolity, provided that they were amusing. That is the sole condition they would impose, but that is a *conditio sine quâ non*.

So it comes that this period, in appearance so deeply devoted to letters, proved one of the least favourable to literature. It cast off Shakespeare ; it ignored the two great epics of Milton and Bunyan. It must be accused of other literary crimes : the word is not too strong. The age condemned Dryden, one of the most powerful and prolific geniuses which England has ever produced, to squander the best years of his intellectual vigour in the hurried concoction of works for which he knew himself to be unfitted [438] ; it drove Otway, with his strong dramatic gifts,

---

[438]   " And Dryden, in immortal strain,
Had raised the Table Round again,
But that a ribald king and Court
Bade him toil on, to make them sport,
Demanded for their niggard pay,
Fit for their souls, a looser lay,
Licentious satire, song and play ;

to wear out on unworthy compositions the pen which was capable of writing *The Orphan* and *Venice Preserv'd* ; and it turned Shadwell, endowed from birth with notable powers of observation and lively comedy, into the reluctant author of contemptible farces.

A society with so base and so narrow a conception of literature could hold its writers in no high esteem. It thought of them only as entertainers and mountebanks, people in whom you took but little interest except so far as they amused you. Such interest as Charles II's Court showed for them, was wholly selfish, superficial and devoid of sympathy. They were praised, it is true, but the patron praised out of vanity to prove his good taste and gain kudos thereby. The society of some was sought, but the host invited them for his own sake, not for theirs, because their friendship was a diploma of wit,[439] because he wanted from them some literary service, because he coveted their praise or simply because he found them merry company. When the patron had praised (or criticized) their work, had invited them to his table, had laughed at their jests or had, in accordance with society custom, flung them a few guineas [440] in payment

---

The world, defrauded of the high design,
Profaned the God-given strength, and marr'd the lofty line."
(Walter Scott, *Marmion*, Introduction to Canto I.)

[439] " There marched the bard and blockhead, side by side,
Who rhym'd for hire, and patroniz'd for pride."
(Pope, *Dunciad*, IV, ll. 99–100.)

[440] Sometimes they got no guineas :
" Sir, I've a Patron, you reply. 'Tis true . . .
Why faith e'en try. Write, Flatter, Dedicate,
My Lord's and his Forefathers Deeds relate :
Yet know he'll wisely strive ten thousand ways,
To shun a needy Poet's fulsom Praise ;
Nay, to avoid thy Importunity,
Neglect his State, and condescend to be
A Poet, tho perhaps a worse than thee.
Thus from a Patron he becomes a Friend ;
Forgetting to reward, learns to commend ;
Receives your twelve long Months successless Toil,
And talks of Authors, Energy and Stile ;
Damns the dull Poems of the scribling Town,
Applauds your Writings, and repeats his own ;
Whilst thou in Complaisance oblig'd must sit
T'extol his Judgment, and admire his Wit ;
And wrapt with his *Essay on Poetry*,
Swear *Horace* writ not half so strong as He,
But that we're partial to Antiquity . . . "
(A Satyr upon the Poets . . . in *Poems on
Affairs of State*, vol. II, pp. 138 ff.)

of some panegyric, he had done all that was due to himself and his position ; he owed them nothing, neither sympathy nor consideration : and he thought no more about them.

When the King admired *Hudibras* it never occurred to him to wonder how Butler contrived to live. When he took unto himself a Poet Laureate—he had to follow his predecessor's example and have a Poet Laureate—little cared he whether the salary was paid or no. He had shown his good taste ; that was enough. On the same principle, Buckingham who fancied himself as a connoisseur, urged Lee to come to London and once he had come, felt no further responsibility for him.[441] Similarly Otway's aristocratic boon-companions let him die in poverty, if not of poverty.[442] Dryden was mercilessly thrashed without one of his patrons turning a hair and Mulgrave looked unconcernedly on while his protégé endured suffering of which he was the cause. Wycherley himself, the special favourite who had mixed on equal terms with the nobility, lay for seven years in prison without any of his dear Court friends appearing to observe his absence, still less dreaming of paying the debts which kept him there.[443] They went on

[441] Spence, p. 62.—Lee went out of his mind and the Duke wrote verses on his madness. See above, note No. 435.

[442] " Otway was more beholden to Captain Symonds the Vintner in whose Debt he died four hundred Pounds, than to all his Patrons of Quality." (Manuscript note by Oldys on Langbaine's article : Otway, p. 398.)—In debt, and dying of hunger he asked alms of a passer-by, crying : " I am Otway, the poet." Moved to pity, the stranger gave him a guinea with which Otway dashed to a baker's. He began to eat so greedily that the first mouthful of bread choked him (April 14, 1685). He was thirty-four. This version of his death has been questioned, but Mr. Gosse, his latest biographer, accepts it as true. However that may be, there is no doubt that he died in the extreme of misery.

[443] Oldham was under no illusions about these fine gentlemen :
" *Bless me ! how great his Genius ! how each Line*
Is big with Sense !
Cries a gay, wealthy Sot, who would not hail
For bare five Pounds, the Author out of Jail."
                              (*A Satire, Dissuading from Poetry.*)
" Chymists and Whores by *Buckingham* were fed,
Those by their honest Labours gain'd their Bread ;
But he was never so expensive yet,
To keep a Creature merely for his Wit ; . . .
Pemb—[roke] lov'd Tragedy, and did provide
For Butcher's Dogs, and for the whole Bankside ;
The Bear was fed, but Dedicating *Lee*,
Was thought to have a larger Paunch than he."
                        (*A Satyr upon the Poets, being a Translation*
                        out of the 7th Satyr of Juvenal ; in Poems on
                        Affairs of State, vol. II, 1703, pp. 138 ff.)

applauding his plays without wondering what had become of the author.[444]

Flattered and made much of to-day while he was amusing, scorned and forgotten to-morrow—such was the writer's fate. Authors were fed on fine words, and that was all. At heart the great looked down on them, as wealthy folk may look down on poor devils whose trade is to amuse them, as the rich landowner of those days, swollen with self-importance, could look down on the serfs who toiled for a living on his land. In short, a poet in the eyes of this gay world was just a variety of buffoon, exercising a skill slightly superior to that of the Court Jester of the good old days, but having no more claim than he to respect or to considerate treatment. Woe betide him when his tricks cease to seem funny! Throw him out, drive him off with contumely, cover him with abuse—without allowing him the right to protest—at need, have him beaten to death! Treat him like a woman of the gutter : enjoy him, then kick him out of doors. The simile is Rochester's.[445]

This is what the fine sentiment of the Court amounted to, and its parade of zeal for literature. Complete neglect would have been of greater value to the poets, for it would have compelled them to rely wholly on themselves and to use their gifts to the best of their power.[446] Instead, they exhausted the bulk of their energy in pursuing a mirage which could lead only to fresh disillusionment. The very fashion for writing affected by elegant society made the poets' position even worse, while evoking more false hopes. It had the result of creating two factions in literature : the patricians and the plebs. The greater the pretensions of the aristocracy, the worse treated was the

---

[444] Pack, *Miscellanies in Verse and Prose*, Some Memoirs of William Wycherley, Esq.,—Spence, pp. 44, 45.

[445]   " For *Wits* are treated just like common *Whores* ;
            First they're *enjoyed*, and then *kick'd out of Doors*."
                              (*Satire against* Man, *Works*, vol. I, p. 2.)

" It is the business of poor Poets to be the diversion of mankind ; pleasure is their being. I think I may call 'em the Mistresses of the World ; which, if granted, I am sure 'tis easie to prove their Gallants very brutish, for they generally loath them as soon as they're enjoy'd."
                              (Lee, Dedication of *Cæsar Borgia*.)

He expresses the same idea with the same comparison in the Epilogue to his *Theodosius*.

[446] We have seen that it was when Dryden felt himself forsaken and alone that he wrote *All for Love*. It is probable that we owe Otway's *Orphan* to the same feeling.

commonalty. Willy-nilly, the author found himself embroiled in the quarrels of his conceited patrons and, as was but natural, suffered the fate of the earthen jar.

It might well seem that so many bitter disappointments would have opened his eyes to the vanity of his hopes. But the King and the Court offered so many allurements that even repeated disappointments could not entirely disillusion him. The English nation had recovered from the Puritan fever only to fall victim to the Royalist, and in enthusiastically recalling Charles II had surrendered itself to him wholeheartedly. Welcomed, flattered, cherished like an idol, the King had become the focus and the symbol of England. Only the Court counted for anything in comparison with him, and the Court was merely the mirror of the King. The citizenry was looked upon askance and kept at arm's length ; the citizens maintained their reserve and acquiesced in being nothing. Even if the Court had not seduced him by so many promises, the author had nowhere else to turn, and no hope from any other quarter.

That was the crux. There was as yet no " public ". Neither the word nor the thing existed.[447] The author saw before him only a coterie, too exclusive not to be all-powerful, too powerful not to command obedience. Whatever way he turned, he could find no one to whom he could appeal against the verdict of Court society. There was nothing to be done but to submit with what grace he could muster. From the moment that a man adopted the career of a writer he was obliged to swear allegiance to fashionable society and make himself a courtier— or die of hunger.[448]

The author of the day became the complete and perfect sycophant. He modelled himself meticulously on his masters

---

[447] Dryden always uses the word " people " where we should now say " public ". See in particular his Preface to *The Mock Astrologer* and note No. 362 above. [The " public " meant " public affairs ". B. D.]

[448]   " The *Poets* who must live by Courts or starve,
              Were proud, so good a Government to serve ;
              And mixing with Buffoons and Pimps profain
              Tainted the Stage, for some small Snip of Gain.
              For they, like *Harlots*, under *Bawds* profest,
              Took all th'ungodly pains, and got the least.
              Thus did the thriving Malady prevail,
              The Court, its Head, the *Poets* but the Tail," etc.
                   (Dryden, Epilogue written for Fletcher's *Pilgrim*.)

and painstakingly sought to acquire an aristocratic polish.[449] In his plays he introduced on the stage none but persons of social standing,[450] and he adopted their ways of speech. The court indulged the affectation of talking French ; he talked French too, and to such purpose that his fellow-countrymen of to-day often require a translation of his jargon,[451] which must assuredly have been unintelligible to the ordinary citizen of his own time. Once caught up in the machinery, he was helpless. Before sitting down to write, he carefully inquired how the wind was blowing among those on high, and dutifully trimmed his sails accordingly, even when he saw clearly where the chosen course was leading him. Dryden wrote what is perhaps the finest appreciation of Shakespeare which English literature possesses,[452] and yet laid sacrilegious hands on Shakespeare ; he worthily praised the epic genius of Milton [453] and yet dressed his heroes in the costumes of Mademoiselle de Scudéry. Shadwell and Otway passed vigorous and just criticism on contemporary comedy, which no plays deserved more thoroughly than their own.[454] All decried current taste [455] and all pandered to it ;

[449] " I have always acknowledged the wit of our predecessors with all the veneration which becomes me ; but, I am sure, their wit was not that of gentlemen," etc. (Dryden, *Defence of the Epilogue to the Second Part of the Conquest of Granada*.)

[450] When they borrow a play of Molière's, they usually suppress the free natural speech of servant to master ; this would evidently have grated on noble ears. Thus in Ravenscroft's imitation of *le Bourgeois Gentilhomme* all Nicole's remonstrances are put into the mouth of M. Jourdain's daughter. It is difficult to see what propriety gained by this device.

[451] See, for instance, Dryden's *Marriage-à-la-Mode*, the scene between Palamede and Melantha (II, i). In his edition of Dryden, Walter Scott frequently explains the French expressions used and Swift used to say that in his day a large number of the words and phrases introduced by Court influence under Charles II were already barely intelligible. (*A Proposal for improving the English Tongue*.)

[This was probably an affectation confined to a few, and Dryden was sure of support in making fun of it. Palamede sizes up Melantha rapidly enough in II, i, and laughs at her, but she is more especially made fun of in III, i, in her scene with Philotis, where, the reader will remember, the new French words she learns " began at *sottises* and ended *en ridicule* ". B. D.]

[452] *Essay Of Dramatick Poesie.*

[453] In his Preface to *The State of Innocence*, he calls *Paradise Lost* " one of the greatest, most noble and most sublime poems which either this age or nation has produced ".

[As *The State of Innocence* was never acted, Dryden can hardly have clothed the characters in any costume. As for laying sacrilegious hands on Shakespeare, see the addition to note 122. Bardolatry had not begun. B. D.]

[454] " Though I have known some of late so Insolent to say, that *Ben Johnson* wrote his best *Playes* without Wit ; imagining that all the Wit in *Playes* consisted in bringing two Persons upon the Stage to break Jests, and

they inveighed against the over-emphasis on scenery and setting, yet wrote tragedies appealing to the eye ; they deplored the debasement of comedy into coarse farce, yet against their better judgment indulged in clowning, garnished with calculated smuttiness.[456] They saw and cursed the current that swept them on, but not one of them attempted to swim against it. Many possessed the necessary strength ; but to risk such a

---

to bob one another, which they call Repartie, not considering that there is more wit and invention requir'd in the finding out good Humor, and Matter proper for it, than in all their smart reparties. For in the writing of a Humor, a Man is confin'd not to swerve from the Character, and oblig'd to say nothing but what is proper to it : but in the *Playes*, which have been wrote of late, there is no such thing as perfect Character, but the two chief Persons are most commonly a Swearing, Drinking, Whoring Ruffian for a Lover, and an impudent ill-bred *tomrig* for a Mistress, and these are the fine People of the *Play* ; and there is that Latitude in this, that almost anything is proper for them to say ; but their chief Subject is bawdy, and profaness which they call *brisk writing*, when the most dissolute of Men, that relish those things well enough in private, are *chok'd* at 'em in publick : and, methinks, if there were nothing but the ill Manners of it, it should make Poets avoid that Indecent way of Writing." (Preface to Shadwell's *Sullen Lovers*).—" And then their Comedies now a days are the filthiest things, full of Bawdy and nauseous doings, which they mistake for raillery and Intrigue ; besides, they have no wit in 'em neither ; for all their Gentlemen and men of wit, as they style 'em, are either silly conceited impudent Coxcombs, or else rude ill-mannerly drunken Fellows—fogh——" (Lady Squeamish in Otway's *Friendship in Fashion*, Act I.)

[455] See, amongst others, Dryden in his Dedication of the *Spanish Fryar* and his *Defence of an Essay of Dramatique Poesie*. See also almost all his Prologues and Epilogues.

> " *Dryden* himself, to please a frantick Age,
> Was forc'd to let his Judgment stoop to Rage :
> To a wild Audience he conform'd his Voice,
> Comply'd to Custom, but not err'd by Choice.
> Deem then the Peoples, not the Writer's Sin,
> *Almanzor's* Rage, and Rants of *Maximin*."
> (Granville, *Essay. Upon unnatural Flights in
> Poetry*, *Works*, I, p. 93 and note.)

[456]
> " Then Courts of Kings were held in high Renown,
> E'er made the common Brothels of the Town : . . .
> The King himself to Nuptial Ties a Slave,
> No bad Example to his Poets gave :
> And they not bad, but in a vicious Age
> Had not to please the Prince debauch'd the Stage."
> (Dryden, *The Wife of Bath, her Tale*, in *Fables
> Ancient and Modern*, p. 481.)

" Posterity is absolutely mistaken as to that great man ; tho' his comedies are horribly full of double entendres, yet 'twas owing to a false complaisance for a dissolute age. He was in company the modestest man that ever convers'd."

(*Gentleman's Magazine*, Feb. 1745.)

venture, to defy fashion before an audience accustomed to lay down the law and closely united as a body, would have been to play for high stakes. Put your audience out of humour, and you had no alternative but—to give up writing. Authors did not think the game worth the candle, they recognized the better path, and chose the worse. Dryden's Prologue to *The Kind Keeper* frankly says :

> Let them, who the rebellion first began
> To wit, restore the monarch if they can,
> Our author dares not be the first bold man.
> He, like the prudent citizen, takes care
> To keep for better marts his staple ware.[457]

Weary of struggle and despairing of victory, authors resigned themselves to murmuring a humble little literary credo :

> You now have habits, Dances, Scenes and Rhymes,
> High Language often : I, and Sense sometimes . . .
> But blame your Selves, not him who Writ the Play ; . . .
> He's bound to please, not to Write well ; and knows
> There is a mode in playes, as well as Cloathes.[458]

If he wins no applause, it is because he has not known how " to lower himself to please his auditors ".[459] Thus driven to make a virtue of necessity, he gave up trying to be himself. In twenty years, only two works are noteworthy as having an intrinsic value : Dryden's *All for Love* and Otway's *Orphan*. And these two plays belong to the close of the period that has been the subject of this first chapter.

Compelled thus to abase themselves in their work, we need not be surprised to see them abasing themselves also in their lives. Powerless to shake off their dependence on those whose

---

[457]   " He who made this, observ'd what Farces hit,
            And durst not disoblige you now with wit."
                         (Dryden, Prologue to *The Assignation*.)

[458] Dryden, Prologue to *The Rival Ladies*
[459] Dryden, Preface to *An Evening's Love*.

    " Th' unhappy Man, who once has trail'd a Pen,
      Lives not to please himself but other Men."
            (Prologue to Lee's *Cæsar Borgia*, written by Dryden.)

    " So should wise Poets sooth an awkard Age,
      For they are Prostitutes upon the Stage :
      To stand on Points were foolish and ill-bred,
      As for a Lady to be nice in Bed ;
      Your wills alone must their Performance measure,
      And you may turn 'em ev'ry way for pleasure."
                         (Lee, Epilogue to *Theodosius*.)

taste governed their writings, they eagerly set about currying their favour and rivalled each other in sycophancy, exceeding all bounds and violating all dignity. Readily donning the livery of Messrs. So and So, they assailed their patrons with flatteries which no one imagined to be sincere.[460] Willingly they made obeisance to folly and to shame provided these were covered by a title. The flattery-competitions which went on among them did nothing to raise them in the eyes of an arrogant society. They grew accustomed to be despised and became despicable.

Their private life suffered. Most of them adopted a devil-may-care philosophy which left little room for self-respect. We have seen the kind of man D'Urfey was ; Lee lived a riotous life in which wine played no small part [461] ; Shadwell was " a brute " in conversation [462] and also drank ; after a week of fashionable orgies with Lord Plymouth, Otway spent whole months with low-caste companies in disreputable taverns [463]; Oldham was of Rochester's gang [464] ; enough said.

Their self-respect being so small, they respected their profession little. They sacrificed their literary pride so cheaply as

---

[460] Dryden wrote to Rochester : " I have sent your Lordship a prologue and epilogue, which I made for our players, when they went down to Oxford. I hear they have succeeded ; and by the event your Lordship will judge how easy 'tis to pass anything upon an university, and how gross flattery the learned will endure."

(*Works*, edited Scott and Saintsbury, vol. XVIII, p. 95.)

[461] " Poor *Nat. Lee* (I cannot think of him without tears) had great merit. In the poetic sense he had, at intervals, inspiration itself : but liv'd an outrageous, boisterous life, like his brethren . . ."

(*Gentleman's Magazine*, Feb. 1745.)

" *Nat. Lee* slept in next, in hopes of a Prize,
Apollo remember'd he had hit once in thrice ;
By the Rubies in's Face, he could not deny,
But he had as much Wit as wine could supply."
(Rochester, *A Scession of the Poets, Works*, I, p. 134.)

[462] " Shadwell in conversation was a brute." (*Gentleman's Magazine*, Feb. 1745) ; *Quarterly Review*, Oct. 1878, p. 314, article on Dryden. Like De Quincey later, Shadwell also used opium. On his drunken habits see Dryden : *The Vindication*, etc., where he is introduced under the name of Og.—The coarseness of his conversation is confirmed by a manuscript note of Oldys on the Shadwell article in Langbaine.

[463] " You'll be glad to know any trifling circumstance concerning *Otway* . . . He gave himself up early to drinking, and like the unhappy wits of that age passed his days between rioting and fasting, ranting jollity and abject penitence, carousing one week with Lord *Pl——th*, and then starving a month in low company at an ale-house on *Tower-Hill*." (*Gentleman's Magazine*, Feb. 1745.)—See also Johnson, *Lives of the English Poets* : Otway.

[464] à Wood, *Athenæ Oxonienses*, s.v. John Oldham.

to subordinate their own judgment to the opinion of any titled or moneyed fool, and not even to resent insults offered them. When the most distinguished of their company was outrageously maltreated not more than one or two had the courage to protest. The others laughed and congratulated themselves that a storm which might have broken over them had burst on a fellow-writer's shoulders. Dryden himself swallowed his indignation for fear of damaging his position. Not only did the writers of the day lack, as a body, all *esprit de corps*, they did not even form small literary groups of friends bound together by sympathy, such as gathered later round Addison, Pope and Samuel Johnson. Each played his own hand careless of his dignity, careless of the dignity of his fellows, without, in short, any of the feelings we associate with the man of letters. From this we draw the conclusion that, just as there was no public, there were at this period no men of letters either.

CHAPTER II

JOHN DRYDEN AND POLITICS
(1680–1688)

I

Re-awakening of political and religious passions : Whigs and Tories.— Political Drama : Dryden, Otway, Lee, Southerne, Crowne, D'Urfey, Shadwell, Settle, Tate, Mrs. Behn, Ravenscroft, Bankes.—Political Prologues and Epilogues

The years immediately following the Restoration had been light-hearted and carefree. The King thought only of leading a gay life and in this the Court wholeheartedly co-operated. His subjects, full-fed with strait-laced Puritanism, drifted gently with the stream or at least, beguiled by the good humour and infectious geniality of a Prince, " young, charming, and a winner of all hearts ", had not the courage to swim against the current. Everything smiled on the new régime ; monarchy and the King were immensely popular, and no dissentient voice sounded a discordant note in the general chorus of gaiety and content.

Good order had been established. Pursued and hunted down, liberty and even life endangered,[1] Puritans and Republicans were forced to take refuge in obscurity, and public opinion kept them there. The fallen government now seemed actually an impious usurpation and Charles I a martyr, Cromwell a parricide, and his supporters hateful hypocrites or detestable fanatics. The terrible reprisals taken against everything connected with the Republic, the horrid treatment meted out to all who had in any measure shared the Protector's political or religious views, seemed only the just reward of unprecedented crimes committed without excuse.[1a] So the Puritans lay low, and because they gave no sign of life they were thought to be well and truly dead.

---

[1] See Neal, vol. IV, chaps. 5 and 6 ; Geffroy, pp. 202–3.

[1a] [This is to exaggerate the very mild retribution visited on the Parliamentarians : there were hardly any executions. The worst sufferers were the many dissenting ministers who were ejected from livings which belonged to the Anglican Church. When one thinks of what happened during the French Revolution, or in many countries in our own generation, one cannot but admire the moderation shown by the victorious royalists. B. D.]

Free from any unwelcome anxieties at home, and firmly determined, whatever happened, not to create trouble for himself either at home or abroad,[2] living in an atmosphere of general approval and unmixed amusement, Charles II had quickly grown accustomed to thinking that life and the exercise of power provided a merry party which would never end.

But the Puritan fires, apparently extinct, were smouldering under their ashes. It was the King himself who blew the embers into flame. First and foremost the excesses of the Court soon re-awakened respect for the stern uprightness of " the Saints ". People had hated exaggerated virtue, they were soon nauseated by exaggerated vice.[3] They were glad to let the King enjoy himself, but when they saw him treat everything as a jest, even the interests of his people, they felt he was carrying merriment too far, and they remembered that if his predecessors had tended to magnify trifles into affairs of State, they had, at least, taken affairs of State seriously, and had not squandered their tax-revenues on enriching mistresses and favourites.[4]

Once people began to make comparisons, they did not stop. Whatever views you might hold about Cromwell, you could not deny that under him England had cut a good figure in Europe.[5] The English had perhaps tended somewhat to forget, but little by little Charles II quickened their memories. The town of Dunkirk had been won from Spain by the Protector's arms, Charles sold it to Louis XIV—for money. Nay, he sold himself to France.[5a] And—unheard-of disgrace—he let the Dutch

---

[2] " It is said the King being one day importuned by the Duke to undertake things which he thought very dangerous, told him, *Brother, I am resolved never to travel again, you may do so if you please.*" (Rapin de Thoyras, vol. II, book 23, p. 725.)

[3] In 1668, the apprentices of London set about " pulling down the bawdy-houses ", saying " that they did ill in contenting themselves in pulling down the little bawdy-houses, and did not go and pull down the great bawdy-house at White Hall." (Pepys, March 24, 25, 1668.)

[4] Macaulay, *History*, chap. II.—" The King hath lately paid about £30,000 to clear debts of my Lady Castlemayn's." (Pepys, Dec. 12, 1666.)

[5] See Geffroy, p. 164.

[5a] [The affair was a little more subtle than that. Charles's ambition, which he pursued stubbornly under the screen of flippancy, was to make himself absolute monarch over a strong England. For this he needed money, and the only way he could get it was by making concessions to Louis. He was playing a dangerous game, but had he lived a few years longer he would probably have succeeded completely, and been in a position to defy France. If his brother had had a tithe of his ability, English history would have been very different. B. D.]

F

fleet sail up the Thames, and for the first time in history the citizens of London heard the sound of enemy guns. Cromwell had inspired the foe with more respect.[6]

What stirred England more profoundly yet, was the King's religious behaviour. In their horror of Puritanism, the English had forgotten their old hatred of Popery. Having calmed their feelings toward the one, Charles succeeded in reviving their feelings against the other. They soon saw, in fact, that while the King treated the Puritans with extreme severity, he and his brother showed much more tolerance to Roman Catholics. The King married a Portuguese princess [7] and allowed his French mistress, the Duchess of Portsmouth, complete dominion over him.[8] The Duke of York was even less discreet and did not hesitate to make public profession of Roman Catholicism (1671), thus arousing acute Protestant anxiety. Similarly, when the King proclaimed a Declaration of Indulgence in 1672—which under cover of giving relief to all Dissenters was in fact designed to give a free field to the Roman Catholics—the Protestants were not deceived. The Nonconformists themselves were the first to protest against the specious liberty offered them. As an understanding was known to exist between Charles II and Louis XIV, the people—still vividly remembering " Bloody Mary "—

---

[6] See Reresby, p. 74.

[7] The Infanta, Dona Catarina, sister of King Alphonso VI of Portugal (1662).

[8] See Reresby, pp. 234 and 276.—The Duchess of Portsmouth was passionately disliked ; there are innumerable satires on the subject. In vol. II alone of the Luttrell Collection in the British Museum, I find three : " A Pleasant Dialogue betwixt Two Wanton Ladies of Pleasure ; Or, *The Dutchess of Portsmouths woful Farwell to her former Felicity* " (1684–5), No. 167 ; " The Dutchess of Portsmouths Farwel " (1684–5), No. 168 ; " Portsmouth Observed and Described," 1684, No. 254.—In *Poems on Affairs of State*, 1703, vol. I, p. 216, I note a piece of verse called *On his Royal Highness's Voyage beyond Sea*, March 3d., 1678, which thus begins :

> " R. H. they say is gone to Sea,
> Design'd for the *Hague*
> But *Portsmouth's* left behind to be
> The Nation's Whorish Plague."

The story goes that Nell Gwyn was driving through the streets of Oxford in her carriage, pursued by the hooting of the crowd, who mistook her for the Duchess of Portsmouth. " She looked out of the window and said, with her usual good humour, ' Pray, good people, be civil ; I am the Protestant whore.' This laconic speech drew upon her the favour of the populace, and she was suffered to proceed without further molestation." (Cunningham, *The Story of Nell Gwynn*, chap. VI, p. 121.)

foresaw a fiery persecution [9] by the Romanists under the direction
of the King of France.   So, day by day, causes of complaint
piled up ; the King's popularity was wearing thin ; the number
of malcontents increased and they dared to make their voices
heard.   Above all, the national conscience took fright—soon one
cry alone was heard throughout the land : the Church in danger !
Since Heaven—endorsing the country's views—had denied
children to Charles's marriage to a Roman Catholic, his brother,
James, Duke of York, was next in the succession, and with him
Romanism in its most fanatic form would mount the throne.
This threat to the future was a spark to tinder.   From words the
nation passed to deeds.   The House of Commons began hos-
tilities, by compelling the King to withdraw his Declaration of
Indulgence, and by passing the Test Act (1673) against the
Roman Catholics, to which—so deep was the people's feeling—
Charles did not dare to refuse the royal assent.   The Duke of
York was obliged to resign his office of Grand Admiral of the
Fleet, but in the same year, as if to defy Parliament and nation,
he took as his second wife a devout Roman Catholic princess,
Maria of Modena, whom the people promptly nicknamed " The
Pope's eldest daughter ".[10]

Such was the mood in England when Titus Oates appeared
with his sensational revelations of an alleged Popish Plot (1678).
The country was in a state of excitement so acute that people
believed the whole story ; they saw themselves encircled by
snares and dangers, prepared themselves for self-defence, and
became literally mad with fear and anger.   Political and religious
passion had seemed dead.   They were now rekindled, to burn
more fiercely than ever before.   It was soon clear that if people
had so long kept silence it was not because they had nothing to
say.[10a]

[9]   " What need I to apologize ?
                  'Tis said, nothing more true is,
              The chiefest part of 's Errand lies
                  To fetch in Cousin *Lewis*.

              That both together, as they say,
                  If one may dare to speak on 't :
              Thro' Hereticks Throats may cut their way,
                  To bring in *James* the Second . . ."
              (*On his Royal Highness's Voyage beyond Sea*, see last note.)

[10] On the state of public opinion at this critical time, see Christie,
Letters Addressed from London to Sir Joseph Williamson, in the Years 1673 and 1674.
    [10a] [The most complete study of the whole affair is Mr. John Pollock's
The Popish Plot. B. D.]

England was once again divided into two hostile camps : on the one hand were those who looked on the Duke of York as a menace to the English constitution and religion and wished at all costs to exclude him from the succession ; on the other, those who held that his right to the throne came from God and could not be questioned on any grounds whatsoever. Here, the champions of the nation's rights—there, the upholders of the royal prerogative. The one party set about sending petitions to the King, demanding that Parliament be immediately summoned to bring in a Bill of Exclusion directed against the Duke of York. The other showered addresses on him expressing their abhorrence of petitions and of parliaments. In a moment politics dominated everything. Everyone was a prey to quite exceptional mental excitement. Normal social relations were at an end. "I know but four men, in their whole [Whig] party," said Dryden, " to whom I have spoken for above this year last past ; and with them, neither, but casually and cursorily. We have been acquaintance of long standing, many years before this accursed Plot divided men into several parties." [11] " Things have got to such a pass," wrote Reresby,[12] " that there are not only divergencies of interest, but there are almost no business or social relations except between people of the same opinions." Henceforth there were in England neither neighbours, nor friends, nor colleagues, nor families ; there were only Petitioners (also known as Exclusionists or Birminghams [13]) and Abhorrers (also called Anti-Birminghams, Yorkists, Irish, Bogtrotters or Tantivies).[14] All these terms speedily gave way to " Whigs " and " Tories " respectively.

Whig-a-more, abbreviated to Whig, was a term applied to the peasants of the Scottish Lowlands, fanatical Presbyterians who had recently risen and assassinated the Primate. Tory was the Romanist outlaw, half vagabond, half bandit, who had sought refuge in the Irish bogs.[15] This unflattering title was given to the adherents of the Duke of York, while his opponents were branded by the equally unflattering name of Whigs.

[11] *The Vindication*, etc.   [12] Reresby, p. 265.
[13] That is to say, " False Protestants " (North, *Examen*, p. 321). The people of Birmingham were reputed to manufacture false coin.
[14] Stephens, *Catalogue* . . . vol. I *passim* ; North, *Examen*, p. 321 ; Reresby, pp. 187 and 190. " To ride tantivy " means " at headlong pace ". The Tantivies were the extremists who were said to be heading full speed for Rome.
[15] Macaulay, *History*, chap. II, vol. I, pp. 256–7 ; Swift, *Works*, edited Walter Scott, vol. III, p. 508, note.

The Court was naturally on the Tory side ; the City, which now re-entered the picture, rallied to the side of the Whigs.[15a] The light-hearted days of irresponsibility and jollity were over. It was impossible for anyone to steer clear of politics, and the writers who had hitherto concentrated only on amusing the Court were compelled, like everybody else, to take sides.

The theatre was still the rage, so it was through the theatre that they first took part in the struggle. Up to now they had ventured no excursions into the political field save by complimentary allusions to the King : [16]

> You, Sir, such blessings to the World dispense,
> We scarce perceive the use of Providence,

or by rhetorical affirmations of the sanctity of royalty : a scarcely veiled protest against republican theories :

> Kings, tho' they err, should never be arraign'd [17] ;

> But make him know it is a safer thing,
> To blaspheme Heav'n, then to depose a king [18] ;

> We ought, when Heav'n's Vicegerent does a Crime,
> To leave to Heav'n the right to punish him.
> Those who for wrongs their Monarchs murther act,
> Worse sins than they can punish they contract.[19]

Politics in the theatre were confined to flattering generalities of this type.

It is true that when England was at war with Holland in 1673 Dryden had written his *Amboyna, or The Cruelties of the Dutch to the English Merchants*, with the evident intention of stirring up public opinion to support the policy of the government. The tragedy was dedicated to Lord Clifford who up to that moment had been a Minister. But in 1673 no one took politics seriously. Mrs. Behn—who was, as the reader will recall, a political spy as

---

[15a] [It is true that the City, the dissenting and trading element, was against the King : but the Court was divided. Many great nobles, e.g. Shaftesbury, fought hard against the royal measures. The battle in the House of Lords over the Exclusion Bill was bitter and long-drawn-out. B. D.]

[16] Crowne, Epilogue to *Calisto*, addressed to the King.

[17] Lee, *Sophonisba* (III).

[18] Crowne, *The History of Charles the Eighth of France* (I, 1).

[19] Earl of Orrery, *Tryphon* (I, 1). In the volume entitled *Two New Tragedies*.

[Such statements are not merely flattery. They are, in a sense, Hobbism, and reflect an attitude of mind understandable in a people who did not want another civil war. B. D.]

well as an author—was simply laughed at when she sent from
Holland the all-too-accurate news of Ruyter's raid up the
Thames.[20]   The drama did not follow up this experiment of
Dryden's but speedily reverted to its normal fatuity.

Now, however, there was no more laughter.   The struggle
raged with fury and it was no longer so easy to side-track political
issues.   Sick as a man might be of them, they were there, they
were full of menace, they thrust themselves on his attention.
The theatre could not escape them.   From 1680 onwards it
echoed every passion and reflected every tiny incident of a stormy
period that was destined to end in a Revolution.[21]

The titles of plays changed suddenly and significantly.   One
after another the stage presented :

> Sir Barnaby Whigg.[22]
> The City Heiress.[23]
> The Royalist.[24]
> The Roundheads, or The Good Old Cause.[25]
> The Loyal Brother, or The Persian Prince.[26]
> Venice Preserv'd, or A Plot Discover'd.[27]
> City Politiques.[28]
> A Common-Wealth of Women.[29]

They even dragged Shakespeare—whose plays they continued
to remodel—into the politics of the day.   In the early days of
the Restoration, when Dryden borrowed his *Troilus and Cressida*,
he encumbered it with a subsidiary and romantic title *Or, Truth
Found too Late* ;   when the actor Lacey rewrote *The Taming of the
Shrew* he rechristened it *Sauny the Scott.*   Crowne now adapted
Henry VI and called it *The Misery of Civil-War* ;   Tate reintroduced

---

[20] Granger, *A Biographical History of England,* s.v. Mrs. Behn.
[21] "All run now into Politicks." (Shadwell, Notice of *The Lancashire Witches.*)—

> "'Tis Faction buys the Votes of half the Pit."
> (Dryden, Epilogue for Southerne's *Loyal Brother.*)

> "The Stage, like old Rump-Pulpits, is become
> The Scene of News, a furious Party's Drum.
> Here Poets beat their brains for Volunteers
> And take fast hold of Asses by their Ears . . ."
> (Shadwell (?) *A Lenten Prologue.*)

[22] By D'Urfey.   [23] By Mrs. Behn.
[24] By D'Urfey.   [25] By Mrs. Behn.
[26] By Southerne.   [27] By Otway.
[28] By Crowne.   [29] By D'Urfey.

Coriolanus as *The Ingratitude of a Common-Wealth*.[30] The gulf between the two periods is revealed by the contrast between the titles current in each.

The titles just quoted all obviously belong to plays directed against the City and the Whigs. There are two reasons for this : first, the playwrights, long vassals of the Court, were naturally for the most part more inclined to sing its praises than to oppose it ; secondly, the Tories, making common cause with the King, had the advantage of being able openly to attack their opponents, while the Whigs enjoyed no such privilege.[31] Such authors as were tempted to take the popular side dare not indulge in provocative titles, but instead of advertising their principles had to content themselves with jests at the expense of the Romanists.[32] Shadwell, for instance, in his *Lancashire Witches* introduces the ridiculous Irish priest Teague O' Divelly ; Settle in the *Female Prelate, the Life and Death of Pope Joan* brings his heroine to bed in the streets of Rome. Whig sympathizers had to confine themselves to general allusions of this kind, and even then the allusions must be neither too obvious nor too cutting. Otherwise the play was suppressed. In a transitory fit of Protestant zeal Crowne had spiced his First Part of Henry VI with " a little Vineger against the Pope " [33] only to see his tragedy " e're it liv'd long . . . stifled by command ".[34] During the whole of

[30] In his Dedication he says : " Upon a close view of this Story, there appear'd in some Passages no small Resemblance with the busie *Faction* of our own time. And I confess, I chose rather to set the *Parallel* nearer to Sight, than to throw it off at further Distance."

[31] " I am no Politician," says Settle in dedicating his *Pope Joan* to Shaftesbury, " for that Scribler must have no prospect to his Interest, who dares affront so numerous a Party, that are so powerful a Support of the Stage."

[32] As early as 1679, on the occasion of the Popish Plot, Oldham had published his *Satyrs upon the Jesuits*. They were extremely successful : First Edition 1679 ; Second Edition 1685 ; Eighth Edition 1782 (Stephens, *Catalogue* . . ., I, p. 649).

[33]   " To-day we bring old gather'd Herbs, 'tis true,
        But such as in sweet *Shakespears* Garden grew.
        And all his Plants immortal you esteem,
        Your mouthes are never out of taste with him.
        Howe're to make your Appetites more keen,
        Not only oyly Words are sprinkled in ;
        But what to please you gives us better hope,
        A little Vineger against the *Pope*."   (Prologue.)

[34] " . . . My aversion to some things I saw acted there (viz. at Court) by great men, carried me against my Interest, to expose Popery and Popish

James II's reign the performance of Dryden's *Spanish Fryar* was forbidden because of the character of Dominick, the Spanish monk.[35] As for direct political allusions, the moment they implied the slightest reflection on the Tories, they were excised. In his *Lancashire Witches* Shadwell had introduced the character of Chaplain Smerk, to poke fun at the Anglican clergy, and in particular at their hatred of Dissenters. This whole part was cut to pieces by the Master of the Revels.[36] Lee's tragedy *Lucius Junius Brutus* was stopped after its third performance, because it talked too much of liberty.[37] In remodelling Shakespeare's *Richard II* Tate had to change the English king into *The Sicilian Usurper*, yet even so the play was banned after the second performance, evidently for political reasons, since he protests in his Dedication that every page of it " breathes loyalty ".[38]

In short, almost the only way by which the Whigs could give vent to their feelings in the theatre, was to hiss whatever the Tories applauded.[39]

The Tories, on the other hand, had more than the privilege of hissing what the Whigs applauded ; the authors who upheld their point of view were on the stronger side, and had therefore complete freedom to air their opinions and attack their opponent's with no beating about the bush. They made full use of their

---

Courts in a Tragedy of mine, call'd *The Murder of Humphry Duke of Gloucester*, which pleas'd the best Men of *England*, but displeas'd the worst ; for e're it liv'd long, it was stifled by command." (Crowne, Dedication of *The English Frier.*)

[35] *Biographia Dramatica*, s.v. Spanish Fryar.

[36] See Shadwell's Preface. In the 1720 edition of his *Works* the excised passages are printed in italics. In one of them Sir Edward Hartford says to Smerk :

" You . . .
   Foam at the mouth when a Dissenter's nam'd."

[37] Cibber, *Apology*, p. 200.

[38] See my Bibliography. " I fell upon the new-modelling of this Tragedy (as I had just before done on *The History of King Lear*) charmed with the many Beauties I discover'd in it . . . After this Account it will be askt why this Play shou'd be supprest, first in its own Name, and after in Disguise ? All that I can answer to this is, That it was *Silenc'd on the Third Day* . . . Every scene is full of Respect to Majesty, and the dignity of Courts, not one alter'd Page but what breathes Loyalty ; yet had this Play the hard fortune to receive its Prohibition from Court."

[39]   " That he shall know both Parties, now he Glories ;
         By Hisses th' Whiggs, and by their Claps the Tories."
                          (D'Urfey, Prologue to *Sir Barnaby Whigg*.)
   " They themselves (the Whigs) owned openly, by their hissings that they were incensed at it (the play)." (Dryden, *The Vindication*, etc.)

opportunities. Their first move was more than ever to enliven their plays with floods of Royalist fervour. They had frequently in the past put warm professions of faith into the mouths of their characters ; but now their passionate loyalty burst all bounds. In any and every context they dragged in such lines as

> . . . Learn here the greatest Tyrant
> Is to be chose before the least Rebellion.[40]

> . . . This Maxim still
> Shall be my Guide (*A Prince can do no ill !*)
> In spight of Slaves, his Genius let him trust ;
> For Heav'n ne'er made a King, but made him just.[41]

D'Urfey's Sir Charles Kinglove is about to make a gift of £20,000 to Charles I. In ecstasy he adds : " Oh, did he want as many drops of blood from the dear Centre of my life, my heart, as he does pounds from my now happy Store, should I not freely bleed ? Strong in my zeal beyond Mortality, with my own hands I'd crush the trembling Lump, until the Noble Loyal Debt was paid." [42]

Down even to the gallants of the comedies, hitherto accustomed to speeches of a very different sort, there was no character who did not feel an urge to utter similar sentiments. Mrs. Behn's comedy *The Roundheads* shows Loveless and Lady Lambert engaged in an amorous *tête-à-tête*. Lady Lambert chooses this moment—it is difficult to see why—to reveal a crown and sceptre lying on an adjacent table, whereupon Loveless cries :

> Have I been all this while
> So near the Sacred Reliques of my King ! . . .
> —Hail Sacred Emblem of Great Majesty, . . .
> —'tis Sacrilege to dally where it is ;
> A rude, a Sawcy Treason to approach it
> With an unbended knee ; for Heav's [*sic*] sake, Madam,
> Let us not be profane in our Delights
> Either withdraw, or hide that Glorious Object.[43]

Frequent and vehement as such passages were, they were not sufficient to satisfy the public's raging appetite for politics.

---

[40] Crowne, *The Misery of Civil-War*, IV. [See also note 19 above. B. D.]

[41] Bankes, *Vertue Betray'd*. These are the last lines of the play, spoken by the king.

[42] *The Royalist*, V, 1.

[43] IV, 2. Lady Lambert is General Lambert's wife. Lady Cromwell and Lady Fleetwood are also among the Dramatis Personæ.

They were too vague, too general.   More outspoken, more direct allusions to current events and people of the day, were needed. Tory authors spared no pains to supply them.   Southerne devoted a whole play, *The Loyal Brother or the Persian Prince* to championing the Duke of York.   In *The Duke of Guise* Dryden and Lee represented Charles II as Henri III of France, the Duke of York as King of Navarre and the Duke of Monmouth as Guise, and that there might be no mistake began their Prologue with the words " Our play's a parallel."   Crowne's *City Politiques* brings on to stage Titus Oates and the venerable Whig lawyer, Maynard.[44]   Dryden's opera *Albion and Albanius* is nothing but a long-winded glorification of Charles II and his successor with a violent satire on their enemies.   For, as we can well believe, not the slightest chivalry was shown in any quarter towards the Whigs.   They were lavishly treated to abuse and the grossest personal insults.   It was the fashion to call them " fanatical rogues " and " seditious rascals ",[45] and Puritan convictions were freely assumed to be synonymous with the most disreputable practices.[46]   " I never knew a religious Fool ", says Craffy in Crowne's *City Politiques*, " that was not a Rogue in my life." [47] " Damn the City," says another.   " Damn all the Whigs, Charles, All the Whigs," is the reply.[48]   The citizenry and their

[44] Maynard was more than eighty years old.   When the Prince of Orange met him for the first time he said to him : " You must have survived all the lawyers of your standing."—" Yes, Sir," replied Maynard, " and, but for Your Highness, I should have survived the laws too."   (Macaulay, *History*, chap. 10, vol. II, p. 576.)   Under the name of *Bartoline* Crowne naturally made him into a corrupt old attorney and his wife—under the name of *Lucinda*—into a coquette.   In the printed version of his play he even went so far as to reproduce Maynard's peculiarities of speech, for old age had not spared him all his teeth.—Titus Oates figured as *Dr. Paunchy*.

[45] D'Urfey's list of Dramatis Personæ in *Sir Barnaby Whigg* contains :

" *Wilding*—A Loyal and Witty Gentleman, only addicted to rail against Women."
" *Sir Barnaby Whigg*—a Phanatical Rascal."

In *The Royalist* D'Urfey describes Captain Jonas as " A Seditious Rascal that disturbs the People with News and Lyes to promote his own Interest ".
[46] Mrs. Behn's *City-Heiress* contains, amongst other characters, one, Mrs. Clacket, " A City-Bawd and Puritan ".
[47] I, i.

[48]   " *Closet*.   The City, you know, Sir, is so censorious . . .
  Sir Charles Meriwell.   Damn the City.
  Sir Anthony Meriwell.   All the Whigs, *Charles*, all the Whigs."
                                        (Mrs. Behn, *The City-Heiress*, IV.)

officials were grossly ridiculed.   The rôles of betrayed husbands
and self-important fools were reserved exclusively for them.
Tate named one of his plays *Cuckolds-Haven or, an Alderman No
Conjuror*.   In *The London Cuckolds* Ravenscroft introduces two
aldermen under the names of Doodle and Wiseacre.   Accusing
Anne Boleyn of adultery, Henry VIII—in one of Bankes's
tragedies—exclaims :

> I have more Horns than any Forrest yields,
> Than *Finsbury*, or all the City musters
> Upon a Training, or a Lord Mayor's day.[49]

The fiercest of the attacks was directed against Shaftesbury,
the leader of the Whig party.   He was the chief target for jest
and abuse.   Playing on his name, the Tories called him " Shifts-
bury " because of his changes of front.[50]   Preachers alluded to
him as Mephistopheles or The Demon,[51] Southerne represented him as a sort of political Iago under the name of Ishmael
in his *Loyal Brother* ;   Otway pilloried him in *Venice Preserv'd* as
an imbecile old senator bearing the suggestive name of Antonio
(Shaftesbury's Christian name was Anthony),[52] and since,
despite his sixty years, he was reputed somewhat over-fond of
women,[53] the poet devoted a long scene to showing him playing
the lapdog to amuse his mistress, barking, biting, yelping, only
to be rewarded for his pains by kicks and whippings.[54]   Vulgarity
went further, publicly alluding to his physical disabilities.   He
had had a serious fall from a carriage which resulted in an
accumulation of fluid that the doctors sought to remedy by

[49] *Vertue Betray'd*, IV.
[50] North, *Examen*, p. 42.
[51] B. Martyn and Dr. Kippis, *The Life of the First Earl of Shaftesbury*,
vol. II, p. 285.
[52] The Dramatis Personæ include " Antonio, a fine speaker in the
Senate ".

[53]   " Next is a Senatour that keeps a Whore,
         In *Venice* none a higher office bore :
         To lewdness every night the Letcher ran,   ⎫
         Shew me, all *London*, such another man,   ⎬
         Match him at Mother *Creswold* if you can.   ⎭
         Oh *Poland, Poland* ! had it been thy lot
         T'have heard in time of this Venetian Plot,
         Thou surely chosen hadst one king from thence
         And honour'd them as thou hast *England* since."
         (Prologue to *Venice Preserv'd*.)   See also note 57 below.

[54] III, 1.

adjusting to his side a silver tap.[55]   Party venom eagerly seized on this subject for jesting.   A newly-invented wine-jar with a turn-cock was baptized a *Shaftesbury* and installed in the royal taverns.[56]   A rumour ran that before the election of John Sobieski Poland had offered the crown to Shaftesbury, who was hence nicknamed *Tapski* or *Potapski*.[57]   The theatre did not scorn to exploit these unsavoury jests.   In the Prologue to *Cuckolds-Haven* Tate speaks of " Treason's Tap ".[58]   Dryden introduces into his opera *Albion and Albanius*, " a Man with a long, lean, pale face, with fiend's wings, and snakes twisted round his body ; he is encompassed by several fanatical rebellious heads, who suck poison from him, which runs out of a tap in his side ".[59]

While tragedies, comedies and operas fought the enemies of the Court with any weapon they could lay hands on, prologues and epilogues carried on a guerrilla warfare in detail.   The most trifling incidents and day-to-day happenings of current politics were brought down on the wing.   In 1681 Shaftesbury was accused of treason before the Grand Jury ; but this Jury, appointed by the City Magistrates, was composed of Whigs. They refused to find him guilty and brought in a verdict of *Ignoramus*.   Prologues and epilogues were forthwith filled with

---

[55] *Biographia Britannica*, s.v. Cooper (Anthony Ashley).—Walter Scott, *A Collection of Scarce and Valuable Tracts* . . . vol. VIII, p. 315, note.
[56] Dryden, *Works*, edited by Scott and Saintsbury, VII, p. 282, note.
[57] " A modest Vindication of the Earl of Shaftesbury : In a Letter to a Friend concerning his being elected king of Poland." (Walter Scott, *A Collection of Scarce and Valuable Tracts* . . . VIII, p. 313.)—The British Museum possesses a Broadside called : *The Last Will and Testament of Anthony King of Poland*.   From it I quote the following lines :

> " My Tap is run ; then *Baxter* tell me why
> Should not the *good*, the great *Potapskie* die ? . . .
> Ye *Mortal Whigs* for Death prepare,
> For mighty Tapski's *Guts* lie here.
> Will his great Name keep Sweet, d'y'think !
> For certainly his Entrals stink . . ."
>   See my Bibliography, s.v. *Anthony*.

[58] And at the end of Act III :

> " The very dregs of Treason's Tap are out."

[59]   " In the Piss and the Spew the poor Cooper did paddle,
To stop up his Tap, but the Knave was not able . . ."
                         (*The Wine-Cooper's Delight*. See my Bibliography, s.v. *Wine-Cooper*.)

thrusts at the *Ignoramus* verdicts of juries.[60]   To avenge himself
for this acquittal, the King declared the City's privileges forfeit
and set over it new Sheriffs and a new Lord Mayor.   Having
thus, so to speak, tasted blood, he started a campaign against
the Municipal Charters of every town suspected of Whig sympathies [61] ;   then it was the Sheriffs' turn to submit to cross-
examination.[62]   During the excitement caused by the Exclusion
Bill, Charles II had thought it wise to despatch his brother to
Scotland in a sort of diplomatic exile.   The Duke returned to
London for a momentary stay in 1680 while Parliament was
prorogued.   Otway's Prologue to *The Orphan* greeted him as he
passed through.   He was gone again before the end of the year
and the Epilogue to *The Royalist* reminded the audience of " the
Gentleman in Scotland ".[63]   In 1682 he came back to London

[60]   " What in my face cou'd this strange Scribler see,
            (Uds Heart) to make an *Evidence* of me ?
            That never cou'd agree with *Ignoramus*,
            But for a *Tender Conscience* have been famous."
                                    (D'Urfey, *The Royalist*, Epilogue.)

         " Pay Juries that no formal Laws may harm us
            Let Treason be secur'd by *Ignoramus*."
                                    (Mrs. Behn, *The Roundheads*, Prologue.)

         " But what provok'd the Poet to this Fury,
            Perhaps he's piqu'd at by the *Ignoramus* Jury . . ."
                                    (Ravenscroft, *The London Cuckolds*, Epilogue.)

         " But, Friends, don't think that you shall longer Sham us,
            Or that we'll Bugbear'd be by your *Mandamus* ;
            You see Dame *Dobsons* Devil long was famous,
            But fail'd at last ;   so will your *Ignoramus*."
                                    (Ravenscroft, *Dame Dobson*, Epilogue.)

         " And then in *Ignoramus Holes* they think,
            Like other Vermin, to lie close, and stink."
                                    (Anon., *Romulus and Hersilia*, Prologue.)

[61]   Cooke, *History of Party*, I, p. 223 ff.

[62]   " Now I dare swear, some of you *Whigsters* say
            Come on, now for a swinging Tory Play.
            But, Noble *Whigs*, pray let not those *Fears* start ye,
            Nor fright hence any of the *Sham Sheriffs Party* ;
            For, if you'l take my censure of the story,   ⎫
            It is as harmless as e're came before ye,   ⎬
            And writ before the times of Whig and Tory."⎭
                                    (Anon., *Romulus and Hersilia*, Prologue.)
   The Prologue Dryden wrote for the King and Queen on the union of
the two theatres expresses the wish that " Whig poets and Whig sheriffs
may hang together ".

[63]   " For who are these among you here that have
            Not in your Rambles heard of *Tory Cave* ;
            That rores in Coffee-house, and wasts his Wealth,
            Toping the Gentleman in *Scotland's* Health."
                                    (D'Urfey, *The Royalist*, Epilogue.)

for good.   Dryden forthwith composed a prologue [64] and Otway an epilogue [65] to celebrate his return ; and Otway added to his epilogue an epistle to the Duchess. [66]   About the same time the Duke of York's portrait at Guildhall was slashed by an unknown hand ; Otway castigated as a " rascal " the " vermin " who had dared to deface this sacred countenance.   In 1684 the Court had temporarily triumphed over its enemies, and prologues and epilogues shared in the rejoicing. [67]   In 1685 the Duke of York became King James II ; the poets lost no time in chanting the long years of prosperity he promised to his people. [68]   The same year saw Monmouth's ill-advised insurrection and D'Urfey armed with a scythe the actor who spoke the prologue to his *Common-Wealth of Women*, for scythes were the weapons carried by many partisans of the Protestant Duke. [69]

[64]
[65] } See my Bibliography.

[66] *Works*, III, p. 368.

[67]
> " Now would you have me rail, swell and look big,
> Like rampant Tory over couchant *Whig*,
> As spit-fire Bullies swagger, swear and roar,
> And brandish Bilbo, when the Fray is o're,
> Must we huff on when we're oppos'd by none ? "
>> (Prologue intended for (Rochester's) *Valentinian*
>> to be spoken by *Mrs.* Barrey.)

> " Since the *Whig-Tyde* runs out, the *Loyal* flows.
> All you who lately here presum'd to bawl,
> Take warning from your Brethren at *Guild-Hall* ;
> The *Spirit of Rebellion* there is quell'd . . .
> Impartial *Justice* has resum'd agen
> Her awful Seat, nor bears the Sword in vain."
>> (Epilogue to Otway's *Atheist*, by Mr. Duke of
>> Cambridge.)

[68]
> " How greatly Heaven has our great Loss supplyed ?
> 'Tis no small Vertue heales a Wound so wide . . .
> Verse is too narrow for so Great a name,
> Far sounding Seas hourly repeat His Fame.
> Our Neighbours vanquished Fleets oft wafted o're
> His Name to theirs, and many a trembling Shore ;
> And we may go, by His great Conduct led
> As far in Fame as our Forefathers did . . .
> These are not all the blessings of this Isle,
> Heaven on our Nation in a Queen does smile,
> Whose Vertue's Grace by Beauty shines so bright . . ."
>> (Crowne, *Sir Courtly Nice*, Prologue.)
See also the Epilogue to Dryden's *Albion and Albanius*.

[69] Prologue, Spoken by Mr. *Hains* with a Western Scyth in his Hand :
> " From the *West* as Champion in defence of Wit,
> I come to mow you Critticks of the Pit . . .

It would be easy to multiply these quotations, for such allusions abound. It is safe to say that if all other historic documents relating to this stormy period were to be lost, it would almost be possible to reconstruct it in minute detail by consulting the prologues and epilogues to which it gave birth.

II

Decadence of Drama.—Newspapers.—The Coffee House ; The Newsletter ;
The Pulpit

Despite the fervour it displayed, and the zeal with which it sought to increase its influence, the theatre could not meet the new demands of the time. First, it was going out of fashion. The public had lost their keenness and become less diligent in their attendance, so much so that the King's and the Duke's Companies had been compelled for lack of spectators to unite their threatened interests in one single royal company in 1682.[70] This decline of the theatre was in the natural course of things. It had been exploited and misused to such a degree that it could not possibly maintain its first brilliance. For twenty years the theatre had been everything. It had exhausted all its resources in order to allure its audiences ; theatre-goers had become blasé, and pampered to saturation-point ; and there were no novel attractions left to offer them.

Secondly, political crises supervened, fatally competing with the theatre in interest. Political sympathies diverged too often for authors to be tempted to write, or directors at vast expense to produce, plays in several acts, which the public were not always in the mood to enjoy or which they listened to with divided attention.[71] Thus, just as Dryden's *Albion and Albanius*—an

---

This Godly Weapon first invented was
By Whigs to cut down Monarchy like Grass ;
But I know better how to use these Tools,
And have reserv'd my Scythe to mow down Fools."

[70] Downes, *Roscius Anglicanus*, p. 39.—Cibber, *Apology*, pp. 57, 58. Cibber is mistaken in dating the union of the two companies 1684.

[Recent histories, giving accurate detail, may be found in Allardyce Nicoll's *Restoration Drama*, which prints many of the relevant documents, and Montague Summers's *The Playhouse of Pepys*. See also Doran, *His Majesty's Servants*. B. D.]

[71]   " And what can Players hope for, in these Days,
When e'r the Idle Youth forsake our Plays ?
The empty Head that never thought before
But on New fashions, or a fresh new Whore: . . .

opera in verse produced with an amazing and reckless use of music, scenery and costumes—appeared on the stage the news reached London that the Duke of Monmouth had landed at Lyme Regis, laying claim to the throne. It can easily be imagined that the public was more deeply stirred by this invasion than by the adventures of Dryden's heroes, and this new work, on which both the poet and the theatre had built great hopes, was given only six performances in all.[72]   But the radical reason for the theatre's receding into the background was that it was a poor instrument for polemics, and polemics now absorbed every man's attention.   The original Puritans who formed the backbone of the Whig party, eschewed the theatre and not even plays upholding their point of view could lure them into it.   As Shadwell put it :

> Our Popes and Fryars on one Side offend,
> And yet alass the City's not our Friend :
> The City neither likes us nor our Wit,
> They say their wives learn ogling in the Pit ;
> They'r from the Boxes taught to make Advances,
> To answer stolen sighs and naughty glances . . .[73]

The theatre therefore could exercise no influence on the Whigs of the City, and the only thing political plays could hope to do, was to strengthen the Tories in opinions of which they were long since the champions : too slight a reward for too much toil.   It was useless to continue the struggle on these lines.   It was absolutely necessary to discover another weapon to seek out the elusive foe, to attack him in his lair, above all to reason with him.   Each new occurrence, each principle enunciated, each

---

> For News he now walks gravely up and down,
> And every Fop's a Politician grown."
>   (Shadwell, Prologue to *The Woman-Captain*.)

" I cannot easily excuse the printing of a play at so unseasonable a time, when the great plot of the nation, like one of Pharaoh's lean kine, has devoured its younger brethren of the stage."
                    (Dryden, Dedication of the *Kind Keeper*.)

[72] " This being perform'd on a very Unlucky Day, being the Day the *Duke of Monmouth*, Landed in the *West* : The Nation being in a great Consternation, it was perform'd but Six times, which not answering half the Charge they were at, Involv'd the Company very much in debt." (Downes, *Roscius Anglicanus*, p. 40.)   Malone says (*Life of Dryden*, p. 186) that if tradition is to be believed the audience withdrew in disorder at the sixth performance and the play was never acted again.

[73] See chap. I, note No. 205, above.

emergent personality, must be discussed with the opponent and with the drifting crowd of waverers—always so important a factor in politics. These are tasks which the theatre can rarely at any time satisfactorily perform, and in which it is bound utterly to fail when auditors are absent, especially those very auditors on whose conversion an author's heart is set.

Nowadays this business of discussion and polemics is handled by the Press. But in the England of those days the Press was embryonic. The first known publications with any resemblance to newspapers were scarcely more than fifty years old.[74] From 1619 onwards [75] modest little pamphlets, not too well printed, had begun to appear, which undertook to supply the curious with news of foreign countries.[76] These news reports were like the famous newspaper of Jérôme Paturot [76a] : they appeared " sometimes ". Most of them probably consisted of the one issue only. Where they had a longer life, their name seems to have varied with each new appearance.

The first English journal which aimed at being a regular periodical would seem to have appeared on the 23rd of May 1622 : *Weekly Newes from Italy, Germanie, Hvngaria, Bohemia, the Palatinate, France and the Low Countries*, printed, as the title indicates, once a week. With constant changes of name and publisher it

[74] For a long time *The English Mercurie* dated 1588 was quoted as the first English newspaper, but in 1839 a remarkable letter from Thomas Watts of the British Museum to Antonio Panizzi, the then Keeper of the Printed Books, conclusively proved that this ancient newspaper was a fake.—See my Bibliography, s.v. Watts.

[75] The British Museum Catalogue of English newspapers begins with 1604. But prior to 1619 I can find nothing save papers relating to affairs of State, royal proclamations officially published with the superscriptions : " Set forth by Authoritie " or " Commanded by his Maiestie to be published in Print ", and usually printed by the King's Printer. These are political documents, not newspapers.

[76] Such are : *Newes out of* Holland : Concerning Barnevelt . . . London : Printed by T. S. for Nathanael Newbery . . . 1619 (British Museum). It consists of 28 small quarto pages including the title. Twelve of these are devoted to France and the Duke of Épernon.—Newes from Poland . . . Published by Authority . . . *At London* 1621. (British Museum)—*Newes from France* . . . Translated according to the French Copie, *printed at Paris. London* . . . 1621 (British Museum).

[76a] [Jérôme Paturot was a character invented by Louis Reybaud in the forties of the last century as a vehicle for political satire in very amusing novels. Paturot became a sort of legendary hero, after the manner of Tartarin, but at the beginning of this century died out as a familiar reference. Paturot was very up to date, and offered his regular subscribers, on their first subscription, the choice of a pair of boots, an overcoat, or a leg of mutton. B. D.]

struggled on haltingly to 1640.[77] Whether intermittent or recurrent, all these newspapers—if we can already use the word—had one characteristic in common : they invariably confined themselves to foreign news, and were content to print their information dryly, without comment or discussion.

With the Long Parliament and the Civil War, political leaflets quickly increased in number and vigour. From 1640 to the execution of Charles I in 1649, more than a hundred seem to have appeared with different titles, and more than another eighty between 1649 and the Restoration.[78]

Every event, in a period when events followed each other thick and fast, found everywhere and immediately its chronicler. One gave news of Great Britain, another of Ireland, Scotland or Wales. There were " Certain Informations from Severall Places ".[79] This, told people what was happening in Oxford;

[77] " *Translated out of the Low Dutch Copie London*, Printed by I. D. for *Nisholas Bourne* and *Thomas Archer* . . ." 1622 (British Museum). On September 25, 1622, Nathaniel Butter and William Sheffard offered for sale : " Newes from most parts of Christendome " ; then we find Butter joining Bourne to publish " A True Relation of the Affaires of *Europe* (Oct. 4, 1622)." Butter and Bartholomew Downes published on October 15, 1622, " A Continuation of the Affaires of the Low-Countries, and the Palatinate ". Endorsements like the following are frequent : " The Continuation of our Former Newes ", " The Continuation of our Forraine Avisoes ", " The Continuation of the Forraine Occurrents for 5 weekes last past ", or sometimes the title " The Weekely Newes Continued ". From the format and the names of the publishers—Bourne, Archer, Butter, Downes and Sheffard—it is clear that we are dealing with one and the same journal throughout.

[78] George Chalmers, *The Life of Thomas Ruddiman*, 114, note *m*. This work (pp. 404–42) contains a chronological list of newspapers that had appeared after the Civil War.—See also Andrews, chaps. III to VI.

[79] " *Mercurius Britannicus* : Communicating the affairs of Great Britaine . . . 1643 " (British Museum).

" The Victorious proceedings of the Protestants in Ireland ; from the beginning of *March* to this present, being the 22. of the same month . . . Printed at London for *John Wright*, in the Old-baily. 1642 " (British Museum).

" *Aprill the first*, 1642. A Continuation of the Tryumphant and Couragious proceedings of the Protestant Army in *Ireland* . . . London Printed for John Wright, 1642 " (British Museum).

" The late Proceedings of the Scotish Army . . . 1644 " (British Museum).

" The Scotish Dove Sent out and Returning . . . April 1646 Num. 129." (British Museum).

" The Welch Mercury . . . 1643 " (British Museum).

" Speciall Passages And certain Informations from severall places, Collected for the use of all that desire to bee truely Informed . . . 1642 " (British Museum).—I give the dates of the earliest issues I have been able to find.

that, what was being done at Westminster; a third reported what
was going on at Court.[80] Similarly each point of view, each
tendency, found its champion. On every side there was an
outburst of Mercurys of every colour : Mercurius-Civicus, Philo-
Monarchicus, Morbicus, Medicus, Bellicus, Pacificus, Problematicus, Veridicus, Candidus, Elencticus, etc.[81] There was even
a Mercury giving news of Hell.[82] *The Laughing Mercury* gave
" genuine news " of the moon and the antipodes.[83] The News-
books, as they were then called, were born—and died, for most
were fairly short-lived—with astounding rapidity.

Each new publication immediately provoked one or more
hostile retorts : *Mercurius Impartialis* attacked *Mercurius
Militaris* [84]; *Mercurius Aquaticus* replied " to all that hath or shall

[80] " Numb. 1. *Mercurius Academicus* : Communicating the Intelligence
and Affairs of Oxford . . . April 1648 " (British Museum).
" The Spie : Communicating Intelligence from Oxford " (1643 ?)
(British Museum).
" *Mercurius Melancholicus* ; or, Newes from Westminster and other parts
. . . 1647 " (British Museum).
" *Mercurius Aulicus*, A Diurnall, Communicating the Intelligence and
Affaires of the Court to the rest of the *Kingdome*. Oxford . . . (date added
by hand) 1642/43 " (British Museum). The *Mercurius Aulicus* was edited
by Sir John Birkenhead.
[81] " *Mercurius Civicus* . . . 1643 " ; " *Mercurius Philo-Monarchicus* May
1649 ; " " *Mercurius Morbicus* . . . 1647 " ; " *Mercurius Medicus* . . . 1647 " ;
Mercurius Bellicus . . . 1647 " ; " *Mercurius Pacificus* . . . 1648 " ; " A new
Mercury. Called *Mercurius Problematicus* . . . 1644 " ; " *Mercurius Veridicus*
. . . 1646 ; " " *Mercurius Candidus* 1646 " ; " *Mercurius Elencticus* . . . 1647."
All these are in the British Museum.—Amidst this flood of Mercurys, some
had difficulty in finding a name. Witness the following title :

> " 17 Jan, 1643. Mercurius, etc. [*sic*]
> Upon my life new borne, and wants a Name,
> Troth let the Reader then impose the same
> Veridicus—I wish thee ; if not so
> bee—Mutus—for wee Lyes enough doe know."
> (British Museum.)

[82] " *Mercurius Diabolicus*, Or *Hells Intelligencer* . . . 1647 " (British
Museum).
[83] " The Laughing Mercury, *or* a True and Perfect Nocturnall, *Communicating many strange Wonders*, Out of the World in the Moon, *The Antipodes,
Maggy-land, Tenebris, Fary-land, Green-land*, and other adjacent Countries.
Published for the right understanding of all the Mad-merry-People of *Great-
Bedlam. From* Wednes day *Octob.* 27 to *Wednes.* Novem. 3. 1652 Numb.
30 " (British Museum).
[84] " *Mercurius Impartialis* : or, An Answer to that Treasonable Pamphlet
Mercurius Militaris, . . . from Tuesday *December* 5 till Tuesday December 12,
1648 " (British Museum).—" Numb. 1. Mercurius Militaris : . . . Beginning
on *Tuesday, October* 10, 1648 " (British Museum).

be writ " by *Mercurius Britannicus* [85] ; *Mercurius Pragmaticus* was countered by *Mercurius Anti-Pragmaticus*,[86] *Mercurius Melancholicus* by *Mercurius Anti-Melancholicus*.[87] If a *Weekly Discoverer* came out, another paper forthwith undertook to " strip it naked " for its readers.[88] There was even a Mercury which threw down the gauntlet to all its brethren at once, under the name of *Mercurius Anti-Mercurius*.[89] Without even troubling to seek a different designation, one publicist would often simply lift his opponent's title, thus catching the eye of the other's habitual readers. And we not infrequently come across two copies of the same paper in the same format, bearing the same date and the same printer's name, in short, identical in every way except that the two sets of news they bring are entirely contradictory and that the persons lauded by the one are violently attacked by the other.[90]

In addition to these papers, a host of pamphlets and leaflets which seem to have been read no less widely and with equal gusto debated political and religious questions. The Library of the British Museum possesses a collection [91] of these pamphlets published between 1640 and 1660 containing no less than 30,000 specimens, which works out to an average of four or five per day. And collections of this kind are always and inevitably incomplete.

But all this publishing did not yet amount to a " Press ". Though passions ran high, though people thirsted after news,

[85] " *Mercurius Aquaticus*, or, the Water-Poets Answer to all that hath or shallbe Writ by *Mercurius Britannicus*. Ex omni ligno non fit Mercurius. Printed in the Waine of the Moone *Pag.* 121, *and Number* 16 *of* Mercurius Britannicus, 1643 " (British Museum).

[86] " Num 1 *Mercurius* Pragmaticus.—Communicating Intelligence from all Parts, touching all Affairs, Designes, Humours, and Conditions throughout the Kingdome. Especially from *Westminster* and the *Head-Quarters*. From Tuesday *Septem.* 14, to Tuesday *Septem.* 21, 1647 " (British Museum). " Num. 1. *Mercurius* Anti-Pragmaticus. Communicating some remarkable Intelligence. From Tuesday *Oct.* 12 to Tuesday *Oct.* 19, 1647 " (British Museum).

[87] " *Mercurius Melancholicus* . . . 1647 ", First No. Sept. 14 (British Museum). " Mercurius Anti-Melancholicus . . . 1647 ", First No. Sept. 18 (British Museum). Note that the reply was prompt.

[88] *The Weeckly Discoverer* and *The Discoverer stript Naked*. These titles are quoted by Disraeli, *Curiosities of Literature*, Origin of Newspapers.

[89] " Numb. 1 *Mercurius Anti-Mercurius*. Impartially Communicating Truth, correcting falshood . . . Sept. 1648 " (British Museum).

[90] Johnson, *Lives of the English Poets*, Addison.—See also *The Athenæum*, 1858, No. 1594, p. 620.

[91] This Collection goes by the name of *The King's Pamphlets* because it was offered to the Museum by George III. It would more justly be described as the *Thomason Collection* after the indefatigable London bookseller to whose zeal we owe it. See *The English Cyclopaedia*. London, 1859, s.v. British Museum. This article was written by Mr. Thomas Watts.

news still reached them in wholly irregular fashion and never daily. At first the News-books appeared at most once a week. Even when the war grew more lively, and impatient readers would not be kept so long waiting, none was published oftener than twice or thrice a week. Notice also that they continued to be very modest, badly-printed pamphlets, that the news was always dry and scanty and that even when comment began to find a place—as yet a very small place—it was, in accordance with the mood of the day, of the most violent character, usually taking the form of invective.[92]

The Restoration sharply put a full stop to such discussion as there had been. The Press, already subjected to a censorship by the Long Parliament,[93] was ridden on a very tight rein by Charles II's government.[94] Nothing was printed without a permit from the Licenser who allowed none but carefully sifted news to reach the public. To ensure the quality of this news, government set up newspapers of its own. Thus in December 1661 there appeared *The Kingdom's Intelligencer* " to prevent false news "[95]; then in January 1662, *Mercurius Publicus*, also " to prevent false news "[96]; in 1663 *The Intelligencer* and *The Newes*[97] both " published for the satisfaction and information of the people "; and in 1665 the mouthpiece of the Court, the *Oxford Gazette*, later known as the *London Gazette*.[98]

No publications were tolerated alongside these privileged

[92] In his *Calamities and Quarrels of Authors*, Disraeli quotes some samples under the title *The Paper-Wars of the Civil Wars*.
[93] Decree of Sept. 30, 1647. See Cobbett, III, p. 780.
[94] See chap. I, note No. 402 above.
[95] " Numb. 2. The Kingdom's Intelligencer of the Affairs now in agitation in *England, Scotland* and *Ireland* ; Together with forrain Intelligence ; *To prevent false Newes*. Published by Authority. From Monday, *January* 5 to Monday *January* 12, 1662 " (British Museum).
[96] " Number 1. *Mercurius Publicus, Comprising* The Sum of all Affairs now in agitation in *England, Scotland* and *Ireland*, Together with Foreign Intelligence ; for Information of the People, and to prevent false News. *Published by Authority. From* Thursday *February* 28 to Thursday *March* 7, 1661 " (British Museum).
[97] " Numb. 1. The Intelligencer ; Published *For the Satisfaction and Information of the People. With Privilege. Monday* August 3, 1663 " (British Museum) ;—" Numb. 1. The Newes, Published *For Satisfaction and Inform-ation* of the People. *With* Privilege. Thursday September 3, 1663 " (British Museum).
[98] It was first called the *Oxford Gazette* because the Court had fled to Oxford during the London Plague (*Biog. Brit.*, s.v. L'Estrange).—" Numb. 1. The Oxford Gazette. Published by Authority Nov. 7. 1665 " (British Museum).—" Numb. 24. The London Gazette. *Published by Authority*. From Thursday, *February* 1, to Monday February 5, 1665 " [o.s.] (British Museum).

newspapers, except sensational gossip-mongerings or fantastic nonsense. A few sample titles will sufficiently indicate the contents and the value of these latter : " Bloody News from Chelmsford : or, A Proper New Ballad, containing A true and perfect Relation of a most barbarous Murther committed upon the Body of a Country Parson who died of a great Wound given him in the Bottom of the Belly, by a most Cruel Country-Butcher for being too familiar with his Wife [99] : For which Fact he is to be tried for his Life at this next Assizes. Oxford. Printed in the Year MDCLXIII " ; or in another vein : " Magnifico Smokentissimo Custardissimo Astrologissimo Cunningmanissimo Rabinissimo Viro Iacko Adams de Clarkenwell Greeno Lanc lovelissimam sui Picturam Hobbedeboody pinxit et scratchabat " [100] ; or again : " The Man in the Moon, Discovering a World of Knavery under the Sun, with a perfect *Nocturnal*, containing several strange Wonders out of the *Antipodes, Magyland, Faryland, Greenland, Tenebris,* and other parts adjacent. *Published for the right-understanding of all the mad-merry-people in* Great Bedlam. 1663 " [101] ; or again : " The Infallible Mountebank or Quack Doctor, 1670 " ; " The Extravagant Prentices with their Lasses at a Taverne Frollick, 1672 " [102] ; " The London Prodigal " [103] ; " A Strange Wonder in Wiltshire, Affirmed by Three Ministers that were Eye-Witnesses of this following Relation " [104] ; " Flos Ingenii vel Evacuatio Descriptionis, Being an Exact Description of Epsam and Epsam Wells " [105] ; " Clod-pate's Ghost : or a Dialogue Between *Justice Clod-Pate*, and his (*quondam*) Clerk Honest *Tom Ticklefoot* ; Wherein *is faithfully related all the News* from Purgatory *about* Ireland, Langhorn, etc.". [106] " New News of a Strange Monster found in Stow Woods near Buckingham, of *Human Shape*, with a Double Heart, and no Hands ; a Head with two Tongues, and no Brains " [107]—and so forth.

---

[99] British Museum, Luttrell Collection, vol. II, No. 144.
[100] Stephens, *Catalogue*, I, No. 1018.   [101] British Museum.
[102] Stephens, *Catalogue*, I, Nos. 1032 and 1043.
[103] ". . . Or the Unfortunate Spendthrift " . . . London . . . 1673 (British Museum, Luttrell Collection, vol. II, No. 131).
[104] 1674 (ibid., No. 245). For other similar titles see Andrews, I, pp. 79, 80.
[105] " *London* Printed in the year 1674. folio." British Museum : 816, m. 19/40).—See my Bibliography, s.v. Flos.
[106] " August 25, 1679. folio." (ibid., 816, m. 19/43).—See my Bibliography, s.v. Clod-pate.
[107] 1699 (Luttrell Collection, vol. III, No. 7).
[These are ballads and broadsides rather than newspapers in any accepted sense of the word. B. D.]

It is true that the censorship no longer existed at the date which we have now reached. The Licensing Act, passed shortly after the Restoration, had expired in 1679, and had not been renewed. Every Englishman henceforward had the right to print whatever he wished—at his own risk and peril. But this new freedom was in a general way of little benefit to political discussion—because the carefully packed juries pitilessly condemned every piece of writing to which the government took exception [108]—and it was of no advantage at all to the newspapers. The judges declared unanimously that this freedom did not in fact extend to the " gazettes " [109] and that no one had the right to print political news without the King's permission, which permission the King granted only to the *London Gazette*. Nevertheless, amid the seething political passions aroused by the fights over the Exclusion Bill, and the acute tensions that were caused by the Popish Plot, some political leaflets contrived to appear—whether because the Crown judged it prudent to turn a blind eye, or because the zeal of the parties succeeded in eluding its vigilance. Among these were, for instance : *Domestick Intelligence* ; *The English Intelligencer* ; *The Friendly Intelligence* ; *The English Currant* ; *Poor Robins Intelligence* ; *The True News* ; *The Protestant (Domestick) Intelligence* ; *The True Domestick Intelligence*.[110]

[108] " Mr. *Benjamin Harris* . . . He sold a *Protestant Petition* in King *Charles's* Reign, for which they fin'd him, Five Hundred Pound, and set him once in the Pillory " (Dunton, *Life* . . . p. 293).—See also Andrews, chap. VI, and my Bibliography, s.v. Smith (Francis).—After the discovery of the Rye-House Plot (1683) censorship was *de facto* re-established and nothing unfavourable to the Court appeared except clandestinely. In July 1685 James II re-established the censorship *de jure*. The best proof of how little weight the Press carried at that date, is the fact that the censorship was reintroduced without the Tories dreaming of rejoicing or the Whigs of complaining (Macaulay, *History*, chap. V).

[109] Hallam, *Constitutional History* III, pp. 4–5.

[110] " Numb. 1. Domestick Intelligence, Or News both from City and Country. Published to prevent false reports. Monday July the 7th 1679 " ;— " The English Intelligencer. Thursday July 24. 1679. Num. 2 " ;—" The Friendly Intelligence. Published for the Accommodations of all sober persons. *Munday, September* 7th 1679. Numb. 1."—" The English Currant. Or, Advice Domestick and Forreign. Published for general Satisfaction. Monday, September 8, 1679 " ;—" Poor Robins Intelligence, Revived ; Published for the Accommodations of all Ingenious persons. Wednesday *November* the 26th 1679 " ;—" The True News : or, Mercurius Anglicus, Being the Weekly Occurrences Faithfully Transmitted. January 1679. Numb. 15 " ;— " The Protestant (Domestick) Intelligence ; or, News both from City and Country. Published to prevent false Reports. Fryday, *January* 16, 1679 Numb. 56 " ;—" The True Domestick Intelligence, *Or* News both from City and Country. Published to prevent false Reports. *Feb.* 1680 Numb. 69." —All these papers are in the British Museum.

Some of these papers even introduced themselves with titles like echoes of the Civil War : *A Pacquet of Advice from Rome* ; *Mercurius Anglicus* ; *The True Protestant Mercury* ; *The Impartial Protestant Mercury* ; *Mercurius Civicus* ; *The London Mercury* ; *Mercurius Infernus* ; *Jesuita Vapulans* ; or, *A Whip for the Fool's Back and a Gag for his Foul Mouth*. There was even a revival of the *Weekly Discoverer* to which retorted, just as under the Republic, *The Weekly Discoverer, stript Naked*.[111]

At this critical moment Government thought it necessary to take an active part in the discussion and to find another medium than the *London Gazette* to convey sound, twenty-four-carat opinions to the public. The *Gazette* was certainly a poor instrument of propaganda. It appeared on Mondays and Thursdays only, on a single sheet like all its predecessors, and gave the scanty news which the Court thought fit, in the most laconic terms without comment of any kind. It is as if the French Government should hope to guide public opinion through *le Journal officiel* or *le Bulletin des lois*. A newspaper was therefore required to provide an orthodox commentary on the news published by the *Gazette*. The Court called its new paper *The Observator*[112] and summoned one, Roger L'Estrange,[113] a prolific and most devoted Royalist scribbler, to edit it.

During the Civil War, L'Estrange had fought in the ranks of the Royal Army. He was captured and condemned to death

111 " Numb. 1. A Pacquet of Advice from Rome : or, The History of Popery. Begun to be Published on *Tuesday* the 3. of *December*, 1678. and thence to be continued " ; Edited by Henry Care ;—" Mercurius Anglicus : or, The Weekly Occurrences Faithfully Transmitted. Nov. 1679. Numb. 3 " ;—" Numb. 1. The True Protestant Mercury, or Occurrences *Forein* and *Domestick*. Beginning Tuesday the 28 Decemb. 1680 " ;—" Numb. 11. The Impartial Protestant Mercury, or Occurrences *Foreign* and *Domestick*. *May* 31. 1681 " ;—" Mercurius Civicus : or, a True Account of Affairs both Foreign and Domestick *Monday* 29 March, 1680, Numb. 3 " ;—" Num. 1, The London Mercury. *London* Thursday April 6. 1682." These papers are all in the British Museum except the four last, which are quoted by Andrews. I, pp. 73 and 80.

112 " Numb. 1. The Observator. In *Question and Answer*. Wednesday April 13 1681." (British Museum and Bibliothèque Nationale : Nd. 85.) This paper appeared twice a week, on Wednesdays and Saturdays, occasionally three times, as in the week April 10–17, 1682. It consisted of a single sheet only. The opening of the first issue is a good indication of its aims :

" Q. Well ! They are so. But do you think to bring 'um to their Wits again with a *Pamphlet* ?

A. Come, come ; 'Tis the *Press* that has made 'um Mad, and the *Press* must set 'um Right again."

113 On L'Estrange, see *Biographia Britannica*, and Stephens, *Catalogue*, I, No. 1083.

by the Parliamentarians, but escaped after four months' imprisonment. Later, people said, Cromwell had pardoned him and
set him at liberty, thanks to his skill in playing the violin.[114]
This did not prevent his noisily demanding at the Restoration,
reward for his devotion to the good cause. Charles II was quick
to notice him and gave him a confidential post : making him
Licenser of the Press.[115] From this moment L'Estrange became
the Court's literary maid-of-all-work—supervising and directing
the Press, editing newspapers [116] and pro-Government pamphlets
as required.[117] As an ever-ready writer he could not refuse to
assume responsibility for the *Observator*. It must be admitted
that he was not without a certain gift for brutal argument, and
though his style is vulgar and pretentious it does not lack life and
vigour. He placed at the service of the Tories all his pamphleteering skill and all the resources of a not over-scrupulous [118]

[114] The pamphlets of the day call him " Cromwell's Fiddler ". In a
drawing of 1680 he is represented holding a violin and bow and wearing
round his neck this inscription : " Touzer old Nol's Fidler " (Stephens,
Catalogue, I, No. 1085. See also No. 1110). In volume III of the Luttrell
Collection, No. 138, he figures as a dog called Towzer with a violin attached
to his tail.

[115] L'Estrange had, so to speak, brought these duties on his own head
by publishing in 1663 " Considerations and Proposals in Order to the Regulation of the Press : *Together* with Diverse *Instances of Treasonous*, and *Seditious
Pamphlets*, Proving the *Necessity* thereof ". See my Bibliography.

[116] Amongst others, *The Intelligencer* and *The Newes* already mentioned
and *Heraclitus Ridens*.—" Numb. 1. Heraclitus Ridens : *Or*, A discourse
between Jest and Earnest, where many a True Word is spoken in opposition
to all Libellers against the Government . . . *Ridentem dicere verum Quis
vetat* . . . Horat. *London*, Printed for the Use of the People, *Tuesday*, Feb. 1.
1681 " (Bibliothèque Nationale, No. 61, complete collection).

[117] See a long list of his writings in Watt and in *Biographia Britannica*.—
L'Estrange is the *Sheva* of the second part of Dryden and Tate's *Absalom and
Achitophel* :

> " Than Sheva, none more loyal Zeal have shown,
> Wakeful as *Judah's* lion for the Crown,
> Who for that Cause still combats in his Age,
> For which his Youth with danger did engage,
> In vain our factious priests the Cant revive,
> In vain seditious Scribes with Libels strive
> T' enflame the Crowd, while He with watchful eye
> Observes, and shoots the Treasons as They fly :
> Their weekly frauds his keen replies detect ;
> He undeceives more fast than they infect.
> So *Moses*, when the pest on *Legions* prey'd,
> Advanc'd his Signal, and the Plague was stay'd."

[118] He wrote a pamphlet against Milton entitled *No blind Guides*
(Johnson, *Lives of the English Poets*, Milton). Dunton held no very favourable
opinion of L'Estrange. This is what he says of him (*Life* . . . p. 349) :

enthusiasm, and from 1681 to 1687 his paper passionately upheld all the views dear to the Tory heart.

All his zeal achieved little. In spite of every effort, the Press was not yet in a position to yield the results hoped of it. It did its best : to little purpose. There is no use running a political journal—unless someone reads it. Now the newspaper was still in its infancy and had few readers, for the newspaper habit was as yet no part of English daily life.[119] Its sphere of influence was therefore very limited, and it was not through newspapers that the general public could be reached.

Besides, public opinion flowed through other more important channels.

There were, first, in London the Coffee Houses. They were new to the city—the first dated from 1652—but they had quickly taken root and grown and multiplied with amazing rapidity. By the end of Charles II's reign, there was no class of society, and no profession, which had not its own Coffee House. In the City proper there was one for merchants ; society gentlemen had one near St. James's Park ; men of letters went to The Rose near Covent Garden—later known as Will's Coffee House, where Dryden had an armchair always reserved for him, in winter by the chimney-corner, in summer on the balcony.[120] The Coffee House had gradually come to play an important part in the Londoner's life. It was there that he met his friends, that he made business appointments, that he had his letters addressed, and that he often spent his evenings.[121]

When politics again came to the fore, the Coffee House was there, a ready-made focus for news. People dropped in as a

---

"A Man that betrays his Religion, and Country, in pretending to defend it . . . That was made Surveyor *of the Press*, and wou'd wink at unlicens'd Books, if the Printer's Wife would but————" [*sic*].

[119] Pepys, who talked of everything, mentions the words News-book or Gazette only two or three times in the whole course of his diary.

[120] In 1709 *The Tatler* is dating its articles from the various Coffee Houses according to the subject dealt with. Its first issue says : " *All Accounts of* Gallantry, Pleasure *and* Entertainment, *shall be under the Article of* White's Chocolate-House ; Poetry *under that of* Will's Coffee-house ; Learning *under the Title of* Graecian ; Foreign and Domestick News, *you will have* from St. James's Coffee-house." (Numb. 1.)

[121] " And we may judge the time as well spent there (at the Booksellers') as (in later days) either in Tavern or Coffee-House ; though the latter has carried off (after 1683) the spare hours of most people." (Roger North, *The Life of the Honourable and Reverend Dr. John North* a sequel to *The Life of the Honourable Sir Dudley North.*)—See how large a place the Coffee House takes in the life of Pepys.—Swift had his letters addressed to St. James's Coffee House (Journal to Stella, Oct. 14, 1710).

matter of course to read the News-books,[122] to gather the rumours that were going round, to hear the latest events of the day, to argue, to hammer out their own opinions. Politics ere long enjoyed pride of place. The Coffee House became a sort of small-scale Club [123] where people read newspapers and pamphlets aloud, or where impromptu orators held forth for or against Whigs or Tories. In all these places, views and opinions were poured forth with a freedom which the Press, supervised and spied upon as it was, could not know.[124]

So the Coffee House exercised a most important influence. Hitherto, people holding the same opinion were scattered here

[122]   " Syrrop of Soot, or Essence of old Shooes,
          Dasht with Diurnals, and the Books of News."
               (A Cup of Coffee : or Coffee in its Colours, 1663.)

See my Bibliography, s.v. Coffee.

[123]   " I' the Coffee house here one with a grave face
          When after salute, he hath taken his place,
          His Pipe being lighted begins for to prate
          And wisely discourses the affairs of the state."
               (A New Satyricall Ballad of the Licentiousness
                    of the Times . . . London, Printed in the
                    Year 1679. British Museum, Luttrell
                    Collection, vol. II, No. 116.)

     " There's nothing done in all the World,
          From *Monarch* to the *Mouse*
     But Every Day or Night 'tis hurld
          Into the *Coffe*-house . . .
     You shall know there, what Fashions are ;
          How Perrywigs are Curl'd
     And for a Penny you shall heare,
          All Novells in the World . . . "
               (News from the Coffe-House ; . . . London
                    . . . 1667.   With Alowance.   British
                    Museum, Luttrell Collection, vol. II,
                    No. 145.)

     " Each Coffee-house is fill'd with subtile Folk,
     Who wisely talk, and politickly smoke."
               (Shadwell, Prologue to *The Woman-Captain*.)

     " *Bak'd* in a pan, *Brew'd* in a pot,
     The third device of him who first begot
     The Printing Libels, and the Powder-plot."
               (A Satyr against Coffee. British Museum,
                    Roxburghe Collection, vol. III, No. 831.)

[124] On Coffee Houses, see Macaulay, *History*, chap. III.— The *Spectator*, No. 305, calls them " our *British* Schools of Politics ".
     [For a good account, see Leslie Stephen's *English Literature and Society in the Eighteenth Century*.   1904.   He puts the first appearance of the coffee house in 1657.   B. D.]

and there.   There existed, so to speak, only a multitude of
individual opinions, isolated units who but rarely, and only in
exceptional circumstances, could find an opportunity of meeting
and forming a group.   Nowadays, the newspapers link together
in groups people sharing the same outlook and give these groups
cohesion.   But as we have just seen, the newspapers of the late
seventeenth century were wholly unqualified to do this.   What
the newspaper could not compass, was achieved, at least in
London, by the Coffee Houses.   These eating-places provided
rallying-points.   People met, exchanged opinions, formed groups,
gathered number.[125]   It was through them, in short, that a
public opinion began to evolve, which thereafter had to be
reckoned with.   The Government were so fully conscious of this
that they began to feel uneasy and the Danby Government would
fain have suppressed these hot-beds of political opinion.   But
the Coffee Houses had already become so indispensable to
Londoners that the outcry was violent and general, and Government had to abandon the project.[126]

If London opinion was formed by coffee-house discussion,
the provinces found a partial equivalent in a peculiar type of
literature known as *Newsletters*, of which we must here take
notice.

Outside the capital there were at this time no newspapers in
England.[127]   The post, as yet barely organized, brought London
papers only after much delay,[128] and we already know that they
were in any case miserly even of expurgated news.[129]   Opposition
papers led a precarious existence ;   of Government papers the
London Gazette offered no comment, and the *Observator* ventured
on discussion only with approval from above.   Such a press was
lenten fare to people hungry for news, far from the centre of
affairs and happenings, and lacking the frank interchanges of

[125] Aubrey, quoted by Disraeli, *Curiosities of Literature*, vol. II, *Introduction
of Tea, Coffee and Chocolate*, boasts " the modern advantage of coffee-houses
in this great city, before which men knew not how to be acquainted except
with their own relations and societies ".

[126] North, *Examen*, pp. 138–41.

[127] The first provincial paper was the *Mercurius Caledonicus* which was
published in Edinburgh in 1660 and ran to ten issues.   The second Edinburgh
paper was *The Edinburgh Gazette* of 1699 (George Chalmers, *The Life of Thomas
Ruddiman*, pp. 118, 119) :—See chap. I, note No. 402 above.   Outside London
no printing-press was authorized except at York and at the two universities.
James II had this law re-enacted.

[128] On the post of those days, see Macaulay, *History*, chap. III.

[129] " Gazetts no News can tell." (*Clod-pate's Ghost*, already quoted,
p. 158 above.)

the Coffee House. Provincial readers found compensation in the Newsletters. These were hand-written letters which important county people, the nobility, the upper middle classes, the clergy, the magistrates, the universities had despatched to them from London at least once a week.[130] There were people—ancestors of our " reporters "—who made a profession of writing Newsletters.[131] They went from Coffee House to Coffee House and to the Law Courts, they prowled about the Court and the City, their ears cocked to gather news and rumours. Fearless of the Censor's watchful eye—in this having the advantage of the newspapers,—they hastened to record everything in detail with their own personal comments in the letter which their provincial correspondent impatiently awaited, for during many long years people in the country had no other news from London.

Another important factor in the formation of public opinion remains to be mentioned : the pulpit. Though the clergy at the beginning of Charles II's reign had to so large an extent resigned themselves to playing a worldly and complaisant part, there were nevertheless among them men of high character who had kept alive the tradition of virtue and hard work : men like Jeremy Taylor, a survival from a preceding age, like Tillotson, Barrow, Stillingfleet, whose sermons and books bear witness to activity and zeal, and who had been able to maintain real and well-deserved influence over an important section of Church-people.[132] When religious and political questions came again to the fore, when the nation realized that despite the reaction against Puritanism it was still stoutly Protestant, the zeal and influence of such men increased, and when the clergy intervened

[130] I have handled a collection of these Newsletters, addressed between March 26, 1723 and December 31, 1730, to the Right Honourable Viscount Percivall. In the British Museum Catalogue of Manuscripts they bear the numbers " Additional 27,980 and 27,981 ". The first begins with this sentence which proves that we are dealing with a real manuscript newspaper : " In order to Inform our Readers with ye great Application, and Diligence of ye Ministry in ye Discovery of ye Plot, we shall insert . . . " These missives were written every second day on three large unsigned sheets and were con-scientiously filled with political and general news including the winning numbers in the lottery.

[131] See in the *Spectator*, No. 625, a letter from one of these newsletter writers.—See also Aubrey, *Letters of Eminent Men*, I, p. 15, and North, *Examen*, p. 133.

[132] Barrow's works run to four folio volumes. Stillingfleet, whom we shall presently see at work, produced six folio volumes (Watt, *Bibliotheca Britannica*). Tillotson's sermons (the earliest dating from 1664) were bought in 1694 for 2,500 guineas (Macaulay, *History*, chap. XX).

in the struggle they proved themselves neither the least ardent
nor the least effective of fighters.   It goes without saying that
the whole body of the clergy rallied to the side of the Tories.[133]
First, the clergy formed an integral part of the royal establishment ; secondly, their old enemies, the Dissenters, were in the
popular camp ; a double reason for their lending their support
without chaffering to the Court party.   Thus, when once battle
was joined, Church preachers vied with each other in protestations of loyalty and in invectives against the Whigs.[134]   Everywhere they preached passionately in favour of *passive obedience* and
non-resistance to the King,[135] and expressed their horror of Dissenters and Republicans.   We can imagine how great an effect
such propaganda was bound to exercise on public opinion when
repeated every Sunday in thousands of churches by a unanimous
clergy.   This effect was particularly strong in the provinces, in
the little towns and villages where no newspaper or newsletter
ever penetrated, where the clergyman was consequently the first
to break the news of events to minds unprepared, telling them at
the same time what they ought to think, with all the authority
of words pronounced *ex cathedra*.   The country clergyman thus
wielded great influence over public opinion, and Macaulay has
no hesitation in attributing to him a large share in the lively
reaction against the Whigs which set in towards the end of
Charles II's reign.[136]

This refers of course only to the clergy of the Church of
England.[137]   The Dissenters had no pulpits, and could preach
only surreptitiously in their " conventicles ", as their secret
meetings were called.   If they were caught, as Bunyan and
Baxter allowed themselves to be, they were banished or thrown
into prison.[138]   But if oral preaching was for them attended

---

[133] There were, naturally some exceptions, like Burnet.

[134] We have already seen that they dubbed Shaftesbury " the Demon "
and " Mephistopheles ".—They drank to the health of the Duke of York
with cheers and cries of " to the confusion of all his enemies ! "   (Burnet,
History of my Own Times, I, p. 509, suppressed passage restored.)

[135] Rapin de Thoyras, vol. II, chap. XXIII.

[136] *History*, chap. II.

[137] We must except, however, the brief respites granted by Charles II's
Act of Indulgence and the two *Declarations of Indulgence* of James II, April 4,
1687, and April 27, 1688.

[138] *Biographia Britannica*, s.vv. Bunyan and Baxter ;—Macaulay, *History*,
chap. II.—" I saw several poor creatures carried by, by constables, for being
at a conventicle.   They go like lambs, without any resistance.   I would
to God they would either conform, or be more wise, or not be catched "
(Pepys, August 7, 1664).

with peril, the Dissenters still had the written word at their disposal, books and more especially little religious tracts : which are still amongst their favourite weapons. Bunyan continued his work even in prison, writing *The Pilgrim's Progress* in his cell. It will not be forgotten that the catalogue earlier quoted shows that half the writings published between 1666 and 1680 were separate sermons or tracts, the majority of which may safely be ascribed to the Dissenters, who were always distinguished by the tenacity with which they clung to their own views and the burning zeal with which they defended them. Howe, " the Puritan Plato ", wrote twenty-five books, three of them in two volumes ; Calamy and Owen, two other famous Nonconformists of the day, were the authors of thirty-five and over eighty works respectively, Baxter of more than a hundred and twenty.[139] A religious group possessing apostles like Bunyan and workers like Howe, Calamy, Owen and Baxter, could not—as long as they had the means of fighting—allow their opponents to be the only people to spread ideas. Compelled though they were to lie low, the Puritans had in fact never ceased to teach or to enlist recruits. The bookseller, John Dunton, who set up in London about 1680, counted over fifty Nonconformist ministers (Baxter amongst them) with whom he was in touch, and all of them were writers.[140] During the whole of the early part of Charles II's reign, while on the surface the Court indulged its merry gambollings, and the theatre and frivolous literature appeared to monopolize attention, there was evidently here an underground literature, so to speak, of which we get imperfect glimpses only,[141] but which must have been considerable and which, without noise and without rest, performed its slow and silent task. Not in vain. For there is no doubt that Puritan publications found readers in no negligible number. One fact alone would suffice

[139] See Watt and *Biographia Britannica*, s.vv. Howe & Calamy ; Allibone s.vv. Owen and Baxter.

[140] Dunton says of his patron : " Mr. Tho. Parkhurst (My Honoured Master) the most eminent Presbyterian Bookseller in the Three Kingdoms . . . He has printed more *Practical* books, than any other that can be named in *London* . . . I have known him sell off a whole Impression before the Book had been almost heard of in London " (*The Life and Errors, etc.*, p. 281).

[141] Here are two titles which sufficiently indicate the Puritan view of the Restoration carnival ! " A just and seasonable reprehension of naked breasts and shoulders " (with a preface by Baxter).—" New instructions unto youth for their behaviour, and also a discourse upon some innovations of habits and dressing ; against powdering of hair, naked breasts, black spots (or patches) and other unseemly customs. 1672." (Quoted by Disraeli, *Anecdotes of Fashion* in *Curiosities of Literature*.)

to prove this : the Court ignored the very name of Bunyan, yet his *Pilgrim's Progress* which appeared in 1678, read by Puritans alone, ran through eight editions in four years, a success unheard of for any fashionable publication of the time.[142]

III

Political Literature under Charles II : Dryden's " Absalom and Achitophel " ; replies of Settle, Buckingham, Pordage, etc.—Dryden's poem " The Medal " ; replies of Hickeringhill, Pordage, Shadwell, etc.—Dryden's Mac Flecknoe.— " Absalom and Achitophel, Part II ", by Nahum Tate and Dryden.— Dryden's " Religio Laici ".—Shadwell and Hunt's replies to Dryden and Lee's " Duke of Guise " ; Dryden's Vindication of " The Duke of Guise " ; Dryden's Translation of Maimbourg's " History of the League "

We now see how the land lay : writers devoted to the Court could not avoid joining in the battle of polemics, but the weapons in their ordinary arsenal were inadequate. Less than ever was the theatre equal to the task ; the newspaper had no appreciable influence. The factors that went to forming public opinion were too many and too complex for the budding Press, still working under restraint, to deal effectively with them all. The newspaper was no less impotent than the theatre to produce those great waves of opinion, those burning expressions of feeling which make a party conscious of its power, which compel opponents to waver, and waverers to think.

Yet something had to be done. The crisis caused by the Popish Plot and by the resurgence of anti-Romanism, was big with menace. Shaftesbury was a doughty champion ; the Duke of Monmouth, whom he had skilfully thrust into the foreground, was winning a disturbing popularity ; the Duke of Buckingham had lent the Whigs the prestige of his powerful name. Unless some means were found to turn the tide, who could foresee how many like deserters [142a] might swell the ranks of the City party,

---

[142] See my Bibliography.

[William Penn might be added to the list of prolific writers who were not members of the Church of England, and whose peculiar position at Court did not save him from imprisonment. In the seventies of the century he produced a spate of pamphlets, some very fat, such as *New Witnesses Prov'd Old Hereticks*, and was copiously answered by dissidents of opposed sects, such as Thomas Hicks, John Faldo, and John Perrot. B. D.]

[142a] [There had always been a group of powerful nobles determined not to be the King's pawns. They were not deserting the Court ; they, and not the King, were to be the Court as far as politics went, and very soon they were. Just as the King made use of French subsidies, so they used the financial power of the City. The Civil War had been fought to counter

how greatly its self-confidence might grow ? Who could prophesy the result of the struggle now begun ?

The King happily recalled that he possessed a Poet Laureate and begged him to come to the rescue.[143] For some time past the King had given Dryden little cause for gratitude. Charles, who now so opportunely bethought him of his poet, had ignored him during the most painful episodes of his struggle with Rochester. Temporarily sickened of the theatre by the Rochester affair, Dryden's thoughts were turning to epic poetry. He had confided this intention to the King and his brother, and had received fair words from them, but no largesse.[144] Perhaps it was at that very moment—whether because of Mulgrave's disgrace or because of an empty treasury—that the payment of his Laureate's salary had ceased.[145] Weary of struggle, he had detached himself from the Court and had written *The Spanish Fryar* against the Roman Catholics : a play highly distasteful to the Duke of York. But however great and well-founded his grievances, Dryden—like all his fellow-authors—was too much the courtier to resist a royal smile, and the King did not need to woo him over-long in order to obtain what he wanted.[146]

Since 1667, when he had addressed his *Annus Mirabilis* to the City of London, Dryden had given up writing poems or verses. The theatre was financially more profitable, and he had devoted himself entirely to the theatre. Now that the theatre was in eclipse and politics took the first place, he gladly took up verse again and with his political poem *Absalom and Achitophel*, he forthwith showed that the Court was well advised to remember him. For while Dryden unhappily pandered too slavishly and too completely to the taste of his time, he had the redeeming merit of carrying to perfection every literary style he attempted. We have seen him take the first place among the authors of

---

the arbitrary power of the King in finance, as much as in religious matters. Charles tried to neutralize the results of the Civil War, which were real enough, though seemingly cancelled by the Restoration. This struggle signalized the emergence of the Whig oligarchy which was to rule England for over a century. B. D.]

[143] See Tonson's Notice for the second part of *Absalom and Achitophel* in *Miscellany Poems*, 1716 ; and Spence, p. 172.

[144] *Discourse concerning. . . Satire*, dedicated to the Earl of Dorset.

[145] See chap. I, note No. 431.

[146] He very quickly recaptured the Duke's favour by amending *The Spanish Fryar* and writing a political Prologue " to His Royal Highness upon his first Appearance at the Duke's Theatre since his Return from Scotland, April 21, 1682 ".

heroic plays, of prologues, and of literary criticism.   Once again he showed that he possessed the rare gift—by no means to be despised—of doing exactly what was wanted exactly when it was wanted, of planting, in fact, " the right thing in the right place at the right time ".   Without models, without precursors, he created the political poem, and at the first attempt produced a masterpiece.

It would have been difficult to strike a note more perfectly in tune with the prevailing mood.   The choice of an allegory was in itself a happy inspiration.   Allegory challenges curiosity by its veil of mystery ;   the puzzled reader tries to lift the veil, every discovery he makes flatters and delights him.   Admiring the author's wit, he is able to admire also his own shrewdness, and the good opinion of himself thus engendered is reflected back on to the work to which he owes it.[147]   But to choose a biblical allegory from the store of allegories available, was a master-stroke.   The very title *Absalom and Achitophel* was a find. To French readers it seems strange.   The name of Absalom awakes in us, it is true, the memory of an unusual form of death, but Achitophel suggests just nothing at all, and we are tempted to exclaim with Boileau :

> Oh, an ignorant poet's ridiculous plan ! [147a]

It is far worse when we begin to read, and come across Barzillai, Ishbosheth, Zimri, Issachar and the Jebusites : these names defeat and frighten us.   But Dryden had good reasons for his choice.   To conduct a political discussion under cover of Old Testament characters, was to fight the Puritans with their own weapons, to command their attention, to compel them to read and to recognize in Absalom their Duke of Monmouth,[148] in his counsellor Achitophel their Shaftesbury, and to wonder what modern persons were concealed behind so many names so familiar to their ears.[148a]

---

[147] See *The Spectator*, No. 512.—" Poems of this *Nature have seldom fail'd of Reception ;   A Veil drawn over the Design in Poetry creates a Curiosity if not a Reverence*." (Preface to *Uzziah and Jotham.   A Poem 1690*.)   See my Bibliography, s.v. Uzziah.

[147a] [*O le plaisant projet d'un poète ignorant !*]

[148] The Duke of Monmouth had already been compared to Absalom in *Absalom's Conspiracy ;   or, The Tragedy of Treason*. London, 1680.   See my Bibliography, s.v. Absalom.

[148a] [It was not, of course, the Puritans alone who would be familiar with the Bible.   Even now, anybody born before 1900 would be familiar enough with the names to find no difficulty in following the allegory.   This

The work was equally well calculated to succeed in the other camp. For one thing, it was acutely pleasing to see the enemy's own arrows fired back at him ; for another, the Court rejoiced in the literary quality of a satire which on so admirable a plane continued the lampoon tradition dear to the courtier's heart. Furthermore, the brevity of the poem allowed it to circulate easily in the Coffee Houses and to scour the provinces in the wake of the Newsletters. The rhymed couplets, well-turned and sonorous, were bound to produce an impression and to linger in the memory, and the biblical subject, while attracting the Puritans, was well calculated to breathe new life and warmth into the sermons of the loyal clergy.[149]

Public opinion, thus catered for, secured for *Absalom and Achitophel* such a welcome as was before unheard of. Johnson's father, who was a bookseller at Lichfield in Staffordshire, told his son that in all his experience he had never known such sales " equalled but by Sacheverell's trial ".[150] This testimony has peculiar importance as showing the provinces entering on the scene and taking part with the Press in a movement of opinion.[151] The poem appeared on November 17, 1681 ; before the end

---

was not, one need hardly say, the first political poem in the language ; even *The Faery Queen* is in some measure a political allegory. Yet the application of Dryden's work was so immediate, the allegory so readily understood, that *Absalom and Achitophel* deserves to be regarded as a literary invention. B. D.]

[149] " Surely a *Politician and a Divine* are scarce Commodities, when we *fly for Refuge to Hakney Poets* and *Hireling Pamphleteers*, with their Juniper-Lectures of *Politicks and Divinity*, to instruct the *Tantivy Clergy*, every Week, against the time that Sunday comes and to Tutor the *Corporations* and *Country Justices*, and Country *Commission-Officers* ! " (Hickeringhill, Post-Script to *The Mushroom*).—Malone (*The Prose Works of John Dryden*, II, p. 293) quotes two sermons inspired by Dryden's poem. The allegory set a general fashion ; see Walter Scott's Preface to *Absalom and Achitophel*. In the Roxburghe Collection (vol. III, p. 916) I have found " Good News in Bad Times : or *Absaloms* Return to *David's Bosome*, 1683 ".

[150] Johnson, *Lives of the English Poets*, Dryden.

[151] The success of the poem in the provinces is confirmed by the following quotation : " What sport it is to see an *old Country Justice* (with his *eager* Chaplain at his Elbow) putting his *Barnacles on his nose* (Bless us !) *How he gapes* and admires when he reads *Nat. Thompson*, the Addresses in the *Gazette, Abhorrences, Heraclitus* or the *Observator*? But, shew him but—*Absalom and Achitophel*—oh—then the *man's horn mad*, there's no holding him, then he *Hunts up* (and though in his *Dining-Room*) how he spends *with double mouth*, and whoops and hallows (just *as he hunts his Doggs* when at *full Cry*) That—That—That—That *Rattle—Towzer—Bull-Dog—Thunder*—That—That—whilst the little Trencher-Chaplain *Ecchoes* to him and crys—*Amen*—" (Hickeringhill, Post-Script to *The Mushroom*.)

of December a second edition was called for.[152] Two further editions appeared in 1682.

The reason was, not only that the author had had the skill to take up a favourable theme, but that the poem itself was amazingly well executed. In satire Dryden was on his own home ground. No one can argue better in verse than he, and this time he had a double source of inspiration : the first, the wish to please his King ; the second, the personal pleasure of being on active service against his old enemy Buckingham, on whom he had so far been unable to take vengeance. So he had the satisfaction of serving his own private ends at the same time as the King's, and he made the author of *The Rehearsal* pay dearly for ten years of enforced resentful silence, by painting Buckingham in the immortal character of Zimri :

> In the first rank of these did Zimri stand,
> A man so various that he seemed to be
> Not one, but all Mankind's epitome :
> Stiff in opinions, always in the wrong,
> Was everything by starts and nothing long ;
> But in the course of one revolving moon
> Was chymist, fiddler, statesman and buffoon ;
> Then all for women, painting, rhyming, drinking,
> Beside ten thousand freaks that died in thinking.
> Blest madman, who could every hour employ
> With something new to wish or to enjoy !
> Railing and praising were his usual themes,
> And both, to show his judgment, in extremes :
> So over violent or over civil
> That every man with him was God or Devil.
> In squandering wealth was his peculiar art ;
> Nothing went unrewarded but desert.
> Beggared by fools whom he still found too late,
> He had his jest, and they had his estate.
> He laughed himself from Court ; then sought relief
> By forming parties, but could ne'er be chief :
> For spite of him, the weight of business fell
> On Absalom and wise Achitophel ;
> Thus wicked but in will, of means bereft,
> He left not faction, but of that was left.[153]

---

[152] This second edition appeared with four sets of verses, one of them by Nahum Tate in praise of Dryden.

[153] Dryden probably borrowed the name Zimri (or Zambri) from the 25th chapter of Numbers where Zimri " a Prince of the chief house among the Simeonites ", was slain in adultery with the " daughter of a Prince of Midian ". He wished no doubt to recall Buckingham's liaison with the Countess of Shrewsbury.

[It is much more likely that Dryden took the name Zimri from I Kings 16, where Zimri " conspired against (Tirzah, his king) . . . and

The whole poem has remained one of the most valued show-pieces of English literature. The portraits are remarkable both for sureness of line and richness of colouring. The argument is lively and skilful, and produced on contemporary polemics an effect such as no piece of political writing had produced before.

The wrath of the Whigs was proof that Dryden had scored a bull's eye. Replies spurted out from every quarter. Settle, who had recently become a vassal of the City, took up again the pen that had written *The Empress of Morocco* to pit himself once more against Dryden by writing a poem too. He called it *Absalom Senior: Or Achitophel Transpros'd*.[154] Buckingham published some poor *Poetical Reflections*[154a] on the work which had treated him so unkindly. At the same time a wretched dramatist called Samuel Pordage[155] brought out *Azaria and Hushai* (i.e. Monmouth and Shaftesbury) ; Henry Care, editor of an anti-Catholic paper, *A Packet of Advice from Rome*, produced *Towser the Second* and a Nonconformist minister two replies : *A Whip for the Fools Back*, who styles *Honorable Marriage a Curs'd Confinement in his profane Poem of Absalom and Achitophel* and *A Key (With the Whip) To open the Mystery and Iniquity of the Poem call'd Absalom and Achitophel*.[156]

---

smote him and killed him ". Everyone would be familiar with the still well-known query " Had Zimri peace who slew his master ? " in II Kings ix, 31. The main story, of course, comes from II Samuel xv seq. B. D.]

[154] Spence, p. 67, says that Settle was assisted by Matthew Clifford, Sprat and several of the best writers of the day. No one would think it. This is how Settle repaints Zimri's portrait as a likeness of Dryden :

> " Besides, lewd Fame had told his plighted Vow
> To *Laura's* cooing Love percht on a dropping Bough ;
> *Laura* in faithful Constancy confin'd
> To *Ethiops* Envoy, and to all Mankind.
> Laura, though Rotten, yet of Mold Divine,
> He had all her Cl—ps, and She had all his Coine.
> Her Wit so far his Purse and Sense could drain,
> Till every P—x was sweetn'd to a Strain.
> And if at last his Nature can reform,
> A weary grown of Loves tumultuous storm,
> 'Tis Age's Fault, not His ; of pow'r bereft,
> He left not Whoring, but of that was left."

[154a] [Wood says he is sure that Buckingham either " wrote, or caus'd to be wrote " the *Poetical Reflections*. These are, as Beljame says, very poor stuff, and are almost certainly not by Buckingham. Thorn-Drury ascribed them to Ned Howard. See *Review of English Studies*, Jan. 1925. B. D.]

[155] See Genest, I, 171 and 213.

[156] See my Bibliography, s.vv. Whip and Key.

The extraordinary success of *Absalom and Achitophel* proved beyond a shadow of doubt that Dryden had hit the nail on the head and that no one could do better than follow his example. It also brought home to Court and King the great advantage of alliance with an author.   When, before long, a second occasion arose for appealing to Dryden, Charles II's eagerness betrayed that he now attached quite a new value to his Laureate's goodwill.

It will be remembered that Shaftesbury, who had been accused of treason and committed to the Tower, was acquitted by the Grand Jury.   Intoxicated by this victory, his adherents kept up for an hour their shouts of triumph, lit bonfires of rejoicing, and finally to commemorate the happy event struck a medal with the inscription *Lætamur* which they ostentatiously displayed.[157] It was an ugly shock to the Court.   They must deal an immediate counterstroke to minimize the ill effects.   Who could do this better than Dryden?   So the King's affection for his Poet Laureate was suddenly redoubled, and seeing him in the Mall one day, he drew him aside and said to him in friendly wise : " Mr. Dryden, if I were a poet, and I believe I am poor enough to be one, I should write a poem on such a subject in the following manner." [158]   Dryden was not slow to take the hint.   *The Medal, a Satire against Sedition*, appeared anonymously in March 1682 with this motto :

> Per Graium populos, mediæque per Elidis urbem
> Ibat ovans ; Divumque sibi poscebat honores.

This satire produced immense effect, and the anger of the Whigs again vented itself in numerous replies.   Hickeringhill, the enlightened pamphleteering preacher who had sent the verses of his *Mushroom* [159] to the printer the very day that Dryden's

---

[157] See Christie's *Life of Anthony Ashley Cooper*, II, pp. 427 ff.   Mr. Christie has reproduced this medal on the cover of his book.—See also Cooke, I, pp. 208 ff.

[158] Spence, p. 171.

[159] " God grant that this *Mushroom* be not like Jonas (his) Goard, *that sprung up in a night* and perished *in a night*.   *Mushrooms* though they spring up in a night, yet (*well drest and Cook'd*) are served up, for *Daintyes*, and last *long*, not withstanding their *hasty Birth*, like this, far from the Authors Library, his *Notes*, and his *Books*.   And if any man *think or say* that it is a Wonder, if this Book and Verses were compos'd and writ in *One Day*, and sent to the Press, since it would employ the *Pen of a ready Writer*, or nimble Scrivener, *to Coppy* this Book *in a Day* (it may be so).   But *it is a Truth as certain* and stable as *the Sun* in the Firmament, and which (*if need be*) the Bookseller, Printer and other *Worthy Citizens*, that are privy to it, can *Avouch*, for an *Infallible* Truth.—*Deo soli Gloria*." (Post-Script to *The Mushroom*.)—See also the full title in my Bibliography.

Medal appeared, attributed this important poetic coincidence to divine inspiration. Samuel Pordage launched *The Medal Revers'd a Satyre against Persecution* : while Shadwell contributed *The Medal of John Bayes : a Satyr against Folly and Knavery* and *The Tory Poets a Satyr*. There were further two poems whose authors have remained unknown : *The Loyal Medal Vindicated*[160] and *Dryden's Satyr to his Muse*.[161] Finally, to all these retorts we must add one which was assuredly the wittiest and happiest of all : a reprint of the verses which Dryden had written in other days in praise of Cromwell.[162]

In writing *The Medal* the poet had worked for the King only. He now felt moved to work a little for himself, while continuing to serve the royal cause. He had squared his long-standing account with Buckingham, but there were still two fellow-authors in the Whig camp whose attacks had been peculiarly galling : his old rival Settle—and Shadwell.

In earlier days Shadwell had been one of Dryden's old friends ; the reader will remember that the two had collaborated (with Crowne also) to write *Notes and Observations* on the *Empress of Morocco* ; again in 1679 Dryden wrote the Prologue for Shadwell's comedy, *A True Widow*. But politics had come between them and, as is so often the case, the old friend had become the most violent of enemies. In *The Medal of John Bayes* Shadwell made the most odious accusations against Dryden in the most outrageous language.[163] Dryden could not leave all these attacks unanswered ; and since, amongst all his enemies, Shadwell was not merely the ablest but the only one of any ability at all, he concentrated on him—reserving Settle for a later occasion—and published *Mac Flecknoe*,[164] *or a Satyr upon the true-blew-protestant poet T. S.* (namely Thomas Shadwell). It is a delightful specimen of literary banter which Pope had still in mind when he wrote *The Dunciad*, and it proved a blow to Shadwell from which his reputation has never recovered.[165]

[160] See my Bibliography, s.v. Medal.

[161] Attributed to Somers.

[162] " Three Poems upon the Death of the Late Usurper Oliver Cromwell : " and also " A Panegyrick On the Author of Absolom [*sic*] and Achitophel." See my Bibliography, s.vv. Dryden and *Panegyrick*.

[163] I have not the nerve to quote them, even in a foreign tongue.

[164] That is to say, the son of Flecknoe, the poet already mentioned on pp. 78 and 119. Flecknoe appears to have been the butt of his fellows, for Marvell, III, p. 280, like Dryden, makes him a laughing-stock.

[165] Let me hasten to say that it was most unjust, for Shadwell's work was very much better than Dryden allows.

This successful elimination of a dangerous opponent gave the Court a taste for blood, and Dryden—who up to now had practically confined his attacks to the chiefs of the popular party, Shaftesbury, Monmouth and Buckingham—was urged to administer a little castigation to the mongrel curs who barked to order at their leaders' heels, by writing a further series of Absalom and Achitophel portraits.[166]

But so many repeated efforts had wearied the Laureate ; he called in his friend Nahum Tate who had just demonstrated his Tory zeal by writing verses in praise of Dryden's political poems. As soon as they had together laid down the general lines to be followed, Tate got to work to maltreat as best he could the infinitely minor lights of the Whig party ; most of them to-day forgotten. He wound up with a pretentious eulogy of the friends of the Court, more especially Dryden and L'Estrange.[167]   Dryden reserved for himself only the opposition writers like Pordage, whom he pictured under the name of Mephibosheth, and above all his dear enemies Settle and Shadwell—Doeg and Og—at whom he lashed out vigorously. Shadwell, the only one to attempt a retort, prefixed a bitter Preface against Dryden to a translation of the tenth Satire of Juvenal.

In the same year Dryden, the versatile, brought out a poem of less combative and calmer tone, *Religio Laici, or a Layman's Faith*, in which he upholds the Church of England and seeks to gather both Romanist and Dissenter once more into her arms.

Poems and literary polemics soon superseded theatre and newspaper. This is not to imply that newspapers or theatre held their peace and ceased to function ; the dates quoted above sufficiently prove that they did not, and passions ran too high for any means to be neglected. But the theatre dropped back into the second place in public regard, and the newspaper, try as it might, shared at best this second place. The type of writing of which Dryden was the pioneer exercised the sole serious influence. So much was this the case that the play which at this time made the most lively impression on the public mind, *The Duke of Guise* by Dryden and Lee, was impressive not by reason of its own merit, but because of the controversy it evoked. Shadwell brought out *Some Reflections upon the Pretended Parallel in the Play Called The Duke of Guise* and probably also a Prologue

---

[166] The Second Part of *Absalom and Achitophel*.

[167] See above, chap. II, note No. 117. Dryden appears in the poem as Asaph.

claiming to have been "refused by the actors". A lawyer called Thomas Hunt produced *A Defence of the Charter and Municipal Rights of the City of London*. Dryden replied to both by a long *Vindication* (of sixty pages) of his play, and the excitement roused by this battle of words was so great that Hunt, threatened with prosecution, was compelled to take refuge in Holland,[168] and Shadwell in the Dedication of his play *Bury-Fair* maintains that his life was in danger and that for several years he was obliged to give up writing.[169]

Such an expenditure of effort did not fail to bear fruit. Dryden was the first to flutter and halt the Whigs in their triumph, and to revive the flagging courage of the Tories. Hearing his voice, all friends of the Court, foremost among them the clergy, felt their zeal redoubled and gained renewed strength from confidence. Little by little the Whigs lost ground and showed themselves less daring and less self-assured. The discovery of the Rye-House Plot (1683) dealt them a final blow. This Whig conspiracy inspired a horror—skilfully exploited by the Royal party—which immediately hurled back into the Tory camp the numerous proselytes who had flung themselves into the opposition ranks in terror of the Popish Plot. The popular party ceased to be popular. Shaftesbury had already fled and died in Holland (1682).[170] The Rye-House Plot provided a convenient opportunity, which was not missed, for eliminating two other leaders of the Whigs : Lord Russell and Algernon Sidney were executed. The King became once more undisputed master of the situation. Nevertheless Charles felt that there was more to do and the

---

[168] *Biographia Britannica*, s.v. Shadwell and à Wood, *Athenæ Oxonienses*, IV, columns 81 ff.

[169] "I could never recant in the Worst of Times, when my Ruine was design'd, and my Life was sought, and for near Ten Years I was kept from the exercise of that Profession which had afforded me a competent Subsistence." (Dedication of *Bury-Fair* to the Earl of Dorset.)

> "Our *Author*, then opprest, would have you know it
> Was Silenc'd for a *Non-conformist* Poet . . ."
>   (Prologue to the same.)

Shadwell did not begin to write again for the theatre till 1688, the year in which he produced *The Squire of Alsatia*. His last preceding play had been *The Lancashire Witches* in 1681.

[170] " . . . The king's influence increasing every day both in London and the country. A loyal lord mayor was this day chosen for the city of London, and two very good sheriffs. My Lord Shaftesbury stole oversea into Holland, and the charter of London was likely to stoop to the *quo warranto* brought against it." (Reresby, p. 263, Nov. 20, 1682.)

writers' work was not yet done. He bade Dryden translate *The History of the League* by the Jesuit Maimbourg. Obviously the aim of bringing out this translation at this particular moment was to increase the unpopularity of the Whigs by comparing them to the French Leaguers who, clothing themselves in a garment of noble religious zeal, attacked the royal power and plunged their country into a long and bloody civil war. It was, in short, a repetition of the tragedy of the *Duke of Guise*, and the Dedication was designed to make its purpose clear even to purblind eyes. This new work of Dryden's was published with particular care, and this time the title-page bore his name and openly proclaimed that it was written at the King's command.[171]

IV

Political Literature under James II : Sprat's Account of the " Horrid Conspiracy against the Late King " (Rye-House Plot).—Dryden and Stilling-fleet discuss religion.—The Anglican Clergy join in polemics against the King.—" The Hind and the Panther " by Dryden.—Montague and Prior's " The Country Mouse and the City Mouse ".—Overthrow of James II

This was destined to be literature's last service to Charles II. In the following year, while Dryden under the royal supervision was working on his opera *Albion and Albanius* to celebrate the King's victory over the Whigs, the Merry Monarch died, leaving his throne to the man who had been the cause of all the heated political feeling of his last years.

The period of hope and calm which normally follows the accession of a new king was this time of short duration. With the accession of James II political passions speedily rekindled. The poets had scarcely time to pay the customary mourning tributes to the deceased monarch, and hail the elevation of his successor,[172] before polemics were again raging more fiercely than ever.

---

[171] Preceding the text was an engraving representing the King on his throne ; the heaven opened slightly to reveal a hand holding a crown. A ray of light from the crown illumined the King's head and in it was written : *Per me reges regnant*. Round the throne stood Justice and nobles with a magistrate in the foreground at whose feet were inscribed the words : *Sibi et successoribus suis legitimis*.

[172] Dryden, *Threnodia Augustalis* ; apotheosis of James II at the end of *Albion and Albanius* ; D'Urfey, *Joy to Great Cæsar* ; *An Elegy upon . . . King Charles II*, and two panegyricks upon . . . *King James and Queen Mary* . . . ; Charles Montague, *On the Death of His Most Sacred Majesty Charles II.* Montague's verses figure in a collection of poems on the death of Charles II

Blinded by zeal, James II seemed in haste to fan the flames of political passion, by ordering Sprat, the newly appointed Bishop of Rochester, and one of the authors of *The Rehearsal*, to compose a narrative of the Rye-House Plot; the fire of religious passion, by asserting that his brother had died a Roman Catholic, and by publishing two documents—said to have been found in Charles II's safe—which maintained the superiority of the Roman to the Protestant Church.[173]

Stillingfleet, Dean of St. Paul's, promptly replied to this letter.[174] Though his name did not appear on the title-page of his *Answer*, the fact that a distinguished member of the English Church should intervene in opposition to the King deserves attention, for it indicated that under James II discussion was from the start to assume a wholly different complexion from discussion under Charles, and in particular that the clergy were to play a different part.

Up to this point the clergy, passionately devoted to the doctrine of passive obedience, had unanimously supported the King. Whatever doubts might privately be entertained about his personal religious convictions, Charles II throughout his reign remained a Protestant, and the head of the Protestant

---

published by the University of Cambridge (*Biographia Britannica*, s.v. Montague) —Here is a specimen of D'Urfey's enthusiasm :

The Kings Health, *set to* Farinel's *Grounds.*

First Strain.

Joy to Great *Caesar*,
Long Life, Love and Pleasure ;
'Tis a Health that Divine is,
Fill the Bowl high as mine is . . .

Second Strain.

Try all the Loyal
   Defy all
   Give Denial ;
Sure none thinks Glass too big here,
Nor any *Prig* here,
Or sneaking *Whig* here
Of Cripple *Tony's* Crew
That now looks blew.
His Heart akes too
The *Tap* won't do . . .
   (*A Collection of One Hundred and Eighty Loyal Songs.*)

See my Bibliography, s.v. Thompson, N.)

[173] See my Bibliography, s.v. James II.
[174] See my Bibliography, s.v. Stillingfleet.

religion in England. The clergy's interest and the royal interest were therefore one. The situation was now radically altered. James II had not only divorced himself from the Church of England but had clearly shown his determination to smash it. The Anglican clergy correspondingly changed their point of view.

So long as persecution and oppression had hit none but Roman Catholics and Dissenters, they had with one voice maintained that God's law forbade resistance. But as soon as the blast of persecution veered in their direction, as soon as their own interests were threatened, they changed their attitude, if not their manner of speech, and made a duty of vigorously challenging the King's pretensions.[175]

This change of clerical allegiance was serious, for it robbed the King of a very loyal and very influential ally ; it was all the more serious because the point at issue had become almost entirely a religious question, and here the clergy were manifestly in strength on their own ground. The consequences were soon seen in the sequel to this first controversy.

It was no light matter to reply to so authoritative a writer as the Dean of St. Paul's. Fortunately, in throwing in his lot with James II, Dryden had become a convert to Roman Catholicism. At the King's request he undertook to answer Stillingfleet. He set to work with heat—with too much heat, for he went so far as to accuse the Dean of disloyalty and " foul dealing " [176]—and devoted all the resources of his skill to the cause of his new religion. But a theologian is not made in a moment. It was not enough to be the best writer of his age, Dryden was no match in battle for a consummate controversialist who had made a life-study of religious questions. Stillingfleet vigorously retorted and easily won the day.

For the writers of the Court, the day of brilliant reply and easy victory was over. They no longer had to contend only with fellow writers, that is to say with their equals, or with political fanatics turned author, whose prose and verse were

---

[175] Amongst the Church of England clergy who at one point had unanimously preached passive obedience, there were not more than 400 who refused allegiance to the revolutionary government of William III. (Macaulay, *Essay on Hallam.*)

[176] " . . . I hope I shall discover the foul Dealing of this Author, who has obscur'd, as much as he is able, the Native Lustre of those Papers, and recommended by a false Light his own sophisticated Ware ; part of which may certainly deserve the clearest Light which can be given it by the Hands of the Under-Sheriff, or of somebody, whom I will not name." (*A Defence of the Papers Written by the Late King of Blessed Memory : Preface.*)

little to be feared. Though but a few years had passed, the blissful days were far distant when Dryden, almost single-handed, had kept at bay the Shadwells and Settles, not to mention the Pordages, Hunts and Hickeringhills. The Court writers of old went into battle on familiar ground, wielding well-tried weapons against a foe with whom they were wont to fight. Now, the terrain was new, and not only were they the novices in this type of warfare, but they were face to face with adversaries weighty by the authority alike of their speech and of their position.

In the wake of Stillingfleet we find the most distinguished ecclesiastics joining the fray, some of whom have left their mark in literature apart from their religious learning, men like Tillotson, Prideaux, Burnet, Atterbury.[177] It was in fact the clergy who now seized the initiative and became masters of the argument. While from one end of England to the other every Church of England clergyman passionately preached in protest against James II's religious leanings, the eminent men whose names I have just quoted, took the cue from Dryden and with unwearied vigour—adopting in their varied writings [178] every tone and style in turn, to appeal now to the people, now to society, now to the learned—they expounded, argued, and studied from every angle, the comparative merits of the Roman Catholic and Protestant religions.[179] Here was a formidable army arrayed against the King, attacking every day, every moment, and from every point of the compass at the same time.

Much as he might have wished, it was impossible for him to silence such a multitude of redoubtable opponents. He could do nothing through the Courts, for he would have had to prosecute every clergyman of the National Church ; he was equally powerless to do anything against their publications, for though in the very first year of his reign, he had re-established a Press Censorship,[180] the Act contained a clause exempting the two Universities of Oxford and Cambridge, and authorizing the printing of theological works approved by either the Bishop

---

[177] Dryden himself said he had learned to write prose by reading Tillotson. (Congreve, Dedication to Dryden's *Dramatick Works*, 1717.)

[178] Macaulay, *History*, chap. VI, says : "Those which may still be found in our great libraries make up a mass of near 20,000 pages. This I can attest from my own researches. There is an excellent collection in the British Museum."

[179] Neal, IV, chap. XI ; Stoughton, vol. II, pp. 117 ff.

[180] Keble, I, p. 1511.

of London or the Archbishop of Canterbury.[181] Now the two Universities were playing a very active part in the fight against Roman Catholicism, and both Compton, Bishop of London, and Sancroft, Archbishop of Canterbury, were far from approving of the King's beliefs.

There was one course only open to James II : to meet argument with argument. To this end he set his machinery in motion. He had his own printing presses in London and Oxford and even at Holyrood in Scotland, and from them he bombarded the whole country with printed matter.

But the writers at his disposal were not of the right calibre to stand up against the Protestant clergy ; they were second-rate Roman Catholic priests, not one of whom won distinction in this war of words. Even if they had had more ability, they could not have turned it to full account owing to their imperfect knowledge of English.

For many years the English climate had been inhospitable to Roman Catholics, and the more devout Romanists in England had sent their children to be educated abroad, either at Rome or Douai. When large numbers of these expatriates returned to England on the accession of James II, they came home knowing Italian or French much better than their mother tongue. One of them, Andrew Pulton, was even driven to request Dr. Tenison to write in Greek or Latin, so that the controversial battle between them might be waged on equal terms.[182] Yet another, one William Clenche, writing an English tract on *St. Peter's Supremacy*, reverted in haste to Italian to write his Dedication to the Queen, thus from the first deterring his readers by many pages in a language they could not understand.[183]

Such allies were willing and eager enough no doubt, but of little value. The only serious reading-matter which the King

---

[181] See paragraph III of the Act, already alluded to, chap. I, note 402, in Keble II, 1250 ff.

> "But *Imprimatur*, with a Chaplain's name,
> Is here sufficient licence to defame."
> (Dryden, *The Hind and the Panther*, part III, 11, 256/7.)

[182] "A. P. having been eighteen years out of his Country, pretends not yet to any Perfection of the *English* expression or Orthography, Wherefore for the future he will crave the favour of treating with the Dr. in *Latine* or *Greek*, since the Dr. finds fault with his *English*. (Notice printed on the reverse of the title page of *A True and Full Account of a Conference*, etc.)

[183] See Macaulay, *History*, chap. VI, where samples of their English style are given.—William Clenche's Dedication : "Alla Serenissima Principessa Maria d'Este Reina d'Inghilterra" is twelve pages long.

could offer to confound the Protestants, was some translations of Bossuet [184]—which would have been more effective if they had not been so miserably translated—and Dryden.

Dryden had not emerged too happily from his recent controversy with Stillingfleet. He hoped to recapture his usual success with a return to verse. He fled the noise of London to find a country retreat favourable to study, and there—slowly, painstakingly, with mature thought—he composed his allegoric poem, *The Hind and the Panther*. The unspotted, milk-white Hind is the Church of Rome, contrasted with the mottled Panther, the Church of England. Around these two animals in the same forest, Dryden groups the Independent Bear, the Anabaptist Boar, the Presbyterian Wolf, the Quaking Hare and the Socinian Fox. All the Protestant sects are thus metaphorically reviewed while the Freethinkers are represented by the Ape. Though this poem suffers from a grave fault which Dryden's opponents were not slow to detect, it nevertheless contains some of the most eloquent and powerful passages he ever wrote. The King himself had it printed at his own Holyrood Press and took pains to circulate it through the whole of England. Thanks to such fostering, *The Hind and the Panther* quickly ran into three, if not four editions. Despite all this, however, Dryden failed to recapture the success of earlier days.

No degree of talent, not even of genius itself—for *Absalom and Achitophel* had earned its author the right to this word—can win a struggle against the convictions of a nation. The further things went, the less was England inclined to accept the views of which Dryden had made himself the champion.

How far he had forfeited his early dominion over public opinion is well shown by the fact that a simple reply by two amateurs sufficed to destroy the whole effect of the famous veteran's poem.[185] The two authors of *The Country Mouse and the City Mouse*, Charles Montague and Matthew Prior, collaborated to produce this retort, and though both possessed wit and

---

[184] See my Bibliography, s.v. Bossuet. It is believed that Dryden undertook to translate Bossuet's *Exposition de la Doctrine de l'Église catholique*. He had also been commanded by the King to translate Varillas's *Histoire des révolutions en matière de religion;* this translation was never published. (Malone, *Life of Dryden*, p. 194.)

[185] There were other replies too : *Reflections upon the Hind and the Panther* by Tom Brown ; *The Laureat* ; *A Poem in Defence of the Church of England* ; *The Revolter. A Trage-Comedy Acted between the Hind and the Panther and Religio Laici.* See my Bibliography, s.vv. Brown (Thomas), *Laureat, Poem* and *Revolter*.

talent, their work looks paltry enough in comparison with the fine verse of Dryden. Their sole merit lies in having detected and revealed the error of design which mars *The Hind and the Panther*. Dryden makes the two animals converse together ; now, since each represents a Church, what can they talk about save religion ? Here we see to what strange incongruities the allegory leads. The Hind is afraid to go to the common stream to drink, for fear of being attacked by the beasts of the forest. A moment after, she speaks of Jesus Christ as her Saviour, and attempts to convert the Panther by arguments about the Real Presence, the authority of the Popes, the Test Act, the Popish Plot, Stillingfleet's writings and Burnet's conjugal prowess. The Panther who in friendly wise ranges the forest with the Hind, carries a crozier and wears a mitre on her head. Montague and Prior had no difficulty in showing how incongruous and laughable it all was, and having made merry over the form of the poem, they stayed their hand and refrained from discussing the basic problems raised. What good would it have done anyhow ? Public opinion had crystallized ; no one needed to be convinced. Those who enjoyed a laugh needed no further inducement to join their side.[186] The applause which hailed their literary banter was so great that Dryden, cut to the quick, bitterly complained : " for two young fellows that I have always been very civil to, to use an old man in so cruel a manner ! "[187] and *The Country Mouse and the City Mouse* laid the foundations of Montague and Prior's political fortunes.

From this point onwards it was clear that James II was

[186]   " But to conclude, blush with a lasting Red,
     (If thou'rt not mov'd with what's already said)
     To see thy Boars, Bears, Buzards, Wolves and Owls,
     And all thy other Beasts, and other Fowl's,
     Routed by two poor Mice : (Unequal fight)
     But easie 'tis to Conquer in the Right."

(*The Laureat.*)

" If you have not yet Mr. Dreydens celebrated poem of the Hinde and Panther wth the no less admired answer to it call'd the Poem of the Panther and Hind transprosed done by a young gentleman Mr. Montagu I will send them both to you."

(Manuscript letter of July 19, 1687 ; British Museum, Additional : 28,569, p. 65 reverse.)

[187] " Dryden was most touched with ' The Hind and the Panther Transversed '. I have heard him say : ' for two young fellows, that I have always been very civil to ; to use an old man in so cruel a manner ! '— And he wept as he said it." (Spence, p. 61.)

striding towards his fall with seven-league boots, and that nothing could prevent the collapse of his tottering throne.[188] The war of words continued with the same result to the end : whatever was written in the King's favour missed its mark, whatever was written against him was read throughout England with delight. When James II endeavoured to win over the Puritans by his first Declaration of Indulgence in 1687, a broadside called *Letter to a Dissenter*, which was attributed to Sir William Temple or alternatively to the Marquis of Halifax,[189] warned the country of the King's true intentions and deeply stirred public opinion. Twenty-four replies appeared in the King's interest, one of them by L'Estrange,[190] but did not succeed in weakening the *Letter's* effect.

The King had no grip on the minds of his subjects ; he was powerless to stay the current that was sweeping him away. Clandestine publications followed hard on each other without his being able to stop them. He could not discover the author of the *Letter to a Dissenter*. Similarly in 1688 when he issued his second Declaration of Indulgence and seven bishops presented a famous petition against its being read in the churches, this petition was printed—no one has discovered how—that very evening, cried in the streets, and bought up with extraordinary avidity,[191] despite anything that could be done to suppress it.

Yet so infatuated was the King, that he was unaware how close he was to the abyss. The authors supporting his cause shared his blind confidence. When a son [192] was born to him

---

[188] See Reresby, from Feb. 10, 1685, to Dec. 28, 1688.

[189] Macaulay (*History*, chap. VII) has no hesitation in deciding on Halifax.—George Savile, Marquis of Halifax, must not be confused with Charles Montague, just mentioned, whom we shall soon see appearing as Baron Halifax and later Earl of Halifax.—*The Letter to a Dissenter* is printed in Walter Scott's *Collection of Scarce and Valuable Tracts*, vol. IX.

[This brilliant work, which Temple could not have accomplished, is now universally conceded to be by Halifax, and is to be found in any edition of his works, e.g. Miss Foxwell's or Sir W. Raleigh's. B. D.]

[190] See my Bibliography, s.v. L'Estrange.

[191] " It was said that the printer cleared a thousand pounds in a few hours by this penny broadside. This is probably an exaggeration but an exaggeration which proves that the sale was enormous." (Macaulay, *History*, chap. VIII.)

[192] The Queen's pregnancy, in which England refused to believe, was the subject of innumerable pamphlets. See in *Poems on Affairs of State*, II, p. 184 : " The Miracle ; how the *Dutchess of Modena (being in Heaven)* prayed the *B. Virgin* that the Queen might have a Son, and how our Lady sent the Angel *Gabriel* with her Smock ; upon which the Queen was with *Child* " ; idem, III, p. 267 : " An excellent new Song, call'd, *The Prince of Darkness* :

on June 10, 1688—the son and heir so long desired—Dryden triumphantly exclaimed : "Britannia Rediviva ! " [193] Five months later, the man who was soon to be William III landed on the English coast and James II took flight while his subjects sang their heads off with Lillibulero. [194]

V

Conclusion : Authors' services are better appreciated.—The City as counter-weight to the Court.—Reciprocal influence of City and Court.—Political com-petes successfully with frivolous literature.—Jacob Tonson, the first English publisher, tries his strength.—Profits from the theatre increase.   This gives promise for the future ; meantime the spiritual and material lot of authors does not improve.—They are " courtiers " in politics as in literature.—Their political changes of front.—Wycherley, Haines and Dryden converted to Roman Catholicism.—Violence of their political passion

The eight years whose stormy history we have been considering and which were so important from the political point of view, were not without some happy turns of fortune for literary men. Let us first note that a shade more importance was being accorded to them, and a shade more consideration shown. When people realized that the author was capable of being something more

---

Showing how three Kingdoms may be set on fire by a *Warming-Pan* " ;— Stephens, Catalogue I, Nos. 1156/7 : " The Warming-Pan, Portraits of the Pretenders, etc."—The story was that another woman's new-born infant was smuggled into the Queen in a warming-pan.

[193] *Britannia Rediviva.*   Mrs. Behn congratulated " Her Most Sacred Majesty on the Universal Hopes of all Loyal Persons for a Prince of Wales." See my Bibliography.

[194] " A foolish ballad was made at that time, treating the Papists, and chiefly the *Irish,* in a very ridiculous manner, which had a burden said to be *Irish* words, *lero lero lilibulero,* that made an impression on the Army, that cannot well be imagined by those that saw it not. The whole Army, and at last all the people both in city and country, were singing it perpetually. And perhaps never had so slight a thing so great an effect." (Burnet, *History* . . . , III, p. 319.)   See also Macaulay, *History,* chap. IX. This song can be found on p. 9 of *A collection of the Newest and Most Ingenious Songs . . . against Popery.* See my Bibliography, s.v. *Collection.*—In a rhymed broadside of 1688 called *An Epistle to Mr. Dryden* (see my Bibliography, s.v. *Epistle*) I note this couplet :

" Dryden, thy wit has caterwauld too long,
    Now *Lero, Lero,* is the only Song . . . "

[Lord Wharton was said to have been the author of this famous song, set to music by Purcell as A New Irish Tune, which is now well known, and has found favour as a regimental march. Wharton boasted that he had " sung a king out of three kingdoms ", but at least as much credit must be given to Purcell's catching lilt, to whistle which was always Uncle Toby's retort to any statements he felt smacked of Toryism or Popery. B. D.]

than an amusement-monger, and that his work might on occasion serve a more useful purpose than pleasantly killing time, they no longer always waited for him to make advances, but began to approach him on their own behalf. The Court laid claim to the services of L'Estrange and Sprat. Charles II personally intervened with Dryden and tried on him the effect of that seductive voice hitherto chiefly used for wooing his mistresses. James II commissioned writings from several writers and printed them himself. Authors were little accustomed to such attentions. They were beginning to be valued. This is the first sign of the changing times.

Another fact carries weight and in part explains the former : The Court was no longer everything. The City had come again into its own, it had its politics, its coffee houses and its newspapers, and for it Whig authors wrote poems and plays. The citizens were not content with this, they coveted authors of their very own. They were wont every year to burn the Pope in effigy ; in 1680 they engaged Settle to preside over this ceremony which they wished to make a particularly brilliant one.[195] They aimed even higher ; they made Dryden offers of money to come over to their side.[196]

The number of readers increased with the resurgence of the City : the closed and narrow circle of the Court opened, to make way for the middle classes who had too long remained aloof but were at last bent on making their existence felt. Up to now there had been, in fact, two groups of readers of radically different tastes, separated from each other and without mutual intercourse, one of which seemed almost non-existent. While the Court, like a noisy and frothy torrent, filled eye and ear with the boisterous fret of its tumultuous waters, the Puritan river, unseen, unheard, pursued unobserved its clear and tranquil course. The two were now united into a single stream and flowed together between wider shores.

Henceforward we can say that the Court no longer has a monopoly of reading ; we may even add that after *Absalom and Achitophel* reading was no longer confined to London.[197]

It was not only the number but also the calibre of readers

---

[195] Nichols, *Literary Anecdotes*, I, 41 ; note ; Disraeli, *Quarrels of Authors*, Pope's Earliest Satire.

[196] See his letter to the First Lord of the Treasury quoted below, p. 196.

[197] The impetus once given, it did not die down. The *Letter to a Dissenter* was circulated through the post to the tune of 20,000 copies. (Macaulay, *History*, chap. VII.)

which rose. Each of the two components of the enlightened public contributed its qualities and made them felt. Amidst all its frivolity and corruption, we must recognize that the Court had the merit of taste and a desire for refinement, thanks to which English polemics, by care for literary form, acquired a polish and seemliness which had hitherto been almost completely lacking.

Consider the famous wranglings of Milton and Salmasius [198] ; without even going back so far, recall the quarrels—wholly literary though they were—between Dryden and Settle. Each of the champions was bent simply on defeating the other, without overmuch concern for the methods by which victory was won. They overwhelmed each other with violent insults and thundering words ; they fought with bludgeons. The infuriated assailant launched savage blows that made his victim's body quiver ; his antagonist without flinching repaid them with equal weight and vigour. The onlookers applauded the cracked skulls and fractured limbs, and even the most fortunate fighters emerged from the combat a mass of wounds and bruises. The presence of ladies and the atmosphere of the drawing-room now put such brutal struggles out of court, and the foil replaced the bludgeon. The duel now demanded sprightliness and elegance ; the attack must be quick, the defence smart and neat. The audience delighted to see skilful passes skilfully parried, and even if the wounds drew blood, at least they did not disfigure the fencers. Rhymed satire became the vehicle of argument and all readers found so much pleasure in a well-turned phrase that versified polemics had the best chance of success. I would not imply that all violence was henceforward banished from discussion. There were plenty of excesses and plenty of vulgarities [199] in the replies which Dryden's political writings brought upon his head, and plenty even in Dryden's work. But however furiously anger might rage—and we shall presently see the extremes of which it was capable—literary considerations moderated the form if not the content. We have seen Dryden's portrait of Zimri which confirms this view. Here is another sample of Dryden's art directed against Shadwell :

Og may write against the king, if he pleases, so long as he drinks for him, and his writings will never do the government so much harm,

---

[198] Taine, II, pp. 357-8 ; Geffroy, pp. 152-4.
[199] See above, chap. I, note No. 315, and chap. II, note No. 154.

as his drinking does it good ; for true subjects will not be perverted by his libels ; but the wine duties rise considerably by his claret. He has often called me an atheist in print ; I would believe more charitably of him, and that he only goes the broad way, because the other is too narrow for him. He may see, by this, I do not delight to meddle with his course of life, and his immoralities, though I have a long bead-roll of them. I have hitherto contented myself with the ridiculous part of him, which is enough, in all conscience, to employ one man ; even without the story of his late fall at the Old Devil, where he broke no ribs, because the hardness of the stairs could reach no bones ; and for my part, I do not wonder how he came to fall, for I have always known him heavy : the miracle is, how he got up again. I have heard of a sea-captain as fat as he, who, to escape arrests, would lay himself flat upon the ground, and let the bailiffs carry him to prison, if they could. If a messenger or two, nay, we may put in three or four, should come, he has friendly advertisement how to escape them. But to leave him, who is not worth any further consideration, now I have done laughing at him,—would every man knew his own talent, and that they who are only born for drinking, would let both poetry and prose alone ! [200]

It would be possible to cite other similar passages ; *Mac Flecknoe* might almost be quoted *in extenso*. We have, however, quoted enough to show how much milder were the forms polemics now favoured, thanks to a Court which had made literature the fashion.

If the Court had taught the ruder Puritan middle classes to appreciate polish and elegance, they for their part had introduced a wholesome and sustaining element into the courtier's dissolute and superficial life.

We have seen that despite appearances, other matter than plays and songs had been finding readers. This subterranean stream of readers now found its way into the open, happily overwhelming the superficial and degraded, and was soon swelled by the serious-minded Royalists. For there were serious-minded men also in the Royalist camp—though the empty-headed had so long prevented serious voices being heard—if it were only the group of thinkers who, feeling the need of quiet study after the disturbances of the Civil War, founded the Royal Society in 1662. [201]

From this point of view the revival of politics had a fortunate effect. Compelling people to give up the sole pursuit of enjoy-

[200] *The Vindication*, etc.
[201] Amongst them were Dryden, Cowley, Denham, Evelyn, Barrow, Waller and Sprat.

ment it turned their minds to wholesomer, more vigorous thought. As regards the reign of James II in particular, we must add that the King's more frigid temperament and the fact that he had passed the age of sensual passion and was wholly preoccupied in seeking the triumph of his religious views, gave far less encouragement to licence than Charles II had done, and thus imposed a measure of restraint.

It would obviously be untrue to imply that the general tone had suddenly improved all at once. A society which for twenty years has devoted itself wholly to pleasure and cast aside all modesty and self-respect, cannot purify itself in a day. Plays in particular—even political plays—were not less licentious or less disgusting than in the first years of Charles II. Ravenscroft's *London Cuckolds*, Rochester's *Valentinian*, Otway's *Souldiers Fortune* and his *Atheist*, Crowne's *City Politiques*, Lee's *Princess of Cleve*, Sedley's *Bellamira* and Mrs. Behn's new comedies, were in no way behind the most audacious of the early Restoration plays in daring and indecency.[202]   Prologues and Epilogues likewise were no less shameless than in the past.[203]

[202] I shall confine myself to a few quotations : [Rochester d. 1680, B. D.]

> " The Love of Women moves even with their Lust.
> Who therefore still are fond, but seldom just :
> Their Love is Usury, while they pretend,
> To gain the Pleasure double which they lend.
> But a dear Boy's disinterested Flame
> Gives Pleasure, and for meer Loves gathers pain ;
> In him alone Fondness sincere does prove,
> And the kind tender Naked Boy is Love."
>
> (Rochester, Valentinian, II, 1.)

" *Beauregard* : Would the Lady of my Motion make haste, and be punctual ; the Wheels of my Nature move so fast else, that the weight will be down before she comes." (Otway, *The Atheist*, II, 1.)   His father speaks to him of " brawny-bum'd Whores " (III, 1).

> " *Nemours :*   Let's try how our lips fit.
> *Marguerite :*   Is that your fitting ?
> *Nemours :*   'Fore Heaven she's wond'rous quick ; Nay, my Dear,
>   and you go to that, I can fit you every way——
> *Marguerite :*   You are a notorious talker.
> *Nemours :*   And a better doer ; prithee try."
>
> (Lee, Princess of Cleve, II, 3.)   And she tries.

> " *Poltrot :*   . . . When you were little Girls of Seven, you were so
>   wanton, your Mothers ty'd your hands behind you——
> *Elianora :*   All this we confess to be true," etc.
>
> (Id., IV, 1.)

The whole play is in this tone, especially Nemours' part.

[203] See, amongst others, the Epilogue to Crowne's *Sir Courtly Nice* ; the Epilogue by Dryden for Lee's *Constantine the Great* ; the Prologue (spoken

Nevertheless we seem to detect some promises of improvement even in the theatre. We begin to hear protests raised against the immoralities displayed on the stage and we see authors compelled to give heed to these protests.[204] From Ravenscroft himself we learn the *The London Cuckolds* did not fail to rouse complaints.[205] Comedy showed a slight, a very

---

by a woman) and the Epilogue to Southerne's *Loyal Brother*, both of them written by Dryden ; the Prologue (also by Dryden) and the Epilogue to Southerne's *Disappointment*.

[204] " Of all the things which at this *Guilty time*,
　　Have felt the honest *Satyr's* Wholsome *Rhime*,
　　The *Play-house* has scap't best, being most forborn,
　　Though it, of all things, most deserves our scorn . . .
　　First to the *Middle-Gallery* we'll go . . .
　　Where reeking *Punks* like Summer Insects swarm,
　　And stink like *Pole-cats* when they are hunted warm : . . .
　　In the *Side-box Moll H . . . n* you may see,
　　Or *Coquet Moll*, who is as lewd as she :
　　That is their Throne ; for there they best survey
　　All the salt Sots that flutter to the *Play* . . .
　　As the *New-River* does from *Islington*,
　　Through several pipes supply ev'n half the Town ;
　　So the Luxurious lewdness of the *Stage*,
　　Drain'd off, feeds half the *Brothels* of the Age.
　　Unless these ills, then, we could regulate,
　　It ought not to be suffer'd in the State."
　　　　　　　　(*The Play-House, a Satyr* . . . by Robt. Gould.)

" Baudy the nicest Ladies need not fear,
The quickest fancy shall extract none here.
We will not make 'em blush, by which is shown
How much their bought Red differs from their own."
　　　　　　　　(Shadwell, *The Squire of Alsatia*, Prologue.)

[205] " Gallants, I vow I am quite out of heart,
　　I've not one smutty Jest in all my part.
　　Here's not one Scene of tickling Rallery ;
　　There we quite lose the Pit and Gallery.
　　His *London Cuckolds* did afford you sport.
　　That pleas'd the Town, and did divert the Court.

　　But 'cause some squeamish Females of renown
　　Made visits with design to cry it down,
　　He swore in 's Rage he would their humours fit,
　　And write the next without one word of Wit.
　　No line in this will tempt your minds to Evil,
　　It's true, 'tis dull, but then 'tis very civil.

　　No double sense shall now your thoughts beguile,
　　Make Lady Blush nor Ogling Gallant smile.
　　But mark the Fate of this mis-judging Fool !
　　A Bawdy Play was never counted Dull,
　　Nor modest Comedy e're pleas'd you much
　　'Tis relish'd like good Manners 'mongst the *Dutch*.

slight tendency to cease to serve as a market-place for debauchery. Politics had drawn off no small number of its male and female addicts.[206] Southerne, who began his dramatic career in 1682, actually has the courage to introduce virtuous women into his plays, even into his comedies.[207] All these things are of course but straws in the wind, but when you have long been floundering in a cess-pool, stirring up septic filth at every step, the tiniest trickle of pure water rejoices your eye and uplifts your heart.

We find, besides, another indication of mental progress—in the appearance of less frivolous reading matter. Political writing had begun seriously to compete with light literature. Religious discussions in which the most eminent people in the country bore a part and which found readers all over England, had prepared people's minds to accept and demand better fare than stale plays, prologues and songs. The " publisher ", just on the point of emerging from the chrysalis of printer-bookseller, would be on the watch for the more substantial work. Jacob Tonson, taking the first steps in publishing, was busy as early as 1683 preparing with Dryden a volume of a new type : a collection of translations from Virgil, Ovid, Horace, etc., and of " original poems by the most eminent hands ", a collection

---

In you, Chast Ladies, then we hope to day,
This is the Poets *Recantation* Play.
Come oft to't that he at length may see
'Tis more than a pretended Modesty :
Stick by him now, for if he finds you falter,
He quickly will his way of writing alter ;
And every Play shall send you blushing home.
For, tho you rail, yet then we're sure you'll come . . . "
(Ravenscroft, Prologue to *Dame Dobson*, spoken
by Mrs. *Currer.*)

[206]   " Here's such a Rout with Whigging and with Torying,
That you neglect your dear-lov'd sin of Whoring :
The Visor-Mask, that ventur'd her Half-Crown,
Finding no hopes but here to be undone ; . . .
Turns Godly streight and goes to Church in spight ;
And does not doubt, since you are grown so fickle
To find more Cullies in a Conventicle."
(Bankes, Epilogue to *Vertue Betray'd.*)

" Our Prologue-Wit grows flat : the Nap's worn off ;
And howsoe'ere we turn and trim the Stuff,
The Gloss is gone that look'd at first so gaudy ;
'Tis now no Jest to hear young Girls talk Baudy.
But Plots and Parties, give new matter birth ;
And State Distractions serve you here for mirth ! "
(Shadwell(?), *A Lenten Prologue.*)

[207] Notably in *The Disappointment.*

still known as Dryden's or Tonson's Miscellany. It appeared in 1684.[208] The experiment justified itself, for in 1685 the two partners launched a second, similar volume which was soon followed by a third.[209] Already in 1683 Tonson had foreseen a probable revulsion in the taste of readers and had been courageous enough to buy from his fellow-bookseller, Brabazon Aylmer, half the rights in Milton's *Paradise Lost*. Without haste—obviously not yet feeling quite sure of his ground—he got ready a new edition which he published in 1688. This was the first worthy recognition of the great, under-appreciated poet. This edition was published by subscription with the encouragement of Atterbury, later Bishop of Rochester, and of Somers, a young literature-loving lawyer, destined to fill ere long the highest offices of state.[210] Henceforward the bookseller was no longer content to be merely a seller of books ; assured of a reading public on whom he could count, he developed ambition and a spirit of enterprise ; he set about seeking out authors and potential books ; he was on the alert for new ideas—in short, he became a publisher.

Such were, in brief, the changes we can note in matters which were of concern to writers : the Court was devoting more attention to them and making approaches to them ; the City was offering them a new market ; the number of readers was growing ; literary taste was spreading ; finally, the publishing firm was born. At the same time certain profits from the theatre were proving more remunerative : the author's fee for a prologue

---

[208] In the same year of 1684 Dryden (see his Letters) advised Tonson to reprint Roscommon's *Essay on Translated Verse* and to run off 1,000 copies. He also revised and reprinted his own *Essay of Dramatick Poesie* in 1684, dedicating it to Dorset.

[209] The first volume is called *Miscellany Poems*, the second *Silvæ*, and the third *Examen Poeticum*. See my Bibliography, s.v. Dryden.

[210] Professor Masson's Edition of the Poetic Works of Milton, *Introduction to Paradise Lost*.—The list of over 500 subscribers, printed at the end of the volume includes, in addition to Somers and Atterbury already mentioned, the names of Dryden, Waller, Lord Dorset, Sir Robert Howard and L'Estrange. It was for this edition that Dryden wrote his verses on Milton :

> " Three *Poets*, in three distant Ages born,
> *Greece*, *Italy* and *England* did adorn.
> The *First* in loftiness of thought Surpass'd,
> The *Next* in Majesty ; in both the *Last*.
> The force of *Nature* cou'd no further goe ;
> To make a *Third* she joynd the former two."

Tonson later had his portrait painted by Kneller holding his Milton in his hand.

went up, from 5 to 10 guineas [211]; the third performance of *The Squire of Alsatia* brought Shadwell the remarkable sum of £130, a fact which was duly remarked on.[212]

All this is far from being without significance, but it would be a mistake to suppose that these fortunate improvements immediately altered the author's position for the better. These improvements were rather promises for the future than realities of the present. The theatre was going down, and while in detail paying more, was earning less; publishing was still tentative and timid, and only preparing for future expansion. As for the City, it offered a dangerous lure to writers, as many who entered its service discovered to their cost. The reader will remember that after the controversy provoked by Dryden's *Duke of Guise*, Hunt was obliged to quit the country and Shadwell to renounce the theatre which had been his source of livelihood. Another Whig pamphleteer, Robert Ferguson, was likewise compelled to seek refuge in Holland.[213] Henry Care, who had edited *A Packet of Advice from Rome* and was the author of *Towser the Second*, ill satisfied with the support given him by the City, turned his back on the Whigs and rallied in 1687 to the banner of James II.[214] Even Settle, whom the City had more particularly enlisted, having quitted the Court for the City, found his illusions shattered and was driven into quitting the City and returning again to the Court.[215]

[211] " Dryden's price for a prologue had usually been five guineas, with which sum Southerne presented him when he received from him a prologue for one of his new plays; Dryden returned the money and said to him, ' Young man, this is too little; I must have ten guineas.' Southerne observing his usual price had been five guineas, ' Yes,' answered Dryden, ' it has been so; but the players have hitherto had my labours too cheap : for the future I will have ten guineas.' " (Life of Southerne, prefixed to his *Works*, p. 5.)

The biographer does not mention the date; but the first prologue Dryden wrote for Southerne was of 1682 (*The Loyal Brother*); the last was 1684 (*The Disappointment*). Pope's lines, *To Mr. Thomas Southern on his Birth-day*, 1742, prove that Dryden's example was applauded by his fellows. Pope calls Southerne

". . . Tom sent to raise
The price of prologues and of plays."

[212] " Note. The Poet receiv'd for his third Day in the House in *Drury Lane* at single Prizes 130l. which was the greatest Receipt they ever had at that House at single Prizes." (Downes, p. 41.)

[213] à Wood, *Athenæ Oxonienses*, s.v. Cooper (Anthony Ashley).

[214] Ibid., s.v. James (Thomas).

[215] See below, p. 201. Settle himself says : " Alas, I was grown weary of my little Talent in Innocent *Dramaticks*, and forsooth must be rambling

All things considered, there was in fact—just as in the past —no harbour of refuge for the author save the Court. Yet the Court, while showing more respect for him than heretofore, still failed to provide practical assistance. Amid all the political difficulties which surrounded the close of his reign, Charles II remained as feather-headed and carefree as at the beginning. Now and again he was seized by an attack of generosity and when Dryden had, at his command, written his poem, *The Medal*, the King suddenly flung him a gift of a hundred " broad pieces " say between £115 and £125.[216] But these noble impulses were exceptional, not recurrent. Whatever hopes the resurgence of politics may have aroused in them, authors were soon compelled to realize that the reign of indifference—at least to all that personally concerned them—was not over. After having collaborated with Dryden in writing *The Duke of Guise*, Lee was driven out of his mind by hope deferred, and was consigned to Bedlam in 1684.[217] Otway, the author of *Venice Preserv'd*, the ardent Tory who turned Shaftesbury to ridicule and wrote such impassioned prologues for the royal cause, died of hunger [218]; Crowne on such good terms with Charles, Crowne, author of *City Politiques*, voiced in 1685 his view of poetry as " a pleasant but barren country " [219]; weary and disheartened by the precariousness of success in the theatre, he begged a post of the King : in vain.[220] The Merry Monarch remained the same to the end. In 1683, when Dryden had just shown himself the gallant champion of the Court, and stunned the triumphant

into *Politicks* ; And much I have got by 't, for, I thank 'em, they have undone me." (Dedication of *Distress'd Innocence*.)

> " Recanting Settle . . .
> Protests his Tragedies and Libels fail
> To yield him Paper, Penny-Loaves and Ale,
> And bids our Youth by his Example fly
> The Love of Politicks and Poetry."
> (Poems on Affairs of State, *A Satyr upon the Poets*, II, pp. 138 ff.)

[216] Spence, p. 172. " Broad piece, a golden Coin some worth 23 shillings and others 25." (Bailey, *English Dictionary*, 1736.)

[217] Spence, p. 62.

[218] See above chap. I, note No. 442.

[219] See above chap. I, note No. 398. He was still of the same opinion in 1694 : " How many Kings and Queens have I had the honour to divertise ? And how fruitless has been all my Labours ? . . . a maker of Fires at Court has made himself a better Fortune, than Men much my Superiors in Poetry could do, by all the noble Fire in their Writings." (Dedication of *The Married Beau*.)

[220] Dennis, *Original Letters*, I, pp. 49 ff.

Whigs by writing in breathless succession *Absalom and Achitophel*, *The Medal*, and *The Duke of Guise*, not to mention *Mac Flecknoe* and *Religio Laici*, his salary as Poet Laureate and Historiographer Royal was four years in arrears, and he was driven to writing the following melancholy letter to the First Lord of the Treasury [221] :

My Lord ;—I know not whether my Lord Sunderland has interceded with your lordship for half a year of my salary : but I have two other advocates, my extreme wants, even almost to arresting, and my ill health, which cannot be repaired without immediate retiring into the country. A quarter's allowance is but the Jesuit's powder to my disease : the fit will return a fortnight hence. If I durst, I would plead a little merit, and some hazards of my life from the common enemies ; my refusing advantages offered by them, and neglecting my beneficial studies for the King's service ; but I only think I merit not to starve. I never applied myself to any interest contrary to your lordship's, and on some occasions, perhaps not known to you, have not been unserviceable to the memory and reputation of my lord your father.[222] After this, my lord, my conscience assures me, I may write boldly though I cannot speak to you. I have three sons growing to man's estate ; I bred them all up to learning, beyond my fortune ; but they are too hopeful to be neglected, though I want. Be pleased to look on me with an eye of compassion. Some small employment would render my condition easy. The King is not unsatisfied of me ; the Duke has often promised me his assistance ; and your lordship is the conduit through which they pass ; either in the Customs, or the Appeals of the Excise, or some other way, means cannot be wanting, if you please to have the will. 'Tis enough for one age to have neglected Mr. Cowley and starved Mr. Butler ; but neither of them had the happiness to live till your lordship's ministry. In the meantime, be pleased to give me a gracious and speedy answer to my present request of half a year's pension for my necessities. I am going to write somewhat by his Majesty's command,[223] and cannot stir into the country for my studies, till I secure my family from want. You have many petitions of this nature, and cannot satisfy all ; but I hope from your goodness to be made an exception to your general rules, because I am with all sincerity

Your lordship's most obedient humble servant

JOHN DRYDEN.

In reply to this petition the poet was given a post in the Customs from which the income was fluctuating and uncertain.

---

[221] This letter has neither address nor date. Malone has supplied both. He believes the date to be August 1683. Both his hypotheses seem fully justified.

[222] That is to say Clarendon. The First Lord of the Treasury, Lawrence Hyde, Earl of Rochester, was his second son. Dryden is no doubt referring to the verses he had in earlier days addressed to the Lord Chancellor. See above, p. 26.

[223] Probably his translation of Maimbourg's *History of the League*.

As for his salary they remitted to him in 1684—as a favour—
—not half a year's but a quarter's arrears. Fifteen quarters
remained unpaid. It is true that some years before, the King
had graciously accorded him a supplementary pension of £100,
but this was paid like his salary, and at the end of 1683 four years
of it also were still owing. It was on the same lines that Dorante
discharged his debt to M. Jourdain.

Dorante : How much does that come to ?
M. Jourdain : That makes a total of 15,800 francs. Add to that
another 200 louis which you are going to give me and that will make
it exactly 18,000 francs which I shall pay you at the first opportunity.

So much for Charles II.[224] As for his brother, he had neither
time nor taste for literature. Even if his fight for Roman
Catholicism had left him the necessary leisure, he was of too
stern and gloomy a temperament to be moved by art. By
nature he was insensitive to the charms of literature, and saw
nothing in it but its political value. His interest in writers was
measured only by the service they could render towards the
triumph of his views. We have seen that he employed many,
and we may safely assume that he paid them punctually for
the work he commissioned. Being, however, neither cultured
nor generous, he confined himself to paying his debt at the just
price, as a man pays his tailor or his shoemaker, feeling the
transaction ended once the cash had changed hands.[225] Charles,
the slave of pleasure and always penniless, loved literature
without paying for it ; James, frigid, miserly, and fanatically
taken up with his religious task, purchased literature without

---

[224] In his poem *Threnodia Augustalis*, written to mourn the death of
Charles II, Dryden could not refrain from including lines like these :

" Tho little was their [the poets'] Hire, and light their Gain,
  Yet somewhat to their share he threw ;
  Fed from his Hand, they sung and flew,
  Like Birds of Paradise, that liv'd on Morning Dew.
  Oh never let their Lays his Name forget !
  The Pension of a Prince's Praise is great."

[225] How niggardly he was with money, we see from the fact that Dryden,
while rendering him services such as no other man could render, was driven
to interlard his political writing with more remunerative work, to grind out
prologues and epilogues and partner Tonson in his first publishing ventures.
It is true that James II knighted L'Estrange and Etherege and gave Southerne
a commission in the army (*Biographia Britannica*, s.vv. L'Estrange, Etherege ;
Life of Southerne prefixed to his works) ; but these marks of favour cost him
nothing. Talking of Etherege, let me relate his end. He went as English
Plenipotentiary to Ratisbon, got drunk, fell down the well of the staircase
and killed himself. A splendid finale, and a fine text for a sermon !

caring for it.   So great was his contempt of it that it amounted
to ingratitude.   If any man in England had a claim on his
gratitude, assuredly Dryden was that man.   Dryden, who during
the furious controversies over the Bill of Exclusion had struck
a staggering blow at the Whigs, rallied the terrified Tories and
perhaps—it is not too much to say—secured the Duke of York's
accession to the throne.[225a]   Yet one of the first acts of this
same Duke of York when he became James II was to practise
his economies on the author of *Absalom and Achitophel* by can-
celling the supplementary pension of £100 granted him by
Charles II, and—miracle of meanness—the tierce of Canary
wine from the royal cellars which since the days of Ben Jonson
the King of England had annually sent his Poet Laureate.

In short nothing, or very little, had radically altered.   Writers
had to fend for themselves as best they might amid the same old
difficulties as in the past, with the result that they continued
to be courtiers as they had been before.   They remained vassals
of the Court and having previously obliged by producing fashionable drama, they now equally obligingly produced fashionable
politics.   Some of them no doubt overdid the sycophancy a
trifle, but it would be unfair to blame them overmuch.   It is
obvious that they could not yet aspire to independence, as was
proved by the unhappy fate of those who tried to emancipate
themselves in premature reliance on the City ;   they dare not
yet attempt to walk alone, for the ground under their inexperi-
enced feet was too unstable.   *Nolens volens*, they could but accept
their fate, cling to the skirts only of the Court, and adapt
themselves to its opinions as they had earlier adapted themselves
to its tastes.   It is easy to imagine that this compulsion always
to follow some one, did not help to raise their moral qualities.
This subordination, this necessity of winning approval from on
high—under pain of getting sacked—compelled them to stifle
their own individuality and aim solely at pleasing.   Their only
ambition was to be a faithful echo ;   far from seeking to develop
their own personal views they tailored their opinions according
to those of the people in power and painstakingly strove to avoid
running counter to them.

As a sort of compensation, they were wholly unembarrassed

[225a] [This is an exaggeration, if a pardonable one.   The issue was fought
out in the House of Lords, while Charles lounged by the fireplace pretending
amusement.   The Exclusion Bill was defeated largely by the efforts of Halifax,
and *Absalom and Achitophel* can have had little effect on this crucial point. B. D.]

by their own inconsistency. We have already seen Dryden
producing his comedy, *The Spanish Fryar*, calculated to please
the Whigs rather than the Court,[226] and then to please the
Court fling off his coat to give the Whigs a drubbing. Other
authors acted likewise. After having in 1681 produced his
tragedy of *Lucius Junius Brutus*, which was promptly suppressed
because the over-frequent recurrence of the word " liberty "
grated on courtly ears, Lee hastened the next year to make
amends by joining Dryden in writing *The Duke of Guise*. In 1679
Crowne was a Tory passionately preaching passive obedience [227];
in 1681 he was a Whig attacking the Roman Catholics [228] ; by
1683 he was a Tory again savaging the Whigs and Protestants [229];
after the Revolution he was a Whig once more.[230] Nahum

[226] About this time his reputation as a Whig was so well established
that in the anti-Shaftesbury pamphlet above quoted (chap. II, note No. 57)
he is named with Shadwell as designated to accompany Shaftesbury to Poland
to be an official of his government. His name is followed by this description :
" Our poet laureat, for writing panegyrics upon Oliver Cromwel, and libels
against his present master, King Charles II of England."

[227]   " Duke—Princes are sacred,
            What e're Religious Rebels may pretend,
            Murderers of Kings are Worshippers of Devils
            For none but Devils are worshipt by such Sacrifices . . .
                          . . . No Sacrilege
            Greater, than when a Rebel with his Sword
            Dare's cut the hand of Heaven from King's Commissions
            To hide the Devils' mark upon his own.
            I lifted up my Arm against the Dauphin,
            It ought to have dy'd and rotted in the Air."
                          (*The Ambitious Statesman*, V, last scene.)

[228] *Henry the Sixth*, see above, p. 143.
            " Pagan and Popish priests
            Are but two names for the same bloody beasts . . .
            Then halter priests and tye 'em to the racks,
            If you will keep the Devil off their backs."
                          (*Thyestes*, Epilogue.)

[229]   " There is in every true *Protestant* Breast ⎫
            A *Heraclitus Ridens*, his Contest,   ⎬
            A Knave in Earnest, and a Saint in Jest ⎭
            The Saint looks up to Heaven, the Knave that while
            Your Pocket picks and at the Cheat does smile . . . "
                          (*City-Politiques* I, i.)

See also above, p. 146.
[230] In his *English Frier* he attacks James II's Court and the Roman
Catholics ; in the Prologue he reproaches those who
            " . . . are so Mad, they'd give up *Englands* Glory,
            Only to keep the wretched Name of *Tory*."

In the Dedication of his *Caligula*, he celebrates the Revolution, and acidly
criticizes Charles II and James II : " . . . this Revolution, which has been

Tate, whose *Sicilian Usurper* was banned by the Court, produced indubitably Tory work in *The Ingratitude of a Common-Wealth* and *Cuckolds-Haven*, and in collaborating in the Second Part of *Absalom and Achitophel*. This did not prevent his accepting from William III the post of Poet Laureate. D'Urfey, who under Charles II and James II had put his dramatic and lyric gifts at the service of the Tories, employed the same gifts against them after the Revolution.[231]   Sprat, who had begun his literary career with lines in praise of Cromwell, having obeyed James II's command to write a narrative of the Rye-House Plot, found it simple and natural to disclaim and excuse this work when William III became King.[232]   L'Estrange was the complaisant tool of royal politics, whoever might happen to be King. He attacked all Nonconformists under James II. So far did he go in this direction that people thought he had turned Roman Catholic and he had publicly to deny the report. Hunt undertook to defend the City's rights only after having written first in favour of the Court in the hopes of securing an important post and finding it awarded to another aspirant.[233]   Henry Care, after violently abusing the Roman Catholics in his news-

---

so happy to England, and the greatest part of Europe. Had not this change been, almost all Europe had been overrun by France ; England, for certain, had lost its Rights, Liberties and Religion, and perhaps, been no more a Kingdom, but a Province to France, a Vassal to Vassals, and for all its Wealth had nothing but a Wafer . . . And what a glorious Figure does England now make in Comparison of what it did some years ago ?   It lay one Reign becalm'd in Luxury : In another Fetter'd : In this Reign it has not only freed it self, but humbled France, and protected Germany, Spain and Holland, and appears one of the greatest Powers in Christendom."

[231]   " Let's leave this Scene of Death, and to the People,
With kind Oration, settle our new Royalty ;
Pull down the Fabrick of ill Government,
And found one upon Justice, Truth and Honour
Whilst all good Subjects, glorying in their Change,
Reflect on Ills from Tyranny did grow,
And bless the happy Revolution now."
                    (*The Grecian Heroine.* These are the closing
                          lines of the tragedy.)

See also the characters of Lady Addleplot and Lady Stroddle in *Love for Money*. They are thus described : " *Lady Addleplot*, A lusty flaunting imperious Lady, a highflown Stickler against the Government, and always railing at it and talking of Politicks.—*Lady Stroddle*, Her Companion, a Papist and Grumbler."

See also Addison, *The Guardian*, No. 67.

[232] Johnson, *Lives of the English Poets*, Sprat ; *Biographia Britannica*, s.v. Sprat.

[233] à Wood, *Athenæ Oxonienses*, s.v. Hunt (Thomas).

paper, did a right-about-turn under James II and abused the Protestants.[234] Settle—having renounced the plaudits of the Court to link his fortunes to the Whigs', having presided over the burning of the Pope's effigy in the City, having written a reply to Dryden's loyal poems and, at Shaftesbury's dictation, *The Character of a Popish Successor*,[235]—became convinced that the City was not going to prove the stronger party, and forthwith unblushingly forswore his Whig convictions in a recantation published in 1683,[236] brutally attacked his former friends, fired off a pamphlet against Russell after his execution, concocted a heroic poem on the coronation of James II, composed a panegyric on the odious Jeffreys, and wound up by enlisting in the army of the " Popish Successor " mobilized on Hounslow Heath. After the Revolution he refurbished his friendship for the City and became its Poet Laureate.[237]

On the accession of James II, when the sole way of currying favour with the King was to adopt his religion, there were many who had no hesitation in staging a conversion.

It seems probable that Wycherley was one of these. The information about him that has come down to us is scanty ; but we know for certain that his creditors had detained him in prison for seven years, that James II procured his release by paying his debts, and that he died a Roman Catholic.[238] Are we wronging the Duchess of Cleveland's protégé if we assume that these two facts are related, and that other considerations than his soul's salvation won him for the Roman Church ? Are we misjudging James II if we assume that it was not the pure love of literature which loosed his purse-strings—normally so firmly tied—for the sake of a man whose heart seemed promising soil for the good seed ? No one can be in much doubt about the answer.

A companion of Wycherley's in opportune conversion was

[234] Ibid., s.v. James (Thomas).
[235] North, *Examen*, p. 96.
[236] A Narrative.—See also *The Present State of England In relation to Popery*.
[237] à Wood, *Athenæ Oxonienses*, s.v. Settle ; Scott and Saintsbury, *Works of John Dryden*, IX, p. 355 ff. ; Nichols, *Literary Anecdotes*, I, p. 41, note ; Disraeli, *Calamities and Quarrels of Authors* : Pope's Earliest Satire ; Pope, *Dunciad*, III, ll. 277 ff. ; *Biographia Dramatica*, s.v. *Pageants* ; see also my Bibliography.
[238] Spence, p. 2 ; Pack, *Miscellanies*, p. 181 ff. ; Allibone, article Wycherley.—Wycherley had first, in France, been a Roman Catholic ; when he came back to England he turned Protestant, finally to die as a Roman Catholic.

H

the author-actor Joseph Haines—known to his intimates as Joe Haines—who was famous for the prologues and epilogues he wrote and himself delivered with great success. When James came to the throne, Haines made a great to-do about a vision he had had of the Virgin Mary, proclaimed himself a convert, was promptly distinguished by the new King and selected as one of the suite to accompany the noble consort of Lady Castle-maine as Ambassador to Rome.[239]

But the most famous and the saddest of these conversions was John Dryden's.

In his case we should prefer to doubt; it is painful to accuse this great genius of a bogus conversion for material advantage. But we seek in vain for sound and convincing reasons to acquit him, and can only exclaim with André de Chénier :

> I'd have liked to believe him, I vow to the skies
> I'd rather have doubted the facts and my eyes.
> But alas, it's not true that outstanding parts
> Cannot flourish in other than high-minded hearts.
> A mortal may strike most sublimely the lyre,
> Yet be weak-kneed, and narrow, and lacking in fire ;
> Unskilled in the virtues his songs so well praise,
> In words he extols them, in practice betrays.[240]

It looks sorely as if Dryden went over to Rome out of faint-heartedness.

Johnson and Walter Scott [241]—swayed by their admiration for the poet and perhaps not uninfluenced by their own political sympathies,—believed, and have tried to prove, that his conversion was the result of genuine conviction and untainted by worldly considerations. Unfortunately it is difficult to accept their special pleading. The damning fact remains that Dryden's

---

[239] *Biographia Dramatica,* s.v. Haines ; Tom Brown, *The Reasons of Mr. Joseph Hains the Player's Conversion and Re-Conversion.*

[240]   " Ah ! j'atteste les cieux que j'ai voulu le croire ;
     J'ai voulu démentir et mes yeux et l'histoire.
     Mais non ! il n'est pas vrai que des cœurs excellents
     Soient les seuls, en effet, où germent les talents.
     Un mortel peut toucher une lyre sublime,
     Et n'avoir qu'un cœur faible, étroit, pusillanime ;
     Inhabile aux vertus qu'il sait si bien chanter,
     Ne les imiter point et les faire imiter."
                    (André de Chénier, edited by Gabriel de
                         Chénier, Paris, 1874, II, p. 150.)

[241] Hallam, Professor Masson, Robert Bell, John Skelton and George Saintsbury follow suit. Saintsbury is the author of an admirable Life of Dryden and an excellent edition of his works, both of which have appeared

conversion was extremely opportune. Even while defending him, Johnson is compelled to admit that people will always suspect the worst, where a person derives personal advantage from a change of faith. Now, the moment of Dryden's conversion coincided on the one hand with the King's reinstatement of Roman rites in Westminster after an interval of 127 years, and on the other with the retrenchment of his pension at James's command. The immediate result of his conversion was the restoration of his income in full.[242] If his change of faith was bona fide, how could he bear even to appear to accept a cash reward for it ? One wonders.

Dryden had hitherto shown no marked interest of any kind in religious matters. He shared the comprehensive scepticism of the Restoration and its cynical contempt for priests of every church and of every country. A casual glance at any of his plays, tragic or comic, confirms this view of his mental attitude.

If we trace his expressed views on Roman Catholicism and Protestantism, from the moment when the two came into conflict, we shall find him alternately backing the one or the other according as his personal interest or the success of his work seemed to dictate. The Duke of York had chosen a moment when a wave of Protestant feeling was at its height to make public profession of his Roman faith ; Dryden promptly exploited

---

since the first edition of this book. He defends Dryden without reserve and yet his view is not fundamentally very different from my own when he says : " It is fully believable that a sense that he was about to be on the winning side may have assisted his rapid determination from Hobbism or Halifaxism to Roman orthodoxy." (G. Saintsbury, *Dryden*, p. 103.)—See the next note. Macaulay (*History*, chap. VII) and W. D. Christie take the other line.

[242] According to Bell's calculations Dryden's conversion took place at the close of 1686 while his pension was restored in full in 1685-6. But Bell himself admits that the conversion probably soon followed, shrewdly adding that if Dryden changed his religion for a pension, the transaction does not become more edifying by proving that he wanted to make sure of the pension before admitting his conversion. I would myself add that it is clear that Dryden did not crudely sell his soul for £100 of pension but that he was certainly influenced by the hope of winning the royal favour.

[Dryden's conversion to Roman Catholicism exposed him to many attacks during his lifetime, as did many of the events of his life (see *Essays and Studies*, xxi, 1936, the article by Hugh Macdonald). In the matter of his religion posterity until lately has not treated him generously. Recent researches, especially by Professor L. Bredvold, have shown that the conversion took place some time before the death of Charles ; but his change of faith need cause no surprise. Like many others of his day, permeated by the scepticism made agreeable by Montaigne, he in the end turned to the old faith : his conversion is really implicit in *Religio Laici*, from which it is only a short step to *The Hind and the Panther*. B. D.]

the prevalent emotion by giving the subsidiary title of *Love in a Nunnery* to his new comedy *The Assignation*.

That was as early as 1672. This second title indicated a definite anti-Papist bias which the epilogue reinforced by very outspoken comments on convents in general.[243] The obvious aim was to attract public attention to the new play. When all England was at fever-heat over the Popish Plot in 1681, Dryden sought to curry favour with the mob by a new attack on the Romanists and wrote his *Spanish Fryar* [244] with evident enjoyment. This was ill calculated to please James II—sensitive as he was in such matters—who banned its performance during his reign. That no one might this time mistake his intention Dryden dedicated this play to Lord Haughton, " recommending a Protestant play to a Protestant patron "—the phrase is worth noting. Then, observing that in playing to the gallery he had somewhat compromised his position with the King's brother, he reversed his engine and softened down the anti-Papist tone of his comedy. But he was not yet aware that the King had secret leanings towards the Roman Church, and he continued to make anti-Romanist allusions as occasion offered, and amongst other delicacies he slipped into *Absalom and Achitophel* a fairly vulgar view of transubstantiation.[245] In *Religio Laici* he is still

[243]   " Some have expected from our bills today,
    To find a *Satire* in our *Poet's Play*.
    The *zealous Rout* from *Coleman-Street* did run
    To see the Story of the *Fryer* and *Nun*
    Or *Tales*, yet more ridiculous to hear,
    Vouch'd by their Vicar of ten pounds a year ;
    Of Nuns, who did against Temptation Pray,
    And Discipline laid on the Pleasant Way :
    Or that to please the Malice of the Town,
    Our *Poet* should in some close Cell have shown
    Some Sister, Playing at Content alone : " . . .

[244] See above, chap. I, note No. 431. In the first Act he ridicules processions ; in the second, the invocation of saints ; in the third, auricular confession. The Epilogue is supposed to be written by a friend of the Author's, but is in fact too good to be from any other hand than Dryden's own. It contains the line :
    " Well may they give the God they can devour."

[245]   " Such savory Deities must needs be good,
    And serv'd at once for Worship and for Food."

It is amusing to compare this passage with *The Hind and the Panther* (part I, ll. 134 ff.) :
    " Could He his Godhead veil with flesh and Bloud,
    And not veil these again to be our food ?
    His Grace in both is equal in extent,
    The first affords us life, the second nourishment."

a Protestant and an orthodox one and is anxious only to lead back into the Anglican fold Roman Catholics [246] and Nonconformists alike. Yet in the very same year his *Vindication of the Duke of Guise* warmly championed the right of a Roman Catholic heir to succeed to the throne in defiance of Protestant prejudice. These two mutually contradictory pieces of special pleading date from 1682. Charles II died in 1685 and the champion of the English Church bade farewell to Protestantism and adopted the religion of his new King. In 1687 he wrote *The Hind and the Panther*, the very negation of *Religio Laici*.

It might well seem that his waverings now were ended, and that in future his path would be undeviatingly straight. [247] Yet even while he was writing *The Hind and the Panther* his point of view shifted on a question of religious sympathy if not of doctrine. When the poem opens, the English Church is flattered and courted ; she should make common cause with Rome to silence the dissenting sects. At the close and in the Preface— written last—the suggestion of an alliance is made instead to the Protestant Dissenters, who are now invited to form a common front with the Roman Catholics against the Anglicans. The

[246] Neither Preface nor poem shows much tenderness towards Roman Catholics. Witness the following lines (ll. 370–93) :

> " In times o'ergrown with Rust and Ignorance,
> A gainfull Trade their Clergy did advance ;
> When want of Learning kept the *Laymen* low,
> And none but *Priests* were *Authoriz'd* to *know* :
> When what small Knowledge was, in them did dwell ;
> And he a *God* who cou'd but *Reade* or *Spell* ;
> Then *Mother Church* did mightily prevail :
> She parcel'd out the Bible by *retail* :
> But still *expounded* what She *sold* or *gave* ;
> To keep it in *her Power* to *Damn* and *Save* :
> *Scripture* was *scarce*, and as the Market went,
> Poor *Laymen* took *Salvation* on *Content* ;
> As needy men take Money, good or bad :
> *God's* word they had not, but the *Priests* they had.
> Yet, whate'er *false Conveyances* they made,
> The *Lawyer* still was *certain* to be paid.
> In those dark times they learn'd their knack so well,
> That by long use they grew *Infallible* :
> At last, a knowing Age began t'enquire
> If *they* the Book, or *That* did *them* inspire :
> And, making narrower search they found, tho late,
> That what they thought the *Priest's* was *Their* Estate :
> Taught by the *Will produc'd*, (the written Word)
> How long they had been *cheated on Record*."

[247] He himself declared : " My doubts are done." (*The Hind and the Panther*, I, line 78.)

dramatist offers them the rôle of victors instead of vanquished.[248]
Why? Because, while the poem was still a-making, the King
had without warning switched his religious policy, and since he
despaired of winning over the Anglican clergy, was ogling the
very fanatics whom he had so recently abhorred. The poet,
faithful echo of his master, finished his song on a different note
from that he had struck at the beginning.

Such was the man whose admirers would persuade us that
genuine conviction prompted his conversion to Rome. But it
is impossible to blink the fact that Dryden was perpetually
changing, not for those intimate and conscientious reasons which
command from everyone a tribute of respect, but for purely
worldly motives. It is impossible not to observe that the wind
which veered his weathercock, was always his direct and immediate personal advantage.

It is true that his admirers lay weight on the fact that on
the accession of William III he remained faithful to his new
religion. But surely it was in his own interest not to change
again. There is a limit to everything—even to inconstancy.
In turning Roman Catholic he had alienated the Whigs but
secured the favour of the Tories. If he had turned Protestant
again, he would have alienated the Tories without recapturing
the confidence of the Whigs. Instead of being despised by one
party only, he would have been despised and rejected by both.[249]
After the Revolution, the Tories had of course lost the innings,
but for many years to come they were by no means without
influence, still less without hope. It has been stressed that
Dryden " brought up " his sons in the Roman faith,[250] but
there are games which you must play to the end or not at all,
and in playing a given rôle you may eventually arrive at deceiving
even yourself. Besides, at the time of their father's conversion
the boys had nearly arrived at manhood, and were of an age to
shoulder the responsibility and claim the merit of their own acts.

[248] This has been remarked by Walter Scott in his *Life of Dryden* and
by Macaulay in his *History* (chap. VII). Robert Bell, who is violently against
Macaulay, has made no comment on this important point.

[249] Joe Haines de-converted himself all right. He publicly displayed
his penitence in the theatre, robed in white and bearing a candle in his hand.
But Dryden was not Haines. Haines had long since had no character of
any kind to lose.

[250] " Brought up " is no apt phrase for children, the youngest of whom
was at least sixteen and the eldest nineteen years old. Charles was born in
1666, John in 1667 or 1668, and Erasmus-Henry in 1669. I borrow these
dates from Robert Bell, one of the most eager defenders of Dryden.

Lastly, there is something in the last years of Dryden's life which shows that even if he succeeded in taking himself in on the subject,[251] his conversion was not one of those reformations in the presence of which all questioning is silenced. When a man who has long been indifferent or sceptical is suddenly—if belatedly—illumined by the light of faith, his daily life henceforth reflects the new radiance of his soul. Be it Protestant or Roman Catholic, true religion honourably practised imposes respect for certain things, things which Dryden had hitherto treated with scant reverence. To minister to the taste of his contemporaries he had pandered to vice and brought a blush to the cheeks of modesty. He was himself sufficiently aware of the duties which his conversion laid upon him to exclaim : " Good life be now my task." [252] We should therefore expect to see him repenting of his evil ways and turning his back on them for ever. When Racine after the success of *Phèdre*—his genius being then at the height of its power—felt called to the serious practice of his religion, he put aside once and for all the work that had been his glory, and did so with an inflexible determination under which his letters groan. Dryden, who had far graver faults to reproach himself with than Racine, remained precisely the sinner he had been before. He staged Molière's *Amphitryon* but packed it full of lasciviousness [253] and in his translation of Roman classics contrived to out-Juvenal Juvenal in daring, to change the outspokenness of Lucretius into disgusting coarseness, and to insinuate indecency even into the *Georgics*.

However reluctantly, and sorely though it be against our will, we are driven to the conclusion that Dryden was no disinterested, single-minded convert. I have dwelt at so much length on this question of Dryden's conversion only because his motives have been so hotly debated. They have been the subject of controversy only because—or so it seems to me—the

[251] Professor Masson, a scholar sympathetic to Dryden, justly says : ". . . In consequence of the very obloquy which his change of religion drew upon him from all quarters, he hugged his new creed more closely, so as to coil round him, for the first time in his life, a few threads of private theological conviction." (*Essays*, p. 127.) I am willing to believe that Dryden deceived himself more quickly and more completely than he deceived others, and with a poet's gift of adaptation came to believe himself, and even to be, sincere.

[252] *The Hind and the Panther*, I, l. 78.

[253] It is true that in 1700 he honourably admitted that in many things Collier's indictment of the immorality of the stage had " taxed him justly ". I should reckon his true conversion from this date.

disputants have failed to take due account of the general position of writers at this time.

Thinking of Dryden alone, our minds are dazzled by his genius and chivalrously refuse to believe that his character was unworthy of our homage. Every suspicion of him seems a detraction from his literary glory and we indignantly reject it. Admiration is a jealous mistress ; when she falls in love with a man she would fain possess him wholly.

But if we refuse to be hypnotized by a famous name, and extend our researches beyond Dryden himself to the period in which his lot was cast, if we cross-examine his contemporaries, we find that the question solves itself. What was it that Dryden did ? Exactly what all his fellow writers of the period did— neither less nor more.[254] Like them, he was unable to make a living by his pen ; like them, he was inevitably condemned to seek the patronage of the great ; like them, his allegiance changed according to the fortune of the day ; like them, he was a writer of his time. The worst we can reproach him with, is that he was not an exception.

But why should he have been an exception ? He made no claim to be of other stuff than they. Had he made himself conspicuous by strength of character ? Far from it. In politics as in religion his convictions were fluid. He started life as a Republican singing the praises of Cromwell ; within two years he was a Royalist enthusiastically hailing the advent of Charles II. In 1673 he wrote *Amboyna* to stir up patriotic feeling in the Dutch War ; then in *Absalom and Achitophel* and in *The Medal* he violently attacked Shaftesbury for having been accessory to this war. Even in literary matters we have seen him abase himself —albeit with reluctance—before the gods of fashion and the day.

It is true that he was the greatest of all the living writers of his time. But his temptations were the greater in proportion as his place was the more exalted, and the urgencies of the time pressed on him the more severely. Poet Laureate he might be, but none the less a poet : that is to say a fragile, vulnerable

---

[254] Amongst professional writers I can find none but Shadwell who remained faithful to his political convictions. But Shadwell himself tells us (see above, p. 112 and note No. 396) that he could not give all his time to writing but was " forced to mind some other business of Advantage ". I do not know what form this business of advantage took, but whatever it was it probably was his refuge and salvation during the stormy years with which this second chapter deals.

member of society, unable to be self-sufficing, a prey to circumstance.

It is not for us then to be surprised that he gave way as others did : Lee, Crowne, Tate, D'Urfey, Sprat, Hunt, Care, L'Estrange, Settle, Wycherley and Haines. His humiliation, the more striking for the rank he held, should simply throw into relief for us the sorry fate of the writers of his day.

One last touch to the picture will show into what depths they were plunged by the wretched state of dependence to which they were helplessly condemned. Merely to live, they had perforce to adopt the opinions welcome in higher quarters, to ensure attention they had also to prove outstanding zeal. As they had earlier gone to the extreme of indecency to gratify degenerate theatre-goers, so now they exploited political passion—with how little conviction—to the very limit. They had trimmed their sails to one wind, they now trimmed them to another. They championed every violent suggestion ; they showed themselves harsh and cruel ; they trampled under foot all conceptions of friendship, compassion and humanity. The Duke and Duchess of Monmouth had been Dryden's protectors at a time when friends were few and very precious ; yet Dryden boldly attacked the Duke in *Absalom and Achitophel*. He went further. He brought his old patron on the stage in the character of the Duke of Guise rebelling against his father Henry III (that is Charles II), nor did he shrink from following the historic parallel to its end, he showed Henry III murdering the Duke of Guise, thus seeming to advise the royal father to assassinate his son.

After this it is superfluous to go back and re-emphasize the odious forms of his polemic against Shaftesbury. We must dwell, however, on one detail of it. In the Prologue to *Don Sebastian* Dryden had proudly told his fellow-countrymen :

> The British nation is too brave to show
> Ignoble vengeance on a vanquished foe.

When he gave voice to this noble sentiment Dryden was himself on the losing side. As victor, he changed his tune, as did his fellows. They had no chivalry even towards the dead. The coarse allusions to Shaftesbury quoted above from Dryden's *Albion and Albanius* and from Tate's *Cuckolds-Haven* date from 1685, that is to say they appeared after the death of the Whig leader. In the Prologue to the same play Tate thinks it witty to make merry over the Duke of Monmouth, lying under sentence

of death if he had not already been executed.[255]   Settle attacked
Russell after his execution.[256]

The same harshness permeates all they write : they call for
the hangman, they cry out for blood.   In dedicating to the King
his translation of the *History of the League*, Dryden volunteers some
political advice.   Hark to his counsels :

> Pardons are grown dangerous to your safety, and consequently to
> the welfare of your loyal subjects . . . you are still forgiving [your
> enemies] and they still conspiring against your sacred life ;   your
> principle is mercy, theirs inveterate malice ;   when one only wards,
> and the other strikes, the prospect is sad on the defensive side.
> Hercules, as the poets tell us, had no advantage on Antæus, by his
> often throwing him on the ground ;   for he laid him only in his mother's
> lap, which, in effect, was but doubling his strength to renew the
> combat.   These sons of earth are never to be trusted in their mother-
> element ;   they must be hoisted into the air and strangled.

There is here nothing ultra-humane, yet this is weak compared
with the sinister jesting of the Epilogue to the *Duke of Guise* which,
to crown all, was recited by a woman.   Just as the dramatists
heightened the effect of their indecencies by putting them into
the mouths of young actresses, they seem to have sought to
emphasize the cynicism of political hatreds by allowing women
to give them brutal expression.   In this Epilogue the actress
Mrs. Cook records a dialogue with a representative of the new
party of Trimmers (approximately the type which in French is
known as the *Juste-Milieu*).   She has just indicated how little
love she bears the Whigs, when the Trimmer interjects :

> " Fie, Mistress Cook ! faith, you're too rank a Tory !
> Wish not Whigs hanged, but pity their hard cases ;
> You women love to see men make wry faces."—
> " Pray Sir," said I, " don't think me such a Jew ;
> I say no more, but ' give the devil his due.' "—
> " Lenitives," says he, " best suit with our condition."—
> " Jack Ketch," [257] says I, " 's an excellent physician."—
> " I love no blood."—" Nor I, Sir, as I breathe ;
> But hanging is a fine dry kind of death."—

---

[255]   " Our Trinculo and Trapp'lin were undone
                When Lime's more Farcy Monarchy begun "

Trinculo is the buffoon in Shakespeare's *Tempest* ;   Trappolin is one of
the characters in a play of Tate's :   *A Duke and No Duke.*

[256] See above, p. 201.

[257] The executioner of the day.   He had been with Judge Jeffreys during
the Bloody Assizes and had executed Lords Russell and the Duke of Monmouth.
His name proverbially denotes a hangman.

" We Trimmers are for holding all things even."—
" Yes ; just like him that hung 'twixt Hell and Heaven."—
" Have we not had men's lives enow already ? "—
" Yes, sure : but you're for holding all things steady.
  Now since the weight hangs all on one side, brother,
  You Trimmers should, to poise it, hang on the other."

The need to gratify political passion thus led authors to forswear all tolerance, to renounce all humane feeling.

The tragedy is that this could not be otherwise. Appearances notwithstanding, the hapless author had no one he could turn to but the Court. Hence followed two almost fatal results : on the one hand, he must at all costs please the King and Court and in so doing set his feet upon a slippery slope ; on the other hand, though the Court his mistress may value his services a trifle more than of old she makes little effort to reward him, for there he is, for ever thrusting himself on her, and when she wants him she is sure to find him waiting, as submissive as ever, as eager as ever to do her bidding. She may fling him now and then a careless smile, but so little fear has she of losing his devotion that she has no mind to make any sacrifices for his benefit. It is a vicious circle : the more he needs the Court, the more he humbles himself to woo her ; the more he abases himself, the less his graceless mistress does for him.

It is this preponderating influence of the Court which explains why the improvements in the author's lot which we have noted, have as yet borne so little fruit. None the less, these improvements were real, and after the Revolution we shall find them developing in a new atmosphere and beginning to prove effective.

CHAPTER III

JOSEPH ADDISON

(1688–1721)

I

The revolution changed many things in England. The sovereign no longer wielded absolute and unquestioned authority by right of birth ; his authority rested on the nation's confidence. The royal power, begotten of public opinion, was obliged to heed the parent's will. Having set up the throne, the public could also overturn it ; and the Jacobite party was there, ever on the alert, awaiting the moment when friction should arise between the King and his subjects.

Those at the head of affairs were therefore continually concerned to preserve harmony and to avert friction. Their task was not merely by their own effort to conciliate public opinion, but to enlist the co-operation of everyone who was in a position to sway people's minds. The King chose ministers who had the ear of Parliament, the ministers sought everywhere to find support for their views and their administration. This being so, they were compelled to enlist the service of authors, who had in recent days so effectively demonstrated the weight their pen could throw into the political scales, and whose importance daily increased with the growth of the Press.

True, the new King whom the Revolution placed on the English throne was no literary connoisseur. William III had but a moderate knowledge of English, and even if he had known enough to appreciate the literature of his new home, we may fairly doubt his having been likely to show much sympathy for writers or to have valued highly the services they could

render him. He believed in two things : war and diplomacy.[1]
Charles II loved literature without paying for it ; James II paid
for it without loving it ; William III neither loved nor paid.[2]

The authors were thereby the gainers. William's ministers
appreciated them instead, and with much fuller understanding
than the King could have shown.

For amongst the first men whom William III summoned to
aid him in the tasks of government, there were many warm
friends of literature. Some of them had by their pen helped to
ensure the success of the Revolution, and owed no small share
of their reputation and influence to their writings. There was
Halifax, for instance, head of the Trimmers and probably the
author of *Letter to a Dissenter* [3] ; there was Somers, the learned
lawyer who encouraged Tonson to re-publish *Paradise Lost*, who
had collaborated in a translation of Plutarch for which Dryden
wrote a life of the Greek historian, and to whom were attributed
many pro-Whig political pamphlets that appeared under James II.[4]
Finally there was Dorset, who had put aside the follies of his
Buckhurst days, but had retained the courteous manners and fine
literary taste of his youth,[4a] and become the discriminating and

[1] When he met Swift at Sir William Temple's he offered to make him
a Captain in his cavalry. (Forster, *Life of Jonathan Swift*, p. 66.)
[But at that time Swift had hardly begun to write, and nothing noteworthy had come from his pen. It is unlikely that William III would
have made him such an offer in 1712, had he been alive, or even in 1704.
B. D.]

[2] Yet the story goes that when Dorset presented Montague (one of the
authors of *The Country Mouse and City Mouse*) to the King, saying : " Sir, I
have brought a *Mouse* to wait on your Majesty ", William replied : " You
do well to put me in the way of making a *Man* of Him ", and ordered him a
pension of £500. The anecdote is certainly apocryphal, and in any case
it is Dorset who is cast in it for the principal part. Dr. Johnson's comment
is : " The king's answer implies a greater acquaintance with our proverbial
and familiar diction than King William could possibly have attained." (*Lives
of the English Poets*, Halifax.)

[3] Another political publication, *The Character of a Trimmer*, is attributed
sometimes to Halifax and sometimes to Sir William Coventry. (Stephens,
Catalogue, I, p. 751.)
[*The Character of a Trimmer*, admirable reading even to-day, and which
contains many famous passages, is undoubtedly by Halifax. See any edition
of his *Works*. B. D.]

[4] Malone, *Life of Dryden*, p. 180 ; *Biographia Britannica*, s.v. Somers.—" In
defense of these *ignoramus* juries, it was said that . . . a book was wrote . . .
it passed as writ by Lord Essex, though I understood afterwards it was writ
by Somers, who . . . writ the best papers that came out in that time."
(Burnet, *History of my Own Times*, II, p. 290.)—See also above chap. II,
note No. 161.

[4a] [" Dorset, the grace of Courts, the Muses' pride." B. D.]

open-handed Mæcenas of two reigns.[5]   Later, Charles Montague, one of the lucky authors of *The Country Mouse and the City Mouse*, became a Minister, and since he owed his advancement entirely to literature he could not be indifferent to its fortunes.[6]

These men had seen with their own eyes how powerfully public opinion might be influenced by a happily conceived, well-timed poem or pamphlet.   They remembered how Dryden had called a halt to the triumph of the Whigs, and himself had in turn been rendered impotent by their replies.   They themselves had personally contributed by their writings to his defeat.   They were bound to feel, and did in fact evince, a peculiar sympathy for authors.   They succeeded in setting up in ministerial circles a tradition of patronage towards literature which their successors maintained for thirty years to come.

This Whig tradition was promptly adopted by the Tories. The Opposition could ill afford to allow the Revolution to monopolize the credit and the advantage of patronizing writers. If Dorset and Montague were the great Whig patrons of literature, the Tories Harley and Bolingbroke, both in Parliament and in office, rivalled them in munificence and zeal.

The happenings that attended the first appearance of Addison's *Cato* are a good indication of the party attitudes to literature.   The author, who was one of the glories of the Whig camp, produced his play at a time when the Tories were temporarily victorious and in power.   The Whigs applauded it with an enthusiasm compounded of vexation at their defeat and pleasure in a friend's success.   They saw in it a means of scoring off the enemy.   But the Tories had no mind to let them do so.   They countered the Whig applause by applauding even more loudly,

---

[5] Halifax, who was already Leader of the House of Lords, was made Lord Privy Seal ; Somers became Solicitor-General ; Dorset was Lord Chamberlain.—The Queen's Vice-Chamberlain was also an author, though one of dubious repute.   He was John Howe, popularly known as Jack Howe, the putative author of many recent lampoons.   (Macaulay, *History*, Chap. XI.) —Ferguson (see above chap. II, note No. 213) also held a fat sinecure in the Excise (Macaulay, *History*, chap. XI ; Stephens, *Catalogue*, I, p. 703).

[6] " Wit and Learning have from your Example fallen into a new Æra . . . it is to you we owe, that the Man of Wit has turned himself to be a Man of Business."   (Steele, Dedication to Charles, Lord Halifax of the fourth volume of the *Tatler*.)

[It is, to say the least of it, an exaggeration to say that Montague owed his advancement entirely to literature.   The Montagues were a powerful family, and he himself had a brilliant financial brain.   The first, and so far the only, person in this country to be ennobled purely for literary merit, is Tennyson.   B. D.]

and spared no effort to convert the play into a Tory gain. On the evening of the first performance Bolingbroke, Secretary of State and leader of the Tory party, summoned to his box the actor who had played Cato and ostentatiously handed him a purse of fifty guineas, publicly thanking him " for defending the cause of liberty so well against a perpetual dictator ". And Queen Anne, whose sympathies were naturally Tory, sent a message to Addison the Whig, to say that she would be happy to permit the play to be dedicated to her.[7] Each side was eager to claim the author for itself.

It sometimes happened that each party chose a different champion. Addison had sung the glories of the great victory of Blenheim, so that Tories entrusted John Philips with the task of celebrating it on their behalf and the rival poem was written under Bolingbroke's roof.[8]

The author was thus being sought after by Ministers—who, thanks to the daily-increasing importance of the House of Commons, were gradually becoming the real rulers of the country —and at the same time sought after by a powerful and sometimes victorious Opposition, which was in a position to offer him more solid benefits than the City had provided for Settle and his friends. He had henceforward no need to beg for favours, they rained down on him unsolicited. He was being courted and could afford to lie back and enjoy the wooing.

As soon as politics began to come to the fore and his potential power was understood, advances had been made towards him, but the eager warmth he was now meeting with was something entirely new. Godolphin, Lord High Treasurer, personally begged Addison to celebrate the victory of Blenheim, and the Chancellor of the Exchequer himself went to the young poet's modest lodging to present the Minister's request.[9] The Whig, Thomas Parnell,

---

[7] The " perpetual Dictator " was Marlborough.—See Johnson, *Lives of the English Poets*, Addison ; Spence, pp. 46, 47 ; Pope's Letter to Sir William Trumbull, Elwin's Edition of the *Works*, VI, p. 7.

[8] Bolingbroke was at this date plain Henry St. John. See Johnson, op. cit., s.v. J. Philips.

[The skies at that time snowed poems on Blenheim, anonymous and signed. Addison's is the best of a thoroughly mediocre display. B. D.]

[9] See Johnson, *Lives of the English Poets*, Addison ; Budgell, *Life of Lord Orrery*, quoted in *Addisoniana*, p. 683 ; Addison's *Works* edited by Hurd, vol. VI ; Aikin, I, 168–9.

[Godolphin consulted Halifax, who suggested Addison, insisting that the poet should be personally approached. Godolphin did not go himself, but sent Boyle, who, as Chancellor of the Exchequer, would convey honour enough. See Eustace Budgell, *Memoirs of the Life and Character of the Earl of Orrery and* transferred his political allegiance to the then triumphant Tories. When Harley, Earl of Oxford, was informed that Dr. Parnell was among the crowd waiting in his antechamber, he allowed Swift to persuade him to bid welcome to the new recruit. With his Treasurer's staff in his hand he went out in person to find and bring him in.[10]   On the accession of George I, Parker, the new Lord Chancellor, as soon as he received the seals of office, appointed the poet Nicholas Rowe to be Secretary of the Presentations without Rowe's even having applied for the post.[11]

This last example shows that the authorities now not only smiled on authors and anticipated their desires, but offered them solid advantages. Pensions (now punctually paid) and remunerative posts fell to their lot, and they were not precluded from aspiring to even higher honours.

Shadwell was Poet Laureate and Historiographer Royal,[12] Tate,[13] Rowe and Eusden [14] were all in their turn Poets Laureate, and Rowe was in addition one of the Land Surveyors of the Port of London, Clerk of the Prince of Wales's Council and, as we have seen, Secretary of Presentations.[15]   Edmund Smith, whose sole literary glory was his tragedy of *Phaedra and Hippolitus* [*sic*] which was a miserable failure, had no one but himself to thank for missing the chance of a post worth £300 a year.[16]   A brother writer Hughes—brother also in obscurity—was more careful of his own interests and secured himself a place in the Ordnance Office, besides being secretary to various commissions for purchasing lands required for the Royal Docks, and finally secretary to the Commission of the Peace.[17]   Ambrose Philips was Lottery Commissioner.[18]   Parnell, who was in orders, was given a

---

the family of the Boyles. 1732. Budgell, as a protégé of the Boyles, and one of Addison's " little Senate " would be in a position to know. B. D.]

[10] Johnson, ibid., Parnell ; Swift, *Journal to Stella*, Jan. 31, 1712–13.

[11] Johnson, ibid., Rowe.

[12] The title-page of his comedy *The Scowrers* bears both these titles.

[13] Chalmers, *Biographical Dictionary*, s.v. Tate (Nahum).

[14] Drake (Nathan), *Essays . . . Illustrative of the Tatler, Spectator and Guardian*, III, pp. 280–5.

[15] Johnson, *Lives of the English Poets*, Rowe.

[16] Ibid., Smith.   Halifax was awaiting Smith with the book the dedication of which he had accepted and was prepared to reward the poet with a post at £300 a year.   Smith kept procrastinating about the dedication and had to be vigorously egged on by his publisher before he brought himself to write it.   Having at last got it written, he was too lazy or proud or bashful to take it in person to the expectant patron.   He was a fantastic type of Bohemian.   His friends called him " Captain Rag ".

[17] Ibid., Hughes.   [18] Drake, *Essays . . . Illustrative, etc.*, III, p. 268.

prebend and later presented to a vicarage worth £400 a year.[19]
Arbuthnot was appointed Physician in Ordinary to Queen Anne.[20]
Garth and Blackmore were knighted.[21] Budgell was First
Secretary to the Lords Justices in Ireland, Deputy Clerk to the
Council, Member of Parliament and Controller of Revenue.
This last post alone brought him in £400 a year.[22] Granville
was an M.P., Knight of the Shire for Cornwall, Secretary at
War, raised to the peerage as Lord Lansdowne, and became
Controller, and later Treasurer, of Queen Anne's Household,
and a Privy Counsellor.[23]

Stepney was entrusted with several important diplomatic
posts.[24] Arthur Maynwaring was Commissioner of Customs,
Auditor of the Imprests and Member of the House of Commons.[25]
Walsh was also an M.P. and Gentleman of the Horse to Queen
Anne.[26] Henry Martyn was Inspector-General of Imports and
Exports.[27] Tickell was Under-Secretary of State.[28] After so
many obscure and semi-obscure names, we are not surprised to
find John Locke figuring as Commissioner of Appeals and of the
Board of Trade, and Sir Isaac Newton with a knighthood as
Director of the Mint.[29] Steele was Chief Editor of the *London
Gazette*, Gentleman Waiter to Prince George of Denmark, Com-
missioner of Stamps, M.P., Governor of the Royal Comedians,
Judge and Deputy Lieutenant of the County of Middlesex,
Surveyor of the Royal Stables at Hampton Court, Commissioner
of Forfeited Estates and a knight.[30] If Swift had not written
A Tale of a Tub and called the Duchess of Somerset " Carrots ",
he would have been a bishop ; and even as it was, he was made
Dean of St. Patrick's in spite of these misdemeanours.[31] Defoe

[19] Johnson, *Lives of the English Poets*, Parnell.
[20] Chalmers, *Biographical Dictionary*, s.v. Arbuthnot (Dr. John).
[21] Johnson, *Lives of the English Poets*, Garth, Blackmore.
[22] Drake, *Essays . . . Illustrative*, etc., III, pp. 1–25.
[23] Johnson, *Lives of the English Poets*, Granville.
[24] The long list of these diplomatic posts will be found in Johnson,
ibid., Stepney.
[25] *Biographia Britannica*, s.v. Maynwaring (Arthur).
[26] Johnson, ibid., Walsh.
[27] Drake, *Essays . . . Illustrative*, etc., III, p. 287.
[28] Johnson, ibid., Tickell.
[29] *Biographia Britannica*, s.vv. Locke, Newton.
[30] For Steele I have consulted (in addition to his own works) : *The
Epistolary Correspondence of Sir Richard Steele* ; Drake, *Essays . . . Illustrative*,
etc., and Forster, *Biographical Essays*, Steele.
[31] See *The Windsor Prophecy* (Scott's Edition of Swift, XII, p. 297 ff. ;
The Author upon Himself, 1713 (ibid., XII, pp. 315–18). In addition, I have

held a post as Accountant to the Commissioners of Glass Duty and was entrusted with various diplomatic missions.[32]   After publishing his first comedy—shortly after his 24th birthday— Congreve was appointed Commissioner of Hackney Coach and Wine Licences, and held also posts in the Treasury and Customs. On the accession of the House of Hanover he was made Secretary for Jamaica.[33]   Vanbrugh discharged the duties of " Clarenceux King at Arms ", was despatched by Queen Anne to Hanover to convey to the future George I the insignia of the Garter, appointed Controller of the Council of Public Works and Inspector of the Royal Gardens.   He was also given a knighthood.[34]   Gay, who began life as a silk-merchant's apprentice, became Secretary to an Embassy at the age of 25.[35]   After having filled several political posts Addison was made Secretary of State and ultimately retired from public life with a pension of £1,600 a year.[36] The less famous author of *Country Mouse and City Mouse*, Matthew Prior, was appointed successively Secretary to the Earl of Berkeley, Ambassador at the Hague, Gentleman of the Bed Chamber to King William III, Secretary to the Embassy at the Treaty of Ryswick, Ambassador to Versailles, Commissioner of Customs and M.P.[37]   His more fortunate collaborator, Montague, who became—as we have seen—a Minister, was made Baron, then Viscount and finally an Earl, and received the Order of the Garter.[38]

Never had writers found life so easy or so brilliant.   Almost

---

consulted Lives of Swift by Johnson (*English Poets*), by Scott (prefixed to the edition of his Works), by Forster and by Craik, also Professor Masson's Essay on Swift in *Essays Biographical and Critical*.

[32] On Defoe (in addition to his own works listed in my Bibliography), I have consulted the lives by Wilson, William Lee and Minto and Forster's study in his volume of *Biographical Essays*.

[33] On Congreve, see Drake, *Essays . . . Illustrative*, etc., III, pp. 307 ff. ; Johnson, *Lives of the English Poets* ; and Gosse, *Life of William Congreve*.

[34] *An Account of the Life and Writings of the Author* prefixed to Vanbrugh's *Works*, 1776, and *Biographia Dramatica*, s.v. Vanbrugh.

[35] Drake, *Essays . . . Illustrative*, etc., III, pp. 23-4 ; Johnson, *Lives of the English Poets*, Gay.

[36] On Addison I have consulted (in addition to his own works) Miss Aikin's *Life of Addison* ; Johnson, *Lives of the English Poets* ; Drake's *Essays . . . Illustrative*, etc. ; *Biographia Britannica* ; Tickell's Preface to his edition of Addison 1721 ; Steele's letter to Congreve prefixed to Addison's Comedy, *The Drummer* ; Macaulay's Essay on Addison.

[37] Johnson, *Lives of the English Poets*, Prior.

[38] Ibid., Halifax.—Voltaire comments : " In France Addison might have been Member of some Academy and might have obtained, through some woman's good offices, a pension of 1200 *livres* . . . in England he became Secretary of State.   Newton was Comptroller of the Mint ; Congreve held

without transition, they leapt from a precarious and despised position to secure and honourable posts, and found themselves courted on every side. They gained a footing in society which they had never before enjoyed, and which a few short years before they would not have dared to dream of attaining even in the distant future.[38a]

II

Happy results of the writers' new status.—They acquire and deserve respect.—
They take a share in the reform of manners

This marked change in their position brought the happiest results.

First, their profession rose in public estimation. As soon as it was clear that literature might be the road to wealth and dignity, it was no longer scorned and looked down upon.

Hitherto literature had seemed—not unjustifiably—a career which led only to endless disillusionment, if not to irretrievable misery. The luckless wight who was trying to live by his pen met only with contempt—tempered, in exceptional cases only, by the respect which talent commands—such contempt as the world

---

an important post ; Prior has become a Plenipotentiary ; Dr. Swift is a Dean in Ireland and is there accounted a much more important person than the Primate . . ." (*Lettres Philosophiques*, Letter XXIII, Garnier's Edition, XXII, pp. 179–80.)

[38a] [While this picture is in the main true, a few cautions may be suggested. Many of the authors named received their posts for reasons other than literary. Montague was a brilliant financier ; Granville, later Lord Lansdowne, owed his advancement to the fact that he was an able man and member of a rich and powerful family which had many Cornish boroughs in its pocket ; Vanbrugh became Controller of Public Works not because of his plays, but because he was a brilliant architect ; Lord Carlisle obtained for him the post of Clarenceux King at Arms because he was building Castle Howard for him. He was the first knight made by George I mainly as a reward for being a stout Whig, and a protégé of the Duke of Marlborough, for whom he had built Blenheim. He, as herald, had presented the King with the Garter in 1706. Defoe got his post in the glass office because he was a man of business and a manufacturer ; at that time he had no fame as a writer, his chief work at that date being his *Essay on Projects*, a business hand-book. Many, such as Walsh and Maynwaring, were simply amateur writers who would have held the posts they did even if they had never written a line. But it is true that men such as Addison, Congreve, Steele, Prior, etc., obtained their posts, many of them sinecures, solely because they were writers. It was certainly a golden age for authors, but even they had to be efficient in their posts, under pain of losing them, as Gay did his. Ability in literature alone was not enough, social charm counted for a good deal, and there were plenty of writers who got nothing. B. D.]

is wont to bestow on those whose livelihood is painfully and precariously earned, if not actually won by subterfuge and dishonour.

The moment that the author became eligible for high employment and fat salaries, he was looked on with another eye and granted what he had never enjoyed before : respect and esteem.[39] Writing was no longer a trade but a career—a career leading to riches and honour ; and this new respect for literature inspired a new attitude to authors. They no longer formed a class apart, they were received in high society not as protégés but on terms of full equality with the greatest.

Prior invited Harley to his house.[40] Swift was on terms of intimacy with the most important figures of his day ; Harley and Bolingbroke habitually addressed him by his Christian name.[41] Congreve's friendship with the Duke of Marlborough's daughter is well known. Addison married the Dowager Countess of Warwick. Commoners such as Vanbrugh, Congreve, Addison, Garth, Steele, Maynwaring, Stepney, Walsh [42] took their seats in the Kit-Cat Club alongside politically-minded peers like the Earls of Dorset and Sunderland, the Dukes of Somerset, Newcastle and Marlborough. In the Scriblerus Club, Swift, Pope, Arbuthnot and Gay rubbed shoulders with Harley and Bolingbroke.[43] Without having to abase themselves as of old, authors

---

[39] " What most encourages men of letters in England is the esteem in which they are held . . . " (ibid., p. 180).

[40] See " An Extempore Invitation to the Earl of Oxford, Lord High Treasurer ", 1712, in his *Poems on Several Occasions*, p. 286.

[41] See his Correspondence, *Works*, XVI, pp. 108, 143, 150, 367, 454, and his *Journal to Stella*, Feb. 17, 1710–11.

Swift sometimes treated Harley pretty cavalierly, sending him into the House of Commons one day to inform the Secretary of State " to let him know I would not dine with him if he dined late " (*Journal to Stella*, Feb. 12, 1710–11). On July 29, 1711, he wrote to Stella : " I was at Court . . . today . . . I generally am acquainted with about 30 in the drawing-room, and am so proud I make all the lords come up to me : one passes half an hour pleasant enough." Again he writes (Oct. 7, 1711) : " The Duchess of Shrewsbury came up and reproached me for not dining with her. I said that was not so soon done ; I expected more advances from ladies, especially duchesses : she promised to comply with any demands I please ; and I agreed to dine with her tomorrow, if I did not go to London too soon, as I believe I shall before dinner. Lady Oglethorpe brought me and the Duchess of Hamilton together today in the drawing-room and I have given her some encouragement, but not much . . . Lord Keeper . . . said : ' Dr. Swift is not only all our favourite, but our governor.' "

[42] *Addisoniana* in vol. VI of Hurd's edition of Addison, p. 676 ; Spence, pp. 46 and 338.

[43] *Life of Swift* prefixed to Scott's edition of his *Works*, p. 200. [For Scriblerus read Brothers'? B. D.]

were introduced and received into every grade of society and all hastened to bid them welcome.

The natural consequence was that literature attracted more recruits than ever before. It was no longer the pastime of the idle rich, the refuge of the outcast, or the dream of the young enthusiast. As soon as he realized that it offered its votaries not the chance of dubious fame but of assured fortune, a hope of rising not falling in the social scale, everyone who felt he could handle a pen, aimed at a literary career. There was now no reason why any man of talent should hesitate to enter the lists.[44] If other periods of English literature can boast of greater names than this, none can show a larger galaxy of authors famous in so many varied styles. Thinking only of Addison, Swift, Defoe, Steele, Congreve, Farquhar, Vanbrugh, Locke and Newton, we have here famous names enough to make the glory of any literature, and yet we have only skimmed the cream of the brilliant period which has long been known as the Augustan Age of English literature.

We see literature held in greater honour and writers more highly esteemed, but this is by no means the whole story. Exalted in others' eyes by the position accorded them in society, authors themselves rose higher in their own estimation. They acquired a loftier conception of their profession and a better opinion of themselves, and as a natural consequence they became more worthy of popular esteem. Well-paid posts released them from the daily struggle for mere subsistence. They were no longer reduced to the degradation of scheming and self-abasement. Life was not only regular but honourable.[45] They played a dignified part in society and in the posts they held, and one

[44] Vanbrugh held the rank of ensign when he began writing (*An Account of the Life and Writings of the Author* prefixed to his *Works*, p. 4) ; Farquhar was a captain *(Some Memoirs of Mr. George Farquhar* prefixed to his *Works)* ; Steele was a captain ; Addison was about to take Orders ; Swift was in Orders ; Parnell was Archdeacon of Clogher in Ireland (Johnson, *Lives of the English Poets*, Parnell) ; Rowe had an income of £300 a year (Spence, p. 257).

[45] A correspondent addressed the following question to the *Spectator* :

" Sir,—Pray be so kind as to let me know what you esteem to be the chief qualification of a good poet, especially of one who writes plays ; and you will very much oblige, Sir,

Your very humble Servant,
N. B."

The *Spectator* answered : " To be a very well-bred man." (No. 314.)

amongst them, Joseph Addison, still remains the model of an English gentleman in the noblest sense of the term.

The new position of the political parties contributed not a little to this happier state of affairs, for it permitted a writer to hold his personal opinions and remain faithful to them, without fear of being plunged into penury. He was no longer face to face with an omnipotent Court to whose whims he must submit or starve, but with two great parties equally balanced which offered him approximately equal advantages. He was not compelled by material considerations to let his views be swayed by his interest, but was at liberty to choose his own road. In short, he was free to be himself and not the mouthpiece of another. Henceforward such weaknesses as he might betray were such as are at all times inherent in human nature.

The only influence an author had previously wielded—and that rarely—was the influence due to talent. He now enjoyed the influence of position and of character.

He was thus able to take a share, an authoritative share, in the great revolution of manners and morals which was coming.

III

Current Manners.—Manners reflected in the drama : Dryden, Shadwell, D'Urfey, Southerne, Congreve, Vanbrugh, Mrs. Manley, Granville, Dennis

The reader will remember the type of manners and morals that had prevailed under Charles II, and will remember too that during the Merry Monarch's last years, and under James II, people were beginning to weary of so much licence and of so much shame, and that many circumstances combined to heighten this weariness : political preoccupation, the dour temperament of James II and even the King's age.

The Revolution of 1688 and the accession of William III encouraged the nation's return to decency and morality. Politics continued to exercise a wholesomely counter-active effect on impulses of unbridled enjoyment, while the King's personal character and Queen Mary's influence combined to calm and steady people's minds.[46] William was cold and by nature

---

[46] In dedicating *The Mourning Bride* to Princess Anne, the Queen's sister, Congreve writes : " It is from the example of princes that virtue becomes a fashion in the people ; for even they who are averse to instruction will yet be fond of imitation." (*Works*, 1752. The oldest edition in the British Museum—noted in my Bibliography—lacks this Dedication.)

taciturn, and more taciturn than ever in England owing to his very imperfect knowledge of the language. The Queen's life was so entirely beyond reproach that it inspired respect even amid the passion of politics. With two such people on the Stuart throne the Court inevitably ceased to be the haunt of pleasure which Charles II had made it : no more gay festivities, no more gaming, no more theatrical performances, no more " gallantry ". William was not the man to be his courtiers' comrade in revelry, and the Queen's example imposed on the ladies of Whitehall at least the semblance of virtue, and of respect for seemly behaviour.[47] So the Court changed completely in character, and its attractions were further diminished by the fact that the King's health com- pelled him to leave the capital and emigrate to Kensington. It was in very truth an " emigration ", for Kensington, which is nowadays a part of London, was then in open country [48] and thus less easily accessible than Whitehall, a circumstance which in itself made Court entertainments less frequent and less brilliant.

William and Mary were succeeded by Queen Anne and she by George I. It was not a woman—particularly not a thrifty and puritanical woman like Anne [49]—nor yet a foreign prince of fifty-five like George I, who knew not a word of his new sub- jects' tongue and who was bourgeois even in his royal amours,[50] who could revive the Restoration days. Thus the English court tradition of irresponsible gaiety was broken : for ever.

[47] We shall presently see that almost all the protests against the excesses of the theatre come from women. In this I divine the influence of Queen Mary. Hampton Court possesses a collection of portraits of Charles II's Court, most of them painted by Lely, and another collection of William and Mary's Court almost all by Kneller. It is interesting to compare the two sets of women's portraits. The " beauties " of Charles II's time are voluptuous courtesans clad—as scantily as possible—in lustrous materials of bright colour. Under William III the ladies' dress has become most markedly more modest and more discreet.

[48]
　　" Where *Kensington* high o'er the neighb'ring lands
　　　'Midst greens and sweets, a Regal fabrick, stands,
　　　And sees each spring, luxuriant in her bowers,
　　　A snow of blossoms, and a wilde of flowers,
　　　The Dames of *Britain* oft in crowds repair
　　　To gravel walks, and unpolluted air.
　　　Here, while the Town in damps and darkness lies
　　　They breathe in sun-shine, and see azure skies . . . "
　　　　　　　　(Tickell, *Kensington Garden*, 1772. See my
　　　　　　　　　　　　Bibliography.)

[49] See Swift, *Journal to Stella*, Aug. 8 and Sept. 2, 1711.
[50] See Lecky, I, p. 221.

The reform was, however, superficial only. Debauchery was no longer acceptable in high places ; that was an important point. But it is obvious that the basis of manners and morals could not be transformed in a night. A whole society cannot switch over from unbounded licence to the worship of moral purity, or—since this is scarcely to be found on earth—let me rather say to respect for virtue and honourable conduct.

After the Revolution, everything, or almost everything, still remained to be done. It is true that some reassuring signs had indicated that people were tired of irregularity and licence, some genuine protests had made themselves heard, but momentum in the wonted direction was too powerful to be immediately brought to a standstill. Objectors were not yet numerous enough, or sufficiently confident of their strength, at once to silence the din of libertines and scatter-brains. Morality was still looked on as bad form and the same set of people still held the centre of the stage.[51] Fashionable diversions remained unaltered and such as we have seen : young sparks scoured the streets at night to the terror of passers by,[52] they cheated at cards,[53] they drank, they

---

[51] " . . . 'Tis to be hop'd this once wise and sober Nation will awaken from its Lethargy. That notwithstanding the present Popularity of Vice, Levity and Impiety, it may one Day recover its Relish of solid Knowledge and real Merit. That Buffoons themselves may one Day be expos'd, the Laughers in their turn become ridiculous, and an Atheistical Scoffer be as much out of Credit as a sober and religious Man is at present . . . 'Tis great Pity that in so noble a Cause any should shew such Poorness of Spirit as to be asham'd of asserting their Religion, and stemming the Tide of Impiety, for fear of becoming the Entertainment of scoffing Libertines." (Blackmore, *Creation*, Preface.)

[52]   " Now is the Time that Rakes their Revels keep ;
          Kindlers of Riot, Enemies of Sleep.
          His scatter'd Pence the flying *Nicker* flings,
          And with Copper the Show'r the Casement rings.
          Who has not heard the *Scowrer's* Midnight Fame ?
          Who has not trembled at the *Mohock's* name ?
          Was there a Watchman took his hourly Rounds,
          Safe from their Blows, or new-invented Wounds ?
          I pass their desp'rate Deeds, and Mischiefs done
          Where, from *Snow-Hill* black sleepy Torrents run ;
          How Matrons hoop'd within the Hogshead's Womb,
          Were tumbled furious thence ; the rolling Tomb
          O'er the Stones thunders ; bounds from side to side :
          So Regulus to save his Country dy'd."
                                        (Gay, *Trivia*.)
                                        [Book III, l. 321.]

See also the *Spectator*, Nos. 324, 332, 335, 347 ; Swift, *Journal to Stella*, March 8, 9, 12, 15, 16, 18, 22, 26, 1711–12 ; and my Bibliography, s.v. Mohocks.

got drunk,[54] women were as brazen as ever.[55] If we search the drama for indications of morality, we find that licentiousness and the extravagances of debauched imaginations still hold the stage. The old comic authors remained faithful to the old tradition : Dryden's *Amphitryon*,[56] D'Urfey's *Don Quixote*, Shadwell's *Scowrers* and his *Volunteers* are no less outrageous than earlier comedies by the same authors.[57] Newcomers followed faithfully in their footsteps. To be fully convinced on this score, it is enough to cast a glance on Southerne's *Sir Anthony Love* or the

---

[53] " Mrs. *Foresight* : . . . do you think any Woman honest ?
  Scandal : Yes, several, very honest ; —they'll cheat a little at Cards,
    sometimes, but that's nothing."
      (Congreve, *Love for Love*, III.)

 " *Sir Ruff Rancounter* : Madam, I have some Doctors in my Pocket,
    if you please to use 'em.
 Lady *Malepart* : What Doctors, Sir ?
 Sir *Ruff* : Why, don't you know the Doctors ? The Dice that
    only run the high Chances. I'll put 'em into your
    Box, and no body the wiser.
 Lady *Mal* : You shou'd ha' don 't without telling me.
 Sir *Ruff* : So I can still, Madam——"
    (Southerne, *The Maids Last Prayer*, III, 1.)

See also Southerne's *Wives Excuse*, IV, 1.

[54] The first Mutiny Bill, passed in 1689, contained a clause forbidding any Court Martial to pass sentence of death after dinner. It was foreseen that " a gentleman who had dined could not safely be trusted with the lives of his fellow creatures ". (Macaulay, *History*, chap. XI, vol. III, p. 45.)— See also Rémusat, vol. L, p. 285 ; Swift, *Journal to Stella*, April 9 and 21, 1711 ; Oct. 29, 1711 ; Feb. 17, 1711–12.

[55] See their dialogues in the Comedies.

[56] See especially I, 2.

[57] In *The Scowrers* Lady Maggot ranges the streets alone looking for gallants to oblige her. Tope, a Scowrer, accosts her saying : " Pray Heaven she be sound—she's of Quality—hah ! may be ne'ere the sounder for that neither." In *The Volunteers* Nickum is described in the list of Dramatis Personæ as " Mrs. *Hackwell's* Stallion ; a Sharper, which is a new name for a Rogue and a Cheat."

" *Teres.*—Here *Mary*, prithee thread my Needle, good girl, whilst I turn
  down this Selvidge here.
 Mar.— Ay, come, let's see 't. (*rises from the Stool*), And so, Mother,
  you say you had a main deal of Prate about me with Vather
  and my Man that is to be—hoh, hah, hoh, hah—What a
  dickins, I think I Can't do't here—I'm blind, I think, with
  living so long a Maid, hoh, hoh. D'ye think I shall thread
  it better tomorrow, Mother ? Hoh, hoh, hoh.—
 Teres.—Ay, ye Jade," etc.
    (D'Urfey, *The Comical History of Don Quixote*,
     part III, II, 1. See also I, 1.)

comic parts of his *Oroonoko*,[58] or to skim the early plays of Congreve and Vanbrugh.   Comedy paints the same manners with the same lack of restraint.[59]   Tragedy took a slight pull on the

[58] As a specimen, let us take a fragment of *Oroonoko*, the first scene of Act IV between the Widow Lackitt, her son Daniel and his wife Lucy (whom he had married in Act II) :

"*Dan :* I am alter'd for the worse mightily since you saw me ; and she has been the cause of it there.
Wid : How so, Child ?
Dan : I told you before what wou'd come on't, of putting me to bed to a strange Woman : but you would not be said nay.
Wid : She is your Wife, now, Child, you must love her.
Dan : Why, so I did, at first.
Wid : But you must love her always.
Dan : Always ! I lov'd her as long as I cou'd, Mother, and as long as loving was good, I believe, for I find now I don't care a fig for her . . . She may call me Hermophrodite, if she will, for I hardly know whether I'm a Boy or a Girl . . . I have no more Manhood left in me already, than there is, saving the mark, in one of my Mother's old under Petticoats here."

See also I, 1, and II, 1.
See the character of the Abbé in *Sir Anthony Love* and the comments on him in II, 1.—This character in conjunction with Coupler in Vanbrugh's *Relapse* (especially I, 3) would seem to indicate that English society had sunk to the very depths of despicable vice. Among the arguments in favour of the theatre which Dennis brings forward in his *Usefulness of the Stage* is the following (p. 26) : "And now lastly, for the Love of Women, fomented by the . . . Stage . . . it may be in some measure excus'd . . . Because it has a check upon the other Vices, and peculiarly upon that unnatural sin, in the restraining of which the happiness of mankind is in so evident a manner concern'd." Tom Brown, too, says : ". . . *Sue Frousie* that came hither the other day, assures me . . . that the practical Vices of the Town boaded an eternal breach betwixt the Sexes, while Each confin'd itself to the same Sex, and so threatened a cessation of Commerce in Propagation betwixt 'em." (*Letters from the Dead to the Living*, p. 64 : From Julian, Late Secretary to the Muses, to Will. Pierre of Lincolns-Inn Fields *Play-House*.)

[59] "*Belinda.* . . . my Glass and I could never yet agree what Face I should make when they come blurt out with a nasty thing in a Play : For all the Men presently look upon the Women, that's certain ; so laugh we must not, tho' our Stays burst for 't, because that's telling Truth, and owning we understand the Jest : and to look serious is so dull when the whole House is a laughing . . . For my part, I always take that occasion to blow my Nose.
Lady Brute : You must blow your Nose half off, then, at some Plays."
(Vanbrugh, *The Provok'd Wife*, III, 3.)

" While our Authors took the extraordinary Liberties with their Wit, I remember the Ladies were then observ'd, to be decently afraid of venturing bare-fac'd to a new Comedy, 'till they had been assur'd they might do it, without the Risque of an Insult, to their Modesty ; or, if their Curiosity were too strong, for their Patience, they took care, at least, to save Appearances and rarely came upon the first Days of Acting, but in Masks (then daily worn, and admitted, in the Pit, the Side-Boxes, and Gallery) which Custom, reins, the worship of Mademoiselle de Scudéry began to make way for an imitation of the great writers of tragedy, but there was still an eager welcome for sensuous scenes and daring descriptions. Congreve did not stint such things in his *Mourning Bride*.[60]   Mrs. de la Rivière Manley, who inherited the mantle of Mrs. Behn, introduced into *The Royal Mischief* a love scene which her model would not have disclaimed.[61]   Granville's *Heroick Love* has passages which are amongst the most risky that anyone had so far ventured to offer to the English stage.[62]   The songs,[63]

---

however, had so many ill Consequences attending it, that it has been abolish'd these many Years."

(Cibber, Apology, p. 154.)

See also *Spectator*, No. 51.

[60] Act III, Scene 6.   Enter Osmyn and Almeria :

" *Osmyn :*   Then *Garcia* shall lie panting on thy Bosom,
                Luxurious, revelling amidst thy Charms
                And thou perforce must yield, and aid his Transport."

[61] At the close of a love scene between Homais and Prince Levan, Acmat, one of the characters, says :

" We'll not intrude into a Monarch's Secrets,
    The God of Love himself is painted Blind ;
    To teach all other Eyes they shou'd be vail'd
    Upon his Sacred Misteries."   (*Shuts the Scene*.)
                                    (*The Royal Mischief*, III, 1.)

[62] Briseis has been stolen from Achilles during his absence.   When he sees her again he says to her :

" The stain of violation is upon thee . . .
    Didst thou resist ? or didst thou early yield ? . . .
    Met'st thou with willing warmth his brutal lust ?
    Had'st thou thy share of Bliss ?   With amorous rage
    Improving Joy with Art ? . . . "

(V, 1.)

[63]

I

" As *Amoret* and *Thyrsis* lay
    Melting the Hours in gentle Play ;
    Joining Faces, mingling kisses
    And exchanging harmless Blisses
    He trembling cry'd, with eager haste
    O let me feed as well as taste,
    I die, if I'm not wholly blest.

II

The fearful Nymph reply'd—*Forbear* ;
    I cannot, dare not, must not hear :
    Dearest Thyrsis, *do not move me*,
    Do not—do not—if you Love me.
    O let me—still the Shepherd said ;
    But while she fond Resistance made,
    The hasty Joy, in strugling fled.

epilogues and prologues remain as indelicate as ever [64] and one of D'Urfey's epilogues surpasses in audacity anything heard before.[65]

Nevertheless, there really was something in the air. Free and reckless as his plays are, the greatest writer of comedies at this time, William Congreve, betrays by his diction a change of taste. Whatever you may reproach his characters with, they have the new virtue of being a trifle more restrained in their expression ; bullying scoundrels and frequenters of brothels they remain, but they do not use the language of the brothel. They set no good example, but at least they are good company. Voltaire's phrase hits them off exactly : they act like rascals but talk like honest men.[66] The same may be said of the characters in Southerne's comedies.

III

Vex'd at the Pleasure she had miss'd
She frown'd and blush'd, then sigh'd and kiss'd
And seem'd to moan in sullen Cooing
The sad miscarriage of their Wooing :
But vain alas ! were all her Charms ;
For *Thyrsis* deaf to Loves allarms
Baffled and senseless, tir'd her Arms.

(Congreve, *The Old Batchelour*, III, 2.)

See also Congreve's *Love for Love* (III, 1), and the song which closes Vanbrugh's *Provok'd Wife*.

[64] Notably the Epilogue of *A Plot and no Plot* by Dennis. It was spoken by a woman :

" . . . The Poet was inclin'd to chuse
Your humble Servant to sustain his Muse :
He knew, if I would beg, I should not want
A favour, who you know have one to grant.
I've kept it long ; There's an old Dame—Pox on her,
An old, morose, damn'd grinning Jade, call'd Honour ;
Who with her coldness checks my forward Nature,
Else should I quickly prove—The happiest creature !
I'll throw her off, if possibly I can,
Throw the grim Goddess off, and put on Man . . .
Now who shall first be my man ? He, I swear,
Who for this Play most warmly shall declare . . . "

[65] *The Comical History of Don Quixote*, part I. The Epilogue is spoken by Sancho, mounted on a donkey called Dapple :

" But for some other Gifts—mind what I say,
Never compare, each *Dapple* has his Day,
Nor anger him, but kindly use this Play
For should you, with him, conceal'd Parts disclose,
Lord, How like Ninneys, would look all the *Beaus*."

[66] " In them [viz. Congreve's comedies] you find everywhere the speech of honest men and the actions of rascals." (*Lettres philosophiques*, Letter XIX. On Comedy. *Works*, XXII, p. 160.)

The public too were no longer willing to tolerate the smuttinesses for which they had earlier shown so much appetite. Protests were frequent. Downes tells us that Granville's *She-Gallants* had but a short run, though " extraordinary witty and well Acted " for " offending the Ears of some Ladies who set up for Chastity, it made its Exit ".[67] D'Urfey's *Don Quixote* [68] and Congreve's *Double-Dealer* [69] also shocked some of the audience. A play of Fletcher's, which a certain Thomas Scott in 1697 worked over in Restoration style, also gave offence.[70] Mrs. Manley's tragedy of which I spoke just now and Vanbrugh's *Relapse* were not—if we can trust their Prefaces—immune from reproach. An Epilogue, also of 1697, sadly complains :

> Once only smutty Jests would please the Town,
> But now (Heav'n help our Trade) they'll not go down.[71]

It seems as if authors no longer felt themselves on firm ground. There was a scene in *Sir Anthony Love*—fairly scandalous, it must be admitted—between his priest and his heroine [72] which Southerne did not dare to put on the stage. In dedicating *The Mourning Bride* to Princess Anne, Congreve eloquently pleads extenuating circumstances for drama, hoping, as he says, " to convince your Royal Highness that a play may . . .

[67] Downes, *Roscius Anglicanus*, p. 45, on " *The She-Gallants*, a Comedy, wrote by *Mr. George Greenvil*, when he was very Young ".
[68] J. Collier, *A Short View*, etc., p. 204.
[69] " His Double Dealer is much censur'd by the greater of the Town : . . . The women think he has expos'd their Bitchery too much ; and the gentlemen are offended with him for the discovery of their follyes : and the way of their Intrigues, under the notion of Friendship to their Ladyes Husbands." (Letter from Dryden to Walsh, probable date 1693 ; first published in R. Bell's *Life of Dryden*, p. 76.) Congreve himself says in his Dedication, " Some of the Ladies are offended."
[70] " The last Scene in the Third Act had the Misfortune to offend some . . . " (Preface to *The Unhappy Kindness*.)
[71] Hopkins, *Boadicea, Queen of Britain*. The Epilogue was spoken by Mrs. Bowman.—In the Prologue to *Sir Anthony Love*, spoken by Mrs. Bracegirdle, Southerne says :

> " O ! would our peaceful days were come agen ; . . .
> When once the Child was turn'd into her Teens,
> You cou'd not find a Maid behind the Scenes.
> But now your Keeping humor's out a door,
> We must dye Maids : or marry to be poor."

[72] V, 1. See the Preface. It was in order not to offend the ladies that he suppressed it, so he tells us. It is printed in the 1774 Edition of his *Works*.

become sometimes an innocent, and not unprofitable entertainment ".[73]

All these signs evidently foreshadow a coming revolution in
taste. At last, thirty years after the Restoration, people had the
courage to mention the words modesty and restraint. This was
much : but still too little. Protests were still too vague and too
weak to be effective. The Anti-Puritan reaction had been too
acute and too vigorous to yield to such hesitant attacks.

IV

*Jeremy Collier's " Short View of the Immorality and Profaneness of the
English Stage".—What Collier was.—Analysis of his book : its faults,
merits, effect.—Replies by Congreve, Vanbrugh, D'Urfey, Wycherley, Dennis,
Settle, Filmer, Drake, Farquhar, etc.—Collier's triumph : reform of the
theatre*

In 1698 a little book of less than 300 pages opportunely came
to speak for, and to rally, the opposition : Jeremy Collier's *Short
View of the* Immorality *and* Profaneness *of the English Stage.*[74]
A zealous clergyman of the Church of England and an ardent
Tory, Collier refused to swear allegiance to King William. He

---

[73] *Works*, 1752 Ed. See also above chap. III, note No. 46.

[74] On Collier, see *Biographia Britannica* ; Allibone, and Macaulay's
Essay on the *Comic Dramatists of the Restoration.*—Before Collier, an estimable
but intolerable writer, Richard Blackmore, had begun the attack on the
stage. As early as 1695 in the Preface to a heroic poem called *Prince Arthur*
he wrote : " Our poets seem engaged in a general *Confederacy* to ruin the
End of their own Art, to expose *Religion* and *Virtue*, and bring *Vice* and
Corruption of Manners, into Esteem and Reputation. The Poets that write
for the Stage (at least a great part of 'em) seem deeply concern'd in this
Conspiracy." Here he added five folio pages of well-aimed criticism.—In
1697 he returned to the attack in the Preface to his *King Arthur* : " The Reasons
which induc'd me to make the former, did likewise engage me in this second
Attempt in *Epick* Poetry ; and among the rest, particularly this, that the
young Gentlemen and Ladys who are delighted with Poetry might have a
useful, at least a harmless Entertainment, which in our Modern Plays and
Poems cannot ordinarily be found . . . that leud and abominable way of
writing which was encourag'd in the late Reigns . . . And tho' these mischievous ways of Writing are still endur'd to the great prejudice of Religion
and good Manners, yet if ever the *English* Nation recovers it's ancient Vertue
and a just Tast of these Matters, I do not doubt but most of those Writers
who have been esteem'd and applauded in the late loose and vicious Times,
will be rejected with Indignation and Contempt, as the Dishonour of the
Muses, and the Underminers of the Publick Good." This is all sensibly
and justly said ; but Blackmore had not lung-power enough to sound a
trumpet round the walls of Jericho.

resigned his offices in the Church, and being a born controversialist girded his loins for battle. He prepared himself for his
task by wide reading—more extensive perhaps than well digested
—and then flung himself heart and soul into the political and
religious fray with a Loyalist passion which earned him several
months' imprisonment in Newgate.[75]

Restored to liberty and not a whit repentant, he set himself
with increased vigour to maintain the rights of James II and to
attack the usurper. Suspected of being a party to Jacobite plots,
he was imprisoned again in 1692. He was not long in bringing
graver trouble on himself. Sir John Friend and Sir William
Parkyns were condemned to death in 1696 for a plot against King
William's life. Collier stood by them to the last and at the foot
of the scaffold publicly and solemnly gave them absolution.
This created no small scandal. He was accused from every side
of having absolved unrepentant assassins and of thus having
appeared to cloak a crime with the mantle of the Church. The
Bishops rebuked him in due form.[76] He was summoned before
the Court of King's Bench, but refused to give obedience to an
illegal tribunal, and was thereupon outlawed. He was under
this ban, that is to say threatened and hunted, when he published
his book against the contemporary theatre. This fact alone is
enough to show the mettle of the man, and the spirit he was
bringing to his attack on the English stage. He was of the
breed of the apostles. Neither his personal danger, nor the
fame of the authors whom he was attacking, nor the brilliance
of recent dramatic triumphs could halt him in his course, or for
an instant delay him. He believed that he had a mission to
fulfil, and he set out to war against the theatre as the Crusaders
of old took the Cross against the Infidel.

Plunging head foremost into battle, he launched a vigorous
frontal attack. Striking ahead of him, striking to right of him,
striking to left of him, he let fly uncounted blows of his brawny
arm, returning perpetually on his tracks as if he feared to have
let his foes escape too lightly. He called to his aid Aristotle,

[75] Allibone gives a list of his political writings. The work for which
he was imprisoned was *The Desertion Discuss'd*. See my Bibliography.

[76] " Mr. *Collier* the absconding, absolving Parson, has been so bold as
to print a second Vindication of the practice of himself and his Comerades
at Tyburn, wherein he pretends to prove the Lawfulness [*sic*] of his and their
practice, by Councils and Fathers, in answer to the Declaration of our Bishops."
(The London News-Letter Numb. 13. From Monday, May 25th, to Wednesday, May 27th, 1696 : *British Museum*.)—See also my Bibliography, s.v.
Letter.

Plato, Horace, Tacitus, Boileau, Rapin, the Ancients and the
Moderns, philosophers, orators and historians, poets, Greek
tragedians and Latin comedians, Athenians, Lacedæmonians and
Romans, the Law, the Councils, the Fathers of the Church down
even to Minutius Felix. With these allies he pushed his charge
home, strewing his path with the mangled remains of authors
and their plays. Pretty well every English dramatist was more
or less battered in the fray, but his severest blows were aimed at
his contemporaries, at Dryden, Wycherley, Congreve, D'Urfey
and Vanbrugh, especially in their latest works. To prove that
they were no models of virtue and chastity was an easy task.
He piles up quotations from their plays, he singles out each passage
which outrages religion, morality, and seemliness, and even
(while he's on the job) each which offends orthodox literary
convention.[77] One by one in full detail he picks out every fault
—even the minutest peccadillo. Every page lengthens the indictment against them. Pressing in turn into his service indignation,
sarcasm, contempt, anathema, he thunders out his fiery speech
for the prosecution, leaving his victim no chance to plead
extenuating circumstances.

Criticisms in plenty may be made against this passionate and
uncompromising attack. Its form is anything but attractive.
Its style is heavy and verges on the brutal, though it does not
lack energy or a certain felicity of phrase. As a whole the book
is nothing but a monotonous sermon, a long homily, scrupulously
divided into sections, many of which are again minutely sub-
divided. The effect on the reader is markedly wearisome, and
fatigue is increased by a laborious erudition which obscures rather
than clarifies the argument. Collier never allows you to forget
that he was in his day a student of Cambridge University, and at
every turn of his discourse he pedantically and coquettishly
displays his knowledge of Greek and Latin authors if he does
not hark back to still older authority. So dear is his hobby-
horse to him, that he often lets her take the bit between her teeth
and completely forgets—and the reader forgets of course even
more completely—the destination he was heading for. While he
devotes, for instance, thirteen pages to proving that the English
drama treats the clergy badly,[78] he spends twenty-eight pages in

---

[77] The passages in Section III, for instance, that are particularly devoted
to Vanbrugh's *Relapse* reproach the dramatist with failure to observe the
unities of time, place and action.

[78] In Chapter III.

discussing the part which priests play in the works of Homer and
Virgil, in Greek tragedy, in Aristophanes, Plautus, Terence,
Corneille and Molière,[79] in Racine, Shakespeare, Ben Jonson,
Beaumont and Fletcher, etc. Then, like M. Jourdain's teacher,
he gives three reasons why it is a duty to respect the clergy :
namely, the first, the second and the third. Next, he fine-combs
history for proof that they have always and everywhere commanded respect from the days of Jews, Egyptians and Persians
down to French and Muscovite times. It must be admitted that
in a discussion devoted to the clergy of the Church of England,
arguments from foreign civilizations and pagan—or at any rate
non-Protestant—religions, are unexpected and not exactly cogent.
This notwithstanding, every step in his logic is supported anew
by a review of the ancients, equally uninteresting, equally out
of place.

Apart from this craze for erudition, Collier is the victim of
another obsession, no less damaging to his book. If he can never
forget that he is a Cambridge man, still less can he forget that he
is in Holy Orders. We have just seen how elaborately he insists
that the drama should respect the cloth, but his sensitivity on
this point rises to almost unimaginable heights. If he were
content to plead merely for respect, he would win his case too
easily ; but he is not content to protest against the coarse and
vulgar jokes perpetually levelled at the clergy and at religion by
the Restoration drama, he must, if you please, deny that any
dramatist in tragedy or comedy has the right to stage any scene
implying that any parson could be subject to any human passion,
fault or eccentricity.[80] He lays claim to absolute immunity, not
limited, as we might expect, to clergymen of the English Church
but extended—a most remarkable fact when we remember the
religious hatreds of his day—to Roman Catholic priests [81] and
Nonconformist ministers.[82] Nor is this enough. He grows
indignant to think of a mufti or a priest of Jupiter [83] being represented in an ugly light, and he cannot forgive Dryden for having
spoken lightly of Muhammad or taken the names of Phœbus and
Mercury in vain, and for having applied disrespectful adjectives

[79] All that he can say about clerics in the plays of Corneille and Molière
is that there are none.
[80] Vanbrugh retorts—justly if somewhat brutally—" A Clergyman is not
in any Country exempted from the Gallows : . . . A Hangman then may
jerk him ; Why not a Poet ? " (*A Short Vindication* . . . p. 54.)
[81] Pp. 98 and 99.   [82] Pp. 101 and 102.
[83] Pp. 103, 105, and 120.

to the bull Apis.[84] He goes even further in retrospective zeal and picks a quarrel with Aristophanes for showing lack of reverence towards Neptune, Bacchus and Hercules.[85]

Worst of all, Collier's book suffers from two grave defects : want of perception and injustice.

He is completely lacking in artistic feeling.[86] His pages contain not one word of admiration for any of the authors ancient or modern that he names. It is clear that he has no spark of sympathy for dramatic literature of any kind—which frequently prevents his judging it fairly. Because Shakespeare has at times used phrases which he—like everyone else—considers too vigorous, he puts Shakespeare on the same level as the comic dramatists of the Restoration.[87] He does not understand that the flavour of words alters with time,[88] that it is not the word but the under-lying meaning which is dangerous and that no sane moralist could hesitate to prefer the outspoken crudities of Shakespeare to the ingeniously veiled vileness of some of his successors. Collier never judges things from the dramatic point of view but focuses his mind on the words alone, and thus makes the dramatist personally responsible for every syllable uttered by his characters. If a rascal or a libertine enters and speaks as suits his character, the author is accused of himself deliberately attacking honesty and virtue.[89]

The root of Collier's injustice is that he considers the theatre, and the theatre alone, guilty of the vices of his time and makes it the scapegoat of his contemporaries' sins. If licence is the fashion, that is the theatre's fault ; if irreverence reigns, the theatre only is the cause ; if high principle is at a discount, the

---

[84] Pp. 61, 184 and 105.

[85] Pp. 38 and 45.

[86] On p. 123 he praises " the famous Corneille " for not having intro-duced Tiresias into his *Oedipus*, tho' he himself admits that this omission is injurious to the tragedy.

[87] Pp. 10, 50 and 125.

[88] Collier himself uses words of which an English writer would to-day be chary. (See particularly, pp. 70 and 73.)

[89] Vanbrugh admirably countered this point : " . . . his Lordship's Words [i.e. Lord Foppington's in *The Relapse*] which he [Collier] quotes about St. *James's* Church, are beyond all dispute on the Minister's side, though not on his Congregation's . . . For though my Lord *Foppington* is not supposed to speak what he does to a Religious End, yet 'tis so ordered, that his manner of speaking it, together with the Character he represents, plainly and obviously instructs the Audience (even to the meanest Capacity) that what he says of his Church Behaviour, is design'd for their Contempt, and not for their Imitation . . . "

(*A Short Vindication* . . . pp. 16 and 17.)

theatre is the villain of the piece. It would seem that Collier
had never met undesirable people off the stage, that the theatre
had deliberately invented vice in order to set an evil example.
He would imply that all England was peopled with innocent
and simple souls who would have been to the world a model of
all the virtues, if dramatists had not, out of pure wickedness,
turned them from the straight and narrow way and hunted them
along the road to perdition. This was to shut his eyes to the
broader issues and oddly to misplace responsibility.[90]

But having made these reservations—as we are bound to do—
we must concede that Collier's book is the sincere testimony of
a brave and honest man. How brave he was, he had already
proved. He proved it yet again—obscure writer as he was—by
boldly attacking the greatest authors of his day, then at the
zenith of their powers and popularity. Honest he was, for
though a partisan in every fibre of his being, he banished every
trace of party spirit from his work. This fervent Tory, who
chose to embrace the cause of James II at the very moment when
loyalty to it could spell for him nothing but risk and danger,
this passionate politician, lays aside all political sympathies when
his task is to defend outraged morals. He does not hesitate to
lash out at such Tories as he encounters in his course and even
those works of theirs which had performed the greatest service
to the cause so near his heart.[91] This burning sincerity gives
his *Short View of the Immorality and Profaneness of the English Stage*
a value of which no criticism can rob it. Each page is steeped
in sincere conviction and impresses even the most recalcitrant
reader. One-sided and violent as was the attack, it had the
merit of being radically just and singularly opportune. It would
be unreasonable to ask of a controversialist the stern and impartial

[90]   " Perhaps the Parson stretch'd a point too far,
            When with our *Theatres* he wag'd a War.
            He tells you, That this very Moral Age
            Receiv'd the first Infection from the Stage.
            But sure, a banisht Court, with Lewdness fraught,
            The Seeds of open Vice returning brought.
            Thus Lodg'd (as Vice by great Example thrives)
            It first debauch'd the Daughters and the Wives . . .
                        (Dryden's Epilogue to Fletcher's *Pilgrim* ; see
                                the lines that follow, quoted above
                                chap. I, note No. 448.)

    Dennis in *The Usefulness of the Stage* (chap. III), like Dryden, replaces re-
sponsibility on the right shoulders.
    [91] P. 183 violently attacks Dryden's *Absalom and Achitophel*.

detachment of a historian. Collier sounded the call to action stations, and sounded it at the right moment. No doubt he lacked a sense of proportion in attacking the theatre only ; but it is only fair to recognize that the theatre was one of the last fortresses in which fashionable vice was entrenched and also the most glaring symbol of the country's demoralization.[92]

With these various merits, the author of the *Short View* combined another which contributed not a little to the success of his book : the advantage of being incontestably Anglican and Tory. For more than forty years—we have seen why and how— virtue had in England been considered Puritan, and we know what reactions the term " Puritan " evoked. These anti- Puritan prejudices, firmly held and violently expressed during the first post-Restoration years, had been somewhat modified by time which had assuaged the ancient hatreds.

Those who had witnessed and those who had taken part in the Civil War had almost all passed on. The Puritans had mellowed both in politics and religion, and had gradually become assimilated in the Whig party and the various dissenting bodies. But a match to the tinder of slumbering prejudice and the old passions would have blazed up as furiously as ever.[93] If Collier had been even slightly suspect of being a Whig or a Dissenter— let alone a Puritan—people on hearing him play the moralist would have begun by shouting " fanatic " and ended by dubbing him " regicide ". He would have been accused of concealing beneath a hypocritical display of virtue the wish to restore the reign of " The Saints " and violently to overthrow the monarchy.[94]

---

[92] " The Seat of Wit, when one speaks as a Man of the Town and the World, is the Play-House ", so says No. 65 of *The Spectator*.

[93] Note how comedy still represents the Puritans and their friends : Fondlewife in Congreve's *Old Batchelour* and Saygrace in his *Double-Dealer*.

[94] D'Urfey made the attempt. See the lines of a song called *The New Reformation*, which he introduced into his comedy, *The Campaigners* (IV, I) :

> " Cuckolds and Canters,
> With Scruples and Banters,
> Th' Old Forty One peal against Poetry ring.
> But let State revolvers,
> And *Treason-Absolvers*,
> Excuse if I sing,
> The Scoundrel that chooses
> To cry down the Muses,
> Would cry down the King."

Congreve's *Way of the World* also ranks Collier among the Puritans : " There are Books over the Chimney—*Quarles* and *Pryn*, and the *Short View of the Stage*, with *Bunyan's* Works to entertain you." (III, I.)

It is easy to guess how the moral question would have been side-tracked amid such recriminations. It would have been swamped under an avalanche of accusation and insult of every kind.

Fortunately for the cause he was championing, Collier was a Tory and a Church of England clergyman of such quality that every misinterpretation of this kind fell to the ground in advance. So people kept to the point at issue and the book produced its full effect.

The effect was great. The theatre world and the literary world were immediately shaken to their foundations. On every side authors and playwrights girded on their armour to give battle to the foe. Congreve, Vanbrugh and D'Urfey, directly indicted, hastened to reply : Congreve and Vanbrugh in specially-written vindications, D'Urfey in a " Familiar Preface " and a Prologue to *The Campaigners*.[95] Wycherley no doubt also replied.[96] Others who had not been pilloried by name, or were not personally interested in the controversy—Dennis, Settle, Drake, Filmer, Motteux, Tom Brown [97]—took up the defensive : not to mention those who wrote anonymously.[98] Two newcomers to drama hastened to enrol themselves under the war-banner of their fellow-playwrights : Farquhar with the Epilogue to his first play *Love and a Bottle* and Cibber with the Prologue to his tragedy of *Xerxes*.[99] A hail of missiles—pamphlets, dissertations, prologues, epilogues, prefaces—rained down on Collier from every side,

[95] See my Bibliography, s.vv. Congreve, Vanbrugh and D'Urfey.

[96] See Macaulay's Essay, *Comic Dramatists of the Restoration*, and Allibone, s.v. Collier (Jeremy). Neither gives a clue that would have enabled me to trace Wycherley's reply.
[Wycherley's answer may be the anonymous *A Vindication of the Stage*, a light, amusing, ineffective piece of writing. Others ascribe it to Gildon. The only really good answer was Dennis's *The Usefulness of the Stage* ; he could meet Collier on his own ground as far as erudition went, but his argument is rather above the head of the general reading public. B. D.]

[97] See my Bibliography, s.vv. Dennis, Drake (J.), Filmer, Motteux, Tom Brown. Macaulay and Allibone quote Settle as amongst those who replied, but give no more clue than in the case of Wycherley. The British Museum Catalogue is silent on all three.

[98] *The Immorality of the English Pulpit* ; *A Vindication of the Stage* ; *Some Remarks upon Mr. Collier's Defence* . . . ; *The Stage Acquitted*, edited by A. D. See my Bibliography, s.vv. Pulpit, Stage, Remarks, A. D.

[99] The Epilogue to *Love and a Bottle* was by the actor Haines who got himself up in mourning to recite it :

> " Royal Theatre, I come to *Mourn* for thee . . .
> Oh Collier, Collier ! thou'st frighted away *Miss C—s* . . . "
> (Farquhar's *Works* 1760 ; the British Museum
> has no separate edition of this play.)

and coming from men who were nearly all fighting *pro aris et focis*, we can well understand that the defence was not less lively than the attack. They attacked the enemy at close quarters. He was spared neither heavy blows nor coarse abuse.[100] Another man might have been dazed by so much noise and so many assaults, might have been bewildered, might have hesitated ; but not Collier. Trifles of this kind could not move him. Controversy was the breath of his life. He had the temperament of the political orator who far from being flustered by interruptions is stimulated thereby to greater eloquence. All these replies merely spurred him to exertion. He parried every blow and let fly his return blows in every direction at once. For ten consecutive years, with inexhaustible energy, he held his own against all comers.[101]

It was he who remained master of the field. This result of the battle might from the outset have been easily foreseen by any attentive observer. It had indeed immediately been evident that public opinion was behind Collier, and would ensure his final victory.[102] We may go so far as to say that his ultimate

---

For the Prologue to *Xerxes* (1699), see Genest, II, p. 169. The British Museum has no separate edition of this play and it is not included in Cibber's *Works*.

[100] " I have no intention to examine all the Absurdities and Falshoods in Mr. *Collier's* Book ; . . . I will remove 'em (the passages quoted by Collier from his plays) from his Dunghil, and replant 'em in the Field of Nature ; and when I have wash'd 'em of that Filth which they have contracted in passing thro' his very dirty hands, let their own Innocence protect them." (Congreve, *Amendments*, etc., pp. 2 and 4.)—" In reading this Gentleman's Book I have been often at a loss to know when he's playing the Knave, and when he's playing the Fool . . . But this I'm sure, *Young Fashion* is no more the Principal Person of the Play, than He's the best Character in the Church." (Vanbrugh, *A Short Vindication*, p. 58.)—In his " Familiar Preface " D'Urfey's wit consists solely in calling Collier " the *Absolver* ", " Doctor Absolution ", " Doctor *Crambo* ", " Hypocrite " and " canting Fool ". The anonymous author of *The Immorality of the English Pulpit* is vulgar and stupid from end to end ; here is one of the phrases he hurls at Collier : " A wicked Parson is the most potent Villain upon Earth " (p. 7).

[101] *A Defence of the Short View* . . . 1699, reply to Congreve and Vanbrugh ; *A Second Defence* . . . 1700, reply to Drake ; *Dissuasive from the Play-House* . . . 1703 (Dennis replied to this last by " The Person of Quality's Answer to Mr. Collier's Letter : *Containing a Defence of a Regulated Stage* " ; (see his *Original Letters*, II, p. 228) ; *A Farther Vindication* . . . 1708, reply to Filmer. See my Bibliography, s.v. Collier. This controversy did not prevent his writing on other subjects ; see *Biographia Britannica*.

[102] He was himself confident of this from the start. In the preliminary notice of *A Defence of the Short View* he already said : " Notwithstanding the singular Management of the *Poets* and *Play-House*, I have had the satisfaction to perceive, the Interest of Virtue is not altogether Sunk, but that Conscience and Modesty have still some Footing among us."

success was manifest from the very manner of his opponents' replies to his attack. The man who might have proved his sturdiest antagonist, Dryden, was weary of the theatre and had already reached the age at which a man looks back on his life to survey the road he has travelled. Convinced that his road had been the wrong one, and that he had squandered his genius, Dryden at first kept silence and then in 1700 in the Preface to his *Fables* he passed judgment on himself with a candour which did honour to him at the end of his career. (He died the same year.) He frankly admitted that in many things Collier had " taxed him justly " : " I have pleaded guilty ", he writes, " to all thoughts or expressions of mine that can be truly accused of obscenity, immorality, or profaneness, and retract them. If he be my enemy, let him triumph ; if he be my friend, as I have given him no personal occasion to be otherwise, he will be glad of my repentance." Vanbrugh cleared his conscience in some sixty pages where a few telling retorts are drowned in colourless and tedious argument. We might have expected a brilliant reply from a man of Congreve's wit, but he writes like an incompetent attorney defending a bad case. He raises minor points only, counters Collier's learning with Greek and Latin quotations of his own, argues about Collier's style [103] and indulges in irrelevant personalities unworthy of his own talent.[104] In a word, he was neither able to establish his innocence nor honest enough, like Dryden, to confess his faults. Even where Collier laid himself open to easy refutation, Congreve contrived to put himself in the wrong by concocting ridiculous evasions. Collier had for instance reproached him for giving the name of Mr. Prig to a chaplain. We might think that on such a point Congreve might have thrown himself on the mercy of the court ; it was not a hanging matter. He preferred to deny having had any ulterior motive whatever in the choice of this name rather than another : " Well, but supposing his name really had been Mr. Prig ? " [105] says he. This is typical of the whole style of his defence.

It is clear that the accused conducted their defence without conviction. They felt at heart that they were in the wrong, and the ground gave way under their feet. Public opinion

[103] Pp. 15, 28–9 and 94 (wrongly numbered 84).
[104] Pp. 21 and 106 (wrongly numbered 96).
[105] P. 58.

which had immediately taken sides for the prosecution [106] exerted
a pressure to which everybody gradually yielded. Approval was
so strong and so unanimous that William III was willing to forget
that Collier was politically his enemy, and issued a *nolo prosequi*
quashing all legal proceedings against him. [107] Eager recruits
flung themselves passionately into the Crusade whose Peter the
Hermit was Jeremy Collier. [108] Morality was the watchword of
the day. Societies for the Reformation of Manners, which during
the reign of James II had been born in obscurity in London, now
came to the fore with ardour and with zest. They lay in wait
for every word uttered on the stage that might be at variance
with morals or religion, they sent their spies to the performances
and brought actors and theatres into court. [109] William III
insistently renewed the orders he had already issued in 1697

[106] By 1699 his book had already reached its fourth edition. See my
Bibliography.

[107] Cibber, *Apology*, p. 159.

[108] Defoe, *The Poor Man's Plea*, 1698 ; *The Stage Condemn'd*, 1698 ;
Some Considerations about the Danger of going to Plays, 1698 and 1704 ; *Animadversions on Mr. Congreve's Late Answer to Mr. Collier*, 1698 ; *A Representation of
the Impiety and Immorality of the English Stage*, 1704 ; *Some Thoughts Concerning
the Stage*, 1704 ; *Plain English, A Sermon . . . for Reformation of Manners*, 1704,
by William Bisset ; Four Pamphlets by Arthur Bedford ; *Serious Reflections on
the Scandalous Abuse and Effects of the Stage*, 1705 ; *A Second Advertisement concerning
the Profaneness of the Play-House*, 1705 ; *The Evil and Danger of Stage Plays*, 1706 ;
*A Serious Remonstrance in Behalf of the Christian Religion, against the Horrid Blas-
phemies and Impieties which are still used in the English Play-Houses*, 1719. See
my Bibliography, s.vv. Defoe, Stage, Considerations, Animadversions, Plays,
Bisset and Bedford (Arthur).—Collier's book was even translated into French.
See my Bibliography, s.v. Collier.

[109] Lecky, II, pp. 546–7. According to their 40th Annual Report
these societies had by 1735 instituted 99,380 proceedings in London and
Westminster alone. At a certain point Queen Anne was obliged to temper
their passion for prosecutions (Genest, II, p. 124). These Societies for the
Reformation of Manners are frequently mentioned in the literature of the
time, notably in John Dunton's *Life and Errors* (passim) ; in *A Representation
of the Impiety and Immorality of the English Stage*, pp. 6–7 ; in Collier's *Dissuasive
from the Play-House*, p. 9 ; in Swift's *Advice to a Young Poet* ; and in Tom Brown.
Amongst other passages here is what Tom Brown has to say : " There has
a terrible enemy arose to the Stage ; an abdicated Divine, who when he had
escaped the Pillory for Sedition and reforming the State, set up for the
Reformation of the Stage ; the Event was admirable . . . one grave Citizen
. . . laid out Threescore Pound in the Impression to distribute among the
Saints . . . There is yet a greater mischief befall'n the *Stage* ; here are
Societies that set up for *Reformation of Manners* : Troops of *Informers* . . .
serve God for Gain, and ferret out Whores for Subsistence " (*Letters from the
Dead to the Living* : Will. Pierre's Answer (to Julian), Lincoln's Inn Fields,
Novem. 5, 1701. Behind the Scenes).—These societies published numerous
pamphlets, etc. Some are mentioned in my Bibliography, s.v. Reforma-
tion.

suppressing immoral or irreligious passages in any play,[110] and the Master of the Revels, whose duty it was to authorize a play, could pass it only after rigorous scrutiny.[111] At the beginning of her reign Queen Anne impressed on actors the need for the greatest self-restraint, forbade the admission behind the scenes of anyone, of whatever rank, unconnected with the theatre, and forbade women to come masked to performances.[112]

There was, however, little need of threats and law-givings. The seed Collier had sown germinated of itself, and the change spontaneously brought about by the exercise of men's free will, produced more far-reaching and speedier results than could have been achieved by the wisest of laws or the fear of serious punishment.

The theatre voluntarily reformed its erring ways. Authors flung into the melting-pot plays that had already been acted, to recast them in finer mould : Congreve deleted several phrases

[110] " His Majesty has been pleased to Command that the following Order should be sent to both Playhouses.

" *His Majesty*, being informed, That, notwithstanding an Order made the 4th of *June*, 1697, by the Earl of *Sunderland*, then Lord Chamberlain of his Majesty's Household, to prevent the Prophaneness and Immorality of the Stage [Note that these are the very words of Collier's title] ; several Plays have lately been Acted, containing Expressions contrary to Religion and good Manners : And whereas the Master of the Revels has represented, That, in Contempt of the said Order, the Actors do often neglect to leave out such Prophane and Indecent Expressions, as he has thought proper to be omitted. These are therefore to signify His Majesty's Pleasure, That you do not hereafter presume to Act anything in any Play contrary to Religion and good Manners, as you shall answer it at your utmost peril. *Given under my Hand this 18th of* February 1698. In the Eleventh year of His Majesty's reign. *Pere. Bertie.* [Peregrine Bertie was Vice Chamberlain. B. D.]

" An Order has likewise been sent by His Majesty's Command to the Master of the Revels, not to License any plays containing Expressions contrary to Religion and good Manners, and to give Notice to the Lord Chamberlain of His Majesty's Household, or in his absence to the Vice-Chamberlain if the Players presume to Act anything which he has struck out." (*The London Gazette*, No. 3,474, Monday, Feb. 27, 1698-9.)

On Dec. 11, 1699, he returns to the charge : " Whitehall, Dec. 11. This day was Published, His Majesty's Proclamation for Preventing and Punishing Immorality and Prophaneness." (*The London Gazette*, No. 3,557 of 11-14th Dec. 1699.)

[111] Cibber, *Apology*, pp. 159, 160.

[112] See Genest, II, pp. 296-7. In order to court Queen Anne's favour, Swift published in 1707 *A Project for the Advancement of Religion, and the Reformation of Manners. By a Person of Quality*. One important passage in it is devoted to the theatre. See Scott's Edition of his *Works*, VIII, pp. 79 ff. and Forster, *The Life of Jonathan Swift*, p. 213.—Similarly Tate published in 1712 *The Monitors. Intended for the Promoting of Religion and Virtue, and Suppressing of Vice and Immorality*. See my Bibliography.

in his *Double-Dealer*,[113] and in *The Mourning Bride*,[114] and *Love for Love* [115] amended passages which had shocked Collier. In *The Provoked Wife* Vanbrugh rewrote a scene in which Sir John Brute, dressed as a parson, was found by the Watch drunk and brawling in the streets, and was taken before a Justice of the Peace whom he scandalized by his language. In the new version the parson's frock is exchanged for a woman's.[116] At the same time new plays were written to a new recipe. Congreve in *The Way of the World* and Vanbrugh in *The Provok'd Husband* [117] were

[113] " This day was played a revived comedy of Mr. Congreve's called ' The Double Dealer ' . . . In the play-bill was printed.—" Written by Mr. Congreve ; with several expressions omitted." (Dryden, *Correspondence*, letter to Mrs. Steward, 1698.)

[114] Genest, II, p. 121.

[115] Genest, II, p. 125.—Congreve had no luck with Collier : for a second time he unnecessarily put himself in the wrong. Valentine is pretending to be mad and Congreve makes him say : " 'Tis strange ! but I am Truth . . . " (IV, 6). Collier scented blasphemy as if Valentine were claiming to be God. Quite evidently he was not, but Congreve substituted the words : " I am honest." [This alteration is not noted in Leigh Hunt's Edn.]

[116] IV, 6. See Genest, II, p. 347, and III, pp. 171–2.

[117] The Prologue to *The Provok'd Husband* was written by Cibber and begins :

" This Play took Birth from Principles of Truth,
To make Amends for Errors past, of Youth.
A Bard, that's now no more, in riper Days,
Conscious review'd the Licence of his Plays :
And though Applause his wanton Muse had fir'd,
Himself condemn'd what sensual Minds admir'd.
At length, he own'd, that Plays should let you see
Not Only, What you Are, but Ought to be :
Though Vice was natural, 'twas never meant,
The Stage should shew it ; but for Punishment !
Warm with that Thought, his Muse once more took Flame,
Resolv'd to bring licentious Life to Shame.
Such was the Piece his latest Pen design'd . . . "

As early as 1702 Vanbrugh wrote in the Prologue to *The False Friend* :

" You dread Reformers of an Impious Age }
You awful Catta-nine-Tailes, to the Stage, }
This once be Just, and in our Cause engage. }
To gain your Favour, we your Rules Obey, }
And Treat you with a Moral Piece to Day ; }
So Moral, we're afraid 't will Damn the Play . . ." }

Farquhar also paid honourable tribute to Collier : " I have not displeas'd the Ladies, nor offended the Clergy, both which are now pleased to say, that a Comedy may be diverting without Smut or Profaneness." (Preface to *The Constant Couple* ; see also the Prologue.)—" The Success and Countenance that Debauchery has met with in Plays ; was the most Severe and Reasonable Charge against their Authors in Mr. *Collier's Short View* : and indeed this Gentleman had done the *Drama* considerable Service, had he both more guarded than they had been before. The later comedies of Farquhar and Vanbrugh mark a gradual transition. These plays were still daring enough, but their natural high spirits and frank merriment carried off anything that was at times a trifle too audacious.[117a] Little by little the English drama sobered down, mended its ways and grew calmer, till we ultimately sail into the quiet waters of Addison's *Cato*, of Rowe's monotonous and sentimental tragedies and of Steele's moral comedies.[118]

V

The Danger of Collier's Attack.—The Danger averted by Addison's " Specta-
tor ".—The Difficulties of Addison's Task

There are some who think that the theatre overdid its reformation.[119] According to them, the English drama after Collier's day partakes too much of Florian's pastoral fables, and they

---

Arraign'd the Stage only to Punish it's Misdemeanours, and not to take away it's Life ; but there is an Advantage to be made sometimes of the Advice of an Enemy, and the only way to disappoint his Designs, is to improve upon his invective, and to make the Stage flourish by vertue of that Satyr, by which he thought to suppress it." (Preface to Farquhar's *Twin-Rivals*.)

Lastly, Cibber wrote in 1708 : " A Play, without a just Moral, is a poor mercenary Undertaking ; and 'tis from the Success of such Pieces that Mr. *Collier* was furnish'd with an Advantageous Pretence of laying his unmerciful Axe to the Root of the Stage." (Dedication of *The Lady's Last Stake*.)

[117a] [The best account of the Collier controversy may be found in *Comedy and Conscience after the Restoration*, by J. W. Krutch. 1924. See also the chapter on Vanbrugh in *Essays in Biography* by B. Dobrée.

However much Collier, together with the sentiment of the time, may have influenced the way in which plays were written, and hastened the decline of the drama by depriving it of its satirical bite, the theatres did not change much, nor the taste of the audiences. In about 1706 the author of *Hell upon Earth, or the Language of the Playhouse* bewailed the fact that the public was still enticed by " horrid comedies ". " The more they have been exposed by Mr. Collier and others," he groaned, " the more they seem to be admir'd." The controversy rumbled on through half the century, the stage being attacked by numerous Societies for the Prevention of Other People's Enjoyment. But the plays continued to be acted. For instance, I have before me a *Daily Post* of 1743, advertising *The Plain Dealer*, *The Country Wife*, and *The Constant Couple*, while offering the playgoer little else, except farce and pantomime.

For the stage history of Restoration and early eighteenth-century plays, see the Notes in the Nonesuch Editions of the principal playwrights. B. D.]

[118] See in particular Steele's *Lying Lover* and *The Conscious Lovers*.—In Fielding's *Joseph Andrews* (book III, chap. XI) Parson Adams says : " I never heard of any plays fit for a Christian to read, but *Cato* and *The Conscious Lovers* ; and I must own that in the latter there are some things almost solemn enough for a sermon."

[119] Hazlitt amongst others. He expresses this opinion in a few pages

would fain cry with Lebrun : " Oh, how welcome a little wolf would be ! "

There is some justification for these regrets, though they are unnecessarily acute. They are, besides, actuated by an admiration for Restoration drama which we cannot easily share, and by a contempt for Collier which we cannot justly endorse. It is, however, fair to say that if Collier—or, worse, his friends—had had their way, that would have been the end of English drama and of many other things besides.[120] Their way led straight back to Puritanism. Collier was not himself a Dissenter, but he had a Dissenter's puritanical ideas about many things, and above all he had re-kindled puritanic fires slumbering in many a fanatic heart. Some were already talking of suppressing the theatre altogether.[121] That would have meant a return to the views of Prynne. If these plans had been carried out, England would have been put back for nearly a century, and her whole moral progress would have had to start again from scratch.

I have neither the wish nor the intention here to say anything against the Puritans. Whatever objections I might raise, I cannot but recognize in them the firm, honest and energetic core of the English nation. It is nevertheless certain that in pushing their principles to the furthest extreme, in seeking to deny to

---

of delicate wit and of sound judgment to boot. (*Lectures on the English Poets, and the English Comic Writers*, part II, pp. 117 ff.)

[120] Filmer in a *Defence of Plays* rightly contends : ". . . Many great and Unexpected Events do frequently flow from very slight and trivial Beginnings. We, or our Fathers, have seen Three flourishing Kingdoms brought to the very Brink of Ruin, a great, good and pious King murder'd on a Scaffold . . . and all by the Unnatural Violence of some hot-headed Zealots, who ran their first Heat indeed against Lawful Sports after Evening Service on *Sundays*, against Wakes, Feasts, Garlands and Maypoles on Holy-Days, and other such like innocent Diversions of the Vulgar ; but never stopp'd in their Career, 'till in Contempt of the Laws, both Divine and Human, they had utterly, and as they thought, irrecoverably, overthrown both Church and State . . . had those strait-lac'd Gentlemen (Collier's over-zealous partisans), with Mr. *Collier's* charitable Assistance once gain'd their Point against Plays, we should find them quickly nibbling at most our other Diversions, and giving our Ladies as frightful an Idea, perhaps of *Hidepark* or the *Mall* as Mr. *Collier* has already done of the Play-house . . ." By 1711 Bedford was tilting at Music. See my Bibliography, s.v. Bedford (Arthur), *The Great Abuse of Musick*.

[121] The anonymous author of *A Representation of the Impiety and Immorality of the English Stage* proposed " a total suppression of the Play-house " (p. 4).—Bedford wrote : " It is high Time to suppress such Places of *Iniquity*." (*The Evil and Danger of Stage-Plays*, p. 218.)—In 1726 William Law published a book called : *The Absolute Unlawfulness of the Stage Entertainment Fully Demonstrated*, to which Dennis replied by : *The Stage defended from Scripture, Reason*, etc.

human nature the most innocent relaxation, and especially in trying to impose by force their own asceticism on everyone, they had exercised a tyranny over the consciences of their fellow-countrymen, and had seriously compromised the very cause of virtue and morality. You cannot establish the empire of Virtue on a sure foundation by making of her a scowling and repellent monster ; Virtue can be a kindly, humane, responsive goddess. The only logical ascetics are the folk who withdraw from the world. If you live in society, you must be genial, and not demand of other men inflexible and unrelaxing self-discipline. Those who fail to understand this truth, and seek to banish from life that beneficent and wholesome element which we call joy, defeat themselves—as do those English sabbatarians of to-day who deny the people Sunday recreation, and thereby encourage drunkenness.[121a] People who are cut off from innocent pleasures take refuge in vicious ones, and the more they are restrained in one direction the more they let themselves go in another. Outraged human liberty reacts against constraint : by licence. That is what happened at the Restoration. That is what would have happened again. If England had had to undergo another spell of exaggerated rigour, she would inevitably have reacted with a new outburst of exaggerated libertinism. The pendulum having been insanely forced to the right, would have swung with equal violence to the left, and Englishmen would have squandered their strength in perpetual oscillations from one excess to the other.

Happily, a man stepped forward at this very juncture to save English society from the threatening danger, to teach men moderation, and introduce them to a safe and level road, to link together in unique and lasting union the two admirable elements in the nation which had so long been striving against each other for supremacy, to fuse the best qualities of Puritan and Cavalier. This man was Addison. The work which confirmed and established England's moral reformation was the periodical which he modestly christened *The Spectator*.

The task which Addison undertook was one of supreme difficulty and delicacy. The urgent need was, not to oppose Collier's campaign, but to carry it on, while moderating its ruthlessness and guiding it into less narrow paths. The immorality

[121a] [It must be remembered that Beljame was writing some fifty years ago ; Sundays are less grim now than they were then, but the battle still goes on. B. D.]

and corruption which had been poisoning the whole social fabric must be attacked and driven out—and here Collier was an ally—but many things must be protected from the iconoclastic zeal of Collier and his disciples : all the genuine manifestations of literature and art, all the subtle pleasures which lend courtesy and charm to social intercourse, and in so doing ennoble and refine man's soul.   The virtue of the Puritan must be reconciled with the elegance of the Cavalier.   The one must be won over to a moral life by finding there good fellowship and pleasant company, the other must be won over to good manners by being shown that these were not incompatible with good morals.

That is to say—and herein lay the major difficulty of Addison's task—he had to distribute praise and blame to each of the two parties ; he had to be with the Puritans, but not in their excess of rigour ; he had to part company with the Cavaliers when their fine manners turned to licence.   In other words, he had to try to find the golden mean.   Now, at all times the golden mean is a thing most difficult to find.   The man who has a foot in both camps can satisfy neither.   Both are against him.   Neither party can tolerate his criticism, neither can bear that he should praise the other.   A mediator in such a case has been wittily compared to the French National Guard during the civil wars, where the first rank was exposed both to the fire of the insurgents and the fire of their comrades behind.[122]

To escape this fate, to succeed merely in making himself heard ; still more, to succeed in convincing his readers, a man needs gifts of persuasiveness, of tact and of impartiality such as are rarely united in one person, and he needs also to enjoy—a thing equally unusual—an authority which is recognized and respected, alike by friend and foe.

Every one of these conditions was fulfilled by Addison.   No writer has ever had to the same degree so many attractive and delightful qualities, and none has more admirably devoted all his gifts to the service of the cause he had at heart.   His own personal character and his position in the government invested him with an authority such as no English author had ever exercised before.

Joseph Addison was the son of an eminent clergyman of the

---

[122] A. Mézières, *le Spectateur d'Addison*, in the *Revue des cours littéraires*, Paris, March 19, 1870.   This essay contains another very pertinent observation : " The part to be played in such a case is far from brilliant.   If your sole aim is to mediate, and to temper excessive zeal, you cannot let yourself indulge in sounding phrases and telling effects."

Church of England, and distinguished himself at Oxford. His intention was to take Orders. His early literary efforts, however, won him admittance to the circle of which Dryden was the presiding genius. He was introduced to Montague and Somers, who shrewdly perceived his unusual talent and sought to enlist him for the service of their party. They persuaded the young Oxonian to give up the idea of the Church and embark on a political career. Through their good offices he was given a pension of £300 a year to enable him to travel in Europe. Poems addressed to his two benefactors proclaimed his allegiance to the Whig party.[123] William III's death, entailing the fall from power of his political friends, seemed for a moment likely to impair the young writer's prospects. But Queen Anne's ministers were semi-Tories, constrained to preserve the outward semblance of a Whig policy, and they turned to him (as we have seen above) to sing the victory of Blenheim. His poem, *The Campaign*, written for this occasion, immediately proved that the apprentice had become the master. Godolphin was so greatly delighted by *The Campaign* that he made its author Commissioner of Appeals in the Excise. He was next given the duty of accompanying Montague (now Lord Halifax) to Hanover, to convey to the Prince Elector the insignia of the Garter ; then appointed Under Secretary of State, and finally Secretary to the Marquis of Wharton,[123a] Lord-Lieutenant of Ireland. This last post brought him in close on £2,000 a year. The Queen made him in addition Keeper of the Irish Records, with an annual salary of £400 a year, and the Irish electors voted him into the Irish Parliament.

Such was Addison's standing when he undertook the work which has deserved the undying gratitude of his fellow-country-men. After *The Campaign*, he had published an account of his travels in Italy,[124] accompanied by some graceful verses, all of which had won him the attention of the cultured public. His public posts gave him a status which was enhanced by his personal reputation. His attachment to the Whig party, with which his career had begun, never flagged through fair weather or foul, and this earned him general respect. He had addressed verses to Montague the minister, he was no less the friend of Montague

---

[123] A Poem to his Majesty, presented to the Lord-Keeper (Somers), 1695 ; *Pax Guglielmi Auspiciis Europae reddita*, dedicated to Montague, 1697.

[123a] [At this time, Dec. 1708, Wharton was an Earl, having been made such in 1706. He was not created Marquis until 1715. B. D.]

[124] *Remarks on Several Parts of Italy*, dedicated to Lord Somers, 1705.

out of office.[125] He was made a member of the Kit-Cat Club even after his party had fallen from power.[126] He inspired so much respect by his principles—moderate without weakness, and firm without ostentation—that when the Tories were inclining towards a Whig policy he was one of the first to whom they turned. He was therefore well qualified to speak to the English public as a whole, and to exercise serious and lasting influence on his compatriots.

Before we proceed further, we must show what tools lay ready to his hand, and pay a just tribute to those who, by preparing the way for his journal, made his path straight and enabled him successfully to carry out his task.

VI

The periodical press after the Revolution.—Abolition of the Censorship.— Its consequences.—Birth of the literary journal : John Dunton's " Athenian Mercury " ; Defoe's " Weekly Review of the Affairs of France " ; Steele's " Tatler "

One of the great reforms consequent on the Revolution of 1688, and one of the most fruitful, was the emancipation of the Press. Except for rare intervals of liberty, Censorship had existed in one form or another under every English Government, royal or republican. On May 3, 1695, it passed away, never to be reinstituted. Parliament refused—almost certainly without suspecting the future consequences of its decision—to renew a law which subjected the Press to any man's good pleasure.[127]

William III's accession had already brought a measure of release to the Press. The new political situation encouraged writers to resume a certain freedom of expression, and some thirty

[125] *A Letter from Italy*, 1701, dedicated to Charles (Montague), Lord Halifax.

[126] In 1704. [It is not quite correct to say that in 1704 the Whigs had fallen from power. Queen Anne's first House of Commons was Tory, and her ministers were such ; but by 1704 the Tories had suffered a decline, while the House of Lords continued strongly Whig. In 1705 the Whigs were returned to power, and did not fall until 1710. But in any event the Kit-Cat was a Whig social club with no political aims, and whether the Whigs were in or out made no difference to membership. Addison was introduced to the club by his friend and patron Halifax. Whig though he was, Addison did not mind taking a place under so firm a Tory as Sir Charles Hedges. B. D.]

[127] Macaulay, *History*, chap. XXI ; Hallam, *Constitutional History of England*, III, chap. XV.

new journals had appeared between 1688 and 1694.[128] But their existence had always been uneasy and precarious, and their anxiety was to escape, rather than to attract, attention. During the early years of William's reign, the only paper which provided serious political information was still the *London Gazette*, published as before under the eye of Government and supplying only favourable news, and none too much even of that. The *Gazette* was so dull that though it had no rivalry to fear, it circulated 8,000 copies only, not even one apiece for every parish in England. Other papers were shy of handling news, and when they did, it was usually copied from the *Gazette*.[129] The Coffee-Houses, which were growing in number and importance and beginning to develop into clubs,[130] remained, with the Newsletters,[131] the chief sources of information and the foci of political debate.

The abolition of the Censorship changed all that. A trusty old Whig, Harris by name, had been publishing a paper called *Intelligence Domestick and Foreign* during the last years of Charles II's reign, and had been obliged to discontinue it and go into voluntary exile. Within a fortnight of the abrogation of the Censorship he announced that his paper, sometime suppressed by " the violators of both the Laws and Liberties of England ", was about to reappear.[132] Ten days after Harris's *Intelligencer*,

[128] See a chronological list of these papers in George Chalmers, *Life of Thomas Ruddiman*, pp. 404–42.

[See also *Government and the Press, 1695–1763*, by L. Hanson. 1936. B. D.]

[129] Macaulay, *History*, chap. XXI.—Some years later Steele was made editor of the *Gazette*. He vowed that in this capacity he had never transgressed the rules observed by every administration : to keep the *Gazette* very harmless and very tame.

[130] On Coffee-Houses, see the *Spectator*, Nos. 1, 49 and 403 ; on Clubs, id., No. 9.

[See also Leslie Stephen, *English Literature and Society in the 18th Century* : 1904. Ashton, *Social Life in the Reign of Queen Anne*. T. H. S. Escott, *Club Makers and Club Members*. E. Ward, *A Compleat and Humorous Account of all the Remarkable Clubs and Societies in the Cities of London and Westminster*. Printed anon. : 1756. B. D.]

[131] Especially noteworthy are the Newsletters of a certain Dyer, which were much to the taste of Tories and High Churchmen. See Macaulay, *History*, chap. XX : *The Lancashire Prosecutions* ; Steele's *Tatler*, No. 86 ; the *Spectator*, No. 45.

[132] Benjamin Harris in the first number of the new *Intelligence Domestick and Foreign* dated Tuesday, May 14, 1695 (in the British Museum) writes : " Some time since I Published an *Intelligence*, with the like Title, wherein upon all Occasions, I Vigorously Asserted, the Laws and Liberties of *England*, against the Bold and Open Violators of both, which Procur'd me so many Inveterate Enemies, that to Save my Life, and my Family from Ruin, I was Compel'd to be an *Exile* from my Native Countrey, for above *Eight Years* : But being now Return'd, I know no reason, why, I may not endeavour, in some Measure,

appeared the first issue of *The English Courant.*[133] Then there poured out in rapid succession *The Post Man*, *The Post Boy*, *The Harlem's Courant*, *The Weekly News-Letter*, *Foreign and Domestick News*, *The London News-Letter*, *With* Foreign *and* Domestick *Occurrences*, *Pegasus*, *The Old Post-Master*, *Lloyd's News*, etc.[134]

So far, these newspapers were nothing much to boast of. They invariably consisted of a single sheet only, and that often printed only on one side.[135] Even *The Post Boy* and *The Post Man*, which were amongst the best produced and the most prosperous (*The Post Man* brought its editor in £600 a year),[136] were miserably printed on dirty paper, sometimes adorned with primitive engravings like those of the French *Liège Almanach.*

---

to Retrieve my Losses, and Misfortunes, by the same Methods, under the Happy Government of His Present Majesty, who hath so Gloriously Restored and Confirmed, our Rights and Privileges to us . . . I shall Write nothing but Truth, and certainty, and if I thereby Disoblige my Old Implacable Adversarys, the Care is taken ; since I doubt not but to Please my Old *Protestant Friends*, whose Zeal for their Freedoms of the Land of their Nativity, in the Worst of Times, I shall have a Just Value for ; While I am, Benjamin Harris."—On Harris, see above, chap. II, note No. 108.

[133] " The English Courant. Numb. I. *To be published every* Wednesday *and* Saturday . . . Saturday, May 25, 1695." (British Museum.)

[134] "Numb. 72. The Post Man, and the Historical Account, etc. From Tuesday, October 22d. to Thursday, Oct. 24th 1695."—"Numb. 9. The Post Boy. With Foreign and Domestick News. From Saturday, June 1. to Tuesday, June 4. *London*, Printed for *A. Roper*, *E. Wilkinson* and *R. Clavel* in *Fleetstreet*, 1695."—" Numb. I. The Harlem's Courant, *Publish'd at* Harlem Saturday, May 28. 1695. *N.S.*" " Numb. 4. The Weekly News-Letter : or, An Exact and Impartial Account of the most Remarkable Occurences. Foreign and Domestick . . . From *Saturday*, June 29. to *Saturday*, *July* 6. Printed for *J. Whitlock* near *Stationers-Hall*. 1695."—" (Numb. I). Foreign and Domestic News : with the Pacquet-Boat from Holland and Flanders . . . Tuesday, July the 2. 1695."—" Numb. I. The London News-Letter. With *Foreign* and *Domestick* Occurrences, Wednesday, April 29 1696."—" Numb. I. Pegasus, With *News*, an *Observator*, and a *Jacobite Courant*. Monday June the 15th 1696." (printed by John Dunton).—" (Numb. I.) The Old Post-Master. With the Occurrences of Great Britain and Ireland, and from Foreign Parts ; Collected and Published. From Saturday *June* the 20th. to Tuesday *June* the 23rd. 1696."—" Numb. 43. Lloyd's News. London, Tuesday. December 8, 1696. *Printed for Edward Lloyd (Coffee-Man) in Lombard Street.*"—All these papers are in the British Museum.

[135] No. 12, for instance, of *The Post Boy*.—It should be said, however, that sometimes even both sides of one printed sheet did not suffice, and supplements were issued like : " A postscript to the Post Boy, in n°. 23 *Wednesday* July 3ᵈ, 1695."

[136] Dunton, quoted by Andrews, I, p. 103.—". . . my most ingenious and renowned Fellow-Labourer, the *Post-Man*." (*Tatler*, No. 178) [but surely this is said ironically ?]. "The Post-Man, who is one of the most celebrated of our Fraternity." (*Tatler*, 204.)

They never appeared oftener than three times a week, and each issue contained about as much matter as would fill one column of a modern newspaper. They were anything but venturesome, and their excursions on to political ground were cautious in the extreme.

They were in fact still mindful of the unanimous pronouncement of Charles II's legal advisers, that the liberty of the Press did not imply liberty to print political news, for which royal permission was always necessary. What would be the judges' ruling on this point now? No one knew, and no one was anxious to challenge them on the question, lest their decision should be unfavourable. It is amusing to see how careful every editor was not to commit himself; though the papers continued to publish none but foreign political news, he always contrived to keep open a way of retreat by prefacing his statements with some precautionary formula like " it is said that . . ." or " people say . . ." or " it is thought that . . ." [137]

The proof that readers were not entirely satisfied by this procedure, is that the years 1695 and 1696 saw the birth of a hybrid type of paper intended to give the newspaper something of the attractive quality of the news-letter. The first specimens of this were *The Flying Post* and *Dawks's News-Letter*. Like other papers, these provided the current news, but they left a good proportion of their paper blank, so that anyone posting a copy to a friend could add by hand the latest information available, and more especially those items which the editor thought it more expedient not to print. [138]

[137] See Andrews, I, p. 101.—" The *Daily Courant*, says he, has these Words, *We have Advices from very good Hands, That a Certain Prince has some Matters of great Importance under Consideration.* This is very mysterious ; but the *Post-Boy* leaves us more in the Dark, for he tells us, *That there are private Intimations of Measures taken by a certain Prince which Time will bring to Light.* Now the *Post-Man*, says he, who used to be very clear, refers to the same News in these Words ; *The late Conduct of a certain Prince affords great Matter of Speculation.*" (*Tatler*, No. 155.)

[138] Andrews, I, p. 86 : " The *Flying Post* thus announces its design : ' If any gentleman has a mind to oblige his country friend or correspondent with this account of public affairs, he may have it for twopence . . . on a sheet of fine paper, half of which being blank, he may thereon write his own private business, or the material news of the day.' "

The earliest issue I have been able to find in the British Museum is " Numb. 281. The Flying Post : or, The Post Master. From Saturday February 27 to Tuesday March 2 1697. Printed for John Salusbury at the *Rising Sun* in *Cornhill*." By this date the *Flying Post* had become just an ordinary newspaper of the time.—The earliest issue of *Dawks's News-Letter* I have been able to get hold of has no title. It begins " *London* S^r 7 January 1698." Like the other

Nevertheless, despite uncertainty and hesitation, the free Press speedily took root in England, and when a bill to subject it anew to regulation was introduced in the House of Commons in 1697, it was defeated by 200 votes to 16.[139]

The painful and trying years of childhood and adolescence were past, the newspaper had attained its majority and achieved emancipation. The first daily newspaper was published in London on March 11, 1702. It was called *The Daily Courant*. At first it found some difficulty in filling both sides of the single sheet on which it was printed, and left one side blank [140]; but after a dozen numbers or so, it regularly appeared fully printed on both sides, and it succeeded in surviving till 1735.[141]

The number of newspaper readers in England must have multiplied mightily in a few years to ensure from the very start the successful survival of a daily paper, and we may fairly attribute a large share of this progress to the emancipation of the Press. This was not the only happy consequence that followed the change of policy. The freedom and development of the Press regularized and moderated its ways.

During the first years of William III's reign, political controversy, and more especially the ventilation of Jacobite sympathies, could not be carried on save by clandestine methods. The only means were secret printing presses, anonymous pamphlets surreptitiously smuggled from the printer's and circulated on the sly. Such a state of affairs produced the inevitable consequences. Reputable people of the opposition party, finding that they could not express their views without transgressing the law, and having recourse to endless subterfuge, held their peace and left their cause at the mercy of fanatics. These folk, who staked liberty and even life on every illegal publication, naturally wanted value for the risks they ran, and no scruple deterred them from any violence which lent weight to their blows. A baser

---

numbers which I have seen in the Newspaper Collection of the British Museum (1698, vol. II), it is printed in italics and consists of two and a half pages of print ; half of the third and the whole of the fourth page are left blank. This part is filled with hand-written news. This copy bears the post-mark and is addressed : " To Me Dorothy Day in Oxon." The earliest numbered copy (No. 358) in the British Museum Collection bears the title : " Dawks's News-Letter " and is dated October 1, 1698. On Dawks and his paper, see the *Tatler*, No. 178.

[139] Macaulay, *History*, chap. XXII.

[140] " Numb. 1. *The Daily Courant*. Wednesday, March 11, 1702." (British Museum.)

[141] Andrews, I, p. 101.

type still, was the low-caste scribbler dealing in witless platitude, who was prepared to sell his pen to anyone for a consideration, and use it to spread stupid and filthy slanders. These things gave rise to a virulent and cynical literature exploiting lies and abuse, and circulating in shameless language the most odious accusations and the coarsest invective.[142] In a few years there had assembled in the attics and outhouses of Grub Street—a street whose name was henceforth a literary symbol—a sort of beggars' nest of all the starveling quill-drivers of London, outlaws and social outcasts, ready to write anything for the most trifling payment[143] and pouring forth a host of minor pamphlets nicknamed " Grubstreets ", so despicable that the adjective has passed into English as a synonym for mean and vile.[144]

The emancipation of the Press happily altered this state of affairs. As soon as everyone was at liberty freely to print what he thought, clandestine publishing lost its attraction and all reason for its continued existence. The Grub-street gradually died out, supplanted by the newspaper. With their future secure, the newspapers grew and developed and soon won a recognized place of their own. Hitherto political controversy

[142] See Macaulay, *History*, chap. XVI : The Jacobite Press ; chap. XX : Jacobite Libels : William Anderton, Writings and Artifices of the Jacobites ; chap. XXI : Effect of the Emancipation of the English Press.

[143] They were commonly known as " Grub-street hacks ".—Grub Street is frequently mentioned in writings of the time ; see Addison, *The Freeholder*, No. 35. Also, Swift's *Journal to Stella*, Aug. 21, Dec. 5 and 18, 1711, Nov. 15 and Dec. 12, 1712 ; likewise Swift's *Answer to Bickerstaff* . . . *By a Person of Quality* ; *A Letter of Advice to a Young Poet* ; to Dr. Delany, *On the Libels written against him* ; *A Scheme to make an hospital for incurables*. The earliest allusions I have met to Grub Street are of 1685 and 1689 : the Prologue to Rochester's *Valentinian*, written for Mrs. Barrey, speaks of " Grub-street *Pens* " and the Prologue to Shadwell's *Bury-Fair* of " *Silly* Grub-street *Songs* ".—The following sketch applies no doubt to one of the denizens of this street : " Mr. Ames, originally a *Coat-seller* . . . You might engage him upon what Project you pleas'd, if you'd but conceal him, for his *Principles* did never resist in such Cases . . . *Wine and Women* were the great Bane of his Life and Happiness." (John Dunton, *Life and Errors* . . . p. 247).—See also Dunton's portrait of Mr. Bradshaw (ibid., p. 241).

[144] *The Imperial Dictionary* (London, 1882) defines the adjective Grubstreet as " mean, low, vile ".

[" Originally the name of a street near Moorfields in London (now Milton-Street), ' much inhabited by writers of small histories, dictionaries, and temporary poems ' (Johnson) ; hence used allusively for the tribe of mean and needy authors, or literary hacks." *N.E.D.* This is the sense in which it is now, and has always been, used. The name was first used by Taylor, the Water Poet, in 1630, the term by Shadwell in 1689. Beljame is a little harsh here, and has slightly misunderstood the term, which does not necessarily convey a moral stigma. B. D.]

had not been confined to one branch of literature ; it was liable to break out anywhere : in the theatre, in prologues and epilogues, in verses, in leaflets or in pamphlets. It now made a home for itself in the newspaper, and tended more and more to stay at home. It formed a new branch of literature and ceased, so to speak, to trespass on its neighbours. Every type of literature was thereby the gainer : drama, poetry and above all, controversy. In becoming centralized, controversy attained self-mastery, coherence and discipline ; it recruited its own specialists, and organized regular discussion. "Journalism" came into being, where previously there had been only individual newspapers ; and journalism lived in the public eye, open to the criticism of the nation : a fact which moderated and humanized debate. The change was, naturally, neither immediate nor complete. It was long before the English press wholly purged itself of baseness and violence ; Grub Street did not give up the ghost without a prolonged death rattle. But from the moment the Press was free, disreputable pamphleteers no longer called the tune of political discussion ; their sober rivals daily won a larger and larger circle of readers. Now that journalism had become a recognized and responsible branch of literature, it ceased to draw recruits from the dregs of society, but attracted able men who had something of value to say. After a few years, journalists numbered in their ranks writers, divines and statesmen of the calibre of Addison, Swift, Steele, Defoe, Garth, Kennet, Berkeley, Atterbury (the last three later to become bishops), Bolingbroke, Prior, and so on.[145]

Thus launched, the English newspaper grew in strength and made its power felt. It had a large and reliable reading public ; the most distinguished men in the country used it to address their fellow countrymen. But it was still one-sided ; it dealt exclusively with politics and was at the service of the parties. It is Addison's glory that he had vision to perceive that the time was come when the reading public, whom the controversialists had enlisted, might be invited to consider other

[145] Addison in *The Tatler, The Whig Examiner, The Medley, The Guardian, The Freeholder, The Old Whig* ; Swift in *The Examiner* ; Steele in *The Tatler, The Medley, The Guardian, The Englishman, The Plebeian* ; Defoe in *The Review,* etc. (See the Bibliography prefixed to William Lee's *Life and Writings of Defoe*) ; Garth and Kennet in *The Medley* (Andrews, I, p. 111) ; Berkeley in *The Guardian* (N. Drake, *Essays Illustrative*, etc., III, pp. 50 ff.) ; Atterbury, Bolingbroke and Prior in *The Examiner* (Swift, *Memoirs relating to that Change which happened in the Queen's Ministry in the Year 1710*).)

subjects than day-to-day politics, and when a paper might handle wider and more fertile themes.

It is a bookseller of those days—a fantastically-minded but inventive fellow—who can claim credit for having been the first to divine that a paper might serve to purvey other things than news. On Tuesday, March 17, 1690, John Dunton of the Black Crow in Gracechurch Street brought out a penny paper first called *The Athenian Gazette*. The second issue, however, was—" to oblige Authority "—rechristened *The Athenian Mercury*.[146] It was an odd production, proceeding by question and answer, and aiming at " Resolving Weekly all the most Nice and Curious Questions Propos'd by the Ingenious ". It would be impossible to conceive a more extraordinary collection of infantile queries and quibblings. Most of the questions relate to the casuistries of light love-making [147] or to microscopic and obscure points of religion and natural history, which are generally further obscured by the replies. " Whether the Torments of the damn'd are visible to the Saints in Heaven ? And vice versa ? "—" Whether 'tis lawful for a Man to beat his wife " ;—" Where was the soul of Lazarus for the four days he lay in the grave ? " ;—" Suppose Lazarus had an estate, and bequeathed it to his Friends, whether ought he or his Legatees to enjoy it after he was rais'd from the Dead ? " ;—" Where extinguish'd Fire goes ? " ;—" What became of the Waters after Noah's Flood ? " ;—" Why a Horse with a round Fundament emits a square Excrement ? " [148]

The editorial board or, as Dunton calls it, " The Athenian Society ",[149] replied to all these questions, and to others odder

[146] My information about *The Athenian Mercury* is drawn from the paper itself, and from Dunton's own *Life and Errors*, pp. 256 ff.

[147] No. 13, amongst others, is devoted entirely to questions of love and marriage. [A good deal of the correspondence in *The Tatler* and *The Spectator* is given to such matters. B. D.]

[148] The first three of these questions occur in the first issue ; Lazarus's estate in the fourth ; Fire in the sixth ; the Flood waters in the sixteenth and the Horse in the twenty-third. On the subject of wife-beating the paper dare not frankly say " yes " for fear of alienating its woman readers. But it argues thus : man and wife are one ; now, a man often inflicts suffering on himself : he lets the surgeon bleed him or amputate a limb, therefore, etc. Congratulations on such skilful tight-rope-walking !—The Horse question is a quaint specimen.

[*The Athenian Mercury* was not really quite so silly as Beljame suggests. It interested Temple, and Swift was all cock-a-whoop at having his early verses published in it. But see Beljame later. B. D.]

[149] It was composed of Dunton himself, Richard Sault, a Cambridge theologian, the Reverend Dr. John Norris and Dunton's brother-in-law Samuel Wesley, father of the future founder of Methodism.

still, with imperturbable gravity and a conscientious industry that never flagged.[150]

This eccentric paper demonstrates better than anything else how willing to learn were the readers of those days, and how much remained to be done towards their education. And nothing shows more clearly how the Press had already penetrated into daily life and how ready and willing people were to read other subjects than politics. For *The Athenian Mercury*, whose origin we have just seen, was a great success. It had begun as a modest weekly, but its third number already announced that so many questions had poured in that it would appear twice a week—and so in fact it did. After two years of life, it tried the experiment of four issues a week [151]; but this was too much, and the attempt had promptly to be given up.[152] Its success soon raised up rivals and imitators : *The Lacedemonian Mercury* edited by the prolific and commonplace Tom Brown,[153] *The Ladies Mercury*,[154] *The British Apollo*.[155] Dunton proudly quotes testimonies of approval

[150] They received this request one day : " Since in your Advertisement you make it known that a *Chyrurgeon* is taken into your Society, I have thought fit to propound the following Question, withal assuring you that the matter of the Fact is true. A Sailor on board the Fleet by an unlucky Accident broke his Leg, being in Drink, and refusing the assistance of the Surgeon of the Ship, called for a piece of new *Tarpauling* that lay on the Deck, which he rolled some turns round his Leg, tying up all close with a few Hoop-sticks, and was able immediately after to walk round the ship, never keeping his Bed one Day. I would know whether the Cure is to be attributed to the Emplastick Nature of the tarr'd and pitch'd Cloth bound on strait with the Hoop-sticks etc. or rather whether it may not be solved according to the *Cartesian Philosophy* ? " The Athenian Society solemnly replied with a discourse on fractures of the focile and of bones in general, on the catagmatic properties of tarred cloth and on Copernicus, without perceiving that they were dealing with a practical joker and a wooden leg. (No. 16.)—Some replies are of more value, this, for instance : " What is Platonick Love ? "— " Nothing at all, unless it be Friendship " (No. 16).—Let us note to the credit of Dunton's paper that it contains notices of new books, both English and foreign.

[151] No. of March 1, 1692.

[152] No. of March 14, 1692.

[153] A. Wood, *Athenæ Oxonienses*, s.v. Browne (Thomas). See also my Bibliography.—Dunton records how he compelled Tom Brown to resign from this paper by threatening to publish his life.

[Tom Brown may be commonplace, but he is by no means flat (*plat* is Beljame's phrase for him). The *Amusements Serious and Comical*, reprinted in 1927, are full of vigorous idiom and lively description. B. D.]

[154] " Vol. I. Numb. 1. *The Ladies Mercury*, Munday, *February* 17, 1693." (British Museum.)

[155] " Numb. 1. The British Apollo or *Curious Amusements for the Ingenious*. To which are added the most material Occurrences Foreign and Domestick *Perform'd by a society of Gentlemen*." (British Museum.)—The collected numbers

which reached him from various quarters : the Marquis of Halifax, " The great and learned nobleman ", read *The Athenian Mercury* regularly and said he " had received great satisfaction from many of the answers " ; Sir William Temple, " a man of clear judgment and wonderful penetration ", sent frequent letters and questions ; Dunton received verses from Tate, Defoe and Motteux, and " Mr. Swift, a Country Gentleman " sent the Athenian Society an Ode which " being an ingenious poem was prefixed to the Fifth Supplement of the Athenian Mercury ".[156] Thus encouraged, the paper continued its bi-weekly appearance until 1696. At that point the competition of politics became too acute, and Dunton decided that it would pay better to issue quarterly numbers. He continued until the collection ran to twenty folio volumes. This did not satisfy readers' demands, and he had to publish a three-volume selection, under the title of *The Athenian Oracle*.

Dunton's idea had been a happy one, and odd as his *Mercury* may seem to us, we cannot deny him the honour of having successfully founded the first literary journal in England.

Dunton's example was not lost on Defoe. We tend too much to think of Daniel Defoe as the author of *Robinson Crusoe* only, and to forget that among many other titles to fame, he has the honour of being the founder of the English literary press. Born of dissenting parents, young Defoe early and passionately flung himself into politics and religious controversy. At twenty-four he was fighting under the banner of Monmouth, " the Protestant Duke ", and it was only by a happy chance that he escaped the fierce reprisals of the Bloody Assizes. In 1688 he was one of the strongest supporters of William III and in 1700 he wrote a poem, *The True-Born Englishman*, to defend the King against those who reproached him with his foreign birth and his Dutch friendships. Eighty thousand copies of the poem were sold.[157] Under Queen

---

of this paper form three volumes, beginning Feb. 13, 1708 and ending March 23, 1711. Note that it includes political news.

[156] This Ode is reprinted in Swift's *Works*. It was when he saw these verses that Dryden said to their author : " Cousin Swift, you will never be a poet."

[It is true that on the whole the Ode deserved Dryden's comment ; but it contains a great deal of characteristic Swiftian philosophy, and, in a wrong form (he should not have followed the fashion of the Pindaric), many of the poetic virtues he was later to use so effectively. B. D.]

[157] See my Bibliography.

[It is impossible to do more than guess at the circulation of *The True-Born Englishman* because of the many pirated editions. At any rate it was huge. B. D.]

Anne, Defoe was again on the war-path. To satirize the intolerant pretensions of the Church of England, he wrote in 1702 a pamphlet, *The Shortest Way with the Dissenters*, which created as great a stir as his poem, but for which he was sentenced to a fine, to the pillory, and to imprisonment during the Queen's pleasure.[158] On the very day that he was subjected to public disgrace he brought out *A Hymn to the Pillory* [159] and in his Newgate cell [160] he began the publication of a weekly paper, the first number of which appeared on Saturday, February 19, 1704, under the title : " A Weekly Review of the Affairs of *France* : Purged from the Errors and Partiality of *News-Writers* and *Petty-Statesmen*, of all Sides ".[161]

Possessed as he was by the spirit of controversy, Defoe was incapable of producing a non-political paper. This makes it the more noteworthy that he did not feel it possible to confine it to purely political topics. Following in Dunton's footsteps, he introduced a literary section which he called " Mercure Scandale : or, Advice from the Scandalous Club : Being A Weekly History of Nonsense, Impertinence, Vice and Debauchery ".[162] This programme clearly points to more ambitious aims than Dunton's. While imitating Dunton, he did more, and did it better, than his predecessor. For one thing, a new spirit was abroad. Since *The Athenian Mercury* was launched, Jeremy Collier had called public attention to more serious matters than those dealt with by the Athenian Society. Defoe, who had already crossed swords with Collier, did not neglect to handle moral questions in his

---

[158] In this anonymous pamphlet Defoe posed as a die-hard High-Churchman and suggested the complete suppression of the Dissenters, by force and violence if need be. Churchmen loudly applauded, but they soon learned the author's name, and the trap into which they had fallen. *Inde iræ.*

[159] I am here mentioning only the most important of Defoe's early works. He was one of the most prolific of English writers. The *Review of the Affairs of France* was his 67th publication [at least. B. D.]. According to William Lee he was the author of 254 works.

[160] He spent more than a year in prison.

[Investigations undertaken since Beljame wrote show that Defoe was in prison for only five and a half months (20th May–4th Nov. 1703), so the *Review* was not begun while he was in gaol. See additions to Defoe bibliography. B. D.]

[161] As its title indicates, the *Review* was at first a weekly, but from the eighth issue onwards it came out twice a week, on Tuesdays and Saturdays, and by 1705 it was appearing three times, on Tuesdays, Thursdays and Saturdays, the days on which the post went out from London to the provinces. It was sold at a penny. Defoe reverted to the size and lay-out of the Newsbooks ; his *Review* consisted of eight small quarto pages instead of a folio sheet.

[162] I take this title from No. 3 of the *Review*.

literary section. He discusses several aspects of contemporary manners, attacks drunkenness, swearing, marital unfaithfulness, the licence of the theatre, and duelling. His Scandalous Club accepts questions and letters [163] and offers varied and often ingenious advice on the reforms of which social life appeared to stand in need.[164] Here was already in outline the sketch of what the literary and moral Press was to be. But the detail had still to be filled in. Many and great as his qualities were, Defoe lacked those which would have enabled him successfully to address the majority of his fellow-countrymen. He was not a man of the world. His robust, straightforward style was without grace or art, and was not calculated gently to inculcate lessons of virtue and the good life in his contemporaries. What most seriously restricted Defoe's influence, was the fact that he was a Dissenter, and therefore suspect to that considerable section of English society to whom every form of Puritanism was hateful and intolerable. The influence of the *Review*, which was one of the most important and widely-read papers of its day,[165] was therefore chiefly political, and practically limited to Whig circles.

Nevertheless, Defoe was on the right tack, and it is thanks

[163] The issue dated Tuesday, September 19, 1704, contains, for instance, a letter from a correspondent signed " Arabella " to the Scandalous Club.— In the same year Defoe started " A Supplementary Journal, to the Advice from the Scandal Club ; *for the Month of* September 1704. To be Continued Monthly." This part of the *Review* consists of questions and answers like Dunton's paper, of verses, etc.

[164] Forster's *Biographical Essays* (Defoe) and Walter Wilson's *Memoirs of Daniel De Foe* (chap. XVI) contain interesting extracts from this section of the *Review*.

[The Review is now easily consulted in the facsimile reprint edited by Arthur W. Secord. Columbia University Press. 1938. B. D.]

[165] Bolingbroke's *Examiner* was founded largely to counter the *Review* (Andrews, I, p. 104). In *A Letter from a Member of the House of Commons in Ireland to a Member of the House of Commons in England Concerning the Sacramental Test*, 1708, Swift says that the *Review* was an indispensable item of Coffee-House furniture. But all the same, Swift had no love for Defoe ; in the same letter he alludes to him as " that fellow who was put in the pillory—I forget his name ". The influence of the *Review* spread quickly in the provinces. *Notes and Queries* (April 3, 1875) quotes some correspondence between Defoe and one John Fransham of Norwich. In it I find this passage dated Nov. 10, 1704 : " It was with no small Satisfaction that I read your Justification in your Review . . . I had read it to several Gentlemen . . . in the chief Coffee-house here where we have it as oft as it comes out and is approv'd as the politest paper we have to entertain us with. I had some difficulty to prevail with the Master of the house to take it in but now he finds I advis'd him well there being no paper more desir'd . . ."—Defoe edited his *Review*, single-handed, for over nine years.

to him that his imitators were able to do better. Imitators were
not long in making their appearance. As early as 1708, while
the *Review* was still going strong, Richard Steele—writing under
the pseudonym of Isaac Bickerstaff [166]—published the *Tatler*,
which like the *Review* appeared tri-weekly and on the same days.
Steele possessed many of the qualities in which Defoe was deficient.
He had been to Oxford, he was a soldier, a playwright, a Government office-holder and a man of the world. Having tasted of
life pretty freely, he had studied men and things from many
angles, and was able with his well-tried, smoothly-running pen
to tackle the most varied subjects in such a way as to interest
the great majority of the reading public. He belonged to the
same political party as Defoe, but his attitude was less tainted
with proselytizing intolerance. Defoe (I speak here only of his
early days) was one person only and that a controversialist, while
Steele was a many-sided character. In him politics had not
swallowed up the man of the world nor the lover of literature.
His views were strong and decided, but they were genial. He
belonged to the new Whig generation to which no odour of
Puritanism clung.

Steele embarked at once on a comprehensive programme,
taking for the motto of his paper :

Quicquid agunt homines nostri farrago libelli.

In his first issue he announced that articles on questions of
gallantry, pleasure and entertainment, poetry and learning would
come from different Coffee-Houses ; while he would write on
various other subjects " from my own apartment " ; and he

[166] The year before, Swift had been campaigning against the Almanack
makers, especially a certain Partridge, an ex-cobbler who successfully retailed
his prophecies in London. Taking the name of Isaac Bickerstaff, Swift gave
himself out to be a genuinely learned astrologer who maintained the wholesome
ancient traditions of his art. As such he blushed at the productions of his
would-be co-astrologers and wished to recapture for Astrology its old-time
brilliance and prestige. He began by predicting that Partridge would die
on the 29th of March of a raging fever, and on the 30th he announced with
the most circumstantial detail the precise manner of Partridge's death on the
predicted day. Partridge vigorously protested that he was still alive. Bickerstaff replied with cogent proof that he was on the contrary well and truly
dead, and to the great delight of London, Rowe, Steele, Addison, Prior,
Congreve and Yalden amused themselves by prolonging the jest. The
Stationers' Company gravely walked into the trap, and officially forbade the
publication of further Almanacks bearing Partridge's name, because no one
had a right to misuse the name of a dead writer. It is easy to picture the
wrath of the unfortunate cobbler-prophet. London's laughter had not died
away when Steele bethought him of publishing his *Tatler* under the popular
name of Isaac Bickerstaff.

would deal also with home and foreign news. In common with Defoe, Steele did not banish politics,[167] but whereas the *Review* gives them the major space and the post of honour, the *Tatler* treats them as accessory and thrusts them into the background. Little by little even news became less important and scantier, and from the eighty-third issue onwards it disappeared entirely. Thus it came about that in the course of his progress Steele recruited an unexpected and invaluable collaborator. Addison was at the time in Ireland, and presently discovered that the name of Bickerstaff cloaked his old school and college friend Richard Steele. His co-operation, warmly and eagerly accepted, rapidly made his influence on the paper felt.[168] The *Tatler* brought Addison the revelation of his true vocation, and new-comer though he was, he was soon taking the lead. " I fared," says Steele, " like a distressed Prince, who calls in a powerful Neighbour to his Aid ; I was undone by my Auxiliary ; when I had called him in, I could not subsist without Dependance on him." [169] And, true enough, Addison's inspiration soon pre-ponderated in the *Tatler* and little by little changed its character in the happiest way. Steele had wit, observation and imagina-tion, and he wrote with ease and elegance. The pages of his paper for which he alone is responsible, provide many most pleasing passages, and the reader will there find in embryo the whole programme which the two friends developed in the later numbers of the *Tatler* and in the *Spectator*.[170] But everything with Steele is tentative and vague. We get flashes of light rather than illumination. His invention is happy and fertile, but he

[167] He was at the moment editor of the *London Gazette* and thus had all the political news at first hand.

[168] Addison's collaboration begins with No. 18. He detected Steele's hand in a comment on Virgil which he himself had once made to his friend. This remark in *Tatler* No. 6 relates to Virgil's good sense in substituting the epithet *Dux Trojanus* for the usual *Pius Æneas* and *Pater Æneas*, either of which would have been out of place when Æneas and Dido sought the shelter of the cave for their love-making.

[169] Preface to fourth vol. of the *Tatler*.

[170] See, for instance, No. 3, where he condemns the dubious morality of Wycherley's *Country-Wife* and at the same time confesses that he cannot endorse the severity towards the theatre shown by his friends and " collabora-tors ", the reformers of manners. The same number contains this passage : ". . . if a fine Lady thinks fit to giggle at Church, or a Great Beau come in drunk to a Play, either shall be sure to hear of it in my ensuing Paper : for meerly as a well-bred Man, I cannot bear these Enormities." Here Steele anticipates the programme and the tone of Addison.—See also No. 8 with Steele's criticism of Ravenscroft's *London Cuckolds*.

does not in practice turn it to full account ; his genius deserts him halfway. He gropes and taps in every direction like a man uncertain where he wants to go, or rather, like one who wants to go to several different places at once. This uncertainty of aim is very marked in the first issues of the *Tatler*. The paper, seeking to be at once literary and political, ends by being neither. Steele touches on everything and handles nothing exhaustively. He had promised his readers too much, and each number is a medley of odds and ends in which nothing stands out and nothing is emphasized. The final impression is confused and blurred.

Addison made a clearance of the undergrowth and brought air and light to the saplings. He clearly saw that the *Tatler* must decide whether it was to be a political or a literary paper, and he saw that politics were amply catered for in a period wholly given over to party strife. He saw too—what his predecessors had but dimly suspected—that a literary paper had a special part to play and a new influence to exert on surrounding society.[171] So, little by little, politics disappeared from the *Tatler* and left the field free for other developments. The delineation of character and social eccentricities, the discussion of literary works, discreet and witty dissertations on morals, claimed every day more and more space. In proportion as the two friends' collaboration grew more intimate and Addison's gifts developed, gaining confidence and strength,[172] the *Tatler*

---

[171] " I must confess I am amazed that the press should only be made use of in this way (i.e. in periodic sheets) by news-writers, and the zealots of parties : as if it were not more advantageous to mankind to be instructed in wisdom and virtue than in politics ; and to be made good fathers, husbands, and sons, than counsellors and statesmen. Had the philosophers and great men of antiquity, who took so much pains to instruct mankind, and leave the world wiser and better than they found it ; had they, I say, been possessed of the art of printing, there is no question but they would have made such an advantage of it, in dealing out their lectures to the public. Our common prints would be of great use were they thus calculated to diffuse good sense through the bulk of a people, to clear up their understandings, animate their minds with virtue, dissipate the sorrows of a heavy heart, or unbend the mind from its more severe employments with innocent amusements. When knowledge, instead of being bound up in books, and kept in libraries and retirements, is thus obtruded upon the public ; when it is canvassed in every assembly, and exposed upon every table, I cannot forbear reflecting upon that passage in the *Proverbs* : ' Wisdom crieth without ; she uttereth her voice in the streets : she crieth in the chief place of concourse, in the openings of the gates : in the city she uttereth her words, saying, How long, ye simple ones, will ye love simplicity ? and the scorners delight in their scorning, and fools hate knowledge ? ' " (*Spectator*, No. 124, and Proverbs i, 20–22.)

[172] Addison's best essays occur fairly late in the *Tatler*. Afterwards he grew surer of himself and did even better, but some are charming and deserve

became what has been justly called a " journal of manners ",[173] a gallery of delightful subject-pictures, a faithful but kindly mirror of society, ever mindful quietly to drive home some delicate and useful lesson in pleasing and attractive guise. With glad surprise, Steele confessed that he scarcely recognized his own child.[174]

VII

The " Spectator ".—A Non-political Daily.—Appeal to new Readers.— Readers' Response.—Moral Rôle of the " Spectator ".—Its Attitude to Cavaliers and Puritans.—Addison's special Qualifications for his Task.— Moral Value of his Paper.—Its Literary and Educational Value.—Its Success.—Contemporary Testimony to the Influence of the " Tatler " and " Spectator "

Let us, however, not linger over the rough sketch, when the finished masterpiece is calling us. The two friends soon became conscious that however skilfully they retouched and elaborated their first draft it would remain an imperfect patch-work and could never be turned into a first-class picture. There was nothing to be done but leave this first experiment as it stood, for what it in itself was worth and start work on something new. On January 2, 1710–11, Isaac Bickerstaff made his exit from the literary stage, where for nearly two years he had played no undistinguished part, and in the following March Addison and Steele—no longer Steele and Addison [175]—the richer by

to be quoted : The politically-minded Upholsterer, Nos. 155, 160, 178, 232 ; Tom Folio, Nos. 158, 160 ; Ned Softly, No. 163 ; The Political Barometer, No. 214 ; The Adventures of a Shilling, No. 249 ; The Court of Honour, Nos. 250, 252, 253, 256, 259, 261, 262, 265. It will be noticed that most of these subjects take up several numbers. Addison taught Steele the art of keeping the reader's interest from one day to the next.

[173] Rémusat, I, p. 195.

[174] " He (Tickell) very justly says, the occasional Assistance Mr. *Addison* gave me in the Course of that Paper [the *Tatler*] did not a little contribute to advance its Reputation especially when, upon the Change of the Ministry, he found leisure to engage more constantly in it. It was advanced, indeed, for it was rais'd to a greater thing than I intended it." (A letter of Steele's prefixed to *The Drummer*, addressed " To Mr. *Congreve* Occasion'd by Mr. *Tickell's* Preface to the Four volumes of Mr. *Addison's* Works ".)

[This Preface of 1721 is, however, an angry reply to Tickell for claiming too much for Addison. Steele, bountifully generous, gave Addison more than his due. See *Essays in Biography*, B. Dobrée, pp. 339 seq. B. D.]

[175] While Steele had written 188 and Addison 42 (and the two friends jointly 36) of the 271 *Tatlers*, Addison wrote 250 and Steele only 240 out of the 555 *Spectators*.—In reckoning 555 *Spectators* I am not counting in the eighth volume of the *Spectator*, which was in fact an entirely new venture.

experience gained, made their bow to the public in the *Spectator*.

Encouraged by the success of the *Tatler* they ventured on two daring innovations : from the beginning the new paper was to be solely literary and it was to appear daily, except on Sundays, instead of only three times a week. The experiment was plucky and arduous. While editing the *Tatler* Steele had already groaned over the difficulty of supplying the public regularly with the promised reading matter :

> When a Man has engaged to keep a Stage-Coach, he is obliged, whether he has Passengers or not, to set out : Thus it fares with us weekly Historians.[176]

How much greater would be the difficulty of running a daily paper which denied itself the advantage of utilizing political news ! In renouncing politics, the editors were forgoing not only a sure and easy means of daily filling up blank spaces in the paper, but at the same time the faithful circle of partisan readers on whom a party journal can always safely count.

There were other potential subscribers to whom the *Spectator* deliberately scorned to appeal : those who had been wont to devour the lampoons and comedies of the Restoration, and were now greedily fattening on pamphlets and Grub-streets. These readers could easily have been wooed and won, if the new paper had been willing to bespatter its pages with slanders, scandals and uncharitable personalities. But Addison would not purchase success at the price

> of those seasonings that recommend so many of the writings which are in vogue among us.[177] As, on the one side, my paper has not in it a single word of news, a reflection in politics, nor a stroke of party ; so, on the other, there are no fashionable touches of infidelity, no obscene ideas, no satires upon priesthood, marriage, and the like popular topics of ridicule ; no private scandals, nor anything that may tend to the defamation of particular persons, families, or societies.

This dual ordinance of self-denial was highly creditable,[178]

---

[176] *Tatler*, No. 12.

[177] *Spectator*, No. 262. See also Nos. 33 and 355.

[178] The merit was all the greater that from every side pressure was brought to bear on the *Spectator* to take up politics and personalities. This is Addison's simple and dignified reply : " There is another set of correspondents to whom I must address myself . . . I mean such as fill their letters with private scandal, and black accounts of particular persons and families. The world is so full of ill-nature, that I have lampoons sent me by people who cannot spell, and satires composed by those who scarce know how to

for, as Addison says, " there is not one of the above-mentioned subjects that would not sell a very indifferent paper ". Nor was this self-denial without its dangers, for, more than any other literary product, a paper which does not immediately command readers, is doomed to speedy and inevitable death.

The truth is that Addison had the courage to disregard the normal supporters of his brother-editors because he divined that there existed, ready and waiting, the makings of another reading public, to whom no one had hitherto given thought. Poets and playwrights had written for the Court and for Society (with a capital S) ; Church of England clergymen and dissenting ministers had written tracts and sermons for their

---

write. By the last post in particular I received a packet of scandal which is not legible ; and have a whole bundle of letters in women's hands that are full of blots and calumnies, insomuch that when I see the name Caelia, Phillis, Pastora, or the like, at the bottom of a scrawl, I conclude of course that it brings me some account of a fallen virgin, a faithless wife, or an amorous widow. I must therefore inform these my correspondents, that it is not my design to be a publisher of intrigues and cuckoldoms, or to bring little infamous stories out of their present lurking-holes into broad daylight. If I attack the vicious, I shall only set upon them in a body ; and will not be provoked by the worst usage I can receive from others, to make an example of any particular criminal. In short I have so much of a Drawcansir * in me, that I shall pass over a single foe to charge whole armies. It is not Lais or Silenus, but the harlot and the drunkard whom I shall endeavour to expose ; and shall consider the crime as it appears in a species, not as it is circumstanced in an individual. I think it was Caligula who wished the whole city of Rome had but one neck, that he might behead them at a blow. I shall do out of humanity, what that Emperor would have done in the cruelty of his temper, and aim every stroke at a collective body of offenders. At the same time, I am very sensible that nothing spreads a paper like private calumny and defamation ; but as my speculations are not under this necessity, they are not exposed to this temptation.

" In the next place, I must apply myself to my party correspondents, who are continually teasing me to take notice of one another's proceedings. How often am I asked by both sides, if it is possible for me to be an unconcerned spectator of the rogueries that are committed by the party which is opposite to him that writes the letter. About two days since, I was reproached with an old Grecian law that forbids any man to stand as a neuter or looker-on in the divisions of his country. However, as I am very sensible that my paper would lose its whole effect, should it run into the outrages of a party, I shall take care to keep clear of everything which looks that way. If I can any way assuage private inflammations, or allay public ferments, I shall apply myself to it with my utmost endeavours ; but will never let my heart reproach me with having done anything towards increasing those feuds and animosities that extinguish religion, deface government, and make a nation miserable." (*Spectator*, No. 16.)

* A character in Buckingham's *Rehearsal* :
" Others may boast a single man to kill,
But I the blood of thousands daily spill."

respective followings ; scholars had written for the universities, and newspapers had written to gratify the passions of one party or another.   But outside the radius of the Court, the Churches and the Universities, outside political cliques, were there not somewhere other readers, possibly even women readers ? [179] Might there not be, perchance, in the professions, in commerce, amongst provincial folk, some persons ready to welcome intelligent mental fare ? [180]   In a society where the Court had first

[179] " But there are none to whom this paper will be more useful than to the female world. I have often thought there is not sufficient pains taken in finding out proper employments and diversions for the fair ones. Their amusements seem contrived for them rather as they are women than as they are reasonable creatures, and are more adapted to the sex than to the species. The toilet is their great scene of business, and the right adjusting of their hair the principal employment of their lives. The sorting of a suit of ribbons is reckoned a very good morning's work ; and if they make an excursion to the mercer's or a toy-shop, so great a fatigue makes them unfit for anything else all the day after. Their more serious occupations are sewing and embroidery, and their greatest drudgery the preparation of jellies and sweetmeats. This, I say, is the state of ordinary women ; though I know there are multitudes of those of a more elevated life and conversation, that move in an exalted sphere of knowledge and virtue, that join all the beauties of the mind to the ornaments of dress, and inspire a kind of awe and respect, as well as love, into their male beholders. I hope to increase the number of these by publishing this daily paper, which I shall always endeavour to make an innocent if not an improving establishment, and by that means at least divert the minds of my female readers from greater trifles. At the same time, as I would fain give some finishing touches to those who are already the most beautiful pieces in human nature, I shall endeavour to point out all those imperfections that are the blemishes, as well as those virtues which are the embellishment of the sex. In the meanwhile I hope these my gentle readers, who have so much time on their hands, will not grudge throwing away a quarter of an hour in a day on this paper, since they may do it without any hindrance to business." [No. 10—not 50 as in the text. E. O. L.]— Addison kept the promise here made to give attention to his woman-readers. See No. 205 for a list of 24 numbers devoted to women's affairs. Swift was of the opinion that he overdid it : " I will not meddle with *The Spectator*," he writes to Stella, Feb. 8, 1711-12, " let him fair-sex it to the world's end."

[180] " I would recommend this paper to the daily perusal of those gentlemen . . . who live in the world without having anything to do in it, and either by the affluence of their fortunes or laziness of their dispositions, have no other business with the rest of mankind but to look upon them. Under this class of men are comprehended all contemplative tradesmen, titular physicians, Fellows of the Royal Society, Templars that are not given to be contentious, and statesmen that are out of business ; in short every one that considers the world as a theatre, and desires to form a right judgment of those who are the actors in it.

" There is another set of men that I must likewise lay a claim to, whom I have lately called the blanks of society, as being altogether unfurnished with ideas till the business and conversation of the day has supplied them. I have often considered these poor souls with an eye of great commiseration, when I have heard them asking the first man they have met with whether

made literature fashionable, where, next, the development of the
Press had spread the habit of reading, ought there not to exist—if
it could be discovered—a whole army of intelligent, open-minded
people who might be attracted without too great difficulty?
Who could tell? Perhaps among newly-won readers, in
drawing-rooms, amongst scholars, amid the congregations of
church or even of dissenting chapel, perchance even amongst
those whose interest had hitherto been wholly monopolized by
politics,[181] there might be found some whose minds had been

---

there was any news stirring? and by that means gathering together materials
for thinking. These needy persons do not know what to talk of till about
twelve o'clock in the morning, for by that time they are pretty good judges
of the weather, know which way the wind sits, and whether the Dutch mail
be come in. As they lie at the mercy of the first man they meet, and are
grave or impertinent all the day long, according to the notions they have
imbibed in the morning, I would earnestly entreat them not to stir out of their
chambers till they have read this paper, and do promise that I will daily
instil into them such sound and wholesome sentiments as shall have a good
effect on their conversation for the ensuing twelve hours." (No. 10.)

[181] " There is no humour in my countrymen which I am more inclined
to wonder at, than their general thirst after news. There are about half a
dozen ingenious men, who live very plentifully upon this curiosity of their
fellow-subjects. They all of them receive the same advices from abroad, and
very often in the same words ; but their way of cooking it is so different,
that there is no citizen, who has an eye to the public good, that can leave
the coffee-house with peace of mind, before he has given every one of them a
reading. These several dishes of news are so very agreeable to the palate
of my countrymen, that they are not only pleased with them when they are
served up hot, but when they are again set cold before them, by those penetrat-
ing politicians who oblige the public with their reflections and observations
upon every piece of intelligence that is sent us from abroad. The text is
given us by one set of writers and the comment by another.

" But notwithstanding we have the same tale told us in so many different
papers, and if occasion requires in so many articles of the same paper ; notwithstanding in a scarcity of foreign posts we hear the same story repeated,
by different advices from Paris, Brussels, the Hague, and from every great
town in Europe ; notwithstanding the multitude of annotations, explanations,
reflections, and various readings which it passes through, our time lies heavy
on our hands till the arrival of a fresh mail. We long to receive further
particulars, to hear what will be the next step, or what will be the consequences
of that which has been already taken. A westerly wind keeps the whole
town in suspense, and puts a stop to conversation.

" This general curiosity has been raised and influenced by our late wars,
and, if rightly directed, might be of good use to a person who has such a
thirst awakened in him. Why should not a man, who takes delight in reading
everything that is new, apply himself to history, travels, and other writings
of the same kind, where he will find perpetual fuel for his curiosity, and meet
with much more pleasure and improvement, than in these papers of the week ?
An honest tradesman, who languishes a whole summer in expectation of a
battle, and perhaps is balked at last, may here meet with half a dozen in a
day. He may read the news of a whole campaign, in less time than he now
bestows upon the products of any single post. Fights, conquests, and revolu-

influenced by the course of events, and who would no longer
be content with the only reading up to now supplied them :
books, tracts, pamphlets, broadsides, Grub-streets, which, when
not blazing with political passion, had been either wholly
frivolous or wholly ascetic.

Addison was the first to formulate these questions clearly
to himself. He divined the existence of such a public and
marched forth to conquer it with clear-cut ideas and a well-
defined plan of campaign.

The first problem to be faced was how to catch the ear of
this multiple and scattered audience ; how to capture the
interest of so many diverse listeners distributed through every
stratum of society. From his first entry on the scene Addison
succeeded by an ingenious stage-device.[182]

His paper was supposed to be edited by a Club in which
people of the most varied characters and professions were represented.[183] Chief amongst them towers the Spectator, a calm
and meditative person who goes through life as a silent observer.
The gravity of his behaviour was remarked even in babyhood ;
before he was two months old he threw away his rattle and
would not use it till they had removed the bells from it. At
the University, apart from College exercises, he did not during

---

tions lie thick together. The reader's curiosity is raised and satisfied every
moment, and his passions disappointed or gratified, without being detained
in a state of uncertainty from day to day, or lying at the mercy of sea and
wind. In short, the mind is not here kept in a perpetual gape after knowledge,
nor punished with that eternal thirst, which is the portion of all our modern
news-mongers and coffee-house politicians.

" All matters of fact, which a man did not know before, are news to him ;
and I do not see how any haberdasher in Cheapside is more concerned in
the present quarrel of the Cantons, than he was in that of the League. At
least, I believe every one will allow me, it is of more importance to an Englishman to know the history of his ancestors, than that of his contemporaries,
who live upon the banks of the Danube or the Borysthenes." (No. 452.)

" Is it not much better to be let into the knowledge of one's self than
to hear what passes in Muscovy or Poland, and to amuse ourselves with such
writings as tend to the wearing out of ignorance, passion, and prejudice, than
such as naturally conduce to inflame hatreds, and make enmities irrecon-
cilable ? " (No. 10.)

[182] I shall henceforward speak of Addison as if he were the sole author
of the *Spectator*, partly for brevity but more because he is obviously its life and
soul and it is he who gives it all its value. But I am not forgetting Steele
who has been unduly eclipsed by his friend's lustre. He deserves an ample
share in the applause showered on Addison and it is pertinent and only fair
here to recall that he had his part in staging the *Spectator*.

[183] See Nos. 1 and 2. The idea of Addison's Club existed already in
embryo in Dunton's Athenian Society and Defoe's Scandalous Club. No. 132
of the *Tatler* contains a foreshadowing of the *Spectator* Club.

the space of eight years utter more than a hundred words. But if he kept his mouth shut, his eyes and mind were open, and there were few celebrated books, either in the learned or modern tongues, which he did not read and ponder during his student years. Having arrived at man's estate, he travelled over all the countries of Europe to satisfy his thirst for knowledge, and even made a special journey to Cairo to take the measure of a pyramid. Returning to London to settle down, he continued to observe men and things with curiosity. There was no place of general resort where his face was not known : the coffee-houses, the theatres, the Exchange, were in turn recipients of his long and silent visits. Having slowly and perseveringly accumulated such a mass of observations he made himself, as he says, " a speculative statesman, soldier, merchant, and artisan, without ever meddling with any practical part in life ". He goes on to say :

I am very well versed in the theory of a husband, or a father, and can discern the errors in the economy, business, and diversion of others, better than those who are engaged in them, as standers-by discover blots which are apt to escape those who are in the game. I never espoused any party with violence, and am resolved to observe an exact neutrality between the Whigs and Tories [184] . . . In short,

---

[184] He scrupulously keeps his word. Not more than once or twice are the Whig sympathies of the author allowed an airing, and then a slight one : in No. 3 for instance the vision of the Bank of England presided over by the beautiful maiden Public Credit on her throne of gold, and No. 139 (by Steele) in eloquent praise of the Duke of Marlborough. But this latter may fairly be considered patriotic rather than political. The only excursions the *Spectator* makes into politics are counsels of tolerance and moderation. How evenly he holds the balance in offering good advice alike to Whigs and Tories, may be judged from the following quotations :

" My worthy friend, Sir Roger, when we are talking of the malice of parties, very frequently tells us of an accident that happened to him when he was a school-boy, which was at the time when the feuds ran high between the Roundheads and Cavaliers. This worthy knight being then but a stripling, had occasion to inquire which was the way to St. Anne's Lane, upon which the person whom he spoke to, instead of answering his question, called him a young popish cur, and asked him who had made Anne a saint ? The boy being in some confusion, inquired of the next he met, which was the way to Anne's Lane ; but was called a prick-eared cur for his pains, and instead of being shown the way, was told, that she had been a saint before he was born, and would be one after he was hanged. ' Upon this,' says Sir Roger, ' I did not think fit to repeat the former question, but going into every lane in the neighbourhood, asked what they called the name of that lane.' By which ingenious artifice he found out the place he inquired after, without giving offence to any party." (No. 125.)

History repeats itself ; the following anecdote sounds like an echo from the French Revolution. Four Indian kings had come on a visit to England

I have acted in all the parts of my life as a looker-on, which is the character I intend to preserve in this paper.[185]

This unusual being was known only to " not above half a dozen select friends " and it was only in their company tha his tongue was loosed, and he consented to allow others a glimpse of the treasure he had accumulated from day to day by observation and reflection.[186] His friends frequently urged him to permit his fellow citizens to benefit by the fruits of his experience. As it was a question not of speaking but of writing, he yielded to their importunity and resolved to " publish a sheetful of thoughts every morning " with the assistance and collaboration of his friends, whom he then introduces to us one by one.[187]

The first is " a gentleman of Worcestershire of ancient descent, a baronet, his name Sir Roger de Coverly ", who divides his time between London and the country. In his early days Sir Roger was " what you call a fine gentleman " who moved in the society of the Rochesters and the Ethereges. But being " crossed in love by a perverse beautiful widow " he has long since grown careless of his dress, and " continues to wear a coat and doublet of the same cut that were in fashion at the time of his repulse, which, in his merry humours, he tells us has been

---

and one of them is giving his impressions of their stay : " The queen of the country appointed two men to attend us that had enough of our language to make themselves understood in some few particulars. But we soon perceived these two were great enemies to one another, and did not always agree in the same story. We could make a shift to gather out of one of them that this island was very much infested with a monstrous kind of animals, in the shape of men, called Whigs ; and he often told us that he hoped we should meet with none of them in our way, for that if we did, they would be apt to knock us down for being kings. Our other interpreter used to talk very much of a kind of animal called a Tory, that was as great a monster as the Whig, and would treat us as ill for being foreigners. These two creatures, it seems, are born with a secret antipathy to one another, and engage when they meet as naturally as the elephant and the rhinoceros. But as we saw none of either of these species, we are apt to think that our guides deceived us with misrepresentations and fictions and amused us with an account of such monsters as are not really in their country." (No. 50.)

I should like to go on and quote his advice to political women (No. 57), his witty No. 81 on the use of " patches " in politics, and a host of others. As it is, I refer the reader to A. Mézières, le Spectateur d'Addison in the Revue des cours littéraires, March 19, 1870.

[185] No. 1.

[186] Nos. 1 and 4.—This peculiarity was certainly characteristic of Addison himself. He was shy and unwilling to talk except in a circle of intimate friends. He used himself to say that he could write a cheque for £1,000 but never had a guinea in his pocket.

[187] In No. 2.

in and out (of fashion) twelve times since he first wore it ". He is now in his fifty-sixth year and devotes himself entirely to his friends and the care of his estates which he administers with paternal kindness, looking on all around him, tenants, servants and guests, as his family, happy to be beloved by his own circle. He is both a good man and a genial companion, " cheerful, gay, and hearty ", with certain eccentricities of character which are no less lovable than his virtues and good qualities.

The gentleman next in esteem and authority to whom the Club introduces us is " another bachelor, who is a member of the Inner Temple ", who has, however, taken up Law only to satisfy his father's whim. If filial duty compels his residence in the Temple, his tastes carry him elsewhere. He prefers to study the passions themselves rather than the lawsuits to which they give rise, and is more diligent in attendance at the theatre than in the Courts. He is besides a man of wide reading and fastidious taste. The next member is " a merchant of great eminence in the City ", Sir Andrew Freeport, a convinced believer in trade and commerce, and an equally convinced enemy of war. Next to him sits a retired Army officer, Captain Sentry, a man " of great courage, good understanding but invincible modesty " ; then " a clergyman . . . of general learning, great sanctity of life and the most exact good breeding " ; and lastly, " that our society may not appear a set of humorists unacquainted with the gallantries and pleasantries of the age we have among us the gallant Will Honeycomb ", who has always kept himself up to date in matters of elegance and fashion [and who " where women are not concerned is an honest worthy man ". B. D.].

How skilful this preamble is ! Every class of society is repre-sented in this Club [188] over which the Spectator presides as detached and impartial arbiter : landed interests, commerce, the Army, the Church, the Law. Literature and art are repre-sented in some degree by all the members, who are all men of taste and culture. Amorous dalliance—note that Addison never

---

[188] " The club of which I am a member is very luckily composed of such persons as are engaged in different ways of life, and deputed, as it were, out of the most conspicuous classes of mankind. By this means I am furnished with the greatest variety of hints and materials, and know everything that passes in the different quarters and divisions, not only of this great city, but of the whole kingdom. My readers, too, have the satisfaction to find that there is no rank or degree among them who have not their representative in this club, and that there is always somebody present who will take care of their respective interests, that nothing may be written or published to the prejudice or infringement of their just rights and privileges." (No. 34.)

forgets the ladies—has its advocate in Will Honeycomb.   Every type of reader will therefore find some one in whom to take an interest ;   each will feel curiosity about one member or another whose character and outlook, developed from one number to another, [189] will challenge his attention and keep it constantly on the alert.   In the wake of one or another we visit in turn the theatre,   the coffee-houses, society,   the streets of London, the courts, the church, the Exchange, the army, and when Sir Roger visits his estates he will take us with him into the country.

This variety of personalities supplies another element of interest.   The same problem is approached from different angles, and opposing points of view give rise to discussion, made more attractive and more stimulating by the clash of opinions. [190]

The whole paper in its variety fulfils—and that right royally —the promise of its opening numbers.   Every day, with amazing fertility and elasticity, the subject changes, and in each subject Addison is at home.   Following him from page to page, the reader is astounded at the ease with which he handles one after another the most varied material, and leads perpetually and smoothly " from grave to gay, from lively to severe ".   A character sketch is followed by an episode of history ;   a witty fantasy by a moral discussion or a literary criticism ;   a tale of country life by a story of the town ;   a picture of social whimsicalities by a discourse on the most profound matters of religion. After a disquisition on anger comes a chat about dancing [191] ; after a discourse on modesty, a discussion about dreams [192] ; from the consideration of envy and effrontery we are led straight on to an appreciation of trade and commerce [193] ;   from luxury and avarice to the immortality of the soul [194] ;   from matters of dress to gardens. [195]   I must pull myself up ;   I should have to quote everything.   For the truth is that no one who has not

---

[189] These portraits built up by successive strokes contain the germ of the English character novel.   The Sir Roger de Coverly articles have been reprinted in one volume ;   they make the most delightful reading.   See my Bibliography, s.v. Addison.

[190] See, for instance, No. 34.—Addison enjoys giving play to opposing views. See in particular Nos. 88, 96, 107 and 137, where the servant question is treated in its different aspects.   [All these four papers are Steele's.]

[191] Nos. 438 and 466.

[192] Nos. 484 and 487.

[193] Nos. 19, 20 and 21.—The praise of commerce is again taken up in No. 69—one of the best of the essays—and in No. 174.

[194] Nos. 55, 56 and 111.

[195] Nos. 129, 360, 477 and 478.

read the 555 numbers of the *Spectator*, and read them consecutively, can possibly imagine the infinity of resource they display, the wealth of invention and exposition which varies and sustains the reader's interest, leading him irresistibly on from one essay to the next. It is not only the choice of varied subjects that is so happy, but also the changes of form and modulations of tone. Now a portrait,[196] now a letter or an anecdote, or perhaps a parable,[197] now a conversation ; prose to-day, to-morrow poetry.[198] Addison is master of the art of quickening and holding the attention. Once you have started for a stroll with him as your companion, you follow his lead to the end, enchanted by the beauty and variety of the scenes through which he takes you, delighted and led on by the chat which enlivens the walk, and you never dream of looking back to survey the road you have travelled till you and he have reached your journey's end.

If we, people of to-day, and of another type of society, thus fall under the spell of this versatile mind, how much more magically must that spell have worked on his contemporaries, to whom almost every essay brought a fresh and acutely pertinent line of thought, and who—more fortunate in this than we—were alive to every one of his allusions. They would have been perverse indeed, and hard to please, if they had found nothing to appeal to them in this rich collection. Addison however had another trump card up his sleeve to win them to him. He puts himself into intimate touch with his readers ; he invites their comments,[199] prints and replies to their letters [200] in such a way as to establish and constantly renew mutual intercourse.

This plan of campaign, so skilfully conceived and so brilliantly

[196] Nos. 15, 58, 59, etc. These portraits were evidently inspired by La Bruyère, and here Addison owes a share of his glory to France. In No. 77 he translates the greater part of La Bruyère's *le Distrait*.

[197] It is scarcely necessary here to recall the celebrated *Vision of Mirzah* (No. 159) which Burns called " that glorious paper in the *Spectator* ".

[198] It was in the *Spectator* (No. 378) that Pope's *Messiah* appeared for the first time. See also Nos. 461, 465, 489 and 551.—The *Spectator* even includes passages in French and Italian, Nos. 229, 513, 545.

[199] In the very first number he says : " Those who have a mind to correspond with me may direct their letters to the Spectator, at Mr. Buckley's in Little Britain." See also Nos. 16, 37 and 428. In No. 442 he even suggests to his readers a subject for them to write on : Money. No. 450 is an essay on it by one of them.

[200] Not a week passes without some letter from a correspondent appearing in the *Spectator*. We might suppose that Addison wrote these himself—as was no doubt sometimes the case. But he rebuts the general accusation in No. 271 and we know from Johnson (*Lives* . . .) that Steele often relied on letters received to provide matter for the essays which it fell to his lot to supply.

executed, was successful. He soon found his readers grouping themselves together and thronging round him. As early as his tenth number he was able to say—with an elation he made no attempt to conceal : " It is with much satisfaction that I hear this great city inquiring day by day after these my papers . . . My publisher tells me that there are already 3,000 of them distributed every day, so that if I allow twenty readers to every paper, which I look upon as a modest computation, I may reckon about three-score thousand disciples in London and Westminster." [201]

A woman-reader writes to him :

" Your *Spectator* is a part of my tea equipage ; and my servant knows my humour so well, that calling for my breakfast this morning (it being past my usual hour) she answered, The Spectator was not yet come in ; but that the tea-kettle boiled, and she expected it every moment." [202]

Another reader thus testifies to his approval : " I love and thank you for your daily refreshments. I constantly peruse your paper as I smoke my morning's pipe (tho' I can't forbear reading the motto before I fill and light), and really it gives a grateful relish to every whiff." [203]

[201] The sales of the *Spectator* progressively increased from the beginning, as the following statements show :

No. 1 on sale only at one bookseller's ; No. 16 onward on sale at two booksellers' ; No. 29 at six ; No. 39 at seven ; No. 49 at eight ; No. 133 at nine ; No. 135 at ten ; No. 147 at eleven ; No. 221 at twelve.

The first number states " *London* : Printed for *Sam.* Buckley, at the *Dolphin* in *Little Britain* : and Sold by *A. Baldwin* in Warwick-Lane." The 16th adds : " as also by *Charles Lillie*, Perfumer, at the Corner of *Beauford-Buildings* in the *Strand*."—We shall later see how considerable the sales became.

[202] No. 92. The *Spectator* was daily taken in to Queen Anne with her breakfast.

[203] No. 134.—These were not the only encouraging signs which he received : see No. 124 : people write him approving letters ; his bookseller tells him that the demand for his paper increases daily ; many readers make separate collections of sets of numbers in which the same subject is dealt with. When the members of the Club begin to disappear, readers fear that it portends the winding up of the paper and " some of the most out-lying parts of the kingdom are alarmed " (Nos. 542 and 553). The *Spectator* found its way even as far as Scotland. " Rare as was the intercourse between the capital and the highlands of Scotland, the Spectator soon found its way regularly to that part of the kingdom. Mr. Stewart, of Dalguise, a gentleman of Perthshire, of very great respectability, who died near ninety, about twelve or fourteen years ago [this was written in 1803] informed us, that, when as usual in that country, the gentlemen met after church on Sunday to discuss the news of the week, the Spectators were read as regularly as the Journal. He informs us also that he knew the perusal of them to be general through the country." (Hurd's Addison, VI, p. 688.)

Thus the first English literary daily at once recruited readers and, it must be noted, faithful readers. When the Ministry of Oxford and Bolingbroke, hoping thus to rid themselves of the bitter and persistent opposition of the Whig Press, imposed a halfpenny tax on each half-sheet of print, the *Spectator* cheerfully shouldered this extra expense, doubled its price and kept afloat in defiance of wind and wave, while numbers of other papers foundered with all hands.[204]

" Do you know," Swift writes to Stella on August 7, 1712, " that Grub Street is dead and gone last week ? No more ghosts or murders now for love or money . . . Now every single half-sheet pays a half-penny to the Queen *The Observator* is fallen ; the *Medleys* are jumbled together with *The Flying Post* ; *The Examiner* is deadly sick ; *The Spectator* keeps up and doubles its price ; I know not how long it will hold."

The *Spectator* " held " for another hundred issues, and when it ultimately disappeared, its place was immediately filled by another paper, the *Guardian*.[205] Addison's prophetic insight had not been at fault : he had, and held, his audience.

This first victory gained, there remained another, and one in our eyes neither less difficult nor less interesting. If the *Spectator* were nothing more than a paper which succeeeded in finding readers (though the material success of the first literary daily was in itself a fact of major importance), it would not command so large a share of our attention. We must not forget that Addison had a moral and intellectual task to perform.

We cannot better formulate his own conception of this task than by borrowing his very words :

Since I have raised to myself so great an audience, I shall spare no pains to make their instruction agreeable, and their diversion useful, for which reasons I shall endeavour to enliven morality with wit, and to temper wit with morality, that my readers may, if possible, both ways find their account in the speculation of the day. And to the end that their virtue and discretion may not be short, transient, intermitting starts of thought, I have resolved to refresh their memories

---

[204] See No. 445 dated July 31, 1712 (the Stamp tax came into force on August 1st) and also No. 488. The tax on newspapers was introduced indirectly in an Act which also taxed soap, paper, vellum, cloth, silk, calicos, etc. (Andrews, I, pp. 106-9 ; see also *Spectator*, No. 488, and the complaints of the Soap-merchant.)

[205] The last number of the *Spectator* is dated Dec. 6, 1712. The first number of the *Guardian* is March 12, 1713.—On June 18, 1714, Addison tried to revive the *Spectator*. It then came out tri-weekly till the end of the year.

from day to day, till I have recovered them out of that desperate state of vice and folly into which the age is fallen. The mind that lies fallow but a single day sprouts up in follies that are only to be killed by a constant and assiduous culture. It was said of Socrates that he brought philosophy down from heaven to inhabit among men ; and I shall be ambitious to have it said of me that I have brought philosophy out of closets and libraries, schools and colleges, to dwell in clubs and assemblies, at tea-tables and in coffee-houses.[206]

This quotation alone suffices to show the spirit in which Addison approached his work. and his whole programme is comprehended in the two equally important phrases : " to enliven morality with wit—to temper wit with morality ". On fundamental questions he is wholly at one with Collier and with the Puritans. He is as deeply alarmed as they at the relaxation of all moral standards that prevails among his fellow-citizens ; like them, he believes that this state of affairs cannot continue without danger and dishonour. But while his predecessors saw this side of the question only, and consequently only one factor of the problem to be solved, Addison faced it in its entirety. Like them, he stands for religion and morality (which, like them, he considers essentially one), but he avoids their error of making these things cheerless and harsh, and of denying a rightful place to wit and merriment. Wiser and more reasonable than they, he is content to aim at the possible, and he asks only that—after a period of so much folly and licence—merriment and wit should settle down, happily wedded to decency and virtue. Others before Addison had diagnosed the evil, but no one before him had so clearly perceived its causes. Therein lies his originality and undeniable claim to credit. No one else understood as he did, that it was the long divorce of wit from virtue [206a] which had produced in England that profound moral disturbance from which people were now just trying to escape, that if the patient's disease were to be cured without fear of a relapse, if his shaken organism were to recover its equilibrium, it was essential to re-establish harmony between these two necessary elements in life, which according to the decrees of natural law must live together, but which of late had been at variance to the equal injury of both.

[206] No. 10.

[206a] [This is an exaggeration ; wit had not always been opposed to virtue between 1660 and Addison's appearance. To name a few there were Halifax, Garth, Defoe ; and even the most virtuous were sometimes witty, e.g. William Penn. B. D.]

But how was this harmony to be established ? What methods of persuasion or diplomacy could avail to reconcile the two sections of the nation, embittered by the political and religious differences of nearly a century ? Each looked with horror on the other, and when unable to oppress, was ever ready with insult and contempt.

Addison succeeded by reason of neither insulting nor despising anyone whether of Right or Left. He excluded not only party politics from his paper but also partisan and sectarian morality. He never names either the Court or the City, the Puritans or the Cavaliers ; he never contrasts them. If he points out the errors of one side, it is never to the advantage of the other.[207] In short, he introduces moderation, calm and impartiality.

Above all, he takes the greatest care not to pose as a reformer. Before him, the champions of morality, lay or clerical, had been little but cantankerous and monotonous preachers fulminating against sinners, drawing a gloomy picture of their vices and impurity and threatening them—unless they should repent— with the wrath of heaven. Addison does not belong to this surly, bitter school. He does not mount the pulpit. He does not preach. No one was ever less of a pedagogue or sermonizer than he. He does not essay to teach people a lesson. He is content to show them what is desirable and seemly, and lead them to prefer it.

Picture to yourself a man of the world unselfconsciously cultured, serious but not starched, learned without pedantry, loving and savouring intellectual pleasures, a Christian withal, a believing Christian, but not bigoted, not puritanical, not intolerant, practising charity as the foremost element in his religion.[208] Picture such a man chatting informally in a company

---

[207] It is extremely rare for him to make direct allusion to the Puritans. Towards the end of No. 161 he mentions them in connection with certain popular amusements they sought to suppress, and he alludes to them again at the close of No. 458. No. 494 which I quote later on (p. 284 f.) is entirely devoted to their conception of religion ; but he does not mention them by name.

[208] In the dream-allegory of No. 3 Religion makes her appearance among the " very amiable phantoms ", but she is led in by Moderation. In another context the *Spectator* (No. 459), quoting " an excellent author ", says : " We have just enough religion to make us hate, but not enough to make us love one another."—And again : " Without a good grace valour would degenerate into brutality, learning into pedantry, and the genteelest demeanour into affectation. Even religion itself, unless decency be the handmaid which waits upon her, is apt to make people appear guilty of sourness and ill-humour " (No. 292).—See also No. 516 devoted to the virtue of tolerance. In No. 432

of distinguished and cultivated people, and sharing with them his views on all the subjects which may be debated in such a gathering—as the chances of conversation may suggest—on literature, on the amusements and manners of the day, on more serious topics concerning this life and the next. In all these talks, varied as they are in subject and in tone, he is genial, witty, always interesting, often high-minded, but never dogmatic or sententious.[209] He unobtrusively avoids hammering away at the same theme, for he would think it both bad taste and bad policy to bore his hearers. He is averse from all exaggeration ; he uses neither high-sounding phrase nor dramatic gesture ; he is readier to praise than to find fault. If he is compelled to blame, he avoids the wounding word which would be as inconsistent with his natural courtesy as with his religion. He implies his censure by a quiet word, more often by an ironic tone of voice, by the twitch of an eyelid or a curl of the lip. His conversation never has the formal well-prepared character of a lecture, yet it conveys instruction, and no one could live long in communion with his mind without drawing from such intercourse both the most subtle enjoyment and the greatest intellectual and moral advantage. Such are Addison's essays : delightful talks of a man of the world, whose mind is ennobled by reason and knowledge, and mellowed by kindliness.

What makes Addison's essays so peculiarly gracious, is that it cost him no effort to strike the friendly note of good will which makes them so effective. In reading them you do not feel that you are dealing with a self-conscious man, ordering his thoughts and keeping guard over his tongue. The man and the author in him are one. He is the same in public among his fellow men as in the privacy of his diary. With him mental integrity was allied by nature to kindness and courtesy. I have already mentioned the high respect he had won in political circles by the charm and the firmness of his character. This respect was so solidly and securely based, that when the feeling stirred up by the Sacheverell Trial brought about the downfall of the Whigs,[210] Addison, without any concession to his opponents,

he displays tolerance even towards Roman Catholics : " Though I am a firm Protestant I hope to see the Pope and Cardinals without violent emotions."— In 1689 John Locke had published his first *Letter on Toleration*, first in Latin, then in English.

[209] " A man may appear learned without talking sentences, as in his ordinary gesture he discovers he can dance, though he does not cut capers." (No. 4.)

[210] See Lecky, I, pp. 51–9.

escaped the unpopularity which suddenly overwhelmed his
friends. In the 1710 elections, which left so many of his party
in the wilderness, he was once more returned to Parliament.
Swift, whose feelings towards the Whigs were tainted by that
bitterness which a political renegade always feels towards the
friends he is deserting, [210a] wrote to Stella : " . . . new elections,
where the Tories carry it among the new members six to one.
Mr. Addison's election has passed easy and undisputed ; and
I believe if he had a mind to be chosen king he would hardly
be refused ".[211] These remarkable words admirably reveal the
nature of Addison's peculiar influence on his contemporaries.
It was an influence springing from contagious sympathy. He
lived in an aura of seductive charm ; whoever came near him
fell under the spell.

In his immediate circle this influence showed itself in the
unusually deep affection and respect which he enjoyed. Pope
tells us that Steele's friendship for him bordered on veneration.[212]
When Garth lay on his death-bed he sent to ask Addison whether
he ought to believe in the Christian religion.[213] Mediocre
poet though Tickell was, he was inspired to write on his dead
friend one of the finest elegies in the English language.[214] One
particular case will show the kind of tie which bound Addison's
friends to him. Amongst the authors who grouped themselves

[210a] [This scarcely does Swift justice. Though he was Whig enough to
support the Revolution, the dogmatic beliefs which he sincerely held made it
impossible for him to be wholly Whig or to support occasional conformity ;
and he really believed that a Whig triumph would mean ruin to the country
and the Church. He was no renegade, and it was Addison, not Swift, who
turned personally bitter over politics. After all, he tried to keep Steele in
his place of Commissioner of Stamps—hardly the rôle of a party-embittered
man. See the *Journal to Stella*, 22nd and 23rd Oct., 1710, and *passim* till
14th Dec. B. D.]
[211] *Journal to Stella*, Oct. 12, 1710.
[212] Spence, p. 197.
[Steele's schoolboy veneration survived a good many shocks, but not,
ultimately *The Plebeian—The Old Whig* quarrel. Pope, when he reported this
to Spence, was thinking of the Button's days, of the Little Senate, where he
himself was a somewhat strange intruder. B. D.]
[213] Spence, p. 2, note.
[This is an agreeable anecdote of Edward Young's, with little real authority,
being *via* Addison himself, or Tickell, " which is much the same ". Garth
who, being the fattest man in London, died with the comment that life was
hardly worth the bother of bending down to tie one's shoe laces, was far too
confirmed a sceptic to believe in a religion because an Addison told him that
he ought. B. D.]
[214] This Elegy is prefixed to Tickell's Edition of Addison, printed in
1721.

round him was a certain Eustace Budgell, who was distantly related to him, and in whom he had always taken an active interest, bringing him to live in London with him and securing for him various public posts under his wing, allowing him to collaborate in the *Spectator* and the *Guardian*, and even exercising ingenuity in helping him to gain a literary success which he would certainly never have attained without his kinsman's kindly aid.[215] While Addison lived, Budgell's conduct was blameless ; but no sooner was his protector taken from him, than the younger man began speculating in public funds, got himself into debt, and quickly slipping down the fatal incline, attempted to pay his debts by forgery. Finally, detected, despised, consumed with remorse, he decided to end his wretched life by committing suicide in the Thames. It was eighteen years after Addison's death that the unhappy man, reviewing in his last hours the course of his life, still thought of Addison, who if he had lived would undoubtedly have saved him from evil courses. His last thought was for his lost friend, and for the marks of kindness and consideration Addison of old had shown him.[216]

In social relationships Addison's moral and mental qualities combined to cast a spell on his fellows. The charm of his companionship was felt to an extraordinary degree by all, even by the most exacting critics and the most reluctant admirers. He was a " favourite " of Mrs. Steele, a woman by no means easy to please, and inclined to view with jealous eye the place Addison

---

[215] Addison completely overhauled, or perhaps éven himself wrote the whole Epilogue to Ambrose Philips' tragedy *The Distrest Mother*. The Epilogue was much admired and praised and Addison allowed it to pass as Budgell's unaided work.

[216] They found on his desk a sheet of paper with the words :

> " What Cato did, and Addison approv'd
> Cannot be wrong."

See Spence, p. 145 ; Drake, *Essays . . . Illustrative of the Tatler, Spectator and Guardian*, III, pp. 1–25.

[Addison seems to have had a great affection for this most adoring of his " little Senate ", and appears to have had a most disastrous influence on him. He obtained him a post in Ireland, and Budgell did well so long as Addison was there to mother him—but only so long. Later he lost heavily when the South Sea Bubble burst, and tried to retrieve himself by gambling, thinking, as Addison had taught him to think, that fortune would always shower favours on him. It is hardly fair to accuse him of forgery. The affair over Dr. Tindal's will, and *Christianity as Old as the Creation* is ugly enough, but it was not forgery. And by that time he was notoriously lunatic, and was so adjudged by the Coroner's jury. See the *D.N.B.*   B. D.]

took in her husband's life.[217]   Pope, who was filled with bitter malice towards him, Pope who drew the portrait of *Atticus*,[218] vowed that he had never met anyone whose conversation was so delightful.[219]   At the very moment that Swift was openly at war with the Whigs and cold-shouldering Addison, he wrote to Stella : " I yet know no man half so agreeable to me as he is." [220]   Lady Mary Wortley Montagu used to say that she had known all the famous wits of her time, but never one who was better company than Addison.[221]   A private conversation with Addison was for Steele a pleasure beyond all others : it was Terence and Catullus in one, with an added something, indefinable, exquisite and delightful, of which Addison alone held the secret.[222]   Edward Young of the *Night Thoughts* often said that when Addison felt at ease his talk had a splendid flow of thought and expression which captured the attention of all.[223]

These eloquent testimonies show how admirably Nature had equipped the author of the *Spectator* successfully to carry out a task of pure conciliation and persuasion.   With his readers, as with his friends, he had only to be himself to win their ears and their affections.   In writing his paper he simply enlarged the circle of his friends.   Delicate as was the reform he aimed at, formidable as were the passions which lay in his way, he overcame all difficulties with the same ease as enabled him in his more immediate circle to triumph over prejudice and ill will. We shall see how impossible it was for the persons involved not to be won over by advice so tactfully tendered, phrased

[217] See Steele's Correspondence, *passim*, especially vol. I, pp. 158 and 171.
[218] This unfair portrait of Addison occurs in Pope's *Epistle to Dr. Arbuthnot* [usually known as *The Prologue to the Satires*. The worst of the portrait was that it was true—if one-sided. B. D.].   (Warburton's Edition of Pope, vol. IV.)
[219] Spence, p. 50.
[220] *Journal to Stella*, Sept. 14, 1711.   Sheridan reports that Swift was wont to say that a *tête-à-tête* conversation with Addison was the pleasantest he had ever known, and that in all the many hours they had thus spent alone together neither had ever wished for the arrival of a third party.   (*Life of Swift* quoted by Drake, *Essays . . . Illustrative*, etc., III, p. 144.)
[221] Spence, p. 232.
[222] " I have often reflected, after a Night spent with him apart from all the World, that I had the Pleasure of conversing with an intimate Acquaintance of *Terence* and *Catullus*, who had all their Wit and Nature heighten'd with Humour, more exquisite and delightful than any other Man ever possessed." (Letter from Steele to Congreve, prefixed to *The Drummer*.)
[223] Spence, p. 355.

with so much wit and good will, and so strongly backed by reason and good sense.

Here, for instance, are some remarks aimed at those who were carrying on the traditions of Charles II's reign ; they occur at the close of a critical analysis of a play of Etherege's, *Sir Fopling Flutter*, which was still a popular favourite in the *Spectator's* day :

According to the notion of merit in this comedy, I take the Shoe-maker to be, in reality, the fine gentleman of the play : for it seems he is an atheist, if we may depend upon his character as given by the Orange-woman, who is herself far from being the lowest in the play.[224] She says of a fine man who is Dorimant's companion, " There is not such another heathen in the town, except the shoemaker." His pretension to be the hero of the drama appears still more in his own description of his way of living with his lady. " There is," he says, " never a man in town lives more like a gentleman with his wife than I do ; I never mind her motions ; she never inquires into mine. We speak to one another civilly, hate one another heartily ; and because it is vulgar to lie and soak together, we have each of us our several settle-bed." That of " soaking together " is as good as if Dorimant had spoken it himself ; and I think, since he puts human nature in as ugly a form as the circumstance will bear, and is a staunch un-believer, he is very much wronged in having no part of the good fortune bestowed in the last act.[225]

This is no flattering likeness, and no gentleman with aspir-ations after social elegance could easily feel flattered at being thus compared to—a shoemaker. But how kindly and ingenious the satire is ! [225a] How skilfully this irony says all that needs be said without fine phrases or wounding words ! How could anyone whom the cap fitted take umbrage and having once begun to read, fail to read to the end ? And when the *Spectator* returns in another passage to the same subject—one which lies very near his heart—in graver mood, how could the most recal-citrant reader fail to be unwittingly carried away by such calm and temperate language which unpretentiously and easily rises to that natural eloquence which impresses and persuades ?

I know no one character that gives reason a greater shock, at the same time that it presents a good ridiculous image to the imagination,

---

[224] The Shoemaker, the Orange-Woman and Dorimant are characters in the play.

[225] No. 65.

[225a] [The kindly and ingenious satire is, of course, Etherege's rather than Addison's. That the play was still a favourite at this time is no tribute to Collier's success, and scarcely bears out Beljame's earlier contention. B. D.]

than that of a man of wit and pleasure about the town.   This description of a man of fashion, spoken by some with a mixture of scorn and
ridicule, by others with great gravity as a laudable distinction, is in
everybody's mouth that spends any time in conversation.   My friend
Will Honeycomb has this expression very frequently ; and I never
could understand by the story which follows upon his mention of such
a one, but that his man of wit and pleasure was either a drunkard
too old for wenching, or a young lewd fellow with some liveliness,
who would converse with you, receive kind offices of you, and at the
same time debauch your sister or lie with your wife.   According to
his description, a man of wit, when he could have wenches for crowns
apiece whom he liked quite as well, would be so extravagant as to
bribe servants, make false friendships, fight relations ; I say, according to him, plain and simple vice was too little for a man of wit and
pleasure ; but he would leave an easy and accessible wickedness, to
come at the same thing with only the addition of certain falsehood,
and possible murder.   Will thinks the town grown very dull, in that
we do not hear so much as we used to do of these coxcombs, whom
(without observing it) he describes as the most infamous rogues in
nature, with relation to friendship, love, or conversation.

When pleasure is made the chief pursuit of life, it will necessarily
follow that such monsters as these will arise from a constant application
to such blandishments as naturally root out the force of reason and
reflection, and substitute in their place a general impatience of thought,
and a constant pruriency of inordinate desire.

Pleasure, when it is a man's chief purpose, disappoints itself ; and
the constant application to it palls the faculty of enjoying it, though
it leaves the sense of our inability for that we wish, with a disrelish
of everything else.   Thus the intermediate seasons of the man of
pleasure are more heavy than one would impose upon the vilest
criminal.   Take him when he is awaked too soon after a debauch, or
disappointed in following a worthless woman without truth, and there
is no man living whose being is such a weight or vexation as his is.
He is an utter stranger to the pleasing reflections in the evening of a
well-spent day, or the gladness of heart or quickness of spirit in the
morning after profound sleep or indolent slumbers . . .

You may indeed observe in people of pleasure a certain com-
placency and absence of all severity, which the habit of a loose unconcerned life gives them ; but tell the man of pleasure your secret
wants, cares, or sorrows, and you will find he has given up the delicacy
of his passions to the cravings of his appetites.   He little knows the
perfect joy he loses, for the disappointing gratifications which he
pursues.   He looks at pleasure as she approaches, and comes to you
with the recommendation of warm wishes, gay looks and graceful
motion ; but he does not observe how she leaves his presence with
disorder, impotence, downcast shame and conscious imperfection.
She makes our youth inglorious and our age shameful . . .

No, there is not in the world an occasion wherein vice makes so
fantastical a figure, as at the meeting of two old people who have
been partners in unwarrantable pleasure.   To tell a toothless old lady

that she once had a good set, or a defunct wencher that he once was the admired thing of the town, are satires instead of applauses : but on the other side, consider the old age of those who have passed their days in labour, industry and virtue ; their decays make them but appear the more venerable, and the imperfections of their bodies are beheld as a misfortune to human society that their make is so little durable.[226]

Addison, as I have said, holds the balance even, between the two extremes.   Having shown how he speaks to the libertine I must now show his approach to the puritanical.   This time I shall quote not passages merely but an entire number of his paper, so that the student may form an idea of how a *Spectator* was composed.   The reader will gladly forgive me these lengthy quotations and be grateful only that I allow Addison to speak instead of holding the floor myself.

Friday, Sept. 26, 1712.

Ægritudinem laudare, unam rem maxime detestabilem, quorum est tandem philosophorum ? Cic.

About an age ago it was the fashion in England, for every one that would be thought religious, to throw as much sanctity as possible into his face, and in particular to abstain from all appearances of mirth and pleasantry, which were looked upon as the marks of a carnal mind.   The saint was of a sorrowful countenance, and generally eaten up with spleen and melancholy.   A gentleman, who was lately a great ornament to the learned world, has diverted me more than once with an account of the reception which he met with from a very famous Independent minister, who was head of a college in those times.   This gentleman was then a young adventurer in the republic of letters, and just fitted out for the university with a good cargo of Latin and Greek.   His friends were resolved that he should try his fortune at an election which was drawing near in the college of which the Independent minister, who I have before mentioned, was governor. The youth, according to custom, waited on him in order to be examined.   He was received at the door by a servant, who was one of that gloomy generation that were then in fashion.   He conducted him, with great silence and seriousness, to a long gallery which was darkened at noonday, and had only a single candle burning in it. After a short stay in this melancholy apartment, he was led into a chamber hung with black, where he entertained himself for some time by the glimmering of a taper, until at length the head of the college came out to him from an inner room, with half-a-dozen nightcaps upon his head, and a religious horror in his countenance.   The young man trembled ; but his fears increased when, instead of being asked what progress he had made in learning, he was examined how he

---

[226] No. 151.—See also No. 358.

abounded in grace. His Latin and Greek stood him in little stead. He was to give an account only of the state of his soul, whether he was of the number of the elect ; what was the occasion of his conversion ; upon what day of the month and hour of the day it happened ; how it was carried on, and when completed ? The whole examination was summed up with one short question, namely, whether he was prepared for death ? The boy, who had been bred up by honest parents, was frighted out of his wits at the solemnity of the proceeding, and by the last dreadful interrogatory ; so that upon making his escape out of this house of mourning, he could never be brought a second time to the examination as not being able to go through the terrors of it.[227]

Notwithstanding this general form and outside of religion is pretty well worn out among us, there are many persons who, by a natural uncheerfulness of heart, mistaken notions of piety, or weakness of understanding, love to indulge this uncomfortable way of life, and give up themselves a prey to grief and melancholy. Superstitious fears and groundless scruples cut them off from the pleasures of conversation, and all those social entertainments, which are not only innocent but laudable ; as if mirth was made for reprobates, and cheerfulness of heart denied those who are the only persons that have a proper title to it.

Sombrius is one of these sons of sorrow. He thinks himself obliged in duty to be sad and disconsolate. He looks on a sudden fit of laughter as a breach of his baptismal vow. An innocent jest startles him like blasphemy. Tell him of one who is advanced to a title of honour, he lifts up his hands and eyes ; describe a public ceremony, he shakes his head ; show him a gay equipage, he blesses himself. All the little ornaments of life are pomps and vanities. Mirth is wanton and wit profane. He is scandalized at youth for being lively, and at childhood for being playful. He sits at a christening or a marriage feast as at a funeral ; sighs at the conclusion of a merry story ; and grows devout when the rest of the company grow pleasant. After all, Sombrius is a religious man, and would have behaved himself very properly had he lived when Christianity was under a general persecution.

I would by no means presume to tax such characters with hypocrisy, as is done too frequently, that being a vice which I think none but He who knows the secrets of men's hearts should pretend to discover in another, where the proofs of it do not amount to a demonstration. On the contrary, as there are many excellent persons who are weighed down by this habitual sorrow of heart, they rather deserve our compassion than our reproaches. I think, however, they would do well to consider, whether such a behaviour, does not deter men from a religious life, by representing it as an unsociable state, that extinguishes

---

[227] This anecdote is not of Addison's invention. The interview really took place, just as he describes it, between Dr. Goodwin, President of Magdalen College, Oxford, and young Anthony Henley, one of the collaborators of the *Tatler*. See N. Drake, *Essays . . . Illustrative*, etc., III, pp. 340-7.

all joy and gladness, darkens the face of nature, and destroys the relish of being itself.

I have, in former papers,[228] shown how great a tendency there is to cheerfulness in religion, and how such a frame of mind is not only the most lovely, but the most commendable in a virtuous person. In short, those who represent religion in so unamiable a light, are like the spies sent by Moses to make a discovery of the Land of Promise, when by their reports they discouraged the people from entering upon it. Those who show us the joy, the cheerfulness, the good humour, that naturally spring up in this happy state, are like the spies bringing along with them the clusters of grapes, and delicious fruits, that might invite their companions into the pleasant country which produced them.

An eminent Pagan writer [229] has made a discourse, to show that the atheist, who denies a God, does Him less dishonour than the man who owns His being, but at the same time believes Him to be cruel, hard to please, and terrible to human nature. " For my own part," says he, " I would rather it should be said of me, that there was never any such man as Plutarch, than that Plutarch was ill-natured, capricious, or inhuman."

If we may believe our logicians, man is distinguished from all other creatures by the faculty of laughter. He has an heart capable of mirth, and naturally disposed to it. It is not the business of virtue to extirpate the affections of the mind, but to regulate them. It may moderate and restrain, but was not designed to banish, gladness from the heart of man. Religion contracts the circle of our pleasures, but leaves it wide enough for her votaries to expatiate in. The contemplation of the Divine Being, and the exercise of virtue, are in their own nature so far from excluding all gladness of heart, that they are perpetual sources of it. In a word, the true spirit of religion cheers, as well as composes the soul : it banishes indeed all levity of behaviour, all vicious and dissolute mirth, but in exchange fills the mind with a perpetual serenity, uninterrupted cheerfulness, and an habitual inclination to please others, as well as to be pleased in itself.[230]

Addison felicitously groups round these serious subjects of religion and morals an analysis of the main duties of life and expounds them with the same high-principled common sense. It would be easy to extract from his paper a code of practical morality.[231] He writes repeatedly and at length on the question

[228] Amongst others, Nos. 302 and 381.

[229] Plutarch.

[230] No. 494.—Another aspect of the same subject is dealt with in No. 354 ; this time it is the portrait of a she-bigot.—See also the first letter quoted in No. 46 and No. 201, from which I cull this sentence : " The two great errors into which a mistaken devotion may betray us are enthusiasm and superstition."

[231] Professor M. L. Mézières collected from Addison's works, the *Spectator* in particular, an anthology which he justly called *Encyclopédie morale*. See my Bibliography.

of marriage,[232] which it had been the fashion to ridicule and scoff at, on education and instruction [233] which were still gravely neglected.[234] In dealing with important subjects such as these, he does not forget that a host of minor questions arise in daily life which from their constant recurrence in all sorts of circumstances acquire real importance. He does not omit to treat of customary conventions, courtesy, good breeding, and the everyday forms of politeness which contribute so greatly to the pleasure and dignity of life.[235] In short, wherever he detects an error

---

[232] Nos. 149, 170, 171, 203, 261, 299, 364, 437, 479, 482, 486, 490, 500, 520, 522, 525. " Nothing is a greater mark of a degenerate and vicious age ", he says, " than the common ridicule which passes on this state of life." (No. 261.)

[233] Nos. 66, 215, 307, 353, 426, etc. No. 215 opens with a beautiful paragraph on education : " I consider an human soul without education like marble in the quarry, which shows none of its inherent beauties, till the skill of the polisher fetches out the colours, makes the surface shine, and discovers every ornamental cloud, spot, and vein that runs through the body of it. Education, after the same manner, when it works upon a noble mind, draws out to view every latent virtue and perfection, which without such helps are never able to make their appearance.

" If my reader will give me leave to change the allusion so soon upon him, I shall make use of the same instance to illustrate the force of education which Aristotle has brought to explain his doctrine of substantial forms, when he tells us that a statue lies hid in a block of marble ; and that the art of the statuary only clears away the superfluous matter and removes the rubbish. The figure is in the stone, the sculptor only finds it. What sculpture is to a block of marble, education is to an human soul. The philosopher, the saint, or the hero, the wise, the good, or the great man, very often lie hid and concealed in a plebeian, which a proper education might have disinterred, and have brought to light." (This passage was translated by Professor M. L. Mézières, in his *Leçons anglaises de Littérature et de morale.* Paris, 1826, I, p. 300.)—In 1693 Locke had published his *Thoughts Concerning Education.* Following in Locke's footsteps Addison anticipates Rousseau in advising women to suckle their infants themselves (No. 246). In Nos. 157 and 168 he writes pages against corporal punishment in schools, pages which his fellow countrymen of today might still ponder with advantage.

[234] Steele recommended to his readers a certain English Grammar in these terms : " I therefore enjoin all my female correspondents to buy and study that grammar, that their letters may be somewhat less enigmatic ; and on all my male correspondents likewise, who make no conscience of false spelling and false English, I lay the same injunction, on pain of having their epistles exposed in their own proper dress in my lucubrations." (Drake, *Essays . . . Illustrative*, etc., III, pp. 348–9.)

[235] No. 100, on good humour in society ; No. 104, on decorum ; No. 148, on breaches of good taste ; No. 155, on undue licence in conversation ; No. 302, on women's carelessness in indoor dress ; No. 371, against swearing ; No. 430, on the strange freedoms some married people take in company ; No. 503, on the misbehaviour of people at church ; No. 508 (2nd letter), on the way some men behave towards women ; Nos. 242 and 533, against lewd conversation in public conveyances, etc. etc.

to be corrected, a bad habit to be cured, a step forward to be made—however trifling these may be—he mounts guard like a sentinel at his post, fighting against accepted follies, from duelling to vulgar superstitions,[236] on the alert, as he himself says, to serve the public " by reprehending those vices which are too trivial for the chastisement of the law, and too fanatical for the cognizance of the pulpit ".[237]

It would, however, be a grave mistake to picture the *Spectator* as nothing but a monotonous collection of lessons in morals and good manners. Anything but that. And therein lies Addison's originality. Other moralists usually point out the evils of con-temporary ways, laying bare their causes, effects and dangers with more or less justification and vigour, and consider their task then ended. Addison goes further : he is not content to diagnose and locate the malady, he points out and supplies the remedy.

This remedy, as the intelligent reader will already have perceived, is—pleasure. Pleasure, which the Puritans had indis-creetly banned, which the Restoration libertines had dishonoured, must be restored to her due place in social life. Despite her enemies, above all, despite her friends, she must be reinstated. Widely and wisely interpreted, refined intelligent pleasure could supply Puritanism with a most necessary safety valve [238] ; and so-called high society with a wholesome and lasting corrective to its base and vulgar amusements.[239] When once innocent pleasure had taught the " unco guid " to relax, and had extri-cated the licentious from their mire, the most difficult part of her task would be accomplished. So having attacked with just as much warmth as his predecessors—but in another tone and

---

[236] Nos. 84 and 97, against duelling ; No. 7, on the folly of superstitions ; No. 505, against belief in portents, prodigies and the interpretation of dreams. —There are, however, some superstitions which he shares : he is prepared to admit the possibility of apparitions and witchcraft (Nos. 110 and 117).

[237] No. 34.

[238] " Pleasure and reaction of one kind or other are absolutely necessary to relieve our minds and bodies from too constant attention and labour." (No. 258.)

" A man that is temperate, generous, valiant, chaste, faithful and honest, may at the same time have wit, humour, mirth, good breeding and gallantry." (No. 51.)

[239] " Delicacy in pleasure is the first step people of condition take in reformation from vice " (No. 370). For this reason Addison attacks the brutalities of the Mohocks in their nocturnal expeditions (Nos. 324, 332, 335, etc.) ; excessive drinking (No. 474) ; barbarous spectacles (No. 436) ; and so on.

with more moderation—the excesses of the fashionable play,[240] the *Spectator* by no means demands the suppression of the theatre.[241] He asks only that it be chastened and purified that he may commend it to his fellow citizens as a " noble entertainment ".[242] In the same way he continually recommends to his readers everything which can offer pleasurable recreation to mind or body : reading,[243] music,[244] dancing,[245] conversation [246] or painting.[247] Setting an example in his own practice, he hopes to provide recreation for his readers at the same time as he offers useful information. Not only does he enliven his lessons—so pleasant in themselves—by amusing anecdote and witty comment,[248] he often devotes a whole issue to pure mental entertainment, and such numbers are by no means the least happily inspired. Let us consider a sample specimen :

Thursday, April 3, 1712.

'Errat, et illinc
Huc venit, hinc illuc, et quoslibet occupat artus
Spiritus : eque feris humana in corpora transit,
Inque feras noster.

Ovid., Met. XV, 165.

Will Honeycomb, who loves to show upon occasion all the little learning he has picked up, told us yesterday at the club, that he thought there might be a great deal said for the transmigration of souls and that the eastern parts of the world believed in that doctrine to this day. " Sir Paul Rycaut", says he, " gives us an account of several well-disposed Mahomedans that purchase the freedom of any little bird they see confined to a cage, and think they merit as much by it, as we should do here by ransoming any of our countrymen from their captivity at Algiers. You must know ", says Will, " the reason is, because they consider every animal as a brother, or a sister in disguise, and therefore think themselves obliged to extend their charity to them, though under such mean circumstances. They'll tell you ",

---

[240] I have quoted above his criticism of Etherege's comedy, *Sir Fopling Flutter.*—See also Nos. 51, 446, etc.
[241] Steele firmly said to Cibber : " To talk of suppressing the Stage, because the Licentiousness, Ignorance, or Poverty, of its former Professors may have abus'd the proper Ends of its Institution, were, in Morality as absurd a violence, as it would be in Religion to silence the Pulpit, because Sedition or Treason had been preach'd there." (Cibber, Dedication to *Ximena.*)
[242] No. 141.—See also No. 370.   [243] Nos. 37, 80, 92, etc.
[244] No. 405. He recommends, contrary to Puritan ideas, the use of music, even in churches.
[245] No. 67.   [246] Nos. 68, 138, 409.
[247] Nos. 83, 226, 244.
[248] See, amongst others, Nos. 491, 509, 535.

says Will, " that the soul of a man, when he dies, immediately passes into the body of another man, or of some brute, which he resembled in his humour or his fortune when he was one of us."

As I was wondering what this profusion of learning would end in, Will told us that Jack Freelove, who was a fellow of whim, made love to one of those ladies who throw away all their fondness on parrots, monkeys, and lap-dogs. Upon going to pay her a visit one morning, he writ a very pretty epistle upon this hint. " Jack ", says he, " was conducted into the parlour, where he diverted himself for some time with her favourite monkey, which was chained in one of the windows ; till at length, observing a pen and ink lie by him, he writ the following letter to his mistress, in the person of the monkey ; and upon her not coming down so soon as he expected, left it in the window, and went about his business.

" The lady soon after coming into the parlour, and seeing her monkey look upon a paper with great earnestness, took it up, and to this day is in some doubt," says Will, " whether it was written by Jack or the monkey."

Madam,—

Not having the gift of speech, I have a long time waited in vain for an opportunity of making myself known to you ; and having at present the conveniences of pen, ink, and paper by me, I gladly take the occasion of giving you my history in writing, which I could not do by word of mouth. You must know, madam, that about a thousand years ago I was an Indian Brahmin and versed in all those mysterious secrets which your European philosopher, called Pythagoras, is said to have learned from our fraternity. I had so ingratiated myself by my great skill in the occult sciences with a demon whom I used to converse with, that he promised to grant me whatever I should ask of him. I desired that my soul might never pass into the body of a brute creature ; but this he told me was not in his power to grant me. I then begged that into whatever creature I should chance to transmigrate, I might still retain my memory, and be conscious that I was the same person who lived in different animals. This he told me was within his power, and accordingly promised me on the word of a demon that he would grant me what I desired. From that time forth I lived so very unblamably, that I was made president of a college of Brahmins, an office which I discharged with great integrity till the day of my death.

I was then shuffled into another human body, and acted my part so very well in it, that I became first minister to a prince who reigned upon the banks of the Ganges. I here lived in great honour for several years, but by degrees lost all the innocence of the Brahmin, being obliged to rifle and oppress the people to enrich my sovereign ; till at length I became so odious, that my master, to recover his credit with his subjects, shot me through the heart with an arrow, as I was one day addressing myself to him at the head of his army.

Upon my next remove I found myself in the woods under the shape of a jackal, and soon enlisted myself in the service of a lion. I used to yelp near his den about midnight, which was his time of rousing and seeking after his prey. He always followed me in the rear, and when I had run down a fat buck, a wild goat, or an hare, after he had feasted very plentifully upon it himself, would now and then throw me a bone that was but half-picked for my encouragement ; but upon my being unsuccessful in two or three chases, he gave me such a confounded gripe in his anger that I died of it.

In my next transmigration I was again set upon two legs, and became an Indian tax-gatherer ; but having been guilty of great extravagances, and being married to an expensive jade of a wife, I ran so cursedly in debt that I durst not show my head. I could no sooner step out of my house, but I was arrested by somebody or other that lay in wait for me. As I ventured abroad one night in the dusk of the evening, I was taken up and hurried into a dungeon, where I died a few months after.

My soul then entered into a flying-fish, and in that state led a most melancholy life for the space of six years. Several fishes of prey pursued me when I was in the water, and if I betook myself to my wings, it was ten to one but I had a flock of birds aiming at me. As I was one day flying amidst a fleet of English ships, I observed an huge seagull whetting his bill and hovering just over my head. Upon my dipping into the water to avoid him, I fell into the mouth of a monstrous shark that swallowed me down in an instant.

I was some years afterwards, to my great surprise, an eminent banker in Lombard Street ; and remembering how I had formerly suffered for want of money, became so very sordid and avaricious that the whole town cried shame of me. I was a miserable little old fellow to look upon, for I had in a manner starved myself, and was nothing but skin and bone when I died.

I was afterwards very much troubled and amazed to find myself dwindled into an emmet. I was heartily concerned to make so insignificant a figure, and did not know but, some time or other, I might be reduced to a mite if I did not mend my manners. I therefore applied myself with great diligence to the offices that were allotted me, and was generally looked upon as the notablest ant in the whole molehill. I was at last picked up, as I was groaning under a burden, by an unlucky cock-sparrow that lived in the neighbourhood, and had before made great depredations upon our commonwealth.

I then bettered my condition a little, and lived a whole summer in the shape of a bee ; but being tired with the painful and penurious life I had undergone in my two last transmigrations, I fell into the other extreme, and turned drone. As I one day headed a party to plunder an hive, we were received so warmly by the swarm which defended it, that we were most of us left dead upon the spot.

I might tell you of many other transmigrations which I went through ; how I was a town rake, and afterwards did penance in a bay gelding for ten years ; as also how I was a tailor, a shrimp, and a tom-tit. In the last of these my shapes I was shot in the Christmas holidays by a young jackanapes, who would needs try his new gun upon me.

But I shall pass over these and several other stages of life to remind you of the young beau who made love to you about six years since. You may remember, madam, how he masked, and danced, and sung, and played a thousand tricks to gain you ; and how he was at last carried off by a cold that he got under your window one night in a serenade. I was that unfortunate young fellow, whom you were then so cruel to. Not long after my shifting that unlucky body, I found myself upon a hill in Ethiopia, where I lived in my present grotesque shape till I was caught by a servant of the English factory, and sent over into Great Britain : I need not inform you how I came into your hands. You see, madam, this is not the first time that you have had me in a chain ; I am, however, very happy in this my captivity, as you often bestow on me those kisses and caresses which I would have given the world for when I was a man. I hope this discovery of my person will not tend to my disadvantage, but that you will still continue your accustomed favours to

Your most devoted humble Servant,

PUGG.

P.S.   I would advise your little shock-dog to keep out of my way ; for as I look upon him to be the most formidable of my rivals, I may chance one time or other to give him such a snap as he won't like.[249]

The Spectator often offers his readers similar titbits, in the belief that he is contributing to their moral education when he provides their mind with subtle amusement of good quality.   Nor is this all.   Fully and permanently to restore to cultured pleasure its rightful place in life, Addison sets himself to explain and demonstrate its charm and value ; he undertakes in short—and a most interesting element in his work it is—the intellectual education of his fellow-countrymen.

We might even say that he laid the foundation of literary criticism in England.   I have already pointed out that the first tentative but significant steps in this direction were taken by Dryden.   But Dryden never passed beyond slight essays on particular points, chosen according to the mood and interest of the moment, with no defined aim, no sequence, and no attempt to consider any work as a whole.[249a]   He was writing, moreover, for the frivolous Court society, for readers almost incapable of

[249] No. 343. See also the amusing petition of *Who* and *Which* in the second letter of No. 78 and the reply of *That* in the second letter of No. 80.
[249a] [To readers of Dryden this must seem an incredible statement. Think of the *Essay of Dramatick Poesie*, of the *Preface to the Fables*, or half a dozen other critical passages ! It is true that Dryden did not describe what he was criticizing ; he was writing for a more cultivated public, and assumed that they knew what he was talking about.   There had been a good deal of good critical writing in the seventeenth century—not to mention the sixteenth —Hobbes and Rymer, for instance, coming within the period here studied. See Spingarn's edition of *Critical Essays of the Seventeenth Century*. O.U.P.   B. D.]

sustained thought and attention, and his aim was to please rather than to instruct. Graceful and ingenious as his discourses are, they neither had, nor were intended to have, any deep or extensive influence. The author's highest purpose was fulfilled if he had succeeded in providing some new material for the friendly conversations of the Sedleys, the Dorsets, the Mulgraves and their like.[250] Addison's circle had a much wider radius, and his readers were more serious-minded. His conception of a writer's role was entirely different from Dryden's. So it happened that when he came in his turn to cultivate the field where his predecessor had traced the first furrow, he brought to his task more serious intention and a wider vision. He fixed his eyes not on the Court alone, but on society as a whole, and he sought to open Everyman's eyes to literature ; better still, to open his mind, form his judgment, teach him to think and provide him with general ideas on life and art. He made it his business to conduct a course on literature and æsthetics. Not indeed speaking from pulpit or professorial chair, nor taking his readers back to distant origins, nor dogmatically propounding elaborate theories ; such procedure was ruled out by the limited size of each number of his paper and by the novelty of the subjects he handled, new at least to most of his readers.[251] He had, besides, no wish to play the pedagogue. His literary lessons, scattered through the *Spectator*, are much more modest. Like his moral lessons, they are practical and simple. His aim is not to supply accurate and detailed knowledge, but to awaken taste and the power of worthily enjoying the delicate pleasure of which he invites his readers to partake.[252] Nevertheless, by

[250] There had since appeared, of course, Thomas Rymer's letter, *The Tragedies of The last Age consider'd* (1678) and his *Short View of Tragedy . . .* (1693) (see my Bibliography), and above all the Essays of Sir William Temple : I. *Upon* Antient *and* Modern Learning : II. *Upon* the Gardens of Epicurus (in the body of the volume this essay is dated 1685) : III. *Upon* Heroick Virtue : IV. *Upon* Poetry (*Works*, I, pp. 147 ff.).

But these things were still addressed to a limited circle of the learned and fashionable world.

[251] The *Spectator's* method in these matters was so new that he was reproached with " prostituting learning to the Embraces of the vulgar " and making her " a common strumpet " (No. 379).

[252] " As the great and only end of these my speculations is to banish vice and ignorance out of the territories of Great Britain, I shall endeavour as much as possible to establish among us a taste of polite writing " (No. 58).
—In the Dedication of his first volume he speaks of his paper as a work which " Endeavours to cultivate and polish human life, by promoting virtue, knowledge, and by recommending whatsoever may be either useful or ornamental to society."

recurring several times to the same question, from one number to another, he covers the ground little by little, and soon succeeds in providing his readers with quite a respectable outfit of literary ideas. Briefly and without pedantry, he sets forth the principal rules which in his opinion should govern various types of composition,[253] warns them when he thinks their enthusiasm or admiration is wrongly directed,[254] puts them on their guard against specious work, advises them [255] what to read [256] and above all—with catholic taste and infectious sympathy which knows no national boundaries, no limitation of period—he calls their attention to the masterpieces of every country and of every age,[257] introduces these works and puts the reader into a position adequately to appreciate their beauties.[258] From end to end of his paper, he never loses sight of this side of his task. In varying forms, directly or indirectly, he perpetually returns to it, and there is scarcely any subject which does not give him opportunity to introduce a relevant parallel, or a literary fact, or a happily appropriate quotation. The product of a classical education which he had constantly refreshed and increased by reading and conversation, his memory was never at a loss. At the required moment it supplied without fail the author and the passage that he needed. I need no proof beyond the Latin and Greek mottos which he habitually prefixed to each number. These offered his readers a rich and instructive collection of

---

[253] See his remarks on Tragedy Nos. 39, 40, 42. His Essays on Milton which I deal with later formulate the rules for epic poetry.

[254] See in particular his articles against " false wit ", Nos. 58, 59, 60, 61, 62 and 63.

[255] Especially his women readers.

[256] " We know the highest pleasure our minds are capable of enjoying with composure, when we read sublime thoughts communicated to us by men of great genius and eloquence " (No. 146). See also his articles on the pleasures of imagination, Nos. 411-21.

[257] A glance at an Index to the *Spectator* is enough to show how wide and varied is the range of his literary studies. I shall mention only some numbers devoted to then—recent works—the first essays in literary criticism ever published in England : No. 253 on Pope's *Essay on Criticism* which had just appeared (1711) ; No. 290 written after the performance of Ambrose Philips's *Distrest Mother* ; No. 400 on the same author's *Pastoral Verses* ; No. 523 on the *Miscellany* of Pope and Philips (1709).

[258] " The criticisms which I have hitherto published have been made with an intention rather to discover beauties and excellences in the writers of my own time, than to publish any of their faults and imperfections." (No. 262.) " It is a very honest action to be studious to produce other men's merit ; and I make no scruple of saying I have as much of this temper as any man in the world." (No. 532.)

interesting quotations that were never commonplace or hackneyed.[259]

In his literary passages Addison naturally never forgot the theatre which he so greatly valued. To make it the " noble entertainment " of which he dreamed, he demanded many reforms and improvements. The vigorous indictments I have quoted of the licence in which comedy indulged, were far from being the only ones he drew up. From the artistic point of view he made many strictures on contemporary drama, and stated his case with remarkable accuracy and judgment. When you have just been studying Restoration drama, it is a joy to hear him protesting with his usual wit against the use of rhyme in tragedy,[260] and the ridiculous rantings worn so threadbare by the Lees and Drydens,[261] against facetious epilogues gaily terminating a tragedy,[262] and especially against the abuse of stage costumes and decorations.[263] With all these cheap and tawdry devices he contrasts the graver beauties of Greek and French drama, which he himself was to imitate in his *Cato* when he turned his own hand to tragedy.

[259] " When I have finished any of my speculations, it is my method to consider which of the ancient authors have touched upon the subject that I treat of. By this means I meet with some celebrated thought upon it, or a thought of my own expressed in better words, or some similitude for the illustration of my subject. This gives birth to the motto of a speculation, which I rather choose to take out of the poets than the prose writers, as the former generally give a finer turn to a thought than the latter, and by couching it in few words and in harmonious numbers, make it more portable to the memory. My reader is therefore sure to meet with at least one good line in every paper." (No. 221.)

[260] No. 39. [261] No. 40.

[262] Nos. 338 and 341.

[263] I should like to show by at least one example the tone in which he handles these subjects : " Aristotle has observed, that ordinary writers in tragedy endeavour to raise terror and pity in their audience, not by proper sentiments and expressions, but by the dresses and decorations of the stage. There is something of this kind very ridiculous in the English theatre. When the author has a mind to terrify us, it thunders ; when he would make us melancholy, the stage is darkened. But among all our tragic artifices, I am the most offended at those which are made use of to inspire us with magnificent ideas of the persons that speak. The ordinary method of making a hero is to clap a huge plume of feathers upon his head, which rises so very high that there is often a greater length from his chin to the top of his head than to the sole of his foot. One would believe that we thought a great man and a tall man the same thing. This very much embarrasses the actor, who is forced to hold his neck extremely stiff and steady all the while he speaks ; and notwithstanding any anxieties which he pretends for his mistress, his country or his friends, one may see by his action that his greatest care and concern is to keep the plume of feathers from falling off his head." (No. 42.)
—No. 44 on the same subject is also extremely witty.

He formulates another contrast too. However great were the services which Addison rendered to his contemporaries by initiating them into opinions which had up to that time been the privilege of a chosen few, however timely and wise were his literary teachings, he has yet other merits as a critic, and we must recognize to his honour that he helped to rediscover the literary title-deeds of his country and became one of the promoters of a kind of English Renaissance. I must explain myself. At the Restoration the works which are still the greatest achievements of the English genius, fell into neglect, indeed, it may be said into temporary oblivion. Political and religious preoccupations, French culture—which Charles II made fashionable—and frivolous taste, all combined to spread a thick mist of forgetfulness over the fairest flowers which the strength and richness of this genius had brought forth. We have seen how Shakespeare had been brushed aside or, worse, disrespectfully remodelled. The most famous of his predecessors and contemporaries had been equally ill-treated. The only new poet who deserved a place of honour at their side, Milton, author of *Paradise Lost*, had reaped little but silence and indifference. The sound core of truly English literature had been swamped by the futile babblings of the Restoration. So much so, that Saint-Evremond, who lived in England from 1661 to 1703 and moved in the most cultured circles, appears scarcely to have heard Shakespeare mentioned.[264] Sir William Temple, unquestionably one of the most distinguished Englishmen of his day, in his essay *Upon Ancient and Modern Learning* [265] omits all mention of Chaucer, Spenser, Shakespeare and Milton. Swift, in all his writings, only once alludes to Shakespeare [266] and is so ill acquainted with his works that he attributes to him one of Chaucer's.[267] Even Addison, in his versified *Account of the Greatest English Poets*,[268] also forgot to

---

[264] He mentions him once only and then quite casually. Writing to the Duchess of Mazarin : " Hear every evening the comedy of Henry VIII or of Queen Elizabeth " . . . and notes to this passage add :

" *by the famous *Shakspear* who died in 1616 ;

†by *Thomas Heywood* who flourished under *Elizabeth* and *James I.*

All the plays of this period are very long and extremely boring." (*Œuvres meslees*, 1705, II, p. 306.)—This is the first allusion to Shakespeare by any French author.

[265] *Works*, I, pp. 151 ff.   [266] Journal to Stella, Jan. 8, 1711–12.

[267] Letter to Gay dated Nov. 20, 1729 (Elwin's Edition of Pope, VII, p. 167).—In his *Life of Swift* (p. 466) Walter Scott says that Swift does not appear to have possessed a copy of Shakespeare.

[268] *Addressed to Mr. H. S.*, 1694.—We should remember that Dryden, whose magnificent tribute to Shakespeare in his Essay on Dramatick Poesie

include Shakespeare. But when he wrote the *Account* he was young, and was reflecting merely the current valuations of his day. When he came to write the *Spectator*, age and meditation had matured him. Steeped though he was in French literature and criticism [269]; dearly though he loved continually quoting Boileau, Racine, Corneille, even Bouhours and Lebossu [270]; faithfully—too faithfully—though he fashioned his own tragedy of *Cato* on the French pattern, he yet had come to understand that a people cannot safely betray its national genius by imitating a foreign literature however splendid. He saw that the spirit of England was in danger of losing its bearings and, if writers did not beware, of drifting into long stretches of sterile production like that of the Restoration period. His artistic instinct rose above his literary theories and his own poetic predilections, and revealed to him that true English poetry must be English—not foreign-born. Its wealth of glory, too long obscured, must be brought again to light and English genius referred back to its native, undervalued origins. To his readers he spoke with admiration of Shakespeare,[271] of Spenser,[272] of Bacon,[273] of Ben Jonson,[274] and especially of Milton, to whose masterpiece he devoted no less than eighteen articles.[275] Apart from Tonson's edition of *Paradise Lost*, to which I have already referred, this

---

I have spoken of above (p. 81), introduces this tribute with caution and diffidence.—Pope thought " it was mighty simple in Rowe to have written a play (*Jane Shore*) professedly in Shakespeare's style, that is professedly in the style of a bad age ". (Spence, p. 174.)

[269] His admiration for French literature was, however, neither uncritical nor unreserved. See especially No. 44, where he criticizes Corneille's *Horace*.

[270] Nos. 62, 369, 409.

[271] Nos. 22, 39, 40, 42, 44, 45, 48, 116, 141, 160, 206, 208, 210, 218, 230, 235, 279, 285, 346, 360, 370, 396, 397, 400, 419, 468, 474, 484, 485, 541. In some of these numbers (eleven of which are Addison's own) Shakespeare is mentioned several times, and the Spectator's admiration is unstinted : he calls him " the admirable Shakespeare " (No. 210), classes him amongst the " great geniuses " (No. 160) and suggests young men's being set to act scenes from his plays, as well as from Terence and Sophocles (No. 230). He contrasts Shakespeare's plays with the popular plays of the day (No. 208), and finally—this fact is specially noteworthy—vigorously condemns the current practice of " reforming " a play of Shakespeare's at the cost of " half its beauty " (No. 40). A fine passage about Shakespeare also occurs in No. 402.

[272] Nos. 62, 297, 390, 419, 510.

[273] Nos. 10, 19, 160, 411, 447, 554.

[274] Nos. 28, 510, 527.

[275] Nos. 267, 273, 279, 285, 291, 297, 303, 309, 315, 321, 327, 333, 339, 345, 351, 357, 363, 369.—These are not the only articles in which Milton is mentioned ; see also Nos. 12, 33, 62, 89, 160, 173, 304, 425, 472, etc.

was the first reparation England made to the great poet who had died forgotten.[276] Addison went further ; he recalled to mind the old popular ballads,[277] thus anticipating the movement by which Percy later so profoundly and so happily requickened English poetry.[278]

Thus, approaching at once from every point of the compass, Addison entered into, and took possession of, the minds of his fellow-countrymen. By addressing himself to their reason, their conscience and their good taste in turn ; by interesting and instructing them ; by reasoning with them and teaching them to reason ; by awakening or re-awakening them to lofty and sensitive feeling, he gradually won their affection and their confidence. The net of his gracious and irrefutable argument was so well and closely woven, that none of those on whom his heart was set was able to slip through its meshes. Before his time the Cavaliers had one answer ready made for anyone who cast their dissolute manners in their teeth : " He's a fanatic." The Puritans similarly dismissed everyone who challenged their gloomy code with : " He's an infidel ", and with averted face passed by on the other side. In the case of Addison, neither party could file its favourite plea. There was no denying it— here was a man who was both a gentleman and a Christian : as true a gentleman as the most polished of Charles II's courtiers, as sincere a Christian as the most devout Presbyterian apostle.

[276] The *Tatler* had already begun to redirect attention to the authors of the great century.   He speaks of Bacon (Nos. 108, 247), of Spenser (No. 194), of Ben Jonson (No. 267), of Milton (Nos. 6, 40, 79, 98, 114, 137, 149, 237, etc.), of Shakespeare (Nos. 8, 41, 47, 53, 68, 90, 106, 111, 117, 167, 251, 271, etc.). When he wished, however, to quote passages from *Macbeth* in Nos. 68 and 167, he used Davenant's pitiably " modified " version.

[277] Nos. 70 and 74 : Chevy Chase ; No. 85 : The Babes in the Wood. He is of the same opinion as Alceste :

> " Et je prise bien moins tout ce que l'on admire,
> Qu'une vieille chanson que je m'en vais vous dire "

> (Good what the world admires. To me more dear
> The fine old song that I shall let you hear.)

[278] Percy's *Reliques of Ancient English Poetry* was published in 1765. [The Ballads were never wholly neglected. When John Prideaux was made Bishop of Oxford in 1641, a friend wrote to him : " Send me what ballads you have, and I will let *you* see what I have." Various collections were made, e.g. at Shirburn Castle *c.* 1610. Selden (1584–1654) made a collection, as did Anthony à Wood (1632–95), Pepys (1633–1703), not to mention Harley. The manuscript on which Percy founded his edition appears to have dated from about 1650. What Addison did was to make respected by a snobbish middle class, work which might otherwise have remained the delight of the few. B. D.]

So much was this the case, that the reader who was tempted to vote him too pious, was won over by his easy and genial humour, and another who was inclined to think him too worldly, could not resist the genuine moral and religious temper which breathes from every page of his paper. The one forgave his piety because of his wit, the other forgave his wit because of his piety, neither perceiving that he himself was being gradually converted : in the one case to virtue, in the other case to innocent enjoyment. Addison's readers were like an encircled army, whose retreat is cut off, whose resistance is vain ; no course was open to them save surrender.

And surrender they did—with the utmost good will. The moral success of the *Spectator* equalled, or exceeded, its material success. Not only was it read, as no other periodical had ever been read before, but it was not read in vain. The good seed, widely scattered in the soil prepared by Collier, by Defoe and by Steele, was quick to germinate and strike root. Vice, though already shaken and weakened, did not of course immediately disappear for ever and leave a clear field for a Golden Age of purity and innocence. But Vice was thrust aside, and could no longer count on the general admiration of her charms ; immorality was no longer considered fashionable or in good taste. A cheap reputation for wit could no longer be acquired by sneers at everything worthy of respect ; threadbare jests at the expense of religion were no longer considered funny ; well-worn epigrams about marriage and wedded misadventures no longer raised a laugh (the Englishman of to-day doesn't even get the point). New subject-matter for jesting had to be found. True, there were sceptics and free-thinkers still ; but scepticism had gone out of fashion, and serious discussion had taken the place of the sneer that had served as a cheap substitute for thought.[279] True also, there were libertines still, but they no longer openly gloried in their debauchery, and they no longer commanded admiration. In short, no one was compelled to choose between a parade of

---

[279] Toland, *Christianity not Mysterious* (1696), *Nazarenus* (1718), *Pantheisticon* (1720), etc. etc. ; Collins, *Priestcraft in Perfection* (1710), *A Discourse of Free-Thinking* (1713), etc. Tindal, *Christianity as old as the Creation* (1730), etc. ; Bolingbroke, *Letters on the Study and Use of History* (1752) ; etc. etc. See my Bibliography.—The doctrines of scepticism, moreover, proved unable to exert a lasting influence. In 1790 Burke was able to ask : " Who, born within the last 40 years, has read one word of Collins, and Toland, and Tindal . . . and that whole race who called themselves Freethinkers ? " (*Reflections on the French Revolution.*) [But Mandeville ? B.D.]

vice and irreligion or the stigma of being an unmannerly rustic. Society had changed its tone. It was thought neither ridiculous nor strange to hear men talk seriously of serious things. Virtue could show herself openly without a blush, and raise her head —never to lower it again. As Macaulay says, in his Essay on Addison :

" So effectively did he retort on vice the mockery which had recently been directed against virtue, that, since his time, the open violation of decency has always been considered among us as the sure mark of a fool."

It may seem a matter of surprise that I should attribute so much influence to a modest leaflet which London booksellers sold for a penny, and we must not fail to remember that others had prepared Addison's path and that influences of many kinds had inclined men's minds to a moral rebirth.[280] But no one who reads contemporary tributes can for an instant doubt that the *Spectator* and its predecessor the *Tatler* played a major part in this happy reformation, nor that Addison's peculiar merit was, that he brought high principles home to all and made them common currency, at once cultivating men's minds and mending their manners.

As early as 1711, just when the *Spectator* had succeeded the *Tatler*, a writer—believed to be the poet Gay—bore this testimony :

His disappearing (i.e. the Tatler's) seem'd to be bewailed as some general Calamity,[281] everyone wanted so agreeable an Amusement, and the Coffee-houses began to be sensible, that the Esquires Lucubra-

---

[280] There is no doubt that there was in England at this moment an upsurging of virtue, which manifested itself in a general hunger for religious propaganda. Within a few years of each other the learned botanist Ray brought out *The Wisdom of God, manifested in the Works of Creation* (1691), the philosopher, Locke, his *Reasonableness of Christianity, As delivered in the Scriptures* (1695) ; the cleric, Clark, *A Discourse concerning the Unchangeable Obligations of Natural Religion, and the Truth and Certainty of the Christian Revelation* (1706) ; and the journalist, Addison, *The Evidence of the Christian Religion*, a work which appeared after his death. See my Bibliography. It is appropriate to remember also the influence which sermons were to exert, and the writings of clergymen like Tillotson, Stillingfleet, Sherlock and South and of Non-conformists like Matthew Henry whose Bible Commentaries are still popular.

[281] This is corroborated by the following verses :

" When first the *Tatler* to a *Mute* was turn'd,
  Great Britain for her *Censor's* Silence mourn'd ;
  Robb'd of his sprightly Beams, she wept the Night,
  'Till the SPECTATOR rose, and blaz'd as Bright.

tions alone, had brought them more Customers, than all their other News Papers put together.

It must indeed be confess'd that never Man threw up his Pen under Stronger Temptations to have employed it longer ; His Reputation was at a greater height than, I believe, ever any living Author's was before him . . . Everyone read him with Pleasure and Good-Will ; and the *Tories*, in respect to his other Good Qualities, had almost forgiven his unaccountable Imprudence in declaring against them. Lastly it was highly improbable, that if he threw off a Character, the Ideas of which were so strongly impress'd on everyone's mind, however finely he might write in any new form, that he should meet with the same reception.

To give you my own thoughts of this Gentleman's Writings, I shall, in the first place, observe, that there is this noble difference between him and all the rest of our Polite and Gallant Authors : the latter have endeavoured to please the Age by falling in with them, and incouraging them in their fashionable Vices, and false notions of things. It would have been a jest, sometime since, for a Man to have asserted, that anything Witty could be said in praise of the Marry'd State ; or that Devotion and Virtue were in any way necessary to the Character of a fine Gentleman. *Bickerstaff* ventur'd to tell the Town, that they were a parcel of Fops, Fools and Vain Cocquets ; but in such a manner, as even pleased them, and made them more than half inclin'd to believe that he spoke Truth.

Instead of complying with the false Sentiments, or Vicious tasts of the Age, either in Morality, Criticism, or Good Breeding, he has boldly assur'd them, that they were altogether in the wrong, and commanded them, with an Authority, which perfectly well became him, to surrender themselves to his Arguments for Vertue and Good Sense.

'Tis incredible to conceive the effect his Writings have had on the Town ; How many Thousand follies they have either quite banish'd, or given a very great check to ; how much Countenance they have added to Vertue and Religion ; how many People they have render'd happy, by shewing them it was their own fault if they were not so ; and lastly, how intirely they have convinc'd our Fops and Young Fellows of the value and advantages of Learning.

He has indeed rescued it out of the hands of Pedants and Fools ; and discover'd the true method of making it amiable and lovely to all

---

So the first Man, the SUN's first Setting view'd,
And sigh'd, till circling Day his Joys renew'd ;
Yet doubtful how that second SUN to name,
Whether a bright *Successor* or the *Same.*

So we—but Now from this Suspence are freed
Since all must own, who Both with Judgment read
'Tis the Same SUN, and does *Himself* succeed."

(An Epigram on the *Spectator*, in the *Tunbridge-Miscellany*, 1712. See my Bibliography, s.v. Tunbridge.)

mankind : In the dress he gives it, 'tis a most welcome guest at Tea-Tables and Assemblies and is relish'd and caressed by the Merchants on the Change ; . . .[282]

Lastly, His Writings have set all our Wits and Men of Letters upon a new way of Thinking, of which they had little or no Notion before ; and tho' we cannot yet say that any of them have come up to the Beauties of the Original, I think we may venture to affirm, that every one of them Writes and Thinks much more justly than they did some time since . . .[283]

You may remember I told you before that one Cause assign'd for the laying down the *Tatler* was want of Matter ; and indeed this was the prevailing Opinion in Town, when we were surpris'd all at once by a Paper called the *Spectator*, which was promised to be continued every day, and was writ in so excellent a Stile, with so nice a Judgment, and such a noble profusion of Wit and Humour, that it was not difficult to determine it could come from no other hands but those which had penn'd the *Lucubrations* . . .

Mean while, the *Spectator* . . . is in every one's Hand, and a constant Topic for our Morning Conversation at Tea-Tables and Coffee-Houses. We had at first, indeed, no manner of Notion how a *Diurnal Paper* could be continu'd in the Spirit and Stile of our present Spectators ; but to our no small Surprise, we find them still rising upon us, and can only wonder from whence so Prodigious a Run of Wit and Learning can proceed ; since some of our best Judges seem to think that they have hitherto, in general, out-shone even the

---

[282] " How long and happily did *Old Isaac* triumph in the universal Love and Favour of his Readers ? The Grave, the Chearful, the Wise, the Witty, Old, Young, Rich, and Poor, all Sorts, though never so opposite in Character, whether Beaux or Bishops, Rakes or Men of Business, Coquets or Statesmen, Whigs or Tories, All were equally his Friends, and thought their Tea in a Morning had not its Taste without him." (Dedication to Steele of Cibber's *Ximena*.)

[283] " While the World was under the daily Correction and Authority of your *Lucubrations* ; their Influence on the Publick was not more visible in any one Instance than the sudden Improvement (I might say Reformation) of the Stage that immediately follow'd them : From whence it is now apparent, that many Papers (which the Grave and Severe then thought were thrown away upon that Subject) were, in your speaking to the *Theatre*, still advancing the same Work, . . . ; to the end that whenever you thought fit to be silent, the Stage, as you had amended it, might by a kind of substituted Power, continue to Posterity your peculiar manner of making the Improvement of their Minds their public Diversion."

" Nothing but a Genius so universally rever'd could, with such Candour and Penetration, have pointed out its Faults and Misconduct, and so effectually have redeem'd its Uses and Excellence from Prejudice and Dis-favour. How often have we known the most excellent Audiences drawn together at a Day's Warning, by the Influence or Warrant of a single *Tatler*, in a Season when our best Endeavours without it could not defray the Charge of the Performance ? This powerful and innocent Artifice soon recover'd us into Fashion, and spirited us up, to think such new Favour of our Auditors worthy of our utmost Industry, and 'tis to that Industry, so instructed, the Stage now owes its Reputation and Prosperity " (ibid.).

Esquires first *Tatlers*. Most People Fancy, from their frequency, that they must be compos'd by a Society ; I, with all, Assign the first Places to Mr. *Steele* and *His Friend* . . .

Mean time, all our unbyassed well-wishers to Learning are in hopes, that the known Temper and Prudence of one of these Gentlemen, will hinder the other from ever lashing out into Party, and rend'ring that Wit, which is at present a Common Good, Odious and Ungrateful to the better part of the Nation." [284]

A continuation of the *Tatler* that appeared in January 1711 speaks of Steele as " . . . A Gentleman who has so eminently obliged the Publick, and whose Lucubrations have done more Good than all the Moral Discourses that were ever written in our tongue ".[285] An anonymous poet writing in 1712 paid this tribute :

> Improving youth, and hoary age,
> Are better'd by thy matchless page ;
> And, what no mortal could devise,
> Women, by reading thee grow wise . . .
> . . . wedlock by thy art is got
> To be a soft and easy knot . . .
> The ladies, pleas'd with thee to dwell,
> Aspire to write correct, and spell : . . .
>   Maintain, great Sage, thy deathless name,
> Thou can'st no wider stretch thy fame,
> Till, gliding from her native skies,
> Virtue once more delighted flies,
> By each adoring Patriot own'd,
> And boasts herself by thee enthron'd.[286]

While the *Spectator* was still appearing, Tickell warmly congratulated its author on having reformed the fops of both sexes, and restored English society to health :

> . . . Nor harsh thy Precepts, but infus'd by Stealth,
> Please while they cure, and cheat us into Health.
> Thy Works in *Chloe's* Toilet gain a part ;
> And with his Tailor share the Fopling's heart : . . .
> His Miss the frolick Viscount dreads to toast,
> Or his third Cure the shallow Templar boast ;
> And the rash Fool, who scorn'd the beaten Road,
> Dares quake at Thunder, and confess his God . . .[287]

---

[284] *The Present State of Wit* by J. G. (Gay ?). [Now usually assigned to Gay. B. D.]

[285] " The Tatler, with the Character of Mr. Steele, *alias Isaac Bickerstaff*, Esq., No. 272. From *Tuesday, January* 2 to *Thursday, January* 4, 1711." This number is bound in at the close of the *Tatler* in the British Museum copy.

[286] *Bibliotheca : a Poem occasioned by the Sight of a Modern Library*, quoted by Drake, *Essays . . . Illustrative*, etc., III, pp. 394 ff.
[Drake ascribes it to Newcomb : Nichols had given it to Dr. King. B. D.]

[287] *Spectator*, No. 532 : " To the supposed Author of the Spectator." In the Preface to his edition of Addison Tickell says : " The world became

While greatly admiring the *Tatler* and the *Spectator*, Blackmore was at first inclined to question their influence in curing fools of their folly,[288] but was ultimately forced to recognize that their moral value was as evident as their beauty, and that they had taught men to despise irreligious and indecent writing.[289]

Somerville wrote to Addison :

> When panting Virtue her last efforts made,
> You brought your Clio to the virgin's aid :
> Presumptuous Folly blush'd, and Vice withdrew,
> To vengeance yielding her abandon'd crew . . .
> Hard was the task, and worthy your great mind,
> To please at once, and to reform mankind :
> Yet, when you write, Truth charms with such address,
> Pleads Virtue's cause with such becoming grace,
> His own fond heart the guilty wretch betrays,
> He yields delighted, and convinc'd, obeys.[290]

---

insensibly reconciled to wisdom and goodness, when they saw them recommended by him (Addison) with at least as much spirit and elegance, as they had been ridiculed for half a century."

[288] "Let the famous Author of the *Tatlers* and *Spectators* declare his Experience, who, if Wit could have made Men wiser, must certainly have succeeded ; that Gentleman says, in one of his Discourses, *I have many Readers but few Converts* ; I believe he might have said none : For it is my opinion, that all his fine Raillery and Satire, though admirable in their kind, never reclaim'd one vicious Man, or made one Fool depart from his Folly." (*Essays*, vol. I, 1716, Preface.)—". . . The Productions of this Nature, which have of late appeared in this Nation, whether we regard the just and generous sentiments, the fertile Invention, the Variety of Subjects, the surprizing Turns of Wit and facetious Imagination, the genteel Satire, the Purity and Propriety of the Words, and the Beauty and Dignity of the Diction, have surpass'd all the Productions of this Kind, that have been publish'd in any Age or Country. The Reader is no doubt before-hand with me, and concludes, that I mean the *Tatler* and *Spectator*, which for the greatest Part, have all the Perfection of Writing, and all the Advantages of Wit and Humour, that are requir'd to Entertain and instruct the People : And it must chiefly be owing to the great Depravity of Manners of these loose and degenerate Times, that such worthy Performances have produc'd no better Effects." (*Essays*, 1716, I, p. 203.)—Blackmore had been somewhat cruelly handled in the third number of the *Tatler*. This may perhaps account for his scepticism.

[289] " It was with great Pleasure and Satisfaction that Men, who wish'd well to their Country and Religion, saw the People delighted with Papers which lately came Abroad as daily Entertainments ; in which rich Genius and polite Talents were employ'd in their proper Province, that is, to recommend Virtue and regular Life, and discourage and discountenance the Follies, Faults and Vices of the Age ; . . . Nor was it without good Effect, for the People in some measure recover'd their true Relish, and discern'd the Benefit and moral Advantages as well as the Beauties of these daily Pieces, and began to have profane and immodest Writings in Contempt." (*Essays*, II, 1717, p. 268.)

[290] A. Chalmers, *The Works of the English Poets*, XI, p. 190.—Addison's own articles in the *Spectator* are signed by one of the letters of the name Clio.

Another witness, a clergyman, destined later to become a bishop, said : " To him we owe, that swearing is unfashionable, and that a regard to religion is become a part of good breeding . . . He had an art to make people hate their follies, without hating themselves for having them ; he shewed gentlemen a way of becoming virtuous with a good grace." [291]

Yet another testified :

None ever attempted with more Success to form the Mind to Virtue, or polish the Manners of common Life ; none ever touched the Passions in that pleasing, prevailing Method, or so well inculcated the most useful and instructive Lessons. I say, none did ever thus happily perform so important a Work as these illustrious Colleagues, who, by adapting themselves to the Pleasures, promoted the best Virtues of human Nature ; insinuated themselves by all the Arts of fine Persuasion ; employ'd the most delicate Wit and Humour in the Cause of Truth and good Sense ; nor gave Offence to the most rigid *Devotees* or the loosest *Debauchees*, but soon grew popular, tho' advocates of Virtue . . . All the *Pulpit Discourses* of a Year scarce procur'd half the Good as flow'd from the SPECTATOR of a Day. They who were tir'd and lulled to Sleep by a long and labour'd Harrangue, or terrify'd at the Appearance of large and weighty Volumes, could chearfully attend to a single Half-sheet, where they found the Images of Virtue so lively and amiable, where Vice was so agreeably ridicul'd that it grew painful to no Man to part with his beloved Follies ; nor was he easy till he had practis'd those Qualities which charm'd so much in Speculation. Thus good Nature and good Sense became habitual to their Readers. Every morning they were instructed in some new Principle of Duty, which was endear'd to them by the Beauties of Description ; and thereby impress'd on their Minds in the most indelible Characters. [292]

[291] " Anticipation of the Posthumous Character of Sir Richard Steele." By the Rev. Dr. Thomas Rundle. Written about 1720. Quoted in Nichols' Edition of Steele's *Correspondence*, II, pp. 685 ff. Dr. Rundle later became Bishop of Derry.

[292] " *An Essay, sacred to the Memory of Sir Richard Steele,* in The British Journal, or the Censor. *By* Roger Manley, *of* Lincoln's Inn, Esq., No. 89. Saturday, September 13, 1729." (British Museum.)

There are other curious testimonies to the *Spectator's* influence. It is said that a few lines of No. 173 put a stop to a " grinning match " which was to have taken place in a remote county (*Addisoniana*, Hurd's Addison, VI, p. 690). Again, it was considered a matter of pride to have collaborated, even once, in the paper (Boswell, VI, p. 151). But nothing seems to me to redound more to the *Spectator's* honour than the following letter in No. 208 :

" Mr. Spectator,—I have been out of town, so did not meet with your paper dated September the 28th, wherein you to my heart's desire expose that cursed vice of ensnaring poor young girls, and drawing them from their friends. I assure you without flattery it has saved a prentice of mine from ruin, and in token of gratitude, as well as for the benefit of my family, I have put it in a frame and glass, and hang it behind my counter. I shall take care

The salutary effect thus produced, was so obvious that Addison, modest and reserved though he was, when referring in later years to his work, did not hesitate to congratulate himself on the good he had accomplished.[293]

If, therefore, others share with Addison the credit of having laboured for the renewal of England, the greatest of the glory is his alone ; his is the honour of having extended the scope, secured and strengthened the foundations, of this renewal, by robbing vice of its deceptive veneer of elegance ; of having— if the phrase be allowed—brought virtue into fashion. It has been wittily said that he won the laughers over to virtue's side. But this happy phrase does not cover everything. Not only did he bring laughter to the reinforcement of virtue, he brought virtue over to the side of moderation and good sense.[294] While sobering the Cavalier, he humanized the Puritan.[295] He was so successful that ere long his fellow-countrymen marvelled that fashionable society could ever have been so corrupt, and that religious folk could ever have seemed so surly and morose. Since his day, England has had relapses into libertinism and puritanism ;

---

to make my young ones read it every morning, to fortify them against such pernicious rascals. I know not whether what you write was matter of fact, or your own invention, but this I will take my oath on, the first part is so exactly like what happened to my prentice, that had I read your paper then, I should have taken your method to have secured a villain. Go on and prosper."

[293] " There are very good Effects which visibly arose from the above-mentioned Performances [the *Tatlers* and *Spectators*] and others of the like Nature ; as, in the first Place, they diverted Raillery from improper Objects, and gave a new Turn to Ridicule, which for many Years had been exerted on Persons and things of a secret and serious Nature." (*The Free-Holder*, No. 45, May 25, 1716.) See also the remainder of this article. Addison is replying to Blackmore's cynicism quoted just above in note No. 288. The *Spectator's* reputation was not confined to England.—Translations into other languages followed immediately. See L. Mézières (Preface to the *Encyclopédie morale*).

[294] " The last Advantage I shall mention from compositions of this Nature, . . . is, that they show Wisdom and Virtue are far from being inconsistent with Politeness and good Humour. They make Morality appear amiable to People of gay Dispositions, and refute the common Objection against Religion, which represents it as only fit for gloomy and melancholy Tempers. It was the Motto of a Bishop very eminent for his Piety and good Works, in King *Charles* the Second's reign, *Inservi Deo et Laetare, Serve God and be cheerful.*" (The *Free-Holder*, No. 45, May 25, 1716.)

[295]   " Lash'd in thy Satyr, the penurious Cit
          Laughs at himself and finds no Harm in Wit."
                    (Tickell, the *Spectator*, No. 532 : " To the sup-
                    posed Author of the *Spectator* ".)

but since his day two extremes have become alike impossible : the moral tyranny of Cromwell's partisans, and the cynical immorality of Charles II's court.

VIII

Increase in the number and quality of readers.—The influence of politics.— The influence of Addison and his imitators.—An English reading-public is well established

Addison's influence was real and salutary : in yet another way he increased the number and quality of readers.

The emancipation of the Press had already greatly stimulated the habit of reading, and had taught people to feel the need of it. The political circumstances of the day contributed not a little to the same result. Round William III, round Queen Anne, and round George I, a great battle was raging between Whigs and Tories. The battle was feverish and fiery, the issue uncertain. During this period of continuous emotional tension, when England daily wondered anew whether the Revolution of 1688 was final, or whether it was to be erased from English history by a return to the Stuart succession, men's minds were in an extraordinary state of commotion and hyper-excitement. No Englishman was indifferent. No deed could be done, no question be raised, without provoking passionate pro-and-con argument. So violent was discussion that, despite their recent expansion, the newspapers alone could not cope with it. Political pamphlets fought side by side with the papers, and so torrential was the flow of them, that Swift said a man would have to spend the entire day in this kind of reading if he were to keep pace with them.[296]

From time to time Ministers and Parliament, galled and irritated by the unceasing din in their ears, attempted to silence these publications. Bolingbroke sent twelve printers or journalists to prison in one day.[297] William Hart, printer of the

[296] " Meantime the pamphlets and half-sheets grow so upon our hands, it will very well employ a man every day from morning till night to read them, and so out of despair I never read any at all." (Letter from London, dated Sept. 26, 1710 (Scott's Edition of his *Works*, XV, p. 380.) See also Lord Mahon, *History of England*, I, pp. 119, 120 ; Swift, *Journal to Stella*, passim ; Lecky, I, p. 61 ; and Doran, *London in the Jacobite Times*, especially vol. I, chaps. III and V.)

[297] Swift, *Journal to Stella*, Oct. 24, 1711 : and Stanhope, *History of . . . the Reign of Queen Anne*, II, p. 237.

paper called *The Flying Post*, was sentenced by the Court of Queen's Bench to stand twice in the pillory and be imprisoned for two years, besides being fined £50.[298] Not satisfied with individual repressions of this kind, the Tory Government imposed, as we have seen, a heavy general tax on periodicals and pamphlets. For its part, the House of Commons expelled Steele on account of a pamphlet called *The Crisis* and two numbers of his paper *The Englishman*. The House of Lords offered a reward of £300 for anyone who would betray the author of an anonymous pamphlet—actually Swift's—*The Public Spirit of the Whigs*, and not being able to track down the offender himself, they prosecuted the printer.[299] Defoe's book, *The Shortest Way with the Dissenters*, was publicly burnt by order of the House of Commons ; the author was sentenced to a heavy fine and condemned to stand thrice in the pillory and to be imprisoned during the Queen's pleasure. Parliament also ordered Tutchin, of the *Observator*, to be flogged by the hangman. Fleetwood, Bishop of St. Asaph, wrote a Preface expressing in calm and dignified language his respect for the memory of William III, his sermons were consequently burnt. A clergyman named Steevens was fined, and but narrowly escaped the pillory, for having written over-sympathetically of his clerical brethren, the Non-Jurors, who refused to swear allegiance to the Government of the Revolution. Wellwood, editor of *Mercurius Rusticus*, Mist, editor of *Mist's Journal*,[299a] and Dyer, editor of the *Newsletter* that bore his name, were all compelled to attend a session of the House of Commons and do penance on their knees.[300]

All this severity was vain.[301] Papers and pamphlets swarmed

---

[298] Walter Scott's Edition of Swift, II, p. 136, note.

[299] Lord Mahon, *History of England*, I, pp. 67 ff.

[299a] [There may be a certain confusion here in the mind of the forgetful reader : it may be as well to give a few dates. *The Shortest Way with the Dissenters*, 1702. Tutchin's *Observator*, 1702. Leslie's *Observator*, 1702. Bolingbroke's coup, 1711. *The Public Spirit of the Whigs*, 1714. *The Crisis*, 1714. *Mist's Journal*, 1725–8 (it then became *Fog's Journal*). B. D.]

[300] Townsend, *History of the House of Commons*, chap. VII.

[301] " These devils of Grub Street rogues, that write *The Flying Post and Medley* in one paper, will not be quiet. They are always mauling Lord Treasurer, Lord Bolingbroke and me. We have the dog under prosecution, but Bolingbroke is not active enough ; but I hope to swinge him. He is a Scotch rogue, one Ridpath. They get out upon bail and write on. We take them again, and get fresh bail ; so it goes round." (Swift, *Journal to Stella*, Oct. 28, 1712.)

The Stamp Act proved no more efficacious than prosecutions and sentences. Here also, Tory hopes were foiled : Whig papers gained in influence as before, and the pamphlets in particular were bought up with unprecedented avidity.

Within four years Defoe's *True-born Englishman* [1701] went through nine editions on good paper, and twelve cheap pirated editions of which 80,000 copies were sold in the London streets. The famous sermon of Dr. Sacheverell which, at the close of her reign, caused the downfall of Queen Anne's Whig Ministry, and the temporary triumph of the Tories, sold 40,000 copies in a few days.[302] The trial of the too-famous preacher provoked a Whig pamphlet, *A Letter to Sir J(acob) B(anks)*, by one Benson, which enjoyed a sale of 60,000 copies in London alone, and in addition appeared in one Edinburgh and in two Dublin editions.[303] An anti-Sacheverell pamphlet of William Bisset's, *The Modern Fanatick*, ran to at least twelve editions.[304] A small twopenny pamphlet by Swift about Prior's secret diplomatic trip to Paris, sold 2,000 copies in a fortnight, " though the Town is empty ".[305] A more important work of the Dean's, *The Conduct of the Allies*, sold 2,000 copies in two days, and by the end of two months, sales had reached the 11,000 mark, not to mention three Irish editions.[306] One political poem of Tickell's quickly ran into six editions, another into five.[307] The first sermon Sacheverell preached after the three years' compulsory silence that followed his impeachment, sold over 40,000 copies.[308]

These returns are significant. Never before had so many purchasers so faithfully responded to the writer's appeal.

Still, if none but political writings had been in question, we should have been no further on than in James II's day ; we should merely have had to record a marked increase in the

---

what they lost in numbers, and kept the field in triumph. Swift later confessed that the effect of the tax had been " to open the mouths of our enemies and shut our own ". (*History of the Four Last Years of Queen Anne*, *Works*, IV, p. 301.) The net result of the tax was to deal an effective blow at the feeble and detestable publications of Grub Street ; it cleansed the Press.

[302] Burnet, *History of my Own Times*, V, p. 422.

[303] Wilson, III, p. 129. See my Bibliography.

[304] See my Bibliography, s.v. Bisset.

[305] *A New Journey to Paris* ; *Works*, IV, p. 59.—See Swift's *Journal to Stella*, Sept. 11 and 24, 1711.

[306] See my Bibliography and *Journal to Stella*, Nov. 30, Dec. 2 and 5, 1711 ; Jan. 28 and Feb. 8, 1711–12.

[307] *A Poem . . . on the Prospect of Peace* ; *Epistle . . . to a Gentleman at Avignon*. See Johnson, *Lives of the English Poets*, Tickell.

[308] *Journal to Stella*, April 2, 1713.—N. Drake, *Essays . . . Illustrative of the Tatler*, etc., I, p. 91, note.

number of readers. To Addison we owe it that there was at the same time a rise in their quality.

This was primarily his personal achievement. We have seen the zeal with which he devoted himself to the intellectual education of his fellow-countrymen, and the eagerness with which they flocked to his banner. Reading his paper consecutively, it is easy to observe that, as he proceeds, he comes to count more and more on the intelligence of his public, and increases the scope and seriousness of his writing.[309]

It was secondarily the work of Addison's imitators. He had so whetted the public's appetite that demand immediately called forth a swarm of what were known in England as " Essay-papers ", modelled on Addison's happily-inspired articles. For the most part these papers eschewed politics, and supplied short articles of varying tone, on moral and literary subjects, addressed to different classes of society. Apart from many papers which followed the *Tatler* and *Spectator* and simply annexed the names which Steele and Addison had made so popular, there appeared *The Growler, The Whisperer, The Tell-Tale,*[310] *The Female Tatler,*

[309] " I have endeavoured to set my readers right in several points relating to operas and tragedies ; and shall from time to time impart my notions of comedy, as I think they may tend to its refinement and perfection. I find by my bookseller that these papers of criticism, with that upon humour, have met with a more kind reception than indeed I could have hoped for from such subjects ; for which reason I shall enter upon my present undertaking with greater cheerfulness." (*Spectator*, No. 58.)

Addison's eighteen articles on Milton began with No. 267 and were continued every Saturday. His eleven numbers on the Pleasures of the Imagination ran from No. 411 to 421 without a break.

[310] " *The Expiration of Bickerstaff's Lucubrations* was attended with much the same Consequences as the Death of *Melibœus's* Ox in Virgil ; as the latter engendred Swarms of Bees, the former immediately produc'd Swarms of little Satirical Scribblers."

One of these authors called himself The Growler ; " and assur'd us, that to make amends for Mr. *Steel's* Silence, he was resolv'd to *Growl* at us Weekly, as long as we should think fit to give him any Encouragement. Another Gentleman, with more modesty, call'd his paper *The Whisperer* ; and a Third, to Please the Ladies, Christen'd his *The Tell-Tale*. At the same time came out several Tatlers, each of which, with equal Truth and Wit, assur'd us, That he was the Genuine Isaac Bickerstaff . . . some of our Wits were for forming themselves into a Club, headed by one Mr. *Harrison*, and trying how they could shoot in this Bow of *Ulysses* " (*The Present State of Wit*).— Harrison's *Tatler* ran to 52 numbers. (Drake, *Essays . . . Illustrative of the Tatler*, etc.) Swift frequently alludes to Harrison and his *Tatler* in his *Journal to Stella*, especially on Jan. 11 and 13, 1710–11. On the latter date he writes : " You must understand that upon Steele's leaving off, there were two or three scrub *Tatlers* came out, and one of them holds on still, and today it advertized against Harrison's ; and so there must be disputes which are genuine like the straps for razors."—In Walter Scott's Edition of Swift, vol. IX, there are

The Rambler, The Lay Monk, The Historian, The Censor, The Hermit, The Silent Monitor, The Inquisitor, The Pilgrim, The Instructor, The Wanderer, The Freethinker, The Observator, etc.[311] Dr. Drake has counted 106 of these essay-papers between Steele's *Tatler* and the publication of Dr. Johnson's *Rambler* in 1750 and yet his list is probably incomplete.[312] There speedily sprang up, in fact, a whole literature *sui generis*, so prolific and so vigorous, that it has left its characteristic imprint on this period of English letters, which may justly be called The Age of Essayists.

The pattern set by Steele and Addison was so appropriate and so impressively successful, that none of their successors dreamt of adopting any other form than that of their invention. Not only did they steal their very titles, as we have seen, but like them they introduced to their readers characters who were —or would fain have been—near relatives of Isaac Bickerstaff and of the silent gentleman of the *Spectator*. *The Whisperer* was edited by Miss Jenny Bickerstaff,[313] a half-sister of Isaac ; *The Female Tatler* by " Mrs. Crackenthorpe " [314] ; *The Lay Monk*, by a group of the same type as the Spectator Club [315] ; *The Observator*, by " Humphrey Medlecott " [316] ; others, by John Partridge, Walter Wagstaff, Sir Heister Ryley,[317] " Jeremy Quick ", and " Sir John Falstaff ".[318]

I should be reluctant to maintain that all these newcomers

---

some issues of Harrison's *Tatler* which Swift must have retouched.—There was at least one " scrub " *Spectator* (Drake, *Essays . . . Illustrative of the Tatler*, etc., I, p. 348, and *Essays . . . Illustrative of the Rambler*, etc., I, p. 29).

[311] *The Female Tatler*, 1709 ; *The Rambler*, 1712 ; *The Lay Monk*, 1713, edited by Blackmore and Hughes ; *The Historian*, 1713 ; *The Censor*, 1715, edited by Theobald ; *The Hermit*, 1715 ; *The Silent Monitor*, 1715 ; *The Inquisitor*, 1715 ; *The Pilgrim*, 1715 ; *The Instructor*, 1715 ; *The Wanderer*, 1717 ; *The Freethinker*, 1718, edited by Ambrose Philips. (Drake, *Essays . . . Illustrative of the Rambler*, etc., I, pp. 4 ff. ; II, pp. 490 ff.) ; *The Observator*, 1718 (Andrews, I, p. 114).

[312] This number (106 papers) includes those published by Addison and Steele after the *Tatler* : a few deductions should perhaps be made of papers too exclusively political. Dr. Drake continues his list to 1809 and reckons 221 papers which still betray the influence of the *Tatler* and *Spectator*. The list might well be extended beyond 1809.

[313] Drake, *Essays . . . Illustrative of the Rambler*, etc., II, pp. 6 and 7.

[314] Andrews, I, p. 114.

[315] Johnson, *Lives of the English Poets*, Blackmore.

[316] Andrews, I, p. 114.

[317] *Tit for Tat*, 1709-10 ; *Annotations on the Tatler*, 1710 ; *The Visions of Sir Heister Ryley*, 1710 ;—See Drake, *Essays . . . Illustrative of the Rambler*, etc., I, pp. 4-10.

[318] *The Medley, or Daily Tatler*, 1715 ; *The Anti-Theatre*, 1720.—See Andrews, I, p. 114.

were creditable disciples of their masters, or that Bickerstaff, Sir Roger de Coverley and Will Honeycomb would have recognized as of the family, and welcomed with open arms, all the would-be relatives who mustered on every side.[319] The likeness was assuredly remote and superficial.

These over-faithful copies,[320] made for the most part by men lacking both talent and originality, were little more than watered-down imitations of their models. Even the best of them, and those a very few, succeeded in preserving only a faint suggestion of their perfume and savour.[321]

Such as they were, however, they found readers, and per-formed the useful office of maintaining and extending the taste for intellectual reading, especially amongst the middle-classes, who had hitherto taken little heed of literature. Nor did Addison and Steele quit the field. After the *Spectator* had closed down, they still continued their work in various papers, of which at least one, the *Guardian*, can still claim a place of honour along-side their masterpiece.[322]

[319] Without incurring the accusation that he lacked modesty, Addison was justified in saying :

" I cannot but observe with some secret pride, that this way of writing diurnal papers has not succeeded for any space of time in the hands of any persons who are not of our line. I believe I speak within compass when I affirm that above a hundred different authors have endeavoured after our family-way of writing : some of which have been writers in other kinds of the greatest eminence in the kingdom ; but I do not know how it has happened, they have none of them hit upon the art. Their projects have always been dropt after a few unsuccessful essays. It puts me in mind of a story lately told me by a pleasant friend of mine who has a very fine hand on the violin. His maid-servant seeing his instrument lying upon the table, and being sensible there was music in it, if she knew how to fetch it out, drew the bow over every part of the strings, and at last told her master she had tried the fiddle all over, but could not for her heart find where-about the tune lay." (*Guardian*, No. 98.)

[320] " They seem'd, indeed, at first to think, that what was only the *Garnish* of the former *Tatlers*, was that which recommended them, and not those *Substantial Entertainments* which they every were [sic] abound in. Accord-ingly they were continually talking of their *Maid, Night-Cap, Spectacles* and *Charles Lillie*. However there were now some faint endeavours at Humour and *Sparks* of Wit ; which the Town, for want of better Entertainment, was content to hunt after, through a heap of Impertinencies." (*The Present State of Wit*.)

[321] In the four volumes of his *Gleaner*, Drake has collected from these inferior works everything which could possibly survive.

[322] Addison and Steele, singly or together, published successively *The Guardian*, March 12, 1713 ; *The Englishman*, Oct. 6, 1713 ; *The Lover*, Feb. 14, 1714 ; *The Reader*, April 22, 1714 ; the eighth volume of the *Spectator*, Jan. 3, 1715 ; *Town Talk*, Dec. 17, 1715 ; *The Free-Holder*, Dec. 23, 1715 ; *The Tea-Table*, Feb. 6, 1716 ; *Chit-Chat*, March 6, 1716 ; *The Plebeian*, March 14,

I fear that to-day justice is hardly done to these Essayists, even to those who deserve the name of Classics.[323] They are certainly not as much read as they deserve to be.[324] The difficulty of now grasping the allusions of which they are full, no doubt accounts in part for this neglect, but I suspect that people are nowadays inclined to think them too short-winded, and to accuse them of being too sketchy and commonplace.[325] Without lingering to discuss how much exaggeration there is in this complaint, I must confess that it seems to me in certain points not without some justification. I admit that in publishing their opinions fragmentarily and in instalments, they often narrowed their horizon and shut out a comprehensive view. I also admit that in writing with a practical aim, they forewent loftier inspiration on many subjects.

But everything which we of to-day count as a flaw, was a definite asset at the time when they were writing. Their dishes were dressed for delicate or diseased stomachs, accustomed to inadequate or over-sophisticated fare, lacking wholesome appetite or digesting with difficulty. What can the best physician prescribe in such a case? What, but a diet of light and varied meals to tempt the appetite, to sustain and strengthen, without relaxing, an undernourished system, and gradually restore it to normal vigour? What better method could be devised than to serve each item in thin, easily-digested slices and offer every day a new menu to give each meal the charm of novelty?

1719 ; *The Old Whig*, March 19, 1719 ; *The Spinster*, Dec. 19, 1719 ; *The Theatre*, Jan. 2, 1720.

[323] By the term " Classic Essayists ", I personally denote solely Addison and Steele ; but the epithet is generally used to include several authors whose publications are not without interest, since they were born of the success of the *Tatler* and the *Spectator* : Samuel Johnson's *Rambler* (1750–2) ; Hawkesworth and Johnson's *Adventurer* (1752–4) ; *The World* (1753–6) by Dr. Moore with the collaboration of Lord Chesterfield and Horace Walpole ; *The Connoisseur* (1754–6) by George Colman and Bonnel Thornton, with the collaboration of Cowper ; Johnson's *Idler* (1758–60) ; Henry Mackenzie's *Mirror* (1779–80) and *Lounger* (1785–7) ; Cumberland's *Observer* (1785–90) and William Roberts' *Looker-on* (1792–4).

[324] *The Cornhill Magazine* for October, 1876, in an article on Sir Richard Steele laments, that " whereas there was a time when everyone who reads at all was perfectly familiar with the *Spectator*, and when an allusion to a paper would have sufficed without quotation. But time, though it cannot destroy our finest literature, is apt to rust it. Even Sir Roger is known by name only to many well-informed readers."

[325] Jeffrey raised this complaint, with some skill, not against the Essayists alone, but against the whole eighteenth century. See his Contributions to the *Edinburgh Review*, I, pp. 160 ff.

Stout volumes and lengthy treatises would have rebuffed readers so lacking in self-confidence as those of Addison's day. They would not even have been opened.   High-flying speculation and long-drawn-out argument would have uselessly wearied and repelled the reader.   The paper that consisted of short essays tempted the timorous by its brevity and variety, and held them by never overtiring them.   Its unambitious modesty won their confidence.   People who would otherwise never have read at all, unconsciously acquired the habit, and the taste for reading thus became widespread.[326]

After the Restoration, the theatre had become the literature of those who did not read.   Later, politics did indeed compel the Englishman to read—but only in the fever of the moment. Addison's triumph was that he proved that the spice of politics was not indispensable, and that he won for his literary paper at least as many readers as all the party writings of the day put together.   Having begun with a printing of 3,000 copies, the *Spectator* rapidly rose to 4,000, then to 20,000 and often as high as 30,000.[327]   These figures apply to the daily sales ; to these we must add the sale of the volumes.   After the publication in separate numbers, readers immediately demanded a reprint in volumes in two different sizes.   Each of these two issues ran to close on 10,000 copies, and before the daily *Spectator* had ceased to appear, more than 9,000 copies of the first four volumes had been sold.[328]

It is true that the *Spectator* had been obliged to keep each essay brief ; and to offer its physic in small doses.   But gradually and unawares the reading public found its mental power growing stronger, its taste more formed, and its enlightenment greater, and such precautions ceased to be necessary.   The more serious works of English literature were re-edited and read, people

[326] " An *Essay* is an instructive writing, either in Prose or Verse, distinguished from compleat Treatises and voluminous Works, by its shorter extent and less accurate Method . . . the disrelish of such diffusive Pieces in these Times is . . . carry'd so far, that great Books are look'd on as oppressive . . . ; while those in which the principal End, as well as the sentiment of the Author, are contracted into a Narrower Compass, if well writ, meet with general Approbation."   (Blackmore, *Essays*, vol. I, Preface.)

[327] *Addisoniana*, in Hurd's Edition of Addison, VI, p. 688 ; Forster, *Biographical Essays*, Steele ; Drake, *Essays . . . Illustrative of the Tatler*, etc., I, p. 82 and III, p. 326.

[328] See the announcements in Nos. 227 and 283 [I can't see the relevance of either of these two essays. E. O. L.] and Nos. 488 and 555.—The *Tatler* had also had to be immediately reprinted in volume form.

returned to Milton [329] and to Shakespeare.[330] Soon the magazine followed the literary essay, but without supplanting it.[331] The two survived side by side for many years. Finally the novel—not the fantastic romance, but the novel of manners and real life—was born with *Robinson Crusoe* in 1719, and developed with much distinction in the works of Defoe, Richardson, Fielding and Smollett.[332]

The spread of general culture in every direction united all classes of society. Readers were no longer segregated into watertight compartments of Puritan and Cavalier, Court and City, the metropolis and the provinces : all the English were now readers.

[329] Between 1688 and 1730 the Tonsons published twelve editions of *Paradise Lost*, either by itself or in conjunction with other works of Milton (Masson, *The Poetical Works of John Milton*, Introduction to Paradise Lost).

[330] The fourth and last reprint of the 1623 folio edition had appeared in 1685 (the second and third were of 1632 and 1663-4 respectively). In 1709 after the lapse of twenty-four years, Rowe published his edition of Shakespeare (a second edition in 1714) ; then came Pope's edition in 1725 (with a second in 1728) ; Theobald's, 1733 ; Hanmer's, 1744 ; Warburton's, 1747 ; Johnson's, 1765.—In 1741 Garrick made his first appearance on the London stage in *Richard III* and with him there began a brilliant Shakespeare revival.

[All this is slightly exaggerated : Shakespeare never sank very low. Dryden's praise was by no means apologetic ; and if Addison left him out of reckoning that was because it was not in his day the fashion at Oxford to consider him, and Addison always followed the fashion. He did so after Rowe's edition of 1709 was on the stocks. Garrick, and others of his time, " improved " Shakespeare to their hearts' content, and so did Dr. Bowdler, if for other reasons. The Victorians improved him by careful selection, while latterly Robertson, and other " disintegrators " improved him almost out of existence in another way. Why attribute to the Restoration alone what is a habit common to all ages, and, with respect to the Restoration, call it a degrading folly ? B. D.]

[331] " The *Gentleman's Magazine*, For January, 1731 " ; " The *London Magazine*, April 1732 " ; " The *Scots Magazine*, January, 1739, Published in Edinburgh " ; " The *Universal Magazine of Knowledge and Pleasure* : for June, 1747 " ; The *Grand Magazine* : for January, 1758 " ; " The *Town and Country Magazine or Universal Repository of Knowledge, Instruction and Entertainment* : for January, 1769."—These titles are those of the first numbers preserved in the British Museum. On the Magazines and their contents see an article called *Last Century Magazines* in *Fraser's Magazine* for September, 1876, and Cucheval Clarigny, chap. XIV.—The *Gentleman's Magazine* appeared regularly without intermission from 1731 till 1907.

[332] Defoe : *Memoirs of a Cavalier* (1720), *The Life, Adventures and Piracies of the Famous Captain Singleton* (1720), *A Journal of the Plague Year* (1722), *The History and Remarkable Life of the truly Honourable Colonel Jacque* (1722), etc. ; —Swift : *Gulliver's Travels* (1726) ;—Richardson : *Pamela* (1741), *Clarissa Harlowe* (1751), *Sir Charles Grandison* (1754) ;—Fielding : *Joseph Andrews* (1742), *Tom Jones* (1749), *Amelia* (1751), etc. ;—Smollett : *Roderick Random* (1748), *Peregrine Pickle* (1751), *Ferdinand Count Fathom* (1753), *Humphrey Clinker* (1771), etc.

In a word, authors were henceforth provided with a public, that is to say a sufficiently numerous body of readers on whom they could count, and readers sufficiently cultivated to welcome and to purchase every type of literature.

CHAPTER IV

ALEXANDER POPE
(1721–1744)
I

Despite Appearances, Writers are not yet wholly independent.—Patronage now based on Politics.—Writers' Services to Politics : Addison, Steele, Swift, Shadwell, Congreve, Vanbrugh, Rowe, Prior, Gay, Defoe, Locke, Newton, Tate, Eusden, Smith, Hughes, Ambrose Philips, Parnell, Arbuthnot, Garth, Blackmore, Granville, Stepney, Maynwaring, Walsh, Martyn, Tickell.— Why the Political Parties cannot dispense with authors.—Effects of Political Patronage.—Dedications to Statesmen, etc.—The Author's uneasy position

So now we have a reading-public in England. This was a fact of capital importance to the author : an importance impossible to over-estimate. For this reading-public, created by the Essayists [0a], was destined ultimately to emancipate the writer and secure him his independence.

For the moment, however, high though they had climbed in the social scale, honourable as was the position they enjoyed, great as was the respect accorded them, authors were not yet independent.

Queen Anne's reign, the peak of the period we have just been studying, is remembered by Englishmen as a Golden Age of Literature, a writer's paradise of encouragement and patronage. But my reader will probably have noticed that this patronage was by no means wholly disinterested. No doubt one factor therein was pure love of literature. Charles II's reign had sown in high society the seed of literary enjoyment which was now bearing fruit. In this connection it would be unjust to forget that when Dorset's duty as Lord Chamberlain compelled him after the Revolution to cancel Dryden's pension as Poet Laureate and Historiographer Royal, he compensated the poet by generous gifts from his own private purse.[1] It was

---

[0a] [This is to go too far. The essayists no doubt helped the growth to some extent ; but the public was already growing from different causes. See my Introduction. B. D.]

[1] Dryden, Dedication to Dorset of his *Discourse on Satire*, 1693. I should hate to seem cynical, but perhaps the idea was that Dryden should not be driven to extremes. He might have made a dangerous enemy.
[This does indeed seem to be unduly cynical. Dorset, " the grace of courts, the Muses' pride " had been one of the old group of literary roisterers,

Dorset, too, who came to Tate's rescue when nothing further was to be hoped or feared from that aged and impoverished man.[2]   Somers also, enlightened lover as he was of literature and the arts, was not wont to take heed of the personal opinions of those whom he succoured or encouraged.[3]   All the statesmen of the day, in fact, had the admirable virtue of being genuinely cultured men and good judges of literature, which qualities they proved by bringing to light so many valuable men of letters, to the honour of their own memory and the glory of their country.

None the less, the patronage they extended to authors had an entirely political basis.   No crude bargaining took place between statesman and author, nor was the author in any statesman's pay.   But the statesman won the author's attachment, and skilfully contrived to link the latter's interest with his own fortunes. The two formed a sort of mutual-aid society.   The one said : " You stand by me, and I shall see that you do not suffer by it ", the other answered : " You secure me a livelihood and I shall support you."   Thus, no actual demand was made of the author, but he felt himself obliged to give ; he was no mercenary, but he was an ally.   The most distinguished of them, men like Addison, Newton, Locke, Prior and Steele, were entrusted with public office in which they could be directly of value to the party appointing them.   Others were offered posts less in the limelight, in the hope—rarely falsified—that they would render to their patron-friends the type of service which Dryden had performed for Charles II and his royal brother.   Others again were supplied with a comfortable sinecure—a sop, as it were, to Cerberus—to secure at least their silence and neutrality.

At this distance of time, it is easy for us to be taken in by the gracious urbanity of the statesman of those days and his friendly attitude towards the author, an attitude in which lay no trace

---

but had himself great taste and was something of a poet.   He had little to fear from Dryden, and would be glad to help him.   B. D.]

    [2] Chalmers, *Biographical Dictionary*, s.v. Tate.   Tate died hopelessly in debt.   In earlier days Dorset had financed Prior's education.   Prior is said to have been the son of a joiner.   He was early left an orphan, and his uncle, who was a vintner, sent him to school at Westminster.   Visiting the uncle's tavern, Dorset found the boy reading Horace and from that day undertook the care and cost of Prior's further studies.   (Johnson, *Lives* . . . , Prior.)

    [3] Macaulay, *History*, chap. XX, Somers.   He encouraged and protected the antiquary, Hickes " the fiercest and most intolerant of all the Non-Jurors ", and the engraver Vertue, who was a devout Roman Catholic.

    [Somers was known as " the all-accomplisht ".   B. D.]

of patronizing superiority towards a subordinate. This pleasant relationship of equal to equal, is all the more attractive by contrast with the disdainful patronage of men like Rochester and Mulgrave. No wonder that the author welcomed with delight the new régime which suddenly made life so pleasant for him, and recorded it with so much appreciation that we are tempted to see it with his eyes. We are the more inclined to share this illusion, because, while we remember that some writers were frankly political partisans—Steele and Addison were, for instance, zealous Whigs and Swift an ardent Tory— the greater number of names mentioned in the preceding pages are for us nowadays politically colourless, and their connotation is purely and solely literary. We remember only the comedies of Shadwell, Congreve and Vanbrugh, the tragedies of Rowe, the light poetry of Prior, the verses and fables of Gay. How many people connect Defoe's name with anything but *Robinson Crusoe*? Who dreams of inquiring about the political sympathies of Locke or Newton? As for most of the others, their works and their opinions are equally buried in oblivion. Yet, if we look more closely, we note that the writers of the day were one and all involved in political strife and zealously took a more or less active share in it.

Shadwell, who had, as we saw, entered the lists before the Revolution, wrote a poem to commemorate the arrival in England of the Prince of Orange, and another Congratulatory Poem to greet the arrival of " The Most Illustrious Queen Mary ". He also celebrated various events of the reign of William III : the King's return from Ireland, the King's birthday, etc.[4] Congreve, a member of the Kit-Cat Club, mourned Queen Mary's death in a pastoral elegy and " humbly offered " to Queen Anne a Pindaric Ode on the capture of Namur and the victories of Marlborough.[5] Vanbrugh, who knew French well, undertook to keep William III's Government informed of what was going on in France, and did so to such good purpose that he was arrested and spent nearly two years in the Bastille.[6]

[4] See my Bibliography. Queen Mary landed on Feb. 12, 1689 ; Shadwell's verses are dated Feb. 20. Rymer, who later succeeded Shadwell as Historiographer Royal, was even more expeditious : on Feb. 15 he addressed a poem to the Queen on her safe arrival. (Malone, *Life of Dryden*, pp. 207-8.)
[5] See my Bibliography.
[6] Ravaisson, *Archives de la Bastille*, IV, pp. 338-446. It is not expressly stated that he was arrested as a spy. But other documents quoted by Ravaisson show that William III had an excellently-organized system of espionage

Like Congreve, he was a member of the Kit-Cat club. Rowe,
" who was so keen a Whig that he did not willingly converse
with men of the opposite party ",[7] sang the Union of England
and Scotland, the victories of Marlborough, the House of
Brunswick [8] and introduced party allusions into his verses—
even into his translation of Lucan.[9] Prior collaborated in the
Tory *Examiner* and wrote a number of political poems which
he carefully reprinted in his *Works*.[10] The sole reason for Gay's
being appointed Secretary to the Ambassador in Hanover was
that he had dedicated some verses to Bolingbroke ; he also
wrote an Epistle to the Princess of Wales.[11] Defoe, whom we
saw supporting the Revolution of William III with so much

---

in France. Now, in view of the fact that Vanbrugh had a perfect command
of French, that he was a supporter of the English Revolution and on good
terms with people who stood well at Court (see the *Life* prefixed to his Works)
it would seem that his arrival in France without a passport, at a time when
the two countries were at war, made him justifiably suspect to the French
authorities.—See also *Biographia Dramatica*, s.v. Vanbrugh.

[Vanbrugh was arrested at Calais in 1690. At that time he had no
connection with courtly circles ; he may have been known to one or two
senior officers in the army, but that is all. It is most unlikely that he was
directly employed as a spy. He did not go to the Bastille till 1692, and was
not, of course, a Kit-Cat till a good deal later, since the club then hardly
existed, if at all. See Ravaisson, *loc. cit.*, and my Introduction to the Nonesuch edition of Vanbrugh's *Works*. B. D.]

[7] Johnson, *Lives* . . . etc. Rowe.

[8] *Unio*, a little Latin poem, " English'd *by the* Author " in his *Poems on
Several Occasions*, 1714, p. 29 ; *A Poem upon the Late Successes of Her Majesties
Arms*, etc., in his *Works*, II, p. 283 ; *Ode for the New Year*, addressed to George I.
See my Bibliography.

[9] In his *Tamerlane*, Bajazet represented Louis XIV and Tamerlane
William III. See my Bibliography for the quotation from Virgil which
precedes the play.—His tragedy, *The Royal Convert*, 1707, ends with a prophetic
compliment to Queen Anne and the Union of England and Scotland.—
Henry Cromwell wrote to Pope on Nov. 5, 1710 : " I have just read and
compared Mr. Rowe's version of the ninth (book) of Lucan with very great
pleasure . . . He is so arrant a Whig, that he strains even beyond his author,
in passion for liberty, and aversion to tyranny." (Elwin, VI, p. 108.)

[10] See my Bibliography and p. 66 of his *Poems on Several Occasions* :
" Presented to the King, at his Arrival in Holland, after the Discovery of
the Conspiracy, 1696 " ;—p. 133, " *Carmen Seculare*, for the year 1700 ; to
the King " ;—p. 181, " Prologue spoken at Court before the Queen on Her
Majesty's Birth-Day, 1704 " ;—p. 183, A Letter to Monsieur Boileau
Despreaux, occasioned by the Victory at Blenheim, 1704 ;—p. 245, " An
Ode humbly inscribed to the Queen on the Glorious Success of Her Majesty's
Arms, 1706. Written in Imitation of Spenser's Style " ;—p. 285, " To Mr.
Harley wounded by Guiscard, 1711 : An Ode."—On this last item see
Swift's *Journal to Stella*, March 30, 1710–11.

[11] *The Shepherd's Week*, 1714, with a " *Prologue*. To the Right Honourable
the Ld. Viscount of Bolingbroke."—" *Epistle* to a Lady. *Occasion'd by the
Arrival* of Her Royal Highness " in his *Poems on Several Occasions*, II, p. 271.

vigour, left over two hundred political writings.   In 1690 Locke, who was Shaftesbury's friend and collaborator, published two *Treatises of Government* in which he warmly defended the principles of the Revolution against the Tories.[12] Newton, M.P. for Cambridge, actively upheld the rights of the University against the illegal encroachments of James II.[13]

Tate's genuine grief at the death of the sovereigns whom he survived, did not prevent his hailing the accession of their successors and the principal events of subsequent reigns.[14] Eusden's first step on the road to literary success was a Latin verse translation of Lord Halifax's poem on the Battle of the Boyne, and he repaid favours received with several pieces whose subjects were calculated to give pleasure in exalted circles.[15] The interest Lord Halifax displayed in Edmund Smith, was not evoked solely by Smith's tragedy of *Phædra* ; the poet had previously celebrated the accession of William and Mary and the Battle of the Boyne, mourned the death of William III and sung the victory of Blenheim.[16]   Hughes wrote verses on the Duke of Gloucester, the House of Nassau, the Princess of Wales, the Peace of Ryswick and the return of William III in 1699.[17] Ambrose Philips in his *Pastorals* set his shepherds Lobbin, Albino and Lanquet to sing poetic eulogies of Dorset and Queen Anne

[12] See H. R. Fox Bourne, *The Life of John Locke* and Villemain, *Tableau de la littérature au XVIIIe siècle, 5e leçon.*—In his Preface to the *Two Treatises,* Locke says : " These (Papers) I hope are sufficient to establish the Throne of our Great Restorer, Our present King *William* ;   to make good his Title, in the Consent of the People, which being the only one of all lawful Governments, he has more fully and clearly than any Prince in *Christendom.*   And to justify to the World, the People of *England,* whose love of their Just and Natural Rights, with their Resolution to preserve them, saved the Nation when it was on the very brink of Slavery and Ruine."

[13] *Biographia Britannica,* s.v. Newton.

[14] See my Bibliography.—Some verses of his to Queen Anne, " *Britannia's* Prayer to the Queen, 1706.   By Mr. *Tate,* Poet Laureat to her Majesty " may be found in *Poems on Affairs of State,* IV, 1707, p. 129.

[15] See N. Drake, *Essays . . . Illustrative of the Tatler,* etc., III, p. 280, and my Bibliography.

[16] On the Inauguration of *King William and Queen Mary,* An. Dom. 1689 ; On the Return of King William to Ireland, After the battle of the Boyne 1690 (In A. Chalmers, *The Works of the English Poets,* IX, pp. 203–4) ; *A Pindarique Poem Sacred to the Glorious Memory of King William III,* 1702 (see my Bibliography) ;   Ode for the Year 1705 (A. Chalmers, op. cit., p. 207).

[17] *The Triumph of Peace* (see my Bibliography) ;—" The Court of Neptune. On King William's Return from Holland, 1699 " (in his *Poems on Several Occasions,* p. 19) ;—" Song.   Written for the Late Duke of Gloucester's Birthday, 1699 " (A. Chalmers, op. cit., X, p. 24) ;—*The House of Nassau* ; —*An Ode for the Birth-Day of Her Royal Highness The Princess of Wales* (see my Bibliography).

and in his *Life of Archbishop Williams* aired Whig opinions in prose.[18] Parnell, whom Swift introduced to Harley, paid his court with a poem *On Queen Anne's Peace*.[19] At Swift's instigation, Arbuthnot wrote his *History of John Bull* [20] to ridicule Marlborough and turn men's minds to thoughts of peace, and his *Pseudologia Politike* or *The Art of Political Lying* to make merry at the expense of the Whigs.[21] Garth backed the views of his Kit-Cat friends in several poems, in Epistles to Godolphin and to Marlborough, in verses on Queen Anne and on the Jacobin rising of 1715.[22] Blackmore was the author of *A True and Impartial History of the Conspiracy Against the Person and Government of King* William III *of Glorious Memory*, verses in praise of Marlborough, etc.[23] Before being raised to the peerage by Harley's Government, Granville had committed himself to the Tories by poems in honour of Mary of Modena and of James II.[24] Stepney sang in Latin the virtues of Charles II, the Marriage of Princess Anne, and in English the accession of James II, William III's journey to Holland and the death of

[18] See my Bibliography. In Charles I's day Archbishop Williams had been one of the promoters of the Petition of Right.

[19] *On Queen Anne's Peace* (*Written in December*, 1712) (A. Chalmers, op. cit., IX, p. 405).—See Swift, *Journal to Stella*, Dec. 22, 26, 31, 1712 ; Jan. 6, Feb. 19, March 27, 1712–13.

[20] Usually quoted under this title, but the original title is *Law is a Bottomless-Pit*. See my Bibliography.

[21] See Swift, *Journal to Stella*, Oct. 9 and Dec. 12, 1712.—This pamphlet of Arbuthnot's, revised by Swift, is reprinted in Scott's Edition of Swift, vol. VI.

[22] *To the Duke of Marlborough*, on his Voluntary Banishment ; *To the Earl of Godolphin* ; *On Her Majesty's Statue*, in St. Paul's Church-Yard ; *On the New Conspiracy*, 1716 (A. Chalmers, op. cit., IX, pp. 449–50).

[23] *A True and Impartial History*, etc., and *Advice to the Poets* (see my Bibliography) ; "Instructions to *Vander Bank*. A Sequel to the Advice to the Poets. A Poem Occasioned by the Glorious Success of Her Majesty's Arms, under the Conduct of the Duke of Marlborough, the last Year in *Flanders*. Printed in the Year 1709 (In *A Collection of Poems on Various Subjects*. By Sir Richard Blackmore).—In the Dedication of his poem *Alfred* he says : ". . . I had the Honour to contribute more to the Succession of the Illustrious House of *Hanover* to the Crown of *Great-Britain*, than I ever boasted of, contenting my Self with this, that what I had done was for the Service of reformed Religion, and the Good of my Country."

[24] See in his *Genuine Works*, III, pp. 1 and 6–8 : "To the Earl *of* Peterborough, *on his Happy Accomplishment of the Marriage between His* Royal Highness *and the Princess* Mary d'Este *of* Modena" ; "*To the* King *in the First Year of His* Majesty's *Reign*" ; "*To the* King" ; "*To the* King ;—At the age of eighteen he had been eager to fight against the Duke of Monmouth ; in 1688 he had volunteered to maintain in arms the rights of James II ; under William III he remained in retirement." (Johnson, *Lives*, etc., Granville.)

Queen Mary, etc.[25] Maynwaring, having first given rein to his high spirits in verses against the Whigs, allowed them a long canter against the Tories and attacked Swift and Bolingbroke's *Examiner* in the paper known as *The Medley*.[26] Walsh pressed Horace and Virgil into his service to glorify William III's courage and the merits of Whig politics.[27] Henry Martyn actively collaborated in *The British Merchant*, or *Commerce Preserv'd*, a paper founded to oppose the commercial treaty with France which was concluded at Utrecht.[28] Tickell, whom Swift dubbed "Whiggissimus", wrote several sets of verses in favour of the House of Brunswick.[29]

It is not possible to doubt the motives underlying the favour accorded to authors, when we observe that the Whigs reserve it exclusively for Whigs, and the Tories for Tories, and that each triumph of one party or the other is the signal for a distribution of lucrative posts.

On the accession of William III, Dryden, the Tory, was released from his duties and deprived of his salaries, while Shadwell, an over-night Orangeman, was appointed Poet Laureate in his stead. Under William, the Whig Newton was called to be Master of the Mint.[29a] Locke, who by order of Charles II had been driven out of the University of Oxford,

---

[25] *In Obitum* Caroli *Secundi*. He speaks of "Caroli Mores Cœlestibus æquos"; *In Nuptias* P. Georgii et D. Annæ; *To King James II*. Upon his Accession to the Throne. *The Author then of Trinity-College, Cambridge*; On the late horrid Conspiracy (in *The Works of Celebrated Authors, of whose writings there are but small Remains*, II, pp. 58, 56, 3, 11). *An Epistle to Charles Montague, Esq.*; *on his Majesty's Voyage to Holland*; *A Poem Dedicated to the Blessed Memory of Her late Gracious Majesty Queen Mary* (see my Bibliography).

[26] See *Biographia Britannica*, s.v. Maynwaring, which quotes the titles of some fifteen writings of his against the Tories.

[27] *Horace. Ode III. Book III* Imitated 1705; *The Golden Age restored*, 1703. An Imitation of the Fourth Eclogue of Virgil. Supposed to have been taken from a Sibylline Prophecy (A. Chalmers, op. cit., VIII, pp. 417–18).

[28] N. Drake, *Essays . . . Illustrative of the Tatler*, etc., III, pp. 285 ff. See also my Bibliography, s.v. Martyn (Henry).

[29] *The Prospect of Peace* (see my Bibliography). This poem favouring the policy of Harley and Bolingbroke was little calculated to please the Whigs, but the wrong thereby done them Tickell repaired in his later verses: *The Royal Progress*, on the arrival of George I, first published in No. 620 of the *Spectator*, Nov. 15, 1714; *An Imitation* of the Prophecy of Nereus. From Horace, II, Ode XV, on the Jacobite rising of 1715 (A. Chalmers, op. cit., XI, p. 108); *Epistle from a Lady in England to a Gentleman at Avignon*, against the Jacobites (see my Bibliography); *Kensington Garden* in praise of George I (see my Bibliography).

[29a] [But might it not be that Newton's appointment to the Mint was made on technical grounds? B. D.]

had followed Shaftesbury to Holland, and had been unable to return home until he came in King William's train, was appointed Commissioner of Appeals. Blackmore, who had all his life been an Anti-Jacobite, was knighted and appointed Physician to the King. It was to his Tory friends that Swift owed the Deanery of St. Patrick's, and it was likewise the Tories who appointed Gay Secretary to the Embassy in Hanover, who entrusted Prior with important diplomatic missions and elevated Granville to the peerage. Those who throughout the days of Tory triumph had remained faithful to the House of Brunswick, came into their own when George I came to the throne. Addison and Steele, who had been ousted by the previous ministry, were rewarded in overflowing measure. Even before the new King's arrival, Addison was appointed Secretary to the Council of Regency, and was later made Secretary to the Lord-Lieutenant of Ireland and Under-Secretary of State. Steele was made Inspector of the Royal Stables, J.P. and Deputy Lieutenant for the County of Middlesex, Director of the Theatre Royal in Drury Lane and received a knighthood. Garth was also knighted. Tickell was rewarded with a public post in Ireland under Addison.[30] Henry Martyn, who had opposed the Tories' commercial policy, was made Inspector-General of Exports and Imports. It was at this time too that Ambrose Philips, a member of the Hanover Club, secured two of his posts, and that Rowe was made Poet Laureate (before the death of his predecessor, Tate) and provided with other highly remunerative sinecures.

We even see a service reap instantaneous reward. Addison's *Blenheim* had got no further than the simile of the angel, when Godolphin testified his appreciation by appointing him Commissioner of Appeals.

Powerful political motives underlay this eager haste to enlist the author's allegiance and secure his loyalty by every possible device. I have already pointed out how urgently necessary it was for the very existence of any Government after the Revolution, to ensure the support of public opinion, to keep in touch

---

[30] In his *Royal Progress* he prophetically said of George I :

" Now to the Royal Towers securely brought,
He plans *Britannia's* Glories in his Thought,
Resumes the delegated Pow'r he gave,
Rewards the Faithful, and restores the Brave."

[It might also be noted that Vanbrugh was the first man to be knighted by George I. B. D.]

with the nation, and to influence it from day to day. Now-adays, the propaganda indispensable to a constitutional govern-ment, is almost entirely supplied by parliamentary debate. An evening speech by a Minister, or by a leader of the Opposition, is read throughout England next morning, and penetrates into even the tiniest village, to challenge the attention and invite the opinion of millions of readers. But at the period of which I am writing, parliamentary eloquence died within the walls of St. Stephen's, unechoed in the outside world. The publica-tion of debates was strictly forbidden,[31] and the words which swayed the votes of Lords and Commons remained a dead letter in the country at large. Bolingbroke has left a reputation of eloquence unequalled in England, rich as that country is in political oratory, yet not a phrase of any of his speeches has been preserved.[32] It was therefore imperative that the work of discussion, already accomplished in Parliament, should be carried on afresh in the world outside, and contact incessantly renewed with the coffee-houses and clubs and with the provincial electorate. This could be done only by the perpetual publication of fresh matter.[33] The influence nowadays exerted by parlia-mentary speeches then belonged solely to the Press, which means not only newspapers and pamphlets but every literary work, and even verses handling political ideas. It has been justly said that Addison's *Campaign* is merely a rhymed *Gazette*. Every man capable of wielding a pen was a valuable and im-portant ally, and a party chief who neglected to enlist him by flattering attentions, and retain his loyalty by substantial marks

---

[31] See Lecky, I, pp. 442–6, and Andrews, I, pp. 142–9 and 196–203. It was not until 1771 that parliamentary debates began to be freely reported. —In 1745 the *Gentleman's Magazine* was still giving them—and not without risk—under the headline of " Discussions in the Lilliput Senate ". The Lords were the *Hurgoes* : Lord Chesterfield appeared as *Hurgo Castroflet*, Lord Hardwicke as *Hurgo Hickrad* ; the Archbishop of Oxford as Archbishop of *Oxdorf*. The House of Commons became the *Clinabs* and the speakers were *Snadsy, Gamdahm, Feaucs, Pulnub*, that is Sandys, Wyndham, Fox and Pulteney. Europe was *Degulia*, France *Blefuscu*, London *Mildendo*, the Jacobites, *Jacomites*.—The *Scots Magazine* adopted Roman pseudonyms : Sir Robert Walpole was M. Tullius Cicero ; Pulteney, M. Cato : The Duke of Newcastle, Cn. Domitius Calvinus ; and Lord Chesterfield, L. Piso, etc.

[32] Stanhope, *History of . . . the Reign of Queen Anne*, II, p. 175.

[33] We have already seen Bolingbroke collaborating in the *Examiner* ; he was at that time a member of the Ministry. Harley wrote *A Vindication of the Commons in the last Session of Parliament*, 1701 (Townsend, I, p. 157). Watt quotes some dozen political works written by Walpole. On this point, and on the active part played by Walpole and Pulteney in press polemics, see Macaulay's *Essay on Addison*.

of esteem, would have been failing in his duty towards his party
and towards himself. If it was not possible to make the author
an active partisan, it was at least expedient to prevent his swelling
the ranks of the enemy.

So we find both parties on the alert to detect budding talent,
in order to have a nursery of useful collaborators to draw on.
When Congreve called Whig attention to young Addison's
promise, Halifax personally intervened to prevent the young
man's taking orders and to maintain him firmly in his expressed
opinions. It is curious to note Swift recording the solicitude
shown by Harley and Bolingbroke towards the very modest
signs of talent in a Diaper,[34] a Trapp,[35] a Harrison.[36]

For the same reason, turn-coat writers were welcomed with
enthusiasm : there was a double advantage in roping in a
renegade—gain to your own party, loss to the other. We have
already seen the attention lavished on Parnell when Swift brought
him to pay his respects to Harley. Prior also who, under the
wing of his friend and collaborator Montague, had found both
honour and profit in the ranks of the Whigs, went over to the
Tories, who received him with open arms, entrusted him with
negotiations abroad and rewarded him with lucrative posts.
Having won his first literary distinction with a Tory poem, so
good that it was attributed to Dryden, Maynwaring was not
long in showing his appreciation of the courtship of the Whigs.
Halifax hastened to encourage so happy a frame of mind by
securing for him a job in the Customs, and Godolphin's kindness went so far as to purchase from its holder a post worth
£2,000 a year to present it as an offering to the repentant Tory.
Nothing in this mart-and-barter business, however, is more
illuminating than the competition of the two parties to capture
Swift. He was the incumbent of a small Irish parish when he
ventured for the first time into politics with a Whig-flavoured
pamphlet published anonymously in 1701. It was *A Discourse*

---

[34] *Journal to Stella*, March 12, 13, 21, 1711–12 ; Dec. 23, 1712 ; Feb. 12,
13, 1712–13.

[Diaper does not deserve the neglect into which he has fallen : Trapp
and Harrison are not to be mentioned in the same breath with him. It is
extremely difficult to see copies of Diaper's three works, which should be
reprinted. He is beginning to be quoted in anthologies, being far better
than the average ruck of Eusdens, Philips, Hughes, Parnells, *et hoc genus
omne*. B. D.]

[35] Ibid., Jan. 7, 1710–11 ; April 1, 2, 1713.

[36] Ibid., Oct. 13, 1710 ; March 15, 1710–11 ; April 19, 1711 ; March 12,
1711–12 ; Jan. 30, 31 and Feb. 12, 13, 14, 1712–13.

of the Contents and Dissensions between the Nobles and the Commons at Athens and Rome and it produced so much effect that it was popularly ascribed either to Somers or to Burnet. As soon as the author declared himself, Halifax and Somers both expressed a wish to meet him, received him graciously, promised him their support and proposed him for a bishopric.[37] They were unfortunate in being unable to make good their promises, or perhaps they pressed his case too half-heartedly, and Swift, filled with bitter disappointment and resentment, was left to vegetate in his modest benefice. So when the Whig Ministry fell, and the Tories came to power, the disgruntled author hastened across the water and came to London to study the situation.[38] He had meantime written *The Tale of a Tub* which placed beyond all doubt his remarkable talent as a writer, and showed what service he could render to his friends, and how much damage he could inflict on those of the other side.[39] No sooner had he arrived in the capital than the Whigs, anticipating his resentment, laid hold on him and overwhelmed him with compliments and excuses, blaming themselves for having been able to do so little for a man of his calibre. While the Whigs were profuse in compliments, protestations and attentions, the Tories frankly told him that the moment had come to lay the foundation of his fortunes if he had a mind. Harley made personal approaches to him with a courtesy all the more seductive that it was in pleasing contrast to the cold reserve of Somers, one of the Whig leaders. He frequently invited Swift to dine, introduced him to his family circle, treated him as an intimate, called him his friend, and addressed him without formality by his Christian name, till the guest recorded with delight that his position amongst " the people of to-day " was ten times better than with their predecessors and that he was forty times more sought after. So it was " the people of to-day " who won him over and the acquisition of a writer of the first rank was undoubtedly one of the most valuable achievements of the new Ministry. Swift's writings alone did greater service to the Tory

[37] This proposal, previously a matter of conjecture only, has been documented by papers reproduced in Forster's *Life of Jonathan Swift*, pp. 210 ff.

[38] He carried off a book which Halifax had given him [Jolivet's *Poésies Chrétiennes.* B. D.], and wrote in it : " Given me by my lord Halifax, May 3, 1709. I begged it of him, and desired him to remember, *it was the only favour I ever received from him or his party.*"

[39] Bolingbroke later told him : " We were determined to have you ; you were the only one we were afraid of."

cause than all the delicate political manœuvres of Harley and the eloquent speeches of Bolingbroke.[40]

About this same time Harley exerted his diplomacy to retain in neutrality, if he could not win over to an offensive alliance, the two Whig writers, Steele and Congreve. As Editor of the *London Gazette* and Commissioner of Stamps, Steele played an active part in politics. In the hope of securing him, Harley retained him in these two posts, assured him of the high esteem he felt for his character and promised to show practical proof of his wish to be of service to him. Two unpleasing anti-Tory articles which Steele printed in the *Tatler* [41] cost him the editorship of the *Gazette*. But the Tories did not wish to push matters to extremes and Harley sent Swift as his ambassador with general instructions " to clear matters with Steele " and request him to continue " in his office of stamped paper ". Swift's overtures were ill received. Steele, who was always hasty and passionate in politics, resigned his commissionership and launched a merciless campaign against the Tories.[42]

Congreve, who was of milder temper than Steele and appreciative of the easy life which his posts assured him, begged Swift to intercede on his behalf. Delighted to find the dramatist so amenable, Harley sent a gracious reply in Latin :

> Non obtusa adeo gestamus pectora Pæni,
> Nec tam aversus equos Tyriâ sol jungit ab urbe.

This quotation completely won Congreve's heart, and his political muse kept silence through all the remainder of Queen Anne's reign.[43]

[40] For details of Swift's first steps in politics see his own works, especially *Memoirs relating to that Change which happened in the Queen's Ministry in the Year 1710* ; *Imitation of part of the Sixth Satire of the Second Book of Horace 1714* and the *Journal to Stella*.
[What Swift always worked for was the security and betterment of the Church of England. Though as a churchman he would welcome the Revolution as removing the Catholic menace, it was soon pretty clear that the Whigs of Queen Anne's day, with their strong support from the Dissenters, would and could do little for it. Swift had no choice but to be a Tory, which he was from the conviction of a practical man quite apart from his personal ambition. B. D.]
[41] The numbers of June 29 and July 4, 1710. The former contained a portrait of Harley under the name of Polypragmon ; the latter a letter purporting to be by Downes, the prompter, criticizing the new Ministry under the pretence of describing a change of theatrical management.
[42] Swift, *Journal to Stella*, Oct. 22 and Dec. 15, 1710. Harley even offered Steele a better post. See Steele's fine letter to Harley in N. Drake, *Essays . . . Illustrative of the Tatler*, etc., I, pp. 95 ff.
[43] *Journal to Stella* : June 28, 1711, and Swift's *Works*, XVI, p. 349, his letter to Pope from Dublin, dated Jan. 10, 1720-1.

It is clear that Congreve had no illusions about the disinterested kindness of statesmen, but was fully alive to the connection between politics and patronage. His brother-authors were no less wide-awake than he, and the eagerness with which they entered the fray shows that they clearly perceived where their own best interests lay. Those I have so far mentioned all succeeded in securing more or less important posts, and we might assume that special talent prompted them to embark on a career in which they believed themselves destined to succeed. But if we look outside the circle of the specially privileged, we notice that all employed the same procedure for drawing attention to themselves. They understood full well that if they were to derive effective benefit, more was expected of them than proof of purely literary talent. Farquhar—who however died too young to attain distinction—wrote Pindaric verses on the death of General Schomberg, who fell in the Battle of the Boyne, and mourned Queen Mary's death.[44] John Philips also paid his tribute to the memory of the dead Queen,[45] and, as already mentioned, celebrated for the Tories the victory of Blenheim. The critic Dennis composed one poem on Queen Mary's death, another on Marlborough's victories and yet a third, mourning the death of Queen Anne and in the same breath hailing the accession of George I.[46] In 1712 Young made his first literary appearance with a political *Epistle* to Granville newly created Lord Lansdowne ; in 1713 he offered verses to Queen Anne in a political dedication, and in 1714 he wrote a poem on the Queen's death and the New King.[47] Aaron Hill was another who lamented the death of Queen Anne.[48] The Deist, Toland, wrote a pamphlet on the destruction of Dunkirk, and another

[44] *On the Death of General* Schomberg, *Kill'd at the* Boyn ; *On the Death of the late* Queen (*Works*, I, pp. 16 and 41).

[45] *In Memory Of Our Late Most Gracious Lady* (see my Bibliography).

[46] *The Court of Death* : *A Pindarick Poem dedicated to the Memory of her most Sacred Majesty Queen Mary* (*The Select Works of Mr. John Dennis*, I, p. 33) ; *Britannia Triumphans* (see my Bibliography) ; *The Battle of Ramillia* (ibid.) ; *A Poem on the Death of Her late Sacred Majesty Queen Anne, And the Most Happy and Auspicious Accession of his Sacred Majesty King George* (ibid.).—We may note that he obtained a minor post through Marlborough's kind offices. (*Biographia Dramatica*, s.v. Dennis).

[47] *An Epistle.* To the Right Hon. George, Lord Lansdowne, MDCCXII (A. Chalmers, *The Works of the English Poets*, XIII, p. 509) ; *A Poem On the last Day*, dedicated " To the Queen " (see my Bibliography) ; *On the Late Queen's Death. And His Majesty's Accession to the Throne* (ibid.).

[48] The Dream. *Occasioned by the Death of* Q. Anne. *By* Aaron Hill, *Esq.* (In the *Works of Rochester*, M.DCC.XXXI, II, p. 159.)

M

attacking Harley, now Lord Oxford.[49] I could add many other examples, but let these suffice.

In quoting these facts to show that authors had not yet escaped from serfdom, I have no intention of weakening what I have said of their greatly improved position. In proving that they were still dependent on politics, I am far from wishing to imply that they were degrading themselves by taking part in them. No doubt a few trimmed their sails to suit a change of wind and forfeited some self-respect by so doing ; but Newton, Locke, Addison, Steele and many others are no less worthy in my eyes for having taken part in party controversy. I should not even contend that they were wrong to do so or that they would have been better to abstain. It would be absurd to suggest that an author—simply because he is an author—should hold himself aloof from the business of his time and country. There are periods in history, moreover, when no citizen has the right to be a passive spectator of the happenings that are taking place before his eyes. The years which followed the English Revolution of 1688 were a period of this kind. Besides, it is obvious that politics offer a writer natural and frequent opportunity to practise his art and to serve his country. It would be regrettable and unjust to forbid him thus to employ his gifts. I feel therefore no regret that English writers of this time occupied themselves with politics ; but I do regret that circumstances compelled their so doing, and I am bound to record that they owed their new position in society solely to their political activity and that, whether they were aware of the fact or not, this activity was the *sine quâ non* of their very existence. They had, in fact, simply exchanged Court patronage for the patronage of politicians, and they were as powerless to escape the one as the other.

It is manifest that this new form of patronage was pleasanter and less undignified than the earlier. First, because they were not compelled, as of old, to stake all their hopes on Court favour ; they had the choice of allegiance to either of two parties, and this freedom of choice conferred a real liberty of movement. Secondly, the important service they were able to render to their patrons ensured that their value was appreciated. The statesman, wooing the author not for his personal pleasure, nor

[49] Scott's Edition of Swift, XII, p. 305, note. I have been unable to find either of these pamphlets in the British Museum. The second was called *The Art of Reasoning*.

for the fleeting need of the moment, but as a permanent ally
and for serious purposes, was compelled to give thought to
his qualities and qualifications and could not—without danger
to himself and to his party—let a mere whim dictate his choice,
nor afterwards capriciously discard his protégé. Thirdly, since
author and statesman had interests in common, the author
became partner and collaborator rather than client. His
position was no longer the subordinate one of other days.

It is none the less true that he remained dependent on others.
He lived, not by his pen, but by the post he held, and to obtain
it he had to incur certain inevitable obligations. He therefore
still chafed under the inconvenient consequences of dependence.
He still had to pander and pay his court to the influential persons
of the day, to be diligent in his attendance at levées and audiences,
or risk being overlooked, and to spend long hours in antechambers.
" We had much company to-day at dinner at Lord Treasurer's,"
writes Swift to Stella,[50] " Prior never fails : he is a much better
courtier than I ; and we expect every day that he will be a
Commissioner of the Customs." So the author was still constrained humbly to issue his work under the aegis of some famous
name. He had been wont to write dedications ; he went on
writing them, but now to a different address. Instead of offering
them to those in high favour at Court, he sent them now
to Ministers or high officials, or to men influential in public
affairs.

Congreve dedicated one of his comedies to the Right Honourable Charles Montague, one of the Lords of the Treasury ;
another to the Right Honourable Charles, Earl of Dorset and
Middlesex, Lord Chamberlain of his Majesty's Household ; a
collection of his occasional verses again to Charles Montague
now become Lord Halifax. The collection contains a poem
addressed to Halifax, and another to Godolphin, Lord High
Treasurer of Great Britain [51] ; all this without prejudice to the
political works already entered to the author's account. Rowe's
Ulysses was offered to Godolphin ; his *Royal Convert* to Halifax.
Southerne presented his *Wives' Excuse* to The Right Honourable
Thomas Wharton, Controller of His Majesty's Household, his

[50] June 26, 1711.
[51] Poems upon *Several Occasions* (*Works*, III, p. 57) : " The Birth of the
Muse. To the Right Honourable *Charles*, Lord *Hallifax* " ; p. 193 : " To
the Right Honourable the Earl of *Godolphin*, Lord High Treasurer of *Great
Britain*. Pindarique Ode."

Oroonoko to His Grace the Duke of Devonshire, Lord Intendant of His Majesty's Household. Mrs. Manley likewise dedicated *The Royal Mischief* to the Duke of Devonshire. Mrs. Centlivre *The Man's Bewitch'd* to the same, and her *Busie Body* to Somers. Hughes presented his tragedy *The Siege of Damascus* to Cowper, the Lord Chancellor, Ambrose Philips addressed a poetic letter to Dorset [52] and commended his *Pastorals* to his protection. The classical scholar Richard Bentley dedicated an edition of Horace to the Earl of Oxford, and, if we are to believe a footnote of Pope's to the *Dunciad*, he would have dedicated it to Halifax, if the Tories had not meantime come into power. Bentley's nephew, following in his uncle's footsteps, offered yet another edition of the Latin poet to Lord Harley, the new minister's son.[53] John Philips addressed a Latin ode to Bolingbroke,[54] to whom also Gay dedicated *The Shepherd's Week*. Swift laid his *Tale of a Tub* at Somers' feet. Young offered his tragedy of *Busiris* to His Grace the Duke of Newcastle, Lord Chamberlain of His Majesty's household, etc., and his *Paraphrase* of a part of the Book of Job to Parker, the Lord Chancellor.[55] Cibber dedicated *She wou'd and She wou'd not* to the Duke of Ormond who had been commanding the English forces before Cadiz, *The Lady's Last Stake* to the Marquis of Kent, Lord Chamberlain to Her Majesty's household. Addison dedicated his *Remarks on Several Parts of Italy* to Somers, and his opera of *Rosamund* to the Duchess of Marlborough. The third volume of the *Tatler* was inscribed to the Lord Chancellor, Cowper, the fourth to Halifax ; the first volume of the *Guardian* to Lieutenant-General Cadogan, Marlborough's friend and second in command, the second to Pulteney, already a man of influence in the House of Commons. The first volume of

[52] Published in No. 12 of the *Tatler*.

[53] *The Dunciad*, II, line 205, note. The uncle's edition is inscribed to " Nobilissimo et Præstantissimo Viro Roberto Harleio, Baroni de Wigmore, Comiti Oxonii, et Comiti Mortimero, Magnæ Britanniæ Thesaurario " ; the nephew's to " Nobilissimo et Eruditissimo Juveni Edwardo Harleio, Baroni de Wigmore ".

[54] Ad Henricum S^t. John, Armig. 1706 (A. Chalmers, op. cit., VIII, p. 384).

[55] *A Paraphrase* On part of the *Book of Job*. To the Right Honourable Lord Parker, Baron of Macclesfield, Lord High Chancellor of Great-Britain, etc. etc. (A. Chalmers, op. cit., XIII, p. 408).—Johnson (*Lives* . . . Young) wittily remarks : " Parker, to whom it is dedicated, had not long, by means of the seals, been qualified for a patron . . . The Dedication, which was only suffered to appear in Tonson's edition . . . is addressed, in no common train of flattery, to a Chancellor, of whom he clearly appears to have had no kind of knowledge."

the *Spectator* was offered to Somers ; the second to Halifax ; the third to the Right Honourable Henry Boyle, principal Secretary of State ; the fourth to Marlborough ; the fifth to the Earl of Wharton, ex-Lord-Lieutenant of Ireland ; the sixth to the Earl of Sunderland, a former Minister and Marlborough's son-in-law ; the seventh to Methuen, English Ambassador at the Court of Savoy.[56]

These Dedications are unquestionably more dignified than those I have quoted earlier. The Author no longer prostrates himself before his patrons as if they were gods, since he has been rubbing shoulders with them, and no longer sees them merely from a distance, and they have lost for him that aura of religious awe which used to surround them amid the radiance of their inaccessible majesty. The patron has in fact resumed human proportions. You cannot, however, habitually indulge in flattery and compliments without forfeiting some fraction of your self-respect and occasionally lapsing into regrettable ex-aggeration as, for instance, when Addison and Congreve place Halifax on the same plane as Virgil and Homer [57] ; when

---

[56] By a kind of boomerang effect, highly-placed authors became in their turn the target for dedications and petitions. Young dedicated verses to Addison " Secretary to their Excellencies, the Lords Justices " (*On the Late Queen's Death*). See my Bibliography. Swift was courted by a number of his brother-authors (See *Journal to Stella*, especially Jan. 7 and 15, 1712–13).

[57] In *A Letter from Italy* Addison speaks to him of

" . . . lines like Virgil's or like yours."

Congreve writes :

" O had Your Genius been to Leisure born,
And not more bound to Aid us than Adorn !
Albion in Verse with antient *Greece* had vy'd,
And gain'd alone a Fame, which, there, seven States divide " . . .
(Dedication to Halifax of his *Miscellaneous Poems.*)

Compare the verses in which Pope caricatures Halifax as Bufo :

" Proud as *Apollo* on his forked hill,
Sate full-blown *Bufo*, puff'd by ev'ry quill ;
Fed with soft Dedication all day long,
Horace and he went hand in hand in song,
His library, where busts of Poets dead
And a true *Pindar* stood without a head,
Receiv'd of wits an undistinguish'd race,
Who first his judgment ask'd, and then a place :
Much they extoll'd his pictures, much his seat,
And flatter'd ev'ry day, and some days eat : " etc.
(*Epistle to Dr. Arbuthnot, being the Prologue to the Satires.* Warburton's *Pope*, IV, p. 9.)

Ambrose Philips addresses the Honourable Miss Carteret in her cradle [58] ; when Young fills his first verses and dedications with so much extravagant eulogy that he is later ashamed to include them amongst his works. [59]

In addition to this compulsory flattery, the humiliating practice continued of openly offering an author gifts of money. Tickell tells us that Halifax left " no dedicator unrewarded ". [60] When Colley Cibber presented his *Non-Juror* to George I, the King paid him £200. [61] Steele's *Conscious Lovers*, dedicated to the same monarch, earned for its author a purse of £500.

Apart from these drawbacks, the inevitable accompaniment of any form of dependence, and only a repetition of those we have commented on when the author was at the mercy of the Court, the compulsory liaison between literature and politics had its own peculiar inconveniences. In speaking of the *Tatler*, I said that in seeking to be both a political and literary journal it had failed to be either. We may apply the same remark to the writers of this period. They are neither politicians nor authors in the proper sense of either term. Politics and literature were alike the poorer.

Driven to take part in public affairs rather by circumstances than by natural inclination or special talent, the author was not infrequently the victim of the patron's miscalculation. If we are to take Pope's word for it, Prior had little understanding of government or administration. [62] Neither he nor Maynwaring ventured to open his mouth in Parliament. [63] Steele, whose supple and elegant style had tempted his friends to hope that he would prove at least a fluent speaker, made in fact a very poor showing in the House of Commons. Addison failed even

---

[58] See my Bibliography.

[59] For details of these prose and verse flatteries and their suppression, see Johnson's *Lives* . . . Young.

[60] Johnson's *Lives* . . . Halifax.

[61] Genest, II, p. 216.—Note that Cibber was a Whig and had taken up arms for the Revolution of 1688 (Boswell, II, p. 175, note). As its title indicates, the *Non-Juror* was a political work. Cibber was later appointed Poet Laureate and attributed his nomination to this comedy.

[62] Spence, p. 175. [Pope's judgment here is hardly to be relied on. Prior was, as a matter of fact, rather able. B. D.]

[63] " What *Qualities* must we therefore conceive requisite to form a *Publick Speaker* ? When we see such Men as the late Earl of *Orrery*, the late Earl of *Shaftesbury*, the late Mr. *Addison*, Mr. *Prior*, and Mr. *Maynwaring*, sit silent ; while —— and —— and —— and —— hold forth upon every Subject that falls under Debate ? " (Budgell, *Memoirs of the Life and Character of the late Earl of Orrery*, p. 208).

more lamentably. Filling a higher post than his friend, he himself felt how far his performance fell short of what was expected from a Secretary of State and begged leave to resign.[64]

On the other side, the competing interest of politics was unfortunate and harmful to literature. A distinguished contemporary historian [65] justly wrote :

It is, I think, a recognized truth, almost a harmless commonplace, that Liberty is the very soul of Literature. Let us, however, draw a distinction. In antiquity Liberty was a heroic figure who attuned man's soul to the sublime and whose spirit passed from civil life into his works of art and thought. The passions born of her were eloquent and poetic. Such is not the case with that other Liberty, wiser and more self-controlled, regulated and formalized, such as is recognized in one modern society based on constitutional monarchy, Liberty as we have seen her evolving in England since the Revolution of 1688.

This Liberty gives birth rather to vexatious frictions than to mighty battles, rather to intrigue than to passion. No doubt, in its ultimate repercussions and long-term results, this Liberty raises both the dignity of intelligence and the national well-being. But while she establishes and organizes herself, her machinery is too complex and cumbersome not to overwhelm public attention with a thousand details and rob the soul of that creative impulse and undisturbed independence which foster great gifts in literature and art. The mechanism of a constitutional government, if we may use the phrase, makes too great a demand on the mind to be favourable to genius. It fails to provide either the grandeur or the passion of republican liberty or the leisure offered by a peaceful and glorious monarchy.

---

[64] There is a yarn that in 1706 when the Act of Union was being debated in the House, Addison rose to speak and addressing the Speaker began : " Mr. Speaker, I conceive . . . " and stopped short. A second and a third time he started, but could never get beyond the words : " Mr. Speaker, I conceive . . . " Hereupon another Member is reputed to have said : " Mr. Speaker, I regret to note that the honourable member has thrice conceived and brought forth nothing." There is also a story that when it was his business to announce Queen Anne's death to the Elector of Hanover who was to become George I, Addison was so preoccupied with phrase and style that the drafting of the official letter had to be handed over to a clerk who finished it in a few minutes. Both these anecdotes would appear to have been concocted after the event, but, exaggerated though they may be, they are certainly expressing the essential truth.

[" Mr. Addison could not give out a common order in writing, from his endeavouring always to word it too finely."—so Pope in Spence, ed. cit., p. 175. This remark is corroborated in a footnote, but Pope's hearsay evidence in these matters is not to be trusted : we certainly need not take his word that Prior understood little of government or administration, and facts would seem to contradict this. It might be added here that a good writer is not necessarily a good speaker. Gibbon could not speak in Parliament. B. D.]

[65] Villemain, *Tableau de la littérature au XVIII siecle*, 6ᵉ leçon.

From this point of view the parliamentary government of 1688, highly favourable to gifted men of letters whose fortunes it improved, whose influence it created, seems to have been less propitious to the progress of literature.

The demands of parliamentary government, then, absorbed the greater part of a writer's intellectual energy, threw him with no hope of escape into the fever of election contests and political meetings, into pamphlet and newspaper controversy, and thus encumbered literature with a mass of ephemeral work, extravagant political poems, panegyrics, topical and occasional verse, whose futility and banality was patent, most of all to their authors, and whose life was inevitably short. Such political writing or controversial work as allowed its author to put his mark on it might pass muster and survive its maker, if he had been fortunate enough to stumble on some happy stroke of satire or some inspiring subject transcending the petty issues of every day.[66] But are we not entitled to grieve over the time squandered on official duties, the days spent in finding and filing papers, in running offices and appending signatures, and to mourn for the more enduring works of which these occupations have robbed us ? People grieved even at the time : " As for *Comedies*, ther's not great Expectation of any thing of that kind, since Mr. *Farquhar's* Death. The two Gentlemen, who would probably always succeed in the *comick* vein, Mr. *Congreve* and Captain *Steele* having Affairs of much greater Importance to take up their Time and Thoughts."[67] Consider what were the " Affairs of much greater Importance " which in 1707 were taking up the time and thought of Steele and Congreve. Steele was editing the *London Gazette*, Congreve was issuing licences for the plying of hackney coaches and the sale of wines. That is to say, both were doing work which an honest civil service clerk could have done at least as well as they. But what civil

[66] See Swift's witty attack on Marlborough in the *Examiner*, quoted by Villemain in his 6th lesson.

[Nevertheless, it was politics which brought out Swift's best writing, *The Dissensions in Athens and Rome*, the *Tale of a Tub*, *The Conduct of the Allies*, *The Public Spirit of the Whigs*, *The Last Four Years of Queen Anne's Reign* and the *Drapier Letters*. Moreover, *Gulliver's Travels* is largely political. It is likely that but for politics he would not have written at all, except for admirable light verse. B. D.]

[67] *The Muses Mercury*, Sept. 1707, *Of the new Opera's and Plays preparing for the Theatres*. See my Bibliography, s.v. Muses Mercury.

[This is probably true of Steele : but Congreve was not busy, other reasons operated there. B. D.]

service clerk could fill their vacant place in literature ? How many similar cases awake our regret ! Is it not grievous to see Swift harness himself to the party waggon and " toil like a horse " as he phrases it himself,[68] in the daily controversies of Harley and Bolingbroke, leaving a gap of fourteen years [68a] between the *Tale of a Tub* and *Gulliver's Travels* ? Is it not grievous to find amongst Addison's collected works almost a whole volume devoted to administrative scribblings which are rightly reprinted out of respect for his memory, but which usurp the place of unwritten work that would have been worthier of posterity ? We know, moreover, that if Addison's party had remained in power, it is more than probable that we should have forgone the writings that are his glory. We remember that he was in Ireland as Secretary to the Lord-Lieutenant when Steele in London began the publication of the *Tatler*. Even from Ireland Addison came to his friend's assistance, but it was not until the fall of the Whig Ministry relieved him of his official duties, that he was able actively to collaborate on the paper and make his influence felt in it.[69] So we owe the *Spectator* to the enforced leisure thrust on him by the triumph of the Tories. When Queen Anne died, and the Whigs resumed control of the government, Addison gave up working on the English Dictionary he had begun. His last return to politics similarly cost us the tragedy of *Socrates* which he had been planning and left his *Evidences of the Christian Religion* incomplete.

Writers themselves were well aware how ill literature consorted with administration and public business. Prior jestingly complains that " he hates his Commission of the Customs, because it spoils his wit. He says he dreams of nothing but cockets, and dockets, and drawbacks, and other jargon, words of the Custom House." [70] Addison wrote to Swift that " Multiplicity of Businesse and a long dangerous fit of sicknesse have prevented me from answering the obliging letter you honoured me with some time since, but God be thanked I can not make use of either of these Excuses at present being entirely free both of my office and my Asthma." It was Addison also who wrote to Pope advising him " not to content your self with one half

[68] " I toil like a horse, and have hundreds of letters still to read : and squeeze a line out of each, or at least the seeds of a line . . . I have about thirty pages more to write (that is to be extracted) which will be sixty in print." (*Journal to Stella*, Oct. 28, 1712.)   [68a] [Twenty-four. B. D.]
[69] See above, chap. III, note No. 174.
[70] Swift, *Journal to Stella*, March 13, 1711–12.

of the Nation for your Admirers when you might command them all ", and added that " I think you are very happy that you are out of the Fray ". [70a]

But the most serious drawback of the author's position has not yet been mentioned. He was not given his due recognition, he was not appreciated at his true value. " Literature for its own sake had not yet acquired its true place in society." [71] People in those days took no heed of literature as such, but valued only the practical use to which it could be turned. The respect accorded to it was conditioned by circumstance and paid, not to its intrinsic merit, but to its accidental value. It is certain, for instance, that Addison—to quote no other case— owed his success less to his literary gifts than to the first use he made of them, [72] and if he had not been Secretary of State it is unlikely that the Countess of Warwick would have married him. [72a] In short, the writer figured in society not in virtue of being a writer, but as an official and a politician. He was thus himself tempted to consider literature as a means to an end. He devoted himself to his profession, not for its own sake, but for the material advantage it might bring. Swift held his literary reputation cheap, signed none of his works with his name, [73] never thought of publishing a complete edition of them

[70a] [Letter to Swift, March 26, 1717–18, and letter to Pope, November 2, 1713. See Letters of Joseph Addison, ed. Walter Graham, 1941, pp. 692 and 44. B. D.]

[71] Villemain, 5th Lesson. Villemain is speaking of the reign of Charles II, but his comment is no less applicable to the reign of Queen Anne.

[72] " Addison and his Advancement hardly need be mentioned, the Instance is so notorious ; but every body may not so readily recollect that his party-Services contributed more to it than all his laudable Efforts to refine our Manners and perfect our Taste." (Ralph, The Case of Authors by Profession, p. 34.)

[72a] [Lady Warwick married Addison before he became Secretary of State. B.D.]

[73] The one exception in his letter to Oxford A Proposal for Correcting, Improving, and Ascertaining, the English Tongue. " My letter to Lord Treasurer, about the English tongue, is now printing ; and I suffer my name to be put at the end of it, which I never did before in my life." [Journal to Stella, May 10, 1712.)

[This refusal to sign works was hardly indifference. It was possibly because of fear of political pursuit (e.g. A Tale of a Tub) and partly to a sort of pride. He knew that everyone that mattered would be aware of his author-ship, so why expose his name, especially as he was a parson, to the rabble ? Anonymity was by no means singular in those days, even with those who were the most eager for literary fame. Addison loved to write behind a veil, as Gay said (e.g. the Tatlers and Spectators, and The Drummer) and Pope himself often practised it (e.g. The Dunciad). B. D.]

and quite obviously used his gift of writing as a springboard to a bishopric : which he never attained. Even those possessed of means enough to need no man's patronage, and free to put all their ambition into writing worthy of being valued by posterity, men like Rowe and Parnell,[74] had not enough pride to stay at home in lonely independence soliciting no favours. Parnell even stooped to a recantation to win the smiles of men in power. Neither they nor their brother-authors had yet achieved that detachment from outward success that makes a man find honour and satisfaction in his work alone, and concentrate his whole ambition on satisfying himself and his readers, becoming, in a word, a man of letters, living by literature and for literature alone. One even went so far as to affect to despise the work that is now his glory. When Voltaire visited England, eager to see everything, people and places, and to mix in English society, he went to call on Congreve. The young and enthusiastic Frenchman naturally spoke of the dramatist's plays ; but Congreve dismissed these as trifles beneath his dignity, and begged his visitor to see in him nothing but a gentleman who lived very contentedly. " Sir," replied Voltaire, who for his part was a man of letters, " if you had the misfortune to be only a gentleman like any other, I should never have come to see you." [75]

The shadows in the picture are finally darkened by uncertainty and disappointment. The man who relies on the favour of a patron, be he who he may, is building on sand ; and no sand is more shifting than the soil of politics. Many discovered this to their sorrow. Addison's friend Budgell, whose

[74] See above, chap. III, note No. 44.—Apart from his ecclesiastical income Parnell had private means.

[75] *Voltaire, Lettres philosophiques,* Letter XIX, Garnier's edition, XXII, p. 161.—A few years later the English author's attitude was different. In recording this interview Johnson sternly says that Congreve had " treated the Muses with ingratitude " and had displayed a " despicable foppery in desiring to be considered not as an author but a gentleman " (*Lives* . . . Congreve).

[It is time this silly story was scotched ; it will, alas ! never be killed. Voltaire, anxious to meet great authors, visited Congreve some twenty years after *The Way of the World* had been written, and wanted to discuss it with Congreve. Heavens, what a boring prospect for Congreve ! What he said in effect was that he would be delighted to talk generally with Voltaire, as an amateur of letters if you will, but not as an expert. One is inclined to agree with Lamb that " the impertinent Frenchman was properly answered ". For a fuller discussion, see my preface to Vol. II of Congreve's *Works* in the World's Classics Edition, reprinted in *Variety of Ways.* B. D.]

tragic end I have already related, lost the posts he had held
in Ireland because of an untoward attack on the Lord-Lieutenant, and forfeited all hope of office by asserting his independence in criticism of a Government bill. This was the
beginning of his downfall. Opposition to the same bill cost
Steele his directorship of Drury Lane theatre. Like Addison,
he had lost his other posts when Harley and Bolingbroke came
to power. Gay, who had banked on the Tory party, lost his
post as secretary and all chance of serious promotion on the
death of Queen Anne. On the accession of George I, Prior was
accused of treason and imprisoned, forfeiting all his handsome
salaries and retaining only his meagre income as a Cambridge
fellow. Swift, who had hoped by means of politics to win a
bishopric, kept an ever-watchful eye on the health of ailing
prelates,[76] addressed himself first to the Whigs and then transferred his allegiance to the Tories, wearily discharging the
crushing labour of their controversies,[77] haughtily rejecting
their gifts of money, because he hoped for other things at their
hand.[78] Swift, flattered, pampered, consulted, influential—a

[76] In June, 1710, he writes to Halifax : " Pray, my lord, desire Dr.
South " (now on the verge of eighty) " to die about the fall of the leaf, for
he has a prebend of Westminster which will make me your neighbour, and
a sinecure in the country, both in the Queen's gift, which my friends have
often told me would suit me extremely." In November of the same year
he again writes to Halifax " that 'if the gentle winter should not carry off
Dr. South ', perhaps Lord Halifax might so use his credit, that, as Lord
Somers thought of him last year for the bishopric of Waterford so my Lord
President might now think of him for that of Cork if the incumbent died
of the fever he was under ". (Forster, *Life of Jonathan Swift*, pp. 259–61.)
    So much for the Whigs. Now for the Tories : " We hear your Bishop
Hickman is dead ; but nobody here will do anything for me in Ireland,
so they may die as fast or slow as they please." (*Journal to Stella*, May 29,
1711.) " Did the Bishop of London die in Wexford ? poor gentleman ! "
(Ibid., Aug. 24, 1711.) " The Bishop of Gloucester is not dead, and I am
as likely to succeed the Duke of Marlborough as him if he were." (Ibid.,
Feb. 8, 1711–12.) " The Bishop of Dromore . . . has been very near
dying." (Ibid., Jan. 9, 1712–13.)
    [77] See *Journal to Stella*, especially Aug. 25, Nov. 15, 1711 ; July 18,
1712 ; Jan. 1, 1712–13.
    [78] See *Journal to Stella*, Feb. 6, 13 and 16 and March 7, 1710–11.—This
refusal of money is often quoted as an example of lofty disinterestedness.
But Prévost-Paradol shrewdly divined the underlying motive : " Swift ", he
says, " indignantly rejected so unworthy a reward for his services. Humbly
to accept payment from the Ministry would have been to renounce the
hope of a more useful and permanent recognition of his share in its victory.
Swift wanted a bishopric." (*Étude sur Jonathan Swift*, p. 40.)
    [Towards 1714, perhaps earlier, he hankered after a Deanery rather
than a Bishopric—but he wanted it in England. Addison behaved in

small-scale minister in fact—securing posts for his friends but
nothing for himself,[79] not even succeeding in getting audience
of the Queen,[80] let alone a nomination to his coveted bishopric,
ended by becoming only Dean of St. Patrick's in Dublin, and
going over to bury in Ireland his thwarted ambition and his
savage bitterness against others and against himself.

II

*Walpole at the Head of Affairs (1721-42).—Cessation of political patronage
just at the moment when the private patronage of the Great has ceased.—The
writer's trials : Steele, Ambrose Philips, Savage, Dennis, Boyse, Johnson, etc.*

The advent to power of a new Ministry soon showed how
unstable were the foundations of an author's good fortune.

In 1721 Walpole became head of the Government.[81] With
him the patronage extended by statesmen to anyone who could
write, came abruptly to an end.

The motives underlying this new attitude seem to have
been varied and complex. Neither George I nor George II
was the stuff of which an Augustus is made. George I, a stranger
in his own kingdom, was so completely ignorant of English
that Walpole, who did not know a word of German, had to
converse with him in dog Latin. George II made no effort to
conceal his complete contempt for " bainting " and " boetry "
as he called them.[82] Walpole felt no more warmly towards

---

exactly the same way as Swift did in rejecting pecuniary reward when he
hoped for a Secretaryship of State ; see his letter to Halifax of November 30,
1714 (Graham, p. 306). B. D.]

[79] *Journal to Stella*, March 17, 1711–12.

[80] Ibid., Feb. 9, 1710–11.

[81] On Walpole see Coxe, *Memoirs of the Life and Administration of Sir
Robert Walpole* ; Lecky, I ; Lord Mahon, *History of England from the Peace
of Utrecht . . .* ; Macaulay, *Essays, Walpole's Letters to Sir Horace Mann* ;
Walpole (Horace) *Reminiscences.*

[82]   " Alas ! few verses touch their nicer ear ;
               They scarce can bear their *Laureate* twice a year ;
               And justly Caesar scorns the Poet's lays,
               It is to *History* he trusts for Praise."
         (*Satire I. To Mr. Fortescue.* Warburton's *Pope*, IV, p. 57.)

See also Clerk, *The Works of William Hogarth*, I, p. 181 ; and Lord Hervey,
Memoirs, I, chap. XIV and II, chap. XXI.—It is true that Queen Caroline,
wife of George II, showed an interest in writers, but whatever her influence
and intelligence, she could not fill the place left vacant by the King and his
chief Minister.

such matters than did his sovereigns and masters. He was himself indifferently educated and thoroughly unsentimental. Possibly he perceived that political patronage was an artificial system and if continued would give rise to embarrassment. The number of aspiring authors would perpetually increase with the encouragement offered, and the number of jobs available for them would not rise proportionately. Besides, in making a friend of one, you made an enemy of another, and, since spite and malice are emotions more enduring than gratitude, what is precariously gained on one side is lost for certain on the other. Walpole had not failed to notice that no Minister had been more savagely attacked by authors than Halifax, the great patron of men of letters.[83] He decided to ignore the lot, rather than hurt the feelings of one. It is possible that he saw yet another unpleasant result of political patronage : the ambition to achieve distinction, the desire to repay favours received and qualify for greater favour, tempted an author to write and write, and willy nilly to prolong and exacerbate political controversy. This passion for polemics could make little appeal to Walpole, whose maxim of government was *quieta non movere*. Perhaps while constitutional government in England was evolving amid the throes of complex struggle, political controversy had been inevitable and necessary. But once the Hanoverian succession had been accepted, the first difficult phases of its establishment were over; and now the Whig Minister's primary aim was to create an atmosphere of greater calm and stability in public affairs and in the mind of the people. Nor could Walpole overlook the fact that many of the authors who had recently taken a hand in public affairs had been either very ineffective allies—like Addison as Secretary of State, like Prior and Maynwaring in the House of Commons—or even very embarrassing ones, subject to fits of over-independence like Steele and Budgell. He was fond of saying that writers were ill-adapted to practical life, they tended to trust theory rather than experience and were guided by principles invalid in everyday affairs. And in Queen Anne's reign, when he was already a member of the Government but not yet its chief, he was reluctant to endorse Congreve's appointment as Commissioner of Customs, opining that he would prove to have " no head for business ". So when he himself became head of the Government he preferred to choose as collaborators men who were administrators pure and

[83] Macaulay, *History*, chap. XXIV.

simple. If he then needed press-support for his measures, he either did his own writing [84] or entrusted it to hack scribblers whom he crudely hired—men like Concanen, Arnall, Welsted or Henley—who had too little brain to possess opinions of their own, or be tempted to differ from the views of the employer from whom they drew their pay.[85] The main reason, however, which dictated his procedure, was undoubtedly his conviction that the House of Commons was daily growing in power, and was becoming more and more the centre of Government. Walpole was a man of positive and practical views, who possessed great parliamentary gifts. He devoted his entire attention and activity to Parliament [86]; and the result proved how sound his judgment was. Never was Minister pursued with more unrelenting violence or by more distinguished and dangerous opponents; never before had a Minister accorded such freedom of speech to his enemies,[87] and yet despite the freedom and fury of their attacks, despite the strength of an opposition in which were ranged men like Bolingbroke, Carteret, Chesterfield, Pulteney, Wyndham, Pitt, Lyttelton, Swift, Gay, Pope, Fielding, Thomson, Glover—Walpole governed England for more than twenty consecutive years.

[84] I have already mentioned his political writings, chap. IV, note No. 33.
[85] Walpole paid more than £50,000 in the course of ten years to writers supporting his administration (Lecky, I, p. 372). Arnall boasted of having made £10,997 6s. 8d. in four years by his political writing (Scott's Edition of Swift, vol. XII, pp. 103-4).—

> " A pamphlet in Sir Bob's defence
> Will never fail to bring in pence :
> Nor be concerned about the sale,
> He pays his workmen on the nail."
>   (Swift, *On Poetry : A Rhapsody*, 1733. Ibid., XIV, p. 334.)

On Walpole's hireling writers, see also Pope's *Dunciad*, especially II, lines 305–14.
[86] When it was learnt in England that Louis XV had pensioned Crébillon, the following epigram (which I find quoted in Belsham, II, p. 54) became current :

> " At reading this, great Walpole shook his head ;
> How ! wit and genius help a man to bread ;
> With better skill we pension and promote ;
> None eat with us who cannot give a vote."

Swift called Walpole : " Bob, the poet's foe." (*An Epistle to Mr. Gay*, 1731.)
[87] In one of his speeches Walpole remarked that no Government had prosecuted so few pamphleteers and no Government had ever had provocation to prosecute so many.

Whatever were the motives which actuated the new Minister's conduct, the patronage hitherto so extravagantly extended to authors ceased completely. Suddenly they found themselves hurled from their heights of prosperity and success. Everything combined to make the fall a cruel one : it was unforeseen and carried no compensation. But yesterday, Whigs and Tories had alike been the author's patrons. To-day, Tories and Whigs alike failed him. The Whigs, represented by Walpole, offered nothing, and Walpole remained omnipotent Minister from 1721 to 1742. The prolongation of his reign rendered the Tories for their part impotent. Having neither pensions nor posts at their command, the most they could offer was a meagre diet of unfulfilled promises. " St. James's would give nothing ; Leicester House had nothing to give." [88] When he lost the patronage of the politicians, the unfortunate author did not regain the patronage of the aristocracy. The nobleman's importance had yielded to that of the politician and his tradition of literary patronage had been broken.

So there was our author, abruptly planted down to face the facts of existence, thrown back wholly on his own strength and his own resources. His only hope was to get down to business and write for the publishers. But the publishing business was still in its infancy, undeveloped, only half awake, and with but little capital behind it. To make matters worse, the number of authors had been much swollen by reason of the alluring prospects opened to professional literature in the two preceding reigns. The whole crowd of needy and disillusioned writers competed for booksellers' contracts, besieged reviews and magazines with offers of service, and thus put themselves at the publishers' mercy. The publisher naturally took advantage of the position to sweat and exploit the whole scribbling pack. The work he demanded of his victim was often peculiarly laborious and sometimes very odd.

In one of his earliest plays [89] Fielding shows us three luckless devils, Dash, Blotpage and Quibble, whom a publisher lodges in his house and compels to write the livelong day on a starvation

---

[88] Macaulay's *Essays*, Samuel Johnson.—After breaking with his father George II in 1737, the Prince of Wales, in a spirit of opposition set himself up in his little court as a patron of literature. But his means were limited and his protégés but few : I can think of no more than three : Lyttelton, Mallet and Thomson.—Thomson enjoyed £100 a year, Mallet £200, and Lyttelton, who was his secretary probably a little more.

[89] *The Author's Farce* (1730).

diet of " good milk porridge, very often twice a day, which is good wholesome food and proper for students ". Here are some scraps of their instructive conversation :

Dash : Pox on 't, I'm as dull as an ox, tho' I have not a bit of one within me. I have not dined these two days, and yet my head is as heavy as any alderman's or lord's. I carry about me symbols of all the elements ; my head is as heavy as water, my pockets are as light as air, my appetite is as hot as fire, and my coat is as dirty as earth.

Blot : Lend me your Bysshe (i.e. a rhyming dictionary), Mr. Dash, I want a rhime for wind.

Dash : Why there's blind, and kind, and behind, and find, and mind : it is of the easiest termination imaginable ; I have had it four times in a page.

Blot : None of those words will do.

Dash : Why then you may use any that end in ond, or and, or end. I am never so exact : if the two last letters are alike, it will do very well. Read the verse.

Blot : " Inconstant as the seas, or as the wind."

Dash : What would you express in the next line ?

Blot : Nay, that I don't know, for the sense is out already. I would say something about inconstancy.

Dash : I can lend you a verse and it will do very well too.

" Inconstancy will never have an end "

End rhimes very well with wind.

Blot : It will do well enough for the middle of a poem.

Dash : Ay, Ay, anything will do well enough for the middle of a poem. If you can but get twenty good lines to place at the beginning for a taste, it will sell very well.

Quib : So that, according to you, Mr. Dash, a poet acts pretty much on the same principles with an oister-woman.

Dash : Pox take your simile, it has set my chaps a watering.

At this point the publisher arrives on the scene, scolds them all and complains of their sloth. One ought by now to have finished the answer to a letter which was in fact of his own composition. He points out that it is " harder to write on this side the question, because it is the wrong side ". To which his employer retorts : " Not a jot. So far on the contrary that I have known some authors choose it as the properest to show their genius." Another has to finish an account of a murder and is just adding a few moral reflexions as preface to it. Then there is a ghost which must be finished. The last was a pale one, " then let this be a bloody one ". Next, a prospectus for *Bailey's English Dictionary*, but this should not be a lengthy job for it will suffice to copy the proposals for printing *Bayle's Dictionary* —" The same words will do for both." Someone's obituary is also on the stocks, but it seems that the fellow is not dead, so that must be held up pending better news.

Some allowance must of course be made for dramatic exaggeration ; but the accuracy of the main lines of Fielding's picture is established by other contemporary evidence.

Cave, the owner of the *Gentleman's Magazine*, used to buy Boyse's verses at so much a hundred. After some time, gambling on the poet's poverty, he would insist for good measure on having " a long hundred ", that is to say ten or twenty extra lines for nothing.[90] Smollett tells of an author of twenty-four living in an attic who wrote, at a guinea a sheet, historical works which another man published under his own name.[91] In *Joseph Andrews* Mr. Wilson is represented as spending several years in translating for a bookseller, exercising no part of his body but his right arm. The result was illness and disability, and his employer denounced him to his colleagues as a lazy-bones.[92] The hack translators, whom the bookseller Curll kept permanently employed, used to work without remission and to sleep three in a bed.[93] Payment was always precarious. Most writers were reduced to living in misery from day to day, in everlasting anxiety about the morrow, at the mercy of moneylenders to whom they had to pledge their wages, in perpetual dread of the bailiff and the gaol. The chronicle of literature became a collection of strange adventures which far exceed anything to be found in what the French call Bohemia.

Steele, Savage and Ambrose Philips were strolling together in London one evening. A kindly merchant, apologizing for the liberty he was taking, warned them that he had noticed some suspicious characters at the end of the street, who looked uncommonly like bailiffs. If any of them was afraid of bailiffs, he suggested their altering their course. The three asked no questions but made off as fast as they could, without even waiting to thank their benefactor.[94]

[90] Lawrence, *Life of Fielding*, pp. 125–8. See also Boyse's Life in the collection known as *The British Poets* (see my Bibliography, s.v. Boyse) ; and Boswell, VIII, pp. 410–11 ; IX, p. 46 ; X, pp. 63–4.—Boyse was the son of a Nonconformist minister in Dublin. He wrote a poem called *The Deity* which Fielding paid him the compliment of quoting in *Tom Jones* (book VII, chap. I).

[91] *Humphrey Clinker*. This novel came out in 1771, but Smollett began his literary career in 1739.

[92] Fielding : *Joseph Andrews*, book III, chap. III.

[93] Amory, *The Life of John Buncle*, II, pp. 381 ff.

[94] N. Drake, *Essays . . . Illustrative of the Tatler*, etc., I, p. 180.

It was Steele too who once requested Savage to call for him at his house at an early hour. Savage was punctual and found Steele already awaiting him and a carriage at the door. They drove off together and the carriage stopped at a small tavern where the two authors closeted themselves in a private room. Savage was not a little mystified by all this curious procedure, and Steele explained that he wanted to publish a pamphlet and had asked Savage to come and act as his amanuensis. They set to work, Steele dictating and Savage writing until dinner was served. Savage was surprised at the meanness of the entertainment and ventured to ask for wine, which Steele ordered with some reluctance. When dinner was over, they set to work again and completed their task in the course of the afternoon. Savage supposed their work was now done, and expected that his host would call for the bill and set his guest free. But Steele now confessed that he had no money and that he must get his manuscript sold before he could pay for the dinner. So Savage was obliged to scour the booksellers and sell his friend's prose, for which after a good deal of trouble he secured two guineas. Steele had left home solely to evade his creditors and had written his pamphlet to pay for his meal.[95]

Dennis took endless pains to keep clear of the duns and creditors who were a perpetual threat to him, but he imprudently relaxed his precautions one Saturday evening in a wine shop. For two long hours he stayed, not daring to make a movement or to say a word lest he should attract attention to himself, and doing his best to remain concealed. Midnight struck at last and the author rose triumphantly to his feet crying : " Now Sir, bailiff or no, I snap my fingers at you ; you have no hold on me." His distress finally became so acute that his fellow-authors organized a benefit performance for him at the theatre.[96] Of Savage, Johnson writes :

During a considerable part of the time in which he was employed upon this performance (i.e. writing his tragedy of Sir Thomas Overbury), he was without lodging, and often without meat ; nor had he any other conveniences for study than the fields or the street allowed him ; there he used to walk and form his speeches, and afterwards

---

[95] Johnson, *Lives* . . . Savage.—I know of course that Steele was never at any time a model of prudence or economy. But up to the period we are now discussing, his posts had enabled him to avoid any distressing situations. Unemployed, bankrupt and abandoned by his party, he died in poverty and oblivion in 1729.

[96] *Biographia Dramatica*, s.v. Dennis (John).

step into a shop, beg for a few moments the use of pen and ink, and write down what he had composed, upon paper which he had picked up by accident.[97]

He kept alive in the most miserable fashion on sums of money which his poverty or his importunity extorted from one person or another, from actors or fellow-writers, from Lord Tyrconnel, from Walpole, from Queen Caroline. When such succour failed him, he lived from hand to mouth, eating when his friends invited him to share a meal—which the shabbiness of his clothes often prevented their doing—sleeping where he could, in a basement lodging, in a noisome cellar, amongst the dregs of the population. Often he was too poor to afford the luxury of such quarters, and walked the streets of London till fatigue overcame him, and he slept in summer on a bulk in the open air, in winter with thieves and beggars among the warm ashes of a glass-house. He was ultimately arrested and imprisoned at the instance of his creditors —his sole fortune at the time was threepence-halfpenny. He died in prison and had to be buried at the generous keeper's expense.[98]

Boyse would spend whole days in bed for lack of outdoor clothes, when his coat, his shirt and even his sheets were at the pawnbroker's. He used to wrap himself in his blanket, in which he had made a hole so that he could put his arm out to write on his knee. At other times, when important items of his wardrobe were in pawn, he would replace his vanished shirt with paper collar and cuffs, and disguise his lack of breeches by carefully buttoning down his coat. He was often without food for days at a time, witness the following letter and Latin verses which he addressed to his publisher from a sponging-house :

I am every moment threatened to be turned out here, because I have not money to pay for my bed two nights past, which is usually paid beforehand . . . I hope therefore you will have the humanity to send me half a guinea for support, till I finish your papers in my hands. . . . I humbly entreat your answer, having not tasted anything since Tuesday evening I came here, and my coat will be taken off my back for the charge of the bed, so that I must go into prison naked, which is too shocking for me to think of.

> Hodie, teste cælo summo,
> Sine pane, sine nummo,
> Sorte positus infeste,
> Scribo tibi dolens mæste.

---

[97] Johnson, *Lives* . . . Savage.
[98] Ibid.; and Boswell, I, p. 187 ; X, p. 122.

Fame, bile, tumet jecur :
Urbane,[99] mitte opem, precor ;
Tibi enim cor humanum
Non a malis alienum :
Mihi mens nec male grata,
Pro a te favore dato.

Ex gehenna debitoria.
Vulgo, domo spongiatoria.

In the early days of his literary life, Samuel Johnson himself sometimes spent the night wandering through the streets of London for lack of a lodging, and at times went fasting for forty-eight hours on end. At such times he avoided passing near Porridge Lane, for the delicious odours of the cook-shops were intolerably tantalizing to an empty stomach.[100] When he ate, he spent fourpence-halfpenny a day on food. If he was able to allow himself a feast he " dined very well for eightpence with very good company . . . It used to cost the rest a shilling, for they drank wine ; but I had a cut of meat for sixpence, and bread for a penny, and gave the waiter a penny ; so that I was quite well served, nay better than the rest, for they gave the waiter nothing." [101]

Of the authors whom Smollett presents in *Humphrey Clinker*, some have no known domicile, the others go to prison. They eat in nauseating cookhouses, sleep under the stars on a bench, or under a church porch with ladies of the gutter. Their publisher brings them together round his table on a Sunday, the only day when the bailiff has no hold over them. The profession of literature, which a few short years before led a man so easily to prosperity and social position, if not to wealth and honour,

[99] In his Diary Cave called himself " Mr. Urban ".

[100] Mrs. Thrale said to a friend one day, in front of Johnson, that she did not like roast goose, because it smells so when roasting. " But you, Madam," replies the Doctor, " have been at all times a fortunate woman, having always had your hunger so forestalled by indulgence, that you never experienced the delight of smelling your dinner beforehand." " Which pleasure," answered I pertly, " is to be enjoyed in perfection by such as have the happiness to pass through Porridge Island of a morning."——" Come, come," says he gravely, " Let's have no sneering at what is serious to so many : hundreds of your fellow-creatures, dear lady, turn another way, that they may not be tempted by the luxuries of Porridge Island to wish for gratifications they are not able to obtain : you are certainly not better than all of *them* ; give God thanks that you are happier." Mrs. Piozzi, quoted by Boswell, IX, p. 40.—" Porridge Island was a mean street in London, filled with cook-shops for the poorer inhabitants " (Croker's footnote).

[101] See Boswell, *passim*, especially I, pp. 112–14, 151, 187 ; V, pp. 8–9 ; IX, pp. 40 and 235.

now offered nothing but a dreary prospect of struggle, privation and disappointed hope. Under Queen Anne, an author was a gentleman, fashionably dressed, living a regular and reputable life, provided with a fixed income, cutting a figure in the drawing-room, playing a rôle in the state. Now he was a wretched outcast, tattered, dirty and starving,[102] living how or where no one knew. There was practically no distinction between author and beggar. As a natural consequence the writer's trade fell cruelly in public estimation. It seemed a compendium of human misery, one of the most cheerless careers on which a man could embark. When Johnson first arrived in London " Mr. Wilcox, the bookseller, on being informed by him that his intention was to get his livelihood as an author, eyed his robust frame attentively, and with a significant look said, ' You had better buy a porter's knot.' " [103]   Pope writes :

> One Cell there is, conceal'd from vulgar eye,
> The Cave of Poverty and Poetry.[104]

Another contemporary wrote :

Hath Literature been thy choice and thy occupation and hast thou food and raiment ? be contented, be thankful, be amazed at thy good fortune—Art thou dissatisfied and desirous of other things, go and make 12 votes at an Election—It shall do thee more service, than to make a Commentary on the 12 Minor Prophets.[105]

Johnson applied Virgil's lines to the literary profession :

> Vestibulum ante ipsum, primisque in faucibus Orci
> Luctus et ultrices posuere cubilia Curæ ;
> Pallentesque habitant Morbi, tristisque Senectus,
> Et Metus, et malesuada Fames et turpis Egestas,
> Terribiles visu formæ ; Lethumque Laborque.[106]

Finally Hogarth, the painter, in a famous picture [107] showed a poet living in a miserable hovel wrapped in a dressing-gown as he worked, while his wife was mending his only pair of breeches, and interrupted in his work by the demands of a creditor.

The distressing element in such a disorganized life, especially when it overtakes a whole class of people, is, not so much the suffering it inflicts, as the consequences it entails. In the first

[102] See Pope's letter to Burlington and his amusing account of how the bookseller Lintot calmed an irate critic by offering to share his modest dinner with him. Warburton's Edition of *Pope*, VII, p. 336.

[103] Boswell, I, p. 112 note.

[104] *Dunciad*, I, lines 33–4. See ibid., II, lines 419–28.

[105] Jortin, quoted by Genest, I, p. 416.

[106] Boswell, V, p. 43.

[107] *The Distressed Poet*, which dates from 1736.

place, once a man has been divorced from the routine of well-regulated living, he is almost incapable of reconciling himself to it again, unless he has unusual energy or unusual luck. Bitter as is the first experience of uneasy and ill-ordered life, he quickly becomes accustomed to it ; he grows less fastidious ; privation, humiliation even, become less painful ; he resigns himself to them and at last ceases to notice them. Carelessness and improvidence become principles of conduct, and happy-go-lucky irregularity a habit and a tradition. Whatever may be the trials and the uncertainties of an existence unfettered by rule, they are often accompanied by a feeling of independence which is not without a certain charm, and which a man may ultimately learn to prize. We have seen the same thing in France where Bohemian life has found affectionate chroniclers, who even sing its praises.

Boyse's friends, scarcely less poor than he, once clubbed together to redeem his clothes from the pawnbroker (Johnson later says that the sum was made up of sixpenny pieces " at a time when sixpence meant a great deal to me ") only to find him pawning them again two days later. Another time, when he was almost dying of hunger, they gave him money to buy himself a dinner ; but he could not enjoy his meat without kitchen, and he spent half a guinea on mushrooms and truffles which he enjoyed in bed, since he had not at the moment a shirt to his back. Nothing could wean Savage from his irregular life. One day when the Goddess of Wealth smiled on him, he hastened off to buy himself a gold-embroidered cloak in which he proudly masqueraded, though his bare feet were peeping through the holes in his shoes. Lord Tyrconnel took him to live with him and gave him an annual allowance of £200 to boot. Savage turned his host's house into a tavern, acted as if he were the master of his lodging, feasted boisterously with chance acquaintances, wallowing with them in punch and wine, singing and loudly making merry till sunrise, until at last he was naturally shown the door. At another time Queen Caroline granted him a pension of £50 a year, enough in those days to supply him with daily bread. But each time the money was paid, Savage disappeared for two entire months, without telling his friends where he was going, and as soon as the windfall was exhausted he returned penniless to his beloved hand-to-mouth existence. Towards the end of his life, some brother-authors combined to subscribe a considerable sum, sufficient to provide a regular and peaceful existence for him, on condition that he would leave London and settle down quietly by the seaside. Savage set out, but stopped halfway and resumed his usual disorderly way of life in Bristol.

This haphazard way of living has other and graver results. It is rare to find that it does not corrupt the character of those who adopt it. Men of firm principle like Johnson are unaffected ; but others, and inevitably a vastly greater number, yield and become demoralized. Living outside the pale of society, they gradually and unconsciously begin to despise its laws ; irregular life begets easy morals. Living by their wits, they cease little by little to distinguish the line that separates the ingenious expedient from the barefaced fraud. Their self-respect is lowered, their conscience becomes less sensitive, their principles less rigid.

Smollett's *Humphrey Clinker* portrays a group of authors who would appear to have been drawn from life. The philosopher amongst them has been sent down from Oxford as an atheist, and prosecuted for blaspheming the Sabbath in a wine-shop. He undertakes to refute Bolingbroke's metaphysical writings. The Scotsman gives lessons in English pronunciation ; the man from Piedmont writes a satire on the English poets ; a cockney, who is the victim of " agrophobia ", and does not know Indian corn from rice, composes a treatise on agriculture. An Irishman publishes a pamphlet in favour of a Minister in the hope of receiving some token of gratitude ; when disappointed, he passes off his pamphlet as the Minister's own production and writes a reasoned refutation. Another, who has never ventured to show his face outside the privileged quarters where debtors of the day were safe from the bailiff, writes an account of travels in Europe and Asia. In Fielding's portrait gallery [108] there is an author who offers his publisher a pamphlet against the Ministry. This is rejected because two others are already in the press. He then suggests a defence of the Ministry, but this is similarly rejected because it would command no sale. So he falls back on an annotated edition of the *Æneid*. " But I am afraid I am not qualified for a translator, for I understand no language but my own."—" What, and translate Virgil ? "—" Alas, I translated him out of Dryden."—" Lay by your hat, sir—lay by your hat, and take your seat immediately. Not qualified !—thou art as well versed in thy trade as if thou hadst laboured in my garret these ten years ! " In his admiration the publisher becomes familiar and addresses him with " thou ".

" Translators . . ." the publisher Lintot said to Pope, " are

[108] *The Author's Farce.*

the saddest pack of rogues in the world : in a hungry fit, they'll swear they understand all the languages of the universe. I have known one of them take down a Greek book upon my counter, and cry, Ah, this is Hebrew, I must read it from the latter end." One of the translators whom the same publisher had employed and commissioned to make an English translation of Lucretius only wrote the first page himself and then simply copied out an existing translation.[109]

It was not only in literary matters that dishonesty was practised. Authors frequently transgressed the frontiers of professional fraud. They would sometimes publish the prospectus of, and accept subscriptions for, a work which never appeared. Fielding's *Index* sends the publisher *Bookweight* the draft of a prospectus asking him to print five hundred copies with the same number of receipt forms, for a new translation of Cicero's *De Natura Deorum* and the *Tusculan Disputations*. " I am sorry ", says the publisher, " you have undertaken this, for it prevents a design of mine."—" Indeed, sir, it does not ; for you see all of the book that I ever intend to publish. It is only a handsome way of asking one's friends for a guinea." [110]

Savage and Boyse spent part of their lives announcing and discounting new editions of their works. A certain Cooke, who had translated Hesiod, lived for twenty years on a projected translation of Plautus.[111]   These swindles became so general that people of standing formed a defensive alliance against importunate petitioners, and entered into a formal agreement with each other not to subscribe in advance to any work.[112]   Breach of this agreement entailed a fine. Mallet undertook to write a Life of the Duke of Marlborough and on this understanding accepted for many years a pension from his family. But he never wrote a line.[113]   Smollett tells of a certain author who borrowed a horse on the pretext of having to make a journey. He went off at once and sold it and ended by stealing his publisher's riding-boots.[114]   Fielding presents a translator who ultimately found his way to prison for " the rogue had a trick of translating out of the shops as well as the languages ".[115]   Savage helped himself from the shelves of Lord Tyrconnel's library, and his host

---

[109] Pope's *Letter to the Earl of Burlington.*
[110] *The Author's Farce.*   [111] Boswell, IV, p. 26.
[112] Fielding, *Joseph Andrews*, book III, chap. 3.
[113] Johnson, *Lives* . . . Mallet.
[114] *Humphrey Clinker.*   [115] *The Author's Farce.*

used to find handsomely bound books of his, stamped with his arms, displayed for sale in second-hand bookshops. This same wastrel committed manslaughter in a low drinking den and was condemned to death. Thanks to powerful influence, he was let off with six months' imprisonment. It is more than likely that this man—over whose hard lot so many tears have been wasted —was an impostor who deceived innocent Johnson and all his contemporaries by posing as the illegitimate son of the Countess of Macclesfield. We are probably justified in interpreting his dramatic and touching story as nothing but an ingenious fiction cleverly devised to blackmail a great lady by importunity, insult and the threat of scandal.[116]

Having already steeply declined in public favour, the literary profession was on the verge of completely forfeiting all respect and esteem.

III

Dryden and the first English publisher, Jacob Tonson.—The publisher's rôle n literature.—Dryden's translation of Virgil.—His Fables.—Literature increasingly remunerative

While the majority of authors were pleasantly drifting downstream with the placid current of political patronage, there was —fortunately for literature—one amongst them whom the Revolution robbed of all hope of post or pension, and who, thus driven to rely solely on himself, prepared a better future for his brother-writers.

We opened our study with Dryden, and to him we now return. Having, as a Roman Catholic, forfeited his position of Historiographer Royal and Poet Laureate, and also his post in the Customs, being deprived of all useful patronage, now that those whom he had so vigorously opposed had come to power, he set himself to work again with renewed energy—in defiance of shattered hopes and the onset of old age. His genius faltered neither under the weight of years nor the bitterness of trial. He turned first to drama, but with dubious success and inadequate reward. Then, adopting another line, he linked his fortunes with those of his publisher, Jacob Tonson.

[116] See W. Moy Thomas's researches in *Notes and Queries*, Nov. and Dec. 1858, pp. 361, 385, 425 and 445.

I have already mentioned Tonson, an interesting figure, who deserves our closer attention, for with him a new character enters the literary scene.

The production of every literary work involves two distinct processes : an intellectual act and a commercial transaction. As long as the reading public was confined to a restricted circle, the commercial transaction was of little importance. The author was himself responsible for extracting from his labour the reward he was entitled to claim. He relied little on publisher or purchasers ; he dedicated his book and looked for a gift in return. The printer-publisher played an altogether minor part : it was his modest place to print a limited number of copies, without incurring much risk or aspiring to much profit. But as the number and discernment of readers increased, and people began eagerly to look out for and to purchase books, the author saw a vision of more serious and more legitimate advantage and his thoughts turned to the buyers of his books. The more numerous book-buyers became, the more impossible it grew for him to keep directly in touch with them, without squandering thought and energy, which ought properly to be devoted to his writing. The proprietor of a small piece of land can well work it single-handed ; if his property increases, he needs a steward. The author similarly requires an intermediary between himself and his reader, and the reader equally requires an intermediary between himself and the writer of books. It is at this point that the duties of a publisher become changed and enlarged, and he himself a necessary and most important agent for the intellectual producer. It must be his care to study the literary market ; to keep the author informed of the tastes and inclinations of readers ; to seek out for the reader works of value and writers of talent. If he has rivals in the business, he will try to secure good authors to himself by paying them generously. At the same time, foreseeing a certain sale for his publications, he forges ahead, becomes adventurous and risks his capital.

It is to Tonson's credit that he first scented the breath of a new era opening for literature, and at once foresaw that publishing was destined to play an important rôle therein. Taking intelligent advantage of favourable circumstances as they arose, he skilfully contrived to prepare the way for, and ensure the success of, the new development. With him, and largely thanks to him, the publisher proper evolved out of the printer-bookseller.

Jacob Tonson [117] was the son of a London barber-surgeon who at his death bequeathed £100 to each of his children. Jacob set up as a publisher " at the Judge's Head in Chancery Lane, near Fleet Street " in 1678, at a moment when his fellows were cutting a poor enough figure in the world, and when rigorous legislation, and still more the scarcity of readers, imposed such severe limits on their activities that they were solely—and that very modestly—printers and booksellers, occupying a very subordinate place in literature. [118] Divining that the refined literary taste of the Court, combined with the mental awakening produced by political controversy, might prove the herald of better days, Tonson was the first to display serious, though still very cautious, publishing initiative. I have already spoken [119] of his timid ventures with Dryden's plays, his purchase of *Paradise Lost* and particularly of his partnership with Dryden in the publication, before the Revolution of 1688, of two volumes of *Miscellanies*. After the Revolution, the re-establishment of political calm and the success of his first tentative experiments inspired Tonson with courage. He had gained experience, he felt sure of his readers and sure of himself, and his spirit of enterprise gradually grew stronger. In 1688 he published his reprint of *Paradise Lost* and in 1693 translations by Dryden of Juvenal, of Persius and of other Latin authors. At the same time he suggested to Dryden to bring out a third volume of *Miscellanies*, which was soon followed by a fourth. [120] Meantime public opinion was stirring, which ultimately led to the emancipation of the Press. [121] The abolition of restrictive legislation gave new impetus to the book-trade ; the number of booksellers quickly swelled : a few years later Dunton [122] mentioned more than 130 in London alone, which marks a great advance on the figures for Charles II's reign. [123] More and more elated by propitious fortune, Tonson

[117] On Tonson, see Knight, *Shadows of the Old Booksellers*, pp. 48 ff., and Malone's *Life of Dryden*, pp. 523 ff.

[118] See above, pp. 114 ff.

[119] See above, pp. 114 ff. and pp. 192 ff.

[120] *Examen Poeticum* : being The Third Part of Miscellany Poems ; *The Annual Miscellany* : for The Year 1694, Being The Fourth Part of Miscellany Poems. See my Bibliography, s.v. Dryden.

[121] Macaulay, *History*, chap. XXI.

[122] *The Life and Errors* . . . pp. 280 ff.

[123] See above, pp. 114 ff. For all its immense advantages, the abolition of the Censorship had one serious drawback. The preliminary authorization to publish, confirmed the author's property rights in a book. Its abolition left the field open to unauthorized reprints, and there were plenty of people

suggested to Dryden a more ambitious undertaking than they had previously ventured on : a verse translation of the complete works of Virgil.[124] The poet accepted the suggestion, and after three years' work his translation appeared in 1697.

The English Virgil was published by subscription. It was the fourth publication to appear under a new system, which Tonson had successfully adopted in his reprint of *Paradise Lost*.[125] The venture was ingeniously organized to attract subscribers and obviate miscalculations. There were two series of subscribers. The first paid five guineas, the second, two. The five-guinea subscriber was offered a special bait : his copy was enriched with many engravings, under one of which his own coat of arms appeared. The name of the two-guinea subscriber was modestly recorded on a list published with the translation. It is noteworthy that under this subscription system the author was entitled to a proportion of the sums subscribed. It was therefore directly to his interest to recruit as many subscribers as he could, and bring his personal influence to bear on his friends and patrons. The publisher thus enlisted the author as a partner in his enterprise, and made him shoulder a part of the work and of the risk entailed.

In this way, while showing himself more enterprising than his fellows, Tonson continued to display his prudence and commercial acumen. In every venture he proceeded most cautiously, narrowly weighing expenditure and risk, and keeping a watchful eye on his own interest. Dryden, for his part, was no less energetic and alert. We get the feeling that both were exploring uncharted regions, on the look out for surprise and misadventure at every step. This was the beginning of the relations between publisher and author, relations marked at first neither by great mutual confidence, nor by excess of courtesy.

---

eager to take advantage of this loophole in the law. Complaints against the " pirates ", as they were called, were frequent. See in particular Smith, quoted in Johnson's *Lives* . . . John Philips ; No. 101 of the *Tatler* and the Preface to the Second Part of *Robinson Crusoe*. But it's an ill wind that blows nobody good : these pirated editions, by offering readers the opportunity to buy cheap, helped to spread a taste for reading.

[124] In the Dedication of his *Æneid*, Dryden himself states that the idea was Tonson's.

[125] The earlier three were : Walton's *Polyglot Bible*, 1654-7 (Nichols, *Literary Anecdotes*, IV, p. 8) ; the reprint of *Paradise Lost*, 1688, and à Wood's *Athenæ Oxonienses*, 1691 (Malone, *Life of Dryden*, p. 234).

As the following letter shows, the publisher haggled over lines and prices :

Letter from Jacob Tonson to John Dryden, Esq. (probably written in Jan. or Feb. 1692-3 *).

SIR,

I have here returned ye Ovid, wᶜʰ I read wᵗʰ a great deal of pleasure, and think nothing can be more entertaining ; but by this letter you find I am not soe well satisfied as perhaps you might think. I hope at ye same time the matter of fact I lay down in this letter will appear grounds for it, and wᶜʰ I beg you wou'd consider of ; and then I believe I shall at least bee excused.

You may please, Sʳ, to remember, that upon my first proposal about ye 3ᵈ Miscellany, I offer'd fifty pounds, and talk'd of several authors, without naming Ovid. You ask'd if it shou'd not be guyneas, and said I shou'd not repent it ; upon wᶜʰ I imediately comply'd, and left it wholly to you what, and for ye quantity too : and I declare it was the farthest in ye world from my thoughts that by leaving it to you I shou'd have the less. Thus the case stood when you went into Essex. After I came out of Northamptonshire I wrote to you, and reseived a letter dated Monday Oct. 3ᵈ, 92, from wᶜʰ letter I now write word for word what followes :

" I' am translating about six hundred lines, or somewhat less, of ye first book of the Metamorphoses. If I cannot get my price, wᶜʰ shall be twenty guynneas, I will translate the whole book ; wᶜʰ coming out before the whole translation, will spoyl Tate's undertakings. 'Tis one of the best I have ever made, and very pleasant. This, wᵗʰ Heroe and Leander, and the piece of Homer (or, if it be not enough, I will add more), will make a good part of a Miscellany."

Those, Sʳ, are ye very words, and ye onely ones in that letter relating to that affair ; and ye Monday following you come to town.—After your arrivall you shew'd Mr. Motteaux what you had done (wᶜʰ he told me was to ye end of ye story of Daphnis), [Daphne], and demanded, as you mention'd in your letter, twenty guyneas, wᶜʰ that bookseller refus'd. Now, Sʳ, I the rather believe there was just soe much done, by reason ye number of lines you mention in yoʳ letter agrees wᵗʰ ye quantity of lines that soe much of ye first book makes ; wᶜʰ upon counting ye Ovid, I find to be in ye Lattin 566, in ye English 759 ; and ye bookseller told me there was noe more demanded of him for it.—Now, Sʳ, what I entreat you wou'd please to consider of is this : that it is reasonable for me to expect at least as much favour from you as a strange bookseller ; and I will never believe yᵗ it can be in yoʳ nature to use one ye worse for leaveing it to you ; and if the matter of fact as I state it be true (and upon my word what I mention I can shew you in yoʳ letter), then pray, Sʳ, consider how much dearer I pay then you offered it to ye other bookseller ; for he might have

---

* The Third Miscellany was published in July 1693.

had to ye end of ye story of Daphnis for 20 guynneas, wch is in yor
translation 759 lines ;

And then suppose 20 guyneas more for the
same number   .   .   .   759 lines ;

that makes for 40 guyneas . . . . . 1518 lines ;
and all that I have for fifty guyneas are but 1446 ; soe that, if I have
noe more, I pay 10 guyneas above 40, and have 72 lines less for fifty,
in proportion, than the other bookseller shou'd have had for 40, at
ye rate you offered him ye first part. This is, Sir, what I shall take
as a great favour if you please to think of. I had intentions of letting
you know this before ; but till I had paid ye money, I would not
ask to see the book ; nor count the lines, least it shou'd look like a
design of not keeping my word. When you have looked over ye rest
of what you have already translated, I desire you would send it ; and
I own y^t if you don't think fit to add something more, I must submit :
'tis wholly at your choice, for I left it intirely to you ; but I believe you
cannot imagine I expected soe little ; for you were pleased to use me
much kindlyer in Juvenall, wch is not reckon'd soe easy to translate
as Ovid. S^r, I humbly beg yor pardon for this long letter, and upon
my word I had rather have yor good will than any man's alive ; and,
whatever you are pleased to doe, will alway acknowledge my self, S^r,

Yo^r most obliged humble Servt,

J. TONSON.[126]

Tonson, who was in politics an ardent Whig, pestered Dryden
to dedicate his Virgil to William III. The poet, ill-disposed to
change his political allegiance, resisted ; and the subject gave
rise to long argument between them. The publisher, hoping to
carry his point at the last moment, and perhaps to bluff Dryden
by confronting him with a *fait accompli*, had the plates touched
up, which were to form the engravings destined to illustrate the
book, so as to give Æneas the King of England's features. Tonson
lost the trick and his expenses, for Dryden stood firm, but the
poet had to remain on the defensive and fight to the bitter end.[127]

---

[126] This and the following letters will be found in *Dryden's Correspondence*.

[127] " But, however, he (Tonson) has missed of his design in the dedication,
though he had prepared the books for it ; for in every figure of Eneas he
has caused him to be drawn like King William, with a hooked nose." (Dryden.
Letter to his sons.)—Hence this epigram :

" Old Jacob by deep judgment sway'd,
      To please the wise beholders,
Has placed old Nassau's hook-nosed head
      On poor Æneas' shoulders.

To make the parallel hold tack,
      Methinks there's a little lacking ;
One took his father pick-a-pack,
      And t'other sent his packing."

The state of the silver currency in England was at this time deplorable. The country was flooded with clipped and depreciated coins.[128] When a payment was due to Dryden, Tonson usually tried to unload on to him all the most under-weight coins he had at the moment in his till. The unfortunate author had continually to complain :

You know money is now very scrupulously receiv'd : in the last which you did me the favour to change for my wife, besides the clip'd money, there were at least forty shillings brass.

I shall loose enough by your bill upon Mr. Knight * ; for after having taking it all in silver, and not in half-crowns neither, but shillings and sispences, none of the money will go ; for which reason I have sent it all back again, and as the less loss will receive it in guinneys at 29 shillings each.

. . . if you have any silver which will go, my wife will be glad of it. I lost thirty shillings or more by the last payment of fifty pounds, wch you made at Mr. Knights.

When it sometimes happened that Dryden was behind time in delivering his manuscript, the treatment he received was rough and uncivil. One day when St. John (later Bolingbroke) was visiting Dryden, they heard a knock at the front door. " This ", said Dryden, " is Tonson. You will take care not to depart before he goes away ; for I have not completed the sheet which I promised him ; and if you leave me unprotected I must suffer all the rudeness to which his resentment can prompt his tongue." [129]

Dryden was not to be outdone. On one occasion, when Tonson no doubt had pressed some petty calculations on his attention, such as those we have seen above, he wrote acidly :

October the 29th, (f. 1695).

Mr. Tonson,

Some kind of intercourse must be carryed on betwixt us, while I am translating Virgil. Therefore I give you notice, that I have done the seaventh Eneid in the country † ; and intend some few days hence, to go upon the eight : when that is finished, I expect fifty pounds in good silver ; not such as I have had formerly. I am not obliged to take gold,‡ neither will I ; nor stay for it beyond four-and-twenty houres after it is due. I thank you for the civility of your last letter

* A banker or goldsmith, afterwards notorious for his share in the South Sea scheme, to which Company he was cashier.

† At Burleigh, the seat of John, the fifth Earl of Exeter.

‡ Both the gold and silver coin were at this time much depreciated ; and remained in a fluctuating state till a new coinage took place.

---

[128] See Macaulay, History, chap. XXI.
[129] Johnson, *Lives* . . . Dryden.

in the country ; but the thirty shillings upon every book remains with me. You always intended I should get nothing by the second subscriptions, as I found from first to last. And your promise to Mr. Congreve, that you had found a way for my benefit, which was an encouragement to my paines, came at last, for me to desire Sir Godfrey Kneller and Mr. Closterman to gather for me. I then told Mr. Congreve, that I knew you too well to believe you meant me any kindness : and he promised me to believe accordingly of you, if you did not. But this is past ; and you shall have your bargain, if I live and have my health. You may send me word what you have done in my business with the Earl of Derby : and I must have a place for the Duke of Devonshyre. Some of your friends will be glad to take back their three guinneys. The Countess of Macclesfield gave her money to Will Plowden before Christmas ; but he remembered it not, and payd it not in. Mr. Aston tells me, my Lord Chesterfield and my Lord Petre are both left out ; but my Lady Macclesfield must have a place, if I can possibly : and Will Plowden shall pay you in three guinneys, if I can obtain so much favour from you.* I desire neither excuses nor reasons from you : for I am but too well satisfyed already. The Notes and Prefaces shall be short ; because you shall get the more by saving paper.†

JOHN DRYDEN.

Once again he wrote in the same style :

Friday forenoon, (f. Feb. 1695-6).

SIR,
I receiv'd your letter very kindly,‡ because indeed I expected none ; but thought you as very a tradesman as Bentley,§ who has cursed our Virgil so heartily.

. . . Upon triall I find all of your trade are sharpers, and you not more than others ; therefore I have not wholly left you. Mr. Aston does not blame you for getting as good a bargain as you cou'd, though I cou'd have gott an hundred pounds more ; and you might have spared almost all your trouble if you had thought fit to publish the proposalls for the first subscriptions ; for I have guynneas offered me every day, if there had been room ; I believe modestly speaking I have refused already 25. I mislike nothing in your letter therefore, but onely your upbraiding me with the publique encouragement, and my own reputation concerned in the notes ; when I assure you I

---

* From inspecting the plates of Dryden's Virgil, it appears that the Earl of Derby had one inscribed to him, as had Lord Chesterfield. But this wrathful letter made no further impression on the mercantile obstinacy of Tonson ; and neither the Duke of Devonshire, Lord Petre, nor Lady Macclesfield, obtained the place among the first subscribers, which Dryden so peremptorily demands for them.

† This seems to be a bitter gibe at Jacob's parsimony.

‡ Tonson's answer to the foregoing letter seems to have been pacific and apologetical, yet peremptory as to his terms.

§ Richard Bentley, a bookseller and printer, who lived in Russel Street, Covent Garden.

cou'd not make them to my mind in less than half a year's time. Get the first half of Virgil transcribed as soon as possibly you can, that I may put the notes to it ; and you may have the other four books which lye ready for you when you bring the former ; that the press may stay as little as possibly it can. My Lord Chesterfield has been to visite me, but I durst say nothing of Virgil to him, for feare there should be no void place for him ; if there be, let me know ; and tell me whether you have made room for the Duke of Devonshire. Haveing no silver by me, I desire my Lord Derby's money, deducting your own. And let it be good, if you desire to oblige me, who am not your enemy, and may be your friend,

JOHN DRYDEN.

One day when Tonson had refused an advance of money, Dryden sent him the following opening lines of a projected portrait :

> With leering looks, bull-faced, and freckled fair,
> With two left legs, and Judas-colour'd hair,
> And frowzy pores, that taint the ambient air . . .

And in committing the letter to the person entrusted with its delivery, he added : " Tell the dog that he who wrote these lines can write more."

But savage as were these squalls, they passed over : and calm reigned once more. The sky was not continuously fraught with storm.

Dryden wrote :

(Wednesday the 13th of 7 ber f. 1695.)

MY GOOD FRIEND,
. . . I assure you I lay up your last kindnesses to me in my heart ; and the less I say of them, I charge them to account so much the more ; being very sensible that I have not hitherto deserved them.

JOHN DRYDEN.

And again :

August 30, (1693).

MR. TONSON,
I am much asham'd of my self, that I am so much behind-hand with you in kindness. Above all things I am sensible of your good nature, in bearing me company to this place, wherein, besides the cost, you must needs neglect your own business ; but I will endeavour to make you some amends ; . . .

JOHN DRYDEN.

Tonson, for his part, was lavish of minor courtesies. Not content with accompanying the author to the country, he would send him gifts of melons and sherry, both of which were gratefully appreciated.

The truth is that the two men were indispensable to each other. Without Dryden, Tonson would have been nobody, and Dryden had no choice of publishers. However justly founded the complaints to which his behaviour gave rise, Tonson had one virtue—imposed by his own interest—to which Dryden could not be insensible : he was a more solvent debtor than Charles II and a more open-handed giver than Charles's royal brother James. Each volume of the *Miscellanies*, which they jointly produced, brought Dryden £50, and his Virgil some £1,400,[130] that is to say, approximately as much profit as he had reaped in earlier days from fourteen successful plays (counting the sale of the manuscript, the gift evoked by the Dedication and the third-night earnings).[131] Tonson meantime was laying the foundations of his fortune.

Despite their bickerings, author and publisher were in fact so well satisfied with their partnership that after Virgil they undertook yet another joint publication. This was the volume of verse which is known as Dryden's *Fables*. For this volume, the last he was ever to write, Dryden was paid 250 guineas, which for 12,000 lines works out, as Pope calculated,[132] to approximately sixpence a line.

Adversity had opened Dryden's eyes to the fact that henceforth the true patrons of literature would be the publishers. Or, more correctly, that henceforth there would be neither patron nor protégé. The two contracting parties would enter into voluntary collaboration, each making his appropriate contribution : the author his talent, the publisher his commercial experience ; the one risking his labour, the other his capital, and both according to their desert and to their luck, good or ill, would have their share of failure or success. Under these new conditions the author could of course no longer count on pleasant windfalls, on generous gifts, on fortune falling from heaven while he slept. He would have to earn his bread in the sweat of his brow, the

---

[130] Pope (as reported by Spence, pp. 262–3) reckoned it as about £1,200, Malone over £1,300 and Bell about £1,400. A document based on Dryden's personal authority points to the figure of £1,400 (*Notes and Queries*, May 19, 1877, p. 386). Everyone agrees that from a financial point of view the Virgil was a considerable success. The first edition was exhausted in a few weeks. There had been 102 five-guinea and 250 two-guinea subscribers. The second edition appeared early in the following year.

[131] See above, p. 112 f.

[132] Spence, pp. 262–3. Tonson might on this occasion be well content. Dryden had contracted to supply 10,000 lines for 250 guineas and furnished actually another 2,000 over and above the tally.

publisher paying nothing for nothing. But by his work, severe and toilsome though it might be and frequently coupled with rebuffs, the author acquired, if he deserved them, two precious imponderables for which no price is too high—independence and dignity.

Furthermore, in proportion as a reading-public evolved and the publishing trade developed, the opportunity of achieving this independence presented itself more freely to writers, until by slow degrees literature became a remunerative profession.

After the Revolution, dramatists had the benefit not of one performance only, but of two, and sometimes even of three,[133] and the profit of these performances was considerable. With one single play Southerne earned as much as £700, a sum so vastly in excess of those current in the preceding reigns that he was ashamed to confess it to Dryden. True, Southerne had many wealthy and highly-placed friends, and he possessed a quite peculiar gift of arousing their generosity when he hawked his tickets round their great houses.[134] Apart from Southerne, however, we hear of a quite obscure writer who derived £300 from a play that ran only for seven nights.[135] The sale of the manuscript to publishers also became markedly more profitable. The price of a play rose gradually from £20 or £25 to a more serious figure. Dryden sold the text of *Cleomenes* (1691) for thirty guineas,[136] Southerne *The Fatal Marriage* (1695) for £36, Edmund Smith *Phædra and Hippolitus* (1708) for £60.[137] Tonson paid John Philips forty guineas for his little poem on *Cider* (1703).[138] In 1694 Tillotson's *Sermons* were bought for the unheard-of sum of 2,500 guineas, which " in the wretched state in which the silver coin then was ", as Macaulay says,[139] was " the equivalent of at least £3,600 ".[140]

---

[133] Genest, II, pp. 7, 166 and 316 ; Malone, *Historical Account*, pp. 174-5. According to Malone, Farquhar—quite exceptionally—was allowed as many as four performances for *The Constant Couple* in 1700.

[134] Life of Southerne prefixed to his *Works* ; Malone, *Historical Account*, p. 175.

[135] " We have had a poor comedy of Johnson's (not Ben) which held seven nights and has got him three hundred pounds." (Letter of Cromwell to Pope, Dec. 7, 1711. Elwin's Edition of *Pope*, VI, p. 128.)—The author was one Charles Johnson, and the play was called *The Wife's Relief, or The Husband's Cure.*

[136] Malone's *Dryden*, II, p. 230, note No. 2.

[137] Malone, *Historical Account*, p. 180.

[138] Johnson, *Lives* . . . John Philips.   [139] *History*, chap. XX.

[140] The risking of so large a sum on one publication shows how far the spirit of enterprise had already carried the publishers. It must be admitted,

After the appearance of the *Tatler* and the *Spectator* and the definite formation of an English reading-public, the rewards of literary work rose still higher. His publisher paid Sacheverell £100 for the first sermon he preached after his suspension (1713).[141] Rowe received £75 for the manuscript of *Lady Jane Grey* (1715); Cibber £105 for the *Non-Juror* (1718)[142]; Southerne, of whom Pope said that he was

> . . . sent to raise
> The price of prologues and of plays,[143]

got as much as £120 for his *Spartan Dame* (1719).[144] From 1720 onwards the three benefit nights for the author of a play, which had hitherto been an exceptional concession, became the rule.[145] A few years later Gay received more than £1,000 for *The Captives*, and George Jeffreys at least the same sum for his tragedy of *Edwin* (1724). Fenton made more than £1,500 from his tragedy of *Mariamne*.[146] In 1712 Addison and Steele sold half their rights in the first seven volumes of the *Spectator* for £575, which implies a value for the whole copyright of £1,150.[147] In 1716 after his fall from glory, Prior organized the publication of his poems by subscription and made 4,000 guineas[148] by the transaction. In 1720 Gay published his poems in the same way at a profit of £1,000.[149]

If publishers were disposed to be as generous as all this, we may fairly conclude that they had their sound reasons, and that their receipts encouraged them to bold adventure and taught

---

however, that the fact is not of purely literary significance. Tillotson occupied a unique place in England's religious life, and the payment of so high a price for the copyright of his sermons must be attributed more to his fame as an Archbishop than to his gifts as a writer, great though these unquestionably were. His posthumous works run to fourteen octavo volumes.

[141] Swift, *Journal to Stella*, April 2, 1713.

[142] Johnson, *Lives* . . . Dryden, p. 390, Cunningham's note.

[143] See above, chap. II, note No. 211.

[144] Malone, *Historical Account*, p. 181, note. See above chap. II, note No. 211.

[145] Ibid., p. 175.

[146] Young's Letter to Lady Mary Wortley Montagu in her *Works*, II, p. 11.

[147] The record of the sale is in the British Museum : *Additional Manuscripts*, No. 21,110.—The daily sales of the paper had no doubt brought them considerable profits, for we know that Berkeley was paid a guinea for each article he contributed to the *Guardian*, in addition to being given a dinner by Steele. (Nichols' Edition of *Steele's Correspondence*, I, p. 329, note.)

[148] Johnson, *Lives* . . . Prior.

[149] N. Drake, *Essays* . . . *Illustrative of the Tatler*, etc., III, p. 242.

them not to be too sparing of their guineas. The first volume
of *Robinson Crusoe* alone brought in more than £1,000 to its
publisher, who died a few years later worth over £40,000.[150] Soon
after Dryden's death, Tonson bought property in the country,
and was well on the way to a fortune which ultimately rose to
£80,000. The hundred pounds with which he started life had
bred handsomely under his care.

IV

Pope and his publishers Tonson and Lintot.—Pope's Translation of Homer.—
It made Pope's fortune.—Pope breaks the tradition of interested Dedications.—
Preserves a detached attitude to political parties.—Refuses offered pensions.—
Sought by the highest society in England.—The first English man of letters

What was now needed was a man capable of drawing full
advantage from all the recent progress made, and establishing,
on the existence of an enlightened public and on the rivalry of
competing publishers, an author's complete independence.

The man appeared. He was Alexander Pope.[151]

His parents were Roman Catholics, his father, before retirement, a London linen-draper. He spent his childhood and
early boyhood in Windsor Forest, whither his father had prudently
withdrawn with a modest competence, after the fall of James II
and the triumph of the Protestant party, to devote himself to his
son's education.

Delicate and deformed, the boy early showed promise of
great poetic talent. When he came to London to mix in literary
society his verses at once attracted notice, and one of the first
persons whose attention was drawn to them was Dryden's
publisher, Jacob Tonson. Pope had so far published nothing,
and was not yet eighteen when he received the following letter :

GRAY'S INN GATE.
April 20, 1706.

SIR,—

I have lately seen a Pastoral of yours in Mr. Walsh's and Congreve's
hands, which is extremely fine, and is (generally) approved of by the
best judges in poetry. I remember I have formerly seen you at my
shop, and am sorry I did not improve my acquaintance with you.
If you design your poem for the press, no person shall be more careful

---

[150] Spence, p. 340 ; William Lee, *Daniel Defoe*, p. 293.

[151] In addition to Pope's own works, I have consulted especially Johnson,
Carruthers, Dilke, Elwin and Leslie Stephen.

in the printing of it, nor no one can give (a) greater encouragement to it than, sir, your, etc.

(Pray give me a line per post).[151a]

Pope succumbed at once to so courteous and so flattering an overture and his *Pastorals* appeared in 1709 in a new volume of *Miscellanies* published by Tonson.

The first English editor had drawn another ace. Having been the mainstay of Dryden's last years, and helped him to bring out some of his finest work, he rendered literature the further service of encouraging the first steps of a new poet.

So Pope, still a youth, still unknown, entered on the scene, not under the protection of a great lord, nor of a statesman, but under the immediate auspices, and almost at the request, of a publisher.

This fact was bound, or so it seems to me, to have a serious influence on the course of his later life. From the very beginning of his career he saw—what Dryden's latest experiences had no doubt already shown him—that the future of literature lay in the intelligent collaboration of author and publisher, and that he had no need to look further afield for support.

His position was immeasurably more favourable than Dryden's. Dryden had behind him no one but Tonson, which placed him in some sort at the publisher's mercy ; and in Dryden's day Tonson was making, with justifiable caution, his first publishing experiments. Since then Tonson had prospered ; he had become wealthy ; he had become a person of importance, so much so that he had been elected secretary of the Kit-Cat Club. Political and literary authorship had moreover extended its range in every direction, creating a need and a taste for reading, and the publishing trade had consequently expanded. Tonson had not long remained the sole expert in the marketing of books. He was soon confronted by a serious rival, Bernard Lintot.[152] The subsequent competition between the two publishers was a thing wholly new in English literature, and in a host of ways beneficial. There is nothing like competition to make a business man active, clear-sighted and generous. If Tonson brought out an edition of Shakespeare's plays, Lintot capped it with a new edition of his poems. No sooner had Lintot announced the first volume of Pope's verse translation of the *Iliad* than Tonson offered

---

[151a] [Elwin, IX, p. 545. B. D.]
[152] On Lintot, see Knight, *Shadows* . . . pp. 100 ff.

the public Tickell's version of the first book. If Tonson was preparing a translation of Lucretius, Lintot set about finding a translator of the same poet " to publish against Tonson's ".[153] The two of them, hearing that Young had a new work ready for printing, wrote simultaneously to the poet requesting the honour of publishing it.[154] The man whom Pope himself styled " the enterprizing Mr. Lintot, the redoubtable rival of Mr. Tonson ",[155] wasted no time in competing with his brother-publisher for the young poet's work, and in 1712 he secured Pope's collaboration for a collection of *Miscellanies* compiled in imitation of Tonson's.[156] Pope had meantime entrusted his *Essay on Criticism* to another publisher called Lewis. Thereafter his work was divided between Lintot and Tonson. Lintot published *Windsor Forest, The Rape of the Lock, The Temple of Fame* ; Tonson published several poems of Pope's in a volume of his *Miscellanies* which came out under Steele's editorship.[157]

These works, by which the young poet continued to maintain and even increase the promise of his talent, won him an enviable reputation ; but they were far from enriching him. The income from his father's legacy was very modest.[158] He was inclined to try whether his literary reputation and an enlightened public might not between them enable him to conquer fortune.

Dryden had toyed with the plan of following up his Virgil with a translation of Homer. Pope took the idea up again and began to think of tackling the *Iliad*. The publishers hailed

[153] Pope's *Letter to the Earl of Burlington.*
[154] Spence, p. 355 [2nd edn., p. 269].—This double attack gave rise to an amusing blunder. Young wrote to both publishers the same day and in his haste transposed the two addresses so that Lintot got a letter beginning " That Bernard Lintot is so great a scoundrel that . . . "
[155] *Letter to the Earl of Burlington.*
[156] It was called Pope's *Miscellany.* It was in this volume that appeared the first version of the *Rape of the Lock.*
[157] Pope subsequently gave Tonson his edition of Shakespeare, and Lintot his translation of the *Iliad* and the *Odyssey.* His other works he entrusted mainly to Gilliver and to Dodsley. He had given Dodsley £100 to set him up in business.
[158] " . . . The translation of the Iliad. What led me into that . . . was purely the want of money. I had then none ; not even to buy books." Spence, p. 304 [2nd edn., p. 231].—Pope's father had possessed a capital sum of £10,000 ; and when he died in 1717 he left his son an income of between £280 and £400 a year. But Roman Catholics paid double taxes and the uncertainty of their position compelled them to leave a part of their money unproductive or to invest it disadvantageously. After his father's death, Pope wrote to a co-religionist : " He has left me to the ticklish management of a narrow fortune, where every false step is dangerous." (Elwin, VI, p. 377, also VI, pp. 189, 201 and 214.)

the project with enthusiasm, and Lintot outbid all competitors by offering terms more generous than any English publisher had previously ventured on. Like Dryden's Virgil, Pope's *Iliad* was published by subscription. The edition consisted of six quarto volumes at a guinea apiece. Lintot allowed Pope the entire revenue from subscriptions, undertook to bear the cost of supplying the volumes subscribed for, and in addition paid the translator £200 a volume.[159] There were 575 subscribers who took 654 copies and Pope's receipts finally reached the total of £5,320 4s. This success encouraged him to persevere, and he undertook, still with Lintot, the translation of the *Odyssey*.[160] These two translations, which kept him busy for ten years (from 1715 to 1725) brought him a fortune of about £9,000. If we compare this with the £1,400 which Dryden made by his Virgil we can see what great strides have been made in twenty years.[161]

Pope was now thirty-five ; he was rich and, we must hasten to add, independent. His translation of Homer is interesting, not only because of its brilliant financial success, nor because of the intelligence which enabled Pope to acquire by his pen a fortune of that most honourable kind which a man owes to his own labour ; it is interesting also because of the means the poet used to introduce it to the world.

From the moment of his first literary successes Pope had been welcomed into the most distinguished London society. He had been able to count among his friends both writers like

[159] Lintot reserved for himself only the profit from subsequent editions. The *Iliad* by itself made a rich man of him and provided further a considerable income for his heirs.

[160] Pope translated only a part of the *Odyssey* himself. He called in the assistance of two collaborators, Fenton and Broome.

[161] Gay and Swift both commemorated Pope's success, Gay in the verses *Alexander Pope and his Safe Return from Troy. A Congratulatory Poem on his Completing his Translation of Homer's Iliad* (Carruthers, pp. 198 ff.) ; Swift in *A Libel on the Reverend Dr. Delany* (Scott's Edition of *Swift*, XIV, pp. 246 ff.).— It is useful to note that other cases than Pope's confirm the steady rise in literary fees. The performance of *The Beggar's Opera* brought Gay in between £700 and £800 (Letter from Gay to Swift, March 30, 1727–8) (Scott's *Swift*, XVII, p. 181). His opera of *Polly* (1729), a sequel to *The Beggar's Opera*, was banned from the stage, but he published it by subscription and benefited to the tune of at least £2,000 (Johnson, *Lives . . . Gay*). In 1727 Voltaire published in London, by subscription, an English edition of his *Henriade*, dedicated to Queen Caroline, which earned him £6,000 (Garnier's Edition of Voltaire's *Œuvres*, VIII, p. 5). Young made £3,000 by a volume of seven satires on *The Love of Fame* (1728) (*Johnson, Lives . . . Young*). In 1738 Henry Brooke, finding his tragedy of *Gustavus Vasa* banned, published it by subscription, making a profit of £800 (Boswell, I, p. 156, note).

Wycherley, Walsh, Congreve, Granville, Garth, Swift, Steele, Addison, Gay, Arbuthnot, Parnell, and statesmen like Harley, Bolingbroke, Halifax, Somers and Craggs. All of these, authors and politicians alike, were ranged on one side or other in politics. To which party did Pope owe allegiance? Was he a Whig? Or a Tory? [162] Since he was a Roman Catholic, the Tories from the start reckoned him as one of themselves, and towards the close of his poem, *Windsor Forest*, there were some lines in praise of Peace, calculated to please them. But he had written a Prologue for Addison's *Cato* which the Whigs enthusiastically applauded, [163] and the *Spectator* and the *Guardian*, edited by two Whigs, had welcomed his verse and his prose. So each party in turn laid claim to the new-comer : his most trivial actions were noted and criticized from two sides ; his very friendships were analysed ; and each camp showed its longing to annex him, and its still stronger hope that he would not be captured by the other. Some extracts from his correspondence at this time will show the degree to which people were preoccupied with the question of his political opinions :

An honest Jacobite . . . spoke to me the sense, or nonsense, of the weak part of his party very fairly and innocently—that the good people took it very ill of me that I write with Steele, though upon never so indifferent subjects. [164]

The little I have done (for the *Guardian*) and the great respect I bear Mr. Steele as a man of wit, has rendered me a suspected Whig to some of the over-zealous and violent. [165]

I have also encountered much malignity on the score of religion, some calling me a papist and a tory, the latter because the heads of the party have been distinguishingly favourable to me ; but why the former I cannot imagine, but that Mr. Caryll and Mr. Blount have laboured to serve me. Others have styled me a whig, because I have been honoured with Mr. Addison's good word, and Mr. Jervas's good deeds, and of late with my Lord Halifax's patronage. [166]

---

[162] Swift writes to Pope, Aug. 30, 1716 : " I had the favour of yours by Mr. F(ord), of whom before any other question relating to your health or fortune, or success as a poet, I inquired your principles in the common form, 'Is he a whig or a tory?'" (Elwin's *Pope*, VII, p. 14).

[163] " The prologue-writer . . . was clapped into a stanch whig, sore against his will, at almost every two lines." (Letter from Pope to Caryll, April 30, 1713, Elwin's *Pope*, VI, p. 184.)

[164] To the same, June 12, 1713 (ibid., VI, p. 185).

[165] To the same, Oct. 17, 1713 (ibid., VI, p. 197).

[166] To the same, May 1, 1714 (ibid., VI, p. 208).— Caryll and E. Blount were both, like Pope, Roman Catholics ; Jervas was a painter of repute who belonged in politics to the Whig party.

Some modern rumours have been thrown about, which would have represented me as more concerned in party affairs than I ever dreamed on ; in so much that I had the honour to be named in the London Gazette for an enemy to the Grande Société at Button's.[167]

Mr. Phillips did express himself with much indignation against me one evening at Button's Coffee-house, as I was told, saying that I was entered into a cabal with Dean Swift and others to write against the whig interest.[168]

For all that passed betwixt Dr. Swift and me, you know, the whole, without reserve, of our correspondence. The engagements I had to him, were such as the actual services he had done me in relation to the subscription for Homer, obliged me to. I must have leave to be grateful to him, and to any one who serves me, let him be never so obnoxious to any party.[169]

And in the midst of these perpetual commentaries on his conduct inspired by political passion, of these efforts by left and right to capture him, the poet wrote to his co-religionist Caryll :

Yet let me tell you, you can hardly guess what a task you undertake when you profess yourself my friend ; there are some tories who will take you for a whig, some whigs who will take you for a tory, some protestants who will esteem you a rank papist, and some papists who will account you a heretic. I find, by dear experience, we live in an age where it is criminal to be moderate ; and where no one man can be allowed to be just to all men.[170]

Meantime the translation of the *Iliad* appeared.[171] It was an important book, long expected, in which the whole literary world was interested. To which party would it be dedicated ? Dryden, in whose steps Pope was following, had been lavish of his Virgil dedications. He had presented the *Eclogues* to Lord Clifford, the *Georgics* to the Earl of Chesterfield, the *Æneid* to Mulgrave, Marquis of Normanby. What would Pope do ? To whom would he offer his work ? To a Whig or to a Tory ? [172] Neither the one nor the other. He dedicated it to a brother-author, to a famous and honoured man, who, at a time when all men were passionate political partisans, had taken no doubt

---

[167] To the same, Feb. 25, 1714 (ibid., VI, p. 202).—Button's Coffee-House was the Whig rendezvous.

[168] To the same, June 8, 1714 (ibid., VI, p. 209).

[169] To Jervas, August 27, 1714 (ibid., VIII, p. 9).

[170] To Caryll, July 25, 1714 (ibid., VI, p. 215).

[171] The first volume was published in 1715.

[172] It is said that Halifax had expressed the wish that it should be dedicated to him.

a modest part in politics, but with so much calm restraint as to win the favour and goodwill of both parties,[173] and he wrote his dedication in the following simple and straightforward terms :

> I beg to be excused from the ceremonies of taking leave at the end of my work ; and from embarrassing myself, or others, with any defences or apologies about it. But instead of endeavouring to raise a vain monument to myself, of the merits or difficulties of it (which must be left to the world, to truth and to posterity), let me leave behind me a memorial of my friendship, with one of the most valuable men, as well as finest writers, of my age and country : one who has tried, and knows by his own experience, how hard an undertaking it is to do justice to *Homer* : and one, who (I am sure) sincerely rejoices with me at the period of my labours. To him, therefore, having brought this long work to a conclusion, I desire to dedicate it ; and to have the honour and satisfaction of placing together, in this manner, the names of Mr. CONGREVE and of
>
> A. POPE.
>
> *March* 25, 1720.

This dedication is a very important landmark in the history of English literature. It was nothing less than revolutionary. With it Pope shattered at a blow the long tradition of self-seeking dedications, whether political or personal.[174]

To mark still more clearly his wish to remain independent of party, Pope took pains to hold the balance exactly even between Whig and Tory, when expressing in his Preface his gratitude to all who had taken a sympathetic interest in himself or in his great undertaking. Side by side with Addison,

---

[173] Macaulay was the first to point out the motive underlying this dedication from one author to another. In his Essay on *The Comic Dramatists of the Restoration,* he writes : " It was necessary to find someone who was at once eminent and neutral. It was therefore necessary to pass over peers and statesmen. Congreve had a high name in letters. He had a high name in aristocratic circles. He lived on terms of civility with men of all parties."

See also the beginning of Macaulay's Essay on Robert Montgomery.

[174] In the 4th number of the *Guardian,* that is to say, as early as March 16, 1713, Pope had expressed in no uncertain terms his opinion of the fashionable type of dedication :

" To say more to a Man than one thinks, with a Prospect of Interest, is dishonest ; and without it, foolish. And who ever has had Success in such an Undertaking, must of necessity at once, think himself in his Heart a Knave for having done it, and his Patron a Fool for having believed it."

He continued the campaign against dedications : see the *Dunciad,* II, lines 191–206, and IV, lines 101–2.—Before the publication of the *Iliad* Steele had dedicated *The Tender Husband* to Addison (1705) and Gay his *Rural Sports* to Pope (1713) ; but these were both works of slight importance, and the dedications were not designed to catch public attention.

Steele, Garth and Rowe, he named Swift, Parnell and Granville. Finally, amongst the statesmen to whom he offered a tribute of thanks, he particularly singled out Halifax ; but with singular audacity—which did not pass unnoticed [175]—he immediately coupled this name with Bolingbroke's. Now Bolingbroke was at the time an exile and under sentence for high treason, yet Pope was not afraid to write : " Such a genius as my Lord Bolingbroke, not more distinguished in the great scenes of business than in all the useful and entertaining parts of learning." And he closed his paragraph of thanks with the significant remark that the patronage he had received " was the more to be acknowledged, as it is shown to one whose pen has never gratified the prejudices of any party nor the vanity of any man ".[176]

It was no small merit, in an age entirely given over to political struggle, to adopt an attitude so independent as Pope's. First, as we have just seen, it was by no means easy to avoid being sucked into the vortex, and it required both imperturbability and active effort to resist persuasive advances, and even more to resist the temptation of establishing truth by replying to attack and misrepresentation, a course which frequently entangles a man in controversy against his will. Secondly, Pope's aloofness did not spring from indifference. Pope was a Roman Catholic, that is member of a conquered, proscribed and persecuted class, victim of Draconian laws.

[175] Swift wrote to Pope, June 28, 1715 : " You are pretty bold in mentioning Lord Bolingbroke in that preface." (Elwin, VII, p. 11.) And Jervas also wrote on the same date : " The Whigs say Bolingbroke is the hero of your preface. Pray make room for Walpole in your next, to keep the balance of power even." (Elwin, VIII, p. 14. Walpole had been the president and reporter of the commission which decided on the impeachment of Bolingbroke and of Lord Oxford.) Pope replied : " If the whigs say now that Bolingbroke is the hero of my preface, the tories said, you may remember, three years ago, that Cato was the hero of my poetry. It looks generous enough to be always on the side of the distressed, and my patrons of the other party may expect great panegyrics from me (when) they come to be impeached by the future party rage of their opponents. To compliment those who are dead in law, is as much above the imputation of flattery, as Tickell says it is, to compliment those who are really dead, and perhaps too there is as much vanity in my praising Bolingbroke, as in his praising Halifax. No people in this world are so apt to give themselves airs as we authors." (Elwin, VIII, p. 15.)—Tickell had dedicated his translation of the first book of the *Iliad* to Lord Halifax who died a month before it was published.
[176] The Preface was published with the first volume of the *Iliad* in 1715 ; the Dedication with the sixth and last volume in 1720.

Every Roman priest convicted of having celebrated mass or exercised his ministry in any manner whatsoever (unless it were in the house of a foreign ambassador) ran the risk of imprisonment for life. Denunciation was encouraged by a reward of £100. To conduct a boarding-school, or in general to play any part in education, was similarly to incur a life sentence. Young Roman Catholics were not eligible for any public school, college or university, and if a father sent his child abroad to be educated in his own faith, he rendered himself liable to a fine of £100, which became the reward of the man who had denounced him. Every Englishman on reaching the age of eighteen was obliged to take an oath of allegiance to the Crown and another acknowledging its religious supremacy. Nonjurors could neither purchase nor inherit land, which passed by right to the Protestant next of kin. A Roman Catholic paid double taxes. Civil and military service, teaching, the bar and legal professions were closed to him. He was even forbidden to own a horse worth more than £5.[177] If a Roman Catholic was suspected of opposition, two Justices of the Peace could at any moment summon him to take the oaths of allegiance and supremacy, and if he refused, he put himself in the position of a released convict. He had not the right to go to law, to approach within five miles of London or, without a special permit, to travel more than five miles from his home. The penalty for infringement of these regulations was confiscation of goods. He might moreover be challenged either to renounce his errors or to quit the country ; if he did not obey, or if he returned without the royal permission, the penalty was death. It is true that these repressive laws were not applied in all their rigour, but they remained a perpetual menace. If a personal enemy, or a delator tempted by the reward, drew attention to a Roman Catholic, if Government was—rightly or wrongly —apprehensive of some disturbance brewing, these laws could be instantly brought into play.[178]

Pope had suffered, and continued to suffer, for his religion.

[177]　　" Horses by Papists are not to be ridden :
　　　　But sure the Muse's Horse was ne'er forbidden.
　　　　For in no Rate-Book, it was ever found
　　　　That *Pegasus* was valued at Five-pound."
　　　　　　　　　　(Dryden, Prologue to *Don Sebastian*.)

[178] Lecky, I, pp. 272–6 and 303–10. Lecky attributes the laxity with which these laws were enforced, in part at least to the fact that a Roman Catholic was at the time acknowledged leader of English literature.

As a child, he had seen his parents take refuge in the solitude
of Windsor Forest, seeking to be overlooked, hiding themselves
to practise their religion, compelled to give their children an
imperfect education. He had witnessed their sorrow and
anxiety.[179] As a man, he heard the complaints of his co-
religionists, he shared their hourly apprehensions and vexations.[180] Sorrowfully he said : " It is not for me to speak of
England with tears in my eyes. I cannot consider that country
mine where I am not allowed to call a foot of ground my own."

There was therefore good reason, enough and to spare, why
Pope's sympathy did not go forth to the Whigs and the Protestant party, but naturally inclined him towards the Tories, if
not actually towards the Jacobites. His chief personal friends
were in fact Tories, and as he grew older his ideas approximated
more and more to theirs. He frequently expressed in verse the
views they cherished, and in one of his works, his *Epistle to
Augustus*, did so with so much vigour that the poem narrowly·
escaped being proscribed. But his main concern was to be an
author, and not to allow himself in his own despite, to be lured
like his fellows into politics on the slightest provocation. While
neither disguising nor concealing his opinions, he did not wish

[179]   " Bred up at home, full early I begun
            To read in Greek the wrath of Peleus' son.
            Besides, my Father taught me, from a lad,
            The better art, to know the good from bad :
            (And little sure imported to remove,
            To hunt for Truth in Maudlin's learned grove.)
            But knottier points we knew not half so well,
            Depriv'd us soon of our paternal Cell ;
            And certain Laws, by suff'rers thought unjust,
            Deny'd all posts of profit or of trust :
            Hopes after hopes of pious Papists fail'd,
            While mighty William's thund'ring arm prevail'd.
            For Right Hereditary tax'd and fin'd,
            He stuck to poverty with peace of mind ;
            And we, the Muses help'd to undergo it ;
            Convict a Papist he, and I a Poet."
                            (*Satires and Epistles*, VI, Horace 2 Epist. 2,
                            lines 52–69, Warburton's Edition, p. 209.)

[180] See Pope's letters to Caryll dated Aug. 16, 1714, and March 2,
1715–16, and those to Blount, March 24, 1715–16 and June 23, 1716 (Elwin
VI, pp. 217, 238, 372 and 374). In 1730 one of his nephews was prevented,
after fourteen years of preparation, from qualifying as an attorney because
oaths were unexpectedly required of him which his religion forbade him to
take. (Letters to Caryll, Dec. 1730 and Jan. 31, 1732–3. Elwin, VI,
pp. 325, 337.) In 1744 when the Pretender's activities were causing alarm,
a royal proclamation, which Pope was obliged to obey, forbade Roman
Catholics to live in London.

to air them where they had no relevance, but sought to devote himself wholly and freely to his profession, unhampered by any commitment of his own or other people's. This single-minded concentration on his profession, this concern to exercise it in dignity and independence, was the dominating principle of his life. Not only did he bear witness to it in his own conduct but he strove to convert his brethren to it.

One day, for instance, when Gay, cheated of the ambitious hopes he had centred on the Court, haughtily refused as beneath him, a post he was offered in the household of one of the royal children, Pope wrote to him :

> I could find it in my heart to congratulate you on this happy dismission from all court dependency . . . You are happily rid of many cursed ceremonies, as well as of many ill and vicious habits, of which few or no men escape the infection, who are hackneyed and trammelled in the ways of a court. Princes indeed, and peers (the lackeys of princes) and ladies (the fools of peers), will smile on you the less ; but men of worth and real friends will look on you the better. There is a thing, the only thing which kings and queens cannot give you—for they have it not to give—liberty, which is worth all they have, and which, as yet, I hope Englishmen need not ask from their hands. You will enjoy that, and your own integrity . . . While you are nobody's servant, you may be anyone's friend, and as such, I embrace you in all conditions of life.[181]

Similarly when Swift, yearning again to take a hand in politics, seemed for a moment on the brink of yielding to Pulteney's blandishments, Pope offered him this advice :

> Surely, without flattery, you are now above all parties of men, and it is high time to be so, after twenty or thirty years' observation of the great world.
>
> Nullius addictus jurare in verba magistri.
>
> I question not, many men would be of your intimacy, that you might be of their interest : but God forbid an honest or witty man should be of any, but that of his country. They have scoundrels enough to write for the passions and their designs ; let us write for truth, for honour, and for posterity.[182]

---

[181] Letter dated Oct. 16, 1726 (Elwin, VII, p. 427).
[182] Letter dated Nov. 16, 1726 (ibid., p. 87).—On Dec. 1, 1731, he again wrote him :

"I am glad you resolve to meddle no more with the low concerns and interests of parties . . .

Quid verum atque decens, curare, at rogare, nostrum sit."
(Elwin, VII, p. 258.)

It would be wrong to picture Pope's religion as having made this independence of his a compulsory virtue, whose restraint he could not have shaken off even if he had wished. It is true that as a Roman Catholic he was debarred from public office ; but that did not deter either Whigs or Tories from making him tempting offers which he was free to accept had he so desired.

When Harley was in office, he expressed on several occasions his regret at not being able to give Pope a place in the administration, and made it clear that the poet need only turn Protestant to have what he liked for the asking. Pope, who had never been over-zealous in his faith—if indeed he was not all his life more Deist than Papist—had no other reason for not following Dryden's example than the fear of wounding his aged parents, yet he would not even toy with the suggestion : " I could not . . . without giving a great deal of pain to my parents ; such pain, indeed, as I would not have given to either of them, for all the places he could have bestowed upon me." [183]

---

[183] Spence, pp. 304–5 [2nd Ed. of Spence, 1858, the page reference is 231].—The following passage from a letter of Pope's to Caryll, dated May 1, 1714, seems to have reference to Harley's proposal :

" Though I find it an unfortunate thing to be bred a papist, when one is obnoxious to four parts in five as being so too much, and to the fifth part for being so too little, I shall yet be easy under both their mistakes . . . God is my witness, that I no more envy the protestants their places and possessions than I do our priests their charity or learning. I am ambitious of nothing but the good opinion of all good men of all sides, for I know that one virtue of a free spirit is more worth than all the virtues put together of all the narrow-souled people in the world. If they promise me all the good offices they ever did, or could do, I would not change for them all one kind word of yours." (Elwin, VI, pp. 208–9.)

See also letters from Swift to Pope, July 19 and Sept. 29, 1725 (Elwin, VII, pp. 49 and 53).—After the death of Pope's father in 1717, Bishop Atterbury—with the utmost delicacy, be it said—drew Pope's attention to the advantage which would accrue from his conversion. Pope replied in a long letter which deserves to be read in its entirety ; I confine myself to quoting a passage :

" As to the *temporal* side of the question, I can have no dispute with you. It is certain, all the beneficial circumstances of life, and all the shining ones, lie on the part you would invite me to. But if I could bring myself to fancy, what I think you do but fancy, that I have any talents for active life, I want health for it ; and besides it is a real truth, I have less inclination (if possible) than ability. Contemplative life is not only my scene, but my habit too. I began my life where most people end theirs, with a disrelish of all that the world calls ambition. I do not know why it is called so ; for to me it always seemed to be rather *stooping* than *climbing*." (Carruthers, pp. 162–4.)

Again, in a letter to Swift, Nov. 28, 1729, Pope writes :

" Yet am I of the religion of Erasmus, a catholic. So I live, so I shall die ; and hope one day to meet you, Bishop Atterbury, the younger Craggs,

At the beginning of George I's reign, Halifax asked to see the poet. He had, he said, noted with regret that Pope had not received the recognition he deserved. He rejoiced to be now in a position to be of service to him : if Pope felt inclined to accept the offer, he would be granted a pension with no condition attached. Pope thanked him, but, as if he needed leisure for reflection, returned no immediate answer. Later he wrote to Halifax, renewing his thanks, and saying that he had given the offer mature consideration. With the pension, he would no doubt be able " to live more at large in town " and drive his carriage, but that without the pension he could live " happily enough in the country ". His choice was made, and he preferred " liberty without a coach ".[184]

Later, his intimate friend Craggs, happening to have at his disposal a secret fund of public money, pressed him most insistently to accept from this source a pension of £300 a year, which no one would ever know about. This offer also Pope refused. In thanking Craggs for this proof of his friendship he added simply that if he ever needed to borrow money Craggs was the first to whom he would turn.[185]

On another occasion Swift took it upon himself to speak to Carteret of a pension for Pope. No sooner had Pope heard of this, than he wrote with some acrimony to his friend :

I was once displeased before at you, for complaining to Mr. Dodington of my not having a pension, and am so again at your naming it to a certain lord. I have given " some " proofs, in the course of my whole life (from the time when I was in the friendship of Lord Bolingbroke and Mr. Craggs, even to this, when I am civilly treated by Sir R. Walpole), that I never thought myself so warm in any party's cause as to deserve their money ; and, therefore, never would have accepted it ; but give me leave to tell you, that of all mankind the two persons I would least have accepted any favour from are those very two, to whom you have unluckily spoken of it. I desire you to take off any impressions which that dialogue may have left on his lordship's mind, as if I ever had any thought of being beholden to him or any other, in that way. And yet you know I am

---

Dr. Garth, Dean Berkeley, and Mr. Hutchenson, in that place, to which God in his infinite mercy bring us, and everybody ! " (Elwin, VII, p. 175.)

[184] Spence, pp. 305–6 [1858 Ed., pp. 231–2]. See also in Johnson Pope's letter to Halifax, dated Dec. 1, 1714.—Pope was no doubt alluding to Halifax's offer when some years later he wrote to Swift : " Horace might keep his coach in Augustus's time if he pleased. But I will not in the time of our Augustus." (Letter of Oct. 22, 1727, Elwin, VII, p. 104.)

[185] Spence, pp. 307–8 [1858 Ed., p. 232].

no enemy to the present constitution—I believe as sincere a well-wisher to it, nay, even to the church established, as any minister in or out of employment whatever.[186]

Rather than accept as a favour money from other men, Pope preferred to live, with lesser luxury and greater dignity, on what he earned by his own work. He rented on a long lease a house at Twickenham on the Thames in the neighbourhood of London. There he made his home, living in his own house like a landed proprietor, tending his garden, working at his leisure, receiving his friends, caring tenderly for his old mother, and proudly exclaiming :

> But (thanks to Homer) since I live and thrive,
> Indebted to no Prince or Peer alive.[187]

He was thus the first to set a noble example to his fellow-authors. He demonstrated to them that they could at last live as independent men, that literature was now a liberal profession, and that henceforth they need owe their due place in society to nothing but their own talent. This poet, who sought favours from none, was sought after by all, and the house at Twickenham became the trysting-place of a company which would have done honour to a royal palace. There were seen not only distinguished intellectuals like Swift, Atterbury, Gay and Arbuthnot, artists like Jervas and Kneller, politicians like Murray, Pulteney, Lyttelton and Wyndham, but those most eminent by birth, rank and station. Thither came Bolingbroke, the brilliant orator, the statesman who at one moment had held the destiny of England in his hand ; Lord Oxford, colleague and rival of Bolingbroke, and his son, later the inheritor of his title (1724) ; Lord Peterborough, gallant and chivalrous commander of the English army in Spain ; the fashionable and witty Chesterfield ; Lords Burlington, Bathurst and Cobham ; the Earls of Orrery and Marchmont ; the Dukes of Shrewsbury and Argyle, in a word, all the most brilliant stars of aristocratic England. Even the King's son and heir, the Prince of Wales,

---

[186] Nov. 28, 1729 (Elwin, VII, pp. 174–5).

[187] *Satires and Epistles*, VI, Horace 2 Epist. 2, lines 68–9 ; Warburton, IV, p. 209.—Again, in prefacing *The Dunciad* he says : " But it happens that this our poet never had any place, pension, or gratuity, in any shape, from the said glorious Queen, or any of her Ministers. All he owed, in the whole course of his life, to any court, was a subscription, for his Homer, of £200 from King George I, and £100 from the Prince and Princess."

went out of his way to call on the poet and accepted his invitation to dinner.[188]

With all these great folk Pope mixed on the same terms as with his brother authors—on a footing of perfect equality. He took his place among them as of natural right. If they entertained him in their houses, he entertained them in his. All were his friends ; none was his patron. If at one time or another he dedicated one of his books to one of them, it was not to flatter him or invite his support—as had so recently been the accepted practice of writers—it was merely to give public expression to genuine esteem.

On their side the haughty arrogance of other days was completely forgotten : the aristocracy of birth at last paid homage without reserve to the aristocracy of genius. Neither as an act of condescension, nor from motives of self-interest did the great ones of the land seek social contact with the poet. They came out of admiration for his gifts, out of liking for his personality, out of the feeling that it was an honour to be admitted to the circle of his friends.[189] Bolingbroke loved to discuss philosophy and literature with Pope ; Peterborough amused himself by working in the garden [190] ; Bathurst, whose hobby

---

[188] " Oft in the clear, still Mirrour of Retreat,
        I study'd Shrewsbury, the wise and great ;
        Carleton's calm Sense, and Stanhope's noble Flame,
        Compar'd, and knew their gen'rous End the same :
        How pleasing Atterbury's softer hour !
        How shin'd the Soul, unconquer'd in the Tow'r !
        How can I Pult'ney, Chesterfield forget,
        While Roman Spirit charms, and Attic Wit :
        Argyll, the State's whole Thunder born to wield,
        And shake alike the Senate and the Field :
        Or Wyndham, just to Freedom and the Throne,
        The Master of our Passions, and his own.
        Names, which I long have lov'd, nor loved in vain,
        Rank'd with their Friends, not number'd with their Train.
        And if yet higher the proudest List should end,
        Still let me say ! No Follower, but a Friend."
(*Epilogue to the Satires*, lines 78–93. Warburton, IV, p. 324.)

[189] On Nov. 6, 1721, the Earl of Oxford writes to Pope : " I should be glad the world knew you admitted me to your friendship." (Elwin, VIII, p. 189.)

[190] " There, my retreat the best Companions grace,
        Chiefs out of war, and Statesmen out of place.
        There St. John mingles with my friendly bowl
        The Feast of Reason and the Flow of Soul :
        And He, whose lightning pierc'd th' Iberian Lines,
        Now forms my Quincunx, and now ranks my Vines,

was building and plantation, consulted him about his plans. All of them valued his company and his conversation, and if they were cut off from the pleasure of seeing him, they kept up a regular correspondence with him. One and all were eager to do him service ; and the Prince of Wales himself sent him busts for his library.

Finally, nothing shows more clearly the profound change which the Restoration had wrought in the author's status, than the fact that members of the aristocracy addressed to Pope poetic compliments on his work. Among these flattering tributes it is quaint to find verses of Mulgrave's—now Duke of Buckinghamshire [191] (currently known as Duke of Buckingham). The Merry Monarch's brilliant courtier, Dryden's haughty patron, the literary Mæcenas who had seen so many poets bend the servile knee before him, had come to this, that in the reign of George I it was he who paid homage to Alexander Pope.

Alexander Pope, the little, deformed and ailing man, the Roman Catholic, the London linen-draper's son, had become the social equal of the greatest ; and that by dint of minding his own affairs, of wishing to be, and wishing to remain, simply a man of letters.

V

Conclusion

This is a matter in which less than justice has been done to Pope.

First, his biographers have almost always treated his life in isolation, taking too little heed of preceding history. As a

---

Or tames the Genius of the stubborn plain,
Almost as quickly as he conquer'd Spain."
(*Satire* I. To Mr. Fortescue, lines 124–32.
Warburton, IV, p. 69.)

[191] This was Mulgrave's legal title. He formally avoided the title of " Duke of Buckingham " lest it might be claimed by the Villiers family.— The verses by Mulgrave, the Countess of Winchelsea and the Hon. Simon Harcourt, may be found in Elwin's *Pope*, I, pp. 19 ff.—Swift had already tried the Duke's pride severely. In a letter to Stella (May 19, 1711) he writes : " Mr. Secretary told me the Duke of Buckingham had been talking to him much about me, and desired my acquaintance. I answered it could not be ; for he had not made sufficient advances. Then the Duke of Shrewsbury said he thought that duke was not used to make advances. I said I could not help that ; for I always expected advances in proportion to men's quality, and more from a duke than other men."

natural consequence, though they have usually noted his independent attitude, they have failed to appreciate how much
credit he deserved for adopting, and how great service he
rendered by maintaining it.   Themselves rejoicing in their independence, they troubled little to inquire whether their predecessors had in the past enjoyed the same boon, and they saw
nothing remarkable in the conduct of the man who had won
this independence for them.

Pope has suffered in yet another way at his biographers'
hands.   It has become a commonplace to say that a biographer
is usually inclined to conceal or minimize the failings and
mistakes of the man whose life he undertakes to write.   This
disease, to which the biographer is particularly liable, if it be
a disease, is that of over-admiration which Macaulay wittily
diagnosed—after one of the most distinguished sufferers from it
—as *lues Boswelliana*.   But in the case of those who have written
of Pope we find a strange phenomenon : they have been inspired
not by admiration but by the very reverse, a desire to depreciate.
Because Pope has been convicted of sharp practice and bad
faith at certain moments in his life, they would have us believe
that he was capable of nothing but duplicity, perfidy and
treachery.   In the whole of English literature there is perhaps
no figure which has been painted so black as Pope's.   Not
only are his proven frailties displayed with a ruthlessness that
takes no heed of extenuating circumstances, not only is any
ambiguous act of his given the most damaging interpretation
possible, not only is every ugly deed attributed to him by his
enemies, accepted with almost no attempt at verification ; but
his biographers appear to take so much pleasure in the unpleasant side of their task that it exercises a sort of hypnotic
fascination over them which prevents their perceiving even his
most manifest good qualities.

This is not the place to make a detailed study of the accusations with which he has been overwhelmed, or to examine
the exaggeration and even errors which many of them may
contain.   Charles Dilke, one of those who knew Pope best and
perhaps the only man who has been just to him, has already
disproved some of these accusations, and I refer the reader to
his valuable work.   As for me, I have not undertaken to write
the poet's life and I have no mind to counter relentless criticism
with unqualified praise.   There are certain stains on Pope's
character which will unfortunately not wash off.   Yes.   In his

desire to publish his correspondence during his own lifetime Pope played for a long time a curious comedy. The same desire led him to take unfair advantage of his friend Swift when Swift's mental powers were failing. Yes. When asked to explain certain personal allusions in his verse, he had not the courage to answer honestly, and stooped to contemptible and useless evasions. I know these faults of his, and they grieve me the more in proportion as I admire other sides of his character. But who can claim to be without fault? Is it fair that the blame justly incurred by Pope should blot out the praise that he has rightly earned? In any case, not one of the just accusations which besmirch his memory detracts from his independence as a writer, or the faithfulness with which he devoted himself to his profession.

As an example of the injustice with which he has too frequently been treated, I should like, however, to make mention of one reproach that has been levelled at him, because this bears on the subject of my study.

In his life of Pope Dr. Johnson says: " Next to the pleasure of contemplating his possessions, seems to be that of enumerating the men of high rank with whom he was acquainted . . . His admiration of the Great seems to have increased in the advance of life . . . To his later works he took care to annex names dignified with titles."

And in conversation he commented with more asperity:

" How foolish was it in Pope to give all his friendship to lords, who thought they honoured him by being with him! . . . And then always saying: ' I do not value you for being a lord ' ; which was a sure proof that he did." [192]

To which Dilke has vigorously retorted: " So far indeed was Pope from seeking Lords for his acquaintance, that those he did know sought him ; and those who sought him were amongst the most distinguished and intellectual men of his age. Was he to refuse such associates?—was he to refuse such testimony to his worth—such worshippers of his genius—because they were men of distinguished rank and high position? " [193]

I would add that even if we admit that Pope took a certain pleasure in mentioning his noble friends, a spice of vanity was not unnatural. He was the first English writer to be thus

[192] Boswell, VII, p. 208.
[193] *Papers of a Critic*, I, p. 116.—See also his further very just and very eloquent remarks.

honoured. Before his time the great lord and the holder of great office had looked down on the author ; it was only recently that they had condescended to show the writer a modicum of respect, and that in return for services rendered. Pope had rendered service to none ; he had devoted himself wholly to his profession, which was the sole occupation and passion of his life, and despite this, the most highly placed persons had made advances and rendered homage to him. How could he have avoided feeling proud ? We may rather marvel that his head was not turned, as Swift's was in his days of fame.[194] Johnson, himself a great man of letters, ought better than anyone to have understood the justifiable pride of a man who rejoices to note that, thanks to his own merit, and to that alone, he need envy none the advantages conferred by birth or office. When George III sought out Dr. Johnson for a talk, did Johnson not feel himself highly honoured and afterwards remark " he is the finest gentleman I have ever seen " ? Is it not true that " he loved to relate the incident with all its circumstances among his friends " ? And did he not like to boast, as Boswell records, " that he talked to His Majesty with profound respect, but still in his firm manly manner, with a sonorous voice, and never in that subdued tone which is commonly used at the levee and in the drawing-room " ? [195]

Shall we in our turn find fault with Johnson ? Shall we accuse him of vanity ? By no means. He was moved by precisely the same natural instinct as Pope. He was justly proud of the flattering step the King took to meet him ; but he preserved his professional pride, and on principle would not appear to humble himself even before his sovereign.

There is a story that Piron was one day invited to dine at some great seigneur's. As the guests were moving into the

[194] See above, chap. III, note No. 41, and chap. IV, note No. 191.—Nor, for all his grand friends, did he ever forget his fellow-authors. Not to speak of his friendship for Swift, for Gay and for Arbuthnot, he never deserted Savage, who had worn out all his friends in turn. He helped to organize a benefit performance for Dennis who had made savage attacks on him, not sparing even his physical infirmities. He brought strong persuasion to bear on Dodsley, the publisher, to pay a liberal fee to Akenside for a remarkable poem. After reading some verses of Johnson, a man whom he did not know, he wrote spontaneously to Lord Gower commending Johnson to his favour. The Dunciad might seem to belie the benevolence of these acts, but above and beyond personal attacks the Dunciad shows a predominating desire to rid literature of the type of writer who in Pope's opinion brought it into dishonour.

[195] Boswell, III, pp. 19 ff.

dining-room he made way for one whom he did not know; the other refused to take precedence. The master of the house put a stop to this competition in courtesy by saying : " Come on first, Duke, he is only an author."—" Since our ranks are known," retorted Piron, " I claim my own ", and he led the way.

Pope, similarly, claimed his own rank, and his whole profession claimed it with him. Whether or not they recognized their debt to him, his immediate successors, inheriting the rank he had won for them, adopted his attitude and maintained the tradition he had begun.

At present [writes Goldsmith] the few poets of England no longer depend on the Great for subsistence, they have now no other patrons but the public, and the public, collectively considered, is a good and generous master . . . Every polite member of the community, by buying what a man of letters writes, contributes to reward him. The ridicule therefore of living in a garret, might have been wit in the last age, but continues such no longer, because no longer true. A writer of real merit now may easily be rich if his heart be set only on fortune : and for those who have no merit, it is but fit that such should remain in merited obscurity. He may now refuse an invitation to dinner, without fearing to incur his patron's displeasure, or to starve by remaining at home. He may now venture to appear in company with just such clothes as other men generally wear, and talk even to princes, with all the conscious superiority of wisdom. Though he cannot boast of fortune here, yet he can bravely assert the dignity of independence.[196]

Goldsmith's practice harmonized with his theory. When the Earl of Northumberland was appointed Lord-Lieutenant of Ireland he told Goldsmith that he had read his *Traveller* with much enjoyment, and that it would be a great pleasure to him if, in his new capacity, he could do something for him. In recounting this gracious offer, Goldsmith said : " I could say nothing, but that I had a brother there [in Ireland], a clergyman, that stood in need of help : as for myself, I have no dependence on the promises of great men ; I look to the booksellers for support ; they are my best friends, and I am not inclined to forsake them for others." [197]

This testimony is doubly interesting. First, because of the important place Goldsmith occupies in English literature, and secondly because his career as a man of letters was by no means all plain sailing, and was punctuated by long and painful periods

[196] *The Citizen of the World*, Letter 84. *Works*, II, pp. 369–70. These letters first appeared in the paper called *The Public Ledger* in 1760.
[197] Hawkins, quoted by Boswell, II, p. 200.

of hardship. The same interest attaches to a testimony of Johnson's that occurs in a conversation of his with his friends Boswell and Watson :

" Now learning is itself a trade. A man goes to a bookseller and gets what he can. We have done with patronage. In the infancy of learning, we find some great man praised for it. This diffused it among others. When it becomes general, an author leaves the great, and applies to the multitudes." *Boswell :* " It is a shame that authors are not now better patronized." *Johnson :* " No, Sir. If learning cannot support a man, if he must sit with his hands across till somebody feeds him, it is as to him a bad thing, and it is better as it is. With patronage, what flattery ! What falsehood ! While a man is in equilibrio, he throws truth among the multitude, and lets them take it as they please : in patronage, he must say what pleases his patron, and it is an equal chance whether that be truth or falsehood." *Watson :* " But is it not the case now, that instead of flattering one person, we flatter the age ? " *Johnson :* " No, Sir. The world always lets a man tell what he thinks his own way." [198]

Again, in the *Rambler* Johnson repeated the same view but with greater seriousness :

" The Sciences, after a thousand indignities, retired from the palace of Patronage, and having long wandered over the world in grief and distress, were led at last to the cottage of Independence, the daughter of Fortitude ; where they were taught by Prudence and Parsimony to support themselves in dignity and quiet." [199]

So it is clear that Pope had founded a school of thought. It was he who introduced this attitude of proud independence into English literature, a virtue which it has never lost.

I have tried to do justice to his predecessors, and we should not forget how much they did to open and prepare the road. But if it was thanks to their pioneer work that he was able to be an independent man of letters, the personal honour is his, of having desired to be such, and of having invested the literary profession in England with the rank and dignity it enjoys to-day.

[198] Boswell, IV, p. 55.   [199] *The Rambler*, No. 91.

BIBLIOGRAPHY

I. GENERAL WORKS

A. Historical

AUBREY (John).
Letters written By Eminent Persons in the Seventeenth and Eighteenth Centuries : . . . And Lives of Eminent Men, by John Aubrey, Esq. In two Volumes. London : Printed for Longman, Hurst, Rees, Orme, and Brown, Paternoster-Row ; and Munday and Slatter, Oxford. 1813. 8º.

BELSHAM (W.).
Memoirs Of the Kings of Great Britain of the House of Brunswic-Lunenburg. By W. Belsham. Ac mihi quidem videntur huc omnia esse referenda ab iis qui praesunt aliis, ut ii qui eorum in imperio erunt, sint quam beatissimi. Cicero. London : Printed for C. Dilly, in the Poultry. 1793. 2 vol. 8º.

BURKE (Edmund).
Reflections on the Revolution in France, and on the Proceedings in certain Societies in London relative to that event. In a Letter intended to have been sent to a Gentleman *in Paris.* By the Right Honourable *Edmund Burke.* London : Printed for J. Dodsley, in Pall-Mall. MDCCXC. 8º.
[Ed. Sir S. Lee. 1905.]

CHALMERS (George).
The Life of *Thomas Ruddiman,* A.M. The Keeper, for almost Fifty Years, of the Library belonging to the Faculty of Advocates at Edinburgh. To which are subjoined New Anecdotes of *Buchanan.* By George Chalmers, F.R.S.S.A. London : Printed for John Stockdale. Piccadilly : and William Laing, Edinburgh. M.DCC.XCIV. 8º.

CHARLES II.
Copies of two papers Written by the late King Charles the Second. Together with a copy of a Paper written by the late Dutchess of York. Published by his Majestie's special Command. London : Printed by Henry Hills Printer to the Kings most excellent Majesty, for his household and Chappell. 1686. 4º. (This is in manuscript.)

CHRISTIE (W. D.).
Letters addressed from London to Sir Joseph Williamson while Plenipotentiary at the Congress of Cologne in the Years 1673 and 1674. Edited by W. D. Christie, C.B. Author of the Life of the First Earl of Shaftesbury. In Two Volumes. Printed for the Camden Society. M.DCCC.LXXIV. 4º.

CLARENDON (Edward Hyde, Earl of).
The History of the Rebellion and Civil Wars in England, together with an Historical View of the Affairs of Ireland, by Edward Earl of Clarendon now for the first time carefully printed from the original MS. preserved in the Bodleian Library. To which are subjoined the notes of Bishop Warburton. In seven volumes. Oxford, at the University Press. MDCCXLIX. 8º.
[First edition : 3 vols. 1702–4. Ed. W. Dunn Macray. 1888.]

CLARK (G. N.).
[*The Later Stuarts, 1660–1714.* 1934.]

387

COBBETT (William).

Cobbett's Parliamentary History of England. From the Norman Conquest, in 1066, to the Year 1803. From which last-mentioned Epoch it is continued downwards in the Work entitled, " Cobbett's Parliamentary Debates ". London : Printed by T. Curson Hansard, Peterborough-Court, Fleet street. Published by R. Bagshaw, Brydges-Street, Covent-Garden ; and sold by J. Budd, Pall-Mall ; R. Faulder, New Bond-Street ; H. D. Symonds, Paternoster-Row ; Blacks and Parry, Leadenhall-Street ; and J. Archer, Dublin. October 1806. 36 vols. 8⁰.

COOKE (Wingrove George).

The History of Party ; From the rise of the Whig and Tory Factions, in the Reign of Charles II., To the passing of the Reform Bill. By George Wingrove Cooke, Esq., Barrister at Law, Author of " Memoirs of Lord Bolingbroke ", etc. 3 volumes. London : John Macrone, St. James's Square. MDCCCXXXVI. 8⁰.

DORAN (Dr.).

London in the Jacobite Times By Dʳ Doran, F.S.A. . . . In Two Volumes. London, Richard Bentley and Son, New Burlington Street, Publishers in Ordinary to Her Majesty the Queen. 1877. 8⁰.

EVELYN (John).

Memoirs, Illustrative of the Life and Writings of John Evelyn, Esq. F.R.S. Author of the " Sylva ", etc. etc. Comprising his Diary from the Year 1641 to 1705–6, and a Selection of his familiar Letters. To which is subjoined, The private Correspondence between King Charles I. and his Secretary of State, Sir Edward Nicholas, whilst His Majesty was in Scotland, 1641, and at other times during the civil war ; also between Sir Edward Hyde, afterwards Earl of Clarendon, and Sir Richard Browne, Ambassador to the Court of France, in the time of King Charles I. and the Usurpation. The Whole now first published, from the Original MSS. In two Volumes. Edited by William Bray, Esq. Fellow and Treasurer of the Society of Antiquaries of London. London : Printed for Henry Colburn, Conduit Street. And Sold by John and Arthur Arch, Cornhill. 1818. 4⁰.

Diary and Correspondence of John Evelyn, F.R.S., Author of the " Sylva ". To which is subjoined The Private Correspondence between King Charles I. and Sir Edward Nicholas, and between Sir Edward Hyde, afterwards Earl of Clarendon and Sir Richard Browne. Edited from the Original MSS. at Wotton. By William Bray, Esq., F.A.S. A new edition, in four Volumes. Corrected, revised, and enlarged. London : Henry Colburn, Publisher, . . . 1850. 8⁰.

[4 vols. Bohn's Library. 1859. Reprinted : Routledge. 1906.]

GRANGER (J.).

A Biographical History of England, From Egbert the Great to the Revolution : Consisting of Characters disposed in different Classes, and adapted to a Methodical Catalogue of Engraved British Heads. Intended as an Essay towards reducing our Biography to System, and a Help to the Knowledge of Portraits. Interspersed with Variety of Anecdotes, and Memoirs of a great Number of Persons, not to be found in any other Biographical Work. With a Preface, shewing the Utility of a Collection of Engraved Portraits to supply the Defect, and answer the various Purposes of Medals. By the Rev. J. Granger, Vicar of Shiplake, in Oxfordshire. Animam pictura pascit inani. Virg. Celebrare domestica facta. Hor. London, Printed for T. Davies, in Russel-Street, Covent-Garden. 1769–1774. 2 vols. 4⁰.

[3 vols. 1806. Cont. M. Noble.]

HALLAM (Henry).
The Constitutional History of England From the Accession of Henry VII. to the Death of George II. By Henry Hallam, LL.D., F.R.A.S. Foreign Associate of the Institute of France. Seventh Edition. In Three volumes. London : John Murray, Albemarle Street. 1854. 8⁰.

HAMILTON (Antoine).
Mémoires du Chevalier de Grammont. Précédés d'une notice sur la vie et les ouvrages d'Hamilton, par M. Auger, secrétaire perpétuel de l'Académie française. Suivis de la table des noms propres des mémoires de Grammont et d'un choix de ses épîtres en vers et de la correspondance . . . Paris, Librairie de Firmin-Didot, freres, fils et Cᵗᵉ. 1861. 12⁰.

HERVEY (John, Lord).
Memoirs of the Reign of George the Second, from his Accession to the Death of Queen Caroline. By John, Lord Hervey. Edited from the original manuscript at Ickworth, By The Right Hon. John Wilson Croker, LL.D., F.R.S. In Two Volumes. London : John Murray, Albemarle Street. 1848. 8⁰.
[Ed. R. Sedgwick. 3 vols. 1931. With a memoir of the life of Hervey.]

KEBLE (Joseph).
The Statutes at Large in Paragraphs and Sections or Numbers, from Magna Charta To the End of The Reign of King Charles II. (Carefully Examined by the Rolls of Parliament ; with the Titles of such Statutes as are Expired, Repealed, Altered, or out of Use.) Together with the Heads of Pulton's or Rastal's Abridgments in the Margin, And the Addition of above a Thousand New References from other Books of Law. By Joseph Keble of *Grays-Inn*, Esquire. In this Impression are added All the Statutes in the Reigns of King *James* II. King *William* and Queen *Mary*, to the End of the last Session of Parliament, *May* 3. 1695. In the Seventh Year of the Reign of His Majesty King *William* III. All the Statutes of the said Reigns are Alphabetically Tabled with the other Statutes, and the former Table much Improved by Notes on all the Paragraphs or Heads, whereby any Thing that is look'd for may be much sooner found. In Two Volumes. *London*, Printed by *Charles Bill*, and the Executrix of *Thomas Newcomb*, deceas'd, Printers to the Kings most Excellent Majesty, And by the Assigns of *Richard Atkins*, and *Edward Atkins*, Esquires. MDCXCV. folio.

LECKY (William Edward Hartpole).
A History of England in the Eighteenth Century by William Edward Hartpole Lecky. London : Longmans, Green, and Co. 1878–1886. 6 vols. 8⁰.
[8 vols. 1878–90.]

LODGE (Sir Richard).
[*The History of England from the Restoration to the death of William III. 1660–1702.* Vol. VIII of *The Political History of England.* 1910.]

MACAULAY (Thomas Babington, Lord).
The History of England from the accession of James the Second By Thomas Babington Macaulay. Twelfth Edition. London : Longman, Brown, Green and Longmans, 1856. 5 vols. 8⁰.
[Ed. T. F. Henderson. 5 vols. 1931. World's Classics.]

MAHON (Lord). See STANHOPE.

MALCOLM (James Peller).
Anecdotes of the Manners and Customs of London from the Roman Invasion

to the Year 1700 ; including the origin of British Society, Customs and Manners, with a General Sketch of the State of Religion, Superstition, Dresses, and Amusements of the Citizens of London during that period. To which are added, Illustrations of the Changes in our Language, Literary Customs, and gradual Improvement in style and versification, and various particulars concerning public and private libraries. Illustrated by Eighteen Engravings. By James Peller Malcolm, F.A.S. Author of " Londinium Redivivum " ; and of " Anecdotes of the Manners and Customs of London, during the eighteenth century ". *London* : Printed for Longman, Hurst, Rees, Orme, and Brown, Paternoster Row. 1811. 4⁰.

NEAL (Daniel).

The History of the Puritans or *Protestant Non-Conformists*, from the Reformation to the Death of Queen Elizabeth : With An Account of their Principles ; their Attempts for a further Reformation in the Church ; their Sufferings ; and the Lives and Characters of their principal Divines, By Daniel Neal, M.A. *Now all these Things happened unto them for Ensamples ; And they are written for our Admonition.* 1 Cor. x. 11. *London* : *Printed for* Richard Hett, *at the* Bible *and* Crown *in the* Poultry. M.DCC.XXXII. The 2nd volume, dated M.DCC.XXXIII, " from the Death of Queen Elizabeth to the Beginning of the Civil War in the Year 1642 ", has the motto : *But if ye bite and devour one another, take heed ye be not consumed one of another*, Gal. v. 15. The 3rd volume dated M.DCC.XXXVI, " from the Beginning of the Civil War in the Year 1642. to the Death of King Charles I. 1648 ". has the motto : *Think not that I am come to send Peace on Earth, I came not to send Peace but a Sword*, Matth. x. 34. The 4th volume dated M.DCC.XXXVIII, " from the Death of King Charles I. to the Act of *Toleration* by King William and Queen Mary, in the Year 1689 ", has the two following mottoes : *This know also, that in the last Days perilous Times shall come*, 2 Tim. III. 1. *They shall put you out of the Synagogues ; yea, the Time cometh, that whosoever killeth you will think that he doth God Service.* John xvi. 2. 4 vols. 8⁰.

[Ed. J. Toulmin. 1822. With a life of Neal.]

PEPYS (Samuel).

Diary and Correspondence of Samuel Pepys, F.R.S. Secretary to the Admiralty in the Reigns of Charles II. and James II. With a Life and Notes by Richard Lord Braybrooke. The Third Edition, Considerably enlarged. Five Volumes. London : Henry Colburn, Publisher, Great Marlborough Street. 1848. 8⁰.

Diary and Correspondence of Samuel Pepys, Esq. F.R.S., from his MS. cypher in the Pepysian Library, with a Life and Notes by Richard Lord Braybrooke. Deciphered, with additional notes, by Rev. Mynors Bright, M.A. President and Senior Fellow of Magdalene College, Cambridge. With numerous portraits from the Collection in the Pepysian Library, printed in permanent Woodburytype. London : Bickers and Son, 1, Leicester Square. 1875. 5 vols. 8⁰.

The Diary of Samuel Pepys M.A. F.R.S. Clerk of the Acts and Secretary to the Admiralty transcribed from the Shorthand Manuscript in the Pepysian Library Magdalene College Cambridge by the Rev. Mynors Bright M.A. Late Fellow and President of the College with Lord Braybrooke's Notes Edited with Additions by Henry B. Wheatley, F.S.A. London : George Bell & Sons York St. Covent Garden. . . 1893-1896. 8⁰.

[Ed. H. B. Wheatley. 1920.]

[Samuel Pepys. By Arthur Bryant.
  Vol. I. The Man in the Making. 1933.
  Vol. II. The Years of Peril. 1935.
  Vol. III. The Saviour of the Navy. 1938.]

PHILIPS (Ambrose).
  The Life of John Williams, Ld Keeper of the Great Seal, Bp. of Lincoln, and ABp. of York. In the Reigns of King James, and King Charles the First. Wherein *Are related several Remarkable Occurences of those Times both in Church and State.* With an *Appendix* Giving a just Account of his Benefactions to *St. John's* College in *Cambridge.* By *Ambr. Philips*, Fellow of the same College. *Cambridge*, Printed at the University Press, for *A. Bosvile*, at the Sign of the *Dial* over against St. *Dunstan's* Church in Fleetstreet. 1700. 8⁰.

RAPIN de Thoyras.
  The History of England. Written in French by Mr Rapin de Thoyras. Translated into English With Additional Notes, by N. Tindal, M.A. Vicar of Great Waltham, in Essex. The Second Edition. London : Printed for James, John and Paul Knapton, at the Crown in Ludgate-street, near the West-End of St. Paul's. MDCCXXXIII. folio.

RAVAISSON (François).
  Archives de la Bastille. Documents Inédits recueillis et publiés par François Ravaisson. Règne de Louis XIV (1687 to 1692). Vol. IX. Paris, 1877. 8⁰.

RÉMUSAT (Charles de).
  L'Angleterre au dix-huitième siecle. Études et portraits pour servir à l'histoire du gouvernement anglais depuis la fin du règne de Guillaume III, par M. Charles de Rémusat. Paris, Didier et Cie, libraires-éditeurs, 36, Quai des Augustins. 1856. 2 vols. 8⁰.

RERESBY (Sir John).
  The Memoirs of Sir John Reresby of Thrybergh, Bart. M.P. for York, etc. 1634–1689. *Written by Himself.* Edited from the Original Manuscript By James J. Cartwright, M.A. Cantab. Of H.M. Public Record Office. Author of "Chapters of Yorkshire History". London : Longmans, Green, And Co. 1875. 8⁰.

SCOTT (Sir Walter).
  A Collection of Scarce and Valuable Tracts, on the most interesting and entertaining subjects : but chiefly such as relate to the History and Constitution of these Kingdoms. Selected from an infinite number in print and manuscript, in the Royal, Cotton, Sion, and other public, as well as private, libraries, particularly that of the late Lord Somers. The Second Edition, revised, augmented, and arranged, by Walter Scott, Esq. The bent and genius of the age is best known in a free country, by the pamphlets and papers that come daily out, as the sense of parties, and sometimes the voice of the nation. Preface to Kennet's Register. *Judex qui aliquid statuit, una parte audita tantum et inaudita altera, licet aequum statuerit, haud aequus fuerit.* Ld. Cook and Just. Inst. London : Printed for T. Cadell and W. Davies, Strand ; W. Miller, Albemarle-street ; R. H. Evans, Pall-Mall ; J. White and J. Murray, Fleet-street ; and J. Harding, St. James's-street. 1809–15. 13 vols. 4⁰.

SKELTON (John).
  The Impeachment of Mary Stuart Sometime Queen of Scots and other Papers Historical and Biographical. (With this epigraph : "In defence !") By John Skelton Advocate. London, William Blackwood and Sons, 1876. 8⁰.

STANHOPE (Philip Henry, 5th Earl of Stanhope).
    History of England from the peace of Utrecht to the peace of Versailles,
    1713–1783. By Lord Mahon. In seven volumes. Leipzig, Bernhard
    Tauchnitz. 1853. 12⁰.
    History of England comprising the reign of Queen Anne until the peace
    of Utrecht, by Earl Stanhope, 1701–1713, In two volumes. Leipzig,
    Bernard Tauchnitz, 1870. 12⁰.

STOUGHTON (John).
    Ecclesiastical History of England. The Church of the Restoration. By
    John Stoughton. D.D. In two volumes, London : Hodder and
    Stoughton. 27, Paternoster Row, etc. MDCCCLXX. 8⁰.

THORNBURY (Walter).
    Haunted London, by W. Thornbury. *Illustrated by F. W. Fairholt, F.S.A.*
    London : Hurst and Blackett, Publishers, Successors to Henry Colburn,
    13, Great Marlborough Street. 1865. 8⁰.

TOWNSEND (W. Charles).
    History of the House of Commons, from the Convention Parliament of
    1688–9 to the Passing of the Reform Bill in 1832. By W. Charles
    Townsend, Esq. ; A.M., *Recorder of Macclesfield.* London : *Henry Colburn,
    Publisher,* Great Marlborough Street. 1834–4. 2 vols. 8⁰.

TREVELYAN (G. M.).
    [*England under Queen Anne.* 3 vols. 1930–4.]
    [*English Social History : a survey of six centuries, Chaucer to Queen Victoria.* 1944.]

TURBERVILLE (A. S.).
    [*English Men and Manners in the Eighteenth Century.* 1929.]

WALPOLE (Sir Robert).
    Memoirs of the Life and Administration of Sir Robert Walpole, *Earl of
    Orford.* With original correspondence and authentic papers, never
    before published. In Three Volumes. By William Coxe, M.A. F.R.S.
    F.A.S. Rector of Bemerton. *London* : Printed for T. Cadell Jun. and
    W. Davies, in the Strand. 1798. 4⁰.

WILLEY (Basil).
    [*The Seventeenth Century Background.* 1934.]
    [*The Eighteenth Century Background.* 1940.]

                                B. Critical.

ALLIBONE (S. Austin).
    Critical Dictionary of English Literature and British and American Authors
    Living and Deceased From the Earliest Accounts to the Latter End of
    the Nineteenth Century. Containing over forty-six thousand articles
    (Authors). With Forty Indexes of Subjects. By S. Austin Allibone
    . . . Philadelphia. J. B. Lippincott and Co. 1872. 3 vols. 8⁰.

ANDREWS (Alexander).
    The History of British Journalism, from the Foundation of the Newspaper
    Press in England, to the Repeal of the Stamp Act in 1855, with Sketches
    of Press Celebrities, by Alexander Andrews. In two Volumes. London :
    Richard Bentley, New Burlington Street, Publisher in Ordinary to Her
    Majesty. MDCCCLIX. 8⁰.

À WOOD (Anthony).
    Athenæ Oxonienses, an Exact History of all the Writers and Bishops who
    have had their education in the University of Oxford. To which are
    added the Fasti, or Annals of the Said University. By Anthony

à Wood, M.A. of Merton College. A new edition, with additions and a continuation By Philip Bliss, Fellow of St. John's College . . . *Antiquam exquirite matrem.* Virgil. London : . . . 1813–1820. 4 vols. folio.

BATESON (F. W.).
[*English Comic Drama. 1700–1750.* Oxford. 1929.]

BETTERTON (Thomas).
The History of the English Stage, from the Restauration to the Present Time. Including the Lives, Characters and Amours, of the most Eminent Actors and Actresses. With Instructions for Public Speaking ; Wherein The Action and Utterance of the Bar, Stage, and Pulpit are Distinctly Considered. By Mr. Thomas Betterton. Adorned with Cuts. London : Printed for E. Curll, at *Pope's Head* in *Rose-Street, Covent-Garden.* MDCCXLI. Price 5ˢ. Bound. 8⁰. (The attribution of this work to the celebrated actor Betterton was no doubt a convenient guess of bookseller Curll.)

Biographia Britannica.
Biographia Britannica : or, the Lives of the Most eminent Persons Who have flourished in Great Britain and Ireland, From the earliest Ages, down to the present Times : Collected from the Best Authorities, both Printed and Manuscript, And digested in the Manner of Mr. Bayle's Historical and Critical Dictionary. London : Printed for W. Innys, W. Meadows, . . . MDCCXLVII. 6 vols. folio.

Biographia Dramatica.
Biographia Dramatica ; or, a Companion to the Playhouse : Containing *Historical and critical Memoirs, and original Anecdotes* of British and Irish Dramatic Writers, from the Commencement of our Theatrical Exhibitions ; among whom are *some of the most celebrated Actors* : Also an Alphabetical Account, and Chronological Lists of their Works. The Dates when Printed, and Observations on their Merits : Together With *An Introductory View of the Rise And Progress* of the British Stage. Originally Compiled, to the Year 1764, by David Erskine Baker. Continued thence to 1782 by Isaac Reed. F.A.S. *And brought down to the End of November 1811, with very considerable Additions and Improvements throughout, by* Stephen Jones. In three Volumes. London : Printed for Longman, Hurst, Rees, Orme, and Brown, T. Payne, G. and W. Nichols and Son, Scatchard and Letterman, J. Barker, W. Miller, R. H. Evans, J. Harding, J. Faulder, and Gale and Surtis. 1812. 3 vols. 8⁰.

BOSWELL (James).
The Life of Samuel Johnson, LL.D. Including his Tour to the Hebrides, Correspondence with Mrs. Thrale, etc. etc., by James Boswell. With numerous additions, by John Wilson Croker. *Revised and enlarged under his direction by John Wright.* London, Bell and Daldy, York street, Covent Garden. 1868. 10 vols. 8⁰.
[Ed. G. Birkbeck Hill. 6 vols. 1887. Revised L. T. Powell. 6 vols. 1934–40.]

BOYSE (Samuel).
The British Poets. Including Translations. In one Hundred Volumes, LIX. Grainger—Boyse, Chiswick : Printed by Whittingham, College House, for J. Carpenter, J. Booker, Rodwell and Martin. G. and W. B. Whittaker, R. Triphook, J. Ebers, Taylor and Hessey, R. Jennings, G. Cowie and Co. N. Hailes, J. Porter, B. E. Lloyd and Son, G. Smith, and C. Whittingham. 1822. 12⁰.

[*Cambridge History of English Literature.*
Ed. A. W. Ward and A. R. Waller. 1907–27. Vols. VII, VIII, IX, X.]

CHALMERS (Alexander).
The Works of the English Poets, from Chaucer to Cowper ; including
the series Edited with Prefaces, Biographical and Critical, By Samuel
Johnson : And the most approved Translations. The Additional Lives
by Alexander Chalmers F.S.A. In Twenty one Volumes, London :
printed for J. Johnson ; J. Nichols and son ; R. Baldwin ; F. and C.
Rivington ; etc. 1810. 4⁰.
The General Biographical Dictionary : . . . A New Edition, Revised and
Enlarged by Alexander Chalmers, F.S.A. 30 volumes. London : . . .
1812. 8⁰.

CHAPPELL (William).
Popular Music of the Olden Time ; a Collection of Ancient Songs, Ballads,
and Dance Tunes, Illustrative of the National Music of England. With
short Introductions to the different Reigns, and Notices of the Airs
from Writers of the Sixteenth and Seventeenth Centuries. Also A Short
Account of the Minstrels. By W. Chappell, F.S.A. The Whole of the
Airs harmonized by G. A. Macfarren. Two Volumes. Prout sunt illi
Anglicani concentus suavissimi quidem ac elegantes. *Thesaurus Har-
monicus* Laurencini, *Romani*. 1603. London : Cramer, Beale and
Chappell, 201. Regent Street. (1856–59.) 8⁰.

CIBBER (Colley).
[*A Short Account of the Rise and Progress of the English Stage.* 1750. (With
the *Apology*. See Cibber, Section II.)]

CLAVELL (Robert).
The General Catalogue of Books, Printed in England Since the Dreadful
Fire of London MDCLXVI. To the End of *Trinity-Term* MDCLXXX.
Together with the Texts of Single Sermons, With the Authors Names :
Playes Acted at both the Theaters : And an Abstract of the General
Bills of Mortality since 1660. With an Account of the Titles of all the
Books of *Law, Navigation, Musick, etc.* And a Catalogue of School Books.
To which is now added a Catalogue of Latin Books Printed in Foreign
Parts and in *England* since the Year MDCLXX. Collected by *R. Clavell,
London*, Printed by *S. Roycroft* for *Robert Clavell* at the *Peacock* in St. *Paul's
Church-Yard*. 1680. folio.

CUCHEVAL CLARIGNY.
Histoire de la Presse en Angleterre et aux États-Unis, par M. Cucheval
Clarigny, ancien rédacteur en chef du *Constitutionnel*. Paris, Amyot,
éditeur des oeuvres de Napoléon III et de la *Semaine politique*. 8, rue de
la Paix. 1857. in-12.

DILKE (Charles Wentworth).
The Papers of a Critic. Selected from the writings of the late Charles
Wentworth Dilke. With a biographical sketch by his Grandson, Sir
Charles Wentworth Dilke, Bart., M.P., author of " Greater Britain "
and of " The Fall of Prince Florestan of Monaco." In two volumes.
London : John Murray, Albemarle Street. 1875. 8⁰.

D'ISRAELI (Isaac).
Curiosities of Literature. By Isaac D'Israeli. A New Edition, Edited,
with Memoir and Notes, By his Son The Right Hon. B. Disraeli, Chan-
cellor of Her Majesty's Exchequer. In Three Volumes. London :
G. Routledge and Co., Farringdon Street. New York : 18, Beekman
Street. 1858. 8⁰.
        [A selection from the above ed. E. V. Mitchell. 1932.]
Amenities of Literature. Consisting of Sketches and Characters of English
Literature. By Isaac D'Israeli. A New Edition, Edited by his Son,

The Right Hon. B. Disraeli, Chancellor of Her Majesty's Exchequer. In Two Volumes. London : Routledge, Warnes, and Routledge, Farringdon Street, New York : 18, Beekman Street. 1859. 8⁰.

The Calamities and Quarrels of Authors : With some inquiries respecting their moral and literary Characters, and Memoirs for our Literary History. By Isaac D'Israeli. A New Edition, Edited by his Son The Right Hon. B. Disraeli, Chancellor of Her Majesty's Exchequer. London : Routledge, Warnes, and Routledge,. . . . 1859. 8⁰.

DOBRÉE (B.).
[*Essays in Biography 1680–1726*. Oxford. 1925. (Vanbrugh, Addison, Etherege.)]
[*Restoration Comedy*. Oxford. 1924.]
[*Restoration Tragedy*. Oxford. 1930.]
[*Variety of Ways*. 1932. (Dryden, Halifax, Steele, Mandeville.)]

DORAN (Dr.).
" Their Majesties' Servants." Annals of the English Stage, from Thomas Betterton to Edmund Kean. Actors—Authors—Audiences. By Dr. Doran, F.S.A., Author of " Table Traits," " History of Court Fools," " Queens of England of the House of Hanover," etc. Second Edition. (Revised, corrected, and enlarged.) London : Wm. H. Allen and Co., 13. Waterloo Place, S.W. 1866. 8⁰.

DOWNES (John).
Roscius Anglicanus, Or An Historical Review of the Stage : After it had been Suppress'd by means of the late Unhappy Civil War, begun in 1644, till the Time of King *Charles* the IIˢ. Restoration *in May* 1660. Giving an Account of its Rise again ; of the Time and Places the Governours of both the Companies first Erected their Theatres. The Names of the Principal Actors and Actresses, who Perform'd in the Chiefest Plays in each House. With the Names of the most taking Plays ; and Modern Poets. For the space of 46 Years, and during the Reign of Three Kings, and part of our present Sovereign Lady Queen *Anne*, from 1660, to 1706. *Non Audita narro, sed Comperta. London.* Printed and sold by *H. Playford*, at his House in *Arundel-street*, near the Water side, 1708 (date cancelled by hand and altered to 1712). 8⁰.
Roscius Anglicanus, or, An Historical Review of the Stage . . . With Additions, By the late Mr. Thomas Davies, Author of *The Life of Garrick*, and *Dramatic Miscellanies*. London, Printed for the Editor, and Sold at No. 62. *Great Wild-Street*, near *Lincoln's*-Inn-Fields, by Mess. Egerton, *Whitehall* ; Mess. Cox and Phillipson, *James-Street, Covent-Garden* ; R. Ryan. No. 351, Oxford-Street ; H. D. Symonds, No. 20, *Pater-Noster-Row* ; and W. Richardson, under the *Royal-Exchange*. 1789. 8⁰. (Edited by F. G. Waldron.)
[Ed. M. Summers. 1928.]

DRAKE (Nathan). See p. 423.

DYSON (H. V. D.) and John Butt.
[*Augustans and Romantics. 1689–1830*. 1940. Vol. III of *Introductions to English Literature*. Ed. B. Dobrée.]

FORSTER (John).
Oliver Cromwell. Daniel De Foe. Sir Richard Steele. Charles Churchill. Samuel Foote. Biographical Essays. By John Forster. Third Edition. London : John Murray, Albemarle Street. 1860. 8⁰.

GENEST (John).
Some Account of the English Stage, from the Restoration In 1660, to 1830. In ten Volumes.

'Ει δε τι παρωπται, ή ούκ ἀκριβως ἀνειληπται, μηδεις ήμας γραφετω μεμψεως, ἐννοῶν ὡς πεπλανημενην ἱστοριαν συνελεξαμεν.
Evagrius, p. 473. If any thing be overlooked, or not accurately inserted, let no one find fault, but take into consideration that this history is compiled from all quarters. Bath : Printed by H. E. Carrington. Sold by Thomas Rodd, Great Newport Street, London. 1832. 8⁰.

GOSSE (E. W.).
Seventeenth Century Studies A Contribution to the History of English Poetry by Edmund W. Gosse London Kegan Paul, Trench and C⁰, Paternoster Square, 1883, 8⁰. (P. 269–305 : Otway.)

HALLAM (Henry).
Introduction to the Literature of Europe, in the Fifteenth, Sixteenth and Seventeenth Centuries. By Henry Hallam, LL.D., F.R.A.S., Foreign Associate of the Institute of France. De modo autem hujusmodi historiae conscribendae, illud imprimis monemus, ut materia et copia ejus, non tantum ab historiis et criticis petatur, verum etiam per singulas annorum centurias, aut etiam minora intervalla, seriatim libri praecipui, qui eo temporis spatio conscripti sunt, in consilium adhibeantur ; ut ex eorum non perlectione (id enim infinitum quiddam esset), sed degusta-tione, et observatione argumenti, styli, methodi, genius illius temporis literarius, veluti incantatione quadam, a mortuis evocetur. Bacon de Augm. Scient. Fifth Edition in Four Volumes. London : John Murray, Albemarle Street. 1855. 8⁰.

HAZLITT (William).
Lectures on the English Poets, and the English Comic Writers. By William Hazlitt, Author of " Table Talk, or Essays on Men and Manners ; " " Essays on the Literature of the Age of Elizabeth ; " " Characters of Shakspeare's Plays, etc. etc. etc." A New Edition, Edited by William Carew Hazlitt. London : Bell and Daldy, York Street, Covent Garden. 1870. 8⁰.

HETTNER (Hermann).
Geschichte der englischen Literatur von der Wiederherstellung des Königthums bis in die zweite Hälfte des achtzehnten Jahrhunderts. 1660–1779. Von Hermann Hettner. Dritte verbesserte Auflage. Braunschweig, Druck und Verlag von Friedrich Vieweg und Sohn. 1872. 8⁰.

HUNT (J. H. Leigh).
[The Dramatic Works of Wycherley, Congreve, Vanbrugh and Farquhar. 1840.]

JOHNSON (Samuel).
Lives of the most eminent English Poets, with critical observations on their works. By Samuel Johnson. With notes corrective and explana-tory, by Peter Cunningham, F.S.A. In three volumes. London : John Murray, Albemarle Street. 1854. 8⁰.
[Ed. G. Birkbeck Hill. 3 vols. Oxford. 1905.]

KNIGHT (Charles).
Shadows of the Old Booksellers. By Charles Knight. " Now learning itself is a trade. A man goes to a bookseller, and gets what he can. We have done with patronage. In the infancy of learning, we find some great man praised for it. This diffused it among others. When it becomes general, an author leaves the great, and applies to the multitude."—Johnson, in 1773. London : Bell and Daldy, 186, Fleet-street. 1865. 8⁰. [Reprinted 1927.]

KRUTCH (J. W.).
[Comedy and Conscience after the Restoration. New York. 1924.]

LAMB (Charles).
  [*On the Artificial Comedy of the Last Century*. 1821. In *Essays of Elia*.]

LANGBAINE (Gerard).
  An Account of the English Dramatick Poets. Or, Some Observations
  And *Remarks* On the Lives and Writings, of all those that have Publish'd
  either Comedies, Tragedies, Tragi-comedies, Pastorals, Masques, Inter-
  ludes, Farces, or Opera's in the *English Tongue*. By Gerard Langbaine.
  Oxford, Printed by L. L. for George West, and Henry Clements. *An.
  Dom*. 1691. 8⁰.
  [The essay on Dryden is reprinted in *Critical Essays of the Seventeenth Century*.
  Ed. J. E. Spingarn. Vol. III. 1909.]

LOWELL (James Russell).
  Among my Books. By James Russell Lowell, A.M., Professor of Belles-
  Lettres in Harvard College. Boston : James R. Osgood and Company,
  1875. 12⁰.

LOWNDES (William Thomas).
  The Bibliographer's Manual of English Literature . . . revised by Henry
  G. Bohn. London, 1864. 6 vols. 8⁰.

Luttrell Collection
  Vol. I : Eulogies and Elegies. Vol. II : Humorous, Political, and Miscellaneous Ballads. Vol. III : Proclamations and Broadsides. folio.

LYNCH (K. M.).
  [*The Social Mode of Restoration Comedy*. University of Michigan. 1926.]

MACAULAY (Thomas Babington, Lord).
  Critical and Miscellaneous Essays. By T. Babington Macaulay. New
  and Revised Edition. In Five volumes. New York : D. Appleton
  and Company, 346 and 348 Broadway. M. DCCC.LVII. 8⁰.
  [*Critical and Historical Essays*. Ed. F. C. Montague. 3 vols. 1903.]

MALONE (Edmond).
  Historical Account of the Rise and Progress of the English Stage, and of
  the Economy and Usages of the Ancient Theatres in England ; by
  Edmund Malone, Esqur. Basil : Printed and sold by J. J. Tourneisen.
  M.DCCC. 8⁰.

MASSON (David).
  Essays Biographical and Critical : chiefly on English Poets. By David
  Masson. A.M. Professor of English Literature in University College,
  London. Cambridge : Macmillan and Co. 1856. 8⁰.

MEREDITH (George).
  [*An Essay on Comedy*. 1877.]

NICHOLS (John).
  Literary Anecdotes of the Eighteenth Century, Comprizing Biographical
  Memoirs of William Bowyer, Printer, F.S.A. and many of his learned
  friends ; an incidental view of the progress and advancement of literature
  in this kingdom during the last century ; and Biographical Anecdotes
  of a considerable number of eminent Writers and ingenious Artists :
  with a very copious index. By John Nichols F.S.A. in six volumes.
  London, Printed for the author by Nichols, son and Bentley, at Cicero's
  head Red Lion-passage, Fleet Street, 1812. 8⁰.

NICOLL (Allardyce).
  [*A History of Restoration Drama*. 1923.]
  [*A History of Early Eighteenth Century Drama*. 1919.]

PALMER (John).
  [*The Comedy of Manners*. 1913.]

PERRY (H. Ten Eyck).
[*The Comic Spirit in Restoration Drama.* New Haven. 1925.]
PINTO (V. de Sola).
[*The English Renaissance. 1510–1688.* 1938. Vol. II. *Introductions to English Literature.* Ed. B. Dobrée.]
REID (G. W.).
Catalogue of Prints and Drawings in the *British Museum.* Div. I. Political and Personal Satires. Vol. II. June 1689 to 1733. By G. W. Reid. 8⁰.
Roxburghe Collection.
Ancient Songs and Ballads : Written on Various Subjects, and Printed between the Years MDLX and MDCC. Chiefly Collected by Robert Earl of Oxford, and purchased at the Sale of the late Mr. West's Library, in the Year 1773. Encreased by several Additions . . . London, Arranged and Bound in the Year 1774. 2 vols. folio.
SPENCE (Joseph).
Anecdotes, Observations, and Characters of Books and Men. Collected From The Conversation of Mr. Pope, and *Other Eminent Persons of His Time.* By the Rev. Joseph Spence. Now First Published From The Original Papers, With Notes And A Life of The Author. By Samuel Weller Singer.

Apis matinae
More modoque
Grata carpentis thyma.

London : Published By W. H. Carpenter, Lower Brook Street ; And Archibald Constable And Co. Edinburgh. MDCCC.XX. 8⁰.
SPINGARN (J. E.).
[*Critical Essays of the Seventeenth Century.* Ed. J. E. Spingarn. 3 vols. Oxford. 1908–9.]
STEPHEN (Leslie).
[*English Literature and Society in the Eighteenth Century.* 1904.]
STEPHENS (Frederic George).
Catalogue of Prints and Drawings in the British Museum. Division. Political and Personal Satires (No. 1 to No. 1235). Vol. I. 1320 to April 11, 1689. Printed by order of the Trustees. 1870. 8⁰.
SUMMERS (M.).
[*The Restoration Theatre.* 1934.]
TAINE (H.).
Histoire de la Littérature Anglaise, par H. Taine. Paris, Hachette et Cⁱᵉ. 1863. 4 vols. 8⁰.
    [Trans. H. Van Laun. 2 vols. 1871.]
THOMPSON (N.).
A Collection of One Hundred and Eighty Loyal Songs, All written since 1678. And Intermixt with several New Love Songs. To which is Added, The Notes Set by Several Masters of Musick. With a Table to find every Song. The Fourth Edition with many Additions. *London,* Printed, and are to be sold by *Richard Butt,* in *Princess-street* in *Covent-Garden.* 1694. Price Bound 2s. 12⁰.
TIMPERLEY (C. H.).
Encyclopaedia of Literary and Typographical Anecdote : Being a Chronological Digest of the most interesting facts illustrative of the History of Literature and Printing from the earliest Period to the present Time. Interspersed with Biographical Sketches of Eminent Booksellers, Printers, Type-founders, Engravers, Bookbinders and Paper makers, of all ages

and Countries, but especially of Great Britain. With Bibliographical and Descriptive Accounts of their principal Productions and occasional Extracts from them. Including Curious Particulars of the first introduction of Printing into various Countries, and of the Books then printed. Notices of early Bibles and Liturgies of all Countries, especially those printed in England or in English. A History of all the Newspapers, Periodicals, and Almanacks published in this Country. An Account of the Origin and Progress of Language, Writing and Writing Materials, the Invention of Paper, Use of Paper Marks, etc. Compiled and Condensed from Nichols's Literary Anecdotes, and numerous other Authorities, By C. H. Timperley. Second Edition, to which are added, A Continuation to the present Time, Comprising recent Biographies, Chiefly of Booksellers, and A Practical Manual of Printing. London : Henry G. Bohn, York Street, Covent Garden. MDCCCXLII. 8º.

VILLEMAIN.
Cours de Littérature Française, par M. Villemain. Tableau de la Littérature au xviiiᵉ siècle. Paris, Didier et Cⁱᵉ. 1864. 4 volumes 12º.

WALPOLE (Horace).
A Catalogue of the Royal and Noble Authors of England, Scotland, and Ireland ; with *Lists of their Works*. By the late Horatio Walpole, Earl of Orford, Enlarged and Continued to the present Time, *By* Thomas Park, F.S.A. These sheets are calculated for the closest of the idle and inquisitive ; they do not look up to the shelves of what Voltaire happily calls . . . " La Bibliothèque du Monde." See Vol. II, p. 76. *London :* Printed for John Scott, No 442, Strand. 1806. 5 vols. 8º.
Reminiscences : *Written in* 1788, for the amusement of Miss Mary and Miss Agnes B—— Y ; By Horace Walpole, late Earl of Orford. *No wit is needed by the man concerned with past occurrences.* Voltaire. London, Published by John Sharpe, Piccadilly. 1819. 32º.
    [Ed. P. Toynbee. 1924.]

WATT (Robert).
Bibliotheca Britannica ; or A General Index to British and Foreign Literature. By Robert Watt, M.D. In Two Parts :—Authors and Subjects . . . Edinburgh and London. 1824. 4 vols. 4º.

II. AUTHORS

ABSALOM.
Absalom's Conspiracy ; or, the Tragedy of Treason. *London,* Printed in the Year, 1680. folio.

ADDISON (Joseph).
Poems.
A Poem to his Majesty, Presented to the Lord Keeper. By Mr. *Addison,* of *Mag.* Coll. *Oxon.* London : Printed for *Jacob Tonson,* at the *Judge's Head* near the *Inner-Temple-Gate* in *Fleetstreet.* MDCXCV. folio.
The Campaign, A Poem, To his Grace the Duke of *Marlborough.* By Mr. *Addison.*

> Rheni pacator et Istri
> Omnis in hos Uno variis discordia cessit
> Ordinibus ; laetatur Eques plauditque Senator,
> Votaque Patricio certant Plebeia favori.
>   Claud. de Laud. Stilic.

London, Printed for *Jacob Tonson,* within *Grays-Inn Gate* next *Grays-Inn Lane.* 1705. folio.

Dramatic Works.

Rosamond. An Opera. Inscrib'd to Her Grace, The Duchess of Marlborough,

> *Hic quos durus amor crudeli tabe peredit*
> *Secreti celant calles, et myrtea circum*
> *Sylva tegit.*
>
> Virg. Æn. VI.

By the late Right Honourable Joseph Addison Esq. ; Glasgow. Printed and Sold by Robert and Andrew Foulis. M. DCC. LI. 8⁰. [First edition : 1707. 4⁰.]

Cato. A Tragedy. As it is Acted at the Theatre-Royal in *Drury-Lane*, By Her Majesty's Servants. By Mr. *Addison*. *Ecce Spectantibus dignum, ad quod respiciat, intentus operi suo, Deus ! Ecce par Deo dignum vir fortis cum mala fortuna compositus ! Non video, inquam, quid habeat in terris Jupiter pulchrius, si convertere animum velit, quam ut spectet Catonem, jam partibus non semel fractis, nihilominus inter ruinas publicas erectum.* Sen. de Divin. Prov. N. B.   *This book in a fair large Print is Sold by* M. Gunne, at the *Bible and Crown* at Essex-Street *Gate*, and R. Gunne *in* Capel-Street.. 1713. 8⁰.

[In *Five Restoration Tragedies*. World's Classics. 1927.]

The Drummer : or, the Haunted-House. A Comedy. As it is Acted at the *Theatre-Royal* in *Drury-Lane*, By His Majesty's Servants.

> *Falsis terroribus implet.*
>
> *Ut magus.*   Hor.

The Third Edition. With a Preface by Sir *Richard Steele*, in an Epistle Dedicatory to Mr. *Congreve*, occasioned by Mr. *Tickell's* Preface to the Four Volumes of Mr. *Addison's* Works, *London* : Printed for J. Darby : and Sold by Thomas Combes at the *Bible* and *Dove* in *Pater-Noster-Row*. 1722. 12⁰. [First edition : 1716. 4⁰.]

Periodical Essays.

Numb. 1. The Spectator.

> *Non fumum ex fulgore, sed ex fumo dare lucem*
> *Cogitat, ut speciosa dehinc miracula promat.*
>
> Horac.

To be Continued every Day. *March* 1. 1711. folio.

The Spectator. *London* : Printed for *S. Buckley*, at the *Dolphin* in *Little-Britain* ; and *J. Tonson*, at *Shakespear's-Head* over-against *Catherine-Street*, in *the Strand*. 1712. 7 vols. 8⁰. (The first edition to be published in volume form.)

Numb. 1. The Guardian.—*Ille quem requiris*. Mart. To be Continued Every Day. *Thursday*, March 12. 1713. folio.

The Guardian. *London* : *Printed for Mess.ʳˢ Longman, Law, Johnson, Nichols, Dilly, Robinson, Richardson, Baldwin, Rivington, Otridge and Son, Hayes, Wilkie ; W. Lowndes, Ogilvie and Son, J. Edwards, Vernor and Hood, Cadell and Davies, H. Lowndes and Lee and Hurst.* 2 vols. 8⁰. 1714.

The Free-Holder, or Political Essays. London. Printed for D. Midwinter at the *three Crowns* in *St. Paul's Churchyard* ; and J. Tonson at *Shakespear's Head* in the *Strand*. 1716. N⁰. 1. *Friday, December 23, 1715. Rara temporum felicitas, ubi sentire quae velis, et quae sentias dicere licet.* Tacit. 8⁰.

Miscellaneous Prose.

Remarks on Several Parts of *Italy*, etc. In the Years 1701, 1702, 1703. *Verum ergo id est, si quis in caelum ascendisset, naturamque mundi et*

pulchritudinem siderum perspexisset, insuavem illam admirationem ei fore,
quae jucundissima fuisset, si aliquem cui narraret habuisset. Cicer. de
Amic. *London*, Printed for *Jacob Tonson*, within *Grays-Inn* Gate next
Grays-Inn Lane. 1705. 8⁰.

The Evidences of the Christian Religion, By the Right Honourable
Joseph Addison, Esq. To which are added, Several Discourses against
Atheism and Infidelity, and in Defence of the Christian Revelation,
occasionally published by Him and Others : *And Now collected into*
one Body and digested under their proper Heads. With a Preface, containing
the Sentiments of Mr. Boyle, Mr. Locke, and Sir Isaac Newton,
concerning the *Gospel-Revelation. London* : Printed for J. Tonson in
the *Strand.* MDCCXXX. 8⁰.

Sir Roger de Coverley, by the Spectator. The Notes and Illustrations
by W. Henry Wills, London, Longmans, Green and Co. 1 shilling.
12⁰. 1850.

[*The Letters of Joseph Addison.* Ed. Walter Graham. 1941.]
Collected Works.

The Works of the Right Honourable *Joseph Addison,* Esq. : In Four
Volumes. *London* : Printed for Jacob Tonson, at *Shakespear's-Head,*
over against *Katharine-street* in the Strand. MDCCXXI. 4⁰.
(Tickell's edition.)

Bohn's British Classics. The Works of the Right Honourable Joseph
Addison. With Notes by Richard Hurd, D.D. Lord Bishop of
Worcester. A New Edition with large additions, chiefly unpublished,
collected and edited by Henry G. Bohn. London : Henry G. Bohn,
York Street, Covent Garden. MDCCCLIV–MDCCCLVI. 6 vols.
8⁰.

[*Miscellaneous Works.* Ed. A. C. Guthkelch. 2 vols. 1914.]
Biography and Criticism.

Aiken, Lucy.
The life of Joseph Addison. By Lucy Aikin. In two volumes.
London : Printed for Longman, Brown, Green and Longmans,
Paternoster-Row. 1843. 8⁰.

Macaulay, T. B.
The Life and Writings of Addison. Edinburgh Review. July, 1843.

Courthope, W. J.
[*Addison.* 1884.]

AMORY (Thomas).
The life of John Buncle, Esq. ; Containing Various Observations and
Reflexions, Made in several Parts of the World ; and Many extraordinary
Relations.

> *Felix ille animi, Divisque simillimus ipsis,*
> *Quem non mendaci resplendens gloria fuco*
> *Sollicitat, non fastosi mala gaudia luxus.*
> *Sed tacitos sinit ire dies, et paupere cultu*
> *Exigit innocuae tranquilla silentia vitae.*
> Volusenus.

London : Printed for *J. Noon,* at the *White Hart* in *Cheapside,* near the
Poultry. MDCCLVI. 2 vols. 8⁰. [Ed. E. A. Baker. 1904.]

ANTHONY.
The Last Will and Testament of Anthony, King of Poland : Printed for
S. Ward, 1682. folio.

ARBUTHNOT (John).
Law is a Bottomless-Pit. Exemplify'd in the Case of The Lord *Strutt,*

John Bull, Nicholas Frog, and *Lewis Baboon.* Who spent all they had in a Law-Suit. *Printed from a Manuscript found in the Cabinet of the famous* Sir Humphry Polesworth. The Second Edition. *London :* Printed for *John Morphew,* near Stationers' Hall. 1712. Price 3d. 8º. (First edition : 1712.)

[This pamphlet was incorporated into *The History of John Bull.* 1727. In the latter form it is contained in *The Life and Works of John Arbuthnot.* George A. Aitken. 1892.]

Proposals for Printing A very curious Discourse, in two Volumes in *Quarto,* Intitled, ψευδολογα Πολιτικη, or A Treatise of the Art of Political Lying, With An Abstract of the First Volume of the said Treatise. Edinburgh : Reprinted in the Year MDCCXLVI. 8º. (The 1st Edition is dated 1712.) [Ed. George A. Aitken. See above.]

Biography and Criticism.

Beattie, L. M.

[*John Arbuthnot, Mathematician and Satirist.* Cambridge. U.S.A. 1935.]

ARROWSMITH (Joseph).

The Reformation. A Comedy. Acted At the Dukes Theater.

> *Sunt, quibus in Satyra videor nimis acer . . .*
> Horat. lib. 2. Sat. 1.

London, Printed for *William Cademan,* at the Popes-Head, in the Lower walk of the New *Exchange* in the *Strand.* MDCLXXIII. 4º.

BANKES (John).

The Rival Kings Or the Loves of Oroondates and Statira, a Tragedy. Acted at the Theatre-Royal. Written by Mr. Bankes.

> *Divesne Prisco natus ab* Inacho,
> *Nil interest, an Pauper, et infima*
> *De gente sub dio moreris,*
> *Victima nil miserantis Orci.*
> Horat., lib. 2. Ode 3.

London, Printed for *Langley Curtis* in Goat Court on *Ludgate-Hill,* 1677. 4º.

The Destruction of Troy, a Tragedy, Acted at His Royal Highness The Duke's Theatre. Written by *John Bankes.*

> Fortunam Priami cantabo et Nobile Bellum.
> *Quid dignum tanto feret hic Promissor hiatu ?*
> Hor. de Art. Poet.

London, Printed by *A.G.* and *J.P.* and are to be sold by *Charles Blount* at the *Black-Raven* in the *Strand,* near the *Savoy.* 1679. 4º.

Vertue Betray'd : or, Anna Bullen. A Tragedy. Acted at His Royal Highness The Duke's Theatre, Written by *John Banks, Crescit sub Pondere Virtus. London,* Printed for *R. Bentley,* in *Russel-Street* in *Covent-Garden.* MDCXCII. 4º. [First edition : 1682.]

BEDFORD (Arthur).

Serious Reflections on the Scandalous Abuse and Effects of the Stage : in a Sermon preach'd at the Parish-Church of *St. Nicolas* in the City of *Bristol,* on *Sunday* the 7th Day of *January,* 1704/5. By Arthur Bedford, M.A. Vicar of *Temple-Church* in the aforesaid City. *Bristol,* Printed and sold by *W. Bonny* in *Corn-street,* 1705. 8º.

A Second Advertisement concerning the Profaneness of the Play-House. *Bristol.* Printed by *W. Bonny* in *Corn-street.* 1705. 8º.

The *Evil* and *Danger* of Stage-Plays : Shewing their Natural Tendency to Destroy Religion, And introduce a General *Corruption of Manners* ; In almost Two Thousand *Instances*, taken from the *Plays* of the two last Years, against all the *Methods* lately used for their *Reformation*. By *Arthur Bedford*, M.A. Chaplain to his Grace *Wriothesly* Duke of *Bedford* ; and Vicar of *Temple* in the City of *Bristol*.

(Ovid. Metam. lib. 1.)

Cuncta prius tentanda, sed immedicabile vulnus
Ense recidendum est, ne pars sincera trahatur.

Printed and Sold by *W. Bonny*, and the Booksellers of *Bristol* : And by *Henry Mortlock* at the Sign of the *Phoenix* in St. *Paul's Church-Yard*, London, 1706. 8°.

The Great Abuse of Musick. In Two Parts, Containing an Account of the Use and Design of Musick among the Antient *Jews, Greeks, Romans*, and others ; with their Concern for, and Care to prevent the Abuse thereof. And also An Account of the *Immorality* and *Profaneness* which is occasioned by the Corruption of that most Noble Science in the Present Age. By Arthur Bedford, *M.A. Chaplain to His Grace* Wriothesly *Duke of* Bedford, *and Vicar of* Temple *in the City of* Bristol. London : Printed by *J.H.* for John Wyatt at the *Rose* in St. *Paul's* Church-Yard. 1711. 8°.

A serious Remonstrance In Behalf of the Christian Religion, against The Horrid Blasphemies and Impieties which are still used in the *English* Play-Houses, to the great Dishonour of Almighty God, and in Contempt of the Statues of this Realm. Shewing their plain Tendency to overthrow all Piety, and advance the Interest and Honour of the Devil in the World ; from almost Seven Thousand Instances, taken out of the Plays of the present Century, and especially of the five last Years, in defiance of all Methods hitherto used for their Reformation. By *Arthur Bedford*, M.A. Chaplain to the most Noble Wriothesly Duke of *Bedford*, and Rector of *Newton St. Loe* in the County of *Somerset*. *Jer.* 7, 8, 9, 10. *Behold, ye trust in lying Words, that cannot profit. Will ye steal, murder, and commit Adultery, and swear falsly, and burn Incense unto* Baal, *and walk after other Gods whom ye know not ; and come and stand before me in this House, which is called by my Name, and say, We are delivered to do all these Abominations ?* Caetera Deus avertat. To treat Honour and Infamy alike, is an Injury to Virtue, and a sort of Levelling in Morality. I confess, I have no Ceremony for Debauchery ; for to compliment Vice, is but one Remove from worshipping the Devil.—*Preface* to Collier's *Book of the Stage*. *London* : Printed by John Darby, for Henry Hammond, Bookseller in *Bath* ; Richard Gravett, Bookseller on the *Tolzey* in *Bristol* ; and Anth. Piesley, Bookseller in *Oxford*. 1719. 8°.

BEHN (Aphra).

Poems.

A Congratulatory Poem To Her Most Sacred Majesty on the Universal Hopes of all Loyal Persons for a Prince of Wales. By Mrs. *A. Behn*. *London*, Printed for *Will. Canning*, at his Shop in the *Temple-Cloysters*. 1688. 4°.

Fiction.

All the Histories and Novels Written by the Late Ingenious Mrs. *Behn*, Entire in One volume. Viz. I. *The History of* Oroonoko, *or the* Royal Slave. *Written by the Command of King* Charles *the Second*. II. *The* Fair Jilt, *or Prince* Tarquin. III. Agnes de Castro, *or the Force of Generous Love*. IV. *The* Lover's Watch, *or the Art of making Love ; being Rules for Courtship for every Hour of the Day and Night*. V. *The* Ladies Looking-glass *to Dress themselves by, or the whole Art of Charming all Mankind.* VI. *The Lucky Mistake.* VII. *Memoirs of the Court of the King of* Bantam. VIII. *The Nun, or the Perjured Beauty.* IX. *The Adventure of the Black Lady.* Together with The History of the Life and Memoirs of *Mrs. Behn.* By one of the Fair Sex. Intermix'd with Pleasant Love-Letters that pass'd betwixt her and Minheer *Van Bruin,* a *Dutch* Merchant ; with her Character of the Country and Lover : And her Love-Letters to a Gentleman in *England.* The Fifth Edition, Corrected from the many Errors of former Impressions. *London* ; Printed for *R. Wellington,* at the *Dolphin* and *Crown* in St. *Paul's* Church-yard : 1705. 1 vol. 8⁰.

[*The Novels of Aphra Behn.* Ed. E. A. Baker. 1913. Contains all the above novels.]

Dramatic Works.

The Amorous Prince, or, the Curious Husband. A Comedy. As it is Acted at his Royal Highness, the Duke of *York's* Theatre. Written by Mrs. *A. Behn. London,* Printed by *J.M.* for *Thomas Dring,* at the *White Lyon,* next *Chancery-Lane-End,* in *Fleet-street.* 1671. 4⁰.

The Dutch Lover : A Comedy, acted at the *Dukes Theatre.* Written by Mrs. *A. Bhen* [*sic*]. *London* : Printed for *Thomas Dring* at the Sign of the *Harrow* at *Chancery-lane-end,* over against the Inner Temple Gate in *Fleet-Street,* 1673. 4⁰.

The Town-Fopp : Or, Sir Timothy Tawdrey. A Comedy. As it is Acted at his Royal Highness the Duke's Theatre. Written by Mrs. *A. Behn.* Licensed *September* 20. 1676. *Roger L'Estrange. London,* Printed by *T.N.* for *James Magnes,* and *Rich. Bentley,* in *Russel-Street* in *Covent-garden* near the Piazza's. M. DC. LXXVII. 4⁰.

The Rover or the Banish't Cavaliers. As it is Acted at his Royal-Highness The Duke's Theatre. Licensed *July* 2d 1677. *Roger L'Estrange. London,* Printed for *John Amery,* at the *Peacock,* against St. *Dunstan's* Church in *Fleet-Street.* 1677. 4⁰.

Abdelazer, or the Moor's Revenge. A Tragedy. As it is Acted at his Royal Highness the Duke's Theatre. Written by Mrs. *A. Behn, London,* Printed for *J. Magnes* and *R. Bentley,* in *Russel-Street* in *Covent-Garden,* near the *Piazza's,* 1677. 4⁰.

Sir Patient Fancy : A Comedy. As it is Acted at the Duke's Theatre. Written by *Mrs. A. Behn,* the Author of the *Rover.* Licensed *Jan.* 28. 1678. Roger L'Estrange. *London,* Printed by *E. Flesher* for *Richard Tonson,* within *Grays-Inn-gate* in *Grays-Inn-lane* and *Jacob Tonson,* at the *Judge's Head* in *Chancery-lane.* 1678. 4⁰.

The Feign'd Curtizans, or, A Nights Intrigue. A Comedy. As it is Acted at the Dukes Theatre. Written by Mrs. *A. Behn.* Licensed *Mar.* 27. 1679. *Roger L'Estrange. London,* Printed for *Jacob Tonson* at the *Judges Head* in *Chancery-Lane* near *Fleet-street.* 1679. 4⁰.

The Second Part of the Rover. As it is Acted by the Servants of His Royal Highness. Written by *A. Behn. London* : Printed for *Jacob Tonson* at the *Judges-Head* in *Chancery Lane.* MDCLXXXI. 4⁰.

The City-Heiress : or, Sir Timothy Treat-all. A Comedy. As it is Acted At his Royal Highness his Theatre, Written by Mrs. *A. Behn. London* : Printed for *D. Brown,* at the *Black Swan* and *Bible* without *Temple-bar* ; and *T. Benskin* in St. *Brides* Church-yard ; and *H. Rhodes* next door to the *Bear-Tavern* neer *Bride-lane* in *Fleetstreet.* 1682. 4⁰.

The False Count, or, a New Way to play an old game. As it is Acted at the Dukes Theatre. Written by Mrs. *A. Behn. London,* Printed by *M. Flesher,* for *Jacob Tonson,* at the *Judge's Head* in *Chancery-lane,* near *Fleetstreet.* 1682. 4⁰.

The Roundheads or, The Good Old Cause, A Comedy As it is Acted at His Royal Highness the Dukes Theatre. *BY Mrs.* A. Behn. *London,* Printed for *D. Brown* at the *Black Swan* and *Bible* without *Temple bar,* and *T. Benskin* in *St. Brides* Church Yard, and *H. Rhodes* next door to the *Bear Tavern* near *Bride Lane* in *Fleetstreet.* MDCLXXXII. 4°.

The Luckey Chance, or an Alderman's Bargain. A Comedy, As it is Acted by their Majesty's Servants. *Written by* Mrs. A. Behn. This may be Printed, *April* 23. 1686. *R. P. London,* Printed by *R.H.* for *W. Canning,* at his Shop in *Vine-Court, Middle-Temple.* 1687. 4°.

Collected Works.

[*The Plays, Histories, and Novels of the Ingenious Mrs. Aphra Behn.* Ed. R. H. Shepherd. 6 vols. 1871.]

[*The Works of Aphra Behn.* Ed. M. Summers. 6 vols. 1915. (Omits the pindarics.)]

Biography and Criticism.

[*Aphra Behn or the Incomparable Astræa.* V. M. Sackville West. 1927.]

BENSON (William).

A Letter to Sir *J.*—— *B.*—— (Jacob Banks). By Birth a *S*—— (Swede), but Naturaliz'd and now a M——r of the Present p——t : Concerning the late *Minehead* Doctrine which was established by a certain *Free Parliament* of *Sweden,* to the utter *Enslaving* of that Kingdom. Si, mehercle, peccato locus esset, facile paterer vos ipsa re corrigi, sed undique circumventi sumus. Non nunc agitur de Vectigalibus, non de Cociorum Injuriis agitur ; *Libertas* et *Anima* nostra in *dubio* est. *Sallust. Bell. Catilinar.* London : Printed for *A. Baldwin* in *Warwick-Lane.* M. DCC. XI. 8°.

BENTLEY (Richard).

Q. Horatius Flaccus, Ex Recensione et cum Notis Atque Emendationibus Richardi Bentleii. Cantabrigiae. MDCCXI. 4°.

BENTLEY (Thomas).

Q. Horatius Flaccus Ad Nuperam *Richardi Bentleii* Editionem accurate expressus. Notas addidit *Thomas Bentleius,* A.B. Collegii S. Trinitatis Cantabrigienses Alumnus. *Cantabrigiae* : Typis Academicis. Impensis Cornelii Crownfield, Celeberrimae Academiae Typographi. MDCCXIII. 8°.

BISSET (William).

Plain English. A Sermon Preached at St. *Mary-le-Bow,* on *Monday,* March 27. 1704. For Reformation of Manners. With Some Enlargements. By William Bisset, *One of the Ministers of St* Catherine's *by the* Tower, London : Printed for the Author ; and Sold by *A. Baldwin* in *Warwick-Lane.* 1704. 8°.

The Modern Fanatick. With a Large and True Account of the Life, Actions, Endowments, *etc.* Of the Famous Dr. *Sa.....l. Veritas magna est, et praevalebit.* By *William Bisset,* Eldest Brother of the Collegiate-Church of St. *Katherine,* and Rector of *Whiston* in *Northamptonshire, London* : Printed : And Sold by *A. Baldwin,* near the *Oxford-Arms* in *Warwick-Lane* : And *T. Harrison* at the *West* Corner of the *Royal Exchange* in *Cornhill.* 1710. Price Six-pence. 8°.

BLACKMORE (Sir Richard).

Poems.

Prince Arthur. An Heroick Poem. In Ten Books. By *Richard Blackmore* M.D. And Fellow of the College of Physicians in *London.* The Second Edition Corrected. To which is added, An Index, Explaining the Names of *Countries, Cities,* and *Rivers,* etc. *London* : Printed for *Awnsham* and *John Churchil* at the *black Swan* in *Pater-Noster-Row.* MDCXCV. folio.

King Arthur. An Heroick Poem. In Twelve Books. By *Richard Blackmore*, M.D. Fellow of the College of Physicians in *London*, and One of His Majesty's Physicians in Ordinary. To which is Annexed, An Index, Explaining the Names of *Countrys, Citys*, and *Rivers*, etc. *London* : Printed for *Awnsham* and *John Churchil* at the *Black Swan* in *Pater-Noster-Row*, and *Jacob Tonson* at the *Judges Head* in Fleet-street, MDCXCVII. folio.

A Satyr Against Wit. *London* : Printed for *Samuel Crouch*, at the Corner of *Pope's-Head-Alley*, over against the *Royal Exchange* in *Cornhill*. 1700. folio.

Advice to the Poets. A Poem. Occasion'd by the Wonderful Success of her Majesty's Arms, under the Conduct of the duke of *Marlborough*, in *Flanders*. *London* : Printed by *H.M.* for *A.* and *J. Churchill*, at the *Black Swan* in *Pater-Noster-Row*. MDCCVI. folio.

Creation. A Philosophical Poem. In Seven Books. By Sir *Richard Blackmore*, Knt. M.D. and Fellow of the College of Physicians in London.

> *Principio Caelum, ac terras camposque liquentes*
> *Lucentemque globum lunae, Titaniaque astra*
> *Spiritus intus alit, totamque infusa per artus*
> *Mens agitat molem, et magno se Corpore miscet.*
> *Inde hominum, pecudumque genus, vitaeque Volantum,*
> *Et quae marmoreo fert monstra sub aequore pontus.*
>
> Virg.

London : Printed for *S. Buckley* at the *Dolphin* in *Little-Britain* ; and *J. Tonson*, at *Shakespear's Head*, over against *Catherine-street* in the *Strand*. MDCCXII. 8⁰.

A Collection of Poems on Various Subjects. By *Sir* Richard Blackmore, Kt. *M.D.* Fellow of the Royal-College of Physicians. *London* : Printed by *W. Wilkins*, for Jonas Browne at the *Black-Swan* without *Temple-Bar* ; and J. Walthoe, *Jun.* over-against the *Royal-Exchange* in *Cornhill*. MDCCXVIII. 8⁰.

Alfred. An Epick Poem. In Twelve Books. Dedicated to the Illustrious Prince *Frederick* of *Hanover*. By Sir Richard Blackmore. Kt. *M.D.*

> *Tu regere imperio Populos, Romane, memento*
> *(Hae tibi erunt Artes) Paciq; imponere Morem*
> *Parcere Subjectis et debellare superbos.*
>
> Virg., Æneid., Lib. VI.

London, Printed by *W. Botham*, for James Knapton, at the *Crown* in St. *Paul's* Church-Yard. MDCCXXIII. 8⁰.

[*The Works of the English Poets.* Ed. A. Chalmers. 1810. Vol. X. *The Works of the British Poets.* Ed. T. Park. 1818. Vol. 33. Contain poems by Blackmore.]

Prose.

Essays upon Several Subjects. By Sir Richard Blackmore, *Kt. M.D.* and Fellow of the College of Physicians in *London*. *London* : Printed for E. Curll at the *Dial* and *Bible*, and J. Pemberton at the *Buck* and *Sun*, both against St. *Dunstan's* Church in *Fleet-street*. M.DCCXVI. 8⁰.

Essays upon Several Subjects. By *Sir* Richard Blackmore, *Kt. M.D.* and Fellow of the College of Physicians in *London*. Vol. II. *London* : Printed by *W. Wilkins*, for *A. Bettersworth*, at the *Red Lyon* in *Pater-Noster-Row* ; and J. Pemberton, at the *Buck* and *Sun* against St. *Dunstan's* Church in *Fleetstreet*. 1717. 8⁰.

A True *and* Impartial History of the Conspiracy Against the Person *and* Government of King *William* III. Of Glorious Memory, in the Year 1695. By Sir Richard Blackmore, Kt. M.D. *London,* Printed for James Knapton, at the *Crown* in St. *Paul's* Church-Yard. MDCCXXIII. 8⁰.

BOLINGBROKE. See St. JOHN (Henry).

BONNECORSE (Balthazar de).
La Montre. *Par Monsieur* De Bonnecorse. A Cologne Chez Pierre Miceel. M.DC.LXVI. 8⁰.
La Montre. *Seconde Partie.* Contenant La Boëte, et le Miroir. *Par M. de* Bonnecorse. Dédiée à Monseigneur de Vivonne. A Paris, Chez Claude Barbin, au Palais, sur le second Perron de la Ste Chapelle, M.DC.LXXI. *Avec Privilege du Roy.* 8⁰.

BOSSUET (Jacques-Bénigne).
An Exposition of the Doctrine of the Catholic Church in Matters of Controversie. By the Right Reverend *James Benigne Bossuet,* Counsellor to the King, Bishop of *Meaux,* formerly of *Condom,* and Preceptor to the Dauphin ; First Almoner to the Dauphiness. Done into *English* from the Fifth Edition in *French. London,* Printed in the Year 1685. 4⁰.
A Treatise of Communion under Both Species. *By the Lord* James Benigne Bossuet, *Bishop of Meaux, Councellour to the King, heretofore Preceptor to Monseigneur le* Dauphin, *first Almoner to Madame la* Dauphine. Printed at Paris by Sebastian Mabre Cramoisy, Printer to his Majesty. MDCLXXXV. With Priviledge. 12⁰.
A Pastoral Letter From the Lord Bishop of Meaux, To The New Catholics of His Diocess, Exhorting them to keep their Easter. And giving them Necessary Advertisements against the *False Pastoral Letters* of their *Ministers.* With Reflections upon the Pretended Persecution. Translated out of *French,* and Publish'd with Allowance. *London,* Printed by *Henry Hills,* Printer to the King's most excellent Majesty, for His Household and Chappel. 1686. 4⁰.
A Discourse on the History of the Whole World, Dedicated to his Royal Highness the Dauphin, and Explicating the Continuance of Religion with the Changes of States and Empires ; from the Creation till the Reign of *Charles* the Great. Written Originally in French by *James Benigne Bossuet,* sometimes Bishop of *Condom,* and now of *Meaux,* Counsellor of State to the Most Christian King, heretofore Tutor to the Dauphin, and now Chief Almoner to the Dauphiness. Faithfully Englished. *London,* Printed for *Matthew Turner* at the *Lamb* in *High-Holborn.* MDCLXXXVI. 8⁰.
A Conference with Mr. Claude Minister of Charenton, Concerning The Authority of the Church. By *James Benigne Bossuet,* Bishop of Meaux, Councellor to the most Christian King, and formerly Preceptor to the Dauphin : First Almoner to the Dauphiness. *Faithfully done into English out of the French original.* Publish't with Allowance. *London,* Printed for *Matthew Turner,* at the *Lamb* in *High Holbourn.* 1687. 4⁰.

BOYLE (Roger, 1st Earl of Orrery).
Poems.
The following collection contains verse by the Earl of Orrery : A Collection of Poems : Viz. *The Temple of Death* : By the marquis of *Normanby. An Epistle to the Earl of* Dorset : By *Charles Montague,* Lord *Halifax. The Duel of the Stags* : By Sir *Robert Howard.* With Several Original Poems, Never before printed, By the E. of *Roscommon.* The E. of *Rochester.* The E. of *Orrery.* Sir *Charles Sedley.* Sir *George Etherege.* Mr. *Granville.* Mr. *Stepney.* Mr. *Dryden,* Etc. *London* :

Printed for *Daniel Brown*, at the *Black Swan* and *Bible* without *Temple-Bar* : And *Benjamin Tooke* at the *Middle-Temple-Gate* in *Fleetstreet*. 1701. 8°.

Dramatic Works.

The Dramatic Works of *Roger Boyle*, Earl *of* Orrery. To which is Added A Comedy, intitled, *As you find it*. By the Honourable Charles Boyle, Esq ; Afterwards Earl of *Orrery*. Vol. I. Containing : The Black Prince. Tryphon. Henry the Fifth. Mustapha. *London* : Printed for R. Dodsley, at *Tully's-Head*, in Pall-Mall. M.DCC.XXXIX. The second volume is entitled : The Dramatick Works of *Roger Boyle*, Earl of Orrery. Volume II. Containing : Herold the Great. Altemira. Guzman, *a Comedy*. Also as you find it, *a Comedy*. By Charles late Earl of *Orrery*. *London* : Printed for R. Dodsley, in *Pall-Mall*. M.DCC.XXXIX. 8°. (*Henry V*, a historical play, was acted in 1664 ; *Mustapha*, a tragedy, in 1665 ; *The Black Prince*, a tragedy, in 1667 ; *Tryphon*, a tragedy, in 1668 ; *Guzman*, a comedy, between 1667 and 1672 ; *Herold the Great*, tragedy, was not acted ; *Altemira*, tragedy, was acted in 1702 after the author's death. Orrery also wrote a comedy called *Mr. Anthony* which was acted about 1671.)

Two New Tragedies. The Black Prince, and Tryphon. The first Acted at the Theatre Royal *by His Majesties Servants* ; The Other *by his Highness the Duke* of York's *Servants*. Both Written by the Right Honourable the Earl of Orrery. London, Printed for H. *Herringman*, at the Sign of the *Blew Anchor*, in the Lower Walk of the New Exchange. 1672. folio. [First edition : 1669.]

[*The Dramatic Works of Roger Boyle, Earl of Orrery*. Ed. W. S. Clark. 2 vols. Cambridge. U.S.A. 1937. (Includes from MS. *The Tragedy of Zoroastres*.)]

Prose.

Parthenissa That most fam'd Romance : Composed by the Right Hono^ble The Lord *Broghill*, And Dedicated to the Lady *Northumberland*. *London* : Printed for *Richard Lownes* at the *White Lyon* in St *Pauls* Church-yard. 1654. 4°.

A Treatise of the Art of War : Dedicated to the Kings Most Excellent Majesty. *And Written by the Right Honourable* Roger Earl of Orrery. *In the Savoy* : Printed by *T.N.* for *Henry Herringman* at the *Anchor* in the *Lower Walk* of the *New Exchange*. M.DC.LXXVII. folio.

Biography.

Memoirs of the Life and Character Of the Late Earl of *Orrery*, And of the Family of the Boyles. Containing Several Curious *Facts*, and *Pieces of History*, from the Reign of Queen Elisabeth, to the present Times : Extracted from Original Papers and Manuscripts never yet Printed. With A Short Account of the Controversy between the late Earl of Orrery and the Reverend Doctor *Bentley* ; and some *Select Letters* of Phalaris, the famous *Sicilian* Tyrant : Translated from the *Greek*. By Eustace Budgell Esq ;

> *Te, animo repetentem Exempla tuorum*
> *Et* Pater Aeneas, *et* Avunculus *excitet* Hector. Virg.

London : Printed for W. Mears, at the Lamb in the Old Bailey. M.DCCXXXII. 8°.

BRISTOL (Earl of). See DIGBY.

BROWN (Tom). See also DRYDEN and COLLIER.

Numb. 9. The Lacedemonian Mercury. Being A Continuation of the *London Mercury*. Monday March 7. 1692. folio.

Letters from the Dead to the Living. By *Mr.* Tho. Brown, *Capt.* Ayloff,

Mr. Hen. Barker, etc. *Viz. from Jo. Haines* of Merry Memory, to his Friends at *Wills*. *Perkin Warbeck*, to the pretented Prince of *Wales*, *Abraham Cowley*, to the *Covent Garden Society*. *Charon*, to the Illustrious and High-born *Jack Ketch*. *James* the 2ᵈ, to *Lewis* the 14th. *Julian* late Secretary to the Muses, to *Will Peirre* of *Lincolns-Inn* Play-house. *Scarron*, to *Lewis Le Grand*. *Hannibal* to the Victorious Prince *Eugene* of *Savoy*. Pindar of *Thebes*, to *Tom. D.* —— *Catharine of Medicis*, to the Dutchess of *Orleans*. Queen *Mary* to the Pope. *Harlequin*, to Father *Le Chaise*. The Duke of *Alva*, to the Clergy of *France*. *Philip* of *Austria*, to the *Dauphin*. *Juvenal*, to *Boileau*. *Diana of Poitiers*, to Madam *Maintenon*. *Hugh Spencer*, the younger to all the Favourites and Ministers whom it may concern. *Julia*, to the Princess of *Conti*. *Christina* Queen of *Sweden*, to the Women. *Rabelais*, to the Physicians. The *Mitred Hog*; a Dialogue between *Furetiere* and *Scarron*. Beau *Norton*, to his Brothers at *Hippolito's*. Sir *Bartolomew* ——, to Serjeant *S.* —— And several others with their Answers.

> *Infanti Melimela dato, fatuasq; mariscas,*
> *Sed mihi, quae novit pungerem* Chia Sapit. Mart.

London, Printed in the Year, 1702. 8⁰.

Collections.

The Works of Mr. *Thomas Brown*, Serious and Comical, In Prose and Verse. In Four volumes. *The* Fifth Edition, *Corrected from the Errors of the former Impressions.* With the Life and Character of Mr. *Brown*, And a Key to all his Writtings. *Adorn'd with Cuts. London* : Printed for Sam Briscoe, at the *Bell-Savage* on *Ludgate Hill* ; and sold by *R. Smith, A. Bell, J. Round, G. Strahan, E. Symons, J. Osborne, J. Brotherton, A. Bettsworth, W. Taylor, J. Batley, R. Robison, C. Rivington, R. King, J. Pemberton, T. Corbet, D. Browne, W. Mears, F. Clay* and *T. Warner* in Paternoster-Row, 1720. 12⁰. The fifth volume of this edition is entitled : The Remains of Mr. *Thomas Brown*, Serious and Comical, In Prose and Verse. In one Volume. Collected from scarce Papers and Original Mss. never Printed in his Works. With Mr. Brown's Legacy for the Ladies ; or Characters of the Women of the Age. To which is prefix'd, A Key to all his Prophesies, Dialogues, Satyrs, Fables, and Poems, *London*, Printed for *Sam. Briscoe*, at the *Bell-Savage Inn* on *Ludgate-Hill*. 1720. 12⁰. [First edition : 3 vols. 1707. 8⁰.]
[*The Beauties of Tom Brown.* E. C. H. Wilson. 1808.]
[*Amusements Serious and Comical and other works.* By Tom Brown. Ed. with notes by Arthur L. Hayward. 1927. (Contains Letters from the Dead to the Living.)]

Buckhurst (Lord).
Sackville (Charles), Earl of Dorset. See Wilmot (John).

Buckingham (Duke of). See Villiers (George).

Buckingham (Duke of). See Sheffield (John).

Bunyan (John).
The Pilgrim's Progress from this World to That which is to come : delivered under the Similitude of a Dream. Wherein is Discovered, The manner of his setting out, His Dangerous Journey, and Safe Arrival at the Desired Country. By *John Bunyan*, The second Edition, with Additions. *I have used similitudes*, Hosea 12. 10. Licensed and Entered according to Order. *London* : Printed for *Nath.* Ponder, at the Peacock in the *Poultrey*, near *Cornhil*. 1678. 12⁰. [The first edition also 1678.]
[Ed. J. Wharey. Oxford. 1928.]
[Ed., with *Mr. Badman*, G. B. Harrison. Nonesuch. 1928.]

Biography and Criticism.
Brown, J.
[*John Bunyan his Life and Work.* 1885. Revised F. M. Harrison.
1928.]

BURNET (Gilbert). See also WILMOT (John).
Bishop Burnet's History of his own time ; with the suppressed passages of
the first volume, and notes by the Earls of Dartmouth and Hardwicke,
and Speaker Onslow. hitherto unpublished. To which are added the
cursory remarks of Swift, and other observations. Oxford, at the Clarendon Press. MDCCCXXIII. 6 vols. 8°. [First edition : 2 vols.
1724–34.]
[Ed. M. J. Routh. 7 vols. Oxford. 1823. Reprinted 6 vols. 1833.]
[Ed. O. Airy. Oxford. 1897–1900. (Vols. 1 and 2 only.)]

BUTLER (Samuel).
Hudibras. The First Part. *Written in the time of the late Wars.* London,
Printed by *G. J.* for *Richard Marriot,* under Saint *Dunstan's* Church in
Fleetstreet. 1663. 8°.
[Ed. A. R. Waller. Cambridge. 1905. Forming Vol. 1. of *Collected
Works.* Vol. 2 : Characters and passages from notebooks. Ed. A. R.
Waller. 1908. Vol. 3 : Satires and miscellaneous poetry and prose.
Ed. R. Lamar. 1928.]
The Genuine Poetical Remains of Samuel Butler. With Notes, By Robert
Thyer, Keeper of the Public Library, Manchester. With a Selection
from the Author's Characters in Prose. Illustrated with humorous
Wood-cuts, and Portraits of Butler and Thyer. London : Printed for
Joseph Booker, 61, New Bond Street, 1827. 8°.
Biography and Criticism.
Veldkamp, J.
[*Samuel Butler, the author of Hudibras.* 1924.]
Gibson, D.
[*Samuel Butler.* 1932.]

CAVENDISH (William, 1st Duke of Newcastle). See also DRYDEN. *Sir Martin
Mar-all.*
A General System of Horsemanship in All it's Branches : Containing a
Faithful Translation Of that most noble and useful Work of his Grace,
William Cavendish, Duke of *Newcastle,* entitled, the Manner of Feeding,
Dressing, and Training of Horses, for the Great Saddle, and Fitting them
for the Service of the Field in Time of War, or for the Exercise and
Improvement of Gentlemen in the Academy at home : A Science
peculiarly necessary throughout all *Europe,* and which has hitherto been
so much neglected, or discouraged in *England,* that young Gentlemen have
been obliged to have recourse to foreign Nations for this Part of their
Education. With all the original Copper-Plates, in Number forty-three,
which were engrav'd by the best Foreign Masters, under his Grace's
immediate Care and inspection, and which are explained in the different
Lessons. *London* : Printed for J. Brindley, Bookseller to His Royal
Highness the Prince of Wales, in New Bond-street. MDCCXLIII.
2 vols. folio.
[First published Antwerp. 1658. *Méthode et invention nouvelle de
dresser les chevaux.*]
Dramatic Works.
The Humorous Lovers. A Comedy, Acted by His Royal Highness's
Servants. Written by His Grace the Duke of *Newcastle.* London,
Printed by J.M. for *H. Herringman,* at the Sign of the *Blew Anchor* in
the Lower-Walk of the *New-Exchange,* 1677. 4°.

The Triumphant Widow, or the Medley of Humours. A Comedy, Acted by His Royal Highnes's Servants. Written by His Grace the Duke of *Newcastle. London,* Printed by *J.M.* for *H. Herringman,* at the Sign of the *Blew Anchor in the Lower-Walk* of the *New-Exchange,* 1677. 4⁰.

CENTLIVRE (Susanna).
The Busie Body. A Comedy. *Written by Mrs.* Susanna Centlivre.
The Fifth Edition.

> Quem tulit ad scenam ventoso Gloria curru,
> Exanimat lentus Spectator, sedulus inflat.
> Sic Leve, sic parvum est, animum quod laudis avarum
> Subruit aut reficit.
>
> Hor. Epist. Lib. II. Ep. 1.

London : Printed for Bernard Lintot ; and sold by Henry Lintot, at the Cross-Keys, against St. Dunstan's Church in Fleet-street. M.DCC.XXXII. 8⁰. (This play was acted in 1709.)
[Reprinted vol. 4. *Modern British Drama.* 1811.]
The Man's bewitch'd ; or, The Devil to do about Her. A Comedy, As it is Acted at the New-Theatre in the Hay-Market ; By Her *Majesty's Servants.* By Susanna Cent-Livre. *London,* Printed for Bernard Lintott, between the Two *Temple-Gates* in Fleet-street. (1710) 4⁰.
Collected Works.
[*The Works of the celebrated Mrs. Centlivre.* 3 vols. 1761. 3 vols. 1872. (As *The Dramatic Works.*)]
Character.
The Character of A Town-Gallant ; Exposing the Extravagant Fopperies of some vain Self-conceited Pretenders to Gentility, and good Breeding. *London,* printed for *Rowland Reynolds* in the Strand, 1680. folio.

CIBBER (Colley). See also VANBRUGH, *The Provok'd Husband.*
Dramatic Works.
She wou'd, and She wou'd not, or The Kind Imposter. A Comedy. As it is Acted at the Theatre-Royal in *Drury-Lane.* By Her Majesties Servants. *Written by Mr.* Cibber. London : Printed for *William Turner* at the *Angel* at *Lincolns-Inn* Back-Gate, and *John Nutt* near *Stationers-Hall.* 1703. 4⁰.
[Reprinted : vol. 3. *Modern British Drama.* 1811.]
The Lady's last Stake, or, The Wife's Resentment, A Comedy. As it is Acted at the Queen's Theatre in the *Hay-Market,* By Her Majesty's Servants. *Written by Mr.* Cibber. *London :* Printed for Bernard Lintott, at the *Cross-Keys* next *Nando's* Coffee-House in Fleet-street. (1708.) 4⁰.
The Non-Juror. A Comedy. *Written by* Mr. Cibber.

> —*Pulchra Laverna*
> *Da mihi fallere ; da justum, sanctumque videri,*
> *Noctem peccatis, et fraudibus objice nubem.* Hor.

London, Printed for T.J. and are sold by the Booksellers of London and Westminster. M.DCC.XVIII. 8⁰.
[Reprinted : *Plays from Molière by English Dramatists.* H. Morley. 1885.]
Ximena, or, The Heroick Daughter. As it is Acted at the Theatre-Royal By His Majesty's Servants. Written by Mr. *Cibber.*

> *Face nuptiali*
> *Digna, et in omne Virgo*
> *Nobilis Ævum.* Hor.

London : Printed for B. Lintot, between the *Temple-Gates* ; A. Betters-worth, at the *Red Lyon* in *Pater-noster-Row* ; and W. Chetwood, at *Cato's-Head*, in *Russell-street, Covent Garden*. 1719. 8⁰.

Autobiography.

An Apology for the Life of Mr. Colley Cibber, Comedian, and Late Patentee of the *Theatre-Royal*. *With an Historical View of the Stage during his* Own Time. Written by Himself.

Hoc est
Vivere bis, vita posse priore frui. Mart. lib. 2.

When Years no more of active Life retain,
'Tis Youth renew'd to laugh 'em o'er again. Anonym.

London : Printed by John Watts for the Author. MDCCXL. 4⁰. [Reprinted : Everyman's Library. 1906.]

Biography and Criticism.

Senior, Dorothy.
[*The Life and Times of Colley Cibber.* 1928.]

CLARK (Samuel).

A Discourse Concerning the Unchangeable Obligations of Natural Religion, and the Truth and Certainty of the *Christian Revelation*. Being Eight Sermons Preach'd at the Cathedral-Church of St *Paul*, in the Year 1705, at the Lecture Founded by the Honourable *Robert Boyle*, Esq. By *Samuel Clark*, M.A. Chaplain to the Right Reverend Father in God *John*, Lord Bishop of *Norwich*. Isa. 5. 20. *wo unto them that call Evil Good, and Good Evil ; that put Darkness for Light and Light for Darkness ; that put Bitter for Sweet and Sweet for Bitter.* Rom. 1. 22. *Professing themselves to be Wise, they became Fools.* 1. Cor. 2. 10. *But God hath revealed them unto us by his Spirit. London* : Printed by *W. Botham*, for *James Knapton*, at the *Crown* in St. *Paul's* Church-Yard. 1706. 8⁰.

CLENCHE (William).

St *Peter's* Supremacy faithfully discuss'd according to Holy Scripture, and *Greek* and *Latin* Fathers. With a Detection and Confutation of the Errors of Protestant Writers on this Article. Together with A Succinct Handling of several other Considerable Points. *The First Book, Divided into Three Parts.*

Romae nutriri mihi contigit atq; doceri,
Scilicet, ut possem Curvo dignoscere Rectum.

Chryst. 67. Hom. John.

Permissu Superiorum. London, Printed by *Henry Hills*, Printer to the Kings Most Excellent Majesty, for His Household and Chappel. 1686. And are to be sold by *Matthew Turner*, at the *Lamb*, in *Holborn*. 4⁰. (The dedication is signed : Guglielmo Clenche.)

Clod-pate.

Clod-pate's Ghost : or a Dialogue Between *Justice Clod-Pate*, and his (*quondam*) Clerk Honest *Tom Ticklefoot* ; Wherein *Is Faithfully Related all the News from* Purgatory, *about* Ireland, Langhorn, etc. Aug. 25. 1679. folio.

Coffee.

A Cup of Coffee : or, Coffee in its Colours. *London*, Printed in the year 1663. folio, broadside.

Collection.

A Collection of The Newest and Most Ingenious Poems, Songs, Catches, etc. Against Popery. Relating to the Times. Several of which never before Printed, *London*, Printed in the Year MDCLXXXIX. 4⁰.

COLLIER (Jeremy).
   The Desertion discuss'd In a Letter to a Country Gentleman. (1688.)
   8⁰.

The Stage Controversy.
   [For accounts, see *Comedy and Conscience after the Restoration.* J. W. Krutch.
   New York. 1924.
   Essays in Biography, 1680–1726. (Vanbrugh.) B. Dobrée. 1925.]
Works by Collier.
   A Short View of the *Immorality,* and *Profaneness* of the English Stage,
     Together with the Sense of Antiquity Upon this Argument, By
     Jeremy Collier, M.A. *London,* Printed for S. Keble at the *Turk's*
     Head in *Fleet-street,* R. Sare at *Gray's-Inn-Gate,* and H. Hindmarsh
     against the *Exchange* in *Cornhil,* 1698. 8⁰. The Third Edition.
     1698. The Fourth Edition. 1699.
   A Defence of the Short View of the Profaneness and Immorality of the
     English Stage, etc. Being a Reply to Mr. *Congreve's* Amendments,
     etc. And to the Vindication of the Author of the Relapse. By
     Jeremy Collier, M.A. *Fortem animum praestant rebus quas turpiter audent.*
     Juv. Sat. 6. *London* : Printed for S. Keble at the *Turks-head* in
     Fleetstreet, R. Sare at *Gray's-Inn-Gate,* and H. Hindmarsh against the
     Exchange in *Cornhil.* 1699. 8⁰.
     [In reply to Congreve and Vanbrugh.]
   A second Defence of the Short View of the Prophaneness and Immor-
     ality of the *English Stage, etc.* Being *A Reply* to a Book, Entituled,
     The Ancient and Modern Stages Surveyed, etc. By *Jeremy Collier,* M.A.
     London : Printed for *S. Keble* at the *Turk's Head* in *Fleetstreet,* R. Sare
     at *Gray's Inn-Gate* in *Holborn,* and *G. Strahan* against the *Exchange*
     in *Cornhill.* 1700. 8⁰.
     [In reply to Drake.]
   Mr. *Collier's* Dissuasive from the *Play-House* ; in a Letter to a Person
     of Quality, Occasion'd By the late Calamity of the Tempest.
     London : Printed for Richard Sare, at *Grays-Inn-Gate* in *Holborn.*
     1703. 8⁰.
   Mr. *Collier's* Dissuasive from the *Play-House* ; in A Letter to a Person
     of Quality. Occasion'd By the late Calamity of the Tempest. To
     which is added, A Letter written by another Hand ; in Answer to
     some Queries sent by a Person of Quality. Relating to the Irregular-
     ities charged upon the *Stage. London* Printed for Richard Sare, at
     Grays-Inn-Gate in *Holborn.* 1704. 8⁰.
   A Farther Vindication of the Short View of the Profaneness and
     Immorality of the English Stage, In which the Objections of a late
     Book, Entituled, *A Defence of Plays,* are consider'd. By *Jeremy*
     Collier, M.A. *London* : Printed for *R. Sare,* at *Gray's-Inn-Gate* in
     Holborn, and *G. Strahan* at the *Golden Ball* in *Cornhill.* 1708. 8⁰.
     [In reply to Filmer.]
   La Critique du Theatre Anglois, Comparé au Theatre d'Athenes, de
     Rome et de France. *Et* L'Opinion *des Auteurs tant profanes que*
     sacrez, touchant les Spectacles. De l'Anglois de M. Collier. A Paris,
     chez Nicolas Simart, Imprimeur et Libraire ordinaire de Monseigneur
     le Dauphin, ruë S. Jacques, au Dauphin couronné. M.DCC.XV.
     Avec Privilege du Roy. 8⁰. (The *Biographia Britannica* ascribes this
     translation to Pere de Courbeville.)
Works by other hands.
   Brown, Tom.
     The *Stage-Beaux toss'd in a Blanket,* or Hypocrisie Alamode. Expos'd
     in a True Picture of Jerry . . . , a Pretending Scourge to the

English Stage. A Comedy ; with a *Prologue* on *Occasional Con-formity* ; being a full Explanation of the *Poussin Doctor's* Book ; and an *Epilogue* on the *Reformers.* Spoken, at the *Theatre-Royal* in *Drury-Lane. Simulant Curios, et Bacchanalia vivunt.* Juv. *London,* Printed and Sold by *J. Nutt,* near *Stationers' Hall.* 1704. 4⁰.

Congreve, William.

Amendments of *Mr.* Collier's *False and Imperfect Citations,* etc. From the Old Batchelour, Double Dealer, Love for Love, Mourning Bride. By the Author of those Plays.

> *Quem recitas meus est o Fidentine Libellus,*
> *Sed male dum recitas incipit esse tuus.*
>
> Mart.

> *Graviter, et iniquo animo, maledicta tua paterer, si te scirem Judicio magis, quem* [*sic*] *morbo animi, petulantia ista uti. Sed, quoniam in te neque modum, neque modestiam ullam animadverto, respondebo tibi : uti, si quam maledicendo voluptatem cepisti, eam male-audiendo amittas.* Salust. Decl. *London,* Printed for *J. Tonson,* at the *Judge's Head* in *Fleet-street,* near the *Inner-Temple-Gate.* 1698. 8⁰.

[In *Complete Works.* World's Classics. 1925–8.]

Dennis, John.

The Usefulness of the Stage, *To the Happiness of Mankind. To Government,* and *To Religion.* Occasioned by a late Book, written by *Jeremy Collier,* M.A. By Mr. *Dennis. London,* Printed for *Rich. Parker* at the *Unicorn* under the Piazza of the *Royal Exchange.* 1698. 8⁰.

[In *Critical Works.* Ed. E. N. Hooker. 1939–43. Vol. 1.]

Drake, J.

The Antient and Modern Stages survey'd. Or, Mr *Collier's* View of the Immorality and Profaness of the *English* Stage Set in a True Light. Wherein some of Mr *Collier's* Mistakes are rectified, and the comparative Morality of the *English* Stage is asserted upon the Parallel.

> *Rode* Caper *vitem, tamen hic cum stabis ad Aram*
> *In tua quod fundi* Cornua *possit, erit.* Ov.

London : Printed for *Abel Roper,* at the *Black Boy* over against St. *Dunstans* Church in *Fleetstreet.* 1699. 8⁰.

D'Urfey, Thomas.

The Preface to *The Campaigners.* See D'URFEY.

Filmer, Edward.

A Defence of Dramatick Poetry : Being a Review of Mr. *Collier's* View of the Immorality and Profaneness of the Stage. *London :* Printed for *Eliz. Whitlock,* near *Stationer's Hall.* 1698. 8⁰.

A Farther Defence of Dramatick Poetry : Being the Second Part of the Review of Mr. *Collier's* View of the Immorality and Profane-ness of the Stage. *Done by the same Hand. London :* Printed for *Eliz. Witlock,* near *Stationer's Hall.* 1698. 8⁰.

A Defence of Plays : or, The Stage vindicated, From several Passages in Mr. *Collier's Short View,* etc. Wherein is offer'd The most Probable Method of Reforming our Plays. With a Consideration How far Vicious Characters may be allow'd on the Stage. By *Edward Filmer,* Doctor of the Civil Laws. *London,* Printed for *Jacob Tonson* within *Grays-Inn* Gate next to *Grays-Inn* Lane. 1707. 8⁰.

Vanbrugh, John.

A Short Vindication of the *Relapse* and the Provok'd Wife, from

Immorality and Prophaneness. By the Author. *London* : Printed for H. Walwyn, at the *Three Legs* in the *Poultrey*, against the Stocks-Market. MDCXCVIII. 8⁰.

[In *Complete Works*. Ed. B. Dobrée and G. Webb. 1927.]

Anonymous.

Animadversions on Mr. Congreve's Late Answer to Mr. *Collier*. In a Dialogue between Mr. *Smith* and Mr. *Johnson*. With the Characters of the present *Poets* ; And some Offers towards New-Modeling the *Stage*.

> *Sr.* Jos. *Egad, there are good Morals to be pick'd out of* Æsop's *Fables, let me tell you that, and* Reynard the Fox *too*.
>
> Bluff. *Damn your Morals*.
>
> *Sr.* Jos. *Prithee don't speak so Loud*.
>
> Bluff. *Damn your Morals, I must revenge the Affront done to my Honor*.
>
> Old Batch. *Page* 47.

London, Printed for *John Nutt*, near Stationers-Hall. 1698. 8⁰.

Some remarks upon *Mr.* Collier's *Defence of his Short View of the English Stage*, etc. in Vindication of Mr. *Congreve*, etc. In a Letter to a Friend. *London* : Printed for A. Baldwin, near the *Oxford Arms*, in *Warwick-Lane*. 1698. 8⁰.

The Immorality of the English Pulpit, as Justly Subjected to the Notice of the *English Stage*, as The Immorality of the Stage is, to that of the Pulpit. *In a Letter to Mr.* Collier. Occasion'd by the Third Chapter of his Book, Entit'ld, *A Short View of the Immorality of the* English Stage, etc. *London* : Printed in the Year MDCXCVIII. 4⁰.

The Stage Condemn'd, and The Encouragement given to the Immoralities and Profaneness of the Theatre, by the English Schools, Universities and Pulpits, *Censur'd*. King *Charles I*. Sundays Mask and Declaration for Sports and Pastimes on the Sabbath, *largely Related and Animadverted upon*. The Arguments of all the Authors that have Writ in Defence of the Stage against Mr, *Collier, Consider'd*. And The Sense of the Fathers, Councils, Antient Philosophers and Poets, and of the Greek and Roman States, and of the First Christian Emperours concerning the Drama, *Faithfully Deliver'd*. Together with The Censure of the English State and of several Antient and Modern Divines of the Church of *England* upon the Stage. And Remarks on diverse late Plays, as also on those presented by the two Universities to King *Charles* I. *London* : Printed for John Salusbury, at the *Angel* in St. *Paul's* Church-Yard, 1698. 8⁰.

A Vindication of the Stage. With the Usefulness and advantages of Dramatick Representations. In Answer to Mr. Collier's Late Book, Entituled, *A View of the Prophaneness* [*sic*] *and Immorality*, etc. *In a Letter to a Friend. Aut Prodesse volunt, aut Delectare Poetae. Delectant homines, mihi crede, ludi, non eos solum, qui fatentur ; sed illos etiam qui dissimulant.* Cicero. *London* : Printed for *Joseph Wild*, at the Sign of the *Elephant* at *Charing-Cross*. MDCXCVIII. 4⁰.

The *Stage Acquitted*. Being A Full Answer to Mr. *Collier*, and the other Enemies of the Drama. With A Vindication of King *Charles* the Martyr, and the Clergy of the Church of *England*, From the Abuses of a Scurrilous Book, called, *The Stage Condemned*. To which is added, The Character of the Animadverter, and the Animadversions on Mr. *Congreve's* Answer to Mr. *Collier*. *London* :

Printed for John *Barnes* at the *Crown* in the *Pall-mall*, and sold by
M. Gilliflower in *Westminster-hall*, *D. Brown* near *Temple-bar*, and
R. Parker at the *Royal Exchange.* MDCXCIX. 8⁰.

A Representation of the *Impiety* and *Immorality* of the English Stage,
with Reason *for putting a stop thereto* : *and some* Questions *addrest to
those who frequent the* Play-Houses. *London*, Printed, and are to be
sold by *J. Nutt* near *Stationers-Hall*, 1704. 8⁰.

COLLINS (Anthony).

Priestcraft in Perfection : Or, a Detection of the Fraud of Inserting and Con-
tinuing this Clause (*The Church hath Power to Decree Rites and Ceremonys,
and Authority in Controversys of Faith*) In the Twentieth Article of the
Church of *England.* *To forge an Article of Religion, either in Whole or in
Part, and then thrust it upon the Church, is a most heinous Crime, far worse than
Forging of a Deed.* Archbishop Laud's Speech in the Starchamber.
Remains, Vol. 2. pag. 82. Maxime habenda sunt pro suspectis, quae
quomodocunque dependent a Religione. *Baconis Nov. Org. lib.* 2. *Aph.*
29. *London* : Printed for *B. Bragg* in *Pater-noster-Row.* 1710. 8⁰.

A Discourse on Free-Thinking, Occasion'd by The Rise and Growth of
a Sect call'd Free-Thinkers. Mundum tradidit *hominum* disputationi
Deus. Eccl. 3. 11. Vulg. Unusquisque suo sensu abundet. *Rom.* 14. 5.
Ib. Nil tam temerarium, tamque indignum sapientis gravitate atque
constantia, quam, quod non satis explorate perceptum sit et cognitum
sine ulla dubitatione defendere. *Cic. de Nat. Deor.* 1. 1. '*Tis a hard
Matter for a* Government *to settle. Wit.* Characteristicks. *vol.* 1. *p.* 19.
Fain would they confound Licentiousness in Morals *with* Liberty in Thought,
and make the Libertine *resemble his* direct Opposite. Ib. *vol.* 3. *p.* 306.
London, Printed in the Year M.DCC.XIII. 8⁰.

CONGREVE (William). See also COLLIER and DRYDEN.
Poems.

A Pindarique Ode, Humbly Offer'd to the King On His Taking Namure.
By Mr. *Congreve.*

> *Praesenti tibi Maturos largimur Honores :*
> *Nil oriturum alias, nil ortum tale fatentes.*
> > Hor. ad Augustum.

London : Printed for *Jacob Tonson* at the *Judge's Head* near the *Inner-
Temple-Gate* in *Fleetstreet.* MDCXCV. folio.

The Mourning Muse of Alexis. A Pastoral. Lamenting the Death of
our late Gracious Queen Mary Of ever Blessed Memory. By Mr.
Congreve. *Infandum Regina Jubes renovare dolorem!* Virg. *London* :
Printed for *Jacob Tonson*, at the *Judge's Head*, near the *Inner-Temple
Gate* in Fleet Street. 1695. folio.

A Pindarique Ode, Humbly Offer'd to the Queen, On the Victorious
Progress of Her Majesty's Arms, under the Conduct of the Duke of
Marlborough. To which is prefix'd, A Discourse on the Pindarique
Ode. By Mr. *Congreve.*

> *Operosa parvus*
> *Carmina fingo.*   Hor. Ode 2. L. 4.

> *Tuque dum procedis, Io triumphe*
> *Non semel dicemus, Io triumphe*
> *Civitas omnis; dabimusq; Divis*
> *Thura benignis.*   Ibid.

London : Printed for *Jacob Tonson*, within *Grays-Inn* Gate next *Grays-
Inn* Lane. 1706. folio.

Dramatic Works.

The Old Batchelour, A Comedy. As it is Acted at the Theatre Royal, By Their Majesties Servants. Written by Mr. *Congreve.*

> *Quem tulit ad Scenam ventoso gloria Curru,*
> *Exanimat lentus Spectator ; sedulus inflat.*
> *Sic leve, sic parvum est, animum quod laudis avarum*
> *Subruit, aut reficit.* Horat. Epist. I. Lib. II.

The second Edition. *London,* Printed for *Peter Buck* at the Sign of the *Temple* near the *Inner Temple-Gate* in *Fleet-street,* 1693. 4º.

The Double-Dealer. A Comedy. As it is Acted at The Theatre Royal. By Their Majesty's Servants, Written by Mr. *Congreve. Interdum tamen, et vocem Comedia tollit.* Hor. Art. Po. *Huic equidem Consilio palmam do ; hic me magnifice effero, qui vim tantam in me et potestatem habeam tantae astutiae, vera dicendo ut eos ambos fallam.* Syr. in Terent. Heaut. *London :* Printed and sold by *H. Hills,* in *Black-Fryars,* near the *Water-side.* 1694. 8º.

Love for Love. A Comedy. Acted at the Theatre in *Little-Lincoln's-Inn-Fields,* By His Majesty's Servants. Written by Mr. *Congreve.*

> *Nudus Agris, nudus nummis paternis,*
> *Insanire parat certa ratione modoque.*

London : Printed and Sold by *H. Hills,* in *Black-Fryars,* near the *Water-side.* 1695. 8º.

The Mourning Bride. A Tragedy. As it is Acted at the Theatre in *Lincoln's-Inn-Fields.* By His Majesty's Servants. Written by Mr. *Congreve.*

> *Neque enim lex aequior ulla,*
> *Quam necis artifices arte perire sua.*
> Ovid. de Arte Am.

London : Printed and Sold by *H. Hills,* in *Black-Fryars* near the *Water-side.* 1697. 8º.

The Way of the World. A Comedy. As it is Acted at the Theatre in *Lincoln's-Inn-Fields,* By His Majesty's Servants. Written by Mr. *Congreve.*

> *Audire est Operae pretium, procedere recte*
> *Qui Moechis non vultis.* Hor. Sat. 2. L. 1.
>
> *Metuat doti deprensa.* Ibid.

London : Printed for *Jacob Tonson* within *Gray's-Inn-Gate* next *Gray's-Inn-Lane.* 1700. 4º.

Prose.

The Occasional Paper : Number IX. Containing some Considerations about the Danger of going to Plays. In a Letter to a Friend. *London,* Printed for *M. Wotton,* at the Three Daggers in *Fleet-street.* 1698. 8º.

Some Considerations about the Danger of going to Plays. In a Letter to a Friend. *London,* Printed for *M. Wotton,* at the *Three Daggers* in *Fleet-street.* And Sold by *J. Nutt* near *Stationers-Hall.* 1704. Price Three Pence. 8º.

Collected Works.

The Works of Mr. *William Congreve.* In three volumes. Consisting of his Plays and Poems. *The Fifth Edition.* London : Printed for Tonson, in the *Strand.* MDCCLII. 12º. [First edition 1710.]

[*Plays.* Ed. Montague Summers. 4 vols. Nonesuch Press. 1923.]

[*Complete Works.* Ed. B. Dobrée. 2 vols. World's Classics. 1925–8.]

[*Comedies.* Ed. F. W. Bateson. 1930.]

Biography and Criticism.
Gosse, E.
" Great Writers." Edited by Professor Eric S. Robertson, M.A. Life
of William Congreve, by Edmund Gosse, M.A. Clark Lecturer in
English Literature at Trinity College, Cambridge. London, Walter
Scott. 1888. 8⁰.
[Revised edition. 1924.]
Hodges, J. C.
[*William Congreve, the man : a biography from new sources.* 1941. Modern
Language Association of America. General Series II.]
Protopopesco, Dragosh.
[*William Congreve.* 1924.]

COOPER (Anthony Ashley, First Earl of Shaftesbury).
Biography.
Martyn, B., and Kippis, Dr.
The Life of the First Earl of Shaftesbury, from Original documents
in possession of the family. By Mr. B. Martyn and Dr. Kippis.
Now First Published. Edited By G. Wingrove Cooke. Esq. Author
of " Memoirs of Lord Bolingbroke." In two Volumes. London :
Richard Bentley, New Burlington Street. Publisher in Ordinary
to His Majesty. 1836. 8⁰.
Christie, W. D.
A Life of Anthony Ashley Cooper, First Earl of Shaftesbury. 1621–
1683. By W. D. Christie, M.A. Formerly Her Majesty's Minister
to the Argentine Confederation and to Brazil. Two Volumes.
London and New York : Macmillan & Co. 1874. 8⁰.
Traill, H. D.
[Shaftesbury (the first earl). 1886.]

COWLEY (Abraham).
The Works of Mr. Abraham Cowley, Consisting of *Those which were formerly
Printed* : And *Those which he Design'd for the Press.* Now Published out
of the Author's Original Copies. To this Edition are added Cutter of
Coleman-Street : And Several Commendatory Copies of Verses on the
Author, by Persons of Honour. As Also, A Table to the whole Works,
never before Printed. The Eighth Edition. *London,* Printed for *Henry
Herringman* ; and are to be Sold by *R. Bentley, J. Tonson,* F. Saunders,
and T. Bennet. MDCXCIII. folio.
[First edition 1668.]
[Ed. A. R. Waller. 2 vols. Cambridge. 1905–6.]
Biography and Criticism.
Nethercot, Arthur H.
[*Abraham Cowley. The Muse's Hannibal.* Oxford. 1931.]

CROWNE (John).
Fiction.
Pandion and Amphigenia : or the History of the Coy Lady of Thessalia
Adorned with *Sculptures.* By *J. Crowne. London,* Printed by *I.G. for
R. Mills,* at the sign of the *Pestel* and *Mortar* without *Temple-Barr,
Anno,* 1665. 8⁰.
Dramatic Works.
Juliana, or the Princess of Poland. *A Tragicomedy.* As it is *Acted* at His
Royal Highness the Duke of York's Theatre. By *J. Crown,* Gent.
Presto, e bene, di rado riesce bene. Licensed, *sept.* 8. 1671. *Roger L'Estrange.
London,* Printed for *Will. Cademan* at the *Popes-Head* in the lower Walk
in the *New-Exchange,* and *Will. Birch* at the lower end of *Cheapside,*
1671. 4⁰.

The History of Charles the Eighth of France, or the Invasion of *Naples* by the *French.* As it is acted at his Highnesses the Duke of *York's* Theater. Written by Mr. *Crowne, Honestum est secundis tertijsve consistere.* Qu. *London,* Printed by *T.R.* and *N.T.* for *Ambrose Isted,* at the Sign of the *Golden Anchor,* over against St. *Dunstan's* in *Fleet-street.* 1672. 4⁰.

Andromache. A Tragedy. As it is Acted at the Dukes Theatre. *London,* Printed by *T. Ratcliffe,* and *N. Thompson,* for *Richard Bentley,* and Sold by the Book-sellers of *London* and *Westminster.* 1675. 4⁰.

The Countrey Wit. A Comedy : Acted at the Dukes Theatre, Written by Mr. *Crown, London,* Printed by *T.N.* for *James Magnes,* and *Richard Bentley,* at the *Post-Office,* in *Russel-street* in *Covent-Garden.* 1675. 4⁰.

Calisto : or, The Chaste Nimph. The late Masque at Court, As it was frequently Presented there, By several Persons of Great Quality. With the Prologue, and the Songs betwixt the Acts. *All Written by J.* Crowne, *London,* Printed by *Tho: Newcomb,* for *James Magnes* and *Richard Bentley,* at the *Post-Office* in *Russel-street* in *Covent-Garden.* 1675. 4⁰.

The Destruction of Jerusalem by Titus Vespasian. In two Parts. As it was Acted at the Theatre Royal. Written by Mr. *Crowne.* Part the First. *London,* Printed for *R. Bentley,* at the *Posthouse* in *Russel-street* in *Covent-Garden,* 1677. 4⁰.

The Destruction of Jerusalem by Titus Vespasian. The Second Part. As it is Acted at the Theatre Royal By Their Majesties Servants. Written by Mr. *Crown. London,* Printed for *J. Magnes* and *R. Bentley,* in *Russel-street* in *Covent-Garden,* near the *Piazza's,* Anno. Dom. 1677. 4⁰.

The Ambitious Statesman, or the Loyal Favourite. As it was Acted at the theatre *Royal,* by His Majesties Servants. Written by *Mr. Crowne. London,* Printed for *William Abington,* at the *Black-spread-Eagle,* at the West-end of Sᵗ *Paul's.* 1679. 4⁰.

The Misery of Civil-War. A Tragedy, As it is Acted at the Duke's Theatre, By His Royal Highnesses Servants. Written by Mr. *Crown, London,* Printed for *R. Bentley* and *M. Magnes,* in *Russel-Street* in *Covent-Garden.* 1680. 4⁰. (Though it was printed in 1680, this play was not acted till 1681 ; see Genest, I, p. 307.)

Henry the Sixth, The First Part. With the Murder of *Humphrey* Duke of Glocester. As it was Acted at the Dukes Theatre. Written by Mr. *Crown. London,* Printed for *R. Bentley* and *M. Magnes,* in *Russel-Street,* in *Covent-Garden.* 1681. 4⁰.

Thyestes, A Tragedy. Acted at the Theatre-Royal, By their Majesties Servants. *Written by Mr.* Crown. *London,* Printed for *R. Bently* and *M. Magnes,* in *Russel-street,* in *Covent-Garden* near the *Piazza's.* Anno Domini MDCLXXXI. 4⁰.

City Politiques. A Comedy. *As it is Acted* By His Majesties Servants. Written by Mr. *Crown. London,* Printed for R. *Bently* in *Covent-Garden,* and *Joseph Hindmarsh,* Book-Seller to His Royal Highness. M.DC.LXXXIII. 4⁰.

Sir Courtly Nice : Or it Cannot Be. A Comedy. As it is Acted by His Majesties Servants. *Written by Mr.* Crown. *London,* Printed by *H.H.* Jun. for *R. Bently,* in *Russell-street, Covent-Garden,* and *Jos: Hindmarsh,* at the *Golden-Ball* over against the *Royal Exchange* in Cornhill. MDCLXXXV. 4⁰.

[In *Restoration Comedies.* Ed. M. Summers. 1921.]

The English Frier : or, The Town Sparks. A Comedy, As it is Acted by Their Majesty's Servants. By Mr. *Crowne.* London : Printed for *James Knapton,* at the Crown in St. *Paul's* Churchyard. 1690. 4⁰.

The Married Beau : or, the Curious Impertinent, A Comedy : Acted at the Theatre-Royal, By their Majesties Servants. Written by Mr. *Crowne*. London : Printed for *Richard Bentley*, at the Post-House in *Russell-Street* in *Covent-Garden*. 1694. 4°.

Caligula, a Tragedy, as it is acted at the *Theatre Royal*, By His Majesty's Servants. Written by Mr. *Crowne*. London : Printed by *J. Orme*, for *R. Wellington*, at the *Lute* in St *Paul's* Church-Yard, and sold by *Percivil Gilborne*, at the *Harrow*, at the Corner of *Chancery-Lane*, and *Bernard Lintott*, at the *Cross-Keys* in St *Martins-Lane*, near *Long-Acre*. 1698. 4°.

Collected Works.

The Dramatic Works of John Crowne. With Prefatory Memoir and Notes. Edinburgh : William Paterson, London : H. Sotheran and Co. MDCCCLXXIII. 4 vols. 8°.

[In *Dramatists of the Restoration*. Ed. J. Maidment and W. H. Logan. Omits *Andromache, Misery of Civil War, Henry the Sixth*.]

Biography and Criticism.

White, A. F.

[*John Crowne, His Life and Dramatic Works*. Cleveland. 1922.]

D'AVENANT (Sir William).

Poems.

Gondibert : An Heroick Poem, Written by Sr *William D'Avenant*. *London*, Printed by *Tho. Newcomb*, for *John Holden*, and are to be sold at his Shop at the sign of the Anchor in the New-Exchange. 1651. 4°.

[Chalmers, Vol. VI. Also Southey's *Select Works of the British Poets*. 1841.]

Dramatic Works.

The Siege of Rhodes Made a Representation by the Art of Prospective in Scenes, And the Story sung in *Recitative* Musick. At the back part of *Rutland*-House in the upper end of *Aldergate*-Street *London*. *London*, Printed by *J.M.* for *Henry Herringman*, and are to be sold at his Shop, at the Sign of the *Anchor*, on the Lower-Walk in the *New-Exchange*, 1656. 4°.

The Cruelty of the Spaniards in Peru. Exprest by Instrumentall and Vocall Musick, and by Art of Perspective in Scenes, etc. Represented daily at the *Cockpit* in *Drury-Lane*, At Three after noone punctually. *London*, Printed for *Henry Herringman*, and are to be sold at his Shop at the *Anchor* in the Lower walk in the *New-Exchange*. 1658. 4°.

Law against Lovers. (This play, acted in 1662, is not to be found in a separate edition, but is in the following volume :) The Works of Sr William D'Avenant K^t Consisting of *Those which were formerly Printed*, And *Those which he design'd for the Press* : Now Published Out of the Authors Originall Copies. *London* : Printed by *T.N.* for *Henry Herringman*, at the Sign of the *Blew Anchor* in the Lower Walk of the *New-Exchange*. 1673. folio.

Macbeth, a Tragedy. With all the Alterations, Amendments, Additions, and New Songs. *As it's now Acted at the* Dukes Theatre. *London*, Printed for P. Chetwin, and are to be sold by most Booksellers, 1674. 4°.

The Tempest. *See* DRYDEN.

Collected Works.

[*The Dramatic Works*. 5 vols. 1872–4. (*Dramatists of the Restoration*. Ed. J. Maidment and W. H. Logan.)]

Biography and Criticism.

Harbage, Alfred.

[*Sir William Davenant. Poet Venturer. 1606–1668.* Philadelphia, 1935.]

Dowlin, C. M.

[*Sir William Davenant's Gondibert, its preface, and Hobbes' answer : a study in English neo-classicism.* 1935.]

DEFOE (Daniel).

Poems.

The True-Born *Englishman* a Satyr *Statuimus Pacem et Securitatem, et Concordiam, Judicium et Justitiam, inter* Anglos *et* Normannos, Francos *et* Britones, Walliae *et* Cornubiae, Pictos *et* Scotos, Albaniae, *similiter inter Francos et Insulanos Provincias, et Patrias, quae pertinent ad Coronam nostram, et inter omnes nobis Subjectos, firmiter et inviolabiliter observari.* Charta Regis Willielmi Conquisitoris de Pace Publica, Cap. 1. Printed in the Year MDCC. 4°.

A Hymn to The Pillory. *London :* Printed in the Year MDCCIII. 4°.

[Both the above reprinted : E. Arber. *The English Garner.* Vol. VII. 1883.]

Prose.

The Poor Man's Plea, In Relation to all the *Proclamations, Declarations, Acts of Parliament,* etc. Which Have been, or shall be made, or publish'd, for a Reformation of Manners, and suppressing Immorality in the Nation. London : Printed in the Year MDCXCVIII. 4°.

The Shortest-Way With the Dissenters : or Proposals for the Establishment of the Church. *London :* Printed in the Year MDCCII. 4°.

[Reprinted : E. Arber. *The English Garner.* Vol. VII. 1883. Also H. Morley. *Famous Pamphlets.* 1886.]

The Shortest-Way With the Dissenters : Or Proposals for the Establishment of the Church. With its Author's Brief Explications *Consider'd*; His Name *Expos'd,* His Practices *Detected,* and his Hellish Designs set in a true Light, that the Party which stickles for Him, may rightly know Him, and that Which is against Him continue to Triumph over Him. The Second Edition, Corrected and Amended. To which is Added A *Post-Script,* By Way of Answer to some *Malicious and False Aspersions,* etc.

Crimine ab Uno

Disce Omnes.

Nec Defensoribus istis

Tempus eget.   Virg., Æn.

London : Printed in the Year 1703. 4°.

A Weekly Review of the Affairs of *France* : Purg'd from the Errors and Partiality of *News-Writers* and *Petty-Statesmen,* of all Sides. Numb. 1. Saturday, Feb. 19 1704. 4°.

[Facsimile edition : 22 vols. A. W. Secord. New York. 1938.]

Collected Works.

[*Novels and Miscellaneous Works.* 7 vols. 1854–67. (Bohn's British Classics.)]

[*Novels and Selected Writings.* 14 vols. Oxford. 1927–8.]

Biography and Criticism.

Wilson, Walter.

Memoirs of the Life and Times of Daniel De Foe ; Containing A Review of his Writings, and his opinions upon a Variety of important Matters, Civil and Ecclesiastical. By Walter Wilson, Esq. of the Inner Temple. In Three volumes. London : Hurst, Chance and Co. 1830. 8°.

Lee, William.

Daniel Defoe : His Life, and recently discovered writings : extending from 1716 to 1729. By William Lee. London : John Camden Hotten, Piccadilly. 1869. 3 vols. 8°.

Minto, William.

English Men of Letters Edited by John Morley. Daniel Defoe By William Minto. London Macmillan and Co. 1879. 1 vol. 12°.

Trent, W. P.
[*Daniel Defoe. How to know him.* Indianapolis. 1916.]
Dottin, Paul.
[*Daniel De Foe et ses Romans.* 3 vols. Paris. 1924. Trans. Eng. (vol. 1 only). 1929.]
Sutherland, J. R.
[*Defoe.* 1937.]

DENNIS (John). See also COLLIER.
Poems.
Britannia Triumphans : Or the Empire Sav'd, and *Europe* Deliver'd. By the Success of her Majesty's Forces under the Wise and Heroick Conduct of his Grace the Duke of Marlborough. A Poem, By Mr. *Dennis. Ab Jove Principium Musae.* Virg. London : Printed for *J. Nutt near Stationers-Hall.* 1704. 8º.
The Battle of Ramillia : or, the Power of Union. A Poem. In Five Books By Mr. *Dennis. London,* Printed for *Ben Bragg* at the *Raven* in *Pater-Noster-Row,* 1706. 8º.
A Poem Upon the Death of Her late Sacred Majesty Queen *Anne,* And the Most Happy and most Auspicious Accession Of his Sacred Majesty King George. To the Imperial Crowns of *Great Britain, France and Ireland.* With an Exhortation to all True *Britons* to Unity. *Rege incolumi mens omnibus una est.* Virg. Georg. I. 4. *London :* Printed by H. Meere, and Sold by J. Baker at the Black Boy in Pater-Noster-Row. 1714. (Price Six Pence.) 8º.
Prose.
A Plot, and no Plot. A Comedy, As it is Acted at the Theatre-Royal, in *Drury Lane.* Written by Mr. *Dennis.*

> *Militiae quamvis piger et malus, utilis urbi,*
> *Si das hoc, parvis quoque rebus magna Juvari.*
>   Horace Epist.

London, Printed for *R. Parker,* at the Sign of the *Unicorn* under the *Royal Exchange* in *Cornhil : P. Buck,* at the Sign of the *Temple,* near the *Inner Temple Gate, Fleet street :* and *R. Wellington,* at the *Lute* in St. *Paul's* Church Yard. (1697), 4º.
Original Letters, Familiar, Moral, *and* Critical. By Mr. *Dennis.* In Two Volumes. London : Printed for W. Mears, at the Lamb without Temple-Bar. MDCCXXI. 8º.
The Stage defended from Scripture, Reason, Experience and the Common Sense of Mankind, for Two Thousand Years. Occasion'd by Mr. *Law's* late Pamphlet against Stage-Entertainments. In a Letter to . . . By Mr. *Dennis,* London : Printed for N. Blandford, at the *London-Gazette, Charing-Cross* ; and sold by J. Peele, at *Locke's-Head* in *Pater-Noster-Row.* MDCCXXVI. (Price one Shilling.) 4º.
Collected Works.
The Select Works of Mr. *John Dennis.* In Two Volumes.

> *Neque, Te ut miretur Turba, labores ;*
> *Contentus paucis Lectoribus.* Hor.

London, Printed by John Darby in Bartholomew-Close. MDCCXVIII. 8º.
[*The Critical Works of John Dennis.* Ed. E. N. Hooker. 2 vols. Baltimore. 1939–43.]
Biography and Criticism.
Paul, H. G.
[*John Dennis, His Life and Criticism.* New York. 1911.]

DIAPER (William).
[*Nereides : or, Sea-Eclogues.* London. 1712.]
[*Dryades.* London. 1713.]
[Verse translation of the first two books of Oppian's *Halieuticks.* Oxford.
1722.] Ed. in preparation by D. Broughton.

DIGBY (George, 2ᵈ Earl of Bristol).
Elvira : or The Worst not always True. A Comedy, Written by a Person
of Quality. Licens'd *May* 15. 1667. *Roger L'Estrange. London,* Printed
by *E. Cotes* for *Henry Brome* in Little-Britain. 1667. 4⁰.
[Reprinted : R. Dodsley, *A Select Collection of Old Plays.* Vol. XII.
1744. Revised W. C. Hazlitt. Vol. XV. 1876.]

DILLON (Wentworth, Earl of Roscommon.) See also WILMOT (John).
Miscellaneous Works By The Right Honourable. The *Earl of* Roscommon.
London: Printed in the Year MDCCIX, 8⁰.
The Works of the right honourable Wentworth Dillon, Earl of Roscommon.
Glasgow : Printed by Robert and Andrew Foulis. MDCCLIII. 12⁰.
[See Chalmers, Vol. VIII. Also T. Park, *Works of the British Poets.* Vol. 32.]

DOGGET (Thomas).
The Country-Wake : A Comedy. As it is Acted at the New Theatre
in *Little Lincoln's-Inn-Fields* by His Majesty's Servants. *Written by Mr.*
Tho. Dogget, *Comedian. London,* Printed for *Sam. Briscoe* at the Corner
of *Charles-street,* in *Russel-street, Covent Garden* ; Sold by *R. Wellington,* at
the *Lute* in St. *Paul's* Church-yard ; *R. Parker* at the *Royal-Exchange.*
1696. *Price,* One Shilling, Six Pence. 4⁰.

DORSET (Charles Sackville, Earl of). See WILMOT (John).

DRAKE (Nathan).
Essays, Biographical. Critical, and Historical, Illustrative of the Tatler,
Spectator, and Guardian. *By Nathan Drake, M.D.* Author of Literary
Hours, etc. ['Αγαθους ἀγαθοις ἀντεξεταζειν.] Dionysius Halicarnasseus.
In three Volumes.—The second Edition. *London :* Published by
Suttaby, Evance, and Fox. Stationers'-Court, Ludgate-Street ; and
Sharpe and Hailes, Piccadilly. 1814. In-12.
Essays, Biographical, Critical, and Historical, Illustrative of the Rambler,
Adventurer, Idler, and of the Various Periodical Papers which, *In
Imitation of the Writings of Steele and Addison,* have been published between
the Close of the eighth volume of the Spectator, and the commencement
of the year 1809. *By Nathan Drake, M.D.* Author of Literary Hours,
and of Essays on the Tatler, Spectator, and Guardian. Evolvendi
penitus auctores qui de virtute praecipiunt, ut—vita cum scientia
divinarum rerum sit humanarumque conjuncta. Quintilianus. In two
Volumes. Printed by J. Seeley, Buckingham, for W. Suttaby, Stationers
Court. London. 1809. In-12.
The Gleaner : A series of Periodical Essays ; Selected and arranged From
scarce or neglected volumes, with an introduction, and notes, By Nathan
Drake, M.D. Author of " Literary Hours," And of " Essays, on Periodical Literature."

Apis Matinae
More modoque,
Grata carpentis thyma per laborem
Plurimum. Hor.

In four volumes. London : Printed for Suttaby, Evance and Co.
Stationers' Court ; And Robert Baldwin, Pater-Noster Row ; Also for
William Blackwood, Edinburgh, and Michael Keene. Dublin 1811. 8⁰.

DRYDEN (John).

Poems.

Astraea Redux. A Poem on the happy Restoration and Return of His Sacred Majesty Charles the Second. By *John Driden. Jam Redit et Virgo, Redeunt Saturnia Regna.* Virgil. *London* Printed by *J.M.* for *Henry Herringman,* and are to be sold at his shop, at the Blew-*Anchor,* in the Lower Walk of the New-Exchange. 1660. folio.

Annus Mirabilis: the year of Wonder, 1666: an Historical Poem: Containing The Progress and various Successes of our Naval War with *Holland,* under the Conduct of His Highness Prince Rupert and His Grace the Duke of Albemarl. And describing The Fire of London. By John Dryden, Esq.; *Multum interest res poscat, an homines latius imperare velint.* Trajan. Imperator. ad Plin. *Urbs antiqua ruit, multos dominata per annos.* Virg. *London,* Printed for *Henry Herringman,* at the *Anchor* in the Lower Walk of the *New Exchange* : 1677. 8°.
[Facsimile reprint : Clarendon Press. 1927.]

Absalom and Achitophel. A Poem.

> *. . . Si Propius stes*
> *Te Capiet Magis . . .*

London, Printed for *J.T.* and are to be Sold by *W. Davies* in *Amen-Corner.* 1681. folio.

The second part of Absalom and Achitopel. A Poem.

> *Si quis tamen Haec quoque, Si Quis*
> *Captus Amore Leget.*

London: Printed for *Jacob Tonson,* at the *Judges Head* in *Chancery Lane,* near *Fleet-Street.* 1682. folio. (In collaboration with Nahum Tate.)
[Both parts ed. W. D. Christie. Fifth edition revised C. H. Firth. Clarendon Press. 1911.]

The Medall. A Satyre against Sedition By the Author of *Absalom* and *Achitophel.*

> *Per* Graium *populos, mediaeque per* Elidis *Urbem*
> *Ibat ovans :* Divumque *sibi poscebat honores.*

London, Printed for *Jacob Tonson* at the *Judge's Head* in *Chancery-Lane* near *Fleet-street.* 1682. 4°.
[Facsimile reprint : Oxford. 1924.]

Mac Flecknoe, or a Satyr upon the true-blew-protestant poet T.S. London. Printed for D. Green. 1682. 4°.
[Facsimile reprint : Oxford. 1924.]

Three Poems Upon the Death of the Late Usurper Oliver Cromwel. Written by Mr. *Jo. Drydon* [*sic*]. Mr. *Sprat,* of Oxford. Mr. *Edm. Waller. London* : Printed by *William Wilson,* in the Year 1659. And Reprinted for *R. Baldwin* 1682. 4°.
[Originally published as : Three Poems upon the Death of his late Highnesse Oliver Lord Protector of *England, Scotland,* and *Ireland.* By Mr. Edm. Waller. Mr. Jo. Dryden. Mr. Sprat of *Oxford.* 1659. Later reprinted with the above heading by Dryden's enemies, to remind the public of his earlier sympathies. See *Dryden Bibliography.* Hugh Macdonald. 1939. pp. 3–7.]

Religio Laici or a Laymans Faith. A Poem. Written by Mr. *Dryden* : *Ornari res ipsa negat : contenta doceri. London,* Printed for *Jacob Tonson* at the *Judge's Head* in *Chancery-lane,* near *Fleet-street.* 1682. 4°.

Prologue To His *Royal Highness,* Upon His first appearance at the *Duke's Theatre,* since his Return from *Scotland. Written by Mr. Dryden. Spoken by Mr.* Smith. *London,* Printed for *J. Tonson.* (21st April 1682.) folio.

Miscellany Poems. Containing a New Translation of *Virgil's* Eclogues,
Ovid's Love Elegies, Odes of *Horace*, And Other Authors ; With
Several Original Poems. By the most Eminent Hands.

> *Et Vos, O Lauri, carpam, et Te, proxima* Myrte :
> *Sic posita quoniam suaveis miscetis odores.*
>   Virg. *Ecl.* 2.

London, Printed for *Jacob Tonson*, at the *Judges-Head* in *Chancery-Lane*
near Fleet-street, 1684. 8º.
Sylvae : Or, The Second Part of Poetical Miscellanies.

> *Non deficit alter*
> *Aureus ; et simili frondescit virga metallo.*   Virg.

London, Printed for *Jacob Tonson*, at the *Judges-Head* in *Chaneery-lane*
near *Fleet-street*. 1685. 8º.
The Second Part of Miscellany Poems. Containing Variety of New
Translations of the *Ancient Poets* : Together with Several Original
Poems. *By the Most Eminent Hands.* Publish'd by Mr. *Dryden.*

> *Non deficit alter*
> *Aureus ; et simili frondescit virga metallo.*   Virg.

The Fourth Edition. *London* : Printed for Jacob Tonson at *Shakespear's
Head* over-against *Katharine-Street* in the *Strand.* MDCCXVI. 8º.
Examen Poeticum : being The Third Part of Miscellany Poems. Containing Variety of New Translations of the *Ancient Poets.* Together
with many Original Copies, by the *Most Eminent Hands.*

> *Haec potior soboles : hinc Caeli tempore certo,*
> *Dulcia mella premes.*   Virg. Geor. 4.
> *In Medium quaesita reponunt.*   Ibid.

London, Printed by *R.E.* for *Jacob Tonson*, at the *Judges Head* in *Chancery-*
Lane near *Fleetstreet.* MDCXCIII. 8º.
The *Annual Miscellany* : for The Year 1694, Being The Fourth Part of
Miscellany Poems Containing Great Variety of New Translations
and Original Copies by the *Most Eminent Hands.* *London* : Printed
by *R.E.* for *Jacob Tonson*, at the *Judges Head* near the *Inner Temple-*
Gate, in *Fleetstreet.* M.D.CXCIV. 8º.
[For details of the above miscellanies see *Dryden Bibliography.* Hugh
Macdonald. 1939.]
Threnodia Augustalis : a Funeral-Pindarique Poem Sacred to the Happy
Memory of King Charles II. By *John Dryden* Servant to His late
Majesty and to the Present King.

> *Fortunati Ambo, si quid mea Carmina possunt,*
> *Nulla dies unquam memori vos eximet aevo !*

London : Printed for *Jacob Tonson*, at the *Judges Head* in *Chancery-lane*,
near *Fleet-street.* 1685. 4º.
The Hind and the Panther. A Poem. In Three Parts.

> *Antiquam exquirite matrem* } Virg.
> *Et vera, incessu, patuit Dea.*

Holy-Rood-House. Re-printed by *James Watson*, Printer to His most
Excellent Majesties Royal Family and House-hold.
MDCLXXXVII. 4º.
Britannia Rediviva : A Poem on the Birth of the Prince.
Written by Mr. *Dryden.*

> *Dii Patrii Indigetes et Romule, Vestaque Mater.*
> *Quae Tuscum Tiberim, et Romana Palatia servas*

P

Hunc saltem everso Puerum *succurrere saeclo*
Ne prohibete : satis jampridem sanguine nostro
Laomedonteae luimus Perjuria *Trojae.*
Virg. Georg. I.

London. Printed for *J. Tonson* at the *Judges-Head* in *Chancery-Lane* near *Fleet-Street.* 1688. folio.

The Satires of Decimus Junius Juvenalis. Translated into English Verse. By Mr. *Dryden* And Several other Eminent Hands. Together with the Satires of Aulus Persius Flaccus. Made English by Mr. *Dryden.* With Explanatory Notes at the end of each Satire. To Which is Prefix'd a Discourse concerning the Original and Progress of Satire. Dedicated to the Right Honourable *Charles* Earl of *Dorset,* etč. By Mr. *Dryden.*

Quicquid agunt homines, votum, timor, Ira, Voluptas,
Gaudia, discursus, nostri est farrago libelli..

London, Printed for *Jacob Tonson* at the *Judge's Head* in *Chancery-Lane,* near *Fleetstreet.* MDCXCIII. folio.

[The Juvenal satires 1, 3, 6, 10 and 16, and all those of Persius are translated by Dryden.]

The Works of Virgil : Containing His Pastorals, Georgics, and AEneis. Translated into English Verse ; by Mr. *Dryden.* Adorn'd with a Hundred Sculptures. *Sequiturque Patrem non passibus AEquis.* Virg. AEn. 2. The Second Edition. *London,* Printed for *Jacob Tonson,* at the *Judges-Head* in *Fleetstreet,* near the *Inner-Temple-Gate.* MDCXCVIII. folio.

Fables *Ancient* and *Modern* ; Translated into Verse, From Homer, Ovid, Boccace, and Chaucer : with Original Poems. By Mr *Dryden.*

Nunc ultro ad Cineres ipsius et ossa parentis
(Haud equidem sine mente, reor, sine numine divum)
Adsumus. Virg. Æn. lib. 5.

London : Printed for *Jacob Tonson,* within *Gray's Inn Gate* next *Gray's Inn Lane.* MDCC. folio.

Collected Poems.

The Annotated edition of the English Poets. Edited by Robert Bell. Author of ' The History of Russia,' ' Lives of English Poets,' etc. London : John W. Parker and Son, West Strand. The Poetical Works of J. Dryden. 1854. 3 vols. in-12.

The Globe Edition. The Poetical Works of John Dryden Edited with a Memoir, Revised text, and Notes by W. D. Christie, M.A. of Trinity College, Cambridge. New Edition. London : Macmillan and Co. 1870. 8⁰.

The Works of John Dryden. Illustrated with Notes, Historical, Critical, and Explanatory, and A Life of the Author. By Sir Walter Scott, Bart. Revised and Corrected by George Saintsbury. Edinburgh : Printed for William Paterson, Princes Street, by T. and A. Constable, Printers to Her Majesty. 1882-1893. 18 vols. 8⁰. [Contains all the above poems.]

[*Poetical Works.* Ed. G. R. Noyes. New York. 1909.]

[*Poems.* Ed. John Sargeaunt. 1910.]

Dramatic Works.

The Wild Gallant : A Comedy, As it was acted at the Theater-Royal, By His Majesties Servants. Written *By* John Dryden, *Esq.* ; In the Savoy. Printed by *Tho. Newcomb.* for *H. Herringman,* at the *Blew-Anchor,* in the Lower-Walk of the *New-Exchange.* 1669. 4⁰. (Acted in 1662.)

The Rival Ladies. A Tragi-Comedy. As it was Acted at the *Theatre Royal*. Nos. haec Novimus esse nihil. Written by *John Driden* Esquire. *London*, Printed for *H. Herringman*, and are to be sold at his shop in the Lower walk in the *New Exchange*. 1669. 4°. (Acted in 1664.)

The Indian Queen 1664. See HOWARD (Sir Robert).

The Indian Emperour, or, the Conquest of Mexico By the Spaniards. Being the Sequel of the *Indian Queen*. By John Dryden Esq. ;

> *Dum relego scripsisse pudet, quia plurima cerno*
> *Me quoque, qui feci, judice, digna lini.*
> Ovid.

London, Printed for *H. Herringman*, at the Sign of the *Blew Anchor* in the Lower Walk of the *New Exchange*, 1667. 4°. (Acted in 1665.)

Secret-Love, or the Maiden-Queen. As it is Acted By His Majesties Servants at the *Theater-Royal*. Written by John Dryden, Esq ;

> *Vitis nemo sine nascitur ; optimus ille*
> *Qui minimis urgetur.* Horace.

London, Printed for *Henry Herringman*, at the Sign of the *Anchor* on the lower walk of the *New-Exchange*. 1668. 4°. (Acted in 1667.)

Sr Martin Mar-all, or the Feign'd Innocence ; A Comedy. As it was Acted at His Highnesse the Duke of *York's* Theatre. *London*, Printed for *Henry Herringman*, at the Sign of the *Blew Anchor* in the Lower Walk of the *New Exchange*. 1668. 4°. (Acted in 1667.)
[In collaboration with William Cavendish, Duke of Newcastle.]

Sr Martin Marr-all : Or, the Feign'd Innocence. A Comedy. As it is Acted By Their Majesties Servants. By Mr *Dryden*. *London*, Printed for *Henry Herringman*, and are to be sold by *Francis Saunders* at the *Blue Anchor* in the Lower Walk of the *New-Exchange*, 1691. 4°. (From the year 1691, still in Dryden's lifetime, the play has been printed under Dryden's name alone.)

The Tempest, or the Enchanted Island. A Comedy : As it is now Acted At His Highness the Duke of York's Theatre. *London*, Printed by *J. Macock*, for *Henry Herringman* at the Sign of the *Blew Anchor* in the Lower Walk of the *New Exchange*. M.DC.LXXVI. 4°. (In collaboration with D'Avenant ; acted in 1667.)

An Evening's Love. Or the Mock-Astrologer. Acted at the Theatre-Royal By His Majesties Servants. Written by *John Dryden* Servant to His Majesty. *Mallem Convivis quam placuisse Cocis*. Mart. In the *Savoy*, Printed by *T.N.* for *Henry Herringman*, and are to be sold at the *Anchor* in the Lower Walk of the *New Exchange*. 1671. 4°. (Acted in 1668.)

Tyrannick-Love : or, the Royal Martyr. A Tragedy. As it is Acted by his Majesties Servants, at the *Theatre Royal*. By *John Dryden*, Servant to his *Majesty*.

> *Non jam prima peto—neq; vincere certo ;*
> *Extremum rediisse pudet.* Virg.

London, Printed for *H. Herringman*, at the Sign of the *Blew Anchor* in the Lower Walk of the *New Exchange*. 1670. 4°.

The Conquest of Granada by the Spaniards : In Two Parts. Acted at the *Theater-Royall*. Written by *John Dryden* Servant to His Majesty.

> *Major rerum mihi nascitur Ordo ;*
> *Majus Opus moveo.* Virg. Æneid : 7.

In the *Savoy*. Printed by T.N. for *Henry Herringman*, and are to be

sold at the *Anchor*, in the Lower Walk of the *New Exchange*. 1672. 4⁰.
[Acted in 1670.]

Almanzor and *Almahide*. Or the Conquest of Granada. The Second
Part. As it is Acted at the *Theater-Royal*. Written by *John Dryden*
Servant to his Majesty—*stimulos dedit aemula virtus*. Lucan. In the
Savoy, Printed by *T.N.* for *Henry Herringman*, and are to be sold at the
Anchor in the Lower Walk of the *New Exchange*. 1673. 4⁰. [Acted
in 1671.]

The Assignation : Or, Love in a Nunnery. As it is Acted, at the *Theatre
Royal*. Written by *John Dryden* Servant to His Majesty. *Successum
dea dira negat*. Virg. London : Printed by *T.N.* for *Henry Herringman*,
and are to be sold at the *Anchor* in the Lower Walk of the *New Exchange*.
1673. (Acted in 1672.) 4⁰.

Marriage-à-la-Mode. A Comedy. As it is Acted at the Theatre-Royal.
Written by *John Dryden*, Servant to His Majesty.

> *Quicquid sum ego, quamvis*
> *Infra Lucilli censum ingeniumque, tamen me*
> *Cum magnis vixisse, invita fatebitur usque*
> *Invidia, et fragili quaerens illidere dentem*
> *Offendet solido.*   Horat. Serm.

London, Printed by *T.N.* for *Henry Herringman*, and are to be sold at the
Anchor in the Lower Walk of the *New-Exchange*. 1673. 4⁰.

Amboyna : A Tragedy. As it is Acted at the *Theatre-Royal*. Written
by *John Dryden* Servant to His Majesty. *Manet alta mente repostum*.
London, Printed by *T.N.* for *Henry Herringman*, and are to be sold at the
Anchor in the Lower Walk of the *New Exchange*. 1673. 4⁰.

The State of Innocence, and Fall of Man : an Opera. Written in
Heroique Verse, And Dedicated to Her *Royal Highness*, the Dutchess.
By *John Dryden*, Servant to His Majesty.

> *Utinam modo dicere possem*
> *Carmina digna Dea : certe est Dea Carmine digna.*
>   Ovid. Metam.

London : Printed by *T.N.* for *Henry Herringman*, at the Anchor in the
Lower Walk of the *New Exchange*. 1677. 4⁰.

Aureng-Zebe : A Tragedy. Acted at the Royal Theatre. Written by
John Dryden, Servant to his Majesty.

> *Sed, cum fregit subsellia versu,*
> *Esurit, intactam Paridi nisi vendat Agaven.*
>   Juv.

Licensed, *Roger L'Estrange*. London, Printed by *T.N. for Henry Herringman*, at the *Anchor* in the Lower Walk of the *New Exchange*. 1676. 4⁰.

All for Love : Or, the World well Lost. A Tragedy, As it is Acted
at the *Theatre Royal* ; And Written in Imitation of *Shakespeare's* Stile.
By *John Dryden*, Servant to His Majesty. *Facile est verbum aliquod
ardens (ut ita dicam) notare : idque restinctis animorum incendiis irridere.*
Cicero. *In the Savoy* : Printed by *Tho. Newcomb*, for *Henry Herringman*,
at the Blew Anchor in the Lower Walk of the *New-Exchange*. 1678. 4⁰.

Œdipus : A Tragedy. As it is Acted at his Royal Highness The Duke's
Theatre. The Authors Mr. *Dryden*, and Mr. *Lee*.

> *Hi proprium decus et partum indignantur honorem*
> *Ni teneant.*   Virgil.

> *Vos exemplaria Graeca,*
> *Nocturna versate manu, versate diurna.*   Horat.

Licensed, *Jan.* 3. 1678/9. *Roger L'Estrange. London,* Printed for *R. Bentley* and *M. Magnes* in *Russel-street* in *Covent-Garden.* 1679. 4°.
Troilus and Cressida, Or, *Truth Found too Late.* A Tragedy As it is Acted at the Dukes Theatre. To Which is Prefix'd, A Preface Containing the Grounds of Criticism in Tragedy. Written by *John Dryden* Servant to His Majesty.

> *Rectius, Iliacum carmen deducis in actus,*
> *Quam si proferres ignota indictaque primus.* Hor.

London, Printed for *Abel Swall,* at the Unicorn at the West-end of *S. Pauls,* and *Jacob Tonson* at the *Judges-Head* in *Chancery-lane* near *Fleet-street,* 1679. 4°.
The Kind Keeper ; Or, Mr Limberham : A Comedy : As it was Acted at the Duke's Theatre by His Royal Highnesses Servants. Written by *John Dryden,* Servant to his Majesty. Κἢν μεφάγης ἐπὶ ῥίζαν, ὅμως ἔτι καρποφορήσω. ᾽Αντολογία Δευτέρα

> *Hic nuptarum insanit amoribus ; his meretricum :*
> *Omnes hi metuunt versus ; odere Poetas.* Horat.

London : Printed for *R. Bentley,* and *M. Magnes,* in *Russel-Street* in *Covent-Garden,* 1680. 4°.
The Spanish Fryar, Or, The Double Discovery. Acted at the Duke's Theatre.

> *Ut melius possis fallere, sume togam.* Ma.
> *Alterna revisens*
> *Lusit, et in solido rursus fortuna locavit.* Vir.

Written by *John Dryden,* Servant to His Majesty. *London,* Printed for *Richard Tonson* and *Jacob Tonson,* at *Grays-inn-gate,* in *Grays-inn-lane,* and at the *Judge's* Head, in *Chancery-lane,* 1681. 4°.
The Duke of Guise. A Tragedy. Acted By Their Majesties Servants. Written by Mr. *Dryden,* and Mr. *Lee* ῾Οὔτως δὲ φιλότιμοι φύσεις ἐν τᾶις πολιτείαις τὸ ἄγαν μὴ φυλαξάμεναι τοῦ ἀγαθοῦ μεῖζον τὸ κακὸν ἔχουσι. Plutarch. in Agesilao. *London,* Printed by *T.N.* for *R. Bentley* in *Russel-street,* near the *Piazza* in *Covent-Garden,* and *J. Tonson* at the *Judge's Head* in *Chancery-lane.* M. DC. LXXXIII. 4°.
Albion and Albanius : an Opera Perform'd at the Queens Theatre in *Dorset* Garden. *Written by Mr.* Dryden. *Discite justitiam moniti, et non temnere Divos.* Virg. *London,* Printed for *Jacob Tonson,* at the *Judge's Head* in *Chancery-lane,* near *Fleet-street.* 1685. folio.
Amphitryon ; or, The Two Sosia's. A Comedy. At it is Acted at the Theatre Royal.

> *Egregiam vero laudem, et spolia ampla refertis ;*
> *Una, dolo, Divum, si Foemina victa duorum est.* Virg.

Written by Mr. *Dryden.* To which added, The Musick of the Songs Compos'd by Mr. *Henry Purcel. London,* Printed for *J. Tonson,* at the *Judge's Head* in *Chancery-lane* near *Fleet-street* ; and *M. Tonson* at *Grays-Inn-Gate* in *Gray's-Inn-Lane.* 1691. 4°. (Played in 1690.)
Don Sebastian, King of Portugal : A Tragedy Acted at the Theatre Royal. Written by Mr. *Dryden.*

> *Nec tarda Senectus*
> *Debilitat vires animi, mutatque vigorem.* Virgil.

London : Printed for *Jo. Hindmarsh,* at the *Golden Ball* in *Cornhill.* MDCXC. 4°.
Cleomenes, the Spartan Heroe. A Tragedy, As it is Acted at the Theatre Royal. *Written by* Mr. Dryden. To which is prefixt The Life of

Cleomenes. His Armis, illa quoque tutus in aula, Juv. Sat. **IV.** *London*, Printed for *Jacob Tonson*, at the *Judge's-Head* in *Chancery-Lane* near *Fleet-Street*. 1692. 4⁰.

Love Triumphant ; Or, Nature will Prevail, A Tragi-Comedy. As it is Acted at the Theatre-Royal, By Their Majesties Servants.

> *Quod optanti Divum promittere nemo*
> *Auderet, volvenda dies, en, attulit ultro.*   Virg.

Written by Mr. *Dryden. London*, Printed for *Jacob Tonson*, at the *Judges Head* near the *Inner-Temple-Gate* in *Fleet-street*. 1694. 4⁰.

The Pilgrim, a Comedy : As it is acted at the *Theatre Royal* in Drury-Lane. *Written Originally by Mr.* Fletcher, *and now Very much Alter'd with several Additions.* Likewise A Prologue, Epilogue, Dialogue *and* Masque, *Written by the late Great Poet Mr.* Dryden *just before his Death, being the last of his Works. London* : Printed for *Benjamin Tooke*, near the *Middle-Temple-Gate*, in *Fleet-street*. 1700. 4⁰.

The Dramatick Works of *John Dryden*, Esq ; in Six Volumes. *London* : Printed for *J. Tonson* : And Sold by *R. Knaplock, W. Taylor, W. Mears, J. Browne, W. Churchill, E. Symon*, and *J. Brotherton.* (With Congreve's Dedication to the Duke of Newcastle.) MDCCXVII. 8⁰.

[*The Dramatic Works.* Ed. M. Summers. 6 vols. The Nonesuch Press. 1931–2. (Contains all the above plays.)]

Miscellaneous Prose.

Of Dramatick Poesie, An Essay. By *John Dryden* Esq ;

> *Fungar vice cotis, acutum*
> *Reddere quae ferrum valet, exsors ipsa secandi.*
>   Horat. de Arte Poet.

London, Printed for *Henry Herringman*, at the Sign of the *Anchor*, on the Lower-Walk of the New *Exchange*. 1668. 4⁰.

[Reprinted : 1928. Etchells and Macdonald. Preceded by T. S. Eliot's *Dialogue on Poetic Drama.*]

The Vindication : or the Parallel of the *French* Holy-League, and the English League and Covenant, Turn'd into a Seditious Libell against the King and his Royal Highness, by *Thomas Hunt* and the Authors of the *Reflections* upon the Pretended Parallel in the Play Called The Duke of *Guise.* Written by Mr. *Dryden.*

> *Turno tempus erit magno cum optaverit emptum*
> *Intactum Pallanta ; et cum spolia ista, diemq;*
> *Oderit.*

London, Printed for *Jacob Tonson* at the *Judges Head* in *Chancery-Lane* near *Fleet-street*. MDCLXXXIII. 4⁰.

Plutarchs Lives Translated *from the Greek* by Several Hands. To which is prefixt the *Life of Plutarch. London*, Printed for *Jacob Tonson*, at the Sign of the *Judges-Head* in *Chancery-Lane* near *Fleet-street.* 1683–1686. 5 vols. 8⁰. (The 1st vol. is headed : The Life of Plutarch, *written by Mr Dryden.*)

[Reprinted : Everyman's Library.]

The History of the League. Written in *French* by Monsieur *Maimbourg.* Translated into *English*, according to His Majesty's Command, By Mr. *Dryden.*

> *Neque enim libertas gratior ulla est*
> *Quam sub Rege Pio.*

London, Printed by *M. Flesher*, for *Jacob Tonson*, at the *Judge's-Head* in *Chancery-lane* near *Fleetstreet.* 1684. 8⁰.

[In the Scott-Saintsbury edition of *The Works.*]

A Defence of the Papers Written by the Late King of Blessed Memory. and Duchess of York, against The Answer made to Them. By Command. *London* : Printed by *H. Hills*, Printer to the King's Most Excellent Majesty for His Houshold and Chappel. 1686. 4⁰.

[Dryden wrote the defence of the third paper, that of the Duchess of York. In the Scott-Saintsbury edition of *The Works*.]

De Arte Graphica. The Art of Painting. By *C. A. Du Fresnoy*. With Remarks. Translated into *English*, Together with an *Original Preface* Containing A Parallel betwixt Painting and Poetry. By Mr. *Dryden*. As also a Short Account of the most Eminent Painters, both *Ancient* and *Modern*, continu'd down to the *Present Times*, according to the Order of their Succession. *By Another Hand. Ut Pictura Poesis erit.* Hor. de Arte Poetica. *London*, Printed by *I. Heptinstall* for W. Rogers, at the Sun against St. *Dunstan's* Church in *Fleet-street*. M.DC.XCV. 4⁰.

[In the Scott-Saintsbury edition of *The Works*.]

[*The Letters of John Dryden*. Ed. Charles E. Ward. Duke University Press. 1942.]

Collected Works (Prose).

The Critical and Miscellaneous Prose Works of John Dryden, now first collected : With Notes and Illustrations ; An Account of the Life and Writings of the Author, Grounded on Original and Authentick Documents ; And A Collection of his Letters, the greater Part of which has never before been Published. By Edmond Malone, Esq. London : Printed by H. Baldwin and Son, New Bridge-street, for T. Cadell, jun. and W. Davies, in the Strand. M,DCCC. 8⁰.

[*The Essays of John Dryden*. Ed. W. P. Ker. 2 vols. Oxford. 1900, 1926.]

Collected Works (Poems, Dramatic Works, Prose).

The Works of John Dryden. Illustrated with Notes, Historical, Critical, and Explanatory, and a Life of the Author. By Sir Walter Scott, Bart. Revised and Corrected by George Saintsbury. Edinburgh : Printed for William Paterson, Princes Street, by T. and A. Constable, Printers to Her Majesty. 1882–1893. 18 vols. 8⁰.

Drydeniana.

Care, Henry.
Towser the Second, a Bull-dog, or a short Reply to Absalom and Achitophel, 10th December 1681. 8⁰.

Hickeringhill, Edmund.
The Mushroom : or a Satyr against *Libelling Tories* and *Prelatical Tantivies* : In Answer to A Satyr against Sedition called The Meddal, by the Author of *Absalom* and *Achitophel*. And here Answered By the *Author* of the *Black Nonconformist*. The *Next Day* after the Publication of the *Meddal* : To *Help the* sale *thereof. Nitimur in vetitum? Quousque?* London, Printed for *Fra : Smith* Jun. at the Elephant and Castle, in *Cornhill*. MDCLXXXII. folio. (The end of the work is dated London, March 17, 1681.)

Villiers, George, Duke of Buckingham.
Poetical Reflections on a late Poem entituled, Absalom and Achitophel. *By a Person of Honour. London* : Printed for Richard Janeway. 1682. folio.

[Ascribed to Villiers by Anthony à Wood.]

Pordage, Samuel.
Azaria and Hushai, A Poem *quod cuique visum est sentiant. London* : Printed for *Charles Lee*. An. Dom. 1682. 4⁰.

The Medal Revers'd a Satyre against Persecution By the Author of Azaria and Hushai. *Laudatur ab his, Culpatur ab illis. London* : Printed for *Charles Lee*, Anno 1682. 4⁰.

Settle, Elkanah.

Absalom Senior : Or, Achitophel Transpros'd. a Poem. *Si Populus vult decipi, etc.* London : Printed for *S.E.* and Sold by *Langley Curtis,* at the sign of Sir *Edmondbury Godfrey,* near *Fleetbridge.* 1682. folio.

Shadwell, Thomas.

The Medal of John Bayes : A Satyr against Folly and Knavery. *Facit indignatio versus,* London : Printed for *Richard Janeway.* 1682. 4º. (Attributed to Shadwell.) [See *Dryden Bibliography.* Hugh Macdonald. 1939. pp. 232–3.]

The Tory Poets a Satyr. 4º. 1682. " A sad paltry performance against Dryden, Otway, etc.," says Oldys in a Ms. note on Langbaine's Shadwell article. Attributed to Shadwell also by Malone. (See *Life of Dryden,* p. 165), who gives the following extract :

> The laurel makes a wit ; a brave, the sword ;
> And all are wise men at a Council-board :
> Settle's a coward, 'cause fool Otway fought him,
> And Mulgrave is a wit, because I taught him.

Some Reflections upon the Pretended Parallel in the Play Called The Duke of Guise. In a Letter to a Friend. *London,* Printed for *Francis Smith,* sen. 1683. 4º.

The Tenth Satyr of Juvenal. English and Latin. The English by *Tho. Shadwell.* With Illustrations upon it. Licensed, *May* 25 1687. *London* : Printed by *D. Mallet,* for *Gabriel Collins* at the Middle-Temple Gate, in *Fleet-street.* 1687. 4º. (This is a reprint ; the satire must have been 1682.)

Somers, John, Lord.

Satyr to his Muse by the Author of *Absalom* and *Achitophel.*

> *Quo liceat libris non licet ire mihi.*
> *Turpiter huc illuc Ingeniosus eat.*

London, Printed for D. *Green* 1682. 4º. (Attributed to Somers.)

Prior, Matthew.

The Hind and the Panther Transvers'd To the Story of the *Country Mouse* and the *City-Mouse.* Much Malice mingled with a little Wit. *Hind. Pan. Nec vult Panthera domari.* Quae Genus. *London* : Printed for *W. Davis,* MDCLXXXVII. 4º. (In collaboration with Charles Montague.)

Brown, Tom.

Notes Upon Mr. Dryden's Poems in Four Letters. By *M. Clifford* late Master of the *Charter-House, London.* To which are annexed some Reflections upon the *Hind and Panther.* By another Hand.

> *Et Musarum et Apollinis aede relicta,*
> *Ipse facit versus.*

> Juv. Sat. 7.

London, Printed in the Year 1687. 4º.

The Reasons of Mr. Bays Changing his Religion. Considered in a Dialogue between *Crites, Eugenius,* and Mr. *Bays.*

> *Quo teneam vultus mutantem Protea nodo ?* . . . Hor.
> *Ante bibebatur, nunc quas contingere nolis*
> *Fundit Anigrus aquas.* . . . Ovid. Met.

London, Printed for *S.T.* and are to be Sold by the Booksellers of *London* and *Westminster.* 1688. 4º.

The Late Converts Exposed : Or the Reasons of Mʳ Bays's Changing his Religion. Considered in a Dialogue. Part the Second. With

Reflections on the Life of St *Xavier*. Don *Sebastian* King of *Portugal*. As Also the Fable of the Bat and the Birds.

Parcite Oves *nimium procedere, non bene ripae*
Creditur, ipse Aries *etiam nunc vellera siccat*.
Virg. Ecl. 3.

Rode Caper *vitem, tamen hinc sum stabis ad aram,*
In tua quod fundi Cornua *possit, erit.*
Ovid, Fast.

Licensed, *January*, 8. 1689. *London*, Printed for *Thomas Bennet*, at the Sign of the *Half-Moon* in St. Paul's Church-Yard. 1690. 4⁰.

The Reasons of Mᣴ Joseph Hains The Player's Conversion and Re-Conversion. Being the Third and Last Part To The Dialogue of Mr. Bays.

Ecce iterum Crispinus, *et est mihi saepe vocandus*
Ad partes. Juv. Sat. 4.
Non compositus melius cum Bitho Bacchius. Hor. Serm.

London, Printed for *Richard Baldwin*, near the *Black-Bull* in the *Old-Baily*. 1690. 4⁰.

Anonymous.
A Key (With the Whip) To open the Mystery and Iniquity of the Poem call'd *Absalom* and *Achitophel* (1682). 4⁰.

A Whip for the Fools Back, who styles Honorable Marriage a Curs'd Confinement in his profane of Absalom and Achitophel. Printed by T. Snowden for the author. 1682. folio.

A Poem, in Defence of the Church of England ; In Opposition to the Hind and Panther. Written by Mr. *John Dryden*. *Omnia Subsidunt, meliori pervia Causae*. Claudian. *London* : Printed in the Year, MDCLXXXVIII. folio.

The Revolter. A Trage-Comedy Acted between the Hind and Panther, and *Religio Laici*, etc. *London*, Printed in the Year 1687. 4⁰.

A Panegyrick On the Author of *Absolom* [*sic*] and *Achitophel*, occasioned by his former writing of an *Elegy* in praise of *Oliver Cromwell, lately Reprinted*. Reprinted in the Year MDCLXXXII. folio.

Biography and Criticism.
Saintsbury, George.
English Men of Letters, Edited by John Morley. Dryden by G. Saintsbury. London : Macmillan and Co. 1881. 8⁰.

Verrall, A. W.
[*Lectures on Dryden*. Cambridge. 1914.]

Nicoll, A.
[*Dryden and his Poetry*. 1923.]

Lubbock, Alan.
[*Character of John Dryden*. 1928.]

Eliot, T. S.
[*Homage to John Dryden*. 1924.]
[*John Dryden*. New York. 1932.]
[*The Use of Poetry and the Use of Criticism*. 1933.]

Van Doren, Mark.
[*The Poetry of John Dryden*. 1931.]

DUFFET (Thomas).
The Spanish Rogue. As it was Acted By His Majesties Servants. *Written by Tho : Duffett*. Hor. Serm.

O bone ! ne te
Frustrere : Insanis et tu, Stultique prope omnes.

London : Printed for *William Cademan* at the *Pope's Head* in the *Lower Walk* in the *New Exchange* in the *Strand.* M.DC.LXXIV. 4⁰.

DUNTON (John).

Numb. 1. The Athenian Gazette Resolving weekly all the most *Nice and Curious Questions* Propos'd by the Ingenious. Tuesday, March 17th 1690. After the first number the title was changed to :
Numb. 2. The Athenian Mercury. Resolving Weekly all the most *Nice and Curious Questions* Propos'd by the Ingenious. *Licensed and Entered according to Order.* Tuesday, March 24*th.* 1690. folio.

The Athenian Oracle : Being an Entire Collection of the Valuable Questions and Answers in the old *Athenian Mercuries.* Intermix'd with many Cases in *Divinity, History, Philosophy, Mathematicks, Love, Poetry,* never before *Published.* To which is Added, An *Alphabetical* Table for the speedy finding of any Questions. By a *Member* of the Athenian *Society.* *London,* Printed for Andrew Bell, at the *Cross-Keys* and *Bible,* in *Cornhill,* near *Stocks Market,* 1704. 3 vols. 8⁰.

The Life and Errors of John Dunton Late Citizen of *London* ; *Written by Himself in Solitude.* With an Idea of a New Life ; Wherein is Shewn How he'd Think, Speak, and Act, might he Live over his Days again. Intermix'd with the New Discoveries The Author has made in his Travels Abroad, And in his Private Conversation at Home. Together with the Lives and Characters of a Thousand Persons now Living in *London,* etc. Digested into *Seven Stages,* with their Respective Ideas.

> *He that has all his own Mistakes confest,*
> *Stands next to him that never has transgrest,*
> *And will be censur'd for a Fool by none,*
> *But they who see no Errors of their own.*
> Foe's *Satyr upon himself,* P. 6.

London : Printed for S. *Malthus,* 1705. 8⁰.
[Ed. J. Nichols. With memoir. 1818.]

D'URFEY (Thomas).
Dramatic Works.

The Siege of Memphis, or the Ambitious Queen. *A Tragedy,* Acted at the *Theater-Royal.* Written by *Tho. Durfey,* Gent. *Non fit sine Periculo facinus magnum et memorabile.* Terent. *London,* Printed for *W. Cademan* at the Popes Head at the entrance of the *New Exchange* in the *Strand.* 1676. 4⁰.

The Fool Turn'd Critick : A Comedy : As it was Acted at the Theatre-Royall. *By His Majesties Servants.* By *T. D.* Gent. *London,* Printed for *James Magnes* and *Richard Bentley,* at the *Post-Office* in *Russel-street* in *Covent Garden,* 1678. 4⁰.

Sir Barnaby Whigg : or, *No Wit like* a Womans. A Comedy As it is Acted by their Majesties Servants at the Theatre-Royal. *Written by* Thomas Durfey, *Gent.*

> *Quidquid agunt homines, votum, timor, Ira, voluptas,*
> *Gaudia, discursus nostri farrago libelli est.*
> Juvenal.

London, Printed by *A.G.,* and *J.P.* for *Joseph Hindmarsh,* at the *Black Bull* in *Cornhill.* 1681. 4⁰.

The Royalist. A Comedy ; As it is Acted at the Duke's Theatre. By *Thomas Durfey,* Gent. *London,* Printed for *Jos. Hindmarsh* at the Sign of the Black-Bull near the Royal-Exchange in *Cornhill,* Anno Dom. 1682. 4⁰.

The Injured Princess, or The Fatal Wager : As it was Acted at the

Theater-Royal, By His Majesties Servants. By *Tho. Durfey*, Gent. *London* : Printed for *R. Bentley* and *M. Magnes* in *Russel-street* in *Covent-Garden*, near the Piazza, 1682. 4º.

A Common-Wealth of Women. A Play : As it is Acted at the Theatre Royal, By their Majesties Servants. By Mr. *D'Urfey*. *Anguillam Cauda tenes*. Eras. Licensed. Sept. 11. 1685. *Roger L'Estrange. London*, Printed for *R. Bentley* in *Russel-street* in *Covent-Garden* ; and *J. Hindmarsh* at the *Golden Ball* in *Cornwell*, over against the *Royal Exchange*. 1686. 4º.

Love for Money : or, the Boarding School. A Comedy, Written by Mr. *D'Urfey*. *London* : Printed for *Abel Roper* at the *Mitre* in *Fleet-street*, and are to be sold by *Randal Taylor* near *Stationers-Hall*. 1691. 4º.

The Comical History of Don Quixote. As it was Acted at the *Queen's Theatre* in Dorset-Garden, By Their Majesties Servants. Part I. *Written by* Mr. D'Urfey. *London*, Printed for *Samuel Briscoe*, at the Corner of *Charles-street*, in *Russel-street*, *Covent-Garden*, 1694, 4º.

The Comical History of Don Quixote, As it was Acted at the Queen's Theatre in *Dorset Garden*. By Their Majesties Servants. Part the Second. Written by Mr. *D'Urfey*. *London*, Printed for *S. Briscoe*, in *Russel-street*, *Covent-Garden*, and *H. Newman* at the *Grashopper* in the *Poultry*, 1694. 4º.

The Comical History of Don Quixote. The Third Part. With The Marriage of Mary the Buxome. *Written by* Mr. D'Urfey. *Non omnes Arbusta juvant humilesq; myricae*. Virg. *London*, Printed for *Samuel Briscoe*, at the Corner of *Charles-street*, in *Russel-street*, *Covent-Garden*. 1696. Where is Also to be had the Songs, set to Musick by the late famous Mr. *Pursel*, Mr. *Courteville*, Mr. *Aykerod*, and other eminent Masters of the Age. 4º.

[Reprinted (three parts) 1889.]

The Campaigners : Or, The *Pleasant Adventures* at Brussels. A Comedy. With a Familiar Preface upon *A Late Reformer of the Stage*. Ending with a Satyrical Fable of *The* Dog *and the* Ottor. Written by Mr. *D'Urfey*. *London*, Printed for *A. Baldwin*, near the *Oxford Arms* Inn in *Warwick Lane*. MDCXCVIII. 4º.

The Grecian Heroine : or, the Fate of Tyranny. A Tragedy, Written 1718. *London* : Printed for William Chetwood, at *Cato's* Head in *Russel-street*, *Covent-Garden*. 1721. 8º.

Poems.

An Elegy upon the late Blessed Monarch King Charles II. And Two Panegyricks upon their Present Sacred Majesties, King James and Queen Mary. Written by Mr. *Durfey*, London : Printed for *Jo. Hindmarsh*, at the *Black Bull* in *Cornhill*. MDCLXXXV. folio.

Criticism.

[*A Study of the Plays of Thomas Durfey*. R. Forsythe. 2 vols. Cleveland. 1916–17.]

EBSWORTH (J. Woodfall).
Westminster Drolleries, Both Parts, of 1671, 1672 ; being a Choice Collection of Songs and Poems, Sung at Court and Theaters : *With Additions made by ' A Person of Quality.'* Now First Reprinted from the Original Editions. Edited, With an Introduction on the Literature of the Drolleries ; a Copious Appendix of Notes, Illustrations, and Emendations of Text ; *A Table of Contents, and Index of First Lines of Songs and Poems* ; By J. Woodfall Ebsworth, M.A. Cantab. R. Roberts, Boston, Lincolnshire. M.DCCCLXXV. 8º.

ETHEREGE (George).

Dramatic Works.

The Comical Revenge ; or Love in A Tub. Acted at His Highness the Duke of *York's* Theatre in *Lincolns-Inn-Fields.* Licensed, *July* 8, 1664. *Roger L'Estrange. London,* Printed for *Henry Herringman,* and are to be sold at his Shop at the *Blew-Anchor* in the Lower Walk of the *New-Exchange.* 1677. 4°.

She Wou'd if she Cou'd, A Comedy. Acted at His Highnesse the Duke of York's Theatre. Written by George Etherege Esq. *London,* printed for *H. Herringman,* at the Sign of the *Blew Anchor* in the Lower walk of the New Exchange. 1668. 4°.

The Man of Mode, or, Sr Fopling Flutter. A Comedy. Acted at the *Duke's Theatre.* By *George Etherege* Esq. Licensed, *June* 3 1676. *Roger L'Estrange. London,* Printed for *J. Macock,* for *Henry Herringman,* at the Sign of the *Blew Anchor* in the Lower Walk of the *New Exchange,* 1676. 4°.

Collected Works.

The Works of Sir *George Etherege* : Containing His Plays and Poems. *London,* Printed for *H.H.* And Sold by *J. Tonson,* within *Grays Inn* Gate, next *Grays-Inn* Lane ; and *T. Bennet,* at the *Half-Moon* in St. *Paul's* Church-yard. 1704. 8°.

[*The Works of Sir George Etheredge. Plays and Poems.* Ed. A. W. Verity. 1888.]

[*The Works of Sir George Etherege.* Ed. H. F. B. Brett-Smith. 3 vols. Oxford, 1927–. (The first two volumes contain the above three plays.)]

[*The Letter-Book of Sir George Etherege.* Ed. Sybil Rosenfeld. 1928.]

Biography and Criticism.

Dennis, John.

[*A Defense of Sir Fopling Flutter.* 1722. In *The Critical Works.* Ed. E. N. Hooker. 1939–43. Vol. 2.]

McCamie, F. S.

[*Sir George Etherege. A Study in Restoration Comedy.* Iowa. 1931.]

EUSDEN (Laurence).

The Royal Family ! A Letter to Mr. *Addison,* On the King's *Accession to the Throne.* By Mr. *Eusden.* London : Printed for *J. Tonson.* And Re-printed and Sold by *E. Waters* in *Essex-street.* 1714. 8°.

A Poem to Her Royal Highness On the Birth *of the* Prince. By Mr. *Eusden.*

> *Ille Deum vitam accipiet, Divisque videbit*
> *Permixtos Heroas, et ipse videbitur illis.* Virg.

London : Printed for *Jacob Tonson,* at *Shakespear's-Head* over-against *Katharine-street* in the *Strand.* MDCCXVIII. folio.

An Ode for the Birth-Day, MDCCXXI. As it was Sung before His Majesty.

> *Aggrederem O ! magnos (aderit jam tempus) honores !*
> *Hic Vir, Hic est, tibi quem promitti saepius audis !*
> Virg.
> *Plurima securi fudistis Carmina Bardi.* Lucan.

Written by *L. Eusden,* Esquire, Servant to his Majesty. *London* : Printed for Jacob Tonson, at *Shakespear's-Head,* over-against *Katharine-Street* in the *Strand.* MDCCXXI. folio.

Three Poems : The First, Sacred to the Immortal Memory of the late King ; The Second, On the happy Succession, and Coronation of His

present Majesty ; And a Third Humbly Inscrib'd to the Queen. By
Laurence Eusden, Servant to His Majesty.

Ille Deum Vitam accipiet, Divisque videbit
Permixtos Heroas, et Ipse videbitur Illis ! Virg.

Strepitus fastidit inanes,
Inque Animis Hominum Pompa meliore triumphat. Claud.
Utinam modo dicere possem
Carmina digna Dea, certe Dea Carmine digna est ! Ovid.

London : Printed for J. Roberts in *Warwick-Lane.* MDCCXXVII. folio.

FANE (Sir Francis).
Love in the Dark, or The Man of Bus'ness. A Comedy : Acted at the
Theatre Royal By His Majesties Servants. Written By Sir *Francis Fane,
Junior*, Knight of the Bath. *Naturam expellas furca licet, usque recurret.*
Hor. In the *Savoy*. Printed by T.N. for *Henry Herringman*, and are to be
sold at the Anchor in the Lower Walk of the *New Exchange.* 1675. 4⁰.

FARQUHAR (George).
The Constant Couple or, A Trip to The Jubilee. A Comedy. By Mr.
George Farquhar.

Sive favore tuli, sive hanc ego carmine famam
Jure tibi grates, Candide lector, ago.
Ovid. Trist. lib. 4. Eleg. 10.

London, Printed in the Year 1710. 8⁰. (Played in 1699.)
The Twin-Rivals. A Comedy. Acted at the *Theatre Royal* by Her Majesty's
Servants. *Written by Mr.* Farquhar. *Sic vos non vobis. London* : Printed
for *Bernard Lintott* at the Post-House in the *Middle-Temple-Gate* in *Fleet-
street.* MDCCIII.
Collected Works.
The Works Of the late Ingenious Mr. *George Farquhar* : Containing all
his Poems, Letters, Essays and Comedies, Publish'd in his Life-time.
In Two Volumes. The Ninth Edition. Corrected from the Errors
of former Impressions. To which are added some Memoirs of the
Author, never before Publish'd. *London*, Printed for J. Clarke, John
Rivington, James Rivington and James Fletcher, S. Crowder and Co.
T. Caslon, T. Lownds, H. Woodgate and S. Brookes. MDCCLX.
8⁰.
[Second edition : 1711. Earlier collections were made up from
various copies of separate works with a general title-page.]
[*Works*. Ed. W. Archer. 1906. (Mermaid Series.) This edition
contains both the above plays.]
[*Complete Works.* Ed. Charles Stonehill. Nonesuch. 1930.]

FIELDING (Henry).
The History of the Adventures of *Joseph Andrews*, And his Friend Mr.
Abraham Adams. Written in Imitation of the *Manner* of Cervantes,
Author of *Don Quixote*. In Two Volumes. *London* : Printed for A.
Millar, over against St. *Clement's-Church*, in the *Strand*. M.DCC.XLII.
12⁰.
[Ed. G. Saintsbury.   1910.   Everyman's Library.]
[Ed. L. Rice-Oxley.   1929.   World's Classics.]
Biography and Criticism.
Lawrence, Frederick.
The Life of Henry Fielding ; with Notices of his Writings, his Times,
and his Contemporaries. By Frederick Lawrence, of the Middle
Temple, Barrister-at-Law.—" Mores Hominum multorum vidit."

Horace. *De Arte Poetica.* London : Arthur Hall, Virtue and Co, 25, Paternoster Row. 1855. 8⁰.

Cross, W. L.
[*The History of Henry Fielding.* 3 vols. New Haven. 1918.]

Blanchard, F. T.
[*Fielding the Novelist. A Study in Historical Criticism.* New Haven. 1926.]

Voorde, F. P. van der.
[*Henry Fielding, Critic and Satirist.* The Hague. 1931.]

Flecknoe (Richard).
Love's Kingdom, A Pastoral Trage-Comedy. Not as it was Acted at the Theatre near *Lincoln's-Inn*, but as it was written, and since corrected By *Richard Flecknoe*. With a short Treatise of the *English Stage, etc.* by the same Author. *London*, Printed by *R. Wood* for the Author. 1664. 8⁰.
[The treatise to the above is reprinted in W. C. Hazlitt's *English Drama and Stage.* 1869. Also in *Critical Essays of the Seventeenth Century.* Ed. J. E. Spingarn. Vol. 2. 1908.]
The Damoiselles à la Mode. A Comedy. Compos'd and Written by Richard Flecknoe. *London*, Printed for the Author. 1667. 8⁰.

Flos.
Flos Ingenii vel Evacuatio Descriptionis. Being an Exact Description of Epsam and Epsam Wells. *London* Printed in the year 1674. folio.

Gay (John).
The Present State of Wit, in a Letter to a Friend in the Country. *London*, Printed in the Year, MDCCXI. (Price 3d.) 8⁰. (Signed J. G. and attributed to Gay.)
[In *Critical Essays.* Ed. J. Churton Collins. 1903.]
The *Shepherd's Week.* In Six Pastorals. *By Mr.* J. Gay.

> *Libeat mihi sordida rura,*
> *Atque humiles habitare Casas.*   Virg.

The Second Edition. London, Printed for *J.T.* and Sold by W. Taylor at the *Ship* in *Pater-noster-Row.* MDCCXIV.
[Ed. H. F. B. Brett-Smith. Oxford. 1924.]
Trivia : or, The Art of Walking The Streets of London. By Mr. *Gay.*

> *Quo te Moeri pedes ? An, quo via ducit, in Urbem ?* Virg.

London : Printed for *Bernard Lintott*, at the *Cross-Keys* between the *Temple* Gates in *Fleetstreet.* (1716.) 8⁰.
[Ed. W. H. Williams. 1922.]
Collected Works.
Poems on several Occasions. By Mr. *John Gay. London* : Printed for Jacob Tonson, at *Shakespear's-Head* in the *Strand,* and Bernard Lintot, between the *Temple-Gates* in *Fleetstreet.* MDCCXX. 2 vols. 4⁰.
[*The Poems of John Gay.* Ed. Francis Bickley. 1923.]
Biography and Criticism.
[*The Life and Letters of John Gay.* L. Melville. 1921.]

Gentleman's Magazine (The).
1731–1833. New Series : 1834–1851 : 138 volumes 8⁰. [–1907.]

Gould (Robert).
The Play-House a Satyr written in the Year 1685. By Robᵗ. Gould. To the Right Honourable Charles Earl of Dorset and Middlesex, etc.

Granville (George, Lord Lansdowne).
The She-Gallants : A Comedy. As it is Acted at the Theatre in Little-Lincoln-Inn-Fields, By His Majesty's Servants. *London* : Printed for

Henry Playford in the *Temple-Change*. And Benj. Tooke at the *Middle-Temple-Gate*, in *Fleetstreet*. 1696. 4⁰.

Heroick Love : A Tragedy, As it is Acted at The Theatre in *Little-Lincolns-Inn-Fields*. Written by the Honourable *George Granville* Esq. ;

> *Rectius Iliacum Carmen deducis in Actus,*
> *Quam si proferres ignota indictaque primus.*
>   Hor. de Arte Poetica.

London : Printed for *F. Saunders*, in the New-Exchange in the *Strand* : *H. Playford* in the *Temple-Change*, and *B. Tooke* at the *Middle-Temple-Gate*, *Fleet-street*. 1698. 4⁰.

Three Plays, *Viz.* The She-Gallants, A Comedy. Heroick-Love, A Tragedy. And The Jew of Venice, A Comedy. Written by the Right Honble *George Granville*, Lord *Landsdowne*. *London* : Printed for *Benj. Took* at the *Middle-Temple-Gate*, and *Bern. Lintott*, between the Two *Temple-Gates*, MDCCXIII. 8⁰.

The Genuine Works in Verse and Prose, Of the Right Honourable *George Granville*, Lord *Lansdowne*. *London* : Printed for J. and R. Tonson, at *Shakespear's* Head in the *Strand*, and L. Gilliver, J. Clarke, at *Homer's* Head in *Fleetstreet.* MDCCXXXVI. 3 vols. 12⁰.

[For verse by Granville, see Johnson, vol. 25 ; Chalmers, vol. II ; Park, vol. 34.]

Biography and Criticism.

Handasyde, Elizabeth.

[*Granville the Polite*. Cambridge. 1933.]

GWYN (Nell).

The Story of Nell Gwyn : and the Sayings of Charles the Second. Related and collected by Peter Cunningham, F.S.A. London : Bradbury and Evans, 11. Bouverie street, 1852. 8⁰.

HALIFAX (Marquis of). See SAVILE (George).

HOGARTH (William).

The Works of William Hogarth (*Including " the Analysis of Beauty "*) Elucidated by Descriptions, Critical, Moral, and Historical (Founded on the Most Approved Authorities). To which is prefixed Some Account of his Life. By Thomas Clerk. In Two Volumes. *London* : Printed for R. Scholey, 46, Paternoster Row ; *By T. Davison, Lombard Street, Whitefriars.* 1810. 8⁰.

HOPKINS (Charles).

Boadicea Queen of Britain. A Tragedy, As it is Acted by His Majesty's Servants at the Theatre in *Lincolns-Inn-fields*. Written by Mr. *Charles Hopkins*. *London,* Printed for *Jacob Tonson,* near the *Inner-Temple-Gate* in *Fleet-street*. 1697. 4⁰.

HOWARD (The Honourable Edward).

The Usurper, A Tragedy. As it was Acted at the *Theater Royal* by his Majesties Servants. Written by the Honourable Edward Howard, *Esq.* Licens'd *August* 2. 1667. *Roger L'Estrange. London,* Printed for *Henry Herringman* at the *Anchor* in the *Lower Walk* of the *New Exchange.* 1668. 4⁰.

HOWARD (Sir Robert).

Poems, Viz.—1. A Panegyrick to the King.—2. Songs and Sonnets.—3. The Blind Lady, a Comedy.—4. The Fourth Book of Virgil.—5. Statius his Achilleis, with Annotations.—6. A Panegyrick to Generall Monck. By the Honourable Sr Robert Howard. London, Printed for *Henry Herringman,* and are to be sold at his shop at the sign of the *Anchor* on the Lower Walk of the New Exchange. 1660. 8⁰.

Four New Plays, viz : The Surprisal, Committee, Comedies, The Indian Queen, Vestal Virgin. Tragedies. As they were Acted by His Majesties Servants at the *Theatre-Royal*. Written by the Honourable Sir *Robert Howard*. Imprimatur, *March* 7 1664/5. *Roger L'Estrange. London*, Printed for *Henry Herringman*, and are to be sold at his Shop at the *Blew-Anchor* in the Lower Walk of the New-Exchange. 1665. folio. (Following, the titles of each of the four plays : The Surprisal, A Comedy. Written by the Honourable Sir *Robert Howard*. Imprimatur, *March* 7. 1664/5. *Roger L'Estrange. London*, Printed for *Henry Herringman*, and are to be sold at his Shop at the *Blew-Anchor* in the Lower Walk of the New-Exchange. 1665.—The Committee, A Comedy. Written by the Honourable Sir *Robert Howard*. Imprimatur, March 7 1664/5, *Roger L'Estrange, London*, Printed for *Henry Herringman*, at the *Blew Anchor* in the Lower Walk of the New-Exchange, 1665.—The Indian-Queen, A Tragedy. *London*, Printed for *H. Herringman*, at the *Blew-Anchor* in the Lower Walk of the New-Exchange. 1665.—The Vestal-Virgin, or the Roman Ladies, A Tragedy, *London*, Printed for H. Herringman, at the *Blew-Anchor* in the Lower Walk of the New-Exchange. 1665.)

[*The Indian Queen* was written in collaboration with Dryden. In *The Dramatic Works of John Dryden*. Ed. M. Summers. 1931–2. *The Committee* is contained in *Modern British Drama*, vol. 3.]

The Great Favourite, Or, the Duke of Lerma, As it was Acted at the Theatre-Royal, by His Majesties Servants. *Written by the Honourable Sir* Robert Howard. *In the* Savoy : Printed for *Henry Herringman*, at the Sign of the Anchor, on the Lower-walk of the New-*Exchange*. 1668. 4⁰.

[See *Critical Essays of the Seventeenth Century*. Ed. J. E. Spingarn. 1908–9. Vol. II includes the prefaces to *Four New Plays* and *The Great Favourite*.]

Five New Plays, Viz. The Surprisal, Committee, Comedies. And The Indian Queen, Vestal Virgin, Duke of Lerma, Tragedies. As they were Acted by His Majesty's Servants at the *Theatre-Royal*. Written by the Honourable Sir *Robert Howard*. The Second Edition Corrected. *London*, Printed for *Henry Herringman*, and are to be Sold by *Francis Saunders*, at the *Blue-Anchor* in the Lower-Walk of the *New-Exchange*. 1692. folio.

Criticism.

Arundell, D. D.

[*Dryden and Howard*. Cambridge. 1929.]

HUGHES (John).

Poems.

The Triumph of Peace. A Poem.

> *Aggredere O magnos (aderit jam tempus) honores*
> *Chara Deum Soboles, magnum Jovis incrementum !*
> *Aspice convexo nutantem Pondere mundum,*
> *Terrasque, tractusque maris, Caelumque profundum*
> *Aspice, venturo laetantur ut omnia Saeclo !* Virg.

London : Printed for *Jacob Tonson*, at the *Judges-Head* in *Fleet street* near the *Inner-Temple-Gate*. 1698. folio.

The House of Nassau. A Pindarick Ode. By *J. Hughes*.

> *Caelo demittitur alto*
> *Chara Deum Soboles.* Virg.

London : Printed for *D. Brown* at the Black Swan and Bible without *Temple-bar*, and *A. Bell* at the Cross-Keys and Bible in Cornhill. M.DCC.II. folio.

An Ode for the Birth-Day of Her Royal Highness The Princess of Wales, St. David's Day, the First of March, 1715/16. Set to Musick by Dr. J. C. Pepusch, And Perform'd at the Anniversary Meeting of the Society of Ancient *Britons*, establish'd in Honour of Her Royal Highness's Birth-Day, and of the Principality of *Wales*. Written by Mr. *Hugues*.

> *Salve laeta Dies ! meliorque revertere semper,*
> *A Populo rerum digna potente coli !*   Ovid.

London : Printed for *Jacob Tonson*, at *Shakespear's-Head* over-against *Catherine-Street* in the *Strand*. 1716. 4⁰.

Poems on Several Occasions, with some Select Essays in Prose. In Two Volumes. By *John Hughes*, Esq ; Adorn'd with Sculptures. *London* : Printed for J. Tonson *and* J. Watts. MDCCXXXV. 8⁰.

[The following collections contain poems by Hughes : Chalmers, vol. 10 ; Anderson, vol. 8 ; Johnson, vol. 22.]

Dramatic Works.

The Siege of *Damascus*. A Tragedy. As it is Acted at the Theatre-Royal in *Drury-Lane* By His Majesty's Servants. *By* John Hughes, *Esq* ; London : Printed for John Watts at the Printing Office in Wild Court near Lincolns-Inn-Fields. MDCCXX. 8⁰.

HUNT (Thomas).

An Argument for the Bishops Right In Judging in Capital Causes in Parliament : For their Right unalterable to that Place in the Government that they now enjoy. With several Observations upon the Change of our English Government since the Conquest. To which is added a Postscript, being a Letter to a Friend, for Vindicating the Clergy, and rectifying some mistakes that are mischievous to Government and Religion. By Tho. Hunt, Esquire. *In Turbas et Discordias pessimo cuique plurima vis Pax et quies bonis artibus indigent.* Tacit. Hist. 1. 4. *London*, Printed for *Thomas Fox*, at the *Angel* and Star in *Westminster-Hall.* 1682. 8⁰.

A Defence of the Charter, and Municipal Rights of the City of London. And the Rights of other Municipal Cities and Towns of *England*. Directed to the Citizens of *London*. By Thomas Hunt. *Si populus vult decipi decipiatur.* *London*, Printed and are to be sold by *Richard Baldwin* near the *Black Bull* in the *Old-bailey.* (1682.) 4⁰.

JEFFREY (Francis).

Contributions to the Edinburgh Review. By Francis Jeffrey. Now one of the Judges of the Court of Session in Scotland. In Four Volumes. London : Printed for Longman, Brown, Green, and Longmans, Paternoster-Row. 1844. 8⁰.

KILLIGREW (Thomas).

Comedies and Tragedies, Written by Thomas Killigrew, Page of Honour to King *Charles* the First. And Groom of the Bed-Chamber to King *Charles* the Second. *London*, Printed for *Henry Herringman*, at the Sign of the *Anchor* in the Lower Walk of the *New-Exchange*. 1664. folio.

Biography and Criticism.

Harbage, Alfred.

[*Thomas Killigrew.* Philadelphia. 1930.]

KILLIGREW (Sir William).

Three Playes Written by Sir *William Killigrew*, Vice-Chamberlain to Her Majesty the Queen Consort. 1664. Viz. *Selindra. Pandora. Ormasdes.* London, Printed by *T. Mabb* ; for *John Playfere*, at the *White Lion*, in the Upper Walk of the *New Exchange* ; and *Thomas Horsman*, at the three *Kings* in the *Strand*, 1665–64 [*sic*].

Four new Playes, *viz* : The *Seege* of *Urbin*. *Selindra*. *Love* and *Friendship*. (The running title is : *Ormasdes* ; Or *Love*, and *Friendship*.) Tragy Comedies. *Pandora* (in the volume the piece has for its second title : Or the Converts). A Comedy. Written by Sʳ William Killigrew. Vice-Chamberlaine to Her *Majesty*. Oxford, Printed by *Hen: Hall*, printer to the University, for *Ric: Davis*, 1666. folio.

KING (Charles). See MARTYN (Henry).

LA CALPRENÈDE (Gautier de Costes, sieur de).

Hymen's Praeludia : or, *Love's* Master-piece : Being the first Part of that so much admir'd *Romance*, intituled, *Cleopatra*. *Written Originally in the French and now rendred into* English By R. Loveday. Whereunto is annexed, A succinct Abridgement of what is extant in the succeeding Story *By the same Hand*.

> Evand. *Quid magis optaret* Cleopatra *parentibus orta,*
>
> *Conspicuis, Comiti quam placuisse Thori ?*

London, Printed for *George Thompson*, at the White-Horse in *Chauncery*-lane, neere *Lincolnes*-Inn. 1652. 12⁰.

Criticism.

Hill, H. W.

[*La Calprenède's Romances and the Restoration Drama*. Chicago. 1910.]

LACEY (John).

Sauny the Scott : or, the Taming of the Shrew : A Comedy. As it is now *Acted* at the Theatre-Royal. *Written by* J. Lacey, *Servant to* His Majesty. And Never before Printed.

> *Then I'll cry out, Swell'd with Poetick Rage,*
> *'Tis I*, John Lacy, *have Reform'd your Stage*. Prol. *to* Rehers.

London, Printed and Sold by *E. Witlock*, near *Stationers-Hall*. 1698. (Acted in 1667.) 4⁰.

Sʳ Hercules Buffoon, Or the Poetical Squire. A Comedy, As it was Acted at the Duke's Theatre. *Written* by John Lacy, *Com. London* : Printed for *Jo. Hindmarsh*, Bookseller to His Royal Highness, at the Black Bull in Cornhill, 1684. 4⁰.

[*Dramatic Works*. Ed. J. Maidment and W. H. Logan. Edinburgh. 1875.]

LANSDOWNE (Lord). See GRANVILLE (George).

Laureat.

The Laureat.

> *Jack Squabbs Hystory in a little drawn,*
> *Down to his Evening, from his early dawn.*

4 pages folio. (1687.)

LAW (William).

The Absolute Unlawfulness of the Stage-Entertainment Fully Demonstrated By *William Law*, A.M. *London* : Printed for W. and J. Innys, at the *West*-End of St. *Paul's*. MDCCXXVI. 8⁰.

[*Works*. 9 vols. Ed. G. B. Morgan. Brockenhurst. 1892–3.]

LEE (Nathaniel).

The Tragedy of Nero, Emperour of Rome : As it is Acted at the Theatre-Royal, By his Majesties Servants. By *Nathaniel Lee*, Gent. *London*, Printed by *T. R.* And *N. T. James Magnus* and *Richard Bentley*, at the *Post Office* in *Russel-street* in *Covent-Garden*. 1675. 4⁰.

Sophonisba, or Hannibal's Overthrow. A Tragedy, Acted at the Theatre-Royal, By their Majesties Servants. *Written by* Nathaniel Lee, *Gent*.

Praecipitandus est liber spiritus, *Petronius.* *London,* Printed for *J. Magnes*
and *R. Bentley* in *Russel-street,* in *Covent-Garden* near the *Piazza's.* Anno
Domini, MDCLXXVI. 4°.
(This edition does not contain the Epilogue which appears, however,
in the following edition :)
Sophonisba : or Hannibal's Overthrow. A Tragedy. Acted at the
Theatre Royal, By Their Majesties Servants. *Written by* Nathaniel Lee,
Gent. Praecipitandus est liber Spiritus. *Petronius. London,* Printed for
Tho. Chapman, at the *Golden-Key* over against the Mews, near *Charing-
Cross.* MDCXCII. 4°.
Gloriana, or the Court of Augustus Caesar. Acted at the Theatre-Royal
By Their Majesties Servants.

> *Quibus haec, sint qualiacunque*
> *Arridere velim, doliturus si placeant spe*
> *Deterius nostra.* Nor. Sat. 10.

By *Nat. Lee. London,* Printed for *J. Magnes* and *R. Bentley,* in *Russel-street*
in *Covent-Garden,* near the *Piazza's.* Anno Dom. MDCLXXVI. 4°.
The Rival Queens, or the Death of Alexander The Great. Acted at the
Theater-Royal. By Their Majesties Servants. By *Nat. Lee,* Gent.

> *Natura sublimis et acer,*
> *Nam spirat tragicum satis, et feliciter audet.*
> Horat. Epist. ad Aug.

London, Printed for *James Magnes* and *Richard Bentley,* at the Post-house in
Russel-street in *Covent-Garden,* near the *Piazza's,* 1677. 4°.
[In *Modern British Drama.* Vol. 1.]
Mithridates King of Pontus. A Tragedy ; Acted at the Theatre Royal,
By their Majestie's Servants. Written by *Nat. Lee.*

> *Hi motus animorum atque haec certamina tanta,*
> *Pulveris exigui jactu compressa quiescent.*
> Virg. Georg. 1. 4.

Licensed March 28 1678. Roger l'Estrange. *London :* Printed by
R. E. for *James Magnes* and *Rich. Bentley,* in *Russel-street* in *Covent-Garden,*
near the Piazza's. 1678. 4°.
Theodosius : or The Force of Love, A Tragedy. Acted By their Royal
Highnesses Servants, At the Duke's Theatre. Written by *Nat. Lee*
With the Musick betwixt the Acts.

> *Nec minus periculum ex magna*
> *Fama quam ex mala.* Tacit.

London, Printed for *R. Bentley* and *M. Magnes,* in *Russell-street* near *Covent-
garden.* 1680. 4°.
[In *Modern British Drama.* Vol. 1.]
Caesar Borgia ; Son of Pope Alexander the Sixth : A Tragedy Acted at
the Duke's Theatre by Their Royal Highnesses Servants. Written by
Nat. Lee. London : Printed by *R. E.* for *R. Bentley,* and *M. Magnes,* in
Russel-street in *Covent-Garden,* near the *Piazza,* 1680. 4°.
The Princess of Cleve, As it was Acted At the Queens Theatre in Dorset-
Garden. By *Nat. Lee,* Gent.

> *Tuque, dum procedis, Io Triumphe,*
> *Non semel dicemus : Io Triumphe,*
> *Civitas omnis, dabimusque divis,*
> *Thura benignis.* Horat.

London, Printed in the Year, 1689. 4°. (Acted in 1681.)

Lucius Junius Brutus ; Father of his Country. A Tragedy. Acted at the Duke's Theater, by their Royal Highnesses Servants. Written by *Nat. Lee.*

> *Caeloque invectus aperto*
> *Flectit equos, curruque volans dat lora Secunda.*
> Virg. lib. 4.

London, Printed for *Richard Tonson*, and *Jacob Tonson*, at *Grays-Inn* Gate, and at the Judges Head in *Chancery-Lane* near *Fleet-street* ; 1681. 4°.
Criticism.
   Ham, R. G.
     [*Otway and Lee*. New Haven. 1931.]

L'ESTRANGE (Sir Roger).

No Blinde Guides. In Answer To a seditious Pamphlet of *J. Milton's* intituled *Brief Notes upon a late Sermon Titl'd*, the fear of God and the King ; *Preached and since Publishd, By* Matthew Griffith, D.D. *And Chaplain to the late King*, etc. Addressed to the Author. *If the Blinde Lead the Blinde Both shall fall into the Ditch. London*, Printed for *Henry Brome April* 20. 1660. 4°. (Attributed to L'Estrange by Samuel Johnson, *Lives of the English Poets*, Milton.)

Considerations and Proposals in Order to the Regulation of the Press : *Together with* Diverse *Instances* of *Treasonous*, and *Seditious Pamphlets*, Proving the *Necessity* thereof. *By* Roger L'Estrange. *London*, Printed by *A. C. June* 3ᵈ M.DC.LXIII, 4°.

An Answer to a Letter to a Dissenter, Upon Occasion of His Majesties Late Gracious Declaration of Indulgence. By Sir *Roger L'Estrange*, Knight. *London*, Printed for *R. Sare* at *Grays-Inn-Gate* in *Holborn.* 1687. 4°.
Criticism.
   Kitchen, G.
     [*Sir Roger L'Estrange : a Contribution to the History of the Press in the Seventeenth Century.* 1913.]
Letter.

A Letter to the Three Absolvers, Mr. *Cook*, Mr. *Collier* and Mr. *Snett*, Being Reflections on the Papers Delivered by Sir *John Friend*, and Sir *William Parkyns*, to the Sheriffs of *London* and *Middlesex* : At *Tyburn*, the Place of Execution, *April* 3. 1696, which said Papers are Printed at Length, and answered Paragraph by Paragraph. *London* : Printed for *R. Baldwin* near the *Oxford-Arms* in *Warwick*-Lane. 1696. folio.

LOCKE (John).

Two Treatises of Government : In the Former, *The False Principles and Foundation* of Sir *Robert Filmer*, and His Followers, are Detected and, Overthrown. The Latter is an Essay concerning the true Original, Extent, and End of Civil-Government. *London* : Printed for *Awnsham* and *John Churchill*, at the *Black Swan* in *Pater-Noster-Row.* 1698. 8°. (Published for the first time in 1690.)
   [Ed. F. W. Carpenter. 1924. Everyman's Library.]

Some Thoughts concerning Education.

> *Doctrina vires promovet infinitas* [sic]
> *Rectiq; cultus pectora roborant :*
> *Utcunq; defecere mores,*
> *Dedecorant bene nata culpae.* Horat. L. IV. Od. 4.

The Fourth Edition Enlarged. *London*, Printed for *A.* and *J. Churchill*, at the *Black Swan* in *Pater-noster-row.* 1699. 8°. (The first edition was published in 1693.)
   [Ed. R. N. Quick. Cambridge. 1880.]

The Reasonableness of Christianity, As delivered in the Scriptures. *London* :
Printed for *Awnsham* and *John Churchil*, at the *Black-Swan* in *Pater Noster
Row*. 1695. 8º.
Collected Works.
[*Works*. 10 vols. 1823.]
[*The Philosophical Works*. Ed. J. A. St. John. 1843-54.]
[*The Educational Writings*. Ed. J. W. Adamson. Cambridge. 1912,
1922 (revised edition).]
Biography and Criticism.
Bourne, H. R. Fox.
The Life of John Locke, By H. R. Fox Bourne. *In Two Volumes*.
Henry S. King and Co. London. 1876. 8º.
Aaron, R. I.
[*John Locke*. 1937.]
MacLean, K.
[*John Locke and English Literature of the Eighteenth Century*. New Haven.
1936.]

MAIDWELL (John).
The Loving Enemies : A Comedy, As it was Acted at His Highness the
Duke of York's Theatre. Written by *L. Maidwell*.

> *Inventum secuit primus qui nave profundum,*
> *Et rudibus remis sollicitavit aquas*
> *Tranquillis primum trepidus se credidit undis,*
> *Littora securo tramite summa legens :*
> *Mox vagus exultat pelago, caelumque secutus*
> *Aegeas hyemes Ioniasque domat.* Claudian.

London, Printed for *John Guy* at the Sign of the *Flying Horse* between St.
Dunstan's Church, and *Chancery* Lane. 1680. 4º.

MANLEY (Mrs. de la Riviere).
The Royal Mischief. A Tragedy, As it is Acted By His Majesties Servants.
By Mrs *Manley*. *London*, Printed for *R. Bentley*, *F. Saunders*, and *J.
Knapton*. MDCXCVI. 4º.

MARTYN (Henry).
The British Merchant ; or Commerce Preserv'd. In Three Volumes.
By Mr. Charles King, *Chamber-Keeper to the Treasury, and late of* London
Merchant, *London* : Printed for John Darby in *Bartholomew-Close*,
M.DCC.XXI. 8º. (Although the title of this edition gives Mr.
Charles King as the author of *The British Merchant*, the preface says :
The Person to whom our Country is chiefly obliged for these Papers,
and who had the Greatest Hand in them, is *Henry Martin* Esq. ; lately
deceased, who, for his great Merit and Abilities, was made *Inspector-
General* of the *Exports* and *Imports*.)
[The British Merchant : or, Commerce Preserv'd in answer to Mercator.
By Charles King, etc., twice a week. 7 Aug. 1713-30 July 1714.
3 vols. 1721, 1743, 1748.]

MARVELL (Andrew).
The Works of Andrew Marvell, Esq. Poetical, Controversial, and Political,
containing Many Original Letters, Poems, and Tracts, never before
printed, With a new life of the author, By Capt. Edward Thompson
. . . In three volumes. London : Printed for the Editor, by
Henry Baldwin, And sold by Dodsley, in Pall-Mall ; . . .
MDCCLXXVI. 4º.
[*Poems and Satires of Andrew Marvell*. Ed. G. A. Aitken. 2 vols. 1892,
1901.]

[*Poems and Letters of Andrew Marvell*. Ed. H. M. Margoliouth. 2 vols. Oxford. 1927.]
Biography and Criticism.
Legouis, P.
  [*André Marvell, Poète, Puritain, Patriote*. Paris. 1928.]
Bradbrook, M. C.
  [*Andrew Marvell*. Cambridge. 1940.]
Medal.
The Loyal Medal Vindicated. A Poem. *Crescit sub pondere Virtus.* London : Printed for R. *Janeway* in *Queen's Head* Alley. 1682. folio.
MILTON (John).
Paradise Lost, a Poem Written in Ten Books by *John Milton.* Licensed and Entred according to Order. *London,* Printed, and are to be sold by *Peter Parker* under *Creed* Church neer *Aldgate* ; And by *Robert Boulter* at the *Turks Head* in *Bishopsgate-street* ; And *Mathias Walker,* under St. *Dunstons* Church in *Fleet-street,* 1667. 4⁰.
Paradise Lost. A Poem in Twelve Books. The Authour *John Milton.* The Fourth Edition, adorn'd with Sculptures. *London,* Printed by *Miles Flesher,* for *Jacob Tonson,* at the Judge's Head in *Chancery-lane* near *Fleet-street.* MDCLXXXVIII. folio.
The Poetical Works of John Milton : *Edited, with Introductions, Notes, and an Essay on Milton's English,* By David Masson, M.A., LL.D., Professor of Rhetoric and English Literature in the University of Edinburgh. Three volumes. London : Macmillan and Co. 1874. 8⁰.
[*The Works of John Milton.* 18 vols. General editor : Frank Allen Paterson. Columbia. 1931.]
Biography and Criticism.
Addison, Joseph.
  [*Notes on Paradise Lost.* In *the Spectator,* 5 Jan.—3 May 1712.]
Geffroy, A.
  Etude sur les Pamphlets politiques et religieux de Milton, par A. Geffroy, professeur d'histoire au Lycée Descartes, à Paris. Paris, Dezobry, F. Magdeleine et Cᵗᵉ, libr.—Editeurs, Rue des Macons-Sorbonne, 1. Stassin et Xavier, 9, Rue du Coq, près le Louvre. 1848. 8⁰.
Masson, D.
  [*Life of John Milton.* 7 vols. 1849–80.]
Cook, A. S. (editor).
  Criticism on Paradise Lost. Boston. 1892.]
Saurat, Denis.
  [*Milton the Man and the Thinker.* 1924.]
Tillyard, E. M.
  [*Milton.* 1930.]
  [*The Miltonic Setting : past and present.* 1938.]
Lewis, C. S.
  [*A Preface to Paradise Lost.* 1942.]
Darbishire, Helen.
  [*Early Lives of Milton.* 1932.]
Mohocks.
The Town-Rakes or The Frolicks of the *Mohocks or Hawkubites.* With an Account of their Frolicks last Night and at several other Times ; shewing how they slit the Noses of several Men and Women, and wounded others : Several of which were taken up last Night by the Guards, and Committed to several Prisons, the Guards being drawn out to disperse them. 1712. folio.

MONTAGU (Lady Mary Wortley).
>   The Letters and Works of Lady Mary Wortley Montagu. Edited by her Great-Grandson Lord Wharncliffe. Third edition, with additions and corrections derived from the original manuscripts, illustrative notes, and a new Memoir By W. Moy Thomas. In two volumes. London : Henry G. Bohn, York Street, Covent Garden. MDCCCLXI. 8º.
>   [3 vols. 1837.]

MONTAGUE (Charles). See DRYDEN. (Collaboration with Matthew Prior in *The Hind and the Panther Transvers'd*. Drydeniana.)

MOTTEUX (Peter Anthony).
>   Beauty in Distress. A Tragedy. As it is Acted at the Theatre in *Little Lincolns-Inn-Fields*, By His Majesty's Servants. Written by Mr. *Motteux*. With a Discourse of the *Lawfulness and Unlawfulness of Plays*, Lately written in *French* by the Learned Father *Caffaro*, Divinity-Professor at Paris. Sent in a Letter to the Author, *By a Divine of the Church of* England. *London*, Printed for *Daniel Brown*, at the *Black Swan and Bible* without *Temple-bar* ; and *Rich. Parker* at the *Unicorn* under the Piazza of the *Royal Exchange*. 1698. 4º.
>   *Biography and Criticism.*
>   [*Peter Anthony Motteux. A Biographical and Critical Study.* R. N. Cunningham. Oxford. 1933.]

MULGRAVE (Earl of). See Sheffield (John).

Muses Mercury (The).
>   The Muses Mercury : or the Monthly Miscellany. Consisting of Poems, Prologues, Songs, Sonnets, Translations, and other Curious Pieces, Never before Printed. By The Earl of *Roscommon*, Mr. *Dryden*, Dr. *G——th*, *N. Tate*, Esquire. Mr. *Dennis*, Dr. *N——n*, Capt. *Steel*. Mr. *Manning*, etc. To which is added An account of the Stage, of the New *Opera's* and *Plays* that have been Acted, or are to be Acted this Season ; And of the New Books relating to *Poetry*, *Criticism*, etc. lately Publish'd. For the month of *January*. To be continued Monthly. *Ex Quovis Ligno non fit Mercurius*. *London*, Printed by *J.H.* for Andrew Bell, at the *Cross Keys and Bible* in *Cornhill*, near *Stocks-Market*. 1707. 4º.
>   [—Jan. 1708. Ed. John Oldmixon.]

NEWCASTLE (Duke of). See CAVENDISH.

NORTH (The Honourable Roger).
>   *Examen* : or, an Enquiry into the Credit and Veracity of a *Pretended Complete History* ; shewing The Perverse and Wicked Design of it, and the Many Falsities and Abuses of Truth contained in it. Together with some Memoirs Occasionally inserted. All tending to vindicate the Honour of the late King *Charles* the Second, and his Happy Reign, from the intended *Aspersions* of that *Foul Pen*. By the Honourable *Roger North*, Esq. ; *London*, Printed for Fletcher Gyles against *Gray's-Inn* Gate in *Holborn*. MDCCXL. 4º.
>   The Life Of the Honourable Sir Dudley North, Kn.t. Commissioner of the *Customs*, and afterwards of the *Treasury* to his Majesty King *Charles* the Second. And of the Honourable and Reverend Dr. John North, Master of *Trinity College* in *Cambridge*, and *Greek Professor*, Prebend of *Westminster*, and sometime Clerk of the Closet to the same King *Charles* the Second. By the Honourable *Roger North*, Esq. ; *Ea complectitur quibus ipse interfuit*. Cic. de Leg. Lib. 1. *London*, Printed for the Editor, And sold by John Whiston, at Mr. Boyle's Head in *Fleet-street*, MDCCXLIV. 4º.
>   [Both lives edited A. Jessopp. 3 vols. 1890.]

OLDHAM (John).

Satyrs upon the Jesuits ; Written in the Year 1679. *upon occasion of the* Plot, Together with the Satyr against Vertue, *and* Some other Pieces by the same Hand. *London* : Printed for *Joseph Hindmarsh*, at the *Black Bull* in *Cornhill*. 1681. 8º.

The Compositions in Prose and Verse of Mr. John Oldham. To which are added memoirs of his life, and explanatory notes upon some obscure passages of his writings. By Edward Thompson.

> Farewell, too little and too lately known.
> Whom I began to think and call my own :
> For sure our Souls were near ally'd, and thine
> Cast in the same poetic Mould with mine.

In three volumes. London : Printed for W. Flexney, opposite Gray's-Inn Gate, Holborn. MDCCLXX. 8º.

[*Poetical Works.* Ed. R. Bell. 1854, 1871.]

ORRERY (Earl of). See BOYLE (Roger).

OTWAY (Thomas).

Poems.

The Poets Complaint of his Muse ; Or, A Satyr against Libells. A Poem. By *Thomas Otway. Si quid habent veri vatum praesagia, vivam.* London, Printed for *Thomas Norman*, at the *Pope's Head* in *Fleetstreet* near *Salisbury-Court.* 1680. 4º.

Dramatic Works.

Alcibiades. A Tragedy, Acted at the Duke's Theatre. Written by *Tho. Otway. Laudetur ab his Culpetur ab illis. Horat : Serm : Lib.* 1st. Sat. 2. *London* : Printed for *William Cademan* at the sign of the *Popes Head* in the Lower Walk of the *New-Exchange* in the *Strand*, 1675. 4º.

Don Carlos Prince of Spain A Tragedy. As it was Acted at the Duke's Theatre. Written by *Tho. Otway. Principibus placuisse Viris non ultima Laus est.* Hor. *The Fourth Edition Corrected.* Licensed, *June* 15. 1676. *Roger L'Estrange. London* : Printed for *R. Bentley* at the Post-House in *Russel-Street*, in *Covent-Garden.* 1695. 4º. (The play was acted in 1676.)

Titus and Berenice, A Tragedy, Acted at the Duke's Theatre. With a Farce called the Cheats of Scapin. By *Tho. Otway.*

> *Grandis Oratio non est Turgida*
> *Sed Naturali pulchritudine exsurgit.* Pet. Arb.

Licensed *Febr.* the 19th 1676–7. *Roger L'Estrange. London* : Printed for *Richard Tonson* at his Shop under *Grays-Inn-Gate*, next *Grays-Inn-Lane.* 1677. 4º.

Friendship in Fashion. A Comedy, As it is Acted at his Royal Highness the Dukes Theatre. Written by Thomas Otway. *Archilochum Rabies armavit Iambo.* Licensed *May* 31. 1678. *Roger L'Estrange. London*, Printed by *E.F.* for *Richard Tonson*, at his Shop within *Grays-Inn-Lane.* 1678. 4º.

The Orphan : or, the Unhappy-Marriage : A Tragedy, As it is Acted At his Royal Highness The Duke's Theatre. Written by *Tho. Otway*

> *Qui Pelago credit magno, se foenore tollit ;*
> *Qui Pugnas et Castra petit, praecingitur Auro ;*
> *Vilis Adulator picto jacet Ebrius Ostro ;*
> *Et qui sollicitat Nuptas, ad praemia peccat :* . . . .
> *Sola pruinosis horret Facundia pannis,*
> *Atque inopi lingua desertas invocat Artes.*
>
> Petron. Arb. Sat.

London, Printed for *R. Bentley* and *M. Magnes*, in *Russel-Street* in *Covent-Garden*, 1680. 4°.

The History and Fall of Caius Marius. A Tragedy. As it is Acted at the Theatre Royal. By *Thomas Otway*. *Qui color Albus erat nunc est contrarius Albo*. London, Printed for *R. Bentley* in *Russel-street, Covent-Garden*. 1692. 4°. (Acted in 1680.)

The Souldiers Fortune : A Comedy, Acted by their Royal Highnesses Servants At the Duke's Theatre. Written by *Thomas Otway*.

> *Quem recitas meus est O Fidentine libellus,*
> *Sed male cum recitas incipit esse tuus.*

London, Printed for *R. Bentley* and *M. Magnes*, at the Post-House in *Russel-Street* in *Covent-Garden*, 1681. 4°.

Venice Preserv'd, or, A Plot Discover'd. A Tragedy. As it is Acted at the *Duke's Theatre*. Written by *Thomas Otway*. *London*, Printed for *J. Hindmarsh* at the Sign of the Black Bull, over against the Royal Exchange in *Cornhill*. 1682. 4°.

The Epilogue. *Written by* Mr. Otway *to his Play call'd* Venice Preserv'd, or a Plot Discover'd ; *spoken upon his Royal Highness the Duke of York's Coming to the* Theatre, *Friday*, April 21. 1682. *Printed for* Joseph Hindmarsh *at the* Black Bull in Cornhill. 1682. folio.

The Atheist : or The Second Part of the Souldiers Fortune. Acted at the Duke's Theatre. Written by *Tho. Otway*.

> *Hic noster Authores* [sic] *habet ;*
> *Quorum aemulari exoptat negligentiam*
> *Potius, quam istorum obscuram diligentiam,*
> *Dehinc ut quiescant porro moneo, et desinant*
> *Maledicere, malefacta ne noscant sua.* Terence.

London, Printed for *R. Bentley*, and *J. Tonson*, in *Russel-street* in *Covent-Garden*, and at the *Judges Head* in *Chancery-Lane*, near *Fleet-street*. MDCLXXXIV. 4°.

Collected Works.

The Works of Mr. Thomas Otway ; In three volumes. Consisting of his Plays, Poems, and Letters. London : Printed for C. Hitch and L. Hawes, D. Browne, H. Lintot, J. and R. Tonson, J. Hodges, C. Bathurst, J. Brindley, C. Corbet, T. Waller, A. Strahan, and T. Longman. MDCCLVII. 8°.

[*2 vols. 1712.*]

[*The Works.* Ed. M. Summers. 3 vols. 1926.]
[*The Works.* Ed. J. C. Ghosh. 2 vols. Oxford. 1932.]

Criticism.

Ham, F. G.

[*Otway and Lee.* New Haven. 1931.]

PACK (Richardson).

Miscellanies in Verse and Prose.

> *Si quis tamen haec quoque, si quis*
> *Captus amore leget* Virgil.

The Second Edition. *London* : Printed for E. Curll in *Fleet-street*. M.DCC.XIX. 8°. (The author's name occurs at the foot of the Dedication.)

A New Collection of Miscellanies in *Prose* and *Verse*. *Quod si non hic tantus fructus ostenderetur, et si ex his studiis delectatio sola peteretur ; tamen ut opinor, hanc animi remissionem, humanissimam, ac liberalissimam judicaretis. Nam cetera neque temporum sunt, neque aetatum omnium, neque locorum. Haec studia adolescentiam alunt, senectutem oblectant, secundas res ornant, adversis perfugium, ac solatium praebent ; delectant domi, non impediunt foris, pernoctant nobiscum, peregrinantur, rusticantur.*

Cicero *Orat. pro* Archia *Poeta.*
Multa satis lusi. Non est Dea nescia nostri
Quae dulcem curis miscet amaritiem. Catull.
London : Printed for E. Curll, in the *Strand.* MDCCXXV. 8º.

PERCY.
Reliques of Ancient English Poetry : Consisting of Old Heroic Ballads, Songs, and other Pieces of our earlier Poets (Chiefly of the Lyric Kind). Together with some few of later Date. Durat Opus Vatum. London : Printed for J. Dodsley in Pall-Mall. MDCCLXV. 8º.
   [Ed. H. B. Wheatley. 3 vols. 1876–7.]
   [Ed. M. M. A. Schroer. 2 vols. Berlin. 1893. (A reprint of the first edition with later variants.)]

PHILIPS (Ambrose).
Poems.
Pastorals, By Mr. *Phillips. Nostra nec erubuit Silvas habitare Thalia.* Virg. Ecl. 6. (In *Poetical Miscellanies : The Sixth Part.* 1709). See POPE.
To the Honourable Miss Carteret. By Mr. *Ambrose Philips. London* : Printed for J. Roberts, near the Oxford-Arms in Warwick-Lane. MDCCXXV. folio.
   [*The Poems of Ambrose Philips.* Ed. M. G. Segar. Oxford. 1937. (Contains a biographical introduction.)]
Dramatic Works.
The Distrest Mother. A Tragedy. As it is Acted at the Theatre-Royal in *Drury-Lane.* By Her Majesty's Servants. Written by Mr. *Philips. London* : Printed for *S. Buckley* at the *Dolphin in Little-Britain* ; and *J. Tonson,* at *Shakespear's Head* over-against *Catherine-street* in the *Strand.* MDCCXII. 4º.
   [In *Modern British Drama.* vol. 2. 1811.]

PHILIPS (John).
Blenheim a Poem, Inscrib'd to the Right Honourable *Robert Harley,* Esq ; *London,* Printed for *Tho. Bennet,* at the *Half-Moon* in *St. Paul's* Church-yard. 1705. folio.
In Memory of Our Most Gracious Lady, Mary Queen of *Great Britain, France,* and *Ireland,* a Poem. By *John Phillips. London,* Printed for John Harris, at the Harrow in the *Poultry.* MDCXCV. folio.
   [*The Poems of John Philips.* Ed. M. G. Lloyd Thomas. Oxford. 1927.]
Poems.
Poems on Affairs of State ; From the Time of *Oliver Cromwell,* to the Abdication of K. *James* the Second. *Written by the greatest Wits of the Age.* Viz. Duke of *Buckingham,* Earl of *Rochester,* Lord *B...st,* Sir *John Denham, Andrew Marvell,* Esq ; Mr. *Milton,* Mr. *Dryden,* Mr. *Sprat,* Mr. *Waller,* Mr. *Ayloffe,* etc. With some Miscellany Poems by the same : Most whereof never before Printed. *Now carefully examined with the Originals, and Published without any Castration.* The Fifth Edition, Corrected and much Enlarged. Printed in the Year 1703. 8º. (This volume composed of two parts, the second having a special title :) State-Poems ; Continued From the time of *O. Cromwel,* to the Year 1697. Written by the Greatest Wits of the Age, *viz. The Lord* Rochester, *The Lord* D——t, *The Lord* V——n, *The Hon,* Mr. M——ue, Sir F. S.——d, *Mr.* Milton, *Mr.* Prior, *Mr.* Stepney, *Mr.* Ayloffe, *etc.* With Several Poems in Praise of *Oliver Cromwel,* in *Latin* and *English,* by *Dr.* South,

Dr. Locke, *Sir* W. G——n, *Dr.* Crew, *Mr.* Busby, *etc.* Also some Miscellany Poems by the same, never before Printed. Now carefully Examined with the Originals, and Published without any Castration. Printed in the Year MDCCIII. 8⁰. [First edition : 1697.]

Poems on Affairs of State, from the Reign of K. *James* the First, to this Present Year 1703. Written by the Greatest Wits of the Age. *Viz.* The Duke of *Buckingham,* The Earl of *Rochester.* The Earl of *D——t.* Lord *J——s.* Mr. *Milton,* Mr. *Marvel.* Mr. *St. J——n.* Mr. *John Dryden.* Dr. *G——th.* Mr. *Toland.* Mr. *Hugues.* Mr. *F——e.* Mr. *Finch.* Mr. *Harcourt.* Mr. *T——n, etc. Many of which never before Publish'd.* Vol. II. Printed in the Year 1703. 8⁰.

Poems on Affairs of State, From 1640, to this present Year 1704. *Written by the greatest wits of the Age,* Viz. The late Duke of *Buckingham,* Duke of *D——re,* Late E. of *Rochester,* Earl of *D——t,* Lord *J——rys.* Ld *Hal——x, Andrew Marvel,* Esq ; Col. *M——d——t,* Mr. *St. J——ns,* Mr. *Hambden,* Mr. *Dryden,* Mr. *St——y,* Mr. *Pr——r,* Dr. *G——th,* etc. Most of which were never before published. Vol. III. Printed in the Year 1704. 8⁰.

A New Collection of Poems Relating to State Affairs, from Oliver Cromwell To this present Time : By the Greatest Wits of the Age : Wherein, not only those that are Contain'd in the Three Volumes already Published are inserted, but also large Additions of chiefest Note, never before Published. The whole from their respective Originals, without Castration. *London,* Printed in the Year, MDCCV. 8⁰.

[This was a pirated edition, repudiated as spurious in vol. II of the genuine edition, 1707.]

Poems on Affairs of State, From 1620, to this present Year 1707. *Many of them by the most eminent Hands.* Viz. Mr. *Shakespear.* Mr. *Waller.* D. of *D——re.* Mr. *Dryden.* Mr. *W——sh.* Mr. *D——y.* Dr. *Wild.* Mr. *Brady.* Mr. *Tate.* Mr. *Hughes.* Mr. *Manning.* Mr. *Arwaker,* etc. *Several of which were never before publish'd. To which is added,* A Collection of some Satyrical Prints against the *French* King, Elector of *Bavaria,* etc. Curiously ingraven on Copper-Plates. Vol. IV. *London,* Printed in the Year 1707. 8⁰.

PHILIPS (Katherine).
Poems By the most deservedly Admired Mʳˢ. *Katherine Philips* The matchless Orinda. To which is added *Monsieur Corneille's* Pompey and Horace Tragedies. With several other Translations out of *French. London,* Printed by *J.M.* for *H. Herringman,* at the Sign of the *Blew Anchor* in the Lower Walk of the New Exchange. 1667. folio.
[In *Minor Poets of the Caroline Period.* Ed. G. Saintsbury. Vol. I. Oxford. 1905.]
Biography.
Souers, P. W.
[*The Matchless Orinda.* 1931.]

POPE (Alexander).
Poetical Miscellanies : The Sixth Part. Containing a Collection of *Original Poems,* With several New Translations. *By the Most Eminent Hands. London,* Printed for *Jacob Tonson,* within *Grays-Inn Gate,* next *Grays-Inn* Lane. 1709. 8⁰.
The Works of Alexander Pope Esq. In Nine Volumes Complete. With his last Corrections, Additions, and Improvements ; As they were delivered to the Editor a little before his Death : Together with the Commentaries and Notes of Mr. Warburton. London, Printed for J. and P. Knapton, H. Lintot, J. and R. Tonson, and S. Draper. MDCCLI. 8⁰.

[For earlier collections supervised by Pope see *Alexander Pope, a bibliography.* R. H. Griffith. Vol. I. 2 parts. 1922–7.]

The Works of Alexander Pope. Including several hundred unpublished letters, and other new materials. Collected in part by the late R^t. Hon. John Wilson Croker. With Introduction and Notes. By Rev. Whitewell Elwin and William John Courthope, M.A. With portraits and other illustrations. London : John Murray, Albemarle Street. 1871–1886. 10 vols. 8°.

[*The Poems of Alexander Pope.* The Twickenham Edition. General editor : John Butt.

Imitations of Horace, with an epistle to Dr. Arbuthnot, and the epilogue of the satires. Ed. John Butt. 1939.
The Rape of the Lock and other Poems. Ed. Geoffrey Tillotson. 1940.
The Dunciad. Ed. J. Sutherland. 1943.]

[*The Prose Works of Alexander Pope.* Ed. Norman Ault. vol. 1. (1711–1720.) Oxford. 1936.]

Biography and Criticism.

Carruthers, Robert.
The Life of Alexander Pope. Including Extracts from his Correspondence. By Robert Carruthers. Second Edition, revised and considerably enlarged. With numerous engravings on wood. London : Henry G. Bohn, York-Street, Covent Garden. MDCCCLVII. 8°.

Stephen, Leslie.
English Men of Letters, Edited by John Morley. Alexander Pope. By Leslie Stephen. London : Macmillan and Co. 1880. 8°.

Warren, A.
[*Alexander Pope as Critic and Humanist.* Princeton. 1929.]

Sherburn, George.
[*The Early Career of Alexander Pope.* Oxford. 1934.]

Root, R. K.
[*The Poetical Career of Alexander Pope.* Princeton. 1938.]

Tillotson, G.
[*On the Poetry of Pope.* Oxford. 1938.]

Printers.

The Case and Proposals *of the Free-Journeymen Printers, in and about* London, *humbly submitted to Consideration.* Licensed *October* 23. 1666. *Roger L'Estrange.* folio.

Prior (Matthew). See also Dryden (Drydeniana).
To the King, An Ode on His Majesty's Arrival in Holland, 1695. By Mr. Prior.

Quis desiderio sit pudor aut Modus
Tam Chari capitis ? Hor.

London, Printed for *Jacob Tonson* at the *Judge's Head* near the *Inner-Temple-Gate* in *Fleetstreet,* 1695. folio.

An English Ballad : In Answer to Mr. *Despreaux's* Pindarique Ode on the Taking of Namure. *Dulce est desipere in loco. London,* Printed for *Jacob Tonson,* at the *Judge's Head* near the *Inner-Temple Gate* in *Fleetstreet.* MDCXCV. folio.

Poems on *Several Occasions. London :* Printed for Jacob Tonson at *Shakespear's Head,* over against *Katharine-Street* in the *Strand,* and John Barber, upon Lambeth-Hill. MDCCXVIII. folio.

[*The Writings of Matthew Prior.* Ed. A. R. Waller. 2 vols. Cambridge. 1905–7.]

Biography and Criticism.
Bickley, F.
  [*The Life of Matthew Prior.* 1914.]
Legg, L. G. W.
  [*Matthew Prior.* 1921.]
PRYNNE (William).
  Histrio-Mastix. The Players Scourge, or, Actors Tragaedie, *Divided into Two Parts.* Wherein it is largely evidenced, by divers *Arguments*, by the concurring Authorities and Resolutions of *Sundry texts of Scripture* ; of the *whole Primitive Church*, both under the *Law and Gospell* ; of 55 *Synodes and Councels* ; of 71 *Fathers and Christian Writers*, before the yeare of our Lord 1200 ; and above 150 *foraigne and domestique Protestant and Popish Authors*, since ; of 40 *Heathen Philosophers, Historians*, Poets ; of many *Heathen*, many *Christian Nations, Republiques, Emperors, Princes, Magistrates* ; of sundry *Apostolicall, Canonicall, Imperiall Constitutions* ; and of our owne *English Statutes, Magistrates, Universities, Writers, Preachers, That popular Stage-playes (the very Pompes of the Divell which we renounce in Baptisme*, if we beleeve the Fathers) *are sinfull, heathenish, lewde, ungodly Spectacles, and most pernicious Corruptions ; condemned in all ages, as intolerable Mischiefs to Churches, to Republickes, to the manners, mindes, and soules of men. And that the Profession of Play-poets, of Stage-players ; together with the penning, acting, and frequenting of Stage-playes, are unlawfull, infamous and misbe-seeming Christians.* All pretences to the contrary are here likewise fully answered ; and the unlawfulness of acting, or beholding Academicall Enterludes, briefly discussed ; besides sundry other particulars con-cerning *Dancing, Dicing, Health-drinking, etc.*, of which the *Table* will informe you. *By* William Prynne, *an Utter-Barrester of* Lincolnes Inne. Cyprian. De Spectaculis lib. p. 244. *Fugienda sunt ista Christianis fidelibus, ut iam frequenter diximus, tam vana, tam perniciosa, tam sacrilega Spectacula : quae, et si non haberent crimen, habent in se et maximum et parum congruente fidelibus vanitate.* Lactantius de Vero Cultu cap. xx. *Vitanda ergo Spectacula omnia, non solum ne quid vitiorum pectoribus insideat, etc. sed ne cuius nos voluptatis consuetudo detineat, atque a Deo et a bonis operibus avertat.* Chrysost. Hom. 38. in Matth. Tom. 2. Col. 299. B. et Hom. 8. De Paenitentia, Tom. 5. Col. 750. *Immo vero, his Theatralibus ludis eversis, non leges, sed iniquitatem evertetis, ac omnem civitatis pestem extinguetis : Etenim Theatrum, communis luxuriae officina, publicum incontinentiae gymnasium, cathedra pestilentiae ; pessimus locus ; plurimorumque morborum plena Baby-lonica fornax, etc.* Augustinus De Civit. Dei. 1. 4. c. i. *Si tantummodo boni et honesti homines in civitate essent, nec in rebus humanis Ludi scenici esse debuissent.* London, Printed for *A.E.* and *W.I.* for *Michael Sparke*, and are to be sold at the Blue Bible, in Greene Arbour, in little Old Bayly. 1633. 4°.
Criticism.
Kirby, E. W.
  [*William Prynne : a Study in Puritanism.* Cambridge. U.S.A. 1931.]
PULTON (Andrew).
  A True and Full Account of a Conference Held about Religion Between Dr. Tho. Tenison and A. Pulton one of the Masters in the Savoy. Pub-lished by Authority. *London*, Printed by *Nathaniel Thompson* at the Entrance of *Old-Spring-Garden*, near *Charing-Cross.* 1687. 4°.
RALPH.
  The Case of Authors by Profession or Trade, Stated. With Regard to Booksellers, the Stage, and the Public. No Matter by Whom. "The question is not to make people read, but to make them think." L'esprit

des Loix, I. Part. p. 183. *London* : Printed for R. Griffiths, Bookseller, in *Paternoster Row.* MDCCLVIII. 8⁰.

RAVENSCROFT (Edward).

The Citizen turn'd Gentleman : a Comedy. Acted at the *Duke's Theatre.* By *Edw. Ravenscroft.* Gent. *London,* Printed for *Thomas Dring,* at the *White-Lyon* next *Chancery-Lane* and in *Fleetstreet.* 1672. 4⁰.

The Careless Lovers : A Comedy Acted at the Duke's *Theatre.* Written by *Edward Ravenscrofts* [*sic*], Gent. *London* : Printed for *William Cademan,* at the *Popes Head* in the Lower Walk in the *New Exchange.* 1673. 4⁰.

Scaramouch a Philosopher, Harlequin a School-Boy, Bravo, Merchant, and Magician. A Comedy After the Italian Manner acted at the Theatre-Royal. *Written by Mr.* Edward Ravenscroft. *Spe Incerta certum mihi laborem sustuli.* Terent. in Hecyram. Printed for *Robert Sollers* at the Flying Horse, in St. *Pauls Church-yard.* MDCLXXVII. 4⁰.

The London Cuckolds. A Comedy ; As it is Acted at the Duke's Theatre. By *Edward Ravenscroft,* Gent. *London,* Printed for *Jos.* Hindmarsh at the Sign of the Black-Bull near the Royal-Exchange in *Cornhill. Anno Dom.* 1682. 4⁰.

[In *Restoration Comedies.* Ed. M. Summers. 1921.]

Dame Dobson : or, The Cunning Woman. A Comedy As it is Acted at the Dukes Theatre, By *Edward Ravenscroft,* Gent. *London,* Printed for *Joseph Hindmarsh,* Bookseller to His Royal Highness, at the *Black Bull* in *Cornhill.* 1684. 4⁰.

Titus Andronicus, or the Rape of Lavinia. Acted at the Theatre Royall, A Tragedy, Alter'd from *Mr. Shakespears* Works, by Mr. *Edw. Ravenscroft.* Licensed, *Dec.* 21. 1686. *R.L.S. London,* Printed by *J.B.* for *J. Hindmarsh,* at the *Golden-Ball* in *Cornhill,* over against the *Royal Exchange.* 4⁰. (Acted in 1687.)

The Canterbury Guests : or A Bargain Broken. A Comedy. Acted at the *Theatre-Royal. Written by* Mr. Edward Ravenscroft, *London,* Printed for *Daniel Brown* at the *Bible* without *Temple-Barr* ; and *John Walthoe,* at his Shop in *Vine-Court, Middle Temple.* 1695. 4⁰. (Acted in 1694.)

RAY (John).

The Wisdom of God, Manifested in the Works of the Creation. Being the Substance of some common Places delivered in the Chappel of *Trinity-College* in *Cambridge.* By *John Ray,* M.A. sometimes Fellow of that, and now of the *Royal Society. London* : Printed for *Samuel Smith,* at the *Princes Arms* in S. *Pauls* Church-Yard. 1691. 8⁰.

Reformation.

An Account of the Societies for *Reformations of Manners,* in England And Ireland. With a Persuasive to Persons of all Ranks, to be Zealous and Diligent in Promoting the Execution of the Laws against *Prophaneness* and *Debauchery,* for the Effecting *A National Reformation.* Published with the Approbation of a Considerable Number of the *Lords Spiritual* and *Temporal,* and Honourable *Judges* of both Kingdoms. The Third Edition. *Who is on the Lord's side, let him come unto me ?* Exod. 32. 20. *Who will rise up with me against the Wicked ? Or who will take my part against the Evil doers ?* Psal. 94. 16. N. Tr. *London,* Printed for *B. Aylmer* and *Bell,* in *Cornhill ; D. Brown* without *Temple-Bar ; T. Parkhurst,* in *Cheapside ; J. Robinson, D. Midwinter* and *T. Leigh,* and *R. Sympson,* in St. *Paul's Church-Yard ; T. Godwin* and *W. Rogers,* in *Fleet-street ; J. Walthoe,* in the *Temple ; Is. Harrison,* at *Lincolns-Inn ; S. Heyrick,* at *Grays-Inn-Gate* in *Holbourn,* and *J. Fox,* in *Westminster-Hall.* 1700. For the more general Benefit of the Publick, this Book is Sold at One Shilling Bound. 8⁰.

The Fifth Edition. *London*, Printed by *J. Downing*, in *Bartolomew Close* near *West-Smithfield* : And are to be Sold by him and *D. Brown*, Bookseller, without *Temple-Bar*. 1701. 12⁰.

A Help to a National Reformation. Containing An Abstract of the Penal-Laws against Prophaneness and Vice. A Form of the Warrants issued out upon Offenders against the said Laws. Directions to Inferior Officers in the Execution of their Office. Prudential Rules for the giving of Informations to the Magistrates in these Cases. A specimen of an Agreement for the Forming of a Society for *Reformation of Manners* in any City, Town, or larger Village of the Kingdom. And Her Majesty's Proclamation for Preventing and Punishing Immorality and Prophaneness ; and the late Act of Parliament against prophane Swearing and Cursing. To which is added, An Account of the Progress of the Reformation of Manners in *England* and *Ireland*, and other parts of the World. With Reasons and Directions for our Engaging in this Glorious Work. And the Special Obligations of Magistrates To be diligent in the Execution of the Penal-Laws against Prophaneness and Debauchery, for the Effecting of a National Reformation. As also, some Considerations offered to such unhappy Persons as are guilty of prophane Swearing and Cursing, Drunkenness, and Uncleanness, and are not past Counsel. *Printed for the Ease of Magistrates, Ministers, and Inferior Officers, and the Direction and Encouragement of private Persons, who in any part of the Kingdom are engaged in the Glorious Work of* Reformation *or are Religiously disposed to contribute their Endeavour for the Promoting of it.* The Fifth Edition with great Additions. London, Printed and sold by *Joseph Downing* in *Bartholomew-Close*, near *West-Smithfield*, 1706. 12⁰.

A Letter to a Minister of the Church of England, Concerning the Societies for *Reformation* of *Manners. London* : Printed and Sold by *Joseph Downing* in *Bartholomew-Close*, near *West-Smithfield*. 1710. 4⁰.

ROCHESTER (Earl of). See WILMOT (John).

Romulus.
Romulus and Hersilia ; Or, The Sabine War. A Tragedy *Acted at the Dukes Theatre. Militat omnis Amans, et habet sua Castra Cupido.* Ovid. *London*, Printed for *D. Brown*, at the *Black-Swan* and *Bible* without *Temple-Bar*, and *T. Benskin* in St. *Brides* Church-yard, *Fleet-street*. 1683. 4⁰.

ROSCOMMON (Earl of). See DILLON (Wentworth).

ROWE (Nicholas).
Poems.
Poems on Several Occasions. By *N. Rowe*, Esq ; Printed for E. Curll at the Dial and Bible against Sᵗ. *Dunstan's* Church in Fleet-street. 1714. 4⁰.

Ode for the *New Year* MDCCXVI. By *N. Rowe*, Esq ; Servant to His Majesty.

> *Custode rerum Caesare, non furor*
> *Civilis, aut vis eximet otium :*
> *   Non ira quae procudit enses,*
> *   Et miseras inimicat urbes.*
>   Hor. Lib. 4. Ode 15.

London : Printed for *J. Tonson*, at *Shakespear's-Head*, overagainst *Catherine Street* in the *Strand*. 1716. folio.

[See Chalmers, vol. 9 ; Park, vols. 32, 53, 54.]

Dramatic Works.

Tamerlane. A Tragedy. As it is Acted at the New Theater in *Little Lincoln's-Inn-Fields.* By His Majesty's Servants. Written by *N. Rowe* Esq ;

> *Magnus ad altum*
> *Fulminat Euphraten bello, Victorque volentes*
> *Per Populos dat jura, viamq; affectat Olympo.*
> Virg. Georg. 4.

London, Printed for *Jacob Tonson,* within *Gray's-Inn-Gate,* next *Gray's-Inn-Lane.* 1702. 4º.

Ulysses : A Tragedy. As it is Acted at the Queen's Theatre in the Hay-Market. By Her Majesty's Sworn Servants. Written by *N. Rowe,* Esq. ;

> *Stultorum Regum et Populorum Continet aestus—*
> *Rursus quid Virtus, et quid Sapientia possit*
> *Utile proposuit Nobis exemplar Ulyssem.*
> Horat. Epist. Lib. I. Epist. 2.

London, Printed for *Jacob Tonson,* within *Grays-Inn* Gate next Grays-Inn Lane. 1706. 4º.

The Royal Convert. A Tragedy. Written by Nicholas Rowe, Esq. ; *Laudatur et Alget. London* : Printed for Jacob Tonson in the *Strand.* MDCCXXXV. 8º. (Acted in 1707.)

The Tragedy of *Jane Shore.* Written in Imitation of Shakespear's Style. By *N. Rowe,* Esq.

> *Conjux ubi pristinus illi*
> *Respondet Curis.* Virg.

The Second Edition. *London* : Printed for Bernard Lintott, at the *Cross-Keys,* between the *Two Temple-Gates,* Fleet-*street,* 1714. 12º. (Acted in 1714.)

[*Three Plays : Tamerlane, The Fair Penitent, Jane Shore.* Ed. J. R. Sutherland. 1929. (With a biographical introduction.)]

Collected Works.

The Works of Nicholas Rowe, *Esq.* ; *London* : *Printed for* H. Lintot, J. *and* R. Tonson *and* S. Draper. MDCCLXVII. 2 vols. 12º. [3 vols. 1728.]

RYMER (Thomas).

The Tragedies of The last Age Consider'd and Examin'd By the Practice of the Ancients, and by the Common sense of all Ages. In a Letter to *Fleetwood Shepheard,* Esq ; By Thomas Rymer, of *Grays-Inn,* Esquire.

> *Clament periisse pudorem.*
> *Cuncti pene patres ; ea quum reprehendere coner*
> *Quae gravis AEsopus, quae doctus Roscius egit.* Hor.

London, Printed for *Richard Tonson* at his Shop under *Grays-Inn* Gate, next *Grays-Inn.* (1678.) 8º.

A Short View of Tragedy ; It's *Original, Excellency,* and *Corruption.* With some Reflections on *Shakespear,* and other Practitioners for the Stage. By Mr. *Rymer,* Servant to their Majesties. *Hodieque manent vestigia ruris.* Hor. *London,* Printed and are to be sold by *Richard Baldwin,* near the *Oxford Arms* in *Warwick-Lane,* and at the *Black Lyon* in *Fleetstreet,* between the two Temple-Gates. 1693.

SAINT-EVREMOND.

Œuvres Meslees de Mr. *de Saint-Evremond,* Publiées sur les Manuscrits de

l'Auteur. A Londres, chez *Jacob Tonson*, Marchand Libraire, à *Grays-Inn-Gate*. MDCCV. 2 vols. 4°.
[The Letters, in translation, were edited by John Hayward, 1927.]

St. John (Henry, Viscount Bolingbroke).
Letters on the Study and Use of History. To which are added, Two other Letters, and Reflections upon Exile. By the late Right Honourable Henry St. John, Lord Viscount of Bolingbroke. In Two Volumes. London : Printed for A. Millar, in the Strand. MDCCLII. 8°.
[Reprinted : 1870. Ed. G. M. Trevelyan. Cambridge. 1935. (Letters 6–8 only.)]
Biography.
Hassall, A.
[*Life*. 1915.]
Petrie, Sir C.
[*Bolingbroke*. 1937.]

St. Serfe.
Tarugo's Wiles : or, the Coffee-House. A Comedy. As it was Acted at his Highness's, the Duke of *York's* Theater. Written *By* Tho. St Serfe, *Gent. London*, Printed for *Henry Herringman* at the Sign of the Anchor, on the Lower-walk of the New-*Exchange*. 1668. 4°.

Savile (George, Marquis of Halifax).
The Character of a Trimmer. His Opinion of I. The Laws and Government. II. Protestant Religion. III. The Papists. IV. Foreign Affairs. By the Honourable Sir *W. Coventry*. The Second Edition, carefully Corrected, and cleared from the Errors of the first Impression. *Licensed* December 27. 1688. *London*, Printed for Richard Baldwin, next the *Black-Bull* in the *Old-Bailey*, MDCLXXXIX. 4°. (For the ascription of this work to the Marquis of Halifax, see text.)
[*Complete Works*. Ed. W. Raleigh. Oxford. 1912.]
Biography.
Foxcroft, N. C.
[*Life and Letters of Sir George Savile, Bart. ; first Marquis of Halifax*. 2 vols. 1898.]

Scott (Thomas).
The Unhappy Kindness : or A Fruitless Revenge. A Tragedy, As it is Acted at the Theatre Royal.

> *Ad Generum Cereris sine Caede et sanguine pauci*
> *Descendunt Reges.*   Juv. Sat. 10.

Wrirten [*sic*] by Mr. *Scot. London*, Printed for *H. Rhodes* in *Fleet-street*, *S. Briscoe* in *Covent-garden*, and *R. Parker* at the *Royal Exchange* : 1697. 4°.

Scudéry (Magdeleine de).
Clelia. An Excellent *New* Romance : Dedicated to *Mademoiselle de Longueville*. Written in *French* by the Exquisite Pen of *Monsieur de Scudery*, Governour of *Nostredame de la Gard. London* [*sic*], Printed for *Humphrey Mosely* and *Thomas Dring*, and are to be sold at their Shop, at the Princes Arms in St. *Pauls* Church-yard, and at the George in Fleet-street, near *Cliffords*-Inne, 1656–61. 5 vols. folio.

Sedley (Sir Charles).
Poems.
The Poetical Works of the Honourable Sir *Charles Sedley* Baronet, and his Speeches in Parliament. With *Large Additions never before made Publick*. Published from the Original M.S. by Capt. *Ayloffe*, a near Relation of the Authors. With a New Miscelany of Poems by several of the most

Q

Eminent Hands. And a Compleat Collection of all the Remarkable Speeches in both *Houses of Parliament* : Discovering the Principles of all *Parties* and *Factions* ; the Conduct of our *Chief Ministers*, the Management of Publick Affairs, and the Maxims of the Government, from the year 1641, to the Happy Union of *Great Britain* : By several Lords and Commoners. Viz. The Duke of *Albemarle*, Earl of *Clarendon*, Earl of *Bristol*, Lord *Wharton*, Earl of *Pembrook*, Lord *Hollis*, Lord *Brook*, Lord *Essex*, Earl of *Argile*, Lord *Melvil*, Lord *Haversham*, Lord *Belhaven*, etc. *Algernon Sidney* Esq. ; Mr. *Waller*, Sir *Francis Seymor*, Mr. *Pym*, *Richard Cromwell*, Mr. *Strode*, Sir *William Parkins*, Sir *William Scroggs*, Sir *J—— P——*, And several other Lords and Commoners. *London*, Printed for Sam. Briscoe, and Sold by *B. Bragg* at the *Raven* in *Paternoster-Row*. 1707. 8⁰.

Dramatic Works.

The Mulberry-Garden, A Comedy, As it is Acted by His Majestie's Servants, At the Theatre-Royal, Written by the Honourable Sir *Charles Sidley*. *London*, Printed for *H. Herringman*, at the Sign of the *Blew Anchor* in the Lower walk of the *New Exchange*. 1668. 4⁰.

Antony and Cleopatra : A Tragedy. As it is Acted at the Dukes Theatre. Written by the Honourable Sir Charles Sedley, Baronet, Licensed *Apr.* 24. 1677. *Roger L'Estrange*. *London*. Printed for *Richard Tonson* at his Shop under *Grayes-Inne-Gate* next *Grayes-Inn-lane*. MDCLXXVII. 4⁰.

Bellamira, or the Mistress, A Comedy : As it is Acted by Their Majesties Servants. Written by the Honourable Sir Charles Sedley Baronet. Licensed, *May* 24. 1687. *Rog. L'Estrange*. *London*, Printed by *D. Mallet*, for L. C. and *Timothy Goodwin*, at the Maiden-Head over against St *Dunstans* Church, in *Fleet-Street*. 1687. 4⁰.

Collected Works.

[*The Poetical and Dramatic Works*. Ed. V. de S. Pinto. 2 vols. 1928. (Contains a complete bibliography.)]

Biography and Criticism.

Pinto, V. de S.
[*Sir Charles Sedley*. 1927.]

SETTLE (Elkanah). See also DRYDEN (Drydeniana.)
Poems.

An Heroick Poem on the Coronation of the High and Mighty Monarch, James II. King of England, etc.

Caesar
Imperium Oceano, Famam qui terminet Astris.

By *E. Settle*. *London*, Printed by *J.L.* for *Benjamin Needham*, in *Duck-Lane*, MDCLXXXV. folio.

Dramatic Works.

Cambyses King of Persia : A Tragedy. Acted by His Highness the Duke of York's Servants. *Written by* Elkanah Settle, *Gent*.

Aut Faman sequere, aut sibi convenientia finge
Scriptor.   Hor. de Arte Poet.

Licensed, *March* 6. 1670. *Roger de l'Estrange*. *London*, Printed for *William Cademan*, at the *Pope's Head* in the Lower Walk of the New-Exchange. 1671. 4⁰.

The Empress of Morocco. A Tragedy with Sculptures. As it is Acted at the Duke's Theatre. Written by *Elkanah Settle*, Servant to his Majesty. *Primos da versibus annos*. Petr. Arb. *London*, Printed for

William Cademan at the *Popes-head* in the Lower Walk of the *New-Exchange* in the *Strand*, 1673. 4°.
[Ed. M. Summers. 1935.]
Notes and Observations on the Empress of Morocco Revised. With some few *Errata's* to be Printed instead of the *Postscript*, with the next Edition of the *Conquest of Granada*.

> *Impune ergo mihi recitaverit ille Togatas ?*
> *Hic. Elegos ?*   Juven.

London, Printed for *William Cademan* at the *Popes*-Head in the Lower Walk of the New Exchange in the *Strand*. 1674. 4°.
Love and Revenge, a Tragedy. Acted at the Duke's *Theatre*. Written by *Elkanah Settle*, Servant to his Majesty. *London*, Printed for *William Cademan*, and are to be sold at the Sign of the *Popes-head* in the *New-Exchange* in the *Strand*. 1675. 4°.
The Conquest of China, By the Tartars. A Tragedy Acted at the Duke's *Theatre*. Written by *Elkanah Settle*, Servant to His Majesty.

> *Multum sudet frustraque laboret*
> *Ausus idem, tantum series juncturaque pollet.* Hor.

London, Printed by *T.M.* for *W. Cademan*, at the *Popes-Head* in the *Lower-Walk* of the *New-Exchange*, in the Strand. 1676. 4°.
Ibrahim The Illustrious Bassa. A Tragedy. Acted at the Duke's Theatre. Written by Elkanah Settle, Servant to His Majesty.

> *Te*
> *Nos facimus Fortuna Deam.*   Juven.

Licensed *May* the 4th. 1676. *Roger L'Estrange*. *London*, Printed by *T.M.* for *W. Cademan*, at the *Popes-Head* in the *Lower* Walk of *New-Exchange* in the *Strand*. 1677. 4°.
The Female Prelate : Being The History of the Life and Death of Pope Joan. A Tragedy. As it is Acted at the Theatre Royal. Written by Elkanah Settle, Servant to His Majestie. *Facit Indignatio Versus.* Juven. *London*, Printed for *W. Cademan*, at the Popes head in the *New Exchange*. 1680. 4°.
[Ed. M. Summers. 1935.]
Distress'd Innocence : Or, The Princess of Persia. A Tragedy. As it is Acted at the Theatre Royal by Their Majesties Servants. *Written by E. Settle.*

> Ut ridentibus arrident, ita flentibus adsunt
> Humani vultus :. Si vis me flere dolendum est
> Primum ipsi Tibi, tunc tua me infortunia laedent
> Telephe vel Peleu . . .   Horat. de Arte Poetica.

London, Printed by *E(?) I.* for *Abel Roper* at the *Mitre* near *Temple-Bar* in Fleet street, 1691. 4°.
Miscellaneous Prose.
The Character of a Popish Successour, and What England May expect From Such a One. Humbly offered to the Consideration of both Houses of Parliament, Appointed to meet at Oxford, On the One and Twentieth of *March*. 1680/1. The Third Edition Corrected. London : Printed for *R. Janeway.* 1681. folio.
A Narrative Written by E. Settle.

> *Humano capiti cervicem pictor equinam*
> *Jungere si velit, et varias inducere plumas*
> *Undique collatis membris, ut turpiter Atrum*
> *Desinat in piscem, Mulier formosa superne,*
> *Spectatum admissi risum teneatis, amici.*

Q*

London, Printed, and are sold by *Thomas Graves* for the Author. 1683. folio.

The Present State of England In relation to Popery. Manifesting the Absolute Impossibility of Introducing Popery and Arbitrary Power into this Kingdom. Being a Full *Confutation* of all Fears and Apprehensions of the Imagined Dangers from thence : And particularly of a Certain *Pamphlet* Entituled The Character of a Popish Successor. By *E. Settle*. London, Printed by *J. Gain*, for *William Cademan*, at the *Popes-Head* in the Lower Walk of the *New Exchange*, in the *Strand* ; anno MDCLXXXIV. folio.

Biography and Criticism.

Brown, F. C.

[*Elkanah Settle : his Life and Works*. Chicago. 1910.]

SHADWELL (Thomas). See also DRYDEN (Drydeniana).

Poems.

A Congratulatory Poem On His Highness the Prince of Orange His Coming into England. Written by T.S. A True Lover of his Countrey. *London*, Printed for *James Knapton*, at the *Sign* of the *Crown* in St. *Pauls* Church-yard. MDCLXXXIX. folio.

A Congratulatory Poem To the Most Illustrious Queen Mary Upon Her Arrival in England. By *Tho. Shadwell*. London : Printed for James Knapton, at the Sign of the Crown in St Paul's Church-Yard. MDCLXXXIX. folio.

Ode On the Anniversary of the King's Birth. By *Tho. Shadwell*, Poet Laureat, and Historiographer Royal.

> *Steriles Transmisimus annos*
> *Haec Ævi prima Dies.*

London : Printed for *James Knapton*, at the Sign of the *Crown* in St. *Paul's* Church-Yard. 1690. folio.

Ode to the King. On His Return from Ireland. By *Tho. Shadwell*, Poet Laureat, and Historiographer-Royal to their Majesties. 1690. folio.

Votum Perenne. A Poem to The King On New-Years-Day. By Thomas Shadwell, Esq ; Poet Laureat, and Historiographer Royal. *London*, Printed for *Samuel Crouch*, at the Corner of *Pope's-Head-Alley*, over against the *Royal-Exchange*, 1692. folio.

Dramatic Works.

The Sullen Lovers : or, the Impertinents. A Comedy Acted by his Highness the Duke of *Yorkes* Servants. Written by Tho. Shadwell.

> *Num satis est dixisse, Ego mira Poemata pango,*
> *Occupet extremum scabies, mihi turpe relinqui est*
> *Et quod non didici sane nescire fateri.*
>
> Hor. de Art. Poet.

In the *Savoy*, Printed for *Henry Herringman* at the Sign of the *Anchor* in the Lower-Walk of the *New-Exchange*. 1668. 4°.

The Royal Shepherdess. A Tragi-Comedy, Acted By his Highness the Duke of *York's* Servants. *Non Quivis videt immodulata Poemata Judex.* Hor. de Arte Poet. *London*, Printed for *Henry Herringman*, at the Sign of the Blew-Anchor, in the Lower-Walk of the *New-Exchange*. 1669. 4°.

The Humorists ; A Comedy. Acted By his Royal Highnesses Servants. Written By Tho. Shadwell, *Poet-Laureat*, and *Historiographer-Royal.*

> *Quis inique*
> *Tam patiens urbis tam ferreus utteneat* [*sic*] *se.*

London, Printed for *Henry Herringman*, and are to be Sold by *Francis Saunders* at the *Blew Anchor* in the *Lower Walk* of the *New Exchange*, and *James Knapton* at the *Crown* in *St. Pauls Churchyard*. 1691. 4⁰. (First edition : 1671. Acted in 1670.)

The Miser : A Comedy Acted by His Majesties Servants, At the Theatre Royal. Written by *Thomas Shadwell. London*, Printed for *Hobart Kemp*, at the sign of the *Ship*, in the upper Walk of the *New Exchange*. 1672. 4⁰. (Acted in 1671.)

Epsom-Wells. A Comedy, Acted at the Duke's Theatre. Written by *Tho. Shadwell*. Μεγάλων ἀπολισθαίνειν ἁμάρτημα εὐγενές. Licensed, *Feb.* 17 1672/3. *Roger L'Estrange. London*, Printed by *J.M.* for *Henry Herringman* at the Sign of the *Blew Anchor* in the Lower Walk of the *New Exchange*. M.DC.LXXIII. 4⁰. (Acted in 1672.)

Psyche : A Tragedy, Acted at the Duke's Theatre. Written by *Tho. Shadwell. London*, Printed by *T.N.* for *Henry Herringman*, at the *Anchor* in the Lower Walk of the *New Exchange*. 1675. 4⁰.

The Libertine : A Tragedy, Acted by His Royal Highness's Servants. Written by *Tho. Shadwell. London*, Printed by *T.N.* for *Henry Herringman*, at the *Anchor*, in the Lower Walk of the *New Exchange*. 1676. 4⁰.

The Virtuoso. A Comedy, Acted at the Duke's Theatre, Written by *Thomas Shadwell*. Licensed *May* 31. 1676. Roger L'Estrange. *London*. Printed by *T.N.* for *Henry Herringman*, at the *Anchor* in the Lower Walk of the *New Exchange*. 1676. 4⁰.

The History of Timon of Athens, The Man-Hater. As it is acted at the *Dukes Theatre*. Made into a Play. By *Tho. Shadwell*. Licensed, Feb. 18. 1677/8. *Ro. L'Estrange*. London, Printed by *J.M.* for *Henry Herringman*, at the *Blue Anchor*, in the Lower Walk of the *New-Exchange*. 1678. 4⁰.

A True Widow. A Comedy, Acted by the *Duke's* Servants. Written by *Tho. Shadwell. Odi profanum Vulgus et Arceo*. Printed for *Benjamin Tooke*, at the *Ship* in St *Paul's* Church-Yard. 1679. 4⁰.

The Woman-Captain : A Comedy Acted by His Royal Highnesses Servants. Written by *Tho. Shadwell. London*, Printed for *Samuel Carr*, at the *King's-Head* in Sᵗ *Paul's Church-yard*. 1680. 4⁰.

The Lancashire Witches, and Tegue O Divelly The Irish Priest. A Comedy. Part the First. The Amorous Bigot, with Second Part of Tegue O Divelly, A Comedy. Both Acted by their Majesties Servants. Written by *Thomas Shadwell* Poet Laureat, and Historiographer Royal to their Majesties. *London*, Printed for *R. Clavell, J. Robinson, A.* and *J. Churchill* and *J. Knapton*, and are to be Sold at the *Crown* in St. *Pauls* Church-yard, 1691. 4⁰. [First edition : 1682. Acted in 1681.]

A Lenten Prologue, Refus'd by the Players. 1683. folio. (Attributed to Shadwell.)

The Squire of Alsatia. A Comedy, As it is Acted by Their Majestys' Servants. Written by *Tho. Shadwell*.

> *Creditur, ex medio quia res arcessit, habere*
> *Sudoris minimum, sed habet Comaedia tanto*
> *Plus oneris, quanto veniae minus.*
>> Hor. Ep. ad Aug. I. lib. 2.

London, Printed for *James Knapton*, at the *Queens-Head* in St. *Paul's* Church-Yard. 1688. 4⁰.

Bury-Fair. A Comedy, As it is Acted by His Majesty's Servants. Written by *Tho. Shadwell*, Servant to His Majesty. *London*, Printed for *James Knapton*, at the *Crown* in Sᵗ. *Paul's* Church-yard : 1689. 4⁰.

The Scowrers. A Comedy, Acted by Their Majesties Servants. Written by *Tho. Shadwell*, Poet Laureat, and Historiographer-Royal. *London* : Printed for James *Knapton*, at the *Crown* in St. *Paul's* Church-yard. 1691. 4°.

The Volunteers, or The Stock-Jobbers. A Comedy, As it is Acted by Their Majesties Servants, At The Theatre Royal. Written by *Tho. Shadwell*, Esq. Late Poet-Laureat. and Historiographer Royal. Being his last Play. *London*, Printed for *James Knapton*, at the *Crown* in St. *Paul's* Church-yard. 1693. Where are also to be had all Mr. *Shadwells* 17 Plays etc. Bound up, or single. 4°. (Played in 1692.)

Collected Works.

The Dramatick Works of *Thomas Shadwell*, Esq ; In Four Volumes. *London* : Printed for J. Knapton, at the *Crown* in St. *Paul's Church-Yard* ; and J. Tonson, at *Shakespear's Head* over-against *Katharine-Street* in the *Strand.* MDCCXX. 12°.

[*The Complete Works.* Ed. M. Summers. 5 vols. 1927.]

Biography and Criticism.

Borgman, A. S.

[*Thomas Shadwell : His Life and Comedies.* New York. 1928.]

SHAKESPEARE (William).

Mézières, A.

Shakspeare, ses oeuvres et ses critiques. Par A. Mézières, Professeur de littérature étrangère à la faculté des lettres de Paris. Deuxième édition. Ouvrage couronné par l'Académie française. Paris, Charpentier, libraire-éditeur, 28, Quai de l'École. 1865. 12°.

Ingleby, Clement Mansfield.

Shakespeare's Centurie of Praise ; *Being* Materials for a History of Opinion on Shakespeare and his Works, *Culled from Writers of the first Century after his Rise.*

> *Praestanti tibi maturos largimur honores,*
> *Jurandasque tuum per nomen ponimus aras,*
> *Nil oriturum alias, nil ortum tale fatentes.*
> *Horat. Epist., lib. ii. ep. i. l.* 73.

London : *For the Editor* : *Printed by* Josiah Allen, of Birmingham, *and published by* Trübner and Co., 57 et 59, *Ludgate Hill.* 1874. 8°.

SHEFFIELD (John), Earl of Mulgrave, Duke of Buckingham and Normanby.

An Essay on Poetry : By the Right Honourable The Earl of Mulgrave. The Second Edition. London, Printed for *Jo. Hindmarsh*, at the *Golden Ball* over against the *Royal Exchange* in *Cornhil.* MDCXCI. folio.

The Works of John Sheffield Earl of Mulgrave, Marquis of *Normanby*, and Duke of *Buckingham.*

> *Nec* Phoebo *gratior ulla est*
> *Quam sibi quae* Vari *praescripsit pagina nomen.* Virg.

London. Printed by John Barber, Alderman of *London.* MDCCXXIII. 2 vols. 4°.

[*Miscellanea from the works of John Sheffield, Duke of Buckingham.* The Haworth Press. 1933.]

SMITH (Edmund).

A Pindarique Poem Sacred to the Glorious Memory of King William III.

> *Ignis utique quo clarius effulsit, citius*
> *Extinguitur, eripit se aufertque ex Oculis*
> *Subito perfecta Virtus.* Cambden de Phil. Syd.

By *M. Smith* Gent. *London*, Printed for *Andrew Bell* at the Cross-Keys and Bible in Cornhil. MDCCII. folio.

Phaedra and Hippolitus. [*sic*]. A Tragedy. At it is Acted at the Queen's Theatre in the *Hay-Market*, By Her Majesty's Sworn Servants. By Mr. Edmund Smith. *London*, Printed for Bernard Lintott at the *Cross-Keys* between the two Temple-Gates in *Fleetstreet*. 1709. (Acted in 1707.) 4⁰.

SMITH (Francis).

An Account of the Injurious Proceedings of Sir George Jeffrey K^{nt}. Late Recorder of London, against Francis Smith, Bookseller. With his Arbitrary Carriage towards the Grand-Jury, at *Guild-Hall*, Sept. 16. 1680. Upon an Indictment then Exhibited against the said *Francis Smith*. For Publishing a Pretended *Libel*, entitled, An act of Common-Council for Retrenching the Expences of the Lord Mayor and Sheriffs of the City of London, etc. Together with an Abstract of very many former Losses, and Publick Sufferings Sustained by Him both in his *Person* and *Estate*. *Humbly submitted to the Consideration of all* True English-Men. *London*, Printed for Francis Smith at the *Elephant and Castle* in Cornhill near the Royal-Exchange. folio.

SMOLLETT (Tobias).

The Expedition of Humphry Clinker. By the Author of Roderick Random. In Three Volumes.

> Quorsum haec tam putida tendunt,
> Furcifer ? at te, inquam.   Hor.

London, Printed for W. Johnston, in Ludgate-Street ; and B. Collins, in Salisbury. MDCLXXI. 12⁰.

[Ed. R. Rice-Oxley. World's Classics. 1925.]

Biography and Criticism.

Hannay, David.

[Tobias Smollett. 1887.]

Lewis Melville.

[The Life and Letters of Tobias Smollett. 1926.]

Some thoughts.

Some Thoughts Concerning the Stage in a Letter to a Lady. *London* : Printed, and are to be Sold by *J. Nutt.* near *Stationers-Hall*. 1704. 8⁰.

SOUTHERNE (Thomas).

The Loyal Brother or the Persian Prince. A Tragedy As it is Acted at the Theatre Royal by their Majesties Servants. By *Thomas Southern*. *I, fuge ; sed poteras tutior esse Domi. Mart.* London, Printed for *William Cademan* at the *Popes Head* in the New *Exchange* in the *Strand*. 1682. 4⁰.

The Disappointment, or The Mother in Fashion. A Play As it was Acted At the Theatre Royal. Written by *Thomas Southerne*.

> *Neque tu divinum Æneada tenta,*
> *Sed longe sequere, et vestigia semper adora.* Stat.

London, Printed for *Jo. Hindmarsh*, Bookseller to his Royal Highness, at the Black Bull in *Cornhil*. 1684. 4⁰.

Sir Anthony Love : Or, The Rambling Lady. A Comedy. As it is Acted at the Theatre-Royal by Their Majesties Servants. Written by *Tho. Southerne*.

> *Artis severae si quis amat effectus,*
> *Mentemque magnis applicat*
> *det primos versibus annos,*
> *Maeoniumque bibat foelici* [sic] *pectore fontem.*
> Petro. Arb. Satyr. pag. 3.

London : Printed for *Joseph Fox* at the *Seven Stars* in *Westminster Hall*, and *Abel Roper* at the *Mitre* near *Temple Bar*. 1691. 4⁰.

The Wives Excuse : Or, Cuckolds make Themselves. A Comedy. As it is Acted at the Theatre-Royal, By Their Majesties Servants. Written by *Tho. Southern*. *Nihil est his, qui placere volunt, tam adversarium, Quam expectatio*. Cicero. *London*, Printed for *Samuel Brisco*, over against *Will's Coffee-house*, in *Russel-Street*, in *Covent-Garden*. 1692. 4⁰.

The Maids last Prayer : or Any, Rather than Fail. A Comedy. As it is Acted at the Theatre Royal, By Their Majesties Servants. Written by *Tho. Southerne*.

> *Valeat res ludicra, si me*
> *Palma negata, macrum ; donata reducit opimum.*
> Hor. Epist. 1. lib. 2.

London, Printed for *R. Bentley*, in *Russell-street* in Covent-Garden, and *J. Tonson*, at the *Judges Head* in *Chancery-Lane*. 1693. 4⁰.

The Fatal Marriage : or the Innocent Adultery, A Play, Acted at the Theatre Royal, By Their Majesties Servants. *Written by* Tho. Southerne. *Pellex ego facta mariti*. Ovid. *London*, Printed for *Jacob Tonson*, at the *Judges Head* near the Inner-Temple-Gate in Fleetstreet, 1694. 4⁰.

Oroonoko : A Tragedy As it is Acted at the Theatre-Royal, By His Majesty's Servants. Written by *Tho. Southerne*.

> *Quo fata trahunt, virtus secura sequetur.* Lucan.

> *Virtus recludens immeritis mori.*
> *Caelum, negata tentat iter Via.*
> Hor. Od. 2, lib. 3.

London : Printed for *H. Playford*, in the *Temple-Change*. *B. Tooke* at the *Middle-Temple-Gate*. And *S. Buckley* at the *Dolphin* against St Dunstan's Church in Fleet-street. MDCXCXVI. 4⁰.

[In *Modern British Drama*. vol. 1.]

Collected Works.

Plays Written by Thomas Southerne, Esq. now first Collected. With An Account of the Life and Writings of the Author.

> Your tributary tears we claim,
> For scenes that Southerne drew ; a fav'rite name.
> He touch'd your fathers heart with gen'rous woe,
> And taught your mothers youthful eyes to flow ;
> For this he Claims hereditary praise,
> From wits and beauties of our modern days.
>
> Hawkesworth.

London, Printed for T. Evans near York-buildings : and T. Becket, corner of the Adelphi, Strand. MDCCLXXIV. 3 vols. 8⁰.

Biography and Criticism.

Dodds, J. W.

[*Thomas Southerne, Dramatist*. New Haven. 1933.]

Sprat (Thomas).

A True Account and Declaration of The Horrid Conspiracy against the Late King, His Present Majesty and the Government : *As it was order'd to be Published by His late Majesty*. The second edition. *In the Savoy* : Printed by *Thomas Newcomb*, One of His Majesties Printers ; and are to be sold by *Sam. Lowndes* over against *Exeter-Change* in the *Strand*. 1685. folio. [First edition also 1685.]

Stapleton or Stapylton (Sir Robert).

The Slighted Maid, A Comedy, Acted with great Applause at the Theatre in Little *Lincolns-Inn-*Fields, *By His Highness the* Duke of York's *Servants.* London, Printed for *Thomas Dring* at the *George* near St. *Dunstan's* Church in *Fleet-street.* 1663. 4⁰.

The Step-Mother A Tragi-Comedy, Acted with great Applause at the Theatre in Little *Lincolns-Inn* Fields, *By His Highness the Duke of* York's *Servants.* Imprimatur, *Decemb.* 26. 1663. *Roger L'Estrange. London,* Printed by J. *Streater* ; And are to be sold by *Timothy Twy* . . . (The rest of the title eroded.)

The Tragedie of Hero and Leander. Written by Sʳ. Robert Stapylton Kt. One of the Gentlemen Ushers of his Majesty's Most Honorable Privy Chamber, Licensed August 25. 1668. *Roger L'Estrange. London,* Printed for *Thomas Dring,* the Younger, at the *White Lyon* next *Chancery-Lane* in *Fleet-street,* 1669. 4⁰.

Star-Chamber.

A Decree of Starre-Chamber, concerning Printing, *Made the eleuenth day of July last past.* 1637. Imprinted at London by *Robert Barker,* Printer to the Kings most Excellent Maiestie : And by the Assignes of John Bill. 1637. 4⁰.

STEELE (Richard).

Dramatic Works.

The Lying Lover : or The Ladies Friendship. A Comedy. As it is Acted at the Theatre Royal by Her Majesty's Servants. Written by Mr. *Steele.* Haec nosse salus est adolescentulis. Tertul. *London* : Printed for Bernard Lintot at the *Middle-Temple-Gate* in Fleetstreet. 1704. Price. 1s. 6d. 4⁰.

The Conscious Lovers. A Comedy. As it is Acted at the Theatre Royal in *Drury-Lane.* By His Majesty's Servants. Written by Sir *Richard Steele.*

Illud Genus Narrationis, quod in Personis positum est, debet habere Sermonis Festivitatem, Animorum Dissimilitudinem, Gravitatem, Lenitatem, Spem, Metum, Suspicionem, Desiderium, Dissimulationem, Misericordiam, Rerum Varietates, Fortunae Commultationem, Insperatum Incommodum, Subitam Laetitiam, Jucundum Exitum rerum. Cic. Rhetor. ad Herenn. Lib. I. *London* : Printed for J. Tonson at *Shakespear's Head* over against *Katharine-Street* in the *Strand.* 1723. 8⁰.

[Ed. M. J. Moses. *British Plays.* Vol. 1. Boston. 1929.]

[*The Plays.* Ed. G. A. Aitken. 1894. (Mermaid Series. 1903.)]

Periodicals. See also ADDISON (*The Spectator* and *The Guardian*).

Numb. 1. The Tatler, By *Isaac Bickerstaff* Esq ; *Quicquid agunt Homines nostri Farrago Libelli.* Tuesday, April 12. 1709. folio.

[Ed. G. A. Aitken. 4 vols. 1898–9.]

The Lucubrations of *Isaac Bickerstaff* Esq ; Οὐ χρὴ παννύχιον εὕδειν βοσληφόρον ἄνδρα. Homer. *London,* Printed : And to be deliver'd to Subscribers, by *Charles Lillie,* Perfumer, at the Corner of *Beauford-Buildings,* in the *Strand* ; and *John Morphew* near *Stationers-Hall.* MDCCXIII. 4 vols. 8⁰.

[Ed. H. R. Montgomery. 1861.]

Encyclopédie Morale, ou Choix des Essais du Spectateur, du Babillard et du Tuteur ; traduits en français, par M. L. Mézières, Docteur ès-Lettres, ancien professeur de Rhétorique . . . Paris, F. M. Maurice, libraire-éditeur, rue de Sorbonne, n⁰ 5. MDCCCXXVI. 2 vols. 8⁰.

Miscellaneous Prose.

The Epistolary Correspondence of Sir Richard Steele ; including *his familiar letters* to his wife and daughters ; to which are prefixed, *fragments of three plays* ; two of them undoubtedly Steele's, the third supposed to be Addison's. Faithfully printed from the originals ; and

illustrated with literary and historical anecdotes, *by John Nichols,*
F.S.A.E. and P. In two volumes. London : Printed by and for
John Nichols and Son, Red Lion Passage, Fleetstreet ; and sold by
Messrs. Longman, Hurst ; Rees, and Orme, Paternoster-Row. 1809.
2 vols. 8º.
[*The Correspondence of Richard Steele.* Ed. Rae Blanchard. 1941.]
[*Tracts and Pamphlets.* Ed. Rae Blanchard. Baltimore. 1944.]
Biography and Criticism.
    Dennis, John.
        [*Remarks on a Play called the Conscious Lovers.* 1723. (In *Critical Works.*
        Ed. E. N. Hooker. 1939. vol. 2.)]
    Dobson, Austin.
        [*Richard Steele.* 1886.]
    Aitken, G. A.
        [*Richard Steele.* 2 vols. 1889.]
    Connely, W.
        [*Sir Richard Steele.* 1934.]

STEPNEY (George).
An Epistle to Charles Montague Esq. ; on his Majesty's Voyage to Holland,
by Mr. *George Stepney.* Licensed *Jan.* 31 1690/1. *J. Fraser. London* :
Printed for *Francis Saunders* at the *Blue Anchor* in the *Lower Walk* of the
New Exchange. 1691. folio.
A Poem Dedicated to the Blessed Memory of Her late Gracious Majesty
Queen Mary. By Mr. Stepney. *London* : Printed for *Jacob Tonson,*
at the *Judge's Head,* near the *Inner-Temple Gate* in *Fleetstreet.* 1695. folio.
[Poems by Stepney are contained in Johnson vol. XII and Chalmers
vol. VIII.]

STILLINGFLEET (Edward).
An Answer to some Papers Lately Printed concerning the Authority of the
Catholick Church In Matters of Faith, and the Reformation of the Church
of England. *London* : Printed for *Ric. Chiswell* at the *Rose* and *Crown* in
Sᵗ *Paul's* Church-yard. MDCLXXXVI. 4º.
A Vindication of the Answer to some Late Papers Concerning The Unity
and Authority of the Catholick Church and the Reformation of the
Church of England. London : Printed for Richard Chiswell, at the *Rose*
and *Crown* in Sᵗ *Paul's* Church-yard. MDCLXXXVII. 4º.

SWIFT (Jonathan).
A Tale of A Tub. Written for the Universal Improvement of Mankind.
Diu multumque desideratum. To which is added, An Account of a Battel
Between the Antient and Modern Books in St. *James* Library. Basima
cacabasa eanaa irraumista, diarbada caëota bafobos camelanthi. *Iren.*
Lib. I. c. 18.

    Juvatque novos decerpere flores,
    Insignemque meo capiti petere inde coronam,
    Unde prius nulli velarunt tempora Musae. Lucret.

The Second Edition Corrected. *London* : Printed for *John Nutt,* near
Stationers-Hall. MDCCIV. 8º. (First edition also 1704.]
    [Ed. A. Guthkelch and D. Nichol Smith. 1920.]
A Letter from a Member of the House of Commons in Ireland to a Member
of the House of Commons in England, Concerning the *Sacramental Test.*
London : Printed for *John Morphew,* near *Stationers-Hall.* 1709. 4º.
[First edition : 1708.]
The W—ds—r Prophecy. Printed in the Year, 1711. folio.
The Conduct of the Allies, and of the Late Ministry, In Beginning and
Carrying on The Present War.

Partem tibi Gallia nostri
Eripuit : partem duris Hispania bellis :
Pars jacet Hesperiae : totoq; exercitus orbe
Te vincente perit. Terris fudisse cruorem
Quid juvat Arctois, Rhodano, Rhenoq; subactis ?
Odimus accipitrem quia semper vivit in armis.
Victrix Provincia plorat.

The Second Edition, Corrected. *London*, Printed for *John Morphew*, near *Stationers-Hall*. 1711. 8⁰. (First edition also 1711.)

A Proposal for *Correcting, Improving* and *Ascertaining* the English Tongue ; In a Letter To the Most Honourable Robert *Earl of* Oxford *and* Mortimer, *Lord High Treasurer* of Great Britain. The Second Edition. *London* : Printed for Benj. Tooke, at the *Middle-Temple-Gate, Fleetstreet.* 1712. 8⁰.

A Letter of Advice to a Young Poet : together with a Proposal for the Encouragement of Poetry in this Kingdom.

Sic honor et nomen divinis vatibus atq;
Carminibus venit. Hor.

By J. Swift. Printed at *Dublin*, Reprinted at *London*, and Sold by *W. Boreham* at the *Angel* in *Pater-Noster-Row*. 1721. 8⁰.

Collected Works.

The Works of Jonathan Swift, D.D. Dean of St. Patrick's, Dublin ; containing Additional Letters, Tracts and Poems, not hitherto published ; with Notes, and a Life of the Author, by Sir Walter Scott, Bart. Second Edition. Edinburgh : Printed for Archibald Constable & Co. and Hurst, Robinson and Co. London. 1824. 19 vols. 8⁰.

[*The Prose Works.* Ed. Herbert Davis. Oxford. 1939–
    1. *The Tale of a Tub.* 1939.
    2. *Bickerstaff papers and Pamphlets on the Church.* 1939.
    3. *Examiner and other pieces (1710–11).* 1939.
    10. *The Drapier's letters and other works (1724–26).* 1941.
    11. *Gulliver's travels.* 1941.]

[*The Correspondence of Jonathan Swift. D.D.* Ed. F. Elrington Ball. 6 vols. 1910–14.]

[*The Letters of Jonathan Swift to Charles Ford.* Ed. D. Nichol Smith. Oxford. 1935.]

[*The Poems.* Ed. Harold Williams. 3 vols. Oxford. 1937.]

Biography and Criticism.

Prevost-Paradol, M.
    Jonathan Swift, his life and his works, by M. Prevost-Paradol : Paris, A Durand, 7, rue des Grès-Sorbonne, near the Panthéon. 1856. 8⁰.

Forster, John.
    The Life of Jonathan Swift. By John Forster. Volume the First. 1667–1711. London : John Murray, Albemarle Street. 1875. 1 vol. 8⁰. (Only this volume ever appeared. The author died after having published it.)

Craik, Henry.
    The Life of Jonathan Swift, Dean of St. Patrick's, Dublin, By Henry Craik, M.A. with Portrait. London, John Murray. 1882. 8⁰.

Stephen, Leslie.
    [*Jonathan Swift.* 1882.]

Moriarty, G. P.
    [*Dean Swift and his Writings.* 1892.]

Van Doren, C.
    [*Swift.* 1930.]

Quintana, R.
[*The Mind and Art of Jonathan Swift.* 1936.]
Newman, B.
[*Jonathan Swift.* 1937.]
Pons, Émile. [*La Jeunesse de Swift.* 1925.]

TATE (Nahum). See also DRYDEN (*The Second Part of Absalom and Achitophel*).
Poems.

On the Sacred Memory Of Our Late Sovereign : With a Congratulation To His Present Majesty.
Non deficit Alter
Aureus.
Written by *N. Tate. London*, Printed by *J. Playford*, for *Henry Playford*, near the *Temple*-Church : 1685. folio.

The Triumph of Union : With the Muse's Address For the Consummation of it in the Parliament of Great Britain. Written by Mr. *Tate* Poet-Laureat to Her Majesty. London : Printed in the Year 1707. 4°.

A Congratulatory Poem To His Royal Highness Prince George of Denmark, Lord High Admiral of Great Britain. Upon the Glorious Successes at Sea. By N. Tate, Esq ; Poet-Laureat to Her Majesty. London : Printed by H. Meere, for J.B. and sold by R. Burrough and J. Baker, at the *Sun* and *Moon* in *Cornhill* ; and J. Morphew, near *Stationers-Hall*. 1708. folio.

An Entire Set of The Monitors. Intended for the Promoting of Religion and Virtue, and Suppressing of Vice and Immorality. Containing Forty One Poems on Several Subjects, *In Pursuance of Her* Majesty's *Most Gracious Directions*. Perform'd by Mr. Tate, Poet Laureat to Her Majesty, Mr. Smith, and Others. This Undertaking was Encourag'd by the *Subscription* of the following Gentlemen of the Clergy (besides *That* of Many of the Nobility, and great Numbers of the Gentry) His Grace my Lord Arch-Bishop of *York*, my Lord Bishop of *Lincoln*, my Lord Bishop of St. *Davids*, my Lord Bishop of *Gloucester*, Dr. *Moss*, Dean of *Ely*, Dr. *Brailsford*, Dean of *Wells*, Dr. *Williams*, Dr. *Bedfourd*, Dr. *Brown*, Dr. *Fog*, Dr. *Pelling*, Dr. *Bray*, Dr. *Hoadley*, Dr. *Blake*, Dr. *Hunt*. Dr. *King*, Dr. *Waugh*, Dr. *Wells*, Dr. *Only*, Dr. *Heath*, with about Fifty more of that Reverend Order. N.B. When the *Authors* had publish'd these Twenty One Papers, they were oblig'd (by being engag'd in other Affairs) to decline further proceeding in this Undertaking. folio.

A Poem Sacred to the Glorious Memory of Her Late Majesty *Queen* Anne. By N. Tate, Esq ; Poet Laureat to King William, Queen Mary, Queen Anne, and to His present Majesty, till the Day of his Decease. Printed in the Year MDCCXVI. 8°.

A Poem. Occasioned by the Late Discontents and Disturbances in the State. With Reflections upon the Rise and Progress of Priest-Craft. Written by *N. Tate.*

Liberius si
Dixero quid, si forte Jocosius, Hoc mihi juris
Cum Venia dabis. Hor.
Vincit Amor Patriae. Virg.

London : Printed for *Richard Baldwin*, near the *Oxford-Arms* in *Warwick-Lane*. MDCXCI. folio.

Mausolaeum : A Funeral Poem On our late Gracious Sovereign Queen Mary, Of Blessed Memory. By N. Tate, *Servant to His Majesty.* London : Printed for *B. Aylmer*, at the *Three Pigeons* against St. *Dunstan's* Church in *Fleet-street*. And *R. Baldwin*, near the *Oxford-Arms* in *Warwick-Lane*. 1695. folio.

A Congratulatory Poem On the New Parliament Assembled On This Great Conjuncture of Affairs. By *N. Tate*, Esq ; Poet-Laureat to His Majesty. London : Printed for W. Rogers, at the *Sun* against St. *Dunstan's* Church in Fleetstreet, MDCCI. folio.

Dramatic Works.

Brutus of Alba : or, the Enchanted Lovers. A Tragedy. Acted at the Duke's Theatre. Written by N. Tate. *Neque ut te miretur Turba, Labores,* Hor. Licensed *July* 15. 1678. *Roger L'Estrange. London,* Printed for *E.F.* for *Jacob Tonson,* at the Sign of the *Judge's-Head* in *Chancery-Lane,* near *Fleet-Street,* 1678. 4°.

The History of King Lear. Acted at the Duke's Theatre. Reviv'd with Alterations. By *N. Tate. London,* Printed for *E. Flesher,* and are to be sold by *R. Bentley,* and *M. Magnes* in *Russel-street* near *Covent-Garden,* 1681. 4°.

The *History* of King *Richard* the Second Acted at the Theatre Royal, Under the Name of the *Sicilian Usurper.* With a Prefatory *Epistle* in Vindication of the Author. Occasion'd by the Prohibition of this *Play* on the Stage. By *N. Tate. Inultus ut Flebo Puer* ? Hor. *London,* Printed for *Richard Tonson,* and *Jacob Tonson,* at *Grays-Inn* Gate, and at the Judges-Head in *Chancery-Lane* near *Fleet-street.* 1681. 4°.

The Ingratitude of a Common-Wealth ; or, the Fall of Caius Martius Coriolanus. As it is Acted at the Theatre-Royal. By N. Tate.

> *Honoratum si forte reponis Achillem,*
> *Impiger, Iracundus, Inexorabilis, Acer,*
> *Jura neget sibi nata, nihil non arroget Armis.* Hor.

London, Printed by T.W. for *Joseph Hindmarsh,* at the *Black-Bull* in *Cornhill.* 1682. 4°.

Cuckolds-Haven : or, an Alderman No Conjuror, A Farce acted at the Queen's Theatre in *Dorset Garden.* By *N. Tate. London,* Printed for *J.H.* and are to be sold by *Edward Poole,* next door to the *Fleece Tavern* in *Cornhill.* 1685. 4°.

A Duke and no Duke a Farce. As it is Acted by Their Majesties Servants. Written by *N. Tate.* With The several Songs set to Music, With thorow Basses for the *Theorbo,* or *Basse Viol. London,* Printed for *Henry Bonwicke,* at the *Red-Lyon* in St. *Pauls* Church-Yard. 1685. 4°.

TEMPLE (Sir William).

The Works of Sir *William Temple,* Bart. In Two Volumes. To which is Prefix'd Some Account of the Life and Writings of the Author. *London* : Printed for *A. Churchill, T. Goodwin, J. Knapton, R. Smith, B. Tooke, J. Round, J. Tonson, O. Lloyd, W. Meres, T. Woodward,* and *F. Clay.* MDCCXX. folio.

[4 vols. Edinburgh. 1814.]

[*Essays of Sir William Temple.* Ed. J. A. Nicklin. 1911.]

Biography.

Marburg, Clara.

[*Sir William Temple.* 1932.]

TICKELL (Thomas). See also ADDISON (Preface to Addison's *Works* 1721, and to *The Drummer*).

A Poem To His Excellency The Lord Privy-Seal, on the *Prospect* of *Peace.* By Mr. *Tickell.*

> *Sacerdos*
> *Fronde super* Mitram *faelici insignis Olivae.* Virg.

London : Printed for J. Tonson, at *Shakespear's-Head* over against *Catherine-street* in the Strand. 1713. folio.

Epistle from A Lady in *England* ; To A Gentleman at *Avignon*. By Mr.
Tickell. The Third Edition. London, Printed for *J. Tonson*, at *Shake-
spear's-Head* over against *Katharine-street* in the *Strand*. 1717. folio.
Kensington Garden. *Campos, ubi Troja fuit.* Virg. London : Printed
for J. Tonson, in the Strand. MDCCXXII. 4⁰.
[*The Poetical Works.* Boston. 1894.]
Biography and Criticism.
    Tickell, R. E.
    [*Thomas Tickell and the Eighteenth Century Poets.* 1931.]

TINDAL (Matthew).
Christianity as old as the Creation : Or, the Gospel, A Republication of the
    Religion of Nature. Est autem jus naturale adeo immutabile, ut ne
    quidem a Deo mutari potest. *Grot. de Jure Belli et Pacis*, 1. 1. C. 1.
    10. n. 5. *The Gentiles, which have not the Law, do by Nature the Things
    contained in the Law.* Rom. ii. 14.—*God is no Respecter of Persons ; but in
    Every Nation, he that feareth him, and worketh Righteousness, is accepted with him.*
    Acts. x. 34, 35, Proinde perfectam illam Religionem quae Christi praedi-
    catione nobis tradita est, non Novam aut Peregrinam, sed si verum dicere
    oportet, primam, solam veramque esse liquido apparet. *Euseb.* Eccl.
    Hist. 1. 1. C. 4. *Valesius's* Transl. Res ipsa quae nunc Christiana Religio
    nuncupatur, erat et apud Antiquos, nec defuit ab Initio generis humani,
    quousq ; ipse Christus veniret in Carne ; unde vera Religio quae jam
    erat, caepit appellari Christiana. *Aug. Oper.* To. 1. p. 17. C. *Retract.*
    1. 1. C. 13. The Religion of the Gospel, is the true original Religion of
    Reason and Nature.—And its Precepts declarative of that original
    Religion, which was as old as the Creation. *Serm. for prop. the Gosp. in
    for. Parts,* by Dr. *Sherlock,* now Bp. of *Bangor,* p. 10. and 13. God does
    nothing in the Government of the World by mere Will and Arbitrariness.
    —The Will of God always determines itself to act according to the eternal
    Reason of Things.—All rational Creatures are oblig'd to govern them-
    selves in ALL their Actions by the same eternal Rule of Reason. Dr.
    S. *Clark's* Unchang. Oblig. of Nat. Relig. Edit. 4. p. 47, 48, 49. *London,*
    Printed in the Year MDCCXXX. 4⁰.

TOLAND (John).
Christianity not Mysterious : or a Treatise Shewing, That there is nothing
    in the Gospel Contrary to Reason, Nor Above it : And that no Christian
    Doctrine can be properly call'd A Mystery. *We need not desire a better
    Evidence that any Man is in the wrong, than to hear him declare against Reason
    and thereby acknowledge that Reason is against him.* ABp. Tillotson. London,
    Printed in the Year 1696. 8⁰.
Nazarenus : Or *Jewish, Gentile,* and *Mahometan* Christianity. Containing
    The history of the antient Gospel of Barnabas, and the modern Gospel
    of the Mahometans, attributed to the same Apostle : this last Gospel
    being now first made known among Christians. Also, The Original
    Plan of Christianity occasionally explain'd in the history of the Nazarens,
    wherby diverse Controversies about this divine (but highly perverted)
    Institution may be happily terminated. With The relation of an Irish
    Manuscript of the Four Gospels, as likewise a Summary of the antient
    Irish Christianity, and the reality of the Keldees (an order of Lay-
    religious) against the two last Bishops of Worcester. By Mr. *Toland.*

   Intacta et Nova ? graves Offensae, levis Gratia. ⎱Plin. lib. 10.
                   ⎰Epistl. 8.

   *Ast ego Caelicolis gratum reor ire per omnes
   Hoc opus, et Sacras populis notescere Leges.*
              Lucan. lib. 10, ver. 197.

London, Printed : And Sold by J. Brown without Temple-Bar, J. Roberts in Warwick-Lane, and J. Brotherton at the Black Bull in Cornhill. 1718. 8⁰.

Pantheisticon : or the Form Of Celebrating the *Socratic-Society*. Divided into Three Parts. Which Contain, I. The Morals and Axioms of the Pantheists ; or the Brotherhood. II. Their Deity and Philosophy. III. Their Liberty, and a Law, neither deceiving, nor to be deceived. To which is prefix'd A Discourse upon the Antient and Modern Societies of the Learned, as also upon the Infinite and Eternal Universe. And subjoined, A short Dissertation upon a Two-fold Philosophy of the Pantheists, that is to be followed ; together with an Idea of the best and most accomplished Man. Written Originally in Latin, by the ingenious Mr. *John Toland*. And now, for the first Time, faithfully rendered into English. *London* : Printed for Sam. Paterson, at *Shakespear's-Head* opposite *Durham-yard*, in the *Strand* ; and Sold by M. Cooper, in *Pater-noster Row*. 1751. 8⁰. (First edition : 1720.)

TUKE (Sir Samuel).
The Adventures of Five Hours. A Tragi-Comedy. *The Second Edition. Non ego Ventosae Plebis suffragia venor.* Horat. Feb. 12. 1662. Imprimatur. *John Berkenhead. London*, Printed for *Henry Herringman*, and are to be sold at his Shop at the Sign of the *Anchor* in the Lower Walk of the *New Exchange*. 1664. 4⁰.
[Ed. B. Van Thal and M. Summers. 1927.]
[*Sir Samuel Tukes Adventures of the Five Hours in relation to the Spanish Plot and to Dryden.* A. Gaw. Baltimore. 1917.]

Tunbridge.
The Tunbridge-Miscellany : Consisting of Poems, etc. Written at *Tunbridge-Wells* this Summer. By Several Hands.

> *Carminibus meritas celebrare Puellas*
> *Dos mea.* Ovid.

London. Printed for E. Curll at the Dial and Bible, against St. *Dunstan's* Church in Fleetstreet. MDCCXII. 8⁰.

Uzziah.
Uzziah and Jotham. A Poem. Licensed and Entred according to Order. *Obscuris vera involvens.* Virg. Æneid. 1. 6. *London* : Printed for *B. Motte*, and are to be sold by *Randall Taylor* near *Stationers-Hall*. 1690. folio.

VANBRUGH (John). See also COLLIER (The Stage Controversy).
The Relapse or Virtue in Danger : Being the Sequel of The Fool in Fashion, A Comedy. Acted at the Theatre-Royal in *Drury-Lane*. By the Author of a late Comedy Call'd *The Provok'd Wife. London*, Printed for S.B. and Sold by *R. Wellington* at the Lute, in St. *Paul's* Church-Yard. 1698. 4⁰. (Acted in 1697.)
The Provok'd Wife : A Comedy. Written by *Mr. Vanbrug. Author of the Relapse.* London, Printed in the Year 1710. (Acted in 1697.)
[First edition : 1697.]
Æsop. A Comedy. With the Addition of a Second Part. Written by Mr. Vanbrug. Printed for T. Johnson. Bookseller at the Hague. MDCCXI. 8⁰. (Acted in 1697.) [First edition : 1697.]
The False Friend. A Comedy. As it is Acted at the *Theatre-Royal* in *Drury-Lane*, By His Majesty's Servants. *London* : Printed for *Jacob Tonson*, within *Gray's Inn Gate*, next *Grays Inn Lane*, 1702. 4⁰.
The Provok'd Husband : or *A Journey to* London, A Comedy, As it is Acted at the Theatre-Royal, By His Majesty's Servants. Written by the *Late Sir* John Vanbrugh, *and Mr.* Cibber, *Vivit Tanquam Vicina Mariti.*

Juv. Sat. VI. *London* : Printed for J. Watts, at the Printing-Office in *Wild-Court* near *Lincolns-Inn Fields.* MDCCXXVIII. 8°.
Collected Works.
Plays, Written by Sir John Vanbrugh. In two volumes. London : Printed for J. Rivington, T. Lowndes, S. Caslon, C. Corbett, S. Bladon, W. Nicoll, T. Evans, and M. Waller. MDCCLXXVI. 12°. [2 vols. 1719.]
[*The Complete Works.* Ed. B. Dobrée and G. Webb. 4 vols. 1927.]
Biography and Criticism.
Ward, W. C.
[Preface to edition of the *Plays.* 1893.]
Whistler, Laurence.
[*Sir John Vanbrugh. Architect and Dramatist. 1664–1726.* 1938.]

VILLIERS (George, Duke of Buckingham). See also DRYDEN (Drydeniana).
Dramatic Works.
The Rehearsal, As it was Acted at the Theatre-Royal, *London,* Printed for *Thomas Dring,* at the *White-Lyon,* next *Chancery-Lane* end in *Fleet-street.* 1672. 4°.
English Reprints. George Villiers, Second Duke of Buckingham. The Rehearsal. First acted 7 Dec. 1671. Published (? July) 1672. With Illustrations from Previous Plays, etc. Carefully edited by Edward Arber, *Associate, King's College, London, F.R.G.S.,* etc., London : Alex. Murray and Son. 30, Queen Square, W.C. *Ent. Stat. Hall.* 2 November, 1868. (*All Rights reserved.*) 12°.
[Ed. M. Summers. 1914. Ed. A. C. Barnes. 1927.]
The Chances, A Comedy : As it was Acted at the Theatre Royal. Corrected and Altered by a Person of Honour. *London,* Printed for A.B. and S.M. and Sold by *Langley Curtis* on Ludgate Hill, 1682. 4°.
Miscellaneous.
Miscellaneous Works, Written by His Grace *George* Late Duke of *Buckingham. Collected in One Volume from the Original Papers.* Containing Poems on several Subjects. Epistles. Characters. Pindarics. The Militant Couple, a Dialogue. And the Farce upon *Segmoor-*Fight. With Letters by and to the Duke of *Buckingham.* By Persons of Quality. Also *State Poems* on the Late Times, by Mr. *Dryden,* Sir *George Etherage,* Sir *Fleetwood Sheppard,* Mr. *Butler,* Author of *Hudibras,* Earl of *D——,* Mr. *Congreve,* Mr. *Otway,* Mr. *Brown,* Capt. *Ayloffe,* etc. Never before Printed. With the late Duke of *Buckingham's* Speeches in the *House of Lords,* upon Conference with the *Commons.* To which is added, *A Collection of Choice remarkable Speeches, that were spoken in both Houses of Parliament, by several Noblemen, and Commoners, in relation to the Government and Liberty of the Subject.* In the Reigns of K. *Charles* I. The Usurpation of the *Rump,* and *Oliver Cromwell.* K. *Charles* II. and K. *William* III, etc. London : Printed for and Sold by *J. Nutt* near *Stationers-hall.* 1704. 8°.

VOLTAIRE.
Œuvres Complètes. *Nouvelle Édition* . . . par Louis Moland . . . Paris, Garnier Frères, Libraires-Éditeurs. 1877–1885. 52 vols. 8°.

WALLER (Edmund).
The Maid's Tragedy altered. With some other Pieces. By Edmund Waller, Esq. ; Not before Printed in the several Editions of his Poems. London, Printed for *Jacob Tonson,* at the *Judges Head* in *Chancery-Lane,* near *Fleet-street.* 1690.
The Works of *Edmund Waller,* Esq. ; in Verse *and* Prose. Published By

Mr. *Fenton*. *London* : Printed for J. Tonson in the *Strand*. MDCCXXX. 12⁰.
    [Ed. G. Thorn Drury. 2 vols. 1905. (Muses Library.)]

WATTS (Thomas).
    A Letter to Antonio Panizzi, Esq. Keeper of the Printed Books in the British Museum, on the reputed earliest printed newspaper, " The English Mercurie, 1588." By Thomas Watts of the British Museum. London : . . . 1839. 8⁰.

WILMOT (John, Earl of Rochester).
    Valentinian : A Tragedy, As 'tis Alter'd by the late Earl of Rochester, And Acted at the Theatre-Royal. Together with a Preface, concerning the Author and his Writings. *By one of his Friends*. *London* : for *Timothy Goodwin* at the *Maiden-head* against St. *Dunstans* Church in *Fleetstreet*. 1685. 4⁰.
    Familiar Letters : Written by the Right Honourable *John*, late Earl of *Rochester*, And several other Persons of Honour and Quality. With letters Written by the most Ingenious Mr. *Thomas Otway* and Mrs. *K. Philips*. Publish'd from their Original Copies. With other Modern Letters, By *Tho. Cheek*, Esq. ; Mr. *Dennis*, and Mr. *Brown*, *London* : Printed by *W. Onley* for *Sam. Briscoe*, at the Corner of *Charles-street*, in *Russel-street*, *Covent-Garden*. 1697. 8⁰.
    Poems on Several Occasions : With Valentinian ; a Tragedy. *To Which is added*, Advice to a Painter. Written by the Right Honourable *John*, late Earl of *Rochester*. *London* : Printed by H. Hills, and Sold by the Booksellers of *London* and *Westminster*. 1710. 8⁰.
    The Works of the Right Honourable The Earls of *Rochester* and *Roscommon*. With some Memoirs of the Earl of *Rochester's* Life, by Monsieur *St. Evremont* : In a Letter to the Dutchess of *Mazarine*. The Third Edition. *To Which is added*, A Collection of Miscellany *Poems*, By the most Eminent Hands. *London* : Printed for E. Curll, at the *Peacock*, without *Temple-Bar*. 1709. 8⁰.
    The Works of the Earls of Rochester, Roscommon, and Dorset. The Dukes of Devonshire, *Buckinghamshire* etc. With Memoirs of their Lives. In Two volumes. Adorned with Cuts. *London* : Printed in the Year M.DCC.XXXI. Price 5s.
    [*The Collected Works*. Ed. John Hayward. 1926.]
    Biography and Criticism.
    Burnet, Gilbert.
        Some Passages of the Life and Death Of the Right Honourable John Earl of *Rochester*, Who died the 26th of *July*, 1680. Written by his own Direction on his Death-Bed, By *Gilbert Burnet*, D.D. *London*, Printed for *Richard Chiswell*, at the *Rose* and *Crown* in St. *Pauls Church-Yard*. 1680. 8⁰.
    Forgues, E. D.
        John Wilmot, comte de Rochester. Revue des Deux Mondes, August and September 1857.
    Prinz, J.
        John Wilmot Earl of Rochester his Life and Writings. Leipzig. 1927.]
    Whitfield, F.
        [*Beast in View. A Study of the Earl of Rochester's Poetry*. Cambridge. U.S.A. 1930.]
    Williams, Charles.
        [*Rochester*. 1935.]
    Pinto, V. de S.
        [*Rochester. Portrait of a Restoration Poet*. 1935.]

Wine-Cooper.

The Wine-Cooper's Delight, To the Tune of, *The Delights of the Bottle* . . . *London*, Printed for the *Protestant Ballad-Singers*. (1681). folio.

Works.

The Works of Celebrated Authors, Of whose Writings there are but small Remains. *London* : Printed for J. and R. Tonson and S. Draper in the *Strand*. MDCCL. 2 volumes 12⁰. (1st volume : *The* Earl *of* Roscommon, *The* Earl *of* Dorset, *The* Earl *of* Halifax, and *Sir* Samuel Garth ; 2nd volume : *George* Stepney, Esq. ; William Walsh, *Esq.* ; and Poems *by Bishop* Sprat.)

WYCHERLEY (William).

Love in a Wood, or St. James's Park. A Comedy. As it is Acted By Their Majesties Servants. Written by Mᵣ *Wycherley.*

Excludit sanos Helicone poetas
Democritus ;   Horat.

London, Printed by *T. Warren* for *Henry Herringman*, and are to be Sold by *R. Bentley, J. Tonson, F. Saunders*, and T. Bennet, 1694. 4⁰.
[First edition : 1672. Acted in 1671.]

The Gentleman Dancing Master. A Comedy, Acted at the Duke's Theatre. By Mr. *Wycherley.*

Horat. *Non Satis est risu diducere rictum*
Auditoris : et est quaedam tamen hic quoq; virtus.

London, Printed by *J.M.* for *Henry Herringman*, and *Thomas Dring* at the Sign of the *Blew Anchor* in the Lower Walk of the *New-Exchange*, and at the Sign of the *White Lyon* in *Fleetstreet* near *Chancery-Lane* end. 1673. (Played in 1672.) 4⁰.

The Country-Wife, A Comedy, Acted at the Theatre-Royal. Written by Mr. *Wycherley.*

Indignor quicquam reprehendi, non quia crasse
Compositum illepideve putetur, sed quia nuper :
Nec veniam Antiquis, sed honorem et praemia posci. Horat.

London, Printed for *Thomas Dring*, at the *Harrow*, at the Corner of *Chancery-Lane* in *Fleet-street*. 1675. (Acted in 1673.) 4⁰.

The Plain-Dealer. A Comedy. As it is Acted at the Theatre Royal. Written by Mᵣ Wycherley.

Horat.—*Ridiculum acre*
Fortius et melius magnas plerumque secat res.

Licensed *Jan.* 9. 1676. Roger L'Estrange. *London*, Printed by *T.N.* for *James Magnes* and *Rich. Bentley* in *Russel-Street* in *Covent-garden* near the *Piazza's* M.D.C.LXXVII. (Acted in 1674.) 4⁰.

[*Complete Works.* Ed. M. Summers. 4 vols. 1924.]

Biography and Criticism.

Perromat, C.
   [*William Wycherley. Sa vie—son Oeuvre.* Paris. 1921.]
Barker, H. Granville.
   [*Wycherley and Dryden.* In *On Dramatic Method.* 1931.]

YOUNG (Edward).

Busiris, King of Egypt. A Tragedy. *By* E. Young, *LL.B.* O triste plane acerbumque funus ! O morte ipsa mortis tempus indignius ! Jam destinata erat egregio Juveni, Jam electus nuptiarum dies ; quod gaudium, quo maerore mutatum est ? Plin. Epist. London, Printed for *T. Johnson.* M.DCCXIX. 12⁰.

A Poem on the *Last Day*. By Edward Young Fellow of *All-Souls* College, *Oxon*. *Venit Summa Dies*, Virg. Oxford. Printed at the Theatre for *Edward Whistler*, MDCCXIII. 8º.

On the Late Queen's Death. And His Majesty's *Accession to the* Throne. Inscribed to *Joseph Addison*, Esq. ; Secretary to their Excellencies the Lords Justices. By Edward Young, Fellow of *All-Souls* College, *Oxon*. *Gaudia Curis*. Hor. *London* : Printed for *J. Tonson*, at *Shakespear's Head* over against *Catherine street* in the *Strand*. 1714. folio.

[*The Complete Works*. Ed. E. J. Doran. 2 vols. 1854.]

Biography and Criticism.

    Mackail, J.
       [*Edward Young*. 1926.]

INDEX

NOTE.—Numbers in brackets and italics refer to notes : thus, the entry 343 (*85*) is a reference to note 85 on page 343. But reference to the subject of the entry is often made in the body of the text on the page concerned, as well as in the note so referred to. Thus, " Arnall, Wm., 343 (*85*) " is to be taken to mean that, while a specific reference to Arnall is made in note 85 on page 343, there may be (and in fact is) also a reference to him in the text of that page.

Numbers in heavy type refer to the pages of the bibliography.

The International Library of
SOCIOLOGY AND SOCIAL RECONSTRUCTION

Editor: KARL MANNHEIM
Late Professor of Education in the University of London

ADVISORY BOARD: SIR HAROLD BUTLER, K.C.M.G., C.B.; SIR ALEXANDER CARR-SAUNDERS, M.A., Director of the London School of Economics; SIR FRED CLARKE, M.A. (Oxon), Chairman, Central Advisory Council for Education; LORD LINDSAY OF BIRKER, C.B.E., Master of Balliol College, Oxford.

PLAN OF THE LIBRARY
Sections

ROUTLEDGE & KEGAN PAUL LTD.
68-74 Carter Lane, London, E.C.4

SOCIOLOGY OF EDUCATION

Education after School
by C. STIMSON
In preparation. About 15s.

The Problem of Punishment in Education
by EWALD BOHM
In preparation. About 21s.

Mission of the University
by ORTEGA Y GASSET. Translated and introduced by HOWARD LEE NOSTRAND
7s. 6d.

Total Education: A Plea for Synthesis
by M. L. JACKS, Director, Department of Education, Oxford University
Second Impression. 10s. 6d.

Education in Transition
A Sociological Analysis of the Impact of the War on English Education
by H. C. DENT
Fourth Impression. 12s. 6d.

The Reform of Secondary Education
by H. C. DENT
About 15s.

Education for Adults: A Study in Transition
by T. MACKAY MURE
About 10s. 6d.

Who Shall Be Educated? The Challenge of Unequal Opportunities
by W. LLOYD WARNER, Prof. of Anthropology and Sociology, Member of Comm. on Human Development, Univ. of Chicago; ROBERT J. HAVIGHURST, Prof. of Education, Member of Comm. on Human Development, Univ. of Chicago; MARTIN B. LOEB, Inst. of Child Welfare, Univ. of California, at Berkeley
10s. 6d.

The Social Psychology of Education: A Sociological Study
by C. M. FLEMING, Ed.B., Ph.D., University of London Institute of Education
Fourth Impression. 7s. 6d.

German Youth: Bond or Free
by HOWARD BECKER, Professor of Sociology, University of Wisconsin
Illustrated. 18s.

The Museum: Its History and Its Tasks in Education
by ALMA S. WITTLIN, Dr. Phil. *In preparation. Illustrated. About 21s.*

Comparative Education
A Study of Education Facts and Traditions.
NICHOLAS HANS, Lecturer in Comparative Education at the University
of London, King's College *About 21s. net*

SOCIOLOGY OF RELIGION

Sociology of Religion
by JOACHIM WACH *30s.*

The Economic Order and Religion
by FRANK KNIGHT, Prof. of Social Sciences, University of Chicago,
and THORNTON W. MERRIAM, Director of U.S.O. Training, Nat.
Council of the Y.M.C.A. *15s.*

SOCIOLOGY OF ART AND LITERATURE

Sociology of the Renaissance
by ALFRED VON MARTIN, translated by W. L. LUETKENS
Second Impression. 8s. 6d

Theatre, Drama and Audience in Goethe's Germany
by W. H. BRUFORD, M.A., Professor of German, University of
Edinburgh *In Preparation. About 25s.*

Chekhov and His Russia: A Sociological Study
by W. H. BRUFORD, M.A., Professor of German in the University of
Edinburgh *16s.*

The Sociology of Literary Taste
by LEVIN L. SCHÜCKING. Dr. Phil. *Second Impression 7s. 6d.*

**Men of Letters and the English Public in the
18th Century, 1660-1744. Dryden, Addison, Pope**
by ALEXANDRE BELJAME. Edited with an Introduction and Notes
by Prof. BONAMY DOBREE. Translated by E. O. LORIMER *25s.*

3

SOCIOLOGICAL APPROACH TO THE STUDY OF HISTORY

The Aftermath of the Napoleonic Wars: The Concert of Europe—An Experiment

by H. G. SCHENK, D.Phil. (Oxon)   *Illustrated.   16s.*

Progress and Disenchantment: A Study of European Romanticism

by H. G. SCHENK, D.Phil. (Oxon)   *Illustrated.   About 21s.*

SOCIOLOGY OF LAW

The Sociology of Law

by GEORGES GURVITCH, Ph.D., LL.D., Prof. of Sociology, University of Strassbourg, France. With an Introduction by ROSCOE POUND, Prof. of Jurisprudence, late Dean of the Faculty of Law, Harvard University

18s.

The Institutions of Private Law and Their Social Functions

by KARL RENNER, President of the Austrian Republic. Edited with an Introduction and Notes by O. KAHN-FREUND, Ll.M., Dr. Jur., Lecturer in Law, University of London   *About 10s. 6d.*

Legal Aid

by ROBERT EGERTON, Hon. Sec. Legal Sub-committee Cambridge House, Solicitor of the Supreme Court. With an Introduction by D. L. GOODHART, K.C., D.C.L., Ll.D., Prof. of Jurisprudence, Oxford

2nd Impression.   10s. 6d.

Soviet Legal Theory: Its Social Background and Development

by RUDOLF SCHLESINGER, Ph.D., London   *2nd Impression.   16s.*

4

CRIMINOLOGY AND THE SOCIAL SERVICES

Theory and Practice of a Family Court
by CARL BIRNBAUM, formerly Professor of Psychiatry, Berlin University, and John Otto Reinemann, Dr. Jur., formerly Municipal Councillor in Berlin   *In preparation. About 15s.*

Juvenile Delinquency in an English Middletown
by HERMANN MANNHEIM, Lecturer in Criminology in the University of London   *In preparation. About 18s.*

Mental Health in a Rural Area
by Dr. MAYER GROSS   *In preparation. About 15s.*

Criminal Justice and Social Reconstruction
by HERMANN MANNHEIM, Dr. Jur., Lecturer in Criminology in the University of London   *15s.*

The Psycho-Analytical Approach to Juvenile Delinquency: Theory, Case Studies, Treatment
by KATE FRIEDLANDER, M.D., L.R.C.P. (Edin.), D.P.M. (Lond.), Hon. Psychiatrist, Inst. for the Scientific Treatment of Delinquency; Clinical Dir., W. Sussex Child Guidance Service   *18s.*

Voluntary Social Services since 1918
by HENRY A. MESS, late Reader in Social Science in the University of London in collaboration with Constance Braithwaite, Violet Creech-Jones, Hilda Jennings, Pearl Jephcott, Harold King, Nora Milnes, John Morgan, Gertrude Williams and W. E. Williams. Edited by GERTRUDE WILLIAMS, Lecturer in Economics, University of London   *21s.*

SOCIOLOGY AND POLITICS

Social and Economic Movements: A Handbook to the Understanding of the Modern Political Scene
by H. W. LAIDLER   *In preparation. About 30s.*

The Analysis of Political Behaviour: An Empirical Approach
by HAROLD D. LASSWELL, Professor of Law, Yale University School of Law   *21s.*

Dictatorship and Political Police

The Technique of Control by Fear by E. K. BRAMSTEDT, Ph.D. (London)

15s.

Nationality in History and Politics

by FREDERICK HERTZ, Author of "Race and Civilisation"

Second Impression. 25s.

FOREIGN AFFAIRS, THEIR SOCIAL, POLITICAL AND ECONOMIC FOUNDATIONS

Patterns of Peacemaking

by DAVID THOMSON, Ph.D., Cantab., Research Fellow of Sidney Sussex Coll., Cambridge; E. MEYER, Dr. rer. pol., and A. BRIGGS, B.A., Cantab.

21s.

French Canada in Transition

by EVERETT C. HUGHES, Professor of Sociology, University of Chicago

15s.

State and Economics in the Middle East

by A. BONNE, Dr. œc. publ., Director, Economic Research Institute of Palestine

About 25s.

Economic Development of the Middle East

An Outline of Planned Reconstruction by A. BONNE, Dr. œc. publ., Director, Economic Research Institute of Palestine

Second Impression. 12s. 6d.

Federalism in Central and Eastern Europe

by RUDOLF SCHLESINGER, Ph.D., London

30s.

The Danube Basin and the German Economic Sphere

by ANTONIN BASCH, Dr. Phil., Columbia University

18s.

The Regions of Germany

by R. E. DICKINSON, Reader in Geography, University College, London

Second Impression. 10s. 6d.

MIGRATION AND RE-SETTLEMENT

Settlement in Underpopulated Areas
by JULIUS ISAAC, Ph.D. (London). *In preparation. About 18s.*

Economics of Migration
by JULIUS ISAAC, Ph.D., London. With an Introduction by Sir ALEXANDER CARR-SAUNDERS, Director of the London School of Economics
18s.

Co-operative Communities at Work
by HENRIK INFIELD, Director, Rural Settlement Inst., New York
15s.

ECONOMIC PLANNING

Retail Trade Associations
A New Form of Monopolist Organisation in Britain, by HERMANN LEVY, Author of "The New Industrial System" *Second Impression. 15s.*

The Shops of Britain: A Study in Retail Trade Distribution
by HERMANN LEVY
21s.

The Price of Social Security—The Problem of Labour Mobility
by GERTRUDE WILLIAMS, Lecturer in Economics, University of London
Second Impression. 12s. 6d.

SOCIOLOGY OF THE FAMILY AND ALLIED TOPICS

The Family and Democratic Society
by J. K. FOLSOM, Professor of Sociology, Vassar College
In preparation. About 30s.

Nation and Family
The Swedish Experiment in Democratic Family and Population Policy
by ALVA MYRDAL
2nd Impression. 21s.

The Sociology of Women's Work
by GERTRUDE WILLIAMS, Lecturer in Economics, University of London
About 15s.

Adolescence
Its Social Psychology: With an Introduction to recent findings from the fields of Anthropology, Physiology, Medicine, Psychometrics and Sociometry
by C. M. FLEMING, Ed.B., Ph.D., University of London Institute of Education *About 15s.*

TOWN AND COUNTRY PLANNING.
HUMAN ECOLOGY

Social Background of a Plan: A Study of Middlesbrough
Edited by RUTH GLASS. Illustrated with Maps and Plans
In preparation. About 30s.

City, Region and Regionalism
by ROBERT E. DICKINSON, Reader in Geography, University College, London. With Maps and Plans *21s.*

The West European City: A Study in Urban Geography
by ROBERT E. DICKINSON, Reader in Geography, University College, London. Illustrated, with Maps and Plans. *In preparation. About 21s.*

Creative Demobilisation
Vol. I. Principles of National Planning
By E. A. GUTKIND, D.Ing.
Vol. 2. Case Studies in National Planning
Edited by E. A. GUTKIND, D.Ing. *Second Impression. 21s. each*

Revolution of Environment
by E. A. GUTKIND, D.Ing. *Illustrated. 30s.*

The Journey to Work
by K. LIEPMANN, Ph.D., London. With an Introduction by Sir Alexander Carr-Saunders, Director of the London School of Economics
Second Impression. 15s.

SOCIOLOGICAL STUDIES OF MODERN COMMUNITIES

Negroes in Britain

A study of Racial Relations in English Society
by K. L. LITTLE, Ph.D., London   25s.

Co-operative Living in Palestine

by HENRIK F. INFIELD, Director, Rural Settlement Inst., New York
Illustrated. 7s. 6d.

ANTHROPOLOGY AND COLONIAL POLICY

The Sociology of Colonies: An Introduction to the Study of Race Contact

by RENÉ MAUNIER. Translated from the French by E. O. Lorimer
In preparation. About 42s.

Malay Fishermen: Their Peasant Economy

by RAYMOND FIRTH, Prof. of Anthropology, University of London
Illustrated. 25s. net

Peasant Life in China

by HSIAO T'UNG FEI, Ph.D., London   *Fourth Impression. Illustrated. 15s.*

A Chinese Village: Taitou, Shantung Province

by Martin C. Yang   *About 15s.*

Hsinlung Hsiang

A Field Study of Peasant Life in the Red Basin, West China
by ISABEL CROOK and YU HSI-CHI   *About 21s.*

A Japanese Village: Suye Mura

by JOHN P. EMBREE, Visiting Assoc. Prof. of Anthropology, University
of Chicago. With an Introduction by A. R. RADCLIFFE-BROWN,
Professor of Social Anthropology, Oxford University
Illustrated. 18s.

The Golden Wing: A Sociological Study of Chinese Familism

by LIN HUEH-HWA, with an Introduction by RAYMOND FIRTH
16s.

SOCIOLOGY AND PSYCHOLOGY OF THE PRESENT CRISIS

War, Love or Money: A Psychological Study of European Culture Patterns
by H. V. DICKS, M.D., M.R.C.P. *In preparation. About 21s.*

Diagnosis of Our Time
by KARL MANNHEIM *Fourth Impression. 10s. 6d.*

Farewell to European History or the Conquest of Nihilism
by ALFRED WEBER *16s.*

The Fear of Freedom
by Dr. ERICH FROMM *Fourth Impression. 15s.*

SOCIAL PSYCHOLOGY AND PSYCHO-ANALYSIS

Psychology and the Social Pattern
by JULIAN BLACKBURN, Ph.D., B.Sc. (Econ.), Lecturer on Social Psychology, London School of Economics *Second Impression. 10s. 6d.*

The Framework of Human Behaviour
by JULIAN BLACKBURN, Ph.D., B.Sc. (Econ.), Lecturer on Social Psychology, London School of Economics *12s. 6d.*

Individual Development in Society
by JULIAN BLACKBURN, Ph.D., B.Sc. (Econ.), Lecturer on Social Psychology, London School of Economics *About 10s. 6d.*
(*Three independent volumes supplementing each other*)

A Handbook of Social Psychology
by KIMBALL YOUNG, Professor of Sociology, Queens College, New York *Second Impression. 21s.*

Sigmund Freud—An Introduction
A Presentation of his Theories and a discussion of the Relationship between Psycho-analysis and Sociology by WALTER HOLLITSCHER, Dr. Phil. *8s. 6d.*

Social Learning and Imitation
by NEAL E. MILLER and JOHN DOLLARD of the Institute of Human
Relations, Yale University   *15s*

APPROACHES TO THE PROBLEM
OF PERSONALITY

The Cultural Background of Personality
by RALPH LINTON, Professor of Anthropology, Columbia University
                                                                          10s. 6d.

The Feminine Character. History of an Ideology
by VIOLA KLEIN, Ph.D., London. With an Introduction by KARL
MANNHEIM.   *12s. 6d.*

The History of Autobiography in Antiquity
by GEORG MISCH. Translated by E. W. DICKES   *About 21s.*

Personality and Problems of Adjustment
by KIMBALL YOUNG   Demy 8vo.   *35s.*

PHILOSOPHICAL AND SOCIAL FOUNDATIONS
OF THOUGHT

Homo Ludens: A Study of the Play Element in Culture
by Professor J. HUIZINGA   *In preparation. About 21s.*

The Ideal Foundations of Economic Thought
by W. STARK, Dr. rer. pol., Dr. Jur.   *Second Impression. 15s.*

**The History of Economics in Its Relation to Social
Development**
by W. STARK, Dr. rer. pol., Dr. Jur.   *Second Impression. 7s. 6d.*

America: Ideal and Reality
The United States of 1776 in Contemporary European Philosophy by
W. STARK, Dr. rer. pol., Dr. Jur.   *10s. 6d.*

The Decline of Liberalism as an Ideology
by J. H. HALLOWELL   *12s. 6d.*

Society and Nature: A Sociological Inquiry
by HANS KELSEN, Formerly Prof. of Law, Vienna and Geneva, Depart
ment of Political Science, University of California   *21s.*

Demographic Material Appearing in the Transactions of the Royal Society in the 17th and 18th Centuries
Edited by Dr. R. R. KUCZYNSKI   *In preparation. About 15s.*

Population Controversies of the Eighteenth Century
Edited by DAVID GLASS, Ph.D.   *In preparation. About 15s.*

GENERAL SOCIOLOGY

A Handbook of Sociology
by W. F. OGBURN, Professor of Sociology, University of Chicago, and
M. F. NIMKOFF, Professor of Sociology, Bucknell University   25s.

FOREIGN CLASSICS OF SOCIOLOGY

Wilhelm Dilthey: Selected Readings from his Works and an Introduction to his Sociological and Philosophical Work
by H. A. HODGES, Prof. of Philosophy, University of Reading   10s. 6d.

From Max Weber: Essays in Sociology
Translated, edited, and with an Introduction by H. H. GERTH and
C. W. MILLS   21s.

DOCUMENTARY

Changing Attitudes in Soviet Russia
Documents and Readings concerning the *Family*
Edited by R. SCHLESINGER, Ph.D., London   *About 21s.*

Changing Attitudes in Soviet Russia
Documents and Readings concerning *National Autonomy and Experiments in Administrative Devolution*
Edited by R. SCHLESINGER, Ph.D., London   *About 21s.*

Changing Attitudes in Soviet Russia
Documents and Readings concerning *Foreign Policy*
Edited by R. SCHLESINGER, Ph.D., London   *About 21s.*

All prices are net

THE WESTMINSTER PRESS, LONDON, W.9